VYBORG

ROZHDESTVENSKAIA

LITEINAIA

Nevskii cotton-spinning factory

OKHTA REGION

ISCOW

ALEKSANDRO-NEVSKAIA

LABOR AND SOCIETY IN
TSARIST RUSSIA

Sponsored by the Russian Institute
Columbia University

LABOR AND SOCIETY IN TSARIST RUSSIA

The Factory Workers of St. Petersburg
1855–1870

REGINALD E. ZELNIK

STANFORD UNIVERSITY PRESS

STANFORD, CALIFORNIA

1971

Stanford University Press
Stanford, California
© 1971 by the Board of Trustees of the
Leland Stanford Junior University
Printed in the United States of America
ISBN 0-8047-0740-5
LC 73-130832

TO ELAINE

Acknowledgments

This study was first undertaken as a doctoral dissertation at Stanford University. The basic research was completed in Leningrad and Moscow on a fellowship from the Inter-University Committee on Travel Grants. I am grateful to the professional staffs of the State historical archives in Leningrad and Moscow (TsGIAL and TsGAOR), the Leningrad regional archives (GIALO), and the Saltykov-Shchedrin Library for their kind assistance. Professor N. G. Sladkevich of Leningrad State University gave me very helpful advice, as did other officials of that institution. I am also indebted to the professional staffs of the Slavic Library of Helsinki University, Hoover Institution, Library of Congress, New York Public Library, and the libraries of Columbia University and the University of California at Berkeley. A Senior Fellowship from the Russian Institute of Columbia University enabled me to complete the manuscript in a congenial and intellectually stimulating atmosphere. Valuable research assistance from Carol Shelly and Gerald Surh was supported by the Center for Slavic and East European Studies at Berkeley, which also subsidized the typing of the manuscript by Mrs. Grace O'Connell. Professors Loren Graham, Leopold Haimson, Martin Malia, Nicholas Riasanovsky, Hans Rosenberg, Irwin Scheiner, Allan Widman, and Isser Woloch have read all or parts of the manuscript and given me helpful advice. I am especially indebted to the original supervisors of my dissertation, Professors Anatole Mazour and Wayne Vucinich, for their advice and encouragement, and to Professor Rose Glickman, who provided invaluable criticisms at almost every stage of the manuscript. I wish to thank the Editor of the *Slavic Review* and the University of Chicago Press, respectively, for allowing me to republish, in reworked and expanded form, my articles "An Early Case of Labor Protest in St. Petersburg: The Aleksandrovsk Machine Works in 1860," *Slavic Review*, XXIV,

No. 3 (Sept. 1965), and "The Sunday School Movement in Russia, 1859–1862," *Journal of Modern History*, XXVII, No. 2 (June 1965), copyright 1965 by The University of Chicago.

My wife Elaine, in addition to sharing in the painful endeavors and dislocations that inevitably surround the preparation of a dissertation and first book, helped enormously in the editing of the manuscript in its earlier stages. The editorial assistance of Betty Smith and Nancy Donovan of Stanford Press has proved invaluable. The Index was carefully prepared by Mrs. Evelyn Thomas. Finally, I am deeply grateful to my parents for their encouragement and support throughout the years.

R.E.Z.

Note on Transliteration and Dates

With a few obvious exceptions, the Library of Congress system of transliteration (without diacritical marks) has been followed. Archaic nineteenth-century spellings of Russian names and titles have been partially modified to conform with modern orthography. Dates follow the Julian ("old style") calendar. A list of abbreviations is provided at the end of the book, before the Notes.

Contents

LABOR AND SOCIETY IN
TSARIST RUSSIA

Introduction

HOWEVER ONE may interpret and evaluate the Russian revolutions of 1917, it is impossible to deny the decisive role in their outcome that was played by industrial workers. Yet, although most Western accounts of 1917 have at least recognized the importance of the attitudes and actions of the workers, it is only recently that American authors have attempted to delve into the earlier history of this segment of Russia's population and its place in Russian society.[1] Except for a handful of articles, even the recent studies have examined the Russian workers only in the narrow context of their relations with revolutionary Marxist intellectuals and political groups.[2] Moreover, few of them look further back than the early 1890's.

This neglect of the history of Russia's industrial workers has been symptomatic of the more general failure to examine the processes of Russian industrialization in the period before the "take-off" of the 1890's. Major studies in this area, covering the first half of the nineteenth century, have appeared only in the past three years.[3] No one to date has tried to examine the situation of the nineteenth-century Russian worker as a part of the context of early industrialization, to assess the impact of the early experiences of Russian laborers upon their subsequent political evolution, or to investigate the interaction between the workers' situation and the attitudes and actions of other segments of society before the 1890's.

This book is intended to be the first step in such an endeavor. The year 1855 has been chosen as a point of departure because the death of Nicholas I in that year, and the termination of the Crimean War in 1856, set the stage for a fresh assessment of government policy toward industrialization and hence toward industrial workers. A new pro-industrial attitude emerged from that assessment, and although there was considerable vacillation in the choice and implementation of particular policies in the years that followed, the tsarist regime would never again revert to the ambiguity about industrialization that had characterized the reign of Nicholas I (1825–55). From this point of view, the years 1855–1917 constitute a discrete and continuous period. It may be subdivided according to such criteria as the vigor with which industrialization was pursued and the degree of success with which it was implemented, but the basic pro-industrial posture assumed by Alexander II early in his reign remained as tsarist policy during the reigns of his successors. The year 1855–56 thus marks an important point from which to begin to follow the evolution of the general context in which the history of the industrial worker transpired. Moreover, the relative relaxation of autocratic control that marked Alexander's advent to the throne opened up new possibilities for public discussion and debate about industry, labor, and related questions, which had been severely restricted during the reign of Nicholas. Anticipation of the forthcoming emancipation of the serfs infused the atmosphere with the spirit of social reform, which was partially transformed into public concern with the situation of factory workers. In turn, public discussion at times spilled over into concrete activity aimed at improving the lot of the industrial laborer.

The year 1870 has been chosen as the terminal point for this book because the following year marked the beginning of a process of cross-fertilization between urban factory workers and the radical intelligentsia. From 1871 until the assassination of Alexander in 1881, there was a fairly steady interaction between radical Populists and a significant segment of the industrial workers of St. Petersburg (and, to a lesser extent, between Populists and workers in other cities) that, despite some interruptions in the 1880's, formed a continuum with the interaction between workers and Marxists in the 1890's. In contrast to the post-1870 period, the first fifteen years of Alexander's reign saw virtually no contact between industrial workers and the radical intelligentsia, whose attention was focused on other areas. These years form a discrete period, then, in that they give us the only opportunity between the Crimean War and 1917 to study the situation of urban workers independently of the history of revolutionary politics. Such a study is essential if we are to reach a fuller understanding of the social and political conditions in which the labor movement and the radical movement of the intelligentsia later began to interact.*

My decision to concentrate this study on the city of St. Petersburg may be questioned by some. Insofar as I deal with such topics as tsarist labor policy and the attitudes toward factory labor expressed in the press, the topic of necessity transcends the boundaries of any particular region. It is true, nonetheless, that both the government and unofficial commentators, to the extent that they expressed concern with the problems of urban factory workers, tended to concentrate their attention on the city of St. Petersburg and its immediate environs during the period under consideration. St. Petersburg was both the seat of government and the center of intellectual life. It was natural for officials, professional journalists, and other writers to be concerned primarily with those workers who were closest at hand, and by the time of the Crimean War, St. Petersburg had become the most highly industrialized city in Russia. Factories and factory workers were simply more visible there than in most other Russian cities. For these reasons, even a study that purported to cover all the urban industrial areas of Russia would necessarily place a very heavy emphasis on the St. Petersburg region. I have found it more satisfactory to focus my study expressly on that region, while drawing attention to other areas or to the Empire as a whole where it seems useful.

Underlying this choice, and perhaps more basic to it, is my feeling that the general state of the field of Russian history in the United States requires more concentration on regional studies, confined within fairly narrow chronological limits. Broad works of synthesis and interpretation, based mainly on the research of Soviet scholars, seem to be yielding a diminishing margin of intellectual profit. Since at least some American scholars can now undertake basic research in the Soviet Union, intellectual history has ceased to be the sole domain in which Americans can add to the building blocks of historical synthesis, as several recent studies attest. By taking advantage of new opportunities, we can examine basic historical problems within manageable regional and chronological limits,

---

* The period 1871–81, the years of Populist-worker interaction, will be the subject of a second volume of this study.

eventually achieving new syntheses and general understandings of Russian history. In my particular undertaking, the hope is that by narrowly focusing on a single but vitally important region during a short but formative period, I may contribute to our ultimate understanding of the role of factory workers in the Russian revolutionary movement, and of the social and political repercussions of industrialization as it was carried out in the context of the Russian autocratic system.

Although Soviet writings on the history of industrial labor in nineteenth-century Russia have been voluminous, the scholarly yield has been rather limited. The most useful Soviet contributions have been the collection and publication of documents dealing with labor unrest, some of which have been indispensable to my investigation, and the publication of some statistical studies. Most interpretive studies, however, the best of which date back to the 1920's, suffer from a predictable tendency to present the history of factory workers in as heroic a light as possible, and to ignore those aspects of Russian labor history that cannot be directly related to the revolutionary struggle. Somewhat like their Western counterparts, Soviet historians have not been much interested in the situation of industrial labor during periods of apparent calm or muted, undramatic struggle. While searching further into the past than American historians, they have tended to restrict the object of their search to moments of unrest and defiance and to magnify the significance of these events in order to foreshadow the heroic revolutionary role that industrial workers were to play in later years. Thus, although a few valuable articles have appeared relating to some of the unspectacular aspects of Russian labor history in the period with which I am dealing, most recent Soviet work in this area has been restricted to the role of labor unrest in the so-called revolutionary situation of 1859–61.[4]

A more significant shortcoming in the work of Soviet historians follows from their overly schematic conception of the historical evolution of the industrial working class. Although there have been significant differences in interpretation, there has been little variety in basic approach.[5] Typically, a strong emphasis is placed on the degree to which the Russian industrial worker underwent a historical evolution similar to that of his Western European coun-

terpart. Differences are recognized, but are usually viewed as epi-
phenomenal. Broadly speaking, Soviet historians postulate a more
or less linear development that began with the penetration of the
industrial revolution into Russian economic life, usually ascribed
to the 1840's, and reached its climax with the conscious revolutionary activity of the fully proletarianized workers in 1917. Seen as important milestones along this path are the emancipation of the peasantry in 1861, which set the stage for completing the process of
proletarianization, and the birth of the Marxist movement in the
1890's, which was the necessary condition for infusing the proletariat with revolutionary consciousness.

This schema has its attractive features, and should not be dismissed out of hand. Many important aspects of Russian labor history can be placed within its framework without doing serious violence to historical accuracy. Yet it fails ultimately, in my opinion,
to provide satisfactory answers to some crucial questions; or perhaps more accurately, it fails to ask them.

Why were the urban industrial workers of Russia inclined toward
revolutionary action in 1905 and 1917? If our response to this question invokes their advanced degree of proletarianization—that is,
their severance from traditional agrarian and craft occupations, extensive specialization and division of labor, psychological acceptance of industrial labor as a permanent way of life—then surely
we have not come to grips with it. For we know that revolutionary
predilections were considerably weaker among the workers of countries where the degree of proletarianization was unquestionably
more advanced. Recent events in France should militate against
the smug assumption by Western historians and sociologists that
industrial advancement has closed the door to the emergence of
radical activism among workers in all highly developed nations.
Nevertheless, the history of the past hundred years compels us to
seek other explanations for labor radicalism than advanced proletarianization, as defined above.

On the other hand the degree of proletarianization becomes germane if approached concretely within the context of the flow of
Russian history, and not as a reflection of any sociological law that
purports to fix a certain level of development as the threshold of
revolutionary activism among industrial workers. Such an approach

has recently been illustrated in a lengthy article by Leopold Haimson, covering the period 1905–17.[6] Here the workers' openness to revolutionary appeals (particularly in St. Petersburg beginning in 1912) is not ascribed to advanced proletarian class consciousness, but to the confluence of a growing stream of semiproletarian workers with close rural ties and a smaller, more articulate group of militant young urban worker-revolutionaries with relatively little experience in the labor movement. This confluence is examined by Haimson within the political context of the period, and the result is a convincing explanation of the processes that led to the radicalization of labor. The approach is clearly inconsistent with the a priori assumptions that have characterized most Soviet work in the field.*

The same problem exists with regard to the period examined in the present study: the basic Soviet schema precludes the posing of an important series of questions. How did the fact that Russia's industrialization took place within an autocratic polity and a traditional social structure condition the evolution of the urban working class? How was this anomalous situation perceived by Russia's ruling circles and by educated society? In the absence of an adequate written record of the workers' own perceptions of their situation, to what extent is it possible to infer the course of development of their consciousness from the attitudes and actions of those members of society with whom their fate was most closely linked? Given the Russian worker's ultimate rejection of political autocracy and industrial capitalism, what important moments in the earlier formation of his environment may help us to understand his later evolution?

In raising these and similar questions, one must be careful to avoid the conceptual pitfall of acting as a sort of retrospective academic consultant to the regime of Alexander II. To reveal, for example, that a more "enlightened" policy toward labor was a real possibility even under the conditions that prevailed in the 1860's, and that the rejection of such proposals contributed to the susceptibility of industrial workers to political radicalism, is, I believe, a

---

* It should be noted that Haimson's study is equally damaging to the belief of some Western historians that a more or less linear progression of working-class integration into modern industrial life was taking place in Russia, only to be interrupted by World War I.

contribution to historical knowledge. But this type of analysis is distorted into special pleading if it is presented in such a way as to suggest the manner in which one would have *liked* the tsarist regime to conduct itself to meet the standards of modern liberal historians. The existence (and rejection) of alternative courses of action is of interest to the historian only insofar as it too, as well as the policy actually adopted, contributes to our understanding of the historical context. It is in this spirit that I have attempted to assess the significance of the period 1855–70 for the evolution of the Russian industrial worker.

ONE

Urban Institutions and Factory Labor
Before 1855

RUSSIA'S INDUSTRIAL development before the Crimean War proceeded along complex and contradictory lines. It is not my intention here to attempt a full presentation of the varied successes and
failures of Russian industrialization in the first half of the nineteenth century, or to examine the institutional forces that both
accelerated and impeded the industrialization process. These tasks
have been admirably performed in the recent work of William L.
Blackwell, who presents the period from 1800 to 1860 as one of
"preparation for more rapid industrial growth."[1] My task in this
chapter will be to outline only those aspects of Russian social, economic, and political life in the first half of the nineteenth century
that have the greatest bearing on the later history of the urban industrial worker. These include the character of the Russian city,
its social structure and class composition insofar as these affected
the recruitment and the environment of industrial workers, and
the attitudes and policies of the tsarist government toward urban
industry in general and industrial labor in particular. After survey-
ing these areas in broad outline, I will turn to a more detailed discussion of the city of St. Petersburg and its environs during the
same period.

The relative weakness of Russian cities before the reign of Peter
the Great, the lack of vitality in municipal institutions and urban
economic life, is too well known to be belabored here. The typical
town of the Muscovite period began as a simple fortified settlement planted in the midst of a predominantly agricultural population. Although some of the towns gradually developed a more
complex and varied economic character, they still lacked any significant degree of administrative distinctiveness or political autonomy before the municipal reforms introduced by Peter the Great.[2]

The central document that provided the basis for Peter's reorganization of Russian municipalities was the so-called *reglament Glavnogo magistrata* (regulation for the Chief Magistrate) of January 16, 1721.[3] Broadly speaking, the regulation constituted an attempt to introduce the municipal institutions that had developed over the past centuries in the towns of Western Europe. A hierarchical municipal governing structure was established, unique to the towns, and the urban population itself was sharply defined in categories that simultaneously set it apart from the bulk of the rural population and delineated the internal juridical structure of the urban population itself.

Despite some minor modifications, and ignoring for the moment the question of actual practices, the structures introduced by Peter remained in force until the new municipal and provincial reforms of Catherine the Great. Catherine's municipal charter of April 21, 1785,[4] though it drastically altered the specific content of the existing municipal structure, continued the general direction initiated by Peter. Indeed, even before the publication of this statute, Catherine was aware of the requirements of the city as a discrete entity, though her policies were confused and contradictory.[5] The charter of 1785 was more precise than the regulation of 1721 in attempting to define the parameters of urban society and to give legal definition to the Russian city as a corporate entity.[6]

Nevertheless, the municipal reforms of the eighteenth century, though they granted administrative distinctiveness to the Russian town, failed to grant it a significant degree of administrative autonomy. Towns were granted an independent tax structure, and distinct services and obligations to the state were imposed on their populations, but no significantly independent political rights were associated with these impositions.[7] The reason for this absence of autonomy may be traced to Peter's original motive in deciding to renovate municipal institutions, which was essentially to revitalize the commercial and industrial life of Russian towns by duplicating the institutional forms of the more economically vital towns of Western Europe. In imposing these forms on the Russian city, Peter was using the central authority of the state to create institutions that had evolved gradually and organically in the West. Never did he display any serious desire to relinquish that centralized control, least of all the control over municipal police powers.[8]

After Peter's death his successors vacillated between maintaining strict central control over the cities and allowing this control to lapse into the hands of the provincial governors (*voevody*) of the regions within which the cities were located. In neither case was administrative or police power effectively exercised by city authorities.[9] The charter of 1785 changed this situation somewhat. Quasi-autonomous local administrative institutions received prerogatives that had been denied them in the past. The creation of the General Municipal Duma and the Shestiglasnaia Duma (Six-Man Council; of greater practical importance than the larger body) placed control over all matters affecting the general welfare of the town in the hands of local representatives, at least in theory. But this new degree of theoretical autonomy was counterbalanced by the continued reluctance of an increasingly bureaucratized central government to relinquish its authority in police matters, whether exercised directly or through the provincial administration that had been established in 1775.[10] An important example, which will shortly be discussed in greater detail, is the control that the government exercised —well into the nineteenth century—over such local matters as a peasant's move into the urban population.[11] In general, then, by the nineteenth century Russian cities contained some of the formal trappings of administrative self-regulation, but the administrative institutions remained exceedingly weak.

To what extent can the corporate existence of the eighteenth-century Russian city be defined by the presence of special associations of urban dwellers, holding a juridical status that distinguished them from the nonurban population?[12] In many Western European cities, such associations of persons pursuing similar economic interests formed the nucleus of what gradually developed into the incorporated community of burghers or citizens. In Russia, however, the sequence was reversed. Urban economic associations or corporations did not strive for and gain recognition by the state, but were created by the state. Before the regulation of 1721, corporate municipal institutions were barely developed. Administratively, the trading-industrial population of towns was subdivided not according to trade or craft but according to geographical area of settlement within the given town, and in some cases, according to specific obligations to the state. This form of division, which was meant primarily to facilitate tax collection, left the urban population atomized and amorphous, and the concept of citizenship almost nonexistent. No significant modifications of this picture were introduced until the act of 1721.*

The effect of Peter's regulation was to divide the urban population into two basic groups; one was placed in a juridical relationship to the new municipal institutions, the other was not. The former group, the so-called regular citizens (*reguliarnye grazhdane*), consisted primarily of merchants engaged in trade or manufacture, skilled practitioners such as physicians and artists, and specialized artisans. The other group, the irregular citizens (*nereguliarnye grazhdane*), consisted of all other persons (excluding nobles, clergy, and foreigners) permanently residing in the city, or more generally, the poor and unskilled. The regular citizens were in turn subdivided into two guilds (*gil'dii*), the first for the wealthy and the practitioners of certain skilled and highly valued crafts, the second primarily for petty tradesmen and the bulk of artisans. Only members of the two guilds were to be actively represented as advisers to the town administration or magistrate.[13]

In a limited and rudimentary form, the concept of citizenship as institutional membership in the urban community was contained in these provisions. It did not apply in any way to those in the irregular category, that is, the vast majority of the urban populace, despite the misleading use of the word "grazhdane" for both groups. This term was simply a broad description of townspeople in general; strictly defined, it meant nothing more than dwellers within the territorial limits of a town. Regular citizens, on the other hand, were those with particular rights and obligations, mainly fiscal, relating to the town and its institutions. Their division into guilds somewhat approximates earlier developments in Western cities, the main differences being that the Russian associations were created from above rather than below, and were more heterogeneous in composition than the associations based on a common economic pursuit that were characteristic of the West.

Peter did, however, introduce another municipal institution that clearly bore the character of an urban economic association. This was the *tsekh* or guild of artisans, which Peter borrowed directly from the cities of Germany. Artisan guilds were not unknown in Russia before Peter's reign, but during the Muscovite period they

* Certain less important changes in municipal institutions were introduced by Peter earlier in his reign, but it was the regulation of 1721 that proved decisive.

had existed only in embryonic form and were not widespread.[14] The regulation of 1721, and related enactments during the years 1720–23, created a new basis for organizing artisans (*remeslenniki*) in the cities. Guilds or corporations of artisans were organized according to uniformity of trade. Internally, each tsekh was structured in accordance with the familiar Western European pattern. The highest position was occupied by the masters (*mastera*, i.e., artisans fully empowered to run their own shops), to whom were subordinated the journeymen (*podmaster'ia*) and apprentices (*ucheniki*). Each tsekh was headed by an elected elder (*al'derman* or *starshina*) and his assistant (*tovarishch*) as well as its own corporate assembly (*tsekhovoe sobranie*). Within each tsekh, the elder supervised internal regulations and standards, the quality of work, and the collection of taxes. Collectively, the elders of a given town formed a sort of advisory council to the city magistrate for matters relating to artisans. In addition, an elder—who was required to be a full-fledged master—was eligible to hold municipal office.[15]

Despite its close formal resemblance to the European artisan guild, the Russian tsekh, reflecting the circumstances of its creation, was unique in some important respects. In addition to their leadership roles within the tsekh, the elders were expected to function as administrative and fiscal agents of the government, thus contravening the concept of the guild as an independent association of producers. Furthermore, in contrast to the guilds of Western Europe, the tsekh was not a truly closed corporation. Not only was its membership not restricted numerically, it was even open to such non-urban categories of the population as manorial serfs if the serf was granted authorization to join by his lord. Within certain limitations, membership was not required of all local artisans. Finally, there were no provisions for limiting the quantity of items produced in each tsekh. In short, the tsekh was not so much a voluntary association for protective and monopolistic purposes as it was a quasi-governmental administrative unit aimed at providing a more rational basis for the organization and stimulation of production and for taxing the urban population.[16] Nevertheless, it more closely resembled a voluntary economic organization than did the gil'dii, the structure of which encompassed but did not define the tsekhi.

Catherine's restructuring of urban society, which began well before the publication of the charter of 1785, delineated the concept

of urban citizenship much more sharply and clearly than the enactments of Peter. Peter's first and second guilds of regular citizens,
which had vaguely combined overlapping criteria of wealth, occupation, and prestige, were abolished. The upper guild was replaced
by the merchant class (*kupechestvo*), consisting of persons engaged
in commerce or industry who possessed certain minimum amounts
of capital. The subdivision of the merchants into three guilds (which
dated back to 1742), again based on possession of capital, rounded
out the structure of what became the upper stratum of the urban citizenry in the 1770's. The lower guild was replaced by the *meshchanstvo* (*meshchanin*, loosely translated, means "petty burgher"), which
consisted of all persons engaged in trade or production who did not
possess sufficient capital to belong to the merchant class.[17] Members
of tsekhi were simultaneously part of the meshchanstvo, just as they
had once been part of the second guild. The remainder of the town
population, the equivalent of Peter's irregular citizens, continued
to be institutionally unrepresented. They were merely dwellers in
the town, and in no sense a part of urban society.

The charter of 1785 substantially broadened the concept of urban
citizenship by extending representative institutions to layers of
population that were not necessarily engaged in commercial-industrial activity. Six urban groups were delineated, each with its own
privileges, obligations, and group organization, and encompassing
many of the persons who had earlier been counted as irregular citizens. Taken together, the associations of the six groups constituted
either the actual or the electoral basis for participation in all the
administrative and judicial institutions of the city, including, of
course, the Shestiglasnaia Duma. As noted earlier, this did not mean
a significant increase in urban autonomy in relation to the state;
but it did mean that within the narrow limits of such autonomy as
existed, the juridical personality of the city was now expressed in
the collective institutions of several associations of urbanites, each
holding a distinct juridical status.

For our purposes, the most important of the six groups were the
merchants (of all three merchant guilds), the members of artisan
tsekhi, and the miscellaneous townspeople who permanently resided and worked in the city but did not meet the requirements of
any of the other classifications. The last-named group, known as
posadskie, extended institutional representation to much of the

lower stratum of urban population that had been previously designated as irregular. The three remaining groups extended municipal
representation to nobles with urban dwellings, certain foreigners,
the educated, and other elements of the old irregular and regular
sectors. Under the new arrangements, posadskie and members of
the meshchanstvo (or meshchane) seem to have become virtually
synonymous, except that members of tsekhi continued to be meshchane in a technical sense. Remaining outside the six groups were,
among others, peasants who temporarily resided and worked in the
city while on leave from their estates.[18]

Under the law of 1785 there were some changes in the position
of the tsekhi, but essentially they retained their former structure.
Their representation in the duma made them a component part of
the urban legal community, whereas previously they had merely
been seen as an economic interest group with representatives who
consulted with municipal authorities. Their internal structure remained approximately the same, although the regulations governing them were spelled out in much greater detail. In one respect
the tsekhi were now given more of the character of a closed corporation: the provisions that had allowed for the temporary enrollment
of peasant craftsmen in tsekhi were eliminated. They were, however, restored by Paul I in 1796.[19]

The urban structure that has just been outlined continued, with
some modifications, to prevail until the municipal reforms of 1870.*
It provided the framework within which the growth of urban
industry took place in the nineteenth century. Ironically, it was a
framework that had originated, in part, as an attempt to duplicate
the more vital economic life of Western European cities, yet it was
introduced just at the time when the medieval organization of the
European city was approaching its demise. On the Continent, the
French Revolution had dealt a violent and destructive blow to the
corporate stratification of urban economic life—to the guild system
in particular—not only in France itself but in many areas of Germany that came under French domination. German cities, which
had provided the model for many of the changes introduced in Russia in the eighteenth century, continued to divest themselves of cor-

---

* For the sake of brevity, I have omitted from the discussion certain changes in urban
policy that were introduced during the brief reign of Paul I, but were essentially
reversed during the reign of Alexander I.

porate monopolistic institutions in the years following the defeat of Napoleon, in part under the pressure of new industrial forms, in part as a result of the official policies of some of the German states. Russia, by contrast, had by the time of the French Revolution just succeeded in establishing those urban forms, or an approximation thereof, which in other parts of Europe were coming to be viewed as obstacles to industrial progress. The Russian city had now been defined, but in terms appropriate to Western Europe's past, not its present and future.

Precisely because the Russian version was weaker than its original models, however, it was a less serious obstacle to industrial progress. No familial or kinship patterns, such as were frequently found in the medieval city, precluded the mobility of urban citizens among the various categories. Thus a master artisan could transfer to the third guild of merchants merely by accumulating the requisite amount of capital, as could a meshchanin who engaged in petty trade. Similarly, a third- or second-guild merchant could rise to the next highest guild on the same basis, and, of course, fall back if his capital diminished. Any meshchanin or posadskii was eligible to enroll in a tsekh and work his way up to the position of a master. Finally, even a serf, provided his lord approved, could temporarily enroll in a tsekh. The Russian tsekh had never been conceived as a force exerted in the restraint of trade to prevent competition outside the guild structure. Hence the type of defensive class struggle waged by German artisans in the post-Napoleonic period against the intrusions of individual capitalists—an important aspect of the revolutions of 1848—was not to be found in the nineteenth-century Russian city.[20]

In view of these circumstances, it is difficult to accept the contention of the historian P. G. Ryndziunskii that the urban structure, that is, the municipal institutions and the corresponding legal relationships, was in serious conflict with the requirements of urban economic development. Among the prominent examples cited by that author arc the fiscal and military obligations that bound the meshchane and artisans to the state, the fiscal obligations of meshchane and merchants to their respective corporate organizations, and the stringent regulations covering the acquisition and use of internal passports, severely limiting mobility between cities.[21] Certainly these and other related aspects of the urban structure were out of phase with the principles of economic liberalism that were coming to dominate the life of Western European cities. Only the elimination of the entire system of fiscal-juridical classification would have opened the Russian city to complete freedom of trade and industrial activity and eliminated the necessity to cross complex bureaucratic boundaries in order to change one's economic status. Yet the examples cited by Ryndziunskii were more in the nature of harassments than basic obstacles to economic activity. The procedures for traversing the barriers between urban juridical groups were time-consuming and even distasteful, but they did not constitute serious impediments. Nor were the corporate fiscal obligations of urban groups of a nature that would prevent capital accumulation or penalize economic success. In short, the alleged contradictions between urban institutions and the requirements of economic progress were more theoretical and formal than real. Merchant guilds, corporations of artisans, and related medieval forms appear anachronistic in the nineteenth-century world of liberal economics, but they were not necessarily structural barriers to economic development.

If Ryndziunskii's argument is on weak ground as it relates to economic activity among the urban citizens, it is on sounder ground in relation to urban dwellers who stood outside those categories, that is, most notably, city-dwelling peasants. It is in this area that one indeed finds a serious conflict between the urban social structure and the process of economic urbanization. Whereas my main concern will be with the relevance of this conflict to factory labor, it is necessary to examine first the broader problem of the position of urban peasants with respect to the institutions of the permanent urban citizenry.

The growth of city populations, both in absolute numbers and in proportion to the population of the country as a whole, is a fundamental, if narrow, aspect of the process of urbanization. Given the poor sanitary conditions and high death rates that prevailed among the lower classes of most pre-modern cities, new immigrations were always a vital source of urban populations.[22] For Russian cities not only to maintain themselves but to grow, in the absence of a natural increase of urban population, they had to and did depend on peasant immigration.[23] Mainly as a result of peasant movement to the cities, Russia's urban population grew substantially in the first half of the nineteenth century. Between 1825 and 1856, the urban population of European Russia increased by nearly two million, or approximately 59 per cent.[24]

Part of this increase took place within the urban citizenry, the rate of growth of which actually exceeded by a slight margin that of the urban population as a whole. This would indicate some degree of penetration into the meshchanstvo and merchant classes by former peasants. But in actual numbers the increase was significantly greater in the noncitizen categories, that is, among the peasant immigrant population; the combined total of meshchanstvo and merchants represented only about seven hundred thousand of the two million figure mentioned above.[25] Thus to a great extent the growth of urban population, although it also involved a growth of the urban citizenry, was primarily manifested among that segment of the population for whom the city was a more or less temporary residence and workplace rather than a permanent legal domicile.

In the absence in Russia of the old Western European concept that "city air makes free," residence and labor in the city in no way transformed the juridical status of the peasants who left their villages in quest of urban employment. The one regular urban group to which the peasants had relatively easy access, in that membership did not require emancipation, was the tsekh; but those who succeeded in joining were considered only temporary members, and did not enjoy the rights and privileges of full membership in the artisan community. It was, of course, possible for liberated and runaway peasants, the former legally and the latter by stealth, to find their way into the meshchanstvo, and I have quoted figures indicating that many managed to do so. But the large majority of furloughed peasants (*otkhodniki*) remained outside the pale of urban citizenship. For all intents and purposes they constituted the nineteenth-century equivalent of Peter the Great's irregular citizens, the main group that Catherine's extension of the concept of urban citizenry failed to encompass.

Nor could it, given the continued existence of serfdom. To break down the barriers to the assimilation of peasants into the urban juridical order would have been tantamount to assaulting the prerogatives of the serf-owning nobility. But herein lay the conflict between the existing order and the process of urbanization, for the maintenance of these barriers also precluded the possibility of achieving a stable urban society. Restrictions on the expansion of the concept of urban citizenry that had begun in the eighteenth century meant that precisely those people who provided the real basis for urban growth would be largely excluded from the corporate life of the city. Even *pomeshchiki* (gentry landlords), in whose interest it was to restrict the transformation of their peasants into urban citizens, contributed to the conflict by encouraging peasant participation in urban economic activity as they became more and more dependent on quitrent (*obrok*) and mixed forms of peasant dues.[26]

Although the government responded to this conflict with some vacillation, fundamentally, as long as serfdom was upheld, the regime could only emphasize the barriers between otkhodniki and the urban classes. Complicated bureaucratic obstacles were placed before peasants who were eligible to enroll in the various urban societies. On the other hand, as peasant economic activity became an increasingly important aspect of city life, new means for taxing, controlling, and therefore defining the peasant population of cities had to be sought. In the course of the first quarter of the nineteenth century, special intermediate classifications, bearing their own special obligations and privileges, were created for peasants who engaged in urban trade. The creation of this new class of *torguiushchie* peasants (with several subdivisions) caused some consternation among the merchants, but their objections were short-lived. The heavy financial obligations placed on the trading peasants reduced their power as an economic threat, and the very existence of the new classification decreased the likelihood of large-scale peasant transfers into either the merchant class or the meshchanstvo. It is true that in the second quarter of the nineteenth century some of the burdens on the trading peasants were lightened, and there was some easing of the restrictions on transfer to urban categories, particularly for state peasants. But the basic structure of the urban population remained unchanged: a full urban citizenry having relative mobility within its ranks, but operating somewhat as a closed caste in relation to other city dwellers; a mass of peasant otkhodniki having no juridical relationship to the city; an intermediate group of trading peasants, heavily burdened and restricted in its economic activity, but granted some recognition as at least a temporary urban group.[27]

It was the masses of otkhodniki that provided the potential recruiting ground for an industrial labor force. Indeed, the entire period from the middle of the eighteenth century to the middle of the nineteenth was marked by the steady displacement, in relative terms, of "possessional" laborers (the descendants of peasants and others who, from the time of Peter the Great, had been transformed into the inalienable property of particular factories) by freely hired workers (workers who, though likely to be serfs, were employed in a factory on a contractual basis).[28] Even in the eighteenth century freely hired labor predominated in Moscow, St. Petersburg, Riga, and other urban areas. By the early nineteenth century freely hired workers were more numerous than possessional workers in the manufacture of finished products throughout the country, and by the advent of Alexander II they constituted more than 80 per cent of the labor force.[29] Some of this number could, in urban areas, be recruited from among the local meshchane, but the most common source in the more industrialized towns was the peasant otkhodniki.[30]

The presence of large numbers of otkhodniki guaranteed a numerically adequate labor supply in the few Russian cities where the market for factory workers increased significantly in the first half of the nineteenth century. But if we examine the position of the otkhodniki with an eye toward the future of industrialization as a process involving the introduction of mechanization, the application of efficient techniques and routinized patterns of employment and training, in short, if we think in terms of industrial revolution rather than mere arithmetic expansion, the position of the otkhodniki must be viewed in another light. In a famous article, Alexander Gerschenkron, in discussing the relationship between industrial backwardness and the available labor supply, writes:

The overriding fact to consider is that industrial labor in the sense of a stable, reliable, and disciplined group that has cut the umbilical cord connecting it with the land and has become suitable for utilization in factories is not abundant but extremely scarce in a backward country. Creation of an industrial labor force that really deserves its name is a most difficult and protracted process.[31]

The otkhodniki, of course, had not cut the umbilical cord. Legal, financial, and familial obligations tied to their villages even those whose sojourns in the city were prolonged. In the absence of membership in any of the urban corporate groups, what countervailing institutional ties did they have to the city?

If we exclude those otkhodniki who were self-employed as tradesmen and those who were temporarily attached to a tsekh, there was only one official municipal institution to which the otkhodnik was in any way attached. This was the so-called address office (*adresnaia kontora* or *ekspeditsiia*), introduced in Moscow and St. Petersburg in 1809 and in other cities soon thereafter. An essential function of the address office was surveillance and control over domicile, movement, employment, and general conduct of those peasant workers, the large majority, who stood outside the jurisdiction of a tsekh. All new arrivals in a city, which meant primarily peasants, were required to register with the address office, where they surrendered their peasant passports. In return for their passport and the payment of a fee, they received a permit or ticket (*bilet*) that entitled them to live in the city for a stipulated time period. Since the peasant could not travel beyond the city limits without surrendering his permit and retrieving his passport, the system had the effect of attaching him to the city and accounting for his whereabouts for the duration of his stay. In a sense the address office thus assumed some of the control functions that were invested in the master-serf relationship when the peasant was in his village. The essentially police character of the functions of the address office was well understood by those government officials who were responsible for maintaining internal order.[32]

The remaining institutions that affected the lives of otkhodniki in the city were not official ones. First, there were the branch offices of the patrimonial or seigneurial administration of the estate from which the peasant came. Pomeshchiki often established such offices in cities where a significant number of their obrok serfs were working. Thereby, not only could the general conduct of the peasants be supervised during their absence from the village, but close track could be kept of the income and expenses of the peasants and their quitrents manipulated accordingly, thus creating a sort of negative sliding scale on the peasants' earning power. It is obvious that only the more well-to-do pomeshchiki could afford to establish and maintain urban offices of this sort, but many of the less well-to-do simply invested the same supervisory duties in the person of a peasant elder. In either case, the pomeshchik was attempting to recreate the traditional patterns of rural authority in an urban setting.[33]

Second, there was the *artel'*. The artel' was the traditional association of peasants, usually from the same rural commune, who worked or sought work together away from the village. If the estate office represented the extension of seigneurial authority, the artel' was the extension of communal custom to the city. Indeed the two institutions sometimes merged, in that it was often the elder chosen by the artel' members who served as the pomeshchik's representative in the city in the absence of an office. Thus the same usurpation of a grass-roots peasant institution that the historian Michael Confino describes as having taken place on the land also took place in the city, where the artel' was partially transformed into a vehicle for extending seigneurial authority. On the other hand, the artel' was the only institution capable of mitigating the isolation of the peasant otkhodnik in a strange city and allowing him to share the burden of his employment and subsistence problems with fellow villagers. The artel', like the estate office, was essentially a rural institution physically relocated in an urban area; in no sense was it an organization with official corporate standing or juridical recognition, on either the municipal or (until 1902) the state level. In short, of the three institutions that affected the city lives of peasant otkhodniki, one was essentially an organ of police control, and the other two actually served to segregate the otkhodniki from existing municipal institutions and to emphasize their extra-urban position.[34] Instead of offsetting the otkhodniki's exclusion from the urban corporate groups, each of the three institutions reinforced that tendency and strengthened the "umbilical cord" that bound the otkhodniki to the land. The otkhodniki, a real and potential source of industrial labor, were far from being integrated into the towns in and near which industry was beginning to develop.

Official Attitudes and Policies

The attitude of the tsarist regime toward urban industrial growth and the urban industrial worker in the first half of the nineteenth century cannot be directly deduced from its attitude toward industrialization in general. Something of a consensus seems to have emerged in recent American and Soviet studies of the economic policies of the regime as they related to industrial development. The formulations, of course, are different: the Americans stress the priorities and subjective attitudes of policy makers, whereas the author of the most recent Soviet work employs the categories of class conflict. Thus Walter Pintner tells us that "the main weight of the evidence is that the men who ran the government did not consider the problem of industry to be very important.[35] N. S. Kiniapina, on the other hand, depicts the government of Nicholas I as attempting to move in the direction of industrialization, but making only limited progress owing to the restraints imposed by the anti-industrial interests of an influential segment of the gentry.[36] Yet despite these differences in interpretation and formulation, scholars in the two countries give strikingly similar impressions of government industrial policy.

Some measures were introduced that were clearly pro-industrial in character and intent: the encouragement of advanced technical education and technical publications; the granting of subsidies, premiums, and privileges to certain industrialists (emphasized by Kiniapina); the mounting of industrial exhibitions; the creation of a Manufacturing Council in 1828. But these measures were very limited both in degree and in kind. Even E. F. Kankrin, who as Minister of Finance (1823–44) was among the most conservative officials with regard to industrialization, was willing to support them. Other measures were introduced that were evidently favorable to at least some branches of industry, although the furthering of industrialization was not necessarily their intent: high tariffs on the importation of certain products; the beginnings of railroad construction; the stabilization of the currency. But whether because these policies were motivated by considerations other than industrial expansion, or because of responses to pressures exerted by the land-owning nobility, they had only a limited and ambivalent effect on industrial growth. The solvency of the nobility and the maintenance of military power took precedence over investment in industry, and military power was still only vaguely seen to be related to industrial development. Whether because of conflicting class interests or simply because of a conservative economic outlook, tsarist policy could play only a minor and hesitant role in the industrial growth of Russia during the first half of the nineteenth century. The full significance of most of the measures taken during that period were not felt until the decades following the Crimean War, when a more fundamental commitment to industrial expansion was made.[37]

But government attitudes toward urban industry and the urban worker, our main concern here, did not flow logically out of the government's general approach to industrialization. Throughout the reign of Nicholas I, various government officials made both positive and negative judgments regarding urban industry that did not necessarily depend upon their respective positions toward industry in general. Indeed, it is possible to speak with accuracy of a widespread official hostility toward the growth of urban industrial centers that was much stronger and clearer than any alleged hostility toward industrialization as such. Whereas industrialization in general was almost never rejected outright, not even by the most confirmed advocates of an agrarian economy, the recently evolved industrial cities of England and parts of Western Europe were almost universally condemned in government circles. No one reacted favorably to the prospect that such cities might be arising in Russia.

Actually, the real division that existed among government officials was not over the undesirability of Western-type industrial cities, about which they all agreed, but over the likelihood of their arising in Russia. Two distinct points of view may be identified, one designated "optimistic," the other "pessimistic," although neither was to become a clear guideline to policy. Briefly, the optimistic view maintained that the existence of factories in Russian cities was at least tolerable since, under existing conditions, they were not likely to be transformed into true factory cities of the undesirable European type. The pessimistic view, which tended to come to the fore at times of revolutionary unrest in the West, was that the only real security against the duplication of Western urban unrest in Russia was the curtailing of urban industry. The key to the difference between the two views lay in the degree of confidence with which one viewed Russia's capacity for counteracting the danger of proletarianization inherent in urban industry.

The pessimists, among whom one must count Nicholas I, lacked such confidence. Although Pintner is correct in denying that fear of the growth of an urban proletariat was a primary factor governing industrial policies, there is ample evidence that this fear did begin to arise in government circles in the 1830's and persisted thereafter as an important consideration in government policy toward industry and labor in the larger, more prominent cities.* The first evidence of official alarm concerning the concentration of industry and industrial workers in large cities dates from 1832.† In that year the Tsar expressed a strong interest in arresting the concentration of industry in the city of Moscow and ordered his Minister of Finance to investigate the feasibility of locating more factories in smaller, district towns. "Isn't it necessary *from a political point of view*," Nicholas remarked, "to halt the further aggregation of factory people in Moscow?"[38] This reference to political considerations suggests the possibility that recent revolutionary events in Europe had provoked the Tsar's new alarm concerning factories and factory workers in Moscow. Kankrin's response to the Tsar confirms this hypothesis while providing us with the first known expression of the optimistic view.

It was precisely the umbilical cord, the legal and institutional ties that bound the otkhodnik to the village and kept him from being fully integrated into the urban structure, that provided the basis for the optimistic outlook. It is ironic that Kankrin, a leading pessimist about Russian industrialization in general, was a prominent representative of the optimistic view of urban industry. Writing in November 1834, Kankrin makes it abundantly clear that the Tsar's initial remarks—and whatever exchanges may have taken place in the interval—were inspired by recent events in Western Europe. In agreeing with the Tsar's general apprehensions concerning the danger of large concentrations of workers, Kankrin refers directly to Lyon ("a completely turbulent city") and to the industrial cities of England as examples. Lyon, of course, had just experienced its second weavers' insurrection in less than three years,

---

* Pintner states that Soviet historians Kiniapina, Rozhkova, and others are "without justification" in suggesting that "a distrust or fear of the urban proletariat appeared very early and rapidly became the primary factor that governed the state's attitude toward industry." This formulation somewhat overstates the positions taken by Kiniapina and Rozhkova. W. M. Pintner, *Russian Economic Policy Under Nicholas I* (Ithaca, N.Y., 1967), p. 98.

† Kiniapina claims that the fear existed as early as 1826, when certain restrictions on the location of urban industry were introduced. She asserts that the considerations of health and sanitation advanced by the government were merely a "pretext," and that the restrictions actually reflected the government's fear of large concentrations of urban workers. However, she does not support this view with any specific evidence. N. S. Kiniapina, *Politika russkogo samoderzhaviia v oblasti promyshlennosti (20–50 gody XIX v.)* (Moscow, 1968), pp. 414–15. Cf. Ryndziunskii, pp. 183–84.

the first revolt having antedated the Tsar's original remarks. The reference to Birmingham "and other industrial cities" of England undoubtedly alluded to the workingmen's agitation that had been recently spreading in various parts of England. Kankrin concedes to the Tsar that these examples demonstrate the general validity of his fears: the poverty of workers inclines them toward despair, impulsiveness, and a "spirit of coalition," making their concentration in cities a serious hazard. But here the two points of view part company, for according to Kankrin, the danger was confined to Western Europe, while Russia remained immune. The situation in Russia was completely different from that in Western Europe because in Russia "the workers in urban factories consist almost exclusively of furloughed peasants . . . who return to their homes when work is suspended; hence a significant increase in the urban population at the expense of the peasantry is impossible." In other words, the concentration of workers in urban areas was a serious danger only if the workers represented a permanent and growing presence in the city, that is, only if the umbilical cord was cut. As Kankrin saw it, the attachment of the peasant worker to the land precluded that danger in Russia. This was the core of the optimistic outlook.[39]

The Tsar's fears were not assuaged by Kankrin's assurances; or, in the words of one Soviet historian, his views were "somewhat more farsighted" than those of his Minister of Finance.[40] Nicholas raised the issue again several times in succeeding years. In 1835 he again ordered an investigation into the feasibility of spreading industry more evenly among provincial towns; in 1836 tax exemptions were granted to manufacturers who constructed their factories in the provinces; in 1840 a commission was formed to examine the desirability of restricting the growth of large mechanized industry in the city of Moscow and the surrounding district. The commission did not recommend restrictions, but it did favor further subsidies for manufacturers who built outside the city. Although it is difficult to pinpoint the degree to which each of these measures was prompted by considerations relating to internal order rather than health and sanitation, it is clear that the problem of "the aggregation of a proletariat" (skoplenie proletariata) played a role in the deliberations of the 1840 commission.[41]

The European revolutions of 1848 reinforced the pessimistic

view and brought it into sharper focus. Apprehensions concerning the formation of an urban proletariat were now stated directly and explicitly, and factory workers in the larger cities—particularly Moscow and St. Petersburg—were watched with special care by the police. The reinforcement of police surveillance over the urban populace began almost as soon as the first news of revolution in Paris reached Russia, and several of the orders issued in this connection by the political police (the Third Section) included special instructions to observe factory workers.[42] It was shortly thereafter that A. A. Zakrevskii, the new military governor of Moscow, a former Minister of Internal Affairs, and a close confidant of the Tsar, made what can be regarded as the classic statement of the pessimistic view. Addressing himself to Minister of Finance F. P. Vronchenko (in October 1848) and then to the Tsar himself (in December), Zakrevskii vigorously renewed the argument against the expansion of industry in Moscow, and left no doubt about his reasons. The existence of thirty-six thousand Moscow factory workers, and of thirty-seven thousand peasant-workers in various other occupations who were probably susceptible to their influence, presented a serious danger to the state. The more they grew in number, the more they would become morally corrupted, tempted by violence and crime. In view of this danger, Zakrevskii cautioned that "for the preservation of calm and prosperity, which at the present time are enjoyed only by Russia [a reference to the European revolutions], the government ought not to permit the aggregation of homeless and immoral people, who readily attach themselves to every movement that is destructive of social or private tranquillity."[43] Although Zakrevskii was unable to convince the government that it should prohibit the expansion of industry in Moscow, a modified version of his proposal was approved by the Tsar and the Committee of Ministers in 1849.*

The optimistic point of view continued to be defended both

---

* Kiniapina, pp. 417–21; M. K. Rozhkova, "Ekonomicheskaia politika pravitel'stva," in M. K. Rozhkova, ed., *Ocherki ekonomicheskoi istorii Rossii pervoi poloviny XIX veka* (Moscow, 1959), p. 378. The regulations of June 28, 1849, prohibited the construction of several categories of factories, including cotton-spinning factories and foundries, in Moscow. Other types of factories could be built, and existing plants expanded, with the approval of local authorities. In practice, the regulations were to have little effect. For the full text of the regulations, see *Polnoe sobranie zakonov Rossiiskoi Imperii*, 2d Series, XXIV, No. 23358.

before and after the events of 1848. A decade after his statement of 1834, Kankrin, having just retired from the ministry, reiterated his belief in the essential difference between the urban workers of Western Europe and Russia:

In Russia factory workers and other workers come from the villages, which ... is of great value in that it prevents the excessive growth of an urban factory class that falls into poverty when work is not available. On such occasions the peasant returns to the village, and even if he has earned nothing, and has not paid his dues, he at least has a roof and his daily nourishment. Our factory class [in contrast to that of Western Europe] does not combine for the purpose of extorting pay raises. ... Work stoppages and riots do not improve the situation of factory workers and still less do they guard them against the wretched circumstances [of their lives in the West] ... It is impossible to foresee how far such people might go in their desperation under such circumstances.[44]

Kankrin's successor, Vronchenko, shared this view. His response to Zakrevskii in 1848 was to express his resentment against any comparison between Russian workers and "the homeless foreign proletarians." He noted with pride that "in Russia, and especially in Moscow . . . , the factory worker is not a native inhabitant of the city, as he is abroad." Hence the curtailment of urban industry was not a political necessity in Russia.[45]

In the early 1850's, similar thoughts were expressed by L. V. Tengoborskii, an influential official of the Ministry of Finance, adviser to Nicholas I on economic matters, and author of a major study of the Russian economy. Tengoborskii's views are of particular interest in that he was only a moderate advocate of industrial development. On economic grounds he strongly favored only those branches of industry that were directly connected to the rural economy, and he looked askance at what he held to be the artificial creation of large industrial complexes away from the villages.[46] Yet there was little question in his mind but that even with the appearance of such complexes Russia was relatively safe from the dangers that beset the social stability of Western Europe. This safety stemmed from the peasant status of the Russian factory worker: "This mixed character of cultivator and artizan [i.e., factory worker] preserves us from proletarianism, which has become the sore of so many other countries, and from the violent crises apt to occur in manufacturing countries, when, from a stagnation in trade, a number of hands are thrown out of employment."[47] Again, having described the "misery and proletarianism" that he had observed in the cotton mills of European towns, Tengoborskii assured his readers that

in regard to the moral consequences of the great development of this industry . . ., for Russia these consequences are mitigated to a certain extent by the peculiar condition of our manufacturing industry in general. A large portion of our operatives being at the same time agriculturists, and being accustomed, after working in the factories during the winter months, to return to their homes for the labors of the field, are from this double resource less exposed to the danger of proletarianism.[48]

The optimistic view, which was not confined to the Ministry of Finance,* persisted in government circles well into the reign of Alexander II. In a sense it was simply a variation on a common theme of nineteenth-century Russian thought: Russia's immunity to the social and political diseases of the West. In this case the disease was the urban industrial center found in Western Europe, invidious in its effects on the health and morality of the "proletariat" (literate Russians were familiar with the term by the 1840's), and therefore a serious threat to industrial peace and political stability. To it was counterposed the health and serenity of the industrial situation in Russia, made possible by the peasant-worker's continued ties to the land, which minimized his dependency on the sale of his labor. It was their belief in this contrast that made it possible for officials who disdained the industrial city of the West to view with relative equanimity, or at least professed equanimity, the superficial manifestations of urban industrial growth that appeared in some regions of Russia in the 1830's and 1840's. Perhaps they thought this development was not desirable—neither Kankrin nor Tengoborskii wished to encourage large urban factories—but it seemed at least to be tolerable in that it shared only the appearance and not the essence of comparable phenomena abroad. Whether in or out of the factory, in or out of the city, the Russian worker was not a proletarian, nor, it was assumed, could he become one.

In practice, however, it appears that no one seriously contemplated following either the optimistic or the pessimistic view to its logical conclusion: total nonintervention by the government in the

---

* For instance, to a greater or lesser degree it was shared by General K. F. Tol', head of the Transportation Administration from 1833 to 1842, and by Prince D. V. Golitsyn, military governor of Moscow from 1820 to 1843. Kiniapina, pp. 385, 415, 417; Rozhkova, p. 378.

situation of the urban factory worker or the prohibition of urban industry. No one seems to have seriously believed that the situation was either as idyllic or as fraught with danger as was sometimes suggested. The effective positions of the defenders of either approach resembled each other, even if their points of departure differed. Pessimists were willing to combat the dangers of proletarianization within the urban industrial context itself, reserving their outright assaults on urban industry to special occasions (as in 1848–49); optimists were generally willing to grant that the forces which naturally worked against proletarianization in Russia needed reinforcement during the period of the peasant's sojourn in the city. When the two approaches converged in the form of intensified police surveillance over otkhodniki, or the applying of existing police controls more specifically to urban factory workers, no special controversies resulted. But the integrity of the two approaches also began to yield to another alternative: the advocacy of certain kinds of labor legislation aimed at governing the relations between workers and their employers. Here were the beginnings of an important paradox.

Inherent in the advocacy of labor legislation was a tacit admission that urban industry, however much it was feared in some government circles, was becoming a permanent feature of Russia's economic and social landscape. More important, the idea of labor legislation implied recognition that the urban factory setting generated social and political problems requiring special measures not applicable to, and perhaps even contradicting, existing social and political relations. Such measures not only undermined the assumptions of the optimistic outlook, they called into question the traditional concept of social relations that were based on juridical status and birth, and substituted a new view of social relations based on contract—a dreaded feature of the West. In other words, as a consequence of its own forebodings concerning the possible formation of an urban proletariat, the government itself, however unwittingly, began to look upon the urban workers as an economic class. The introduction of factory legislation implied the existence of a thoroughgoing division of labor. Given the existing system of agrarian relations and the weakness of the urban structure, division of labor in Russia was still minimal. It was also wholly undesirable from the point of view of both optimists and pessimists. Thus, paradoxically, labor legislation implied the very condition that its advocates still hoped to avert.

There is little evidence of official interest in the contractual relations between urban workers and their employers before the 1830's, when some officials began to look upon urban workers as a potential source of social and political unrest. As the use of freely hired labor began to spread in the second half of the eighteenth century and the early decades of the nineteenth, it was inevitable that some disputes would arise between workers and manufacturers over terms of employment, and in some cases between the manufacturer who employed the peasant-worker and the pomeshchik who remained his legal sovereign. Indeed, as early as 1767 the government had shown some awareness of the contractual problems generated by free labor when the Senate ordered that contracts—which at the time consisted mainly of simple oral agreements—must be in writing and registered with the local police.[49] But this order stands as an isolated and inconsequential incident, with no sequel for several decades to come.

For the remainder of the eighteenth century and the first three decades of the nineteenth, the government continued to look upon the freely hired peasant-worker as essentially no different from any other serf. This was simply a casual assumption, as distinct from the conscious and semi-ideological view of the Russian worker's character that was developed in the 1830's and 1840's in response to events in the West. The contractual relations between peasant-workers and private factory owners in cities were as unregulated as relations between lords and peasants on the estates. Significantly, official policy treated unauthorized departures from factories by freely hired workers not as breaches of contract, but as the equivalent of the crime of flight from the manorial estate.[50]

Since contractual rights and obligations were neglected, seigneurial rights took precedence whenever the two were in conflict. This meant, in effect, that whatever terms of contract the peasant-workers were "free" to conclude in the city, they were always subject to recall to the estate at the will of their lord. Here was a clear example of the workers' ties to the land that would later be celebrated by the optimists for stifling the development of a permanent urban labor force.

The practice of recall by the pomeshchik, and in general the obligation that peasant-workers continued to owe their lords even while under contract to urban manufacturers, was a source of repeated inconveniences to the manufacturers. Only once was serious consideration given to resolving this difficulty by transforming peasant-workers into a separate class of urban industrial workers whose place in the economy and the society would be determined exclusively by their place in the labor market. In 1811 the Ministry of Internal Affairs—then headed by O. P. Kozodavlev, "the first minister in Imperial Russia . . . for whom industrialization was a primary concern"[51]—contemplated creating a new special legal status for freely hired workers who had a special skill. This project would have relieved such workers of their obligations to their lords, thus ending their conflicting peasant-worker status; but, as an obvious threat to the serf-owning nobility, the project never went beyond the discussion stage.[52]

This proposal had been made two decades before the avoidance of proletarianization became a factor in government policy. Once this consideration had come to seem important, a reversion to the 1811 plan was almost inconceivable. If problems relating to contractual obligations were to be attacked at all, it would have to be within a framework that accepted, and even valued, the bifurcation of the peasant-worker's position. When he was a peasant on the land, he would be subject only to the customary practices of master-serf relations; when he hired out to work in the city, he would be subject to a legally regulated system of contractual relations; where the two situations came into direct conflict, that is, when the lord attempted to control the movements of his furloughed serfs in a manner that violated the contractual rights of the manufacturer, it was possible to shift the order of precedence without altering the basic situation. Contractual obligations could be given precedence over seigneurial rights in this limited arrangement, without directly threatening the basic prerogatives of the pomeshchik.

This approach was embodied in a series of proposals composed in December 1832—the year in which the Tsar had first voiced his fears about the concentration of urban industry—by Prince D. V. Golitsyn, military governor of Moscow. The expansion of private industry in the Moscow area was well under way at this time, and with it came an increasing number of disagreements between manufacturers and freely hired workers over terms of employment.

Golitsyn was particularly sensitive to the need for establishing some basic standards by which such disagreements could be regulated and adjudged, and for resolving the conflict between seigneurial and contractual authority over the movement of peasant-workers. Not untypically, his conviction that regulation was needed in these areas did not prevent him from defending the optimistic view that the rural ties of the Russian worker provided the chief guarantee against proletarianization. But supplementary measures were needed. His proposals were designated "measures for the termination of complaints between factory workers and factory owners," and were aimed, in part, at "the gradual improvement of the morality and education of working-class people."[53]

According to Golitsyn's plan, the seigneurial-contractual conflict was to be resolved henceforth in favor of the contractual rights of the manufacturer. A manufacturer would no longer be obligated to release his peasant-workers whenever their lord recalled them, but could count on retaining his freely hired laborers until the expiration of their peasant passports if a valid contract had been concluded. This proposal, which apparently resulted from complaints by Moscow industrialists, meant that within the limited duration of the contract and the passport, the bondage rights of the lord were temporarily suspended, the peasant-worker's ties with the countryside partially severed. Although there was nothing very daring about this plan—it left the basic prerogatives of the serf owner untouched —it did hint at a serious flaw in the optimistic perspective insofar as it temporarily suspended the very ties with the countryside that the optimists counted on to avert proletarianization, and it restricted the peasant workers' freedom of movement, since workers would sometimes use a supposed recall by their lords as an excuse for leaving the factory and returning home. More generally, the plan amounted to recognition that the dual character of the peasant worker was presenting obstacles to the rational operation of urban industries. The proposal was approved and became the first part of a "Statute on the Relations Between Factory Owners and Hired Workers" promulgated on May 24, 1835.[54]

Having proposed a framework within which contractual relations would become dominant, Golitsyn then proposed, for the first time in Russian history, to systematize the procedures governing the contractual relations between private manufacturers and their freely hired workers.* His proposals came at a time when the Moscow region was experiencing an important rise in its industrial growth. The number of factories in the province had increased substantially in recent years, and the number of factory workers had increased by nearly twenty-seven thousand in the six years preceding Golitsyn's initiative (1825–31).[55] Much of this increase was urban and suburban in character, and was particularly notable in the recently incorporated northeastern section of the city of Moscow.[56] Such rapid growth made for a relatively unstable situation, and an increasing number of disputes over terms of employment, particularly wages, were called to Golitsyn's attention at the time.[57] He was not sufficiently alarmed to agree with the Tsar's suggestion that industry be curtailed, but he now saw the need to establish a smoother, more orderly relationship between the factory owner and his employees.

The essence of Golitsyn's plan was to rationalize contractual procedures. All conditions and terms of employment were to be specified in writing; all financial transactions between manufacturers and workers were to be recorded in special workers' booklets (known variously as *raschetnye knigi, knizhki, listy,* or *tetradi*); a list of all the obligations of the workers was to be permanently posted on a factory wall. Employers and workers were to be equally bound by the terms of contract. Workers could neither quit nor ask for higher wages prior to the expiration date; employers could neither fire workers nor alter the terms of employment until that date, although a vague clause permitting the firing of workers for "improper behavior" weakened this part of the proposal. Disputes arising out of alleged violations of these procedures were to be regulated by local police officials. It was this plan, somewhat modified, that constituted the second part of the 1835 statute on relations

---

* Even in the eighteenth century, standards had been established for working conditions at various types of possessional and state factories, the possessional factories being looked upon, essentially, as held in trust for the state (see Reginald E. Zelnik, "The Peasant and the Factory," in Wayne S. Vucinich, ed., *The Peasant in Nineteenth-Century Russia* [Stanford, Calif., 1968], pp. 161–64, 169–72; and Reinhard Bendix, *Work and Authority in Industry* [New York, 1963], pp. 167 ff.). But this phenomenon had little in common with government regulation of the terms of contract between two private parties, manufacturers and freely hired workers, now proposed by Golitsyn.

between factory owners and workers. The statute was at first restricted to Moscow and St. Petersburg, but was gradually extended to other industrial regions as well.[58]

Historians have correctly stressed the practical inefficacy of the 1835 statute, the absence of adequate enforcement provisions, and the minor impact it was to have on the actual lives of workers. Yet the very fact that such measures were adopted or even proposed is significant in that it highlights certain conditions and assumptions. In attempting to systematize contractual relations, Golitsyn—and the government as a whole, to the extent that it approved his proposals—was attesting to the existence of a conflict between the demands of a rationally organized industrial system and the continued nonproletarian character of the urban labor force. The adoption of special measures that suggested the character of the urban worker as seller and the manufacturer as buyer of labor as a commodity, that stressed, in other words, the contractual or "bourgeois" aspects of their mutual relations, logically betrayed the goals of optimists and pessimists alike. Kankrin's image of the docile peasant-worker who would simply retreat to the security of the patriarchal rural community when industrial conditions were unfavorable went hand in hand with an idealized vision of the industrial employer—the patriarchal manufacturer who, through his benevolence and authority, commanded the respect and unquestioning obedience of the peasant-worker, thus assuring uniquely peaceful conditions in the Russian factory during the period of the peasant's industrial employment. The new statute came close to being an outright negation of this vision.

Indeed Kankrin himself, although not an enthusiastic partisan of the 1835 legislation, acted in such a way as to cast doubts on his alleged confidence that the abuses of factory life were bypassing Russia. The same conditions that cast doubts in Golitsyn's mind about the viability of existing relations between employers and workers apparently affected Kankrin as well. In 1835, shortly after the enactment of the Golitsyn law and only a year after his first optimistic statements regarding the situation of the Russian worker, Kankrin submitted a memorandum to the Tsar, based on data about conditions in Moscow factories recently collected by officials of his ministry. In the memorandum (entitled "On Measures Toward the Gradual Improvement of the Situation of Factory Workers") Kankrin used these data to argue that steps ought to be taken to protect factory workers from arbitrary treatment by their employers. This time the method proposed was quiet pursuasion rather than public law. The government should act quietly and with caution, "so as not to excite premature pretensions and the spirit of disobedience and grumbling among the workers."[59] Institutional changes were eschewed lest action in the public domain threaten the prestige of the patriarch-manufacturer in the eyes of the workers and thus contribute to their aggressiveness. But to propose even this cautious approach of applying behind-the-scenes pressure to individual manufacturers was an admission that the peasant-worker ideal could only be maintained if the natural rural-urban rhythm were supplemented by preventive action on the part of the government. It was as if Kankrin, having assured the Tsar that all was well, now felt obliged to take measures in order to reinforce his own confidence in the status quo.

The views expressed in Kankrin's memorandum, and in a second memorandum (1837) that was similar to the first but stressed the plight of child laborers in particular,[60] were approved by the Tsar. Accordingly, Kankrin proceeded to admonish some individual entrepreneurs through secret circulars. Most notably, he cautioned them to improve the sanitary and living conditions of their workers, to attend to the educational and religious needs of the workers' children, and—almost a tacit admission of the corrupting effects of the urban industrial environment—to see to it that workers fulfilled their financial obligations to the families they left behind in the villages.[61] Kankrin's emphasis on behind-the-scenes admonitions suggests a greater awareness on his part than on Golitsyn's that labor legislation and the public regulation of labor disputes implied a weakening of official optimism; yet evidence has recently been uncovered indicating that even Kankrin seriously contemplated introducing a form of open arbitration (as will be seen shortly).

It was the issue of child labor that most dramatically illustrated to government officials that freely hired labor, as it presently existed in Russian cities, did not quite fulfill the idyllic vision of the optimists. The use of child labor in factories, already widespread in certain industries in the eighteenth century, increased substantially in the first decades of the nineteenth. The increase—particularly notable in Moscow, Vladimir, and other provinces of the Central

Industrial Region—was a direct result of the trend toward freely hired labor. The more that industrialists were compelled to include wages as an important factor among their costs, the more they were tempted to turn to the cheapest available source of labor—women, and especially children. By the 1830's and 1840's, this practice had become a marked trend.[62]

Although Kankrin, as noted above, had taken special heed of the plight of child workers as early as 1837, the government as a whole became concerned only after a dramatic incident that occurred in 1844. It was one of the few instances of labor unrest in a privately owned factory employing freely hired labor in the first half of the nineteenth century. At the basis of the conflict at the Voznesensk factory—a cotton-spinning mill located some thirty or forty miles to the north of the city of Moscow—was the continued use of so-called *kabal'nye* (literally, bonded or enslaved) laborers. Technically, these were freely hired workers in the sense that they worked for wages, on a contractual basis; but their contracts, unlike those of other freely hired workers, were concluded not between their employer and themselves but between their employer and their lord. In short, they were, in effect, rented out to the manufacturer by the pomeshchik, who received their wages himself. This thinly disguised form of forced labor had become especially widespread after 1816, when the outright purchase of serfs for possessional labor in factories was prohibited definitively. In 1825 the practice had been outlawed by the government, but the prohibition was easily evaded and kabal'nye workers, including young children, continued to be used.[63]

Kabal'nye workers were still being used at the Voznesensk factory in the 1840's. On the basis of a contract between the factory owners and a certain pomeshchik, peasants were hired involuntarily for periods of four years. In many cases their families were broken up during that time. Matters came to a head in 1844, when several hundred workers announced their refusal to continue factory work under the existing circumstances. The workers were adamant, and only a show of military force by local officials persuaded them to return to the factory rather than to their village.[64]

This incident bore the stamp of traditional peasant protest. The peasants' refusal to work was provoked not by a desire to change their working conditions or wages but by their wish to return to the land; essentially their conflict was with the pomeshchik for having hired them out, rather than with the manufacturer for having hired them. Here was evidence, in other words, that industrial employment of workers with strong ties to the land could be a source of conflict rather than stability.

The government considered the incident serious enough to warrant a thorough investigation of the situation of factory workers in the Moscow area, which led in turn to Russia's first legislation governing the use of child labor in private factories. The relationship between the causes of the original incident and the nature of the legislation it led to lay in the fact that the investigation revealed, among other things, the existence of some three thousand child laborers (most of them farmed out by pomeshchiki on the basis of illegal kabal'nye contracts), of whom more than two thousand were forced to work at night. The result was the promulgation, on August 7, 1845, of a law on child labor, the essence of which was the prohibition of night labor, defined narrowly as labor between midnight and 6:00 A.M., for children under the age of twelve.[65]

Even had it been strictly enforced, the law of 1845 could have made only a minor dent in prevailing practices. Its definition of night labor ignored the hours before midnight; it left daytime working hours unrestricted; and it allowed night labor to continue for minors aged twelve or over, a much more significant group numerically than those under twelve. One historian has even argued that the real significance of the law lay in its indirect endorsement of the exploitation of minors in private industry, which, if it had not been prohibited in the past, had not been sanctioned either.[66] One need not accept this rather strained interpretation in order to see that the law had little positive content. After a few attempts to enforce it in Moscow,[67] the law became a dead letter. Like the workers' booklets and other aspects of the legislation of 1835, the prohibition of night labor for children was looked upon as an innovation when plans for factory legislation were again considered in subsequent years. The real significance of the 1845 legislation—as of the statute of 1835—lay not in its implementation but in the very fact that it was proposed and approved.*

Several other items of labor legislation were proposed and dis-

* Unlike the 1835 statute, the law of 1845 was not even registered in the official digest of Russian laws (Svod zakonov). The common assumption that the child labor law of 1882 was the first in Russian history is technically erroneous, but for practical purposes correct.

cussed in government circles before the Crimean War. They were mainly attempts to strengthen the enforcement and extend the provisions of the statute of 1835.* Between 1836 and 1843 a proposal for establishing special industrial tribunals (*manufakturnye raspravy*) was debated in various government bodies. The tribunals would have had the power to arbitrate disputes between workers and manufacturers, and would therefore have put real teeth in the 1835 statute. But although even Kankrin, despite his preference for secretive noninstitutionalized methods, seems to have viewed it favorably, the proposal was eventually allowed to lapse, in part because of a failure to reach agreement on the composition of the tribunals.[68]

A similar but more daring proposal was put forth in 1845 by the civil governor of Moscow, I. Kapnist, who had played an important role in the investigation that exposed the abuse of child labor. Its most interesting feature, the introduction of arbitrators (*posredniki*) in disputes between labor and management, may be viewed as a new version of the abortive plan to create industrial tribunals. This version, however, was distinguished by the bold and novel notion that workers (elected from among those with "the best moral character") should themselves be included among the arbitrators. No manufacturer was to take action on a disputed matter without the participation of worker-arbitrators from his factory. In the words of one member of the Manufacturing Council, the measure "would have the effect of making the worker into a judge of his own employer." This extremely controversial proposal was heatedly discussed over a three-year period.[69]

Although the plan was supported by the military governor of Moscow, A. G. Shcherbatov (to whom it is sometimes erroneously attributed), it received little sympathy in the two most relevant ministries—Finance and Internal Affairs. In any case, whatever slim chance existed for its approval was finally dissipated by the revolutionary events of 1848. Since the new revolutionary outbreak in the West had the effect of reviving the notion in high government circles that urban industry should be curtailed, it was highly unlikely that as daring a notion as Kapnist's would now be imple-

---

* There was a significant set of proposals in the 1840's that did not fall into this category. It was intended for St. Petersburg alone, and will therefore be discussed in the next chapter.

mented. On October 15, 1848, Minister of Internal Affairs L.A. Perovskii stated revealingly:

At this time—when the unrest in Western Europe has demonstrated how dangerous it is to generate any ideas in the working class about the independence of that class and about the creation within that class of any kind of mediating force [*posredstvuiushchaia vlast'*] between the workers and their employers—I consider it totally excessive not only to grant factory workers the right to choose their own representatives, but even to enter into any discussions of this topic.[70]

After 1848, consideration of the Kapnist proposal was not revived. Between 1850 and 1854, however, there were renewed discussions within and between various government agencies of other, less daring proposals for the strengthening of the 1835 legislation. It is noteworthy that the most important initiator of these proposals was General Zakrevskii, the military governor of Moscow, whom we have cited as an outstanding proponent of the pessimistic view in 1848. Having apparently abandoned his earlier, largely futile efforts to curtail the development of urban industry, Zakrevskii now turned to the logical alternative of attempting to minimize the frequency of contractual disputes within his jurisdiction by reinforcing the 1835 provisions for workers' booklets. More importantly, he proposed that the hitherto haphazardly applied legislation be revitalized by the establishment of a uniform, obligatory model for the booklets, and the extension of their use to all Russian factories.

By 1854 substantial agreement on Zakrevskii's plan had been reached by the Ministries of Finance and Internal Affairs, the Legal and Economic Departments of the Council of State, and the Legal ("Second") Section of the Imperial Chancellory. A tentative decision was made to introduce a uniform booklet in St. Petersburg and Moscow as a three-year experiment, after which the plan would be extended to the rest of the Empire. Although some significant differences did arise with regard to the precise content of the regulations to be included in the booklet, the establishment among these diverse branches of government of a general consensus on the need for greater uniformity and regularity in resolving industrial disputes seems to suggest that both official optimism and official pessimism were about to give way to an unequivocally institutional approach. But just as the events of 1848 had intervened to preclude the further consideration of related measures six years earlier, the tensions engendered by the outbreak of the Crimean War now brought the discussions to a halt. Under wartime conditions, declared the Council of State in the spring of 1854, at a time when "it is essential to maintain a special, augmented surveillance over factory workers, it would be extremely inappropriate to make any changes in the existing order of relations between manufacturers and workers." The Council decided to postpone further consideration of such matters "until circumstances are more appropriate."[71]

A final word needs to be said concerning attempts to give life to the enforcement provisions of the statute of 1835. The proposals mentioned thus far, though of course they contained no guarantee of justice for the worker, were in essence attempts to protect the worker from abuses and violations on the part of the manufacturer. On the other hand, new legislation that strengthened the enforcement provisions against violations by workers was actually enacted. It took the form of two new articles in the 1845 edition of Russia's criminal law code. Article 1791 made any kind of collective disobedience by workers a criminal offense, equivalent to rebellion against the authority of the government. Article 1792 made it a criminal offense for workers to stop working before the expiration of their contracts in order to obtain a raise in wages, that is, to strike.[72] Although there is no evidence that either article was actually invoked before the judicial reforms of the 1860's, we again see here a willingness to enmesh the contractual relations of labor and management into a complicated legal structure that had little in common with official ideals concerning the peasantry's relations with authority.*

All the proposals and abortive measures that marked the period between 1832 and the Crimean War had in common an implicit assumption that urban factory workers were and would remain a fairly distinct social and economic grouping, the very existence of which called for special institutional approaches that were relatively

---

* M. Tugan-Baranovskii, *Russkaia fabrika v proshlom i nastoiashchem* (3d ed., St. Petersburg, 1907), pp. 176–77, saw the new articles as a response to labor unrest in possessional and manorial factories, but failed to produce any direct evidence; he did demonstrate that article 1792 was borrowed from foreign legislation. Kiniapina (p. 409) states flatly that the new articles were a response to the Voznesensk incident, which makes more sense for article 1791 than for 1792. B. N. Kazantsev, "Istochniki po razrabotke zakonov o naemnom promyshlennom trude v krepostnoi Rossii (30-ye-nachalo 60-kh godov XIX v.)," *Problemy istochnikovedeniia*, XI (1963), 92–94, taking a more cautious approach, is inconclusive.

new to Russia: written contracts, labor arbitration, industrial courts, the regulation of child labor in private factories, and the like. Ironically, the advocates of these measures—the real implementation of which would have placed Russia ahead of even England in the field of pioneering labor legislation—included partisans of the optimistic view, for whom the measures should have been superfluous from a logical standpoint, as well as partisans of the pessimistic view, for whom such measures represented a lesser evil at best.

It would be an oversimplification, however, simply to designate the assumption that lay behind the proposals as "realistic," and contrast it with the "illusions" contained in the optimistic or pessimistic extremes. The autocratic regime of Nicholas I certainly had the power to implement the policies that would have followed from the pessimistic view—to curtail industrial development in urban areas, or at least confine it to towns that were less politically sensitive than the two capitals—without in any way weakening the underpinnings of the existing order. One can certainly argue that this approach was more realistic, as long as the peasant-worker remained in bondage, than a policy that attempted to split the personality of the peasant-worker into serf and proletarian. Serfdom as an institution demanded from the peasant docility and passiveness, and precluded his recognition as a legal personality. The legislative proposals, on the other hand, posited a worker with a definite legal personality, with clearly delineated contractual rights vis-à-vis his employer, and, in one case at least, with a mandate to participate actively, even aggressively, in regulating his life as a factory laborer. In short, they came close to positing a free man, unbound to land or lord, able to participate—at least to a limited extent—in the institutional life of the city in which he worked and resided. Emancipation and the integration of the former peasant into the regular urban community were the complementary conditions under which the projected legislation might have been made meaningful. Viewed in this light, the government's repeated retreats from these projects —especially when revolution abroad or involvement in war served to dramatize the dangers of creating "pretensions" in the lower classes—appear as sensible acts of caution by a conservative regime that was based on a system of bondage.

The optimistic view, while illusory in many ways, was realistic in one important respect. Despite occasional instances of serious unrest and an increase in the frequency of lesser disputes over terms of employment, one could still argue plausibly that the freely hired urban worker was conducting himself in apparent conformity with the optimistic ideal. No clear and present danger arose during the reign of Nicholas I that dissatisfied workers in the urban centers might become earnestly rebellious. Such incidents of collective protest as did take place occurred almost exclusively in provincial factories of the possessional or manorial type and in the remote establishments of the Ural mining and metallurgical region.* From this perspective as well it was possible to argue plausibly that the creation of new institutions involving the public enforcement of labor legislation would be unnecessarily provocative. This was a not unreasonable short-range perspective, whereas a long-range perspective was unconvincing as long as there was no comparable long-range commitment to industrial development. The conflicts and contrasts between urban industry on the one hand, and serfdom and an urban class structure that excluded most workers on the other, were disturbing but, for the moment, tolerable. This is why it was possible for an optimist like Tengoborskii to celebrate the rural, nonproletarian character of the Russian worker even while explicitly recognizing the economic drawbacks of using unstable and overly mobile peasant labor in industry, of using a peasant-worker who could "never acquire the same aptitude and dexterity as the one who is constantly employed in the same department of skilled labor."[73]

No overwhelming case could be made, then, for any one of the three different approaches that have been under discussion: placing trust in the unproletarian character of the Russian worker; averting the development of a Russian proletariat by curtailing urban industry; or attempting to control the nature of the development of the urban labor force by institutional and legislative means. Any dramatic external or internal event—revolution in the West, war, the Voznesensk unrest—was capable of shifting the balance of forces

* For a chronicle of labor unrest from 1826 to 1860, see *Rabochee dvizhenie*, I, Part II, pp. 631–49. Kiniapina (pp. 386–90) stresses what she considers to have been the growing importance of labor unrest during the same period, but admits that 1) most incidents were of a local and disorganized character, and differed but little from traditional peasant protests, and 2) they took place mainly at manorial and possessional enterprises, rather than in the more modern factories employing freely hired labor.

within the government, or even the thinking of individual officials, in one direction or another. No single approach prevailed, and the government was left to depend on the one traditional means that all could agree on to cover its vacillations and compensate for the lack of policy—surveillance and intervention by the police, and exclusion of the peasant-workers and the otkhodniki in general from all aspects of municipal life that would identify them as urban citizens as distinct from errant countrymen.

TWO

St. Petersburg Before the Reign of Alexander II

IN 1703 PETER THE GREAT began the construction of the Peter and Paul Fortress on the northern bank of the river Neva. Unaware that he was laying the foundation for what would ultimately become a great industrial center, Peter was mainly concerned with the strategic advantages of the fortress in his military conflict with the Swedes. This military concern, however, soon began to dictate the economic development of the area. Shipbuilding and armaments production kept pace with and even outstripped the growth of the fortress town. Before there was a city there was a shipyard, construction on the Admiralty Wharf having begun in 1704. St. Petersburg was soon to become the biggest shipbuilding center in Russia, as well as an important center of armaments production. These industries naturally attracted others, and soon rope, sails, and gunpowder were being manufactured in St. Petersburg along with foodstuffs and building materials to feed and house the city's growing population of soldiers, sailors, and laborers.[1]

There is evidence of some decline in the industrial development of the region after Peter's death; but the second half of the eighteenth century saw a further expansion of the armaments industry, accompanied by an increase in the production of consumer goods for the local population.[2] Altogether, it is estimated that there were some 110 factories, as distinct from artisan shops, in St. Petersburg by the end of the eighteenth century. This figure is based on a crudely drawn distinction between factories and artisan shops—the presence of sixteen or more workers providing the sole criterion—and undoubtedly gives an exaggerated picture of the extent of the city's industrialization.* Yet the figure gives some indication of the relative importance of St. Petersburg industry in Russia: since the

* Exaggerated estimates that result from use of the figure sixteen are not nearly as misleading as the estimates of pre-Soviet historians such as Tugan-Baranovskii, and even early Soviet historians such as P. Liashchenko, who drew their figures, often

total number of factories, defined in the same manner, was approximately twelve hundred, St. Petersburg accounted for some 10 percent of the total. Only the city of Moscow surpassed St. Petersburg.[3]

The number of industrial enterprises in the St. Petersburg area continued to grow in the first half of the nineteenth century. Beginning in the 1830's, however, qualitative changes began to overshadow growth. The most important innovation was the introduction of steam-driven machinery into St. Petersburg's cotton mills.

As early as 1798 St. Petersburg could boast Russia's first mechanized cotton mill, and by 1805, in the same factory, Russia's first known steam engine (a simple machine of five H. P., probably manufactured in England);[4] but it was in the 1830's that mechanization began to affect the St. Petersburg cotton industry on a significant scale. Between 1830 and the Crimean War several large mechanized and partially mechanized textile plants, mainly cotton-spinning factories, were established in and near the city. These included the factory of Baron Stieglitz (founded in 1833; later known as the Nevskii factory), the Rossiiskii (Russian) factory (1835), the Aleksandro-Nevskii factory (1837), the Novyi (New) factory (1844), and the Samsonievskii factory (1851), to mention only a few. A relatively high degree of mechanization distinguished these and other Petersburg textile factories from the textile industries of other parts of Russia. This mechanization was greatly stimulated by the decision of the English government to lift its ban on the exportation of spinning machinery in 1842; yet even in the late 1830's, the newly

---

uncritically, from official tsarist sources that counted little workshops with only two or three workers as factories. In 1946 an article appeared by a Soviet economic historian, M. Zlotnikov ("Ot manufaktury k fabrike," *Voprosy istorii*, No. 11–12 [1946]), in which he criticized this practice and revised previous figures, applying the sixteen-worker minimum as a corrective (pp. 31–39). This criterion—which Zlotnikov borrowed from Lenin—has been almost universally used by Soviet historians since that time, and though it is difficult to see the magical quality in the number sixteen, this is clearly an improvement over past practices. Lenin chose the figure because it was used in an 1895 statute, along with other criteria, to distinguish factories from smaller enterprises. The figure also appeared as a dividing line in earlier tsarist legislation, for example in the guild statute of 1824, and in an 1857 law that made it mandatory for the owners of artisan shops with more than sixteen workers to register in the third guild of merchants. It was also suggested as a dividing line between artisan shops and factories by the Minister of Internal Affairs in the early 1850's (K. A. Pazhitnov, *Problema remeslennykh tsekhov v zakonodatel'stve russkogo absoliutizma* [Moscow, 1952], p. 109). Zlotnikov, correctly understanding the need for some kind of revision, may have picked sixteen simply in order to buttress his suggestion with Lenin's authority. Cf. William L. Blackwell, *The Beginnings of Russian Industrialization* [Princeton, 1968], pp. 41–42.

founded Rossiiskii and Stieglitz factories were spending hundreds of thousands of rubles on the purchase of spinning machinery. As for weaving, mechanical looms were beginning to play an increasingly important role in the capital at a time when hand weaving still dominated in central Russia.[5]

Perhaps of equal importance to the industrial future of St. Petersburg was the development of the city's heavy industry, most notably, the machine industry. The oldest and most impressive machine works in the capital, the Baird factory, dated back to the late 1780's and gradually became the largest enterprise of its kind in the city, as well as one of the first to use steam as its main source of power. Whereas the Baird factory was privately owned, most of the major machine and metal works in the region were owned by the government, a fact that reflected their direct military importance. Subject to the financial limitations of the heavily strained state budget, this branch of industry was fairly stagnant during the 1830's and 1840's, while the cotton-spinning industry thrived. The State Iron Foundry (later famous as the Putilov works) was even closed by the government in 1834 for economic reasons. However, in the 1850's, under the impact of the Crimean War, the period of stagnation ended. Desperately in need of metal products and machines, the government now turned to private enterprise as a solution. Some government-owned factories, such as the State Iron Foundry (1855), were placed in private hands, and new private machine works were founded (mainly by foreigners) with government encouragement. Lessner's cast-iron foundry and machine works, the San Galli machine works, the Siemens and Halske machine works, the Nevskii shipbuilding and machine factory, the Nobel steamship works, and the factory of MacPherson and Carr (later called the Baltic shipbuilding and machine works) were all founded in St. Petersburg and its suburbs between about 1853 and 1857. The high prices that the government was willing to pay for armaments was the principle cause of the appearance of these new enterprises, as well as of the founding of four new factories producing bronze products in roughly the same period. The production of machines and heavy metal goods was replacing cotton spinning as the most dramatically progressing branch of St. Petersburg industry.[6]

Another important qualitative change in St. Petersburg industry lay in the financial organization of many of the new factories. Several of the cotton-spinning factories mentioned earlier were founded and owned not by rich individuals—as had been the pattern for private factories since the time of Peter the Great—but were organized instead on a financial basis almost completely unknown to Russian industry before the 1830's, that of the European-type stock company (*aktsionernoe obshchestvo*). The first such company in Russia that involved itself in industry (among other things) was the famous Russian-American company, founded in 1799 with a capital of well over a million rubles. This company remained an isolated phenomenon, however, and private industry remained the exclusive domain of individual entrepreneurs, operating within the limits of their personal wealth (or of government subsidies), until the 1830's, when several new companies were founded. The largest and most important of these was the Society for the Organization of a Cotton-Spinning Manufactory in St. Petersburg, founded in 1836. Between 1830 and 1854, 70 stock companies of varying sizes were chartered by the government. While they were chartered to operate in various parts of Russia, the fact that the average company began with a capital exceeding one million rubles was mainly a reflection of the large size of some of the companies founded in the capital. The Novyi and Rossiiskii cotton-spinning factories were among the joint-stock companies in which great sums of capital were invested.[7]

Some of the machine and metallurgical factories founded in St. Petersburg around the time of the Crimean War, even if they bore the name and reflected the initiative of an individual entrepreneur, were also organized as joint-stock companies. In contrast to the companies that had been formed in the textile industries, these new companies were strongly encouraged by the militarily humiliated government, both during and immediately following the war. Lacking resources of its own because of wartime expenditures, but anxious to push ahead with a railroad and shipbuilding program, the government not only came increasingly to see advantages in private enterprise but began to recognize the superiority of the joint stock principle as well. Important examples of machine and metal factories founded on this basis are the Lessner (or Samsonievskii) works (initial capital—three million rubles) and the St. Petersburg metal factory (one million rubles), both of which were to figure among the industrial giants of the region in subsequent years.[8]

Both quantitatively and qualitatively, then, there were signs that the industrial revolution was penetrating St. Petersburg during the reign of Nicholas I. As one of the few centers of industry in an agrarian country, St Petersburg became well acquainted with Western-style stock companies, the importation, manufacture, and use of up-to-date machinery, and the appearance of increasingly large-scale enterprises. The impact of these changes should not be exaggerated, especially since there were whole branches of St. Petersburg industry that were untouched by them. Moreover, if we define industrial revolution broadly, as a phenomenon encompassing overall social and institutional changes, then not only Russia as a whole but even the more industrially advanced St. Petersburg region cannot be said to have experienced an industrial revolution by the end of the reign of Nicholas I. If, however, we understand the concept as applying only to changes in industry and industrial technology, it does have a limited application to St. Petersburg.[9] St. Petersburg was not distinguished from other Russian cities by any general transformation of her economy or social structure in these years, but the series of technological and organizational changes that took place within the city's two most important industrial branches constituted important trends, the significance of which would increase in the years ahead. To what degree were these innovations matched by corresponding changes in the composition and pattern of recruitment of the industrial labor force?

In eighteenth-century St. Petersburg the largest single group of factory workers was to be found in those branches of industry that were directly related to the production of armaments. In the first half of the century—in keeping with the pattern established by Peter the Great—most of these establishments were owned and operated by the state, and most of the workers therefore were state peasants, assigned to compulsory labor in factories. By the second half of the eighteenth century, however, the emphasis on government enterprise initiated by Peter had begun to dwindle, and the relative importance of privately owned factories began to increase. With this change came a corresponding shift in the numerical balance between state peasants and freely hired workers, in favor of the latter. New private metallurgical factories, founded either by individual merchants or members of the nobility, began to make extensive use of freely hired labor, as did most branches of light industry (with some notable exceptions). As a result freely hired workers already represented well over half of the workers in St. Petersburg enterprises by the 1760's, and well over 60 per cent by the 1770's, percentages unmatched in any other region of Russia.[10] The growing predominance of freely hired labor in the St. Petersburg region continued into the nineteenth century, reaching 73 per cent of the factory workers of St. Petersburg province by 1825.[11]

As was the case in other parts of Russia, most of these freely hired workers were recruited from among the peasant otkhodniki and, from the point of view of juridical status, were manorial or state peasants. St. Petersburg was experiencing the growth of urban population through peasant migration that, as discussed in the previous chapter, characterized European Russia as a whole in the first half of the nineteenth century. Between 1800 and 1825, the population of the capital nearly doubled, increasing from 220,000 to 425,000. Although the rate of increase declined sharply thereafter, the population continued to grow, except during the Crimean War, reaching approximately half a million by the eve of the emancipation in 1861.[12] Since the death rate in St. Petersburg either matched or surpassed the birthrate throughout this period, this rise can only be attributed to the arrival of new population from outside the city. The high ratio of males to females in the city, never less than two to one in the first half of the century, is further evidence of the presence of a sizable contingent of otkhodniki living in St. Petersburg more or less temporarily.[13]

The large number of peasant-serfs dwelling in the capital was noticeable as early as the turn of the century. At the beginning of Alexander I's reign, a foreign diplomat compared St. Petersburg to ancient Athens, which according to Herodotus had twenty thousand free citizens to its forty thousand slaves.[14] A more accurate assessment reveals that approximately 38 per cent of the city's population belonged to one or another category of peasants in 1801. By the 1830's and 1840's, the corresponding figure was between 44 and 48 per cent, and by 1858 it had surpassed the 50 per cent mark, while the traditional segments of the urban lower classes—meshchane and tsekh artisans—represented only 12 per cent of the St. Petersburg population.[15] Russia's capital, her leading industrial center, her most Westernized city, was—next to Moscow—the Russian city with the largest population of peasant-serfs living within its borders, and was among the cities with the smallest proportion of meshchane.*

Whereas the otkhodnik population was the main source of freely hired factory labor in St. Petersburg, factory workers represented only a small minority of that population. A government commission that operated between 1840 and 1842 estimated the average annual number of workers of all categories in the city as somewhat below two hundred thousand, about half of whom worked there all year round.[16] Most peasants were employed not in factories, but in construction, transportation, or handicrafts (sometimes as independent artisans, but usually as temporary tsekh members; peasant-artisans in St. Petersburg were more numerous than regular tsekh members and constituted some two-thirds of the artisan population in the 1840's). Many others worked as servants, janitors, laundresses, coachmen, and the like. Around the end of the eighteenth century, between five and six thousand were employed in St. Petersburg's 110 "factories," that is, between 2 and 2.5 per cent of the city population. By 1846 this figure had risen to 11,600, reflecting the expansion of the cotton industry, but it still represented only 2.5 per cent of the population, which had doubled in the intervening period. Comparing the number of factory workers in the 1840's with the annual registration of otkhodniki at the St. Petersburg address office (excluding those who registered for periods of less than six months), Ryndziunskii has come up with a ratio of one to thirteen; and even this figure exaggerates the proportion of otkhodniki in industry, as Ryndziunskii points out, since some industrial workers were meshchane.[17]

To answer the question posed earlier, then, the technological and organizational innovations that were taking place in St. Petersburg industry were not matched by corresponding changes in the composition and recruitment of industrial workers. The displacement of various types of forced labor by freely hired labor proceeded more rapidly in St. Petersburg than elsewhere, but it was nonetheless a characteristic trend throughout Russian industry, irrespective of the degree of technological advancement. More sig-

* In the early 1850's, when meshchane constituted at least half the urban population in almost every other Russian province, they constituted only 10 per cent of the city dwellers in St. Petersburg province and slightly over 9 per cent in the capital itself. I. I. Ditiatin, *Ustroistvo i upravlenie gorodov Rossii*, II (Iaroslavl', 1877), 327–28.

nificantly, the freely hired workers of St. Petersburg continued to be of the sort described in the previous chapter: peasant-serfs whose ties with the city were offset by continuing ties and obligations to lord and village. In many respects their situation can only be understood as part of a broader picture of the peasant population of St. Petersburg, among whom those who worked in factories were only a small drop in a much larger sea.

The vast majority of peasants who came to St. Petersburg were manorial serfs. They came from many parts of Russia, but most commonly from regions where agriculture was relatively unrewarding, such as the non-black-soil provinces of Iaroslavl' and Moscow. They came with the permission and encouragement of their lords, in order to earn money with which to pay off their annual obrok and other obligations.

Since there were no laws in Russia limiting the amount of obrok levied by pomeshchiki, a pomeshchik who maintained close surveillance over the activities of his serfs in St. Petersburg through an estate office or an artel' elder was able to raise obrok dues whenever his furloughed serfs were fortunate enough to increase their earnings. Between 1812 and 1840 some pomeshchiki managed to double or even triple their obrok rates as the earnings of their peasants in St. Petersburg increased. The greater the economic difficulties of the pomeshchik, the more he was likely to tighten his squeeze on the earning of his furloughed peasants. Conversely, the serfs of well-to-do landlords usually paid more reasonable obroks.[18]

The erratic patterns of peasant movement between St. Petersburg and the villages may be clearly seen in the example of a single multi-village estate, that of the wealthy Iusupov family in Iaroslavl' province. Among the thousands of Iusupov serfs, many would head for St. Petersburg with the coming of winter and return to the land for agricultural work in the summer. Many other Iusupov peasants (from different villages) would come to the capital for the summer only, when maritime work was available. When this work ended in the fall, they returned to their villages. Finally, there were some Iusupov peasants who remained in the capital more or less permanently. The arm of the Iusupov estate administration extended into the capital in the form of a branch office where the obrok was actually collected, probably through the arteli, in which at least some of the Iusupov workers were organized while in St.

Petersburg. Thus we find the full array of ties that connected the city-dwelling otkhodnik to the land in one enormous group of St. Petersburg peasants from a single estate.[19]

Within St. Petersburg the otkhodniki—who, it must be remembered, constituted close to half the population—were the least assimilated element. As serfs, they did not have the legal right to own immovable property in the city. Their access to the schools of the capital was almost nil: as late as 1858, only 599 peasants were to be found among the 29,387 children enrolled, and many of these were Finns.[20] And perhaps most important, their rapid numerical growth and the irregular seasonal patterns of arrival and departure meant that even finding a decent temporary shelter was a serious problem, as the following data indicate.

In the early 1840's, 1,007 living quarters, inhabited by various types of St. Petersburg workers, were visited by members of a government commission. Of these only 411 were considered to be in good condition by official standards, that is, not overcrowded, well heated and lighted, clean, and dry; 428 were considered barely adequate by these standards, and 238 were described as being in very bad condition. Overcrowdedness meant, in the area visited by one member of the commission, 3,776 workers inhabiting 199 residences, or an average of nineteen workers to each apartment. Even in quarters that were described as good, the workers slept either on boards or, if the workshop itself served as their living quarters, as was not uncommon, on their own workbenches.[21]

Shortly thereafter, in 1847, some five hundred workers' quarters were examined by a second commission. This time conditions were found to be so unsatisfactory that the commission felt compelled to recommend the establishment of a legal minimum standard for cubic feet of space per worker and the construction of special houses or dormitories in various parts of the city, where homeless workers would always be able to find a temporary shelter at nominal cost. In addition, it recommended measures to reduce fire hazards, eliminate filth, and, in general, establish minimally tolerable living conditions for the working class population.[22] The unhealthful conditions that led to these recommendations were further compounded by the fact that St. Petersburg hospitals, already suffering from an extreme shortage of space, often refused to admit an ailing worker regardless of the seriousness of his illness. On occasion the dead bodies of workers who had been rejected by hospitals could be found on the city streets.[23]

Most of St. Petersburg's otkhodniki population had no real family life within the city. I have already noted the high proportion of males in the St. Petersburg population. Even as early as the middle of the eighteenth century, males had constituted 61 per cent of the city's population of ninety-five thousand.[24] As the population grew through peasant immigration, so too did the proportion of males, which surpassed 69 per cent in 1800 and 72 per cent in 1815. This figure remained rather steady until the outbreak of the Crimean War, when the departure of males for military service reduced it to the 64 to 66 per cent range, where it remained into the late 1850's.[25] In 1858 (the only year in the period under discussion for which there are population figures indicating sex within each juridical class) there were almost as many women as men in St. Petersburg within the three primary urban classes (merchants, meshchane, and tsekhovye), whereas there were two males to every female among the peasant population of the city.[26] That the situation was even more extreme among peasant-laborers than among the city's peasant population as a whole is indicated by the breakdown of the 3,776 workers who inhabited the 199 crowded quarters mentioned earlier: 2,872 men; 36 women; 39 young girls; 829 children.[27]

As was the case in other Russian cities, the peasant population of St. Petersburg remained isolated with respect to the municipal administrative structure that had been introduced by Catherine the Great. If anything, the isolation was more significant in St. Petersburg than elsewhere. Because it was the Imperial capital, its institutions tended to receive greater attention from the tsars and the central government, and the functions and structure of these institutions were subjects of greater interest and controversy. Any experimental changes in the municipal charter of 1785, whether intended to strengthen or weaken it, were likely to be introduced in St. Petersburg first. Thus when Paul I launched his attack on elective municipal institutions in 1797–98, it was the St. Petersburg duma that he chose as his first and primary target.[28] Similarly, Alexander I, having formally reestablished the 1785 charter in St. Petersburg and elsewhere, but wishing to supplement the elective institutions with more effective committees of an executive nature, began by introducing them in St. Petersburg (1802), and later (1820) created special financial committees for the cities of St. Petersburg and Moscow only. Since these committees usurped some of the more important functions of the dumas, municipal self-government, weak as it was in any Russian city, was probably weaker still in the two capitals.[29]

But for the same reasons, when the government finally decided to attempt to strengthen the nearly defunct institutions of municipal self-administration, it was St. Petersburg that was singled out for a new charter (1846). Since the main innovation in the St. Petersburg charter was the increased participation of nobles in the municipal dumas, it only served to dramatize the peasants' lack of the prerogatives of urban citizenship. The 1846 charter[30] provided the occasion for reevaluating and broadening the composition of the St. Petersburg citizenry, but not in the direction of including any of the city's growing peasant population, now over 40 per cent of the total.*

To summarize the general situation of the peasant who came to work in St. Petersburg: he was most typically a manorial serf who paid obrok dues; he was tied to his home estate through membership in an artel', family bonds, the presence of an estate office in the city, or the obrok itself; his earnings in the city could be artificially restricted by increases in the obrok; within the city, he occupied the position of a quasi-outcast with respect to access to property, education, health services, living quarters, participation in municipal class institutions, and family life. Furthermore, he occupied the lowest position in the city when it came to the narrower question of earning power. Once in the city, he was easier to exploit, and was constrained to work for lower wages and under greater restrictions than, say, a meshchanin competing for the same work.[31] He belonged, in other words, to not only the most neglected and least assimilated but also the poorest segment of the St. Petersburg population. Yet it is impossible to imagine that thousands of peasants would leave their village homes in Iaroslavl' or Tver each year and make the difficult journey to the capital in the absence of

---

* Even those peasants (15,000 at the beginning of the 1840's) who came closest to obtaining an urban juridical classification, as temporary members of artisan guilds (vremennotsekhovye), were not given representation in the new St. Petersburg duma. Moreover, they were badly treated by the tsekhi themselves. See P. G. Ryndziunskii, Gorodskoe grazhdanstvo doreformennoi Rossii (Moscow, 1958), pp. 452–53.

fairly strong material incentives. Our knowledge of wage patterns and prices in St. Petersburg in the 1840's is based on very sporadic and unsatisfactory data, but it does enable us to reach some rough and tentative conclusions about the nominal and real earnings of the workers who migrated there.

Two sets of wage figures are available for the 1840's, each uncovered by one of the two government commissions that were mentioned in connection with housing conditions. The figures provided by the first commission were drawn from the beginning of the 1840's and (at least in the form in which they are available to us) do not distinguish between factory workers and other types of laborers; those provided by the second commission apply to the year 1847 and were taken from establishments that the commission called factories, although they included neither state factories nor any of St. Petersburg's larger, better known enterprises.[32]

The first commission, after taking the average between two sets of conflicting figures, estimated that the annual earnings of St. Petersburg workers generally fell within a range of 58 to 133 silver rubles,* with about 70 per cent of year-round workers earning wages in the neighborhood of the lower figure, and 10 per cent earning a wage that approximated the higher figure. On the basis of these figures I will assume that a more or less typical worker made somewhat more than 60 rubles a year.

The figures provided by the second commission make it possible to compare this estimate with the earnings of factory workers only. However, with the exception of five textile factories, the thirty-eight enterprises examined by the commission under the heading of "factory" consisted entirely of soap factories, breweries, food factories of various kinds, and the like, and it is not unlikely, since the commission failed to specify their size, that some of these were little more than tiny workshops. Only nineteen of them actually bore the word "factory" (*fabrika* or *zavod*) in their names. As if to complicate matters still further, the commission confined itself to determining the lowest and highest wage level at each enterprise, with no indication of the distribution of wages between the extremes. Confining our calculations to sixteen of the nineteen factories (data was incomplete for three), we find that the average low

---

* One silver ruble was equal to 3.5 assignat rubles. I have used silver rubles unless otherwise indicated.

wage among them was 66 rubles, the average high wage 151 rubles. This range is not greatly out of phase with the figures produced by the first commission, and suggests no wide discrepancy between the wages of factory workers in St. Petersburg and other types of workers in that city. If, as with the first set of figures, the earnings of most workers were fairly close to the lower limit of the range, the 66-ruble figure (5.5 rubles a month) can be used as an approximation of the earnings of a typical St. Petersburg worker in the late 1840's for the purpose of comparing earnings to living expenses.

At that time, in the capital, one ruble could purchase the equivalent of 57 pounds of rye flour (rye bread was the basic food in a lower class diet) or 13 pounds of low-grade meat; the monthly cost of living quarters, unless provided at no cost by the employer, fell within a range of less than half a ruble to five rubles.[33] Annual obrok payments were usually around ten to twelve rubles, and the annual soul tax was just under one ruble.[34] Subtracting one ruble per month for obrok and soul tax, one finds that the worker was left with 4.5 rubles to cover the cost of food and housing. If devoted to food alone, 4.5 rubles was the equivalent of, say, 13 pounds of meat and 200 pounds of flour (the typical meal of a worker actually consisted of bread, cabbage soup with meat or with peas and potatoes, and kasha). Thus a barely adequate diet cost the entire sum that remained, a judgment that is supported by the first commission's estimate of the value of one month's food for the average worker—4 rubles, 87 kopecks.* It would seem, therefore, that the many workers who earned about 66 rubles a year could only survive if they did not have to pay for housing, that is, if housing were provided by the employer. On the other hand, it often happened that food was provided to poorly paid workers at no cost.[35]

Taking all these factors into account, it seems fair to conclude that even workers whose pay fell into the lowest brackets—apparently the bulk of peasant-workers in St. Petersburg—were able to maintain a poor but sustaining diet, pay the obrok and soul tax, and provide for a squalid shelter. And if, as was often the case, food was provided by the employer, there might be a tiny sum left over for their families in the villages or for vodka in the city. Since the

---

* The commission estimated the monthly value of a worker's food as ranging between 14 and 20 assignat rubles, and averaging 17 assignat rubles.

first half of the nineteenth century was a period of rapidly rising prices and slowly rising wages,[36] the situation of the otkhodnik-worker was certainly less gloomy during previous decades, which probably accounts for the decline in the rate of population growth in St. Petersburg during the second quarter of the century. The real value of a St. Petersburg wage, in other words, had become considerably less attractive to an otkhodnik than it once had been. Yet even at the middle of the nineteenth century, despite the many drawbacks and depressing aspects of the life of the city worker, the minimal rewards of a St. Petersburg wage were sufficiently gratifying to thousands of poor peasants to entice them into leaving their distant village homes.

The factory workers of St. Petersburg, like the rest of the large, amorphous mass of peasant-workers of which they formed a part, had strong ties to the countryside, a weak and tenuous relation to the life of the city, and a not-quite-destitute material situation. Given the optimistic assumptions about peasant-workers in some government circles, one wonders whether any of the officials who inhabited the same city were able to distinguish the problems and characteristics of a distinctive group of industrial workers within the mass. They might have discriminated between factory workers and others either by regarding the aggregation of factory workers in the capital as dangerous (that is, by applying one or another version of the pessimistic view) or by accepting industrial labor as a new sort of presence in the capital that required special legislation —the position that we know the government was groping toward but was as yet unable to implement.

Chief among the elements that one might expect to have contributed to a special awareness of the presence of industrial workers was the visual impact brought about by the emergence of large new factories in the 1830's and after. The physical layout of the city is a topic I will return to later with reference to the 1860's, but a brief sketch here will help to highlight the visual meaning of the presence of new industrial plants.[37]

Since the reign of Catherine the Great, St. Petersburg had been divided into ten administrative or police districts (*chasti*), each of which was subdivided into several wards (*kvartaly*). At that time some 40 per cent of the population was concentrated in the three central districts known as the 1st, 2d, and 3d Admiralty districts.

The 1st district, the most populous of the three, was situated on the southern (left) bank of the arch of the Neva River, with the 2d district immediately to the south. It contained some of the most prominent official buildings of the capital, including the Winter and Summer palaces of the tsars, the Holy Synod and Senate, and the Admiralty. The two districts together constituted a residential settlement for the most privileged layers of St. Petersburg society —mainly the upper nobility and bureaucracy, but also some well-to-do merchants. The only significant industrial activity that took place in the area was at the shipyards owned by the Navy,* and since maritime workers could have accounted for only a small fraction of the area's large population, it was the large number of servants (mainly *dvorovye liudi*) retained by the upper classes that made the two districts so populous. The 3d Admiralty district (later known as Spasskaia chast') was bordered by the 1st and 2d to the north and northwest and by the Fontanka rivulet to the south and east. Though it too contained important government buildings, its social composition was markedly different, including as it did many otkhodniki, meshchane, artisans, and merchants. An area of sharp contrasts, it contained one of the most lively and attractive sections of the city's main boulevard, Nevskii Prospekt, and what became in the nineteenth century St. Petersburg's most decrepit, impoverished, and disease-ridden neighborhood, the Sennaia Ploshchad' (Hay-Market Square), well known through Dostoevsky's novel *Crime and Punishment*.

Across the Fontanka, east of the 3d Admiralty district, were the Liteinaia district to the north and the Moscow district to the south. They were fairly similar in social composition to the 1st and 2d Admiralty districts, but they contained more commercial and industrial establishments, mainly workshops and small factories that catered to the special needs of the upper classes (pianos, officers' uniforms, horse-drawn carriages, etc.). Taken together, these five adjoining districts comprised the heart of St. Petersburg, the center of government, commerce, and aristocratic culture, and, to borrow the words of a contemporary observer, "the kingdom of the best

---

* After 1844 the Admiralty ceased functioning as a shipyard. Thereafter it was used only to house the various offices of the Imperial Navy. See V. V. Pokshishevskii, "Territorial'noe formirovanie promyshlennogo kompleksa Peterburga v XVIII–XIX vekakh," *Voprosy geografii*, Coll. XX (1950), p. 142.

society, the place of the inhabitants of the highest circle, of great, polite, or fashionable society."[38]

The small factories in the Moscow and Liteinaia districts were typical, in their size and in their central location, of most of the hundred or so enterprises spread throughout the interior of St. Petersburg (mainly along the Neva River) at the end of the eighteenth century. Although there were larger factories on the edge of the city even in the eighteenth century, they were very few. Early in the nineteenth century, however, a significant geographical redistribution of St. Petersburg industry began to take place.[39] As factories grew in size and new ones were planned on a larger scale, the locus of industry moved away from the city's crowded center out toward the periphery where land was more abundant and less costly, waterpower was more readily available, and official standards for health and safety had not been set.

This centrifugal tendency received an especially powerful stimulus in the early 1830's, the time of the first upsurge of St. Petersburg's cotton-spinning industry, when the cutting of the Obvodnyi (literally, enclosing or encircling) Canal, begun in 1803, was completed. The canal connected the two extremes of the Neva's arched path through the city—the mouth of the river at St. Petersburg port to the west, on the Finnish Gulf, and the Schlüsselburg (Shlissel'burg) Road stretch of the river to the southeast—almost like a string connecting the two ends of a bow. It thereby greatly facilitated the importation of raw materials (particularly American cotton), fuels (such as British coal), and industrial machinery (after the lifting of the British export ban in 1842) to the industrial suburbs that were developing along the Schlüsselburg Road by the river, just beyond the administrative limits of the capital. This area, which already had a nucleus of factories dating from before the turn of the century, would soon become the most important and advanced industrial center of the St. Petersburg region, abounding with textile plants, machine works and foundries, shipyards, and lesser forms of industry. The Obvodnyi Canal—the southern boundary of the city until the 1850's—also stimulated the growth of industry on St. Petersburg's southern periphery, where the absence of waterpower had previously presented a major obstacle.

Of only somewhat less significance than the growing concentration of industry to the south, southeast, and east was the appearance of new industrial establishments in the Petersburg district (where a nucleus of factories actually dated from the 1790's) and in the Vyborg district, St. Petersburg's northernmost area, where lived an extremely poor element of the city's populace. Vasil'evskii Island (the Vasil'evskaia district), located just across the Neva from the central part of the city, to the southwest of the Petersburg district, was a rather special case. It was perhaps the most diversified of all the districts. On the bank of the Neva just across from the 1st Admiralty district, it was virtually an extension of the city center owing to the location there of the Academy of Sciences, the University, and several magnificent residences. But the island also contained many stores and artisan workshops as well as a large number of factories, mainly but not exclusively of small and medium size. These factories, along with those of the Petersburg and Vyborg districts on the same side of the river, the rapidly developing industrial complex of the Schlüsselburg area, and the new factories that were arising along the Obvodnyi Canal and at its western terminus near the Ekateringof suburb, had begun to form an irregular circle around the hear of the city by the 1840's. As a leading historian of St. Petersburg has put it, "The factories surrounded the city as if they were a ring, squeezing the administrative-commercial center in their embrace."[40]

By the end of the 1830's the new industrial belt, although still in embryonic form, was much too visible to escape public notice. In the first quarter of the nineteenth century, with a single minor exception, it would have been impossible to find a description of St. Petersburg factories in the press.[41] In 1839, by contrast, it was possible for readers of the conservative St. Petersburg newspaper *Severnaia pchela* (Northern Bee, No. 274) to take an imaginary walk along the Schlüsselburg Road from the edge of the city into the neighboring industrial villages, to visit factories where the land had been desolate only ten years earlier, to observe the constant presence of industrial activity, and to learn that the growth of factories had multiplied the value of land.

Silk factories are seen where a thousand persons are working every day ...; a little further along a cotton spinning factory where two hundred people labor. Behind it, notice the huge stone buildings of the father, the animator of all these factories—the Aleksandrovsk cast-iron foundry which builds, among other things, the steam-driven machinery for these factories, as well as for ocean-going steamships. . . .

Soon afterward, we approach an enormous building, a totally new institution in Russia: it is for the manufacture of spinning and weaving machines, which up until now have been imported here from England and Belgium at a high cost in money and time.[42]

The same description was soon repeated in almost all the newspapers and journals of the capital.[43] The large-scale, mechanized industries around St. Petersburg's periphery, with their growing concentration of workers were now a matter of public record, a tableau that every resident of the city, including government officials, could read about and see.

The first significant sign of an especially negative or hostile awareness of the growth of industry in the capital on the part of government officials appeared in the early 1830's. In 1833 regulations were introduced that restricted the location of certain kinds of industry either to parts of the city's three northern districts (Vyborg, Petersburg, and Vasil'evskaia) or to areas belonging to the city but beyond its administrative boundaries.[44] These regulations themselves constituted an important factor contributing to the new geographical constellation of St. Petersburg industry just described. If one accepts the official explanation for the issuing of the new regulations (stated as recently as 1902 in the official centenary history of the Ministry of Finance),[45] they were nothing more than sanitary measures, designed to protect the health of the urban population. If this is true, then the regulations were an innovation in degree only, and not in kind, for specific restrictions on factory construction in St. Petersburg based on sanitary considerations date back at least as far as 1759.[46] Nevertheless, the new regulations, even if so narrowly conceived, constitute evidence of a heightened official concern with some of the effects of the growth of industry in the capital.

The case for the argument that the motives behind the new regulations went beyond considerations of sanitation and involved fear of the growth of an urban proletariat has already been made, for the regulations of 1833 were an experimental step taken in response to the questions first raised by Nicholas I the previous year, and as such were part of the government's flirtation with the pessimistic view that continued, with some vicissitudes, at least to 1849.[47]

Officials who considered curtailing urban industry in the 1840's, however, concentrated less on St. Petersburg than on Moscow, perhaps because the Moscow region still had more industry and a much larger contingent of workers than St. Petersburg (in 1848–49 it may simply have been because the military governor of Moscow was an especially strong partisan of the pessimistic view[48]). It is noteworthy that at no point—including 1833—did the government consider curtailing industry in the vicinity of St. Petersburg altogether, for doing so would have meant foregoing all the economic advantages of the city's special position as a Baltic seaport.

Short of actually distributing factories over a wide area or limiting their numbers, the government could deal with potential danger from factory workers by police surveillance. Though we are told that during the reign of Nicholas I the St. Petersburg police still made no distinction between factory workers and other peasants in their written reports,[49] this fact must be balanced against the fragmentary evidence that there was some sense of potential danger from factory workers within the Third Section during the European crisis of 1848. Shortly after news of the February revolution in Paris had reached Russia, a high official of the Third Section summoned the owner of St. Petersburg's largest machine works, F. Baird, to his office in order (in the words of the official) "to call his attention to workers who are reading newspapers and talking about the revolution in France."[50] A few months later St. Petersburg factory workers again attracted special attention during a three-day period of widespread panic and unrest (June 16–18) precipitated by a cholera epidemic. Although the lower classes of all parts of the city took part in these and subsequent disturbances (which were mainly spontaneous mob attacks on "suspicious" people), the authorities were worried particularly about the intentions of the inhabitants of the industrial suburbs. Panicky rumors to the effect that the Baird workers and others might rise up in arms apparently reached the Third Section, and in one case at least—according to the Third Section's annual report for 1848—cossacks were used to maintain order when word was received that factory workers were threatening to attack a hospital.[51] Although these incidents leave little doubt that by the late 1840's there was some awareness in government circles that St. Petersburg workers posed a potential danger to internal security, their significance should not be exaggerated. The measures taken by the Third Section were part and parcel of a broader surveillance over the lower-class population undertaken during a period of stress, and not a special program directed at industrial workers as such.

Despite the appearance of the city's new industrial physiognomy, there were those who continued to apply the optimistic approach to the Russian peasant-worker in St. Petersburg. In 1840 the official journal of the Department of Manufactures and Internal Commerce of the Ministry of Finance (*Zhurnal manufaktur i torgovli*) singled out the owner of a St. Petersburg tobacco factory, Zhukov, for what it considered to be his singularly inspired treatment of his peasant-workers. Not the least of Zhukov's achievements was to insist that his workers remain in constant touch with their rural origins by visiting their villages each year or by being replaced for a time with fresh peasant-workers. It is useful to hear Zhukov's own explanation of his reasons for this practice, which was quoted in the journal with evident approval, since it was so clear an example of the optimistic vision. The purpose, said Zhukov, was to improve the moral character of the worker by encouraging him:

1) not to stop thinking of himself as a peasant; 2) to carry out the duties of son, husband, and father with piety; 3) not to cling to the luxuries of the capital; 4) to restore, in the country, his understanding of the need for uninterrupted work and moderation in food, drink, and clothing; 5) in general, to bring back from the countryside examples of obedience, humility, and compliance, so that he is satisfied and contented in his present position at the factory.[52]

Zhukov's own description of conditions in his factory, however, unintentionally reveals the inadequacy of this model, for, as it turns out, the workers' proximity to the countryside did not obviate the need for him to employ the most stringent methods of discipline and control over his four-hundred-man work force. Nevertheless, the editors of the journal put out by Kankrin's ministry still preferred to use the nonproletarian peasant character of the worker as their norm for St. Petersburg.

The conviction that urban industrial conditions and the relations between workers and employers were in need of state regulation, the alternative to the optimistic and pessimistic extremes, was, not unexpectedly, considered mainly in relation to St. Petersburg and Moscow. The first seriously conceived labor legislation, that of 1835, was drafted in response to conditions in Moscow, and was meant to apply immediately in St. Petersburg as well. Beginning in 1840, more specific attention was paid to conditions in St. Petersburg—witness the two commissions whose findings I have already had occasion to cite. The initiative for forming the first commission, which was formally established in December 1840, seems to have come from the Tsar or his immediate circles. The project was launched after General A. Kh. Benkendorf, head of the Third Section and a close confidant of Nicholas I, sent a secret message to Minister of Finance Kankrin: "His Majesty the Emporer, having turned his supreme attention to the situation of the working people and artisans located here [i.e., in St. Petersburg], has commanded that it be investigated in detail and that possible ways to improve their situation be sought."[53] Accordingly, the so-called Buksgevden commission was established which, in addition to its chairman, Count P. F. Buksgevden (Buxhoeveden) of the Third Section, included representatives of the Ministry of Finance, the local nobility, and the municipal duma.

As with regard to the police surveillance of 1848, it is important not to exaggerate the extent to which the concerned officials separated factory workers from the rest of the wage-earning lower classes. The Buksgevden commission examined the situation of a broad cross section (nearly twenty-three thousand) of poor temporary and year-round workers, ranging from servants and laundresses to artisans and construction workers, that is, the full gamut of occupations available to otkhodniki. Its broad approach reflected the original impetus for forming the commission, namely, concern over the chronic presence of epidemic disease in St. Petersburg caused by the unsanitary and crowded conditions of lower-class living quarters, a problem that was, of course, in no way restricted to the housing of factory workers.[54]

Factory workers were certainly included among those workers whose situation the commission examined, and were occasionally referred to as a distinct group, although only in passing. When the Committee of Ministers authorized the continuation of the commission in January 1842, it instructed it—apparently on the basis of the commission's earlier revelations (which were in no sense limited to the housing question)—to take steps to ensure that manufacturers, industrialists, contractors, and the proprietors of artisan workshops acted "humanely and conscientiously" toward their workers.[55] Similarly, one of the reports of a commission subcommittee stated: "The richer the owners, the manufacturers, the con-

tractors are, the less attention they pay to the welfare of their workers."[56] Both examples show a tendency toward distinguishing between the problems of factories and those of other forms of production. But though the treatment of workers by industrialists
was duly noted as a problem, it was not clearly differentiated from
the problem of the treatment of workers by contractors and owner-
artisans.

This tendency was only somewhat less marked in the commission
of 1847. For reasons that are unclear, the Buksgevden commission
had been allowed to lapse without having brought its work to a
definitive conclusion. The mandate of the new commission was
similar to that of its predecessor, except for a stipulation that exceeded the bounds of an investigation of material conditions: it
was to propose measures for intensifying surveillance over workers'
behavior. Organizationally, it differed from its predecessor in that
it was administered by the Ministry of Internal Affairs.[57]

The actual conduct of the investigation in 1847—which appears
to have been more meticulous than the previous one—reveals a
slightly greater consciousness of the factory situation as a distinctive
one. The commission made it a point to examine carefully 39 private factories (loosely defined), and its report is sprinkled with specific descriptions of factory conditions.[58] On the other hand, this
singling out of factories was once again largely a distinction without a difference. At least this is the impression one gets from the
commission's long and carefully worked out list of recommendations, each of which was meant to apply to the whole range of enterprises investigated, and none of which suggested that any special
approaches to the factory situation were required.[59]

In light of the absence of any rigorous distinctions between categories of enterprises in the work of the two commissions, it is all
the more striking that each of them—the first indirectly and incon-
clusively, the second explicitly—came around to the basic position
of the legislation of 1835, i.e., that a rational system of easily ad-
judicable contractural relations between workers and employers
should become the basis for labor-management relations. The
Buksgevden commission simply provided data and materials on the
basis of which General Benkendorf and the Committee of Ministers
reached a conclusion that, although it had no sequel in action, is
significant in the outlook it reveals: A permanent committee to improve the situation of workers should be formed, under the chair-

manship of the St. Petersburg military governor, one of the major purposes of which would be to accept and adjudicate the complaints of workers against their employers and at the same time to encourage the workers to be "more obedient and more patient."[60]

More revealing are the sections on employer-worker relations in the report of 1847.[61] Without alluding specifically to the law of 1835, they make it abundantly clear that the law had been thoroughly disregarded in St. Petersburg. Despite the 1835 requirements, most "contracts" in St. Petersburg still consisted merely of oral agreements, with little more than the mutual confidence of the two parties to guarantee their validity. Individual workers' booklets (required by the 1835 legislation) were rarely encountered by the commission, which noted the ease with which illiterate workers could be deceived by dishonest employers.

There are internal contradictions and ambiguities in the report concerning the degree to which the absence of written contracts and workers' booklets, and more generally of a regulatory system, had been the source of any actual conflicts and disputes in St. Petersburg. Be that as it may, although the commission made some disparaging remarks contrasting formal solutions of such problems with the patriarchal relations that prevailed in some enterprises (usually when workers and employers shared common regional origins), when it came to concrete recommendations, the commission strongly favored (again without reference to the 1835 law) written contracts, workers' booklets, the precise delineation of the mutual obligations between workers and their employers, and the introduction of formal judicial procedures for resolving contractual disputes. The commission appears to have reached these conclusions reluctantly, and without a sense of great urgency, yet without equivocation about the steps it favored.

Thus by the eve of the 1848 revolutions, those government officials who had been able to study the situation in St. Petersburg directly had reached the conclusion that neither tight police control nor the peasant nature of the Russian worker and the patriarchal character of his employer precluded the need to regularize worker-employer relations by means of contracts. As we know, none of the recommendations that emanated from their studies was adopted. The life of the 1847 commission did not extend beyond its first year. There can be little doubt that like the proposals of Governor Kapnist of Moscow, the commission and its proposals fell victims to the events of 1848. Even the commission's much less controversial proposals on housing were allowed to remain unimplemented. Minister of Internal Affairs S. Lanskoi was to claim unconvincingly a decade later that it had been felt that such matters were best left to private parties acting "in a spirit of enlightened charity."[62] Equally dubious was the government's claim that the Committee of Ministers' proposed adjudicatory committee was not put into practice because the financial cost was prohibitive.[63] Such explanations strain our credibility when we learn that it was considered "totally excessive" by the Minister of Internal Affairs "even to enter into any discussions" about topics of this kind during the unrest in Western Europe.[64]

By the time of the Crimean War, a microcosmic revolution in the technology and organization of industry was well under way in St. Petersburg. An impressive if not yet spectacular industrial complex had arisen on the periphery of the city, which stood in strong relief against the background of a still agrarian countryside. Within the factories that comprised this complex had emerged a quasi-class of peasant-workers, closely tied to their village homes, yet dwelling in and about a major metropolis, a city that gave them and their thousands of fellow otkhodniki in other trades little comfort and protection and no institutional cohesion, but did give them just enough badly needed rubles to justify their presence.

In a period when the intelligentsia was preoccupied with abstract questions or with the single consuming issue of serfdom, in a period when tight censorship was imposed upon the expression of a wide range of opinions, there was little likelihood that the eyes of the educated public would see into the dimly lighted shops and living quarters where the workers of St. Petersburg could be found and equally little chance that the problems of the workers would be brought to the attention of the public through the press. An occasional article in the journal of the Ministry of Finance describing this or that enterprise, or even the more dramatic article of 1839, could draw attention to the new industrial growth, but to be aware of the presence of a new phenomenon is not necessarily to recognize it as constituting a new kind of problem, a "social question" or a "labor question."[65]

The situation might have been otherwise had it not been for the passivity of the workers themselves. Except in reaction to the cholera epidemic—a unique circumstance that involved far more of the lower classes than just factory workers—the peasant-workers of St. Petersburg had still done nothing to dramatize their plight. With the exception of a single incident in 1850,[66] no strikes or particularly industrial forms of unrest took place in the capital during the reign of Nicholas I. If they had, the outlook of the optimists could not have held sway, and the regime would have been compelled to choose between the pessimistic approach of curtailing the capital's industry or acting firmly to implement the legislative programs that were repeatedly broached and never implemented. The impulse to act decisively was really based on an abstraction, for those who saw the presence of large factories in the capital as a source of danger did so mainly by projecting foreign experiences rather than by observing real events in St. Petersburg. On the pessimistic side, the practical effect of such fears was nothing more or less than narrowly conceived police measures; on the legislative side these fears could only intensify the already existing reluctance to proletarianize the peasant-worker.

The absence of pressure from below, the indifference of the educated public, the submersion of the St. Petersburg worker in a much larger sea of otkhodniki who shared a similar fate, all contributed to the failure of the regime to act decisively, the more so in that this was still a regime that hesitated to put its autocratic powers behind a definite policy of industrial development. Ironically, during a period when the strictest government control was maintained over education and literature, and the ideology of laissez-faire economics still had only a minor impact on Russian thought, a policy that virtually amounted to one of laissez-faire prevailed in the area of industrial relations, formal legislative enactments notwithstanding.

This situation, like serfdom itself, could not withstand the impact of the Crimean War. A new era of Russian history was about to begin, an era that would witness not only the end of serfdom and the introduction of judicial, administrative, educational, press, and military reforms, but also the growth and development of railroads and machine industry, important new developments in banking and finance, the expanded use of joint-stock companies, international economic crises, and finally, the appearance of an incipient labor movement. It was within this context that the labor question first emerged as a topic of public discussion in St. Petersburg.

THREE

The Emergence of the Labor Question

THE AREAS of continental Europe that were the first to experience
the impact of the industrial revolution—parts of Germany, Belgium, and France—began to discern the existence of a "labor question" sometime between the 1820's and the revolutions of 1848.[1]
Its discovery both reflected and contributed to important changes
in conceptualization about the nature of politics and society,
changes that cut across the entire political spectrum and were expressed in the new usages that began to be accorded to old words.
In France an important transformation of consciousness was implied in the movement away from such terms as *classes criminelles*
and *classes dangereuses* toward expressions like *classes laborieuses*
and *prolétariat*. This shift corresponded to parallel changes in such
areas as the collection of urban statistics, social hygiene, and the
conventions of literature, not to mention the more obvious realm
of social and political thought.[2] In various Germanic states during
the same period, similar changes accompanied the shift from *Pöbel*
to *Proletariat* in the public consciousness concerning the laboring
poor.[3]

In the German case—the more useful one for comparison with
Russia—the main factors that brought about a new way of thinking
about the urban poor were (1) a relatively sudden expansion of the
labor supply, caused by the rapid growth of population in regions
such as East Prussia, and (2) the inability of new industries to absorb the expanding population at a satisfactory rate. The difference
between a Pöbel and a Proletariat suggested the difference between
a permanent, static, and relatively small substratum of urban poor,
too destitute and sickly to expand its numbers by natural growth,
and a new and expanding mass of propertyless immigrants from
the countryside, reduced to pauperism because of the restricted
demand for workers in the cities into which they streamed. Accord-

ing to Werner Conze, this "pauperism" (a word borrowed from England) was perceived as a new and frightening phenomenon, something essentially different from the problems that had long been posed by the existence of the traditional population of urban poor (*Armenfrage*). It was this startling and offensive configuration that came to be expressed in the 1830's, and especially in the 1840's, by the concept "proletariat."[4]

The labor question that emerged from this context (sometimes also called the "social question," although this term had broader and more varied implications) reflected: first, consciousness of a new stratum of the urban laboring population (usually, but not necessarily, employed or seeking employment in factories) whose way of life was distinct both from that of the general peasantry and from that of the traditional urban poor; and second, belief that this stratum presented a new challenge, whether dangerous or desirable, to the existing order, and was, therefore, a problem in need of a solution.

A wide variety of approaches to the labor question were possible, ranging from attempts to stem or reverse the tide of proletarianization to enthusiastic acceptance of the proletariat as a force that contained the seeds of a new and revolutionary social order. Liberals sometimes greeted the newly discovered class as a potential political ally against the status quo; conversely, sophisticated Prussian conservatives at times advocated an alliance between the crown and the proletariat against the liberal bourgeoisie. More typically, approaches for improving the lot of the proletariat were not directly political. During the decade that preceded the revolutions of 1848, what one German historian has described as a "flood" of brochures and articles on pauperism and the proletariat were published by middle-class philanthropists, liberals, socialists, and conservatives, replete with proposals and programs for resolving the social question. Discussion of these proposals was initiated and carried on mainly outside official circles, which lagged considerably behind the educated middle classes in this respect. In addition to the traditional and relatively uncontroversial charities for the poor (who in any case were not really part of the labor question, as defined above) and the well-known theoretical programs that emerged from the Left, new proposals recommended emergency funds for workers, privately initiated social insurance programs, special housing projects and educational centers, various kinds of associations and cooperative institutions, and protective labor legislation.[5]

The emergence of the labor question in Russia, despite the existence of certain common features, followed a substantially different pattern from the one just described. As has already been noted, government circles displayed some interest in the special problems raised by urban industrial labor well before these problems began to cause concern among the educated public. With a few minor exceptions, nothing resembling the labor question was publicly discussed during the reign of Nicholas I; the entire problem was in the hands of a few government agencies and the special committees discussed earlier, whose work—like that of Nicholas' committees on the peasant question—was shrouded in secrecy.

It is possible, of course, that the virtual absence of discussion about the labor question in the Russian periodical press was a consequence of censorship rather than indifference. It would indeed be surprising if the revolutions of 1848, while stimulating the interest of government officials in the urban workers, failed to have a similar effect on writers and journalists. The government feared open discussion of this kind of issue, and until the death of Nicholas I, with few exceptions, such discussion was severely restricted by the censors.[6] Nevertheless, whatever analysis of the West European working classes was aborted by censorship, there is no serious evidence that Russian writers anticipated the appearance of the labor question, as here defined, on Russian soil. To put it another way, the growth of the laboring populations of St. Petersburg and Moscow, and the appearance of large concentrations of industries—as described in the previous chapter—in these cities, did not come to be viewed among educated Russians as portending a new and special problem before the end of the Crimean War.

In principle, of course, hostility to the urban industrial life of Western Europe and a strong aversion to the idea of a landless proletariat were common characteristics of Russian intellectuals of almost all persuasions. The Slavophiles of the 1840's, and most pointedly after the events of 1848, are the classical case. Favoring *kustar'* (rural handicraft) production and manorial industries, they distrusted large-scale urban industry on humanitarian and spiritual grounds, and saw communal institutions as Russia's guarantee against the dreadful consequences of allowing a proletarian class to develop. "The proletariat is the root of all the material ills in Europe," wrote A. I. Koshelev in 1849, "just as unbelief is the source of the moral evils."[7]

This attitude was not unlike some of the views we have encountered in government circles, except that official optimists stressed bondage rather than communal institutions as the source of Russia's immunity to proletarianization. It was also an important element in the thinking of the Russian Left, partly because of the direct influence of the Slavophiles on the father of Russian socialism, Alexander Herzen. Indeed Herzen, once having formulated his view of the commune as the peasants' shelter from the fate of the Western proletariat, was able to face the prospect of urban industry with relative equanimity. Like the official optimists, he believed that the urban workers' rural ties fortified them in their relations with their urban employers (1849): "The majority of urban workers belong to poor rural communes, . . . but they do not lose their rights in the commune: manufacturers, therefore, must of necessity pay them somewhat more than their rural labor would bring them."[8] Similar ideas were current in the radical Petrashevskii circle of the mid-1840's. "As for factory workers," wrote one member, echoing the official optimistic view with precision, "when their wages fall too sharply, they all return to the countryside. And so in Russia it can really be claimed that there is no proletariat and no destitution."[9]

Hostility toward the proletarian disease (medical images were commonly invoked), accompanied by confidence, or at least hope, that the commune provided Russia with immunity, was the most common attitude of the Left intelligentsia in the years before the Crimean War. No labor question was perceived as existing in Russia, and such references to the Russian factory workers as the ones just quoted were made only in passing. In Russia the social question was still the peasant question, and the problem of proletarianization was still an abstraction, derived from a general awareness of the state of the labor question in Western Europe, and used by some as a way of stressing, through contrast, the virtues of the commune. Russians of differing political persuasions undoubtedly concurred with the following passage in the widely read assessment of the Russian commune by Baron A. von Haxthausen: "All West European states are sick and weak from *one illness*, which threatens them with destruction and the cure for which remains an insoluble puzzle, [and that is] *pauperism-proletariatism*. Russia does not know this misfortune; she is protected from it by the communal system."[10]

One of the few who would have had reservations about Haxthausen's statement was the economist V. A. Miliutin, younger brother of the more famous reformers of the era of Alexander II: Dmitri and Nikolai. A Westernizer of strong socialist leanings who stood on the periphery of the Petrashevtsy, Miliutin was one of the few Russian thinkers of this period who, even though he looked back at the preindustrial social order with considerable nostalgia and was deeply concerned with the sufferings of the workers under the new industrial system, nevertheless welcomed the emergence of the European proletariat. Like a small number of his contemporaries (among them V. N. Maikov and N. Ia. Danilevskii), Miliutin, rather than rejecting outright the development of an industrial working class in Russia, sought approaches that would guarantee the Russian workers a more enviable future than that of the proletarians of England or France. His views were developed in a series of articles published shortly before the 1848 revolutions, most notably in "Proletarii i pauperizm v Anglii i vo Frantsii," which appeared in 1847 in the journal *Otechestvennye zapiski*. It is impossible to determine whether Miliutin's discussion of these problems woud have evolved into a real debate over the labor question between 1848 and 1855 in the absence of censorship; but the fact remains that exceptional as some of his attitudes were, Miliutin was no different from other members of the intelligentsia in his failure to deal specifically and concretely with the situation of laborers in Russia.[11]

During the reign of Nicholas I the only significant public example of an incipient awareness of the labor question that was based on direct observation of urban conditions in Russia, specifically in St. Petersburg, was a statistical article by K. S. Veselovskii that appeared in 1848 in the journal of the Imperial Russian Geographical Society under the bland and unprovocative title "Concerning Immovable Properties in St. Petersburg." In its approach and its tone, Veselovskii's article occupied an intermediate position between a traditional upper-class concern with the poor as a fixed and static group (Conze's *Armenfrage*) and a sense that the expanding lower-class population of the capital grew out of new conditions and presented a new type of social problem. In justifying his statistical inquiry into the poverty of St. Petersburg's common people (*prostoi narod*), Veselovskii adopted a condescending, aristocratic tone. As depressing as the information presented might be, he wrote, it was valuable in that it "acquaints us with the way of life of our numerous younger brothers, arouses interest in them, and makes it possible to lend them a helping hand in time and at the right time." But Veselovskii's concepts regarding the specific causes and effects of the unhappy conditions he described had a modern ring, suggestive of the labor question as it was then being discussed in the West. He presented the laboring poor of St. Petersburg as victims of a social situation, especially noted the effects of the seasonal influx of peasants into the city, criticized urban landlords for exploiting the poor, and attributed the breakdown of health and morals among the peasant-workers of the city to the terrible living conditions they were compelled to accept. Only the absence of one important element prevents us from viewing Veselovskii's article as a full presentation of the labor question: the drawing of a relationship between the problem he described and the growing presence of urban industry.[12]

It was not until the early years of the reign of Alexander II that the approach hinted at by Veselovskii began to become common currency in the periodical press. The relaxation of censorship during those years was a necessary but not sufficient condition for the emergence of the labor question. Of equal importance, industry and industrialization became subjects of public controversy that extended beyond abstract discussion of Russia's future economic course to specific debate over the new patterns that economic and social life were beginning to take. If anticipation of the impending emancipation of the peasantry contributed heavily to a new sense of social transformation, the economic consequences of the Crimean War helped set the stage for controversy over industrial matters, among them the labor question.

The Crimean War, as was noted in the previous chapter, stimulated the growth of industry in St. Petersburg, especially privately owned machine and metal works, often organized as joint-stock companies, that manufactured the war-related products for which the government was willing to pay so dearly.[13] According to official figures, the number of factories in St. Petersburg rose from 329 in 1854 to 367 at the beginning of 1858; more significantly, the ruble value of the output of these factories rose by more than 50 per cent (from 20.5 million to 31 million silver rubles) during the same period, with a rise of more than 100 per cent in the output of the city's iron foundries.[14] To some extent these figures merely reflected the rising prices that resulted from the inflationary financial policies pursued by the government during and especially immediately after the war. But by 1858 prices were falling again, and even before 1858 the inflation was hardly of a magnitude to account for such large increases in the ruble value of production.[15] Clearly a real and significant rise in industrial production had taken place.

When the war ended, however, industry experienced a serious, if not disastrous, crisis, one that combined domestic and foreign elements. Domestically, the conclusion of peace was followed by a decrease in government orders for military and semi-military industrial products. Some branches of industry, having failed to plan for this contingency, soon found themselves with a stock of unsold goods and sharply curtailed their production. Overproduction was, in part, a consequence of lack of caution in financial circles. Spurred on by the growing availability of commercial capital during and immediately after the war, they greeted the termination of hostilities with a renewed outbreak of entrepreneurial fever, founding more and more joint-stock companies. But the easy availability of capital that was the basis for this activity proved short lived. The financial crisis that began in Europe and America in 1857 soon produced a serious decline in the Russian money market. In 1858, despite the growing money shortage, the forming of companies in Russia, especially in St. Petersburg, went on, though the frenzy was somewhat abated. An ever larger number of new companies were folding soon after they were founded, foreshadowing the end of the period of boom.[16]

The unfolding of this unusual economic crisis, which lasted for over six years, was paralleled by another important development in a closely related area: this was the emergence of what may be called an economic press, that is, periodicals devoted primarily to the elucidation of not only agrarian but also financial, commercial, and industrial problems, including their most controversial aspects. The growth of private industry, the spread of the habit of speculation in stocks, the sequence of economic boom and crisis—all these developments called for a vehicle of public expression and sources of timely information that were readily available to the reading public. This type of press had failed to take root in Russia before the reign of Alexander II. No official journals devoted primarily to this range of problems even existed before the mid-1820's, and the few that appeared thereafter, of which the most notable was *Zhurnal manufaktur i torgovli* (1825–60), were extremely limited in scope and rarely touched controversial issues. Unofficial periodicals dealing with economics were occasionally launched, but were almost invariably short-lived.[17]

This situation changed when Alexander II became Tsar. The relaxation of censorship that characterized the early years of his regime encouraged the founding of new periodicals, and one result was the appearance, beginning in 1857, of new journals and newspapers to fill Russia's vacuum in economic journalism. Some of the new periodicals, like similar endeavors in the past, failed to maintain themselves and soon vanished. This was the fate of the St. Petersburg weeklies *Zhurnal dlia aktsionerov* (1857–60) and *Proizvoditel' i promyshlennik* (1859–61), and the Moscow monthly *Vestnik promyshlennosti* (1858–61). But others, most importantly the St. Petersburg daily newspaper *Birzhevye vedomosti* (founded in 1861), became more or less permanently established.[18]

In addition to the appearance of new periodicals, the postwar years saw a shift in emphasis on the part of some of the older ones. Among official publications *Zhurnal manufaktur i torgovli*, the bimonthly organ of the Department of Manufactures and Internal Commerce, attempted to assume a new identity by changing its title to the less official-sounding *Promyshlennost'* (Industry) in 1861. According to a contributor to the second issue of *Promyshlennost'*, the change in title denoted what had now become the journal's "chief obligation," namely, "to interpret the basic needs of our industry and, wherever possible, to indicate the means that are necessary for and capable of promoting its development."[19]

Furthermore, periodicals of a more general and diverse character, ranging from the radical *Sovremennik* to the quasi-official *Russkii invalid*, increased their coverage of industrial problems. In most cases this was done without fanfare, but the decision of one biweekly newspaper to introduce a special section called "Industrial Chronicle," on the grounds that industrial life had become one of the "most interesting contemporary questions," highlights a general tendency.[20]

Industrial activity stimulated by the war, postwar economic difficulties, and the general mood of reform all contributed to the growing interest in industrial life that was reflected in the press. Once the economic press was under way, the periodicals in turn served to stimulate even greater interest in industrial problems and related questions. In its very first issue *Promyshlennost'* lamented the failures that had been experienced by Russian companies the previous year, 1860, the contraction of the available money supply, and the decline of public confidence that was reflected in a continued fall in the purchases of stocks.[21] All the next year, the year of the official proclamation abolishing serfdom, the press continued to agonize over the worsening of economic conditions, especially the decline of the ruble in foreign money markets and the desperate situation of many Russian companies, which were unable to find purchasers for their stocks.[22] Only at the beginning of 1863 were there sufficient signs of economic recovery for the newspaper *Birzhevye vedomosti* to assume a tone of confidence concerning the economic prospects of the new year.[23] In summary, between 1853 and 1857 modern urban industry, private enterprise, mechanization, and stock companies grew at an extremely rapid pace; Russians came to believe, in the wake of military and diplomatic humiliation, that Russia must become industrially advanced and self-sufficient. Between 1857 and 1863 there was a financial crisis, industries suffered from overproduction, and many recently founded companies folded, providing growing evidence for those who favored industrial modernization that the process would entail many complications and challenges previously considered to be unique to other countries. Among those challenges was the plight of the St. Petersburg poor.

Direct evidence of the effects of the deteriorating economic situation on the lower-class population of the capital was available from about 1858. The stage was already set by a rise in the price of consumer goods, especially rye flour, that occurred in the last year of the war and continued, because of the extravagant issuing of paper money by the government, into 1857. The rise in the price of grain, averaging over 32 per cent in the northern regions from 1855 to 1856, outstripped whatever rise there was in wages, catching the city-dwelling peasant-otkhodnik who paid obrok (i.e., the typical freely hired urban worker) in a double squeeze.[24] In 1857 complaints about the high cost of living were common in most parts of Russia and were particularly vociferous in St. Petersburg, Moscow, and other relatively large cities.[25] With the coming of the economic crisis, St. Petersburg found itself short of bread; even in 1861, despite a general fall in prices, the prices of many foods were still rising in the capital.[26]

Beginning around 1858 opportunities for industrial employment were reduced on account of the contraction in industrial production.* In Russia as a whole, according to figures of the Ministry of Finance, the number of employed factory workers was about 628,-000 in 1858.[27] By the beginning of 1861, the number had fallen to 565,142; it declined to 549,687 at the beginning of 1862, to 512,778 the following year, and continued to fall for over two more years.[28] In 1860 industrial stagnation had reached a point that caused one of the new economic journals to predict that factories might soon be cutting their labor forces in half.[29]

Although St. Petersburg (for reasons to be discussed in Chapter 6) recovered from the crisis earlier than most parts of Russia, it too experienced the industrial stagnation. The Aleksandrovsk cotton mill, for example, one of the largest cotton mills in Russia, after a year of record sales in 1856 underwent a 50 per cent drop in sales in 1857 and a less dramatic decline in the following years.[30] One of the most important St. Petersburg machine works, the property of a prestigious branch of the Imperial family (the Leuchtenbergs) and virtually the sole producer of rolling stock for the railroads during the Crimean War, ceased production altogether in 1857.[31] Another leading St. Petersburg factory, the Wright cotton-spinning factory, an employer of several hundred workers, was forced to suspend operations in the fall of 1860.[32]

Despite the fall in employment opportunities (and contrary to the assumptions of official optimism), the flow of otkhodnik job seekers into the city—now facilitated by the recent completion of the Moscow–St. Petersburg railroad line—continued during the first few years of economic difficulty.† They came "from everywhere, from all populated villages, both those located along the

---

* If, as is sometimes asserted, one purpose of the emancipation was to provide a labor pool for expanding industries, it appears at least somewhat incongruous that the deliberations preceding the emancipation and the first steps in its implementation occurred at a time of rising industrial unemployment.

† Only in the year after the emancipation manifesto was the inflow of otkhodniki significantly (if only temporarily) reduced, a factor that, combined with the beginning of the recovery of St. Petersburg industry, helped to relieve some of the pressure on the local job market. See pp. 204 and 221 below.

railroad and those in areas adjacent to it, and even from Moscow. Throngs of people, flowing to Petersburg by railway, remain here for prolonged periods."[33] These throngs had to compete for jobs on an already glutted labor market. In 1859 it was so difficult for otkhodniki to find employment that a special information bureau was established for their benefit.[34] The journal *Narodnoe chtenie*, commenting on the deteriorating situation, feared the effect new immigrants were having on the housing and health of St. Petersburg's laboring population, already approaching one hundred fifty thousand, which was "often forced to live in crowded, filthy, dark, damp, and cold cellars and room corners."[35]

Discovery of the problem of overpopulation and underemployment was coupled with a growing concern in the press about the wretched conditions that existed within many St. Petersburg factories. The iniquities of factory life were sometimes exposed in official as well as unofficial publications. *Promyshlennost'*, referring to the situation of Russia's factory workers as "one of the vital questions of our times," called the attention of its readers to the problems of factory life in the capital, which "does not present a very comforting picture." Tanneries—one of the most backward branches of industry in the city—were singled out by the journal for their extreme crowdedness, filth, and poor ventilation: one could distinguish between recently hired tannery workers and those who had been around for longer periods just by looking at their faces. But tanneries formed only a part of the bleak picture presented in *Promyshlennost'*. Other St. Petersburg factories, including some textile mills and chemical plants, were portrayed as suffering from crowded and hazardous conditions; low wages and the excessive use of child labor were angrily decried.[36]

Among the unofficial publications, the conventionally liberal "thick journal" *Biblioteka dlia chteniia* published the most vigorous exposé of St. Petersburg factory conditions. Some of the factories it took to task for poor ventilation, filthy and crowded workshops, long hours, and other abuses were the same ones that had been described in *Promyshlennost'*, but *Biblioteka*, in addition to offering richer detail, extended the list to include several prominent mechanized cotton-spinning mills that had escaped criticism in the previous piece: the Rossiiskii factory and the Samsonievskii factory (both joint-stock companies) among others. At the same time certain textile factories—most notably the large, mechanized

Novyi Company—were praised for their excellent conditions. Machine and metal works were discussed in less detail, but the deplorable conditions in some, the good conditions in others, were mentioned in passing.[37]

Other aspects of the plight of the St. Petersburg poor in general and of workers in particular were brought to light through the publication in 1860 of E. Karnovich's statistical study of St. Petersburg life and of Feodor Terner's lengthy discourse *Concerning the Working Class and Measures to Secure Its Well-Being* (first serialized in *Biblioteka dlia chteniia* in 1859), and through the publication of materials unearthed by two official commissions between 1859 and 1863.[38] The information provided by these sources in turn found its way into the exposés just discussed and was further disseminated by reviews published in other periodicals. In particular, *Sovremennik* reprinted excerpts from Karnovich's chapter on "Social Life in St. Petersburg," which it received very favorably, and from Terner's book, which (for reasons to be discussed later in this chapter) it attacked.[39]

These publications—of motley political coloration, from official to oppositional—circulated information that stimulated public awareness of the problems of the Petersburg poor and placed those problems in an industrial context. But the crucial factor that transformed this awareness into a full-fledged discussion of Russia's peculiar version of the labor question was the impending emancipation of the peasantry. Not only did heightened public concern with the fate of the peasantry spill over into the attention being paid to the urban poor, there was a new assumption that the future of the urban worker in Russia would, by dint of the forthcoming emancipation, unfold under conditions of "free labor," an ambiguous but vitally important concept. People with varying political convictions now converged on the belief that the destiny of the Russian laborer stood at a crossroads. One road, rejected by all, led to proletarianization as it existed in Western Europe. It was the destination of the other road that constituted the labor question in Russia.

Approaches to the Labor Question

In reality no clear lines separated the various attitudes toward the labor question. Since open discussion of the labor question was new in Russia, well-defined schools of thought or "camps" had not been formed around this problem, and there was certainly not the neat division into two opposed camps envisioned by one historian.[40] Moreover, it will be evident that two or more of the positions about to be considered were sometimes espoused by a single writer and that the categories I will be employing are themselves quite fluid. Nevertheless, the imprecise nature of the reality does not relieve us of the responsibility of attempting to isolate and identify its various components, and, where possible, to relate them to the corresponding tendencies in Western Europe.

With these reservations in mind, then, it is useful to distinguish between three general positions regarding the labor question. First, there was the position that accepted and even welcomed the growth of urban industry, recognized that this implied the development of an industrial working class, and sought to deal with the problems of that class within an industrial context. People who took this general attitude usually favored one of two rather distinct approaches to the question of proletarianization. Some welcomed full-fledged proletarianization—the creation of a separate industrial labor force with no ties to the land—arguing that if certain measures were taken the Russian proletariat would not have to duplicate the miserable experiences of its Western European counterpart. Only to the extent that the word "proletariat" connoted those miserable experiences did this approach imply hostility to the idea of a proletariat in Russia; but we shall see that the term was sometimes used in a positive or at least neutral sense by adherents to this approach. On the other hand, there were those who, while equally favorable to the formation of a landless industrial labor force, were not quite comfortable with the thought of full proletarianization and preferred to temper the situation of the urban working class by retaining some features of traditional peasant institutions.

Second, there was the position that, for want of a better term, might be called proto-populist. This amounted to an updated and more complex version of the general view held by the Russian Left in the 1840's. It was essentially but not unqualifiedly hostile to urban industry and utterly opposed to proletarianization in any form. Because of the context in which it arose, this position tended to be less didactic and more defensive than the equivalent view a generation earlier, which had not been part of a specific debate over the labor question.

Finally, there was what might be looked at either as a new version of traditional philanthropy or as an early forerunner of "small deeds" liberalism. Its adherents tried to improve the lot of poor urban workers, notably with respect to housing and literacy, through charitable activity. Strictly speaking, this activity was not really an approach to the labor question as I have defined it here. In order to support housing projects for the Petersburg poor and Sunday education for urban workers and their children, for example, it was not necessary to have a position on the labor question or a common vision of Russia's economic future; it was necessary only to recognize the existence of squalor and ignorance in Russian cities and to be willing to try to rectify these conditions. Such efforts were compatible with a wide variety of political outlooks and received correspondingly varied support. In light of Russia's long tradition of officially sanctioned philanthropic activity, participants did not conceive of their actions as fundamentally new, although some among them were aware that the problems they were dealing with were on a new order of magnitude and that they were dealing with new, nontraditional elements of the population. Moreover, because of the period in which they occurred, certain of these activities, especially the Sunday school movement, took on a spirit of self-generated activity not seen before. In the particular case of the Sunday schools, peasant-workers were offered something that simply had not existed in the past: centers of working-class education and culture, which encouraged workers to forge institutional ties within the city, to replace the lifeless institutions that had, under serfdom, amounted to nothing more than an extension of pomeshchik authority.

For these reasons, the philanthropic approach to the problems of urban workers in the early 1860's, however much it resembled traditional attitudes toward the Armenfrage, should not be completely isolated from a discussion of the labor question. It is therefore noted in this context, although a detailed discussion will be postponed until the following chapter, when we take up specific attempts to improve the lot of workers and their interaction with government policies. We turn now to a more detailed discussion of the first two general positions.

What types of people, in the early years of Alexander II's reign, welcomed and supported industrial growth and recognized, at the same time, the need to face the problems of the new class of industrial workers spawned by industrialization? For the most part, they were persons who occupied positions somewhere in the gray border zone where government, liberal journalism, and the academic world overlapped. Their main governmental base was the Ministry of Finance, where they often held middle-level and occasionally even upper-level posts. Their main journalistic base was the pro-industrial publications discussed earlier as well as the economic and financial sections of more general publications, usually of liberal bent. At the universities and other advanced academic institutions, they occupied chairs in political economy and in the more technological fields; others held advanced degrees in these fields but were not in academic life.

As experts on controversial questions of economic policy—tariffs, taxation, railroad construction, and so forth—they not only wrote extensively on these topics in the periodicals of the day, but were also frequently called upon by the government to serve on the various ad hoc commissions on these and related problems that were repeatedly created during the reign of Alexander II. Indeed, so close were their ties to the government that although our concern with them here is in their capacity as publicists, their views will later be reintroduced in discussing official labor policy.

Most prominent among these figures were I. V. Vernadskii, professor of political economy at St. Petersburg University (formerly at Moscow University), founder and editor from 1857 of the new economic journal *Ekonomicheskii ukazatel'*; E. I. Lamanskii, assistant director (1860–66) and then director (1866–81) of the newly established State Bank, and contributor to the then liberal *Russkii vestnik*; V. P. Bezobrazov, government official, author of several important works on economic and financial questions; I. Ia. Gorlov, professor of statistics and political economy at St. Petersburg University, contributor to *Biblioteka dlia chteniia* and other periodicals; F. G. Terner, official of the Foreign Affairs and Finance Ministries, contributor to *Biblioteka dlia chteniia* and *Ekonomicheskii ukazatel'*. In addition, the economic experts included two future Ministers of Finance: M. Kh. Reutern (minister 1862–78), who came to that post via the Justice and Naval Ministries, and

N. Kh. Bunge (minister 1881–86), then professor of economics and rector at Kiev University, but with close ties to the economists in the capital.[41]

During the years under discussion these and other like-minded personalities constituted a loosely organized circle (*kruzhok*) of "economists" in St. Petersburg, which would meet in private quarters to discuss current economic questions.[42] Though far from being uniform in their economic and political judgments, they shared a general outlook that is partially summarized in Lamanskii's decription of the way "educated people" reacted to the early days of the new regime:

The sympathies of the majority of educated people were favorable to the new movement, the liberal movement, and of course, given the strained condition of society, all the most burning questions of Russian life brought themselves to the fore: the emancipation of the peasants, the reform of the judicial system, the stimulation of commerce and industry. All at once there appeared a striving toward independent action [*samodeiatel'nost'*].[43]

More specifically, the economists tended to admire (with some reservations) West European institutions, especially in the economic sphere, to advocate free trade and free labor, to encourage industrialization and railroad construction, and to serve as the leading theorists and implementers of the reorganization of Russian banking and finance that began around 1860. Although, with the exception of Terner, none of the economists emphasized the labor question in their writings and activities during these years,* most of them were generally favorable to the idea of labor legislation, and some played important roles as advocates of far-reaching pro-labor measures before the drafting commissions that were formed in 1859.[44] Perhaps more important, other less prominent discussants of the labor question were infected with their general spirit.

Although a detailed discussion of these economists would take us well beyond the scope of the present study, it is useful to take a closer look at the background and outlook of the one who was the most outspoken writer on the labor question. Feodor Terner[45] was the author of what was in 1860 the most extensive work on the labor question ever published in Russia: *Concerning the Working Class and Measures to Secure Its Well-Being*. His father was a well-to-do

* Bunge's ministry was instrumental in formulating the famous labor laws of 1882–86.

Baltic German physician who attained high social status in the capital by attending some of the more important noble families. His maternal grandparents were a German Lutheran pastor and a Russian girl from a family of Orthodox clergy. This mixed cosmopolitan background, not uncommon among the economists, opened up a rich experience of travel and bilingual education to young Terner, which he put to good use in his later career.

After graduating from St. Petersburg University in 1850 (where his interests vacillated between economics and the natural sciences), Terner, like most of the nonacademic economists, embarked on a bureaucratic career. He began in the Ministry of Foreign Affairs, but most of his working life was spent in the Ministry of Finance where, in the 1880's, after many years of service, he achieved the less than exalted rank of Assistant Minister.*

Most of Terner's active career was divided between more modest positions in the ministries, special assignments to mixed governmental commissions (e.g., the commission on taxation, 1859–64), travel abroad to international statistical congresses,† and a nonofficial career in politico-economic journalism (which he pursued with a voracious appetite for fame and public approval). Beginning in 1853, he published articles on various aspects of economic and social policy in several journals, including the French language *Journal de St.-Pétersbourg* (of which he was also an editor), Vernadskii's *Ekonomicheskii ukazatel'*, and *Biblioteka dlia chteniia* (where his book on the labor question first appeared in serial form). He also served as an officer of various quasi-official learned societies, most importantly as secretary of the Imperial Russian Geographical Society.

The Geographical Society had a significance for the economists that extended well beyond the pursuit of scholarship. It served as their institutional base, as their gathering place, and as their point of contact with non-economists, both in and out of government, who shared their liberal, Western-oriented outlook to a greater or lesser degree. Of the economists already mentioned, both Bezobra-

---

* Perhaps the two high points of Terner's career were a short stint as tutor to Alexander, the tsarevich, in the mid-1860's and his few months as Acting Minister of Finance in the late 1880's, when the Minister was ill.

† The first such congress was held in Vienna in 1857. Among the Russians who attended were Lamanskii, Vernadskii, and Terner. Terner, *Vospominaniia zhizni F.G. Ternera*, I (St. Petersburg, 1910), 143.

zov and Lamanskii, in addition to Terner, served terms as secretary of the Society in the 1850's. Lamanskii was elected to that post in 1853, when he succeeded the ailing V. A. Miliutin who, it will be recalled, was one of the few Russian thinkers of the late 1840's who had been interested in the development of a Russian industrial labor force. Miliutin's older brothers, the famous reformers Dmitri and Nikolai, both served on the council of the Geographical Society; and Terner, an ardent admirer of the liberal circles of the Miliutins, the Grand Duchess Elena Pavlovna, and the Grand Duke Konstantin Nikolaevich, became (in 1859) a frequent visitor to the "evenings" at N. Miliutin's where the forthcoming emancipation and other burning issues were discussed. The Grand Duchess, in turn, was among the notables who sometimes attended the "evenings" of the economists' circles, which were held either at Bezobrazov's home or at the quarters of the Geographical Society.[46]

Lamanskii recalls that in 1855, upon hearing of the death of Nicholas I, members of the Geographical Society were so elated, so confident that the superiority of European science and technology evidenced by the course of the war would push the new regime in a progressive direction, that they embraced each other on the streets.[47] With due allowances for probable exaggeration, this description comes close to capturing the spirit of people like Terner in the early years of Alexander's reign. Looking back on these years with a trace of cynicism, but without bitterness, Terner was later to write: "A new epoch was beginning, full of hopes and illusions. . . . Russian society, having lain without motion for so long, in the seclusion of a heavy slumber, was startled out of its sleep and lept into life." With the relaxation of censorship and the mushrooming of new journals, "it seemed as if only that which could serve as a guidepost to the improvement of social life and the raising of the economic welfare of the people was valued in the eyes of society."[48] Despite the slightly derogatory tone one might sense in these and other statements by Terner, suggesting a lack of practicality in the holders of these attitudes, he—like most of his colleagues and close associates—shared in the spirit of the times.

Like the other economists he firmly believed in Westernization, meaning primarily economic progress and industrial development, which he considered essential both for the strengthening of the state and for the future well-being of the people; he favored judicial reform, administrative rationality, and free expression; and, of vital import with respect to the labor question, he championed not only abolition of serfdom but also the obliteration of all its vestiges, including communal land tenure. As M. Tugan-Baranovskii has correctly stated, the "liberal economists" of this period (whom he identifies primarily with Vernadskii's *Ekonomicheskii ukazatel'*) looked at serfdom "with as great and steadfast a hostility as even the most extreme radicals of that period."[49] But, as I will have occasion to stress, liberal economists and extreme radicals were sharply divided over the question of the commune.

In a sense, then, Terner and the other economists were the intellectual carriers, and the new economic press (together with some general periodicals) the intellectual organs of ascendant economic modernization and industrial capitalism. But it is a serious error to infer from this, as certain historians have done, that they in any sense represented or were spokesmen for the industrial bourgeoisie or industrialists as a class.[50]

On the contrary, they held views on some questions that were—or at least were felt to be—in conflict with the interests and certainly with the wishes of those Russian manufacturers who articulated their views. The most obvious example was the antipathy of Terner, Vernadskii, and their associates to protectionism, their Manchesterian predilections toward free trade. If in the past free trade had been the doctrine of exporters of grains and raw materials, of those most cautious about the development of the industrial sector of Russia's economy, in the postwar period it became the watchword of the pro-industrial economists. Unlike the adherents of the original Manchester School in England, the still insecure manufacturers of Russia—before and after the passage of the tariff of 1857—were the leading advocates of protectionism.[51] At the same time, as was noted earlier, the liberal economists (and, with some exceptions, the economic and liberal press in general), far from sharing the negative views of classical Manchester liberalism on government intervention in the mutual relations between labor and capital and related questions, tended to support measures aimed at protecting industrial workers from abuses by their employers.* Indeed, if any general attitude toward Russian manufac-

* Recognizing that the cleavage between the views of the liberal economists and practicing industrialists made it impossible to explain the outlook of the former in terms

turers emerged, it was hostility toward them as a class, an attitude that Terner and others found to be completely reconcilable with their belief in industrialization. This feeling of antipathy and distrust (from which some of the more enlightened St. Petersburg industrialists were exempted) was an essential ingredient of the evolution of the labor question.

Hostility Toward Manufacturers

It was their position on the tariff question, as has been indicated, that made Russian manufacturers especially vulnerable to attack, particularly in the economic press. The fact that financial crisis and economic difficulties followed closely on the heels of the unusually moderate tariff law of 1857 made it possible for manufacturers to argue during the following years that the absence of protectionism was responsible for the stagnation in some branches of industry, and that higher tariffs were needed as an antidote. *Birzhevye vedomosti* was one of the new periodicals that opened its columns to both sides of the tariff controversy, thus providing literate industrialists access to a public forum. In a series of articles entitled "On the Need to Develop the Internal Productivity of Russia," Sergei Shipov articulated the view of many industrialists that high tariffs on foreign manufactures were essential for both offsetting the current money shortage and providing for the growth of "national wealth" in the face of otherwise unendurable competition from West European industry.[52]

Of interest to us here is not the classical array of economic arguments employed by the pro-industrial opponents of this position, but the way they counterposed the selfishness of manufacturers to the true interests of Russia and the Russian people in the course of presenting their case. The vehemence of their position is illustrated by the response to Shipov's article printed in *Birzhevye*

---

of the interests of the latter, Tugan-Baranovskii has argued, half-heartedly and not very convincingly, that the economists represented the interests of the "financial and stock-exchange" wing of the bourgeoisie. But he granted that in comparison to the free traders of earlier decades, they did not have a very "glaring class coloration." M. Tugan-Baranovskii, *Russkaia fabrika v proshlom i nastoiashchem* (3d ed., St. Petersburg, 1907), pp. 518–24. For a more direct acknowledgment of the need to approach the liberalism of this (and a later) period as a phenomenon that should not be identified with the bourgeoisie as a class, see the very interesting article by I. F. Gindin, "Russkaia burzhuaziia v period kapitalizma, ee razvitie i osobennosti," *Istoriia SSSR* (No. 2, 1963), esp. p. 78.

vedomosti the next month. The author, V. Vladimirov, a free trader who owned shares in several large Petersburg companies, conceded some of Shipov's points; but he responded to the main line of argument with the accusation that Shipov was a typical factory owner in his views, and took him to task for his willingness to sacrifice Russia's long-range interests to "the enrichment of a few manufacturers."[53]

The St. Petersburg industrialist Vasilii Poletika was subjected to a similar attack in the same newspaper. Poletika had risen to great prominence in the industrial world on the basis of government contracts during the Crimean War, but like other manufacturers, he suffered from the reduction of government contracts in the years that followed. Now a leading spokesman for protectionism and other causes of the industrial community, Poletika was severely criticized for basing his position on the tariff question on the interests of "a minority" rather than the interests of the Russian masses.[54] Similarly, articles on the tariff question in other pro-industrial periodicals (economic journals, general liberal periodicals, and quasi-official organs) deplored the enrichment of "a few dozen factory owners at the expense of millions of peasants."[55]

An assault on the selfishness of industrialists in the newspaper *Russkii invalid* is especially interesting in that this paper had been until very recently the official organ of the Ministry of War, and was still closely associated with that ministry when the article in question appeared (1861). The head of the Ministry of War was then Dmitri Miliutin, an important frequenter of the reformist circles that, as has been indicated, overlapped considerably with the circle of economists. The ministry, the newspaper, and Miliutin himself were strong proponents of the development of Russia's industrial self-sufficiency, a cause that was enthusiastically defended by the War Minister in his official report to the Tsar of January 15, 1862.[56] But *Russkii invalid*, like other pro-industrial periodicals, did not hesitate to attack industrialists for narrowly pursuing their self-interests with regard to the tariff and other controversial questions. When, in 1861, an unprecedented organization was formed at the initiative of a group of manufacturers, including Shipov, to further the cause of protectionism and other goals,* the paper launched into a virulent attack on its founders:[57]

* The "Society for the Encouragement of the Prosperity of Fatherland Industry."

The people who founded the society are our old acquaintances. . . . These people have always been opposed to the healthy ideas and conclusions of science, which have been striving to introduce some light into the dark situation of our manufacturing industry. In this desperate struggle, they have resorted to all methods. They have retained hired agents who have written entire brochures for them about the value of the protectionist system for society; before every change in the tariff, they have come to Petersburg by the hundreds and threatened to wreck all machines if the scales of the new tariff tip to the other side.

In the same article Poletika was roundly scored for having made public speeches in St. Petersburg in which he called for high tariffs on imported machinery. In short, leaving aside its hyperbole about the wrecking of machines, *Russkii invalid* was simply stating its opposition to any manufacturers who dared to lobby or organize in favor of goals that the editors considered harmful.

In light of these attacks, it is not surprising that the circles under discussion, once the question of the fate of the Russian worker was in the air, were generally unprepared to rely on the voluntary benevolence of manufacturers to resolve the problem. If in discussing the tariff question the press defended the interests of the Russian masses in their capacity as consumers, how much sharper would be its defense of that section of the lower classes that was most directly exposed to the meanness of manufacturers—the industrial workers!

Thus the exposé-type articles cited earlier—one of which appeared in a journal of which Terner was an editor, the other in an organ of the ministry to which he and several of his economist colleagues were attached—bitterly complained about the mistreatment of workers, singled out the names of St. Petersburg manufacturers considered to be the worst offenders, and (although they noted exceptions) reproached Russian industrialists as a whole for their inhumanity and backwardness (*nerazvitost'*).[58] An article in *Russkaia rech'*, deploring how little attention had been paid in the past by Russian writers and society in general to the plight of factory workers, referred harshly to "our merchant-manufacturers, who exploit the strength and health of the people, drink its blood with impunity, corrupt its children, and acquire enormous fortunes through these methods."[59]

The pervasiveness of this hostility is highlighted by the fact that even some industrialists and the few writers who attempted to defend them felt obliged to concede the validity of some of the criticisms. In a lengthy article in *Birzhevye vedomosti*, written in response to *Russkii invalid*'s attack, D. Skuratov denied that it was the greed of manufacturers that accounted for the high prices and the increased unemployment of "our people" in the winter months when they needed work most. It was the absence of sufficient tariff protection, he argued, that bore the real responsibility. Yet he also conceded that the poor education and "semi-Asiatic" habits of Russia's merchant-manufacturers had some bearing on these problems, and pleaded with his readers in a defensive manner not to blame an entire class for failings that were the result of historically determined laws. Not surprisingly, the editors of *Birzhevye vedomosti* made it a point to inform their readers that Skuratov's views did not represent those of the paper.[60]

One manufacturer, who prudently preferred to remain anonymous, even went so far as to publish a scathing attack against his own class for its maltreatment of workers. He accused his fellows of relating to their workers as despots, perpetrating deliberate violations of contract, and subjecting workers to conditions that would have been harmful even to animals, thus impairing their moral development and reducing their value as laborers. Unlike Skuratov, he did not limit his indictment to uneducated and backward manufacturers, but attacked even those who appeared to be educated and progressive for nonetheless refusing to recognize that "the worker is a human being, and ought to be treated humanely."[61] Along similar lines, the thesis was argued in the columns of *Birzhevye vedomosti* that the Russian manufacturer was actually becoming increasingly crude in his treatment of workers in proportion to his success as a big industrialist.[62]

The Influence of Western Experience

Thus far I have presented the new concern for factory workers and the antagonism toward manufacturers as direct responses to specific conditions in Russia: economic crisis, the tariff controversy, ferment over emancipation, and specific knowledge of conditions in the factories of St. Petersburg and other areas. But although references to these factors by the authors I have cited make it abundantly clear that internal Russian developments played an important role in turning the attention of educated society to what was essentially a new range of problems, the actual views that emerged on the labor question, including assumptions regarding the pernicious role of manufacturers, stemmed from other sources. Specifically, they derived from knowledge about the plight of workers and the conduct of manufacturers in the relatively advanced industrial countries of Western Europe, and from an awareness of proposed or attempted solutions to the labor question in those countries. Indeed it is difficult—given the relatively primitive stage of proletarianization in Russia—to even imagine the emergence of the labor question as a public issue in the absence of the European model. It was mainly in viewing the situation of labor in the West that many who raised the labor question in Russia came to consider solutions other than leaving matters in the hands of industrialists.

This circuitous process of anticipating the plight of the proletariat in one's own country through reading or hearing descriptions of conditions in other more industrially advanced countries was not unique to Russia. French social critics, a leading expert has argued, arrived at their initial understanding of the spreading poverty and squalor of Paris in the 1830's and 1840's as a new and dynamic phenomenon, qualitatively different from the existence of urban poverty in the past, through reading analyses of conditions in industrial England. As Louis Chevalier has put it, "The *Mystères de Londres* . . . helped people to understand the *Mystères de Paris*."[63] Similarly, it is well known that Lorenz von Stein's study of conditions in France assisted many Germans—including Marx—to discover the proletariat in the 1840's.

Since the two agents of influence—specific conditions in Russia and impressions of the situation in other countries—were by no means mutually exclusive, there was a natural interplay between them as changing conditions in Russia stimulated greater interest in the West and knowledge of the West was brought to bear on the situation in Russia. Consciousness of the experience of other countries seems to have been more influential in the formulation of approaches and solutions, precisely because the Russian economists and journalists understood that the labor problem in Russia was still at an incipient stage, whereas in Europe the problem was full blown and therefore instructive. Chevalier's argument with respect to France was that accounts of English conditions opened the eyes of Frenchmen to a situation that already existed in France, but was not yet adequately understood. In Russia, by contrast, where the labor question emerged at a time when the vast majority of actual and potential laborers had still not severed their ties with the land, at a time when the country—it was thought—was about to enter but had not yet entered an imperfectly understood era of free labor, the experiences of more industrialized countries necessarily played a somewhat different role, as may be seen through a closer look at the writings of Terner.

Both a sensitivity to the actual material and spiritual privations of the industrial workers of St. Petersburg and a natural inclination to assess them through comparison with the conditions of workers in Western Europe were manifest in Terner's approach to the labor question. "In Petersburg itself," he wrote, as if to display his knowledge of the European scene, "we can find pictures of life that are dark enough to occupy an honorable position in any novel in the genre of *Mystères de Paris* and *Mystères de Londres*." And he then went on to illustrate this point with several pages of data on conditions in the Russian capital.[64]

Nevertheless, Terner was of the opinion that the horror of full-fledged pauperism and proletarianization could still be averted in Russian cities. Employing the frequently invoked metaphors of pathology and medicine, he wrote:

It is much easier to arrest and cut off the disease at the beginning of an illness than when it already has attained its full development. In this respect we have been placed in a particularly advantageous position. What with the sparseness of our urban population, what with the absence of pauperism, we may easily, through certain reasonable measures, by relatively modest means, move the whole matter in such a direction as to be able to cut off completely the future development of pauperism in this country.[65]

Even within this short citation—as in Terner's work as a whole —there is an element of confusion about whether Russia had yet contracted the disease of pauperism. The logic of Terner's descriptions of the situation in St. Petersburg suggests that he believed the disease had begun to set in but was still reversible. But for practical purposes the distinction was unimportant, the approach in either case being essentially one of preventive medicine. The crucial point for Terner was that whatever the danger signals, Russian industrialization had not yet produced and need not inevitably inflict the same physiological and psychic damage on the laboring masses that English and French society had permitted through decades of inaction.[66]

Terner's analysis should not be mistaken for the related but basically different thesis of the old optimists. A few people, such as Tengoborskii—who had actually had an important and direct influence on the evolution of Terner's economic views, and even on his early career[67]—had maintained that the character of existing Russian institutions would allow an organic industrial growth without proletarianization. Terner, however, was writing at a time when emancipation was imminent and when the contraction of industrial employment opportunities had not been mitigated by a return of the peasant-otkhodniki to their villages (which was counted on by the optimists). There was visible unemployment in St. Petersburg and a continued flow of peasants into the city. To defend the optimistic line under these circumstances would have made little sense, and none at all for a strong advocate of Western industrialization. Perhaps anticipation of the degree to which the terms of emancipation would impede full proletarianization might have led to the revival of a sort of neo-optimism during these years of transition. Something of this sort, as we shall see, did appear within the Left. But the economists neither anticipated nor desired such an outcome. Insofar as the concept of proletarianization carried no normative connotations, that is, insofar as it simply meant the formation of a separate working class without any ties to the land, the economists were outspoken believers in its necessity. Vernadskii made this explicit in 1858, when he wrote in the critical notes to his translation of Tengoborskii's major work:

The more that a [factory] worker is involved in agriculture, the less skillful a worker he will be, and his security decreases to the extent that he is less productive in the factory. . . . If the tiller of soil is a poor worker in the factory, then the factory worker is equally bad behind the plough. Real accomplishment and success lie not in the unification of occupations, but in their division.[68]

Terner, although he still entertained some vestigial romantic notions concerning the special character of Russian peasant institutions, was generally of the same opinion. His thesis with respect to the future of Russia's industrial labor force can be reduced to a flat and uninspired statement: Because it was at a relatively early point in its industrial growth, Russia might avoid the worst evils of proletarianization, but only if the errors of the West were correctly understood and certain of the antidotes (I will return to the question of which ones) that were tried in the West too late to be fully effective were applied in Russia at an earlier point in the country's economic evolution. In a sense, what we have in Terner is a modified, demystified version of the older Herzen-Slavophile theme of the advantage of Russian backwardness, but applied within an explicitly pro-industrial context that discerned solutions as well as problems in the Western experience. It was the evils of proletarianization, sometimes summed up by Terner in the word "pauperism," that he wished to avert, not the emergence of a proletariat as such.

One or another variety of this basic approach may be found— albeit usually in less explicit and more muted form—in almost all the discussions of the labor question during these years by pro-industrial writers. Almost all of them expressed unconstrained sympathy for the plight of the working classes of industrial Europe, but without rejecting the value of an industrial working class as such; almost all, despite their misgivings, found something in recent West European experience with the labor question for Russia to emulate; and many expressed confidence that the necessary steps could still be taken in time.

Perhaps the most widely supported European approach to the labor question among Russians of our period—and certainly the most likely to gain sympathy from the government—was that of labor legislation. As has already been mentioned, several of the leading economists appeared before governmental commissions in the capacity of experts and argued for far-reaching legislative measures aimed at regularizing contractual relations, the disposition of labor-management disagreements, working conditions, and the norms governing child and female labor. Similar arguments were made in various organs of the St. Petersburg press.

The liberal journal *Biblioteka dlia chteniia*, one of the most forthright supporters of factory legislation, published a strong plea for such measures in 1862 (when there was still reason to believe that the government was disposed to act in this area). This was one of the exposés of conditions in St. Petersburg factories cited earlier. The author, having concluded that the essential element determining the state of labor conditions in any given factory was the character of the owner—a factor on which he was completely unwilling to rely—inferred that only legislative measures, enforced by a rigorous system of factory inspection, could remove the element of chance. The idea of inspecting factories through a system of district inspectors, under a central bureau, with free and unannounced access to the records and premises of all factories and the power to fine recalcitrant manufacturers, was borrowed by the author from what he deemed to be the eminently successful English system. Having examined the French system of supervision by local police officials and rejected it on the grounds that such officials were too easily influenced by local manufacturers, he expressed a fervent hope that Russia would follow the English pattern.[69]

The following year, 1863, after a government commission appointed to draw up a new industrial statute had circulated its penultimate draft for comments and criticism, *Biblioteka dlia chteniia* proved to be one of the most important and constructive critics of the controversial section on labor legislation. While other periodicals, including *Birzhevye vedomosti*, were cautiously describing the draft statute without editorial comment, *Biblioteka* published a series of suggestions for strengthening the draft from the standpoint of achieving greater protection for the workers (e.g., broadening the categories of workers eligible for judicial disposition of their contractual disputes with employers). These criticisms were summarized in the published transactions of the commission, and in at least one significant case a criticism raised by *Biblioteka* was incorporated into the commission's final draft.[70]

The economic journal *Promyshlennost'*, published by the Ministry of Finance, was equally enthusiastic about West European factory legislation, particularly as it related to child labor. In contrast to Terner, however, *Promyshlennost'* was not sanguine about the prospects for Russia's anticipating the labor question at a relatively early stage; instead it considered that Russia already was in a worse position than Western Europe, especially with regard to the situation of child workers and the manufacturers' indifference to that situation. Contrasting an almost idyllic picture of labor conditions in industrial England and among "our Western neighbors" with a more realistic and graphic account of the wretched situation of child labor in Russia, the editor of the journal's "Industrial Leaflet" section concluded that Russia was in more dire need of comprehensive legislation for the protection of minors than were other countries, where "public opinion is more attentive to the needs of all strata of society," workers are "more highly developed" and their ways less "crude," wages are much higher and the food "incomparably better."[71] But this deviation from the more common approach, which held the situation to be healthier in Russia than elsewhere, had little operational significance. In either case the stress was on the same desideratum: the prompt introduction of West European (mainly English) methods for dealing with the labor question.

Considerably more daring than the promotion of factory legislation—which by virtue of the existence of the government drafting commissions seemed to bear an official stamp of approval—was the suggestion that the forms of struggle of Western workers with their employers might be models for the Russian worker. A case in point was a controversial four-part article by V. K. Rzhevskii that appeared in *Russkii vestnik* (edited by Mikhail Katkov, still in his relatively liberal period) in 1860: "On Measures that Assist the Development of a Proletariat."[72] The author openly expressed his admiration for the struggles waged by British workers against their employers and related sympathetically the successes they had achieved in establishing mutual aid funds, trade unions, and other autonomous organizations. Another article by a collaborator in the same journal described the famed London construction workers' strike of 1859 with respect and approbation. Although the enthusiasm of the author (E. M. Feoktistov, then a well-known liberal political writer) was dampened by the ease with which, he claimed, "a few agitators" had succeeded in misdirecting the London masons' energies toward "chimerical" goals, he predicted a great future for industrial unions in England.[73]

Such views even found their way into *Promyshlennost'*—over the signature of an official of the Finance Ministry (soon to obtain the important post of State Controller). V. A. Tatarinov, a regular contributor to the "Commercial-Industrial News" section of *Promyshlennost'*, published a description (not unlike Rzhevskii's) of the recent development of the strike movement in England and explained to his readers in the simplest possible terms, as if addressing complete novices, the meaning of such expressions as "strike" and "union." Without any equivocation, Tatarinov expressed his full support of the workers' struggle with manufacturers and stated his case for the justice and value of strikes:

It is not the principle of anarchy that lies at their basis [i.e. at the basis of strikes] but, on the contrary, the principle of community, of mutual aid and common action; the workers in these cases do not wish harm to others, do not encroach upon the property of others, but defend themselves and try to support their own independence; not a wild unruliness but a feeling of human dignity, a feeling of their own social significance is what guides them, although perhaps not completely and not always consciously. Labor would like to become equal with capital, to march with it along one road, to enjoy the same advantages—and it is hard to claim that it does not have this right, since capital itself is formed by labor and from labor. Not to destroy or diminish the significance of capital, but to be equal with it—this is the inalienable right of labor. But labor can achieve the implementation of this right only by combining the forces of the separate working people. Only then, with this combination, will labor be not only potentially but actually of equal strength with capital.[74]

Even *Vestnik promyshlennosti*, the periodical that came closest to outright identification with the interests of Russian industrialists, published an article of this kind, expressing admiration for the British working class and a favorable posture toward the organization of labor unions, but without going so far as to endorse strikes.[75]

Do these examples of support for the union movement in England imply a belief that similar institutions and tactics were appropriate for Russian workers? The absence of any direct statements to this effect in most of the articles cited is inconclusive, given the tightened censorship of 1860–61 and the sensitivity of the topic.[76] Moreover, none of the articles specifically disavowed the relevance of their remarks to Russian conditions, which would have been a simple and obvious thing to do if one wished to avoid ambiguity. Nor is it possible to imagine, given the nature of these periodicals and the period in question, that the authors simply excluded Russia from the framework of their discussion because it was a uniquely agrarian country to which the issues at hand were irrelevant.

In the case of Rzhevskii, there is almost no ambiguity. He concluded his essay by turning his attention away from the West and toward his own country. The Russian peasantry, he argued (echoing Terner), had not as yet developed into a pauperized proletariat, but the possibility of this happening was now clearly present. If it were to be avoided, the government must allow a free interplay between the forces of capital and labor and maintain a completely "hands-off" attitude with respect to relations between workers and employers.[77] Although in part this may well have been an argument against labor legislation, in the context of Rzhevskii's discussion of English labor, it was almost certainly also intended as a plea for non-interference by the government in strikes by Russian workers.*

Tatarinov's discussion of the British labor movement eschewed any direct reference to Russia. But the language of the passage quoted above strongly suggests an attempt to set forth universal principles. The "inalienable right of labor" to equality with capital, achieved through combinations and strikes, would seem—in the absence of any statement to the contrary—to apply to Russia as well as England.

Finally, *Russkii vestnik*'s generally favorable account of the London masons' strike, which foresaw a wonderful future for British unionism, included a cryptic suggestion that the problems raised by that strike were not without significance for "other countries."[78] On the whole, then, one is left with the impression—except in the case of *Vestnik promyshlennosti*, where there is no internal evidence one way or the other—that labor unions, even having the right to strike, were viewed by these writers as appropriate institutions for Russia. Like the advocates of labor legislation, they were acutely aware of and strongly sympathetic toward the plight of the European proletariat; they looked favorably upon certain approaches that had recently developed in the West; and (although this was stated much less directly than in the case of advocates of legislation) they seemed to anticipate the application of these methods in Russia.

Implicit in both approaches was a common view of the future of Russia's industrial workers as a distinct class, no longer leading an urban-agrarian double life. The British unions admired by some were permanent class organizations, far removed from the Russian *arteli* of wandering peasant-workers that had been admired

---

* For the Russian government's policies toward labor unrest during this period, see pp. 163–73 below.

in the past as part of an agrarian social order providing a guarantee against proletarianization even in the face of a modicum of industrialization. The labor legislation admired by others, like the abortive legislation of 1835 and 1845, was not intended for a semipeasant temporary labor force. It presupposed, rather, a permanent labor force resembling the industrial proletariat of England and other parts of the West in its place in the social division of labor and in the contractual forms of its relations with employers, which would be governed by laws. In short, the approaches to the labor question discussed thus far were favorable to the transformation of the Russian labor force into a proletariat, insofar as the word denotes full-time, freely hired workers who had neither ownership nor permanent use of any immovable property, were not tied to the land, depended on their employers for tools, and existed exclusively by the sale of their strength and skills. And indeed the point was sometimes made quite explicitly, as when Vernadskii called for the division of industrial from agricultural labor, and A. I. Butovskii, a member of the economists' circle, advocated (in 1858) replacing communal land tenure by a system of individual freedom and private property on the grounds that this transformation would enable otkhodniki who now worked temporarily in cities to "return to the cities and serve as the nucleus of a class of urban workers," a class he considered to be inadequately developed in Russia.[79]

At the same time, insofar as "proletariat" suggested an undesirable condition of material poverty and moral depravity (sometimes equated with "pauperism") that might or might not result from proletarian status in the sense just described, it was precisely in order to prevent the proletarianization of the Russian worker that these writers looked to labor legislation or labor unions or both. Thus it was perfectly consistent for a Rzhevskii to view the highly independent and proletarianized (in the first sense) English working class as a model, and to seek—as indicated in his title—"measures that assist the development of a proletariat in Russia," while simultaneously wishing to avert the proletarianization (in the sense of pauperization) of Russian workers by allowing them to organize in their own defense without government restrictions.

This splitting of the concept of proletarianization was completely consistent with the logic of the existing situation. A quarter of a century earlier, when some government officials were first beginning to discern a latent social and political problem in the situation of factory workers, Western Europe was instructive mainly in a negative sense, awakening a hostility to any form of proletarianization among optimists and pessimists alike. Especially after the revolutions of 1848, the prevalent assumption was that the permanent separation of the peasant-worker from the land and his transformation into a wholly urban being necessarily led to pauperization and therefore to social and political danger. It was unconsciously assumed that the two senses of proletariat were one.

By the beginning of the 1860's, however, Western Europe—in particular England—also provided some evidence, however inconclusive, that through the existence of well-disciplined and successful unions and the enactment of legislative programs, the emergence of a non-pauperized, permanent proletariat was a genuine possibility. It was now quite natural for those who favored industrialization to seize upon this possibility—for those who advocated free labor in contrast to forced labor, but who distrusted the intentions of manufacturers as a class, to begin to look to Western Europe for positive as well as negative models in their approaches to the labor question.

Association—A Russian Solution

Within the pro-industrial camp, there was also a sub-category of approaches that, though basically sharing the outlook just described, including the belief in an emancipated and independent industrial labor force, could not quite accept the notion that such a class could remain immune from pauperism (that is, from proletarianization in the negative sense) without having recourse to traditional Russian institutions for protection. In other words, instead of combining the concept of free industrial labor with Western institutions that reinforced the contractual relationship, the advocates of this second approach sought a special Russian combination that would fuse the West European notion of free industrial labor with a preindustrial communitarian ethos. Although such an approach did not exclude the use of positive examples from Western Europe, it was inspired less by actual developments there than by the experiments and unimplemented schemes of Western social critics, particularly those whom the modern world has come to call utopian.

The fusing of some of the perspectives of Western utopian social-ists with traditional Russian institutions was not, of course, a new phenomenon. It had occurred in various combinations in Herzen and in the Petrashevtsy, and it would arise again in various mani-festations of Russian Populism. What was unique, however, was its appearance in completely nonradical circles closely connected to the government, where industrial capitalism and economic West-ernization in general were viewed as a positive good, and where—in distinction from the proto-Populism of the same period—no positive value was placed on the commune as such, no negative value on the separation of the industrial worker from the land.

The central argument, which developed under the influence of Robert Owen, was that cooperation and association (more or less vaguely conceived) represented a particularly suitable solution to the labor question in Russia because these concepts had a close affinity to an already functioning traditional institution: the work-ers' artel'. Owen was a complex and even self-contradictory figure whose imprecise thinking, as E. P. Thompson has put it, "made it possible for different intellectual tendencies to co-exist" within the Owenite movement.[80] Consider Thompson's contrast between Owen, the enlightened philanthropist and benevolent owner of New Lanark cotton mills who eschewed class conflict by encourag-ing communitarian forms for his workers, and "Owenism," the inspiration for a young and struggling labor movement that en-visioned cooperation as a substitute for competitive capitalism.[81] It was to the former that some nonradical Russians looked during these years.

In 1861 *Russkii invalid* published an article that openly praised Owen, set forth Owenite arguments for the principle of association, and claimed that the organization of labor on the basis of that prin-ciple represented the most advanced stage in labor's evolution. The author, K. R'ianov, disputed the common claim that the principle of free labor—which he considered (prematurely) to have been already introduced with the recently promulgated abolition of serf-dom—was entitled to that honor. Free labor had many advantages, and was clearly superior to serfdom; but in the last analysis it would not benefit the workers because (according to the quasi-official journal of the Imperial War Ministry) it represented the "exploi-tation" of them by "capitalists" and hence "the eternal struggle of manufacturers and workers, capital and labor," that existed in England.[82]

Whereas this language strongly suggests a conception of association as an alternative system to free enterprise, it turns out on closer examination that the author's terminology is misleading. R'ianov was not really questioning the system of privately owned factories and the hiring of free labor. This becomes clear in connection with his optimistic claim that association already existed in St. Petersburg, an assertion that he based on the example of a privately owned factory in the Schlüsselburg industrial area. There, according to R'ianov, the owner of the factory was organizing his workers in a way that held out the hope that "our manufacturers" were not opposed to "the development of the principles of association among the workers."[83] Association, in other words, was (as at New Lanark) a device for improving the collective life of workers within privately owned industry; it was not meant to be the basis for the organization of production itself. Free labor, then, would continue to exist, but the relation would be between the manufacturer and the collective labor association rather than between the manufacturer and the individual worker; association would become not so much a higher form *than* free labor as a higher form *of* free labor. Free labor would be eliminated only in the same limited sense in which a pauperized proletariat would be eliminated through the enactment of factory legislation or the development of powerful labor unions. Indeed, reduced to these terms, the difference between R'ianov's advocacy of labor associations and, say, Rzhevskii's support of labor unions becomes marginal. (This is why I include both views as sub-categories of an essentially similar approach, rather than lump views like R'ianov's with those of the radical advocates of association to be discussed in the concluding section of this chapter.) Other statements sympathetic to the concept of labor associations that appeared in the economic press of this period did not differ substantially from R'ianov's article, and were restricted by essentially the same boundaries.[84]

The most significant expression of the pro-association approach to the labor question from within the camp of liberal economists appeared in Terner's book. Since Terner was in most respects the very embodiment of the mainstream of Russian thought on politico-economic questions during this period, his unique espousal, among the circle members, of an approach that looked to traditional Russian as well as European institutions for a model is of particular interest. It will be recalled that he had posed the question of what measures could be taken, even while one encouraged the industrial expansion of the Russian economy, in order to "cut off the future development of pauperism" before the "disease" began to spread out of control. He sought his answer both in the West and in Russia. Like Rzhevskii, whom he quoted heavily, Terner rejected a whole series of West European methods—ranging from archaic to contemporary—for alleviating the misery of the lower classes. These included the old English approach of directly subsidizing the poor, as well as the most recent English factory legislation so warmly endorsed by some of Terner's colleagues. All such measures, he argued, were superficial, ineffective, and damaging to the workers' initiative.[85] What he did find in the West—in England, France, and parts of Germany—were two related principles which he considered to be the two great forces that would enable the working class to secure its own well-being "by itself, within its own means," and "with much greater certainty" than if it were to rely "on others, on private charity, or on the benevolence of society, of the state." These principles he identified as "savings" (*sberezhenie*) and "association."[86]

By "savings" Terner meant the combining of the financial resources of individual workers in a common mutual aid or savings fund (*kassa vzaimnogo vspomoshchestvovaniia* or *kassa sberegatel'-naia*) that would provide each contributor with security against unemployment, illness, and old age. "Association" (as used by Terner) in a sense meant the positive uses of this combined capital, including not only cooperative consumption, which lowered the cost of living, but also cooperative production, whereby workers might even become the masters of their factories.[87] It was the last point, the idea of associating for production rather than merely for consumption or collective bargaining, that distinguished Terner's position from that of other liberal advocates of association and made it seem a challenge to individual entrepreneurship.

Although Terner did not specify the precise Western European sources of his ideas, it is clear enough that he was well acquainted with various schools of utopian socialism. In arguing for association, he mentioned Proudhon. Elsewhere he referred to "social-communist" teachings, which he criticized for denying private property but praised for defending the principle of association.[88]

But more important to Terner than any school of social thought were various social experiments, recently attempted in England, France, and Germany. He believed that these experiments would flourish much more richly in the virgin soil of Russia:

With the development of the urban and factory population, whose numbers—as a result of the coming reform [i.e. emancipation]—should increase greatly, the present moment seems to be the most propitious for introducing those institutions for the working class that have proved so useful in other countries, and that once rooted in our soil will develop together with the working class and bear the most beneficial fruits, nipping pauperism in the bud.[89]

The particular experimental institutions Terner had in mind included, among others, Louis Napoleon's *cités ouvrières*, the Schulze-Delitzsch banking institutions for workers in Germany, and various mutual aid societies and consumers' associations in England and France. The exact combination of these programs appropriate to Russia was of much less interest to him than the basic principle that he believed inspired all of them, that served as the foundation of his program for industrializing humanely, and that was the "point of departure for any sort of effort toward a real, essential transformation of the conditions and life of the working-class population"—namely, association.[90]

For the other major source of his program Terner looked to native Russian institutions, where he found what he believed to be a genuine basis on which the principle of association could be grafted successfully. Significantly, it was not in the commune that he found the solution. Although much later in his life he was to become a defender of communal land tenure, in the late 1850's and early 1860's Terner, like Vernadskii and most of the economic liberals, considered himself an enemy of the commune: "As a true economist, I argued heatedly . . . with the defenders of communal tenure and was an absolute champion of the principle of private [*viz.*, individually owned] property in peasant land tenure."[91] His case against communal tenure was based on what were then the standard liberal arguments: it hindered the application of modern technology; it fostered an equality that was founded on poverty; it provided no adequate answer to the Malthusian dilemma of the

pressure of geometrically expanding populations on a fixed or arith-
metically expanding supply of land. But Terner combined this line
of reasoning with a more novel argument, which seems to have been
directed toward partisans of the commune on the political Left.
Stated briefly, his argument was that the repartitional commune
(which from a radical perspective was the quintessential commune,
since only periodic repartition guaranteed equality of holdings)
retained the worst feature of private ownership, i.e. individual cul-
tivation, instead of adopting the one redeeming feature of social-
communist teachings—collective labor.[92]

This line of criticism of the commune helps to clarify Terner's
somewhat ambiguous conception of labor associations and leads us
to the Russian institution in which he did find a parallel. If the commune to Terner meant individual labor on collectively owned
property, labor associations meant collective labor on property or
with tools and machinery to which the members still retained individual title. In principle this was very close to the Russian artel', or
at least to those producers' arteli that served as something more than
a collective device for hiring out to others. From this Russian folk
institution associations might effectively develop—even more effectively than in Western Europe—in the coming post-emancipation
era of free labor and unrestricted mobility.[93]

Earlier in this study I argued that the artel' was, in effect, the
extension of communal custom and seigneurial authority in the city.
It was a rural institution, relocated in an urban area, that tended to
widen rather than bridge the gap between the peasant-otkhodniki
and the regular urban population.[94] Now, in Terner's program,
this situation was given a novel twist. The artel' became the focus
of an interesting but rather ineffectual effort, within the pro-industrial milieu, to salvage something from Russian tradition and folk
custom that would serve to alleviate the sufferings and minimize
the atomization of Russian workers during the period of early industrialization. The commune, it was thought, was destined, quite
properly, to vanish, thus cutting the peasant-workers loose to become a proletariat in the acceptable (for Terner) descriptive sense.
But at the same time, by championing the artel', Terner was attempting, as it were, to cut the umbilical cord at a point somewhat
further from the factory and nearer the village. A vestige of rural

Russia, the artel' would continue to protect the Russian worker against the menace of the modern world of mechanized industry and competitive capitalism, the advent of which Terner and his colleagues, despite their genuine concern for the workers' fate, basically welcomed.

Because of his emphasis on the producers' artel' Terner seemed to be making more sweeping proposals than were other liberal supporters of association: the idea of associations entering the field of industrial production implicitly challenged individual entrepreneurship. But the distance between Terner and the others was more apparent than real. Despite his avowed preferences for collectivism, Terner did not intend for labor associations to become the basic organizational form for Russian industry. He thought of them not as a substitute for but as a supplement to private entrepreneurship, ultimately modifying but never preempting the existing relations of production. Indeed he was outspokenly skeptical regarding the workers' moral and financial capacity to gain control of and administer the larger, more complex forms of industry. In his most far-reaching projection big industrialists would be compelled by the pressure of the competition that producers' associations generated to improve the lot of their workers and to enter into some kind of profit-sharing partnerships with associations of workers.[95]

Clearly Terner's view of Russian industrialists was not sanguine. Left to their own devices, in the absence of pressures from below, that is from labor, they were (in his analysis) as prepared to victimize their employees as were their counterparts in the West. Yet when it came to the point of recommending practical steps to launch the association movement in Russia, when it came to the question of who would provide the initial impetus and financial backing for the transformation of arteli into full-fledged associations, Terner saw the upper classes—rich industrialists most notably—as the only viable source. R'ianov emphasized the virtues of St. Petersburg manufacturers in order to justify his guarded optimism with respect to the future of associations in Russia.* Similarly, Terner looked for patronage to the rich and powerful—those classes which, if they

---

* "Two paths now lie before the manufacturers of Petersburg: the path of progress and the path of the Moscow industrialists. To hesitate is not permissible." *Russkii invalid*, Oct. 10, 1861.

did not act on the basis of enlightened self-interest, would themselves suffer in the end "from those moral and social ills that pauperism engenders."[96]

There was an obvious circularity, if not a clear contradiction, in
Terner's position. It sought support within the very economic group
whose indifference to the situation of workers was presumably one
of the reasons that programs like association were needed in the
first place. Given the general quiescence of urban workers in this
period, their relative social backwardness when it came to any form
of collective organization,[97] any advocate of non-governmental approaches to the labor question was bound to run into the same
dilemma the moment he ventured from general arguments into a
discussion of concrete first steps for effecting a program. Logically,
the difficulty could be resolved only by assuming, as R'ianov had
done, the existence of exceptional industrialists whose attitude
toward the workers was cast from a different mold than that of what
had already become the prototypical industrialist. The same backward qualities that seemed to create the possibility of Russia's resolving the labor question in a timely manner made the search for a
social basis for implementing the solution premature. One could
look to Europe for enlightenment about the problem and for hypo-
thetical solutions; one could look to cities like St. Petersburg for
evidence that the problem was now beginning to spread to Russia;
and one could even look to Russia's past for solutions that could be
merged with those found abroad. But except for the government
itself, no force in Russia appeared capable of attacking the labor
question at this time. Those who were less thoroughly committed
to transforming Russia into an industrial power—especially those
on the Left—did not find themselves at quite the same impasse, but
they were no less perplexed by the problem.

Left Opposition to Proletarianization

The Russian Left, or so-called revolutionary-democrats, had the
same basic attitude toward urban labor in the late 1850's and early
1860's that it had had in the 1840's: it was opposed to the creation
of an urban proletariat. Gone, however, was the confidence that
communal institutions would shelter the peasantry from proletarianization. In an atmosphere that seemed to favor the acceleration
of industrialization, with the emancipation of the peasantry immin-

ent and the prospect of insufficient land for freed peasants looming ever larger, there was less and less reason to believe in the nonproletarian future of the Russian masses. The fate of the workers of Western Europe might be shared by those of Russia after all. Many within the Left believed that Russia now stood at a turning point, and in some cases there was a new note of desperation in their discussions of proletarianization.

In 1861, the following thoughts of an anonymous author were quoted with approval in the radical journal *Sovremennik*: Russia now stood in the precise historical position that England had occupied at the beginning of her industrialization; like English industry before it, Russian industry was embarking on a course of rapid development that would be spurred on by the emancipation of the peasantry from serfdom. "Yet the [Russian] people are in a state of completely rude ignorance . . . , with neither a religious nor a moral defense against all the evils that are necessarily tied to factory industry. I have already seen factories in Russia where children under ten years old worked at night and lived in quarters that even an Irishman would not enter."[98] The same anxious sense that Russia might be on the threshold of a future of proletarianization infected Nikolai Shelgunov's famous illegal manifesto "To the Young Generation,"[99] written in collaboration with the radical poet Mikhail Mikhailov in 1861: "The emancipation of the peasants is the first step either toward a great future for Russia or toward her misfortune —toward political and economic prosperity or toward an economic and political proletariat. Which of the two roads will be chosen depends on us." His anxiety was tempered by hope because, unlike Europe, Russia could still build on old institutions like the agricultural commune: "We are a backward people, and in this lies our salvation. We should praise the fates that we have not lived the life of Europe. Her misfortune, her hopeless situation is a lesson to us. We do not want her proletariat, her aristocratism, her governmental principles, and her imperial power." The liberation of the peasantry that had just been promulgated, however, meant that there were now "twenty-three million liberated people for whom the wide road toward [becoming] a European proletariat was opened"; but the road could still be closed by a joining of forces of the oppressed peasant masses with the youth of all classes.[100]

Shelgunov's fear of impending proletarianization was not expressed solely in this anonymous proclamation, which was aimed at stirring up revolutionary sentiment. Among Russian radicals of the period it was he who attempted most systematically to educate his readers with respect to the iniquities of industrial capitalism. His most ambitious effort was a lengthy essay entitled "The Working Proletariat in England and France,"[101] printed in *Sovremennik* shortly after the dissemination of "To the Young Generation." His avowed aim was to demonstrate to Russian readers the evils perpetrated upon the laboring populations of Europe by its economic systems. His method was to expose the harsh conditions of the working classes of France and England, relying in the latter case on materials drawn from the writings of Friedrich Engels (chiefly *The Condition of the Working Class in England*, first published in 1845).[102] Shelgunov displayed no interest in, nor even any knowledge of, the theories of Marx and Engels that had been developed since the original publication of Engels's study. For him there was no dialectical road to social justice leading through the painful development of industrial capitalism. Engels had used his study of conditions in England as evidence of what was on the verge of developing in Germany; Shelgunov made use of the materials provided by Engels as evidence of what could happen in Russia, but with the primary purpose of strengthening his case against it.

To Shelgunov, then, as to most other radicals of the period who touched on the labor question, concern with the labor question was essentially a corollary of a more fundamental concern with the peasant question: What would be the fate of the peasantry under conditions of emancipation? *Sovremennik*, under the editorial leadership of Nikolai Chernyshevskii, was the publication in which the retention of the commune in the post-emancipation period was most vigorously defended. By contrast, Vernadskii, Terner, and their circle of liberal economists were concerned with the labor question primarily as a function of their desire to achieve economic modernization of the country with a minimum of social dislocation. Not only did they regard retention of the peasant commune as incompatible with a modern industrial economy, they were actually the most vigorous opponents of the commune. It followed logically that despite some friendly personal contacts and occasional journalistic collaboration between members of the two camps,[103] the views of the liberal economists were generally held in contempt by people like Shelgunov and Chernyshevskii.*

Whatever the differences in their proposals for resolving the labor question, all the economists and publicists discussed earlier in this chapter, either specifically or by implication, predicated their arguments on the certain formation of a landless proletariat. This was true—as has been stressed—even of Terner, whose views on association placed him closer to the Left than the other economists. Free labor, to the economists, was not simply the opposite of forced labor, that is serfdom, which both they and the radicals passionately opposed; it implied the eradication of any artificial constraints on the operations of the free labor market, such as those embodied in such residual institutions as the internal passport system, the rural commune, and the urban guild structure. The right of workers to combine in unions and engage in an open economic struggle with their employers presupposed a landless proletariat that existed solely through the sale of its combined labor power; and even labor legislation, though it involved government intervention in the industrial labor market, was an attempt to provide a rational and regularized legal base for an independent and permanent labor force.

This range of views could have little appeal to partisans of the commune, for whom freedom was inseparable from land. It is true that when others argued for specific protective measures, especially with regard to child labor, *Sovremennik* saw no inconsistency in adding its support. Thus the measures advocated before government commissions by "our economists" (Bunge, Vernadskii, Bezobrazov, Lamanskii) were depicted in that journal in a completely positive light.[104] Given their basic sympathies for the poor and the oppressed, it is difficult to imagine the *Sovremennik* radicals doing otherwise. But contradictory or not, expressions of support for such measures were isolated incidents, far from the mainstream of radical thought about Russian social conditions, and difficult to reconcile

---

* Shelgunov, probably with considerable exaggeration, has credited Chernyshevskii's journalistic polemic with Vernadskii and other economists over the commune, in the years preceding the emancipation, with clarifying the issues in a way that contributed decisively to the government's decision to retain the commune. N. V. Shelgunov, *Vospominaniia* (Moscow, 1923), p. 29. For a concise discussion of the evolution of Chernyshevskii's thought on the commune and related matters see Franco Venturi, *Roots of Revolution* (New York, 1960), pp. 147–55.

with a vision of the commune as the first line of defense against proletarianization.

Because of their ostensible proximity to the principles of the Russian Left, solutions to the labor question that were based on the principle of association present us with a more complex problem. At least at first glance there would appear to have been some common ground between the advocates of industrialization who spoke sympathetically of Owen or of association, and Chernyshevskii's circles. The ideas of Owen, Fourier, and Saint-Simon were, of course, well known and admired among the left intelligentsia of the 1860's.[105] N. A. Dobroliubov, *Sovremennik*'s chief literary (really social) critic, had written a lengthy eulogy shortly after Owen's death in 1858 in which he referred to Owen as "one of the most noble and attractive" figures of the century.[106] The article was published in *Sovremennik* in 1859, providing Russian readers with a readily available source of information on Owen during the following years. The protagonists of Chernyshevskii's famous novel *What Is To Be Done?* (1863) were admirers, even disciples of Owen and Fourier, and principles of association were incorporated in the heroine's dressmaking establishment. Even Dmitri Pisarev (1840–68), the guiding spirit of *Sovremennik*'s rival journal *Russkoe slovo* and a man much less sympathetic than other leftists to building socialism on the foundation of communal institutions, was greatly influenced by Owen and Fourier, and wrote of them in glowing terms.[107] And from the early 1860's on, the concept of association—often with specific reference to the Russian artel' as an embryonic form—became an essential element in the populist strain of Russian radical thought.[108]

Why, then, were the instances of sympathy for the principle of association expressed by liberal publicists or economists not welcomed enthusiastically by the Left? Why, specifically, was Terner's book *Concerning the Working Class*, in which he defended the proposition that artel'-based associations were the best solution to the labor question, denounced in the pages of *Sovremennik* by Shelgunov, himself a sympathizer with the principle of associations and a defender of the artel'?[109]

To respond that it was because the Russian Left was anti-industrial whereas economists like Terner were leading spokesmen for industrialization is to fall prey to a facile if comforting half-truth.

Ultimately, the anti-industrialism of the Russian Left is as misleading an oversimplification as the view that Nicholas I and the official
pessimists, or, for that matter, the Slavophiles, were hostile to industry as such. Pisarev, for example, strongly believed that industrialization was intimately related to human progress, and took
pains to stress his conviction that industrial machinery was not responsible for the plight of the European working class.[110] Dobroliubov's eulogy to Owen was filled with admiration for New Lanark, a most advanced factory for its times. Not factory industry
as such, but questions concerning its physical location and internal
structure are what distinguished the Left from even as close a neigh-
bor on the spectrum of economists as Terner.

Pisarev provides us with a particularly instructive example of the
contrast, since he was less concerned than the *Sovremennik* group
with the liberal attack on the commune, and the differences between him and the economists are correspondingly narrowed. Expressing himself in terms that recall the worst fears of official pessimism, Pisarev argued against the single large urban industrial
center, where "all kinds of filth is bred" and where the poor and
hungry come to seek employment but instead find "extreme destitution, complete moral decline, and premature death from ex-
haustion, rotten food, or forced depravity." His alternative, however, was not the avoidance of industry, but rather the development
of a multiplicity of smaller, local industrial centers, each of them
closely meshed with the agrarian economy of the surrounding
countryside.[111] Similarly, Dobroliubov cited with approval Owen's
renunciation of large manufacturing centers, with their "deprav-
ing, demeaning, and destructive influence on the mass of the working-class population," and acclaimed his advocacy of medium-sized
industrial-agricultural communities as the only effective means
for averting the further impoverishment of the proletariat.[112] One
cannot help but be struck by the similarity between these views
and the earlier apprehensions of official pessimists, which were in
sharp contrast to the views of both the old optimists and the liberal
economists, who welcomed the growth of the large industrial center
as a sign of progress, provided that appropriate precautions were
taken.*

* It is impossible to ascertain whether Pisarev and Dobroliubov had the Russian capitals specifically in mind in their warnings against large industrial centers, but both

But the question of physical location was only symptomatic of a more fundamental consideration. Implicit in the stated desire to integrate industrial and agrarian life in the proposals of both Dobroliubov and Pisarev was an entire view of the organization and structure of industrial and agricultural labor that ran counter to the views of liberal economists, Terner not excepted. While full justice cannot be done to this problem without a thorough examination of Russian radical thought that would take us far afield, some insights can be gained through a cursory examination of the radical critique of Thomas Malthus, who received considerable attention during these years.

Although Malthusian pessimism was not a significant phenomenon in Russia, the real and potential problem of population growth and its pressure on the land inevitably brought Malthus into the arena of public controversy. If Malthus was correct, then those who favored the retention of communal landholding, basing their arguments in part on the efficacy of periodic land redistribution as a counterweight to population shifts, were building a house on sand. Short of accepting an unbroken future of destitution and early death for the Russian masses, or pursuing the chimera of "self-restraint," one was left with the choice of arguing that Malthus was basically wrong (the bedrock position of the Russian Left) or that there was validity in his position, but only if there were no industrial development to absorb the expanding population (broadly, the position taken by the liberal economists).

Whatever their differences on other matters, Chernyshevskii and Pisarev—the two most influential radical thinkers of the early 1860's—were completely at one in their rejection of Malthus. In 1861 Chernyshevskii published, in *Sovremennik*, an extensive and detailed critique of Malthus's theories, a critique that Pisarev praised and endorsed without reservation.[113] The essence of their refutation of Malthus was that he had endeavored to provide a rationale for opposing basic changes in the social and economic system by attributing to natural causes phenomena that were actually de-

---

articles were written in a manner which suggested to the reader that censorship prevented the authors from openly relating their ideas to Russian conditions. Dobroliubov wrote that a more detailed presentation of Owen's ideas must await the future, since they were "in sharp contradiction to everything that is usually accepted as the truth in our society" (*Sobranie sochinenii*, IV [Moscow, 1962], 46–47).

termined by the existing organization of labor and distribution of wealth. Poverty, "pauperism," and crime could be viewed as the products of excessive population only to the extent that population growth took place under the existing irrational system. Hence to adopt the Malthusian outlook, to seek solutions by maintaining low wages in order to encourage conjugal self-restraint rather than by attempting to reorganize the economic structure was, in effect, to condone and justify existing social injustice.[114]

To Pisarev, no less than to the *Sovremennik* group, the rational organization of labor would mean eliminating the profit motive and the appropriation of one man's labor by another, replacing them with the control of industry by the producers (i.e. workers), and (despite his avowed belief in the division of labor) blurring the lines between agricultural and industrial work.[115] Only under these conditions would the growth of mechanized industry and industrial technology benefit rather than damage the lives of the growing populations that were the source of such apprehension in the Malthusian analysis.

By contrast, a liberal opponent of the commune such as Terner —his commitment to association notwithstanding—really looked to economic development to resolve the Malthusian dilemma. Terner chided the defenders of the commune for believing that what he facetiously called the mathematical law of endless division was applicable to land. Repartition would reach its natural limit, he argued, echoing Malthus, in the relation between fixed space and expanding population; and the main purpose of the commune, the security of its members, would then be destroyed. The alternative to this disaster was the introduction of private farming on the peasant lands.[116] At this point, of course, Terner ceased to be a Malthusian pessimist. For he believed, as we have seen, that the peasants who would become free men by the abolition of communal ties and be squeezed off the land by the introduction of capitalist farming could be successfully absorbed into an expanding industrial economy, provided that the process could be tempered by the use of associations, as he understood the term. When all was said and done, Terner's answer to the Malthusian dilemma was industrial growth.

With these conflicting approaches in mind, we are now in a

better position to understand Shelgunov's attack on Terner as something more than just another assault from the Left on an enemy of
the commune, although it was that too. It was not merely Terner's
opposition to the commune as such, or even the contradictions in
his concept of association that disturbed Shelgunov and his comrades. It was the total picture of the commune disintegrating, urban
industry burgeoning, and capitalist ownership continuing that
made Terner's associations seem mere palliatives—possibly closer
to what Dobroliubov considered to be English middle-class society's
misreading of Owen as a man who helped workers accommodate to
the new industrialism than to the radical essence of Owenism as an
approach to the full emancipation of labor and a weapon in its
struggle against capital.[117] As the title of Shelgunov's article, "Deli-
cacy in Science," implies, he was taken aback by Terner's readiness
to approach the labor question with calm detachment, to see it
as a problem that could be resolved by applying rational scientific
principles rather than as a burning social issue that involved the
suffering of thousands. Why, he asked, did Terner cautiously employ the term "pauperism" to describe the problem rather than the
more grating term "proletariat"? Why did he repeat the old lies
of the political economists about the development of mechanized
industry having raised the living standards of the working classes,
when in truth only the few had benefitted? Why did he hope for
cooperation from the industrialists in the future, when they had
done so little for their workers in the past? And most to the point,
Why was Terner prepared to accept the type of society that had a
working class at all, instead of seeking ways—primarily by preserving the workers' ties with the land—to prevent Russia from developing a proletariat?[118]

Not all these criticisms were based on a just reading of Terner's
book. Certainly there was more compassion in Terner's writing
than Shelgunov suggested; Terner did at times use the word proletariat, and in any case, Shelgunov's judgment of which was the
more delicate term was questionable; and it was misleading to imply that Terner believed industrialization alone could resolve the
labor question. Had he thought this, then his entire discussion of
associations would have been superfluous.

But on the most important point—prevention versus encouragement of the development of a proletariat—Shelgunov's presentation is sound, once the ambiguity of the term is dispelled. Shelgunov distinguished between "proletarian" and "pauper" as follows: A pauper is one who lacks the power to earn an adequate living, whereas a proletarian is one who has the ability and the will to earn a living but is prevented from doing so by external economic circumstances, for which his "economic enemies" (i.e. employers) are responsible.[119] This distinction—which closely parallels Wolfram Fischer's distinction between the *Armenfrage* and the *soziale Frage*—underscores *Sovremennik*'s general opposition to the development of a new class of urban proletarians whose ranks would be swelled by the influx of uprooted peasants, ripe for exploitation by industrial entrepreneurs. Terner's approach, like that of the other economists, is substantially different: Let the uprooting of the peasantry take place, let the division of labor proceed, let the umbilical cord be cut and the peasants become proletarians, but use associations, based on arteli, to ease the transformation. To a Shelgunov, arteli were desirable if they served to link the worker with communal life; to a Terner, if they made the adjustment to the loss of the commune under industrial conditions more bearable. This is why Shelgunov was prepared to say—if only for effect —that he preferred the "crude frankness" of a Rzhevskii, who openly advocated the creation of a Russian proletariat, to the deviousness of a Terner, who wanted to metamorphose Russian laborers into "real" factory workers but politely referred to this terrible process as "measures to secure their well-being."[120]

The Russian Left of the early 1860's was not "anti-industrial" in the literal sense in which the term is sometimes used, but its general aversion to any solution to the labor question that left an uprooted peasantry to the mercy of palliatives—whether labor legislation, trade unions, or even arteli—gave an anti-industrial cutting edge to some of its polemical writings. The elaboration and detailed consideration of reform-oriented plans for mitigating the effects of industrial life on the peasant-worker were areas of endeavor in which Russian radicals neither could nor wished to act effectively. European industrial life continued to be a negative example to the Russian Left, as indeed it was—albeit in a different sense—both to the liberal economists and to the government. But as a source of positive models for approaching the social problems of industrialization Europe had much more to offer to people like Terner than to proto-Populists like Shelgunov, who had greater goals for Russia than a sweeter version of the industrial revolution and for whom the two senses of proletariat were one.

FOUR

The Government Commissions
of 1857–1864

DURING THE EARLY years of Alexander II's reign the evolution of the labor question within government circles revealed the existence of attitudes that were strikingly similar to those of the economists and journalists discussed in the previous chapter. The desire to borrow Western European methods while time was still working to Russia's advantage, the belief in the possibility of a proletariat without pauperism, and even many of the specific proposals with which we are familiar could all be found among the officials of certain governmental agencies. Indeed no publicist's work on the labor question, including Terner's extensive treatise, went nearly as far as some officials in elaborating a program for industrial labor after emancipation. In its most extensive and carefully honed form, this program was embodied in the 1862 and 1864 versions of a "Draft Statute on Industry" composed by the Commission Established to Examine the Factory and Artisan Statutes (more commonly known as the Shtakel'berg Commission, after its chairman, A. F. Shtakel'berg, a young official of the Ministry of Internal Affairs).[1]

The Shtakel'berg Commission was a reflection and a manifestation of the post–Crimean War progressivism and economic liberalism that penetrated parts of the government after the decision to abolish serfdom was announced. The connecting link between the mood generated by this decision and the creation of the Commission was the question of the future of the *tsekhi*, that is, the artisan guilds. The realization that serfdom was soon to be eliminated was accompanied by, and to some extent nourished a growing conviction that the tsekhi, and the urban administrative system in general, were anachronistic. This conviction, in turn, led the government to undertake a thoroughgoing revision of the industrial code, a code that was becoming increasingly antiquated, in the view of many influential Russians.

Criticism of the Tsekhi

If the imminent emancipation signified the transformation of the agrarian serf into a free peasant, then it was logical that the continued existence of institutions which restricted the freedom and mobility of urban craftsmen and, more generally, all corporate forms which restricted Russian urban life, should also be challenged. Implicit in the idea of abolishing the tsekh system (as in the abolition of serfdom) was the notion that juridical class or estate (*soslovie*) might eventually cease to play a significant role in determining rights, privileges, and economic status. By the late 1850's some influential officials had begun to think about reevaluating Russia's urban class institutions and to move toward a new conception of urban society as (in the words of Ditiatin) "the totality of *all* inhabitants of the city." As Ditiatin has argued, it is unlikely that this conception would have received serious consideration without the knowledge that the age of serfdom was about to end.[2]

The impulse to move against the tsekh system, however, did not originate directly from these rather abstract considerations, but rather from the way specific problems and conflicts in the sphere of industrial production were approached in the postwar atmosphere. The decisive question was whether or not the antiquated and artificial line of division between factory production and crafts—an essential component of the legal class structure of St. Petersburg, Moscow, and other cities—should now be broken down. As the Shtakel'berg Commission was later to explain, the legal-administrative division of industry into factory industry and craft industry had led to "very important inconveniences" because of the difficulty of really distinguishing between the two modes of production.[3] To understand the nature of these inconveniences, it is necessary to examine briefly the evolution of the opposition to tsekhi in government circles.

The first serious discussions about fundamentally revising or abolishing the tsekh system began in the 1850's and became particularly important in St. Petersburg and Moscow in the years 1857–58.* The main issue was the fiscal-administrative status of small

---

* There was some discussion in the late 1840's and early 1850's, but it was unrelated to the issues raised in the postwar period. It centered on problems related to the legal classification of Jews. See *Trudy kommissii uchrezhdennoi dlia peresmotra ustavov fabrichnogo i remeslennogo* (St. Petersburg, 1863–64), I, 30–34.

industrial enterprises—some of them only recently established—that did not fall neatly into the category of either artisan shop or factory, and the owners of which were not required to register in a merchants' guild. In the absence of either a long and respected tradition or a clear legal definition of the scope of competence of the tsekh administration, it was often uncertain whether a new enterprise belonged within the jurisdiction of municipal guild authorities or should be classified as a factory, within the less restrictive jurisdiction of the Ministry of Finance. This uncertainty was reflected in anomalies such as the fact that workshops producing cigars and cigarettes were designated as artisan shops in Moscow, but as factories in St. Petersburg.[4] These were not merely formal distinctions, for tsekh jurisdiction entailed a variety of obligations, fiscal and other, whereas administrative responsibility to the Ministry of Finance made an enterprise eligible for the exemptions and privileges offered by the ministry in order to encourage industrial growth. Under the circumstances, conflicts between local tsekh authorities and the owners of small industrial enterprises of an indeterminate classification (often called *domashnie zavedeniia**) were almost unavoidable. Not surprisingly, it was the Ministry of Finance and its agencies—preeminently the Moscow Section of the Manufacturing Council—that acted to protect the domashnie zavedeniia from the inroads and restraints of the tsekh system.[5]

Most of the postwar debate over this conflict took the form of a series of proposals and counterproposals regarding the proper definition of "factory" and other industrial categories, with the Ministry of Finance and its agencies always striving for definitions that would encompass the broadest possible range of enterprises.[6] In the course of this discussion, the anti-tsekh position was most directly and vigorously expressed by the Moscow Section of the Manufacturing Council, the only agency of the Finance Ministry in which manufacturers as such were represented.† While offering a variety of arguments for this or that line of demarcation between artisan shops and factories, the Moscow Section advocated—in the name of industrial freedom—the complete abolition of the tsekh system.

---

* Literally, "domestic establishments," but more accurately rendered in the context as "small factories."

† Henceforth, the Moscow Section of the Manufacturing Council will simply be called the Moscow Section. This agency is discussed more extensively below (see p. 153).

Emphasizing the pressing need for industrial growth—a power-ful debating point in the light of Russia's recent defeat in war—the Moscow Section accused the tsekh administration of stifling indus-trial growth by preventing domashnie zavedeniia from serving as nuclei for larger factories. Ordinarily, it said, "production in this kind of establishment broadens; it increases its capital and the num-ber of workers employed, and the owner joins a [merchants'] guild. In this way many of the factories that are now very important in our country were formed."[7] But the aspiration of municipal craft ad-ministrations (Remeslennye Upravy)—especially in the two capitals —to include as many domashnie zavedeniia as possible in their sphere of authority was having a braking effect upon this natural process.* "Enclosed in the constricting framework of the tsekhi," the Moscow Section proclaimed, "manufacturing industry . . . is de-prived of the space needed for its further development and prog-ress." The solution: to revise Russia's industrial code so as to "liber-ate factory production from guild regulations and restrictions."[8] Specifically, this meant a much narrower delineation of the guild administrations' area of competence and the removal of restrictions on those master artisans who wished to transform their workshops into factories. But even this proposal was intended only as a tem-porary expedient. The best solution, the Moscow Section stated un-equivocally, was to completely abolish all restrictive guilds and repeal the statutes that provided for them, as had been done in those European countries where it was understood that artisan guilds were incompatible with industrial progress.[9]

The artisan guild structure, as explained in Chapter 1, had been imposed on Russian cities by the central government in order to bring their economic institutions into line with those of Western Europe. Ironically, the guild system had barely taken root in Rus-sia when its Western counterpart began to be uprooted by the forces of economic and industrial freedom. By the middle of the nineteenth century the Russian guild system was starting to shed its relatively unrestrictive character, exemplified in the earlier pro-hibition against a guild's interfering with anyone's attempt to earn

* In St. Petersburg, attempts by the Remeslennaia Uprava to gain administrative control over various domashnie zavedeniia and to bring independent, non-tsekh craftsmen under its wing increased significantly between 1853 and 1859 (see Trudy, II, 124–28, for specific examples).

a living,[10] only to find its new aggressiveness challenged by the rising force of economic liberalism in Russia, which again invoked Western practices as a model.*

The trend toward industrial freedom was not the only force providing an impetus to anti-tsekh sentiment. Officials in the Ministry of Internal Affairs, particularly those in the office of the military governor of St. Petersburg, came to share the reservations about the tsekh system that prevailed in the Ministry of Finance and its agencies, although they began with a somewhat different set of considerations. The governor, General P. N. Ignat'ev (1854–61), an old-guard conservative in certain respects,[11] directed a second line of attack on the artisan economy and administration of St. Petersburg. The immediate provocation for his attack arose from the squalid and brutal conditions that were discovered, or rather rediscovered, in the workshops of the capital, where by Russian standards artisans were heavily concentrated.†

These conditions had been carefully scrutinized by two government commissions in the 1840's, but—as we saw in Chapter 2—the commissions' work had not come to fruition.[12] Shortly after the Crimean War, in 1857, fresh complaints about the mistreatment of young apprentices in St. Petersburg workshops led to the launching of a new investigation. The 1857 commission of inquiry—which differed from its predecessors in that it dealt exclusively with artisan shops—examined as many as 1,525 shops over a three-year period, and was appalled by the situation it uncovered, especially with respect to the abuse of children. It found beating, kicking, and dragging of young apprentices by the hair to be the "most common phenomena." On the basis of these and other abuses, the investigators concluded that "the savagery and cruelty of the masters often reaches extreme limits."[13]

* References to the shallow roots of the guild system in Russia are of course not meant to include the Baltic cities, where guilds dated back to the Middle Ages.

† In 1858, of 331,555 artisans (including journeymen and apprentices) in the 49 provinces of European Russia, 38,508 were located in St. Petersburg province, which was second only to Moscow province (with 44,498) in this respect, and which exceeded Moscow province in the proportion of artisans to total population (3.5 per cent and 2.8 per cent respectively). *Trudy*, II, 326–27. The annual report of the St. Petersburg Remeslennaia Uprava for 1860 listed 12,653 *vechnotsekhovye remeslenniki* (permanent artisans, i.e., not including peasant-artisans with temporary city permits), although most of these did not actually work in artisan shops. "Svod dannykh o primenenii remeslennykh postanovlenii, na praktike, v raznykh mestnostiakh Rossii," in *ibid.*, p. 120.

Although 62 shop owners were subjected to various degrees of punishment as a result of these findings, the commission's 1860 report to General Ignat'ev (to whom it was directly responsible) contained few positive recommendations. Its modest proposals for improving the organization of the existing tsekh system were considered by the military governor to be incommensurate with the problems at hand.[14]

Early in 1861, exactly one week after the emancipation was promulgated, Ignat'ev passed on the report to his superiors in the Ministry of Internal Affairs, together with a general exposition of his own views on the tsekh system. Having studied the report with care, Ignat'ev had arrived at a much deeper criticism of the tsekh administration than had its authors. He attributed the abuses described by the report and the failure of the tsekh administration to correct them not only to the cumbersomeness of that administration, with its overabundance of officials and profusion of administrative subdivisions, but to the very nature of a closed and restrictive system of production that preserved the narrowness and ignorance of the producers. Denouncing the tsekh administrative organization as an artificial import from Germany with no real basis in Russian life, Ignat'ev proposed that artisans be restored the "rights of free labor" they had enjoyed before Peter the Great—rights he equated with those presently enjoyed by independent manufacturers. "Neither knowledge of a skill nor examinations are required of a manufacturer; he may engage in various branches of production, subject only to certain conditions relating to the construction of the [factory] building and to the payment of [merchant] guild taxes." The same should be true of the proprietor of an artisan shop, which in any case, Ignat'ev contended, was nothing other than a "small factory." Freed from tsekh restrictions, artisans, like factory owners, would be able to unite several different crafts into a single, centralized company. Stimulated by such opportunities, they would be eager to work and to educate themselves.[15]

Thus (as the Shtakel'berg Commission noted) the Moscow Section of the Manufacturing Council and the military governor of St. Petersburg arrived at essentially the same conclusion from very different points of departure.[16] The primary concern of the former was to facilitate industrial development, of the latter to eliminate irregularities and abuses that the tsekh administration had failed to control. Ignat'ev's was primarily a police concern, the Moscow Section's an economic one. Yet both found themselves driven toward the conclusion that the tsekh was a stifling and outmoded institution that was inappropriate to the dawning era of emancipated labor and industrial freedom.

The St. Petersburg Commission of 1859

It was primarily for the purposes of assessing the various arguments advanced against the tsekh system and drafting a new industrial code that would be applicable to all branches of industry, without regard to mode of production, that the Ministry of Finance and the Ministry of Internal Affairs decided to establish the Shtakel'berg Commission in 1859.[17] By the time the Commission* began to publish its recommendations in 1862, both the Moscow Section's critique of the tsekhi and Ignat'ev's comments, as well as the more specific findings of the 1857 commission of inquiry, had been easily absorbed into the general outlook of Shtakel'berg and his colleagues.† Indeed, the depiction of the tsekh as an anachronistic, obsolete institution, with no relevance to the new era, became one of the Commission's most basic premises and a decisive element in its approach to the drafting of legislation to deal with the labor question.

Before attempting to demonstrate the precise manner in which the Commission related the critique of the tsekh system to the labor question, it is necessary to retrace a sequence of events and circumstances that directly affected the content of the Commission's deliberations. It will be recalled that the outbreak of the Crimean War had led to the postponement of the government's attempt to strengthen the largely ineffectual factory legislation of 1835 until such time, in the words of the Council of State, as "circumstances are more appropriate."[18] In view of the consensus that had been

---

* For the remainder of this chapter, the term "Commission" refers to the Shtakel'berg Commission unless another commission is specifically indicated.

† The members were: from the Ministry of Finance, G. K. Beze of the Department of Manufactures and P. A. Vasil'ev of the Manufacturing Council; from the Ministry of Internal Affairs, S. I. Gratsinskii and N. I. Vtorov, director and vice-director, respectively, of the Economic Department, and M. P. Veselovskii, a special assistant to the Minister; the Secretary of the St. Petersburg Remeslennaia Uprava, P. P. Stolbin. *Trudy*, I, iv.

achieved by 1854, it is hardly surprising that the Ministry of Internal Affairs, sometime around the end of 1858, asked Ignat'ev for his views on the dormant Zakrevskii plan for making workers' booklets compulsory. Ignat'ev's response was unequivocally affirmative; indeed, he went so far as to recommend a number of modifications in the content of the previous drafts of the workers' booklets that strengthened its orientation toward protecting the interests of the workers.[19] Thus within the span of only a few years two supposedly conservative military governors, the officials responsible for the administration of the regions containing Russia's heaviest concentrations of urban industry, were sufficiently concerned with the irregularity of owner-worker relations in their districts to plead for the regularization of contractual relations in factories.

The thread of prewar deliberations having been thus resumed, Ignat'ev was not content to stop with merely advocating workers' booklets. The same conditions in St. Petersburg factories that outraged some of the publicists discussed in the previous chapter, in particular the mistreatment of child workers, now triggered enough of a reaction in government circles to convince the Tsar to take action. The high rate of industrial accidents and injuries, especially in relatively new, mechanized factories, included a distressingly high incidence of injuries to child workers. Early in 1859, shortly after Ignat'ev had given his views on the workers' booklets to the Ministry of Internal Affairs, a temporary commission was formed by Imperial command to inspect the factories of the city and district (uezd) of St. Petersburg and then, in accordance with its findings, to draft safety regulations for the use of machinery and other measures aimed at reducing the burden on child laborers. Although details regarding the initial decision to create this commission remain obscure, it is clear that Ignat'ev—under whose immediate authority the commission was to operate (its chairman was his immediate subordinate, General A. A. Odintsov, municipal commandant of St. Petersburg)—was a central figure in its making.[20]

Ignat'ev began by designing a lengthy tabulated questionnaire for circulation to all St. Petersburg manufacturers (artisan shops, perhaps because they were covered by the 1857 commission, were explicitly excluded) via the civil governor, who was to collect their responses and turn them over to Odintsov's commission.[21] A circular letter signed by Ignat'ev and appended to the questionnaire was polite but determined in tone.* The questionnaire itself was thorough and detailed. Its 39 separate questions covered such matters as the extent of mechanization and safety precautions, the use of child workers and their importance to the operation of the plant, the wages and hours of both adult and child workers, types of punishments and incentives, the quality of housing, food, and medical assistance, and the methods of hiring child workers (e.g., were they hired directly by the factory administration or by the adult workers? were they hired on a contractual basis, and if so, were the contracts made with their parents, their *pomeshchiki*, or the children themselves?). In addition, a separate form detailing the situation of each child worker (aged fourteen or under) was to be filled out by the factory owner.[22]

The responses to the questionnaires revealed what had already been suspected: the widespread exploitation of minors, particularly in the textile mills. A total of 1,282 minors, it was learned, were employed in the factories of St. Petersburg. The cotton industry alone accounted for the employment of 616 children ranging in age from eight to fourteen (information on minors older than fourteen was not solicited). Six out of twelve cotton mills used children on night shifts (defined as work between eight P.M. and five A.M.), and others worked children as well as adults for a fourteen-hour day.[23] The beating of children, usually carried out by fore-

---

* It was addressed to the manufacturers and their administrative staffs, and read as follows:

"The sovereign emperor has seen fit to establish by supreme command a commission to prepare regulations for the elimination of accidents suffered by workers from careless handling of machines or from the hazards of their work and to investigate the situation of children who work in the factories and plants of St. Petersburg.

"To achieve this goal, the commission has prepared the accompanying questions and tables for Messrs. manufacturers.

"These questions must be answered briefly, clearly, and on the basis of no other means than personal verification through the interrogation of workers or [reference to] documents located at the factories.

"This information is required for the preparation of regulations which, without having a constricting effect on industry, will contribute to the betterment of factory workers.

"When the required data has been obtained, responses to the questions and tables should be turned over to the local police inspectors within three weeks.

"In considering questions that relate to factory workers, the commission is required to invite manufacturers from various branches of industry to its sessions. I am convinced that Messrs. manufacturers will help the commission with its work, particularly inasmuch as the establishment of the commission has the interests of industry as its direct goal." (Ignat'ev circular of March 15, 1859, GIALO, f. 253, *op.* 2, d. 205 [1859 g.], p. 4.)

men, was so accepted a practice in the cotton-spinning mills of St. Petersburg that on at least two occasions—both at major factories —beatings took place even in the presence of investigators from the commission.[24]

Their determination to act decisively reinforced by this alarming information, the commissioners proceeded to formulate a set of draft regulations on factory labor. As is easily seen in the content of the questionnaire, Ignat'ev and the commissioners had recognized from the outset that the specific questions of child labor, safety precautions, and working conditions could not be treated in isolation from more general considerations, such as the nature of contractual relations. Drawing on the experience of Western Europe and the advice of some of the liberal economists with whom we are familiar (e.g., Bezobrazov, Vernadskii, Bunge, Lamanskii, and others),[25] and consulting with some of St. Petersburg's leading manufacturers (three of whom even served on the commission), the commissioners composed a comprehensive and basic program of factory regulations, which it printed as a brochure under the title "Draft Regulations for Factories and Plants in the City and District of St. Petersburg."[26] The brochure was then circulated, via the Ministry of Internal Affairs, to the governors of various provinces, who were instructed to solicit and gather the reactions of "competent and concerned persons."

The decision to circulate the project in the provinces was evidently taken with the intention of extending the scope of the proposed legislation beyond St. Petersburg and into other industrial regions. By this time, however, the Shtakel'berg Commission had already been created, and since its professed goal was the drafting of a new, uniform industrial code for the entire Empire, it made little sense for the St. Petersburg commission to continue to duplicate its efforts. By the same token, after receiving Ignat'ev's memorandum on workers' booklets, the Ministry of Internal Affairs had decided that rather than bring his and related proposals before the Council of State, it was preferable to submit them to the newly formed Shtakel'berg Commission for further consideration.[27] The work of the St. Petersburg commission of 1859, like the work of the commission of 1857, was therefore terminated, and its materials— including its draft regulations and the responses from provincial governors and other sources—were incorporated into the work of the Shtakel'berg Commission. Since, with certain modifications, the St. Petersburg draft and the preceding proposals for a uniform workers' booklet provided the basis for the core program that came to be adopted by Shtakel'berg and his colleagues, it would be superfluous to present separate analyses of the two projects. Instead, let us now turn our attention to the approach embodied in the Shtakel'berg draft, referring to the earlier draft only when the differences seem significant.

The Shtakel'berg Proposals

It was the convergence in the Shtakel'berg Commission of the two seemingly unrelated trends just described that made its work especially interesting and, at times, apparently contradictory. The first trend—the movement in the direction of free labor and free enterprise, nourished in general by the approaching end of serfdom and in particular by hostility toward the tsekhi—accounted for the very creation of the body and, as shall now be shown, for the basic spirit with which it approached the problem of removing the constraints on urban economic life. The second trend—the revival of old schemes for official supervision of labor-management relations, but in forms that were much more supportive of labor than before—accounted for much of the specific content of the Commission's work and thus for the paradoxical situation that concepts of laissez faire and welfare legislation not only were not counterposed, but were considered by a high-powered government commission as natural parts of a single, consistent transformation of Russian institutions.

In its examination and criticism of the tsekh system, the Shtakel'-berg Commission repeated and endorsed most of the arguments that had already been set forth by the Moscow Section, General Ignat'ev, and others.* It also drew upon the writings of liberal Rus-

* Many of the Commission's specific criticisms of the tsekh system are interlaced with its summary of data on the operation of tsekhi in St. Petersburg and other regions. "Svod dannykh," *Trudy*, II, 119–78. In some sections it is difficult to tell whether the Commission is paraphrasing the judgments of the 1857 commission of inquiry or presenting its own interpretation of that body's findings.

Unfortunately, although the Commission was forthright in revealing comments critical of its approach by others, it never revealed what, if any, differences existed among its own members. Although it is perfectly plausible that a general consensus prevailed among them on most matters, it is difficult to believe that Stolbin, Secretary of the St. Petersburg Remeslennaia Uprava, shared the report's hostility to the tsekh system. In this respect it is noteworthy that sometime before January 1864 Stol-

sian economists such as A. Korsak (author of a major study of Russian and West European industry) and V. A. Tatarinov (whose positive views on British strikes were noted in the previous chapter) for support.[28] But the main authorities to which the Commission turned, in this as in so many other matters, were the thought and the practical experience of Western Europe.

The key Western European theoretical work cited by the commissioners (and, not coincidentally, by Tatarinov as well) was Victor Böhmert's *Freiheit der Arbeit: Beiträge zur Reform der Gewerbegesetze* (Bremen, 1858), a book that they were already prepared to dub a "classic" in its field. Böhmert's main thesis was that it was a government's manifest duty to promote the liberty of all its citizens to engage freely in any and all industrial pursuits. All legislation that hindered this goal, such as laws authorizing the privileges and monopolies of guilds, should be repealed. This outlook was adopted in its entirety by the Commission, as were a variety of anti-guild positions taken from John Stuart Mill, the French economist Rossi, and others.[29]

The best models from practical experience used by the Commission were provided by Prussia, Austria, and other German speaking areas that had lagged behind France and England in removing restrictions on industrial freedom. The movement toward industrial freedom in these areas was progressing rapidly during the life of the Shtakel'berg Commission. Thus, for example, laws that advanced the freedom of industrial enterprise and removed corporate restrictions on production were enacted in Austria (December 1859), Nassau (June 1860), Saxony (October 1861), Württemberg (February 1862), and Baden (September 1862) during the first four years of the Commission's work. In Prussia, liberal parliamentarians adopted a program for industrial freedom in January 1861, and the privileges of corporate producers were gradually eroded over the next several years.[30]

These events were carefully followed by the Commission, which summarized some of the anti-guild arguments made in the Prussian parliamentary debates of 1860 in its transactions, and interpreted the new trend as evidence that the last vestiges of corporate restric-

bin made a trip abroad that prevented him from participating in the Commission's final deliberations and the drafting of its final proposals. "Zhurnal Kommisii," *Trudy*, III, 73n.

tions on industrial freedom would soon be eradicated throughout the continent. Convinced that both the most up-to-date scholarship and the most recent practices of advanced nations proved that full industrial freedom should replace the constraints of the guild system, the Commission was not prepared to see Russia—which enjoyed the advantage of a guild system that was relatively recently established, rootless, and therefore easily removed—lag behind her neighbors to the West. It was mainly within the framework of these considerations that the Commission undertook the task of drafting a broad industrial code in which tsekhi, ceasing to maintain a legal identity of their own, would be subjected to laws and administration uniformly governing all major branches of industrial production—crafts as well as factories.[31]

It followed logically, thereby conditioning the Commission's entire approach to the labor question, that master artisans, journeymen, and apprentices would lose their corporate identities and dissolve into the simpler functional classifications of capitalist industry: owner (*khoziain*) and worker (*rabotnik*).[32] Thus, just when emancipation seemed to be threatening to create a proletariat by severing traditional ties in the rural community, a major governmental commission was preparing to encourage the proletarianization of workers already in the cities by abolishing the corporate institutions and identities of artisans and giving full rein to the marketplace to become the chief determinant of economic identity. Although the commissioners would undoubtedly have recoiled from this formulation (and on occasion even bent over backward to avoid it), the code that was to be drafted by them was in most respects intended to be an industrial code for an industrial proletariat.

To clarify this point and, indeed, the Commission's entire approach to the labor question, it is necessary to recall what I have called the "first" general position on the labor question that was held by certain economists and journalists. In Chapter 3 I defined that position as one that "welcomed the growth of urban industry, recognized that this implied the development of an urban working class, and sought to deal with the problems of that class within an industrial context."[33] The acceptance of full-fledged proletarianization (in what was termed the "neutral" sense) was seen as a principal corollary. Although the alternative idea of modifying proletarianization through the use of traditional practices based on the artel' also found its way into the Commission's deliberations, thus adding to their complexity, the basic approach of the Commission was to draft legislation that would provide the most favorable circumstances for the evolution of a new and independent working class—a proletariat.

It is probable that in urging the demise of tsekh institutions, the commissioners were fully aware that they were contributing to the creation of an industrial working force lacking a traditional class or corporate identity and having only its economic situation, rather than juridical status, to define its position in society. Since the emancipation of the peasantry signified the end of most forms of obligatory factory labor,* factory peasants were now being absorbed into the general rural population. By the same token, if tsekh institutions were now abolished, city artisans would merge with the general urban population of *meshchane*. The following passage in the Commission's "Explanatory Report"—although cautiously worded and perhaps intentionally opaque—reveals the commissioners' awareness of the implications of this change:

People of all ranks, without distinction, will [once the tsekhi are abolished] work at trades without losing the rights of their former legal class or obtaining new ones, and as a consequence, working at a [particular] trade will be still less connected with the concept of legal class division [*soslovnaia razdel'nost*] and separate class administration than in the past.[34]

In other words, although traditional legal classes or estates may continue to exist for administrative purposes (a qualification that was more problematical than the Commission suggests here, as shall be seen), their preservation is trivialized by what is really the main point—that they would have no significant connection with one's economic activities.

It is especially revealing that in advocating this change in the structure of urban society, the commissioners felt compelled to deny that they were contributing to the emergence of a Russian proletariat, and hence to the ultimate dangers of socialism and

---

* That is, in manorial and possessional factories; obligatory labor by state peasants in state factories, which was abolished gradually, and mainly not until the second half of the decade, was not included in the Commission's discussion. On the introduction of free labor in state factories in the St. Petersburg area, see below, pp. 259–62.

revolution. Whether this charge was actually leveled against the Commission or was merely extrapolated from recent debates in other countries was not made clear (although the Commission's numerous citations from German sources suggest the latter). In any case, borrowing its main line of argument from Böhmert, the Commission attempted to counter the charge by turning it around, that is, by maintaining that not industrial freedom but its absence presented the real danger:

Industrial freedom not only does not create or develop a proletariat, but on the contrary comprises the only reliable means for averting and eliminating the appearance of a proletariat. Only freedom of labor gives the poor man the right to work at and acquire whatever is most useful and profitable to him; only industrial freedom can transform proletarians into industrious and happy citizens.[35]

Furthermore, the Commission strongly endorsed Tatarinov's conclusion that the guild monopoly system "does not avert a proletariat, but serves as the surest path to one."[36]

In making these and similar assertions, the Commission was obviously using the term "proletariat" in a strictly pejorative sense to evoke an image of mass poverty, depravity, and pauperization. It was in no sense denying that its goal was the evolution of a distinct class of urban industrial workers. On the contrary, it was an urban economy based on corporate exclusion, in the Commission's view, that relegated the mass of city dwellers to nonproductive lives of poverty and sloth, whereas free access to productive work under conditions of industrial growth made it possible for factory workers to become an independent and productive economic class. But the common association between the idea of such a class and the negative sense of proletarianization, particularly in a country where the alleged absence of a proletariat in either sense had long since become a stock idea, compelled the commissioners to emphasize the distinction between their goal and the specter of poverty, revolution, and socialism that haunted Europe.

As distant as its outlook was from that of the official optimists (that is, from those who had once dispelled their fears of urban industrialization by pointing to the Russian worker's dependence on the land), the Commission was unable to resist the familiar and comforting thought that the Russian road to industrial strength would be relatively painless because of the "incomparably more advantageous conditions" with which the country was blessed as compared with other European nations.

> The forces of resistance that industrial reform has encountered in the West do not exist in Russia. Up to this time we still have had neither a real factory population, nor pauperism, nor a proletariat. . . . Our urban and rural populations stand at a much lower level of development than in most European countries; but on the other hand, we do not have those manifestations of general poverty that sometimes strike industrial districts in England.[37]

Unlike other invocations of Russia's uniqueness, this was not intended as an argument for complacency. The point was simply that even though unfettered industrial development might contain the germ of serious social dislocation—as it had in England and elsewhere—Russia at least had the advantage of a less well established class structure to be displaced and a smaller impoverished urban population with which to contend. From this point of view, those who believed that traditional institutions had in the past protected Russia from proletarianization were correct. But the same institutions were also seen as dangerously anachronistic in that they prevented large segments of the population—both rural and urban—from becoming a genuine working class and thereby participating in and reaping the benefits of what would hopefully become the most dynamic sector of the economy.

In its internal logic, this entire line of argument amounted to a justification for government action against tsekhi and any other institutions that restrained the free development of a market economy. Once this issue was resolved, however, virtually all of the Commission's work was devoted to devising a complex set of recommendations for government intervention in labor-management relations. Like the liberal economists of these years, the commissioners, far from being consistent Manchesterians, failed to see any contradiction between free enterprise and factory legislation. It was as if, having provided for the creation of an independent labor force whose identity was based solely on its position in the labor market, the Commission immediately felt obliged to modify the new conditions it was creating in order to uphold the position of the new class and to guarantee that its future development would take place under the least ominous circumstances possible.

As in the case of past proposals, the workers' booklets, together with an efficient system for the enforcement of their provisions, were to be the foundation of the new legislative program. Two new features, however, distinguished the Commission's approach from that of the prewar period, while linking it to that of the St. Petersburg commission of 1859.* First, the Commission recognized that a crucial gap existed between regulations governing worker-owner relations and whatever system might be devised to adjudicate the disputes that arose under those regulations—namely, the absence of an impartial system of inspection. Second, the Commission recognized the need to combine the basic question of contractual relations with the more specific questions of child labor and safety regulations—problem areas that had been approached separately under Nicholas I, but which recent experience in the capital had taught the St. Petersburg commission to treat as a whole. In short, the piecemeal approaches of the past were now abandoned in favor of a comprehensive program befitting the advent of a new era in Russian economic life.

In summary form, the main elements in the Commission's proposed legislative program were as follows:[38]

(1) The affirmation of the freely negotiated contract as the basis for relations between owners and workers in Russian industry. The workers' booklet was to become the basic form of contract and, in the Commission's first draft (1862), the only legal basis for the judicial settlement of disputes. Although oral contracts were permissible, the worker was protected by the requirement that his employer issue a booklet on request. The worker, in turn, was required to accept a booklet if issued by his employer. The booklets —which were to be centrally and uniformly printed—would each contain a summary of the essential laws governing employer-worker relations as well as blank spaces for the recording of the specific terms of employment and individual financial transactions, as they occurred, between the contracting parties.[39]

(2) The enforcement of the provisions set forth in the workers' booklets by an independent body of factory inspectors, appointed by the Ministry of Finance. As conceived by the Commission, the inspectorate was to be an executive agency to supervise compliance with the new law. The inspectors, mainly technical specialists,

* Hereafter "the St. Petersburg commission" means that of 1859.

would be entrusted with broad powers, including the power to bring charges against manufacturers alleged to be in violation of the code.[40]

(3) The adjudication of those disputes that could not be resolved through the factory inspectors by urban industrial courts (*Promyshlennye sudy*). These tribunals were to serve as a civil court of the first instance for all industrial litigation, including the pressing of charges against manufacturers by factory inspectors. An intricate structure and a set of procedures were carefully elaborated in 129 separate articles, and a detailed penal code was drafted to guide the meting out of justice to violators of the new laws. The most striking and controversial feature of the proposal (which was borrowed directly from the St. Petersburg commission) was that the members of the courts in each region were to be elected, in equal number, by the manufacturers and the workers.[41]

Taken as a whole, these measures may almost be said to have constituted a sort of miniature government with its own executive and judiciary for the sphere of industrial relations. In view of the commissioners' professed desire to transform the closed character of Russian industrial life and merge the industrial population with the mass of urban citizenry, it was therefore not unreasonable for critics to raise the question of consistency. It was raised with reference to the separate industrial courts by the governor of the Bessarabian district and by the Moscow Section of the Manufacturing Council, which asked rhetorically why one sphere of society should be set aside where some persons could be punished outside the normal criminal procedures.[42]

But, understandably, the charge of inconsistency carried little weight with the Commission. After all, the most industrially advanced and economically liberal countries of Europe—England, Belgium, and France—had provided the models for the three main phases of the proposed program. Compulsory workers' booklets (*livrets d'ouvriers*), as the Commission pointed out, had recently been introduced in France (1854–55) and Belgium (1860). The proposed inspection system (first espoused by the St. Petersburg commission) was consciously modeled on the British Inspectorate. And industrial courts with members elected by manufacturers and workers were inspired by the French *conseils des prud'hommes* (first introduced in Lyon under Napoleon in 1806), which were most fully operative in France (since 1853) and had recently been em-

ulated in Belgium and parts of Germany.[43] Count P. A. Baranov—
the provincial governor of Tver and a fierce supporter of forceful
labor legislation—had inadvertently expressed the aspirations of
the Shtakel'berg Commission when, in defending the St. Petersburg
commission from its critics, he pleaded for the transformation of
Russian workers into "healthy, intelligent, and capable citizens
[grazhdane]."[44] The Shtakel'berg Commission, regarding other
countries as having much more highly developed conceptions of
citizenship* than Russia,[45] could hardly admit to inconsistency for
having proposed institutions considered progressive in countries
that had gone so much further in dismantling corporate economic
and social life. Not surprisingly, therefore, the Commission responded to the governor of Bessarabia with the countercharge that
it was he, and not the commissioners, whose ideas were confused.[46]

In fact, the apparent contradictions that its critics attempted to
ascribe to the Commission lay more in the situation with which it
was endeavoring to cope than in anyone's ideas as such. In England,
France, and Belgium, and even in parts of Germany, where economic liberalism was already clearly in the ascendant and traditional corporate class institutions either already abolished or clearly
on the wane, the creation of special institutions to supervise the
economic relations of the new industrial classes represented a new
phase of compromise with the unrestrained laws of the marketplace. In England—and to varying extents in other parts of Western Europe—industrial relations had by now become an accepted
sphere of economic and social life. A mass of people had entered
or were entering this sphere, having shed, however, painfully, their
previous juridical and economic identities. To establish special laws
and institutions for them—the objections of some Manchesterians
notwithstanding—was only to confirm the precedence of economic
class over juridical status and deal directly with the problems thus
created. In Central Europe, on the other hand, where the struggle
between economic liberalism and corporate institutions had been
joined only recently, the emphasis among innovators was still on
destroying the old restrictive institutions rather than on creating
new kinds of institutional restraints to mitigate the social and eco-

---

* Neither Baranov nor the commissioners explicitly defined what they understood by
"citizenship," but it is clear from the context that they were counterposing this concept to the servility associated with bondage and the limits placed on the civic and
economic freedoms of groups that are excluded, by birth or otherwise, from full membership in a community.

nomic perils of industrial freedom. Shtakel'berg and his colleagues could not resist the temptation to move in both directions at once, that is, to facilitate the development of industrial capitalism while minimizing its most serious social consequence—the appearance of a dissatisfied and hence dangerous working class. The Commission was therefore compelled to combine the rhetoric of economic freedom with concrete proposals based on governmental restraints, thus exposing itself to the charge of inconsistency.*

What lent some force to the charge was not so much the contradiction between free enterprise and factory legislation, but the attempt to fundamentally change only one area of Russian life, to treat industrial relations as the only sphere in which economic function rather than juridical status would become the basis for new administrative and judicial institutions. The Commission never faced this problem directly, but there is reason to believe that it both recognized the difficulty and anticipated its resolution. It would appear that the commissioners looked to the pending judicial, municipal, and tax reforms, and, more generally, to the effects of emancipation, to begin to reconcile these inconsistencies. If emancipation were to create a truly free and mobile population of laborers (as the commissioners, like some of the liberal economists, erroneously anticipated); if municipal reforms were to put an end not only to the tsekhi, but to the entire corporate class administration of the Russian city, and create in its place a juridically uniform urban citizenry, subject to the same municipal institutions; if the commission preparing recommendations for tax reforms (1859–1864, headed by F. G. Terner[47]) were to substitute wealth rather than juridical class as the main basis for taxation; if the pending judicial reforms were to establish a uniform legal system for all

* See the discussion in T. H. Marshall's essay, "Citizenship and Social Class," in *Class, Citizenship, and Social Development. Essays by T. H. Marshall* (Anchor Books ed., Garden City, N.Y., 1965), esp. pp. 78ff, where the author distinguishes between three phases in the development of citizenship in England: civil (eighteenth century), political (nineteenth century), and social (twentieth century). The civil phase, according to Marshall's scheme, included the right to enter freely into contracts, and was therefore antithetical to the corporate restrictions of earlier centuries. The social phase included the right to economic security irrespective of the market place, and was therefore in part a throwback to medieval and early modern times. Thus during the earlier stages of the rise of citizenship, the civil and social aspects of citizenship were often seen as contradictory. In a sense, then, one might argue that Shtakel'berg and his colleagues were endeavoring to overcome this contradiction by telescoping the two phases. (Marshall's intermediary phase of political citizenship was not even discussable by an official commission in nineteenth-century Russia.)

Russians—then the type of reforms the Commission was proposing for industrial relations could blend readily with the more general transformation of Russian society they thought would follow. Russia would be close enough to having a "citizenry" to make the contemplated industrial code no more of an anomaly than, say, the industrial legislation of England. Various passages in the Commission's report suggest that these were, indeed, the directions in which the commissioners expected, or certainly hoped, Russian society would soon move.[48] Whether or not it also crossed their minds that they were in any sense challenging the autocracy's resistance to any concept of citizenship remains obscure.

A good example of the ways in which the Commission was directly confronted by this type of conflict may be found in the question of internal passports. In our earlier discussion of urban institutions, the point was made that the address office, since its establishment in 1809, was one of the few urban institutions with which otkhodniki-workers had any kind of relationship. Its primary purpose, as we have seen, was to oversee and control the movement and activity of the lower-class population (excluding permanent members of tsekhi).* The main method by which this office exercised its control was the issuing of a so-called address ticket (*bilet*) in return for the surrender of a valid passport and the payment of a cash fee. Since not only the original acquisition of the passport but its duration depended on the peasant's lord, the bilet system was an extension of the long arm of serfdom into the peasant's municipal life.[49]

The ultimate significance of this arrangement to the work of the Commission lay in the degree of extra control over his workers that it gave to the manufacturer. For unless a peasant could present his potential employer with his bilet, signifying that his passport was being held at the address office (in some circumstances he had to present the passport itself), the employer was prohibited by law from hiring him.[50] Since the otkhodnik-worker could not leave the city or change his place of employment without his passport, the arrangement served as a sort of guarantee against the worker's quitting

* Having examined the archives of their ministry for 1809, officials of the Ministry of Internal Affairs later explained the establishment of the St. Petersburg address office in this manner: "A single police goal was kept in mind—the establishment of a kind of surveillance over persons who were privately employed, and the raising of the morality of servants." *Gorodskie poseleniia v Rossiiskoi Imperii*, VII (St. Petersburg, 1864), 205–6.

before the expiration of his contract and as an added weapon in the arsenal of the employer in the event of a dispute over wages.[51] At the same time, however, it acted as a restriction on employers who wished to hire workers—particularly day workers (*poden'-shchiki*) who came from nearby areas to do temporary work without settling in at the factory—who were unable or unwilling to register at the address office.*

Officials whose main responsibility was for local law enforcement (e.g. Zakrevskii, in 1852, and Ignat'ev, in 1859, despite their belief in emphasizing contractual relations) tended to argue for the application of the passport or bilet requirement to all factory workers, including day workers. To them the importance of accountability outweighed all other considerations. On the other hand, officials whose main concern was the unhampered functioning of industry (e.g., the Minister of Finance and the Manufacturing Council, when the question arose in connection with the workers' booklets in the early 1850's) wished to avoid burdening manufacturers with excessive requirements.[52] The latter view was endorsed by the Council of State, with some reservations, before the suspension of deliberations over workers' booklets in 1854.[53]

When the issue of passport requirements in factories finally came before the Shtakel'berg Commission, it seems to have aroused little interest or controversy. The Commission eschewed any detailed recommendations regarding the issue on the grounds (which proved to be inaccurate) that the basic Statute on Passports was about to be completely revised and that, since everyone was obligated to comply with whatever laws were in effect, it would be both superfluous and inconsistent with its goal for the Commission to pronounce on this subject.[54] The goal, of course, was the creation of

---

* It should be noted in passing that the original legislation on these matters had failed to specify just how the system was intended to work in the case of peasant-workers who were not actually quartered on factory premises, that is, whether or not it was intended that the bilet or passport change hands at the beginning and end of each workday. In 1846 the Senate had ruled that Baron A. Stieglitz was justified in hiring day workers for his St. Petersburg cotton mill without demanding their passports or *bilety* and that these workers were exempted from registering with the address office. In part, the Senate justified its ruling on the grounds that it was unreasonably burdensome to require so large a factory (Stieglitz hired seven hundred poden'shchiki daily) to process that many documents each day. Thus, in the interest of industrial efficiency the Senate was willing to run the risk that the factory would be illegally harboring runaway serfs. The Senate decision did not eliminate confusion, however, since it failed to specify whether it was meant to apply to other factories besides Stieglitz's. See *Trudy*, II, 192–94.

a distinct and independent working class, unhampered by the juridical distinctions of the past. The peasant passport, a vestige of
serfdom, was a prime example of the kind of restrictive institution
that the Commission considered incompatible with free contracts
arrived at by free economic agents, and the implication of the commissioners' decision to ignore the issue must be that they anticipated the abolition of internal passports and believed there was no
pressing need to face it in the interim.

Nonetheless, the commissioners clearly, if indirectly, indicated
that they foresaw some pressing problems in the passport system.
For example, they recognized the danger that as long as tight restrictions over peasant mobility persisted, the workers' booklets
on which they staked so much might evolve in a manner that would
invest them with some of the characteristics and functions of passports. Even in France the livret d'ouvriers actually served as a sort
of internal passport that workers had to present to get a new job
and to vote for representatives to the conseil des prud'hommes.
From this arose the danger of the employer actually exerting physical control over the worker's mobility through his control over the
booklet, without which the worker was unemployable. The Commission did try to avert this danger by including in its draft report
a specific provision (originally proposed by Ignat'ev, in 1859) stating that it was the worker, and not the employer, who was to retain
possession of the booklet between financial transactions. And as a
further safeguard against the danger that the employer, "because of
personal animosity toward the worker, or misunderstanding, or in
a momentary passion," might endanger the worker's future by entering detrimental remarks in his booklet, the Commission made it
a point to follow the French example of prohibiting any such entries.[55] It also took the further precaution of inserting the following
provision (art. 51) as an extra protective feature for the workers:
"The employer who retains the passports and address tickets of the
workers is obligated to return them immediately when, financial
accounts having been settled and the contract having expired, they
[the workers] no longer wish to remain." Conversely, for reasons it
never explained, the Commission saw fit to provide for the right
of the employer to deduct the fee for a bilet from a worker's wages
(art. 50), which amounted to an authorization for the employer to
act as the agent of the local address office.[56]

Thus, in the last analysis, its mild protestations to the contrary

notwithstanding, the Commission seems to have been quite cognizant of the difficulties inherent in its effort to free a particular
segment of Russian urban society to live and work under institutions that stood out in stark relief from the institutions of an agrarian society and an autocratic government. But rather than openly
face the fact that its recommendations implied a full-scale transformation of Russian society, the Commission preferred to assume that
the implementation of other reforms then in preparation would
bring the rest of Russian life into line with a reformed industrial
sphere.

But an even deeper contradiction complicated the Commission's
work, a contradiction that lay not in institutions but in the situation of the very people for whom the commissioners wished to leg-
islate. Anxious as it was to introduce institutions that it considered
appropriate for a full-fledged working class, the Commission nevertheless repeatedly acknowledged the "backward," peasant character of the existing labor force, which was the legacy of centuries
of serfdom, and even used it as an argument to justify some of its
proposals. The introduction of certain child labor laws, for example, was defended by the Commission on the grounds (among
others) that many workers were peasants who took factory jobs
only in the intervals between periods of field work; hence it was
specious to argue that the proposed legislation would disrupt the
rhythm of factory life, since no steady rhythm of labor existed in
Russian industry.[57]

In a similar vein, the commissioners noted the weakness of the
bonds among workers, who "very often come to the factories by
chance, because of the lack of other, more profitable employment,
and abandon factory production at the first opportunity to return
to easier work." They used this condition as evidence to bolster the
argument that an independent, salaried inspectorate was needed
in order to achieve a balance between the weak, disorganized workers and their more powerful employers.[58]

It was not by chance that in making this point the commissioners
drew an analogy between the potential value of inspectors as pro-
tectors of vulnerable workers and what they claimed to be the already proven success of the recently created "peace mediators"
(*mirovye posredniki*) in protecting the interests of peasants:

If the majority of peace mediators are fulfilling their duties conscientiously, if they are not sacrificing the interests of the peasants to the

interests of the pomeshchiki, then there is no reason to fear that newly designated inspectors, under good circumstances, would subordinate themselves to the influence of the industrialists and forget about their true purpose—to watch over the interests of their younger brothers.[59]

The sentiment that factory workers were the "younger brothers," the provincial and ignorant objects of government tutelage, who needed to be guided and protected, was a touchstone of much of the Commission's argumentation for its program.

At times the commissioners were so anxious to underline the helplessness of the workers that their language betrayed not only condescension, but even an element of scorn. "Carelessness" and "improvidence" were two of the general characteristics of Russian workers, who were "not distinguished by their good moral conduct," the Commission asserted. "Their depravity has become proverbial. They are themselves responsible for much of what they endure, allowing the owners to take advantage of their weaknesses and exploit their carelessness and vices."[60] Similarly, sympathizers with the Commission's proposals, including Governor Baranov as well as some journalists, cited the ignorance and illiteracy of Russian workers as an argument against the Commission's original plan to allow only written contracts to be used as a basis for adjudication in the industrial courts. Russian workers, argued Baranov, struggling to remove any hint of opprobrium from his point, comprehend "neither the juridical nor the moral force of written contracts and obligations, and they respect the truth only through the voice of conscience and conviction."[61] The Commission was persuaded, and removed from its final draft its original provision against the use of oral agreements as a basis for litigation, explaining that "in light of the weak development of our lower classes, to bar the worker's path to judicial procedures solely because—through either carelessness, ignorance, or the refusal of the employer—he was unable to conclude a written contract, would be unjust and oppressive for the worker."[62]

The commissioners used the weakness and backwardness of the working class not only as an excuse for favoring it, but also as an opportunity for imparting form to its as yet unshaped character. For example, the fact that no full-fledged working class as yet existed—owing to "the special circumstances of our fatherland" (most likely a euphemism for serfdom)—meant that it would be possible to adopt a uniform approach to factory workers and artisans once tsekh restrictions had been abolished. The way would then be clear for raising the workers' "intellectual and moral level and improving their material situation": peasant-workers who had been deprived of legal rights and normal social bonds, had had no way in which to publicize their needs, and had been conditioned by serfdom and the guild system might, if the proposed legislation were introduced, gradually come to formulate their own aspirations and even to press for them.[63] It was never boldly stated, but always close to the surface of the commissioners' thought was a conception of the Russian labor force as a sort of tabula rasa on which legislators could inscribe radically new modes of existence.

In view of the Herculean task the Commission had assigned itself —the transformation of backward and disunited (today one would say "atomized") peasant-workers into independent and at least relatively free worker-citizens—it should come as no surprise that the Commission attempted to find an institution that would bridge the gap between the agrarian past and the industrial future of the peasant-worker. Shtakel'berg and his colleagues were inclined to join the economist Terner in looking to a native Russian institution—the artel'. With one important difference: Terner, it will be recalled, in seeking to avert what he conceived of as the proletarianization of the nascent working class, had considered labor associations as an alternative to the labor legislation that was advocated by his fellow economists. The Commission, although it relied heavily on Terner's writings in formulating its views on association,[64] treated the two approaches as complementary, never even considering the possibility of a contradiction.

Accordingly, the third chapter of the Commission's draft industrial code, entitled "On Industrial Societies and Arteli," was devoted to the legal authorization of voluntary associations of workers,[65] a step that had never before been taken by Russian legislators. Workers might come together in arteli or companies (tovarishchestva) to collectively purchase raw materials and foodstuffs, fill large orders, sell products from communal stores, and carry out related activities. It also specified that members of such workers' cooperatives were to share the profits.[66]

If this seems like a modest program, quite peripheral to the Commission's basic vision of a new industrial order, the accompanying explanatory memorandum revealed a more ambitious goal. In it the Commission connected its ideas about arteli and tovarish-chestva with what it called the "free participation of labor and capital in industrial profits" and the "combining of the small savings and divided forces of workers into one large enterprise," ideas for which it acknowledged its debt to Terner.[67] Perhaps even more than Terner the Commission drew upon the controversies that had developed in Western European social thought in the past decades. Characteristically, it invoked the authority of thinkers such as Frédéric Bastiat and Michel Chevalier and cited the social experiments of the Prussian social reformer Schulze-Delitzsch, in order to convince its readers that association, mutual aid, savings funds, and profit sharing were the proper answers to the threat of Louis Blanc's "communism" and Proudhon's "anarchy." The following words, quoted with approval from a French workers' newspaper, represented the Commission's (as well as Terner's) vision of the internal reorganization of Russian industry in the years ahead: "Let the owners of factories make their workers into co-participants [i.e. co-owners] in their enterprises, and the question of the proletariat will soon be resolved."[68]

What real grounds existed for the hope that the artel' might play the ambitious role assigned to it or that workers' associations might ease the transition to full industrialization for the peasant-worker? One of the Commission's grounds for optimism was purely theoretical, namely that despite its numerous faults, the tsekh had enough traces of collective ownership and cooperative savings to enable it to become a basis for workers' associations. With this hope in mind, the Commission backed away from its sweeping indictment of tsekhi to the extent of offering their voluntary transformation into "industrial societies," with open membership based on "free principles of association," as an alternative to abolition, if the members so desired.[69] But this was little more than a lame parting gesture to the tsekhi (perhaps the only positive concrete reference to Russian guilds in the entire five-volume, two-thousand-page transactions of the Commission), based on extrapolations from recent Central European legislation (e.g., the Austrian *Gewerbegesetz* of December 1859, the Saxon *Gewerbegesetz* of October 1861) and not on any direct observations of local tsekhi.*

---

* Indeed, the Commission quickly took back from the guilds with one hand what it had granted with the other. While it spoke favorably of the replacement of the old

But the Commission also argued on the basis of empirical evidence, claiming to see some actual manifestations of growing artel'-association activity in Russian cities, particularly in St. Petersburg, of which it cited several examples: a recently established artel' of master joiners, based on profit sharing (brought to the Commission's attention through an article by Terner); two typographers' mutual aid funds; and a society to provide workers with cheaper living accommodations.[70]

Despite the Commission's intentions, this little list pointed up the weakness rather than the strength of workers' associations in St. Petersburg. The two typographers' mutual aid societies were in no way involved in production. One was actually a philanthropic establishment set up by the Academy of Sciences for its printers. And the "Society for the Improvement of the Lodgings of the Laboring Population"—as the Commission neglected to say—was a joint-stock company, initiated on a nonprofit (and tax-exempt) basis by Strelitskii, Duke of Mecklenburg, and a group of prominent aristocrats (including no less a personage than the arch-conservative Count P. Shuvalov, provincial marshal of the St. Petersburg nobility) to further "public purposes."[71]

The joiners' artel' was thus the Commission's sole example of an association of worker-producers.* Although its existence was made possible by a thousand-ruble grant from a rich individual, it contained many of the cooperative elements so highly esteemed by Terner and the commissioners, including the pooling of tools and raw materials, profit sharing, and the taking of decisions by majority vote.[72] That it stood in virtually complete isolation, however, was further corroborated by a comprehensive list of associations functioning in St. Petersburg, published in *Birzhevye vedomosti* in 1862, in which the joiners' artel' was the only association of

---

guilds by voluntary, non-exclusionary cooperative associations (*Genossenschaften*) in the new Austrian legislation, it criticized the legislation (and that of other German states) for authorizing the continued regulation of the internal structure of the new institutions. The Commission contrasted this situation unfavorably with the freer character of associations—such as those founded by Schulze-Delitzsch—that were not descended, via legislation, from the old guilds. "Ob'iasnitel'naia zapiska," *Trudy*, I, 198–208, 213–15.

* In the third volume of its transactions, published in 1864, the Commission attempted to strengthen its case by pointing to a "gratifying circumstance" in St. Petersburg's industrial life: the establishment of "Pal'ma," a non-guild association or club for artisans. Pal'ma, however, was composed almost exclusively of German craftsmen who resided in the capital (*Trudy*, III, 86n).

worker-producers listed. All the other associations turned out to be organizations of merchants, clerks, petty officials, and the like.[73] Moreover, even the joiners' artel' had no relation to factory production.

The only evidence of any factory-related association in St. Petersburg in this period was the one in the Schlüsselburg area mentioned in *Russkii invalid* in 1861, where a manufacturer was reported to have organized his locksmith workers on some kind of associational basis.[74] And the indications are—in the absence of any reference to it in either the *Birzhevye vedomosti* list or the Commission's survey—that this locksmiths' association was abortive.

"Arteli," the Commission affirmed in defense of its hopes, "have existed in our country from time immemorial and have entered completely into the mores of the people." Perhaps. But the Commission's sweeping deduction from this premise was little more than wishful thinking: namely, that in view of the powerful force of arteli, there were "good grounds to suppose that the totality of social reforms being undertaken will bring elements of association, inherent in the people, into their new life; and if this thing comes about, then one can expect nothing but beneficial results, both for employers and for workers, from its successful development."[75] Arteli of course existed, as they had in the past, but there was simply no truth to the claim that they were performing anything but their most traditional and dismal functions—procuring work for seasonal groups of unemployed otkhodniki and alleviating their misery and poverty through sharing. Except in the mind of a Shtakel'-berg or a Terner, the artel' was more the vestige of a preindustrial order than the vital nucleus of a coming synthesis of industrialism and cooperation among workers.

Nevertheless, there were some who viewed the proposed authorization of industrial associations as a real and significant threat. The increasingly outspoken Moscow Section of the Manufacturing Council claimed that such organizations were "premature" given the current state of Russian society, and therefore dangerous:

The formation of industrial societies is a new matter in Russia, to which even the owners of industrial establishments are unaccustomed, and journeymen and workers—people who are, for the most part, illiterate—still less so. Instead of using it for their own benefit, striving for the goals proposed by the draft [legislation], the workers—led by some kind of intriguers, who will appear without fail—will soon abuse the right they are granted to form societies. Under these circumstances *strikes will arise*, aimed at compelling the owners to raise wages, and so forth. Such societies will be useless, but the workers will be diverted from their business and, beyond that, will abandon themselves to drunkenness.[76]

This alarmist line of reasoning (which was not shared by all members of the Moscow Section) was rejected out of hand by the Commission. Having dismissed the argument with the simple notation that it was contrary to experience, the Commission retained its original provisions on industrial societies and arteli unaltered in its final draft.[77] Yet the Moscow Section had touched on something that could not be so lightly ignored. Had not the commissioners themselves despaired of the peasant-workers' illiteracy, penchant for alchohol, and generally low intellectual and moral level? Was the Commission really as prepared as it suggested to allow associations of workers to develop freely, exempt from any governmental or upper-class tutelage? And what of the question of strikes, perhaps the most delicate question of all?

The answers to these questions are of necessity ambiguous, since the commissioners evidently had mixed feelings. While taking pains to assert the importance of avoiding "excessive" administrative control and of limiting legislation to measures that would merely provide "full room for the initiative of the working class," the Commission was quite vague about just what it considered excessive: "The upper classes should attempt only to assist the initiative of the people, and in certain cases to evoke that initiative . . . , to direct the workers' first steps . . . with advice and explanation, but not with methods of compulsion, which achieve the goal exactly opposite the one desired."[78] But the Commission went on to say that the new working class would not be mature enough to allow its organizations to develop properly—despite their roots in the Russian past—unless the broad features of their structure were "to a certain extent, determined in advance by law."[79] On the whole, however, the Commission had enough confidence in the workers to refrain from any severe restrictions on their freedom of association other than a stipulation (in art. 29) that the charter of each new industrial association would be subject to confirmation by the Ministry of Internal Affairs.[80]

But combining for the purpose of engaging in strikes was another, more sensitive matter. The Commission's proposals—including the workers' booklets, the inspectorate, and the industrial courts —were, after all, an attempt to preserve Russian factories from the familiar European scenes of mass disorder and unrest by substituting mediation and adjudication for direct conflict and tests of strength. Could the Commission at the same time advocate the institutionalization of the kind of conflicts it was seeking to preempt? In dealing with this dilemma, the commissioners demonstrated a rather nuanced sensibility. The Russian Criminal Code of 1845, it will be recalled, made an act of disobedience by a group of workers the equivalent of a criminal offense against the state (art. 1791) and outlawed strikes as criminal acts (art. 1792).[81] These laws had remained on the books unaltered and apparently unused. Since the composition of the Zakrevskii workers' booklet (where they appeared as arts. 21 and 22 respectively), they had been incorporated into the various draft booklets as a matter of course, without evoking any serious controversy.[82] The Shtakel'berg Commission was the first official body to critically evaluate these two laws.

It attributed the existence of the first to the generally coercive basis of worker-owner relations that prevailed before emancipation, especially in manorial and possessional factories. Since the directors of such factories were, in a sense, *"authorities established by the government*, with respect to whom the law demanded unconditional obedience from factory people,"* an act of defiance against them was tantamount to an act of rebellion against the state. However, with the abolition of serfdom and possessional rights over other persons, the validity of this concept had been nullified, the commissioners argued, and with it the very possibility of a crime like the one in question. They recommended that the statute, being thus clearly incompatible with the new order of free labor, be stricken from the books.[83]

The commissioners approached the law against strikes with considerably greater caution, obviously feeling themselves on shakier ground. Advanced European countries like France and Belgium, after all, still maintained stiff penalties against premeditated strikes, as did most other continental governments. Only England distinguished between strikes accompanied by force and violence, which were illegal, and peaceful strikes, which were tolerated (this distinction had also been gaining support in the industrial circles of Belgium). The Commission's discussion of this problem was written in a spirit that displayed obvious sympathy with the English approach and no overt objection whatever toward workers' strikes as such. Nevertheless, the Commission failed to adopt the formal positive position on "simple" nonviolent strikes that its survey of European legislation seemed to be moving toward. Instead, it adopted a safer, less controversial position, which was almost certainly based on prudential considerations: the existing law against strikes should remain in force, but in the interests of justice it should be balanced by an equivalent provision for sanctions against combinations of employers, as was the practice in other European countries. Thus, with this rather innocuous and evasive proviso, the 1845 sanctions against instigating or participating in strikes remained, almost verbatim, in the Shtakel'berg proposals.[84]

The absence of any published responses to this controversial position among the comments on its draft solicited by the Commission, especially since we know that the strike was not without its supporters in the Russian press, only serves to reinforce the impression that this was an area which the Commission felt unable to discuss with full candor. Given the logic of the entire report, and of the section on strikes in particular, it does not seem unreasonable to infer that if full candor had been possible, the commissioners—who in no other area of industrial relations seemed willing to lag behind the most progressive tendencies in the West—might well have responded to the Moscow Section's warning that the free development of workers' organizations could lead to organized strikes by expressing its approval of that outcome. The real problem in the Commission's logic was the gap between its own negative assessment of the cultural level and organizational solidarity of Russian peasant-workers at the present stage of the country's industrial development and the ambitious civic goals it was attempting to set for them. Like the liberal economists, the Commission found itself enunciating goals and aspirations the achievement of which assumed the existence of a social group that itself constituted one of the goals.

The Fate of the Shtakel'berg Proposals

The proposals of the Shtakel'berg Commission, like those of its predecessors, were not destined to be implemented. In 1863—the year after the completion of its first draft—a few minor changes were made in the statutes governing industry and crafts, but not one of the Commission's controversial proposals were among them. When a new edition of the *Svod zakonov* (Digest of Laws), incorporating these changes, was published a decade later, it was virtually indistinguishable from the legislation that existed before the creation of the various commissions of 1857–64.[85]

Writing in 1880, after at least two more government commissions had come and gone without effecting any significant changes in the industrial code, I. I. Ianzhul (soon to achieve fame as one of Russia's first and most dedicated factory inspectors) stated:

Every reader has certainly repeatedly encountered information in the press about the perennial and fruitless existence of various commissions. ... The most fortunate of these commissions work conscientiously on their tasks, assemble a more or less large mass of material . . . , work up drafts of new statutes, and publish them, together with the materials, for public information. But often just at that point when the work of the commission ought to be crowned with some kind of practical results, they fail to materialize. The old legislation . . . continues to exist with all of its earlier defects and inadequacies. And most curious of all, the very same story is repeated a few years later: a new commission on the old question is formed; it publishes new works, composes new drafts, and in the end is equally unproductive.

The best example [of this pattern] can be found in the recent history of Russian factory legislation.[86]

While Ianzhul offered no explanation for the phenomenon he so accurately described, scholarly works ranging from Tugan-Baranovskii's classical study of the Russian factory to the most recent writings of both Soviet and Western historians have attributed the government's failure to implement the St. Petersburg and Shtakel'berg commissions' proposals to a single cause: the successful counterpressures brought to bear by provincial industrialists.[87] Opposition to some of the proposed legislation by a number of provincial industrialists can indeed be documented. Nevertheless —although an alternative explanation cannot be suggested until we have examined some of the actual practices of the government during the lifetime of the commissions (Chapter 5)—it is, for reasons about to be explicated, not only an unsatisfactory but a highly misleading explanation.

The case for this thesis has rested in large part on information contained in an 1861 memorandum written by Count Baranov, governor of Tver, in response to the St. Petersburg commission's earlier request that certain provincial governors solicit responses from manufacturers and others to its proposals.[88] The Baranov memorandum, which summarized the views of some leading Tver manufacturers (including several who also owned factories in Moscow), revealed virtually unanimous opposition to certain important provisions of the commission's draft—most notably the creation of an independent inspectorate, the prohibition of night labor for minors, and the setting of a twelve-year minimum age for child labor. However, proponents of this thesis have ignored the fact that despite these criticisms, the Tver-Moscow manufacturers, without a single exception, broadly approved the commission's project. The closest any of them came to an objection based on general principle was when one of them argued that to outlaw night labor for minors was to violate their "freedom of labor" (svoboda narodnogo truda)—a classical argument, but one that was still rarely applied in this manner in Russia. The objections raised by the manufacturers were mainly matters of emphasis and degree: they would support an inspection system provided it were administered by the Manufacturing Council; and although they objected to the twelve-year age minimum, most of Baranov's respondents, including the spokesman for the "freedom of labor," were favorably inclined to a minimum age of ten and to the setting of some limit on the length of the workday for minors.[89] In short, the Baranov memorandum, composed by an official who was extremely hostile to manufacturers,* does not, on the face of it, lend much support to the thesis that the commissions were faced with a general onslaught by representatives of industrial capital.

Nor do the comments of other industrialists who responded to the St. Petersburg commission's draft: a group of nineteen manufacturers from Moscow, a smaller group from Tula, individual manufacturers from Orel and Rostov-on-the-Don, and the well-

---

* Witness the following statements from the memorandum: "It is obvious that the manufacturers are defending not the well-being of the workers, but only their own pocketbooks." "... The manufacturers think neither of the national wealth nor of the education of the people's children, but are concerned only with their own pocketbooks. They simply exploit its [i.e. the people's] strength and ability, exploit in the full sense of the word, since they are completely unconcerned with either the health or morality of their workers." Trudy, II, 275, 291.

known Khludov brothers, manufacturers of cotton fabrics in Riazan. Their criticisms tended to overlap those of the Tver industrialists, including similar reservations regarding the inspectorate and
the details of the proposed limitations on child labor. The responses showed significant variations, and none came close to a
sweeping criticism of the proposed legislation.[90]

Perhaps sensing the inadequacy of their case with respect to industrialists as such, Tugan-Baranovskii and his imitators adopted
a fall-back position that makes the Manufacturing Council—particularly its Moscow Section—the villain of the piece. The premise
here is that the Moscow Section acted as a spokesman to the government for the views of the organized manufacturers of the Central Industrial Region. A thorough examination of the history of
the Manufacturing Council and its branches would take us far
afield; but the idea that they represented a sort of organized lobby
for manufacturers would appear to be an exaggeration at best.
Historically, Russian manufacturers had never pressed for an organizational structure through which to influence the government
on a regular basis.[91] When the Manufacturing Council was established in St. Petersburg in 1828, it was at the initiative not of manufacturers but of Finance Minister Kankrin, who gave it the organizational status of nothing more than an advisory branch of his
ministry's Department of Manufactures. A majority of members
were to be manufacturers appointed by the minister, although only
one manufacturer attended the opening session, and the council
was generally dominated by nobles and officials. The avowed purpose of the council was to encourage manufacturing industry, but
in practice its function seems to have been mainly limited to collecting statistical information. In general, neither the council nor
its local branches—all of which remained under tight government
control—played any noteworthy role in the economic life of the
country in the years that followed.[92]

The Moscow Section, it is true, managed to display somewhat
more independence and vitality than other branches over the
years, and merchant-manufacturers took an increasingly active
role in its deliberations. But on the whole, its power of initiative
was slight, and its energies were devoted more to routine matters
such as approving patents than to important questions of policy.[93]
In any case, since its reports were never published, the Moscow

Section could not easily have served as a real rallying point for the manufacturing class even if the intent had been there.

One of the important areas of deliberation in which the Moscow Section did participate during the reign of Nicholas was that of labor legislation. But even a cursory glance at its positions on this question reveals that it was hardly a consistent spokesman for the narrow interests of manufacturers. Thus, for example, in the late 1830's and early 1840's it supported an abortive plan to establish an early version of the industrial courts and even agreed with the argument that participation on the courts by manufacturers would be inappropriate. And in 1850–51, it advocated introducing compulsory safety regulations in private factories.[94] True, although the Moscow Section as such was not an active participant in the 1850–54 deliberations over workers' booklets, five of its members notified Governor Zakrevskii that they favored deleting certain of the proposed provisions, most notably, the right of workers fired for misconduct to two weeks notice. On the other hand, they unequivocally endorsed the proposals as a whole.[95]

Turning to the postwar years, it would seem that neither the Moscow Section nor the council as a whole played a major role in the deliberations of the St. Petersburg commission. After the commission's draft was circulated, however, the Moscow Section did respond with the comment that an independent factory inspectorate would be superfluous in Moscow, where the council was capable of conducting its own surveillance.[96] Moreover, the group of nineteen Moscow manufacturers that criticized the inspectorate included some members of the Moscow Section acting as individuals. The strongest statement that might be ventured on the basis of this evidence is that to certain manufacturers from the central provinces the Moscow Section was becoming a sort of symbol of protection against governmental interference, but there is no evidence whatever of a concerted assault against the St. Petersburg commission's proposals on its part.

Even if such an assault on the St. Petersburg commission had occurred, the content of the 1862 draft of the Shtakel'berg Commission would have demonstrated its ineffectiveness. The Shtakel'-berg Commission not only made the factory inspectorate one of the cornerstones of its proposals, it went even further than the St. Petersburg commission in placing restrictions on child labor (a fact conveniently ignored by those who attributed the demise of the St. Petersburg commission to the opposition of manufacturers).

Once the Shtakel'berg Commission had printed and circulated its first draft, in 1863, the Moscow Section began to become outspokenly critical. Its criticisms bore down on four major points: (1) workers' societies or associations were potentially dangerous; (2) the Commission's proposed limits on night labor and the length of the workday for minors went too far and should be modified; (3) except for minor cases, the need for Industrial Courts was doubtful, since cases serious enough to result in the jailing of employers ought to be adjudicated in the regular courts; (4) the function of surveillance belonged in the hands of the Industrial Council (the proposed new name for the Manufacturing Council) and its Moscow Section rather than a new factory inspectorate. The Moscow Section conceded that some kind of inspection system was needed for the "highly humanitarian" goal of "protecting the interests of the working class from abuse," but it expressed apprehensions lest "interference" by inspectors upset the alleged balance that prevailed in owner-worker relations, "destroy all the bonds between employers and workers, serve as a pretext for abuses, and increase the number of complaints." To the Commission's praise of the British inspection system, the Moscow Section responded simply that unlike Russian workers, English workers had developed a sense of the mutuality of interest between workers and employers, which made an inspectorate a workable institution in that context: "Other customs, other morals!"[97]

These were important and pungent criticisms; in part, they struck at the weak point in the Commission's armor—the contrast between the "backwardness" of the Russian worker and the "advanced" role in society he was being asked to play. But they also left open a reasonably wide area of agreement. The second and third points were essentially questions of degree, and with respect to the second it is noteworthy that the Moscow Section did *not* echo the earlier demands of some manufacturers for a minimum child labor age of ten in lieu of the proposed age of twelve. The first point was a significant challenge to the general outlook of the Commission, but not to the basic structure of its proposals, to which associations were peripheral. Factory inspection remained a key item in dispute. But the Commission's most important recommendation—the use of the workers' booklet, backed by some kind of system of enforcement and adjudication—remained unchallenged.*

But most important, the arguments of the Moscow Section—like the aforementioned objections of provincial manufacturers—did not make the slightest dent in the thinking of the commissioners or their supporters in the Ministry of Finance. In 1863 the Department of Manufactures, which exercised immediate authority over the Manufacturing Council and its branches, published a long article by one of its officials, A. Sherer,[98] in which he discussed the proposals of the recent commissions with the greatest sympathy, extolled the virtues of protective labor legislation in "the educated states of Europe," and praised the commissions for having used that legislation as a model. Confident that the new proposals would soon be implemented, Sherer flattered St. Petersburg manufacturers for their constructive attitudes and concluded with the hope that the draft regulations would be accepted in the spirit "that has always distinguished the Russian manufacturer when the general welfare of his fellow citizens was at stake."[99] At this juncture, in other words, Sherer assumed that the Commission's draft would be enacted into law; apparently cognizant of the existence of some criticism, he expressed his confidence, however patronizingly, that the critics would graciously accommodate themselves. At no point did he imply that they would have any other choice.

Early in 1864, when the Commission itself reconvened to review the responses to its first draft, it continued to proceed as if no obstacles stood in its path, and yielded almost nothing to its critics.[100] While attributing special importance to the comments of the Moscow Section,[101] the participating commissioners (equally divided between representatives of the Ministries of Internal Affairs and Finance) rejected summarily each of its major points and most of its minor ones.[102] Indeed they now went so far as to denounce at-

* One might add here that at various points in its critique the Moscow Section spoke somewhat disparagingly of manufacturers and that it recommended certain admittedly minor changes that appeared to be slightly more favorable to workers than the Commission's original language (see, for example, *Trudy*, III, 24, 26, 30, 32, 53–55, 66). One should probably not make too much of this, since the main thrust of the argument was not affected. It is conceivable that these were merely formal gestures, aimed at demonstrating balance and objectivity.

tempts to reduce the forcefulness of their child labor program as one-sided and based on "personal and class interests," and they equated the counterproposals of the Moscow Section and others regarding factory inspection with "class surveillance (by the manufacturers themselves)." The Commission's only alteration of this part of its draft was to *strengthen* the surveillance system by eliminating an earlier provision that had allowed local authorities a voice in choosing the inspectors.[103]

In sum, the Commission's final response to the Moscow Section amounted to a complete, unmistakable, and in tone rather insolent repudiation. In view of the composition of the Commission, it is not inaccurate to say that the Moscow Section had been rebuffed by its superiors in the governmental hierarchy. If, as has been maintained, the Moscow Section of the Manufacturing Council was indeed "the organ of the Moscow manufacturers,"[104] then it must at least be conceded that the manufacturers were as ineffectual in influencing the Shtakel'berg Commission as they had been in attempting to raise protective tariffs a few years earlier.

Having completed the final, barely modified version of their draft industrial code in February 1864, the commissioners submitted it, together with all the comments and related materials, to the recently appointed Finance Minister, M. Kh. Reutern (who served from 1862 to 1878) for scrutiny.[105] Reutern—a member of the circle of liberal economists, a close associate of Terner, and a protégé of the Grand Duke Konstantin[106]—returned the draft to the commissioners without indicating any reservations, although he included some materials from the Baltic region expressing reservations about the applicability to that area of the proposed abolition of guilds. The final session of the Commission was devoted exclusively to the questions raised with regard to the Baltic region (most of the objections were rejected), after which the entire set of materials was returned to Reutern for further examination.[107] Shortly thereafter—from all indications, with the ministry's approval—the final, slightly amended version of the draft legislation was, as we already know, published as part of the third volume of the Commission's transactions.

Its assigned task having been thus completed, the Shtakel'berg Commission, like the St. Petersburg commission before it, faded into oblivion. There is no documentary evidence that the reports of either commission received any further consideration in government circles during the decade of the 1860's; nor were they given further illumination in the press.* Only in the 1870's, when new commissions were again formed to take up the question of labor legislation and related problems, did some of the proposals of 1859–64 reappear, albeit in modified form.[108]

If the Moscow Section and the manufacturers of Central Russia had failed to affect the thinking of officials of the Finance Ministry, which was the ministry most devoted to industrial growth and the one in which their views came closest to having representation, it is almost inconceivable that the proposed legislation fell victim to their sinister pressures on other branches of government (the Council of State? the Second Section?) after 1864, especially in the absence of even a jot of evidence that such pressures were exerted. Manufacturers at this point in Russian history were still as far from forming a cohesive and aggressive class as were the workers. As a group, manufacturers—and provincial manufacturers more than any others—were still a scorned, disdained, and therefore defensive sector of society, vilified even in the pro-industrial press (as was seen in Chapter 3) and subjected to reproach by the most pro-industrial body ever to have been formed by the government (one, incidentally, that placed a high premium on the need to encourage the cohesive development of the industrial middle class as well as of the working class). Only St. Petersburg manufacturers sometimes managed to gain exemption from the anti-industrialist vilification, in part, no doubt, because they obsequiously supported whatever proposals government commissions put forth.

If we are correct, then, in rejecting the views of Tugan-Baranovskii and like-minded historians, where may we look for a satisfactory explanation of the government's failure to act on the proposals of the Commission, proposals that corresponded to sentiments ex-

* In the spring of 1867, when the newly formed Imperial Russian Technical Society held its first plenary session in St. Petersburg, one member presented a thorough review of the St. Petersburg commission's proposals. He made the curious claim that the government had failed to enact them only because they had not gone far enough in protecting the interests of the workers. See *Zapiski Imperatorskogo Russkogo Tekhnicheskogo Obshchestva* (No. 6, 1867), pp. 397–408. The speaker, and other participants as well, seemed to believe that the introduction of factory legislation was still pending. This was certainly a plausible assumption considering that the government had never issued a public statement explaining the fate of the proposals of either of the earlier commissions. The 1867 meeting of the Technical Society is discussed in greater detail on pp. 289–96 below.

pressed by varied sectors of the press, by several high-ranking police officials in key cities, by representatives of the ministries most directly concerned, and to a limited extent, even by some of their harshest critics? Inertia or sloth may at times be reasonable explanations of the workings of the Russian bureaucracy, but they are shown to be inadequate for this period given the rapidity with which such fundamental reforms as emancipation, reorganization of the judiciary, and the *zemstva* (county councils) were put through during the same years. Although it seems sufficiently clear that the projects in question were deliberately held in abeyance from 1864 until the early 1870's (probably against the will of the Finance Ministry), no document has been uncovered containing orders to suspend them. It may well be that no such specific or direct order was ever issued. But it may be possible, by examining certain events that were actually taking place during the commissions' lifetime—including the interaction between government policy, workers, and worker-oriented members of "society"—and relating them to some of the seeming contradictions we have already encountered in sections of the Shtakel'berg draft, to construct a plausible explanation of the commissions' failure. For the labor question was beginning to emerge not only in the form of ideas and arguments over new proposals, but also in the form of concrete acts directly initiated from below.

FIVE

Labor Unrest and the Sunday School Movement

WE NOW turn from attempts by academics, publicists, and government officials to devise programs in the workers' behalf to attempts by the workers themselves to improve their lot through collective action. The Shtakel'berg Commission and, to a greater or lesser degree, several of the writers treated earlier were of the opinion that self-directed nonviolent protest activities, ranging from the collective presentation of grievances to strikes, were desirable or at least tolerable. To what extent did such activities actually take place? What was their character? And what was the nature of the response they evoked from the officials under whose jurisdiction they fell?

Worker Initiative—Labor Unrest

Some Soviet historians have argued that an unprecedented rise in labor unrest characterized the early years of Alexander II's reign. This rise, they contend, was one of several manifestations of Russia's "first revolutionary situation," the designation once given by Lenin to the years 1859–61.[1] In defining a "revolutionary situation," Lenin had noted a significant heightening in the incidence of mass action as an essential element,[2] and the historians in question have endeavored to demonstrate the applicability of this concept to labor as well as to peasant unrest.[3]

It would be erroneous to dismiss this contention entirely, since some important supporting evidence has been presented. For the purposes of our study, however, it should be noted that the overwhelming majority of the cases of labor unrest brought to light by the historians Ionova and Rutman, and others, did not involve free laborers working in the large private enterprises of urban centers such as Moscow and St. Petersburg. They involved almost exclusively workers employed in the possessional and manorial factories of the Ural mining region and the manorial factories of other parts of European Russia, and on some of the recently undertaken railroad construction projects. Moreover, of the 196 cases of labor unrest identified by Rutman as having occurred from 1857 through 1861, the large majority consisted of either disorganized forms of unruliness and agitation (*volneniia*) or the submission of petitions by workers to those in authority. Only two cases are identified by the word "strike" (*stachka*).[4] That only five of the incidents (including the two "strikes") took place in St. Petersburg and the neighboring region, one of the two most highly developed centers of large-scale capitalist industry in the country, suggests a fortiori the primitive nature of whatever "labor movement" may have existed in Russia during these years.

Incidents of mass unrest, however, represent only the top of an iceberg. There is also evidence of widespread dissatisfaction among the workers of St. Petersburg and Moscow that did not necessarily assume the form of collective action by large groups. Even before the Crimean War, Zakrevskii's interest in the establishment of a uniform workers' booklet had first been aroused by the frequent complaints of Moscow factory workers against employers who failed to pay the wages originally agreed on.[5] Similar complaints were also received by members of the Manufacturing Council's Moscow Section, who claimed that in some cases such disputes had actually led to "disobedience," disorders, machine breaking, and even the temporary disruption of production.[6] In the postwar years, the frequency of complaints lodged by workers against their employers became high enough to move the military governor of Moscow to write in 1860 that their number had reached "huge proportions."[7]

In St. Petersburg, complaints by workers in the postwar years were of sufficient magnitude to convince the government to establish an experimental "Temporary Commission for the Examination of Litigation Between Contractors or Employers and Workers or Craftsmen" in 1858[8] (a similar body was created in Moscow in 1860). Its primary task was to mediate disputes by encouraging compromise settlements, but it also had the authority to impose a settlement if mediation failed. Its procedures were informal, brief, and entirely oral.[9]

During the first three years of the Temporary Commission's

eight-year existence,* it received a staggering total of 2,738 complaints from a total of about sixteen thousand workers, some of them acting individually, others as *arteli*.[10] Although the actual number of workers involved may have been considerably lower than sixteen thousand if one allows for the likelihood of repeated complaints by the same persons, these figures certainly bear witness to the existence of widespread dissatisfaction in St. Petersburg. Unfortunately, there is no solid evidence on the precise nature of the disputes that precipitated these complaints. It is not even clear that any of them originated in real factories, and there is some basis for inferring that most of them did not.

To begin with, some of the terms used in the Temporary Commission's title suggest that its initiators may not have had large factories in mind; the term "employer" (*nanimatel'*) is vague, and could refer to the proprietor of any small enterprise such as an artisan shop or even a store, while the term "contractor" (*riadchik*) is more suggestive of, say, the building trades than of a factory. Second, the commission included representatives from every concerned government agency except the one with chief responsibility for factory industry—the Ministry of Finance. Furthermore, while merchants, *meshchane*, and artisans were represented on the commission, industrialists as such were not. The commission's jurisdiction was restricted to cases in which the dispute was based on oral rather than written contracts, which in practice would have excluded the city's major industrial plants. Nor, it should be added, are there references to any of these cases in Rutman's listing of 196 incidents or in A. Pankratova's comprehensive collection of materials on labor unrest.[11] The Shtakel'berg Commission, without going into any detail, described these cases as consisting typically of "the most trivial of conflicts," usually precipitated by the employer's attempt to make small wage deductions in retaliation for unauthorized absences, damage to materials, and the like.[12] On the basis of all these considerations, and—perhaps more to the point—in view of the apparent contradiction between the government's willingness to establish the Temporary Commission and the intolerance that was simultaneously shown toward even the most peaceful of the five major collective expressions of discontent by St.

* The life of the Temporary Commission expired in 1866, when it was supposedly superseded by the new judicial reforms. See *PSZ*, XLI, Part II, No. 43800 (Oct. 31, 1866).

Petersburg factory workers, it is reasonable to conclude that the cases that came before the Temporary Commission were small scale, distinctively nonindustrial, and, to the extent that no open demonstrations seem to have evolved, basically unthreatening from the point of view of police security. Finally, most of the disputes were easily resolved. Of the 2,129 cases that had been completed as of July 31, 1861, a total of 1,517 were settled by mutual agreement.[13]

A true test of the degree of worker militancy in St. Petersburg, as well as an examination of official reactions to organized labor unrest, must be sought in the five known incidents of mass protest during this period, none of which came before the Temporary Commission for adjudication. With the exception of a single episode in 1850,* the five incidents were the first known cases of mass disturbances in the factories of the region. Listed chronologically, they were: 1857, unrest among 393 workers of the Izhorsk Admiralty factory; 1858, "strike" of 300 spinners at the Wright cotton factory; 1859, unrest among 400 workers of the Maxwell cotton factory; 1859, "strike" of 800 workers at the Golenishchevskaia mechanized weaving factory; 1860, petitioning of government officials by 147 workers of the Aleksandrovsk machine works.[14] The three textile plants were privately owned, while the two machine works—the Aleksandrovsk and Izhorsk factories—belonged to the state. In all other respects the five factories were very similar. They were all large-scale enterprises with at least several hundred employees, they were relatively advanced in mechanization and equipment, and they were located outside the city limits, in the young industrial suburbs along the Schlüsselburg Road and the Neva River.

The two so-called strikes, the only incidents of the period so designated by Rutman and others, differed from the other cases in that they involved more distinct and deliberate work stoppages. These stoppages, however, were neither planned, nor organized, nor prolonged. Contemporary sources referred to them not as strikes but

---

* Little is known of this incident. As recounted in the standard Soviet history of St. Petersburg, it appears that in January 1850 a number of workers of the Stieglitz cotton factory demanded the removal of certain fines that had been leveled against them and requested a raise in wages. When the factory administration failed to meet these demands, some seven hundred workers refused to continue their work. The police arrested sixty-six workers, six of whom were singled out as "instigators," beaten in the presence of the other workers, and then sent back home to their villages. Two weeks elapsed before normal conditions were restored at the factory. Akademiia Nauk SSSR. *Ocherki istorii Leningrada*, I (Moscow, 1955; ed. M. P. Viatkin) 703.

as "disorders" (*besporiadki*) or "mutinies" (*vozmushcheniia*).[15] In four of the five cases, the workers involved were seeking either additional pay or compensation for holidays. Their behavior thus differed from the norm of earlier protests by peasant-workers in that their demands were kept within the confines of the urban industrial context and were not directly related to their juridical status as peasants. Only in the Izhorsk incident, the first of the five, were the workers' demands unrelated to their industrial earnings.

The Izhorsk incident was the least complex of the five. On Saturday, July 13, 1857, a group of 393 workers who had apparently been made to work on Sundays announced to the army officer who supervised their work that they would not be on the job the following day. The workers were promptly beaten with sticks, and their demands, for the moment, were left unsatisfied. However, a special military tribunal was convened to investigate the causes of their dissatisfaction. Although the court determined that the delinquent workers—particularly the three "instigators" who had acted as their spokesmen—should be punished for their defiance, it also ruled in favor of their demands. Sunday labor at the Izhorsk factory was henceforth to be prohibited.[16]

The "strike" at the Wright cotton factory, in April 1858, was the first serious case of labor unrest at a private St. Petersburg factory during the reign of Alexander II, and only the second known case in the history of the city. It began when three hundred of the factory's seven hundred workers, without any previous warning, suddenly stopped work and demanded a raise in their piece wage, thus bringing the operations of the factory to a halt. The timely intervention of the local police inspector, however, led to a quick resumption of work. A subsequent threat by some of the workers to stop working again unless a pay raise was introduced was not carried out. The office of the military governor acted swiftly and firmly against the five alleged "instigators" of the work stoppage (four provincial peasants and one St. Petersburg artisan), who were held in detention for a month and then exiled from the city for two years. The remaining participants agreed to continue working under the previous conditions, renounced their demand for a raise, and disclaimed all association with the "instigators."[17]

The government's disposition of the Wright case followed the pattern of the Izhorsk case. Although punishments were meted out to "instigators" and workers were clearly shown that acts of defiance would not be tolerated, officials expressed concern with the circumstances that had caused the unrest and conducted an investigation of conditions at the factory. In this case the workers' grievances were found to have been unjustified (their daily wage of 70 to 90 kopecks was held to be adequate),[18] but the investigation was carried out in earnest, and officials would have undoubtedly placed pressure on the owners of the factory to make an adjustment in favor of the workers if lower wages had been paid. This, in fact, is precisely what happened in the case of the next St. Petersburg "strike."

Trouble began at the Golenishchevskaia factory in December 1859 when eight hundred workers, the largest number involved in any such incident before the 1870's, refused to work on a certain religious holiday. When payday came, the factory administration deducted one ruble from the wages of each worker for the day missed. On the next day, the workers responded with disorders (*besporiadki* is the word used in General Ignat'ev's report) and again refused to return to work. The local police inspector intervened and succeeded in persuading the workers to return to the job, but his task was somewhat more difficult than in the Wright incident. Another day of work was missed before the workers returned to the factory, which they agreed to do only after the inspector had leveled an additional fine of one ruble against each of them.[19]

Once again police officials looked into the conditions that had led to unrest. This time not only was the factory administration found to be in the wrong, but the police inspector made a general criticism of industrialists for encouraging this type of disorder by their mistreatment of workers. The factory director was ordered by Ignat'ev to declare in writing that he would never again violate existing laws against work on religious holidays. A strict police surveillance over manufacturers who acted in violation of these laws was then instituted.[20]

Little information is available about the 1859 unrest at the Maxwell cotton factory. Apparently some four hundred workers demonstrated tumultuously on the Schlüsselburg Road, demanding higher wages. Without hesitation, General Ignat'ev then brought in military units to force the demonstrators back to work. Once again "instigators," this time eight in number, were singled out and placed under arrest. In this case, however, the record does not show whether any official action against the factory administration was carried out or even contemplated.[21]

In the case of the labor unrest at the Aleksandrovsk machine works in 1860, the preservation of most of the relevant archival materials makes it possible to present a clearer and more detailed picture. The Aleksandrovsk factory was a state-owned enterprise that operated within the jurisdiction of the Transportation Administration. Its workers were state peasants. In practice, however, it was run more like a private factory, with the government playing only a limited role. In 1843, the plant had been contracted out to a group of American entrepreneurs, who were responsible to the Transportation Administration for the actual conduct of factory affairs. The Transportation Administration's direct responsibility was restricted to two areas. First, it set forth the terms under which the contractors administered the factory. These were contained in the 1843 contract, which was renewed in 1850 with a few minor changes.[22] This contract was particularly germane to the events of 1860, in that certain provisions armed the workers with a legal basis for their grievances. The second function of the Transportation Administration was to maintain a police office on the factory premises. The office was headed by a *politseimeister* (chief of police), whose responsibility it was to oversee the behavior of the workers and the safety of government property. He had at his disposal a staff of 56 persons, mainly soldiers.[23]

The 1850 contract had clearly stipulated the rates at which the workers were to be paid. The monthly wages of the most highly skilled workers (*mastery*) ranged between 20 and 33 rubles, while those directly below them (*podmaster'ia*) received from 8 to 21 rubles. The simple workers (*masterovye*), who comprised the bulk of the labor force, were paid at the extremely low rate of 5 to 8 rubles, and the young apprentices (*ucheniki*) were given approximately 2.5 rubles.* In addition, each worker received a firewood and flour ration to supplement his wage.[24]

The events of 1860 were an outgrowth of the situation of the

---

* In St. Petersburg in the 1850's, one ruble had the purchasing power of approximately 36 lbs. of wheat flour or 56 lbs. of rye flour. A. Rykachev, "Tseny na khleb i na trud v S.-Peterburge za 58 let," *Vestnik finansov, promyshlennosti i torgovli*, No. 31 (1911), pp. 201–2.

masterovye, who then comprised about 70 per cent of the labor force.[25] As set forth in the contract, the wages of the masterovye did not even equal the average daily wage of the unskilled "black" workers of other St. Petersburg factories and shops in the 1850's—a meager 52 kopecks.[26] There was, however, one clause in the contract which, if applied conscientiously, would have added substantially to the wages of the workers and perhaps to the efficiency of the factory as well. It stated, in essence, that the wages listed above were intended only as a minimum, and were to be supplemented with cash bonuses based on individual performance and output.[27]

In January 1860, 147 of the factory's 257 masterovye submitted a petition to the Director of Transportation, K. V. Chevkin. The petitioners complained that they had been receiving no more than the 5–8 rubles minimum from the American contractors, a sum that not only was inadequate for the support of their large families, but left them too destitute even to buy the necessary work clothes. A large section of the petition was devoted to flattering Chevkin, lauding his kindness and generosity, praying for his health and well-being, and expressing confidence that he would respond favorably to their just request for higher wages.[28]

The petition proved to be successful in the limited sense that some earlier labor protests had been: that is, the authorities looked into the grievances of the workers and, finding them to be justified, instructed the factory administrators to meet their demands. The investigation, ordered by the Transportation Administration's Department of Railroads, found Winans and Company, the American firm, guilty of having failed to comply with the terms of the contract. With the exception of small bonuses distributed to fifty foundry workers in 1859, Winans and Company had made no bonus payments since renewing the contract in 1850.[29] The complaints of the workers having thus been vindicated, Winans and Company was ordered to introduce appropriate bonuses almost immediately. The next payday found the company distributing 471 rubles in bonuses to 178 workers on the basis of their performance, and an additional 218 rubles to the families of 95 workers purely on the basis of need. On the following payday the sum distributed was even greater, as was the number of workers affected.[30] Almost overnight, Winans and Company had taken on the appearance of conscientious and benevolent employers.

Had the matter been left to rest here, the Aleksandrovsk workers might well have drawn the conclusion that they could count
on government agencies to redress their just grievances when they
made their approach in a proper and orderly manner. But the Transportation Administration would not allow this impression to take
root. Once again, the government acted on the premise that, right
or wrong, the workers had committed a criminal act. In this case
their "crime" was not a work stoppage or even a noisy demonstration. It had amounted to nothing more than the peaceful submission of a carefully worded and flattering petition to a responsible
official, a petition that in effect requested no more than the fulfill-
ment of contractual conditions considered by the government to
be legally binding on the employers. But somehow the workers had
to be apprised that no form of organized activity on their own
behalf—not even a petition—was tolerable. The new benefits had
to be separated from the method used to obtain them. Predictably,
this was accomplished through disciplinary measures. The chief
of factory police was assigned the duty of identifying the persons
chiefly responsible for the petition; the fact that the company had
been found guilty would have no bearing on their fate.

After some initial difficulty, the police were able to identify a
29-year-old worker, Nikolai Morozov, as the moving force behind
the petition. Chevkin and the Director of the Department of Railroads quickly agreed that Morozov, who had been working there
from the age of thirteen, should be removed from the factory lest
he "produce a dangerous movement among the other workers."
The American contractors were quick to concur, particularly in
view of the record of absenteeism, drunkenness, and disobedience
compiled by Morozov over the years.[31]

Despite his full and open confession and his wife's moving appeal
to Chevkin, Morozov was exiled to a factory in Petrozavodsk, in
the Olonets mining region.[32] The purpose of such a stern punishment could only have been to make Morozov into an example for
the other workers, and in the short run it seems to have been a
successful move. Twelve years elapsed before any further sign of
labor unrest was noted at the Aleksandrovsk factory.

Yet a basic contradiction ran through the government's handling of the Aleksandrovsk case and of the cases outlined earlier.
Generally peaceful protest was sometimes allowed to produce con-

crete and beneficial results for the workers, but at the same time their actions consistently resulted in serious punishment. By artificially attempting to isolate labor protest from its beneficial results, the government seemed to be telling the workers both that concerted action on their part could indeed bear fruit—as it did, for example, in the Aleksandrovsk factory—and that such actions were intolerable. Mass action was an effective weapon, but pending the introduction of the type of legislation then being prepared by Shtakel'-berg and his colleagues it was presented as incompatible with the existing political order.

None of the cases of labor unrest that took place in St. Petersburg during the years of "the first revolutionary situation" presented an immediate threat to the government or the social order. Perhaps what was threatened were the old optimistic myth of the special immunity of Russian factories from labor disturbances and the government's confidence in the docility of the peasant-worker. But we have seen that official optimism had begun to disintegrate independently of these events, since the end of the Crimean War if not earlier. As to confidence in the workers' docility, government practice had contradicted official theory at least as early as 1854, when the Third Section (political police) had required St. Petersburg manufacturers to sign a pledge to maintain strict surveillance "over those of their workers whose behavior was suspicious or who, by their intemperate behavior, might disturb the peace of the capital."[33]

The five incidents of 1857–60 undoubtedly served to heighten already existing fears. Nevertheless, they did not yet mark a qualitative change in the conduct of St. Petersburg workers. As protests they were modest in character, and the ease with which they were terminated by dealing decisively with a small number of "instigators" is striking. More importantly, they did not begin a trend; the year 1860 marked the last known occasion of serious labor protest in St. Petersburg for several years to come.

The weakness of the spirit of protest among the Petersburg workers, and the continued dominance of an essentially passive attitude, may be illustrated by the behavior of many workers in response to the emancipation manifesto of 1861. In keeping with the government's basic intolerance of any spontaneous workers' demonstrations, irrespective of their form or content, the local police instructed all manufacturers in the St. Petersburg area to overwork their laborers on the eve of the signing of the manifesto, February 18, so that they would be too tired to do anything but rest the next day. It is noteworthy that this act of interference in the relationships between management and labor was resented by the Petersburg manufacturers, who feared that the assignment of extra night work would stimulate dissatisfaction and unrest.[34] As it turned out, the day passed without incident.

On the other hand, Petersburg manufacturers who were anxious to demonstrate their approval of the emancipation had little trouble in enlisting the cooperation of their workers. Several manufacturers engaged in philanthropic gestures such as erecting new workers' hospitals as a memorial to the emancipation. Some soon took the additional step of having their workers participate in organized expressions of gratitude. Thus the prominent industrialist V. Poletika, who was soon to be attacked in the press for his selfishness, announced that the peasants employed at his factory, the Semiannikovskii works, were anxious to offer thanks to the Tsar for their liberation from servitude. A ceremonial meeting was arranged at which the workers were to present the Tsar with a silver platter. Poletika spared no efforts to make the presentation as elaborate as possible. A speech was written for one of the few literate workers to read, and a declaration was prepared for all of them to sign (mostly with crosses). Other St. Petersburg manufacturers delegated workers to attend the ceremonies, which transformed the occasion into something of a class affair rather than merely the gesture of a single industrialist. In all, some three hundred workers, representing six enterprises, participated.

The ceremonies ended on an embarrassing note. Soon after the Tsar appeared to accept his award, the worker who had been delegated to deliver the speech became flustered and was unable to continue. Furthermore, when asked why they were thanking the Tsar, several workers admitted that they barely understood what the emancipation was all about; they had attended only because they were ordered to do so by their employers. A contemporary observer remarked that this was far from being an isolated incident.[35]

In summary, it can be said that although the labor unrest of 1857–60 represented a significant departure from the past, the factory workers of St. Petersburg still remained relatively docile.

Insofar as the goals of the unrest were not directly related to the dual peasant-worker status of the protestors and did not imply a rejection of the role of industrial laborer as such, it bore a different character from earlier unrest among Russian factory peasants. Yet even this point needs qualifying, since the conflict over holiday labor that figured in some of the episodes suggests a throwback to preindustrial patterns.

This was especially true of the incident that involved the largest number of workers, the Golenishchevskaia unrest, in which the fundamental issue was the workers' refusal to appear on the job on a religious holiday. "The inclination to celebrate holidays," the Shtakel'berg Commission would explain in 1864, "is strongly developed . . . in our people. . . . In the interests of industry as well as morality, it would be more desirable to restrain this tendency than to spread it."[36] The proliferation of traditional Orthodox religious celebrations, so deeply engrained in the culture of the Russian peasantry,* was bound to conflict with the newer industries' requirements for continuity and regularity of production.† Thus while the demand for higher wages provided the main theme of the labor unrest just described, in some cases less "proletarian" demands shaded the picture.

Measured in terms of organization and perseverance in the face of adversity, the degree of militance displayed by the St. Petersburg workers was not particularly impressive. Organizationally, there is not the slightest evidence of any contact or even mutual influence among the workers of the five factories. The ultimate weakness of each of the protests, the relative ease with which police were able to subdue them with minimal use of force, effectively nullified whatever contribution they might have made to stimulating the search for a new approach to the regulation of labor-management relations. For the moment, Ignat'ev's police and the other agencies involved seemingly had an adequate solution: to invoke the coercive powers of the state against employers if particularly flagrant

---

* See Mary Matossian, "The Peasant Way of Life," in Wayne S. Vucinich, ed., *The Peasant in Nineteenth-Century Russia* (Stanford, Calif., 1968), pp. 31ff. An article in *Revue des Deux Mondes* of January 15, 1864, spoke of the ruinous effect on the Russian peasantry of "the incredible number of holidays" they took; cited in *Trudy*, III, 105n.

† This conflict was a growing source of embarrassment and difficulty to industrialists and proponents of industrial progress in the years that followed. See, for example, pp. 292 and 298 below.

abuses were uncovered, but to suppress any attempt by workers to demonstrate for the redress of their grievances, even if their demonstration had been the means whereby the authorities had first become cognizant of the abuses. The isolation of "instigators" and the use of exemplary punishment seemed adequate to the task of cowing the mass of workers. The basic assumption remained that both labor unrest and the conditions that provoked it were inimical to the interests of state security, and the police powers were therefore prepared to act independently on both fronts—against management as well as labor—to preserve internal order.

As our sampling suggests, however, action against workers was more consistently undertaken than action against manufacturers. Moreover, the very nature of the two-pronged policy was such that whatever balance may have been struck in any particular case, the general thrust of the policy could only favor the employers. For to the extent that the intimidation of workers was successful as a prophylactic measure, grievances would remain concealed and abuses uncorrected.

It is true, of course, that both in and out of the government a general consciousness of the harshness of factory conditions in St. Petersburg was growing independently of worker demonstrations. But that consciousness, while it nourished the drafting commissions' deliberations over factory legislation, did not reflect a sufficient sense of urgency to unleash specific and concrete government pressures on individual manufacturers and companies except in those few cases that were dramatized by mass protests.

The only exception to this rule—that is, the only example of direct intervention by St. Petersburg authorities in behalf of workers that was *not* a response to labor unrest—was triggered by the horrible death in 1861 of a seventeen-year-old girl who worked at one of the larger cotton-spinning factories. Her death was attributed to the negligence of the factory administration, which had failed to take adequate safety measures on one of its rolling machines. Two years earlier, safety hazards and the abuse of child workers had led General Ignat'ev to distribute a polite circular letter to manufacturers and to launch the investigation of local factory conditions that was to provide one of the bases for the report of the Shtakel'berg Commission. Now, even while that commission was in session, Ignat'ev's patience was exhausted by the dramatic death of the young girl. He promptly seized the occasion to issue a general notice to all St. Petersburg manufacturers, circulated in the local press, ordering them in no uncertain terms to erect railings around steam-driven machinery and to take other precautionary measures. A period of ten days would be allowed for raising possible objections; thereafter, Ignat'ev warned, compliance would be strictly enforced.[37] But however humanely motivated Ignat'ev's effort may have been, its institutional significance was simply to point up the fact that in the continued absence of an organized framework for the handling of such cases, only an occasional atrocity might replace severely punishable demonstrations as a stimulus to government intervention in the workers' favor.

The entire pattern of official conduct, then, was clearly within the established limits of autocratic tradition. Those representatives of the Imperial authority who were responsible for maintaining order in and about the factories of the capital acted as if they believed themselves to be above the interplay of narrow class conflicts, dealing in a summary manner now with manufacturers, now with workers, as the occasion required. Even Ignat'ev, in principle a supporter of a new legal-administrative structure for the rationalization of industrial relations, continued to act toward workers and manufacturers as if they were conglomerates of atomized individuals, each directly subjected to the benevolent will of the autocrat, rather than collective economic groupings whose legal personalities and institutionalized rights were on the verge of being recognized. The legislation that was then in preparation—just like recognition of the right to petition, demonstrate, or strike—would, in effect, have granted recognition to the workers as a collective economic group possessing legitimate class interests. Nothing in the transactions of the Shtakel'berg Commission even suggested the existence of so wide a gap between the commission's goals and existing practice.

"Society's" Initiative—the Sunday School Movement

In my earlier discussion of the initial appearance of the labor question in St. Petersburg, I referred to one way of dealing with the question that combined elements of traditional philanthropic activity and foreshadowings of the "small deeds" liberalism of later years. Because it partook more of the character of the *Armenfrage* than of the labor question as here defined—and also because it involved activity more than the elaboration of ideas—that approach was not discussed in detail in the chapter on the labor question, but was deferred instead to the present consideration of initiatives from below.

The most significant philanthropic activity oriented toward improving the lot of the urban worker, the so-called "Sunday school movement" of 1859–62, crossed paths with the labor question at what proved to be a critical juncture. Although its partisans came from various walks of life, represented diverse political persuasions, and shared no single attitude toward industrialization in general or the labor question in particular, the movement sprang from the same postwar, pre-emancipation climate of social consciousness and sympathy for the lower classes that we have already seen reflected in the writings and works of economists, journalists, and government officials. Moreover, urban workers and their children, many of them from St. Petersburg factories, constituted one of the primary targets of the movement. Indeed, as it turned out, the fate of the Sunday schools was to some extent decided in the factories of the capital.

Terner, it will be recalled, expressed the hope that the better educated and more well-to-do elements of society would dedicate themselves to the elevation of the working classes by providing the motor force for his labor associations. Similar sentiments with regard to the special obligations of the enlightened and the privileged were voiced, at times, by the Shtakel'berg Commission.[38] While the Sunday school movement did not involve the association of workers in any strict economic sense, it did bring workers together voluntarily for purposes of self-improvement, and it was probably for this reason that the schools were included in the Shtakel'berg Commission's chapter "On Industrial Societies and Arteli"[39] as an example of one of the constructive purposes for which industrial societies should be authorized.* Since the Sunday school movement was by far the most important and widespread effort on the part of educated society to alter the fate of the urban worker, it provides us in microcosm with a test of some of the aspirations and hopes that were then shared within what can loosely be called the prolabor camp. In viewing this short-lived experiment closely, something may be learned about the attitudes of various elements in society—including workers, manufacturers, students, and govern-

* Sunday schools were also endorsed by the St. Petersburg commission of 1859 as an appropriate means for spreading literacy within the working class. *Trudy*, II, 301.

ment officials—toward the first centers of working-class education and culture to replace the restrictive institutions that had for so many years accompanied the peasant-worker to the city.

The Sunday school movement was launched in the city of Kiev in 1859, when educated society was still heady with the news that serfdom was soon to be abolished, and ended abruptly in St. Peters- burg in 1862, a casualty of the crisis that followed the promulgation of the terms of abolition. During this brief period many educated Russians devoted themselves to the ambitious task of raising the low level of literacy of urban workers by establishing and staffing free private schools. The movement, which was entirely secular in inspiration, derived its name from the fact that classes were held on the one day of the week when the worker's time was his own— Sunday. The schools operated in many cities throughout European Russia, but it was in St. Petersburg that they developed most ex- tensively and aroused the greatest controversy. By the end of 1860, barely one year after the opening of the first Sunday school in Kiev, St. Petersburg counted 23 Sunday schools, more than any other city in the Empire.[40]

The spirit of enthusiasm that educated St. Petersburg society brought to the Sunday school activity and to other related projects was personified by N. V. Stasova, sister of the well-known critic, historian, and archeologist, V. V. Stasov. Consumed by concern for the welfare of the poor and the downtrodden, like many of her contemporaries, Stasova was prepared to plunge into almost any philanthropic cause that presented itself. She participated in the St. Petersburg Society for the Improvement of the Lodgings of the Laboring Population (noted with enthusiasm by the Shtakel'berg Commission), in a society for the assistance of women laborers, and in hospital work for the indigent. When presented with an oppor- tunity to collaborate in the establishment of weekly grammar schools for illiterate workers, she did not hesitate to accept the new challenge.[41]

Stasova first heard about the Sunday schools from Platon V. Pav- lov, a former history professor at Kiev University, a "passionate enemy of serfdom," and a great advocate of the cause of popular education.[42] Pavlov had been the chief source of inspiration for the university students who founded the first workers' schools in Kiev. Shortly thereafter, in December 1859, he had moved to St. Petersburg, where he began by devoting himself mainly to establishing schools for women workers.[43] He soon made contact with Stasova and other enlightened intellectuals who shared his enthusiasm for popular causes. Combining his energy with theirs—especially with that of the capital's increasingly restive student youth—Pavlov contributed to the rapid growth of Sunday schools. Thanks to their common efforts, twenty schools were opened in St. Petersburg just during the short period from April 1860 to January 1861.[44] As the emancipation of the peasantry approached, the future of popular education in the capital looked bright.

But despite this encouraging beginning, the promise of the Sunday schools was not to be fulfilled. Before very long the movement began to decline, and by June 1862 it had ceased to exist. The ultimate cause of its demise was closely related to the evolution of official attitudes toward the schools and toward popular initiative in general. But the movement also suffered a loss of vitality, which, while perhaps not contributing to its suppression, raises some question whether it would have succeeded even if the government had chosen to tolerate it. To understand this internal decline it is necessary to examine the attitudes of various social groups toward the schools as they developed.

In some segments of society misgivings about the schools were apparent almost from the outset. The most virulent opposition came from the merchants, shop owners and petty-manufacturers whose employees attended or wished to attend the schools. Their hostility, according to contemporary reports, was based on the fear that education might make their workers less docile and might lead them into more skilled employment.

The first overt cases of this kind of opposition occurred in Kiev, as early as the fall of 1859, when some employers succeeded in restricting the number of their employees attending.[45] In St. Petersburg a similar situation began to develop in the fall of 1860. Here the proprietors of various artisan shops placed obstacles before their workers by assigning them special duties on Sundays and intimidated them by demanding that they produce written evidence of attendance from the schools. When these restrictions began to affect attendance adversely, a conflict arose between the employers and the school administrators, who argued that no proofs of attendance should be required inasmuch as the schools had the official approval of the government.[46]

The more well-to-do manufacturers of St. Petersburg, the owners of the larger, more mechanized industrial establishments, where literacy and advanced skills were highly prized, did not, as a rule, share the attitude of the artisan masters and petty manufacturers. On the contrary, if they had any interest in Sunday school education at all it was almost invariably a positive one. Not only did they often support the schools financially, but in several cases they actually established Sunday educational facilities on the premises of their factories. In the Schlüsselburg Road industrial area, it was the Vargunins, a family of prominent manufacturers, who took the lead in establishing and supporting schools for factory workers. One member of the Vargunin family became the director of the largest school in the area, which was established in 1860 with the collective support of other local manufacturers and took in as many as seven hundred pupils—adults and children—during the first year of its existence.[47]

Other St. Petersburg industrialists, mainly but not exclusively in the Schlüsselburg area, were praised by the journal of the Ministry of Education for their active support of Sunday schools.[48] The Samsonievskaia Sunday school in the Vyborg district—destined to become the center of the controversy that led directly to the termination of the movement—received heavy financial backing from local industrialists, who encouraged the workers from their factories to attend classes.[49] The enlightened attitude of these Petersburg manufacturers caught the favorable attention of a contributor to the organ of the Ministry of Finance's Department of Manufactures. Citing the extreme ignorance of the Russian working class as a leading obstacle to industrial progress, he warmly praised those St. Petersburg manufacturers who, knowing that the growth of national industrial production was in their own self-interest, supported Sunday education for workers.[50]

There is little evidence of enthusiasm for the Sunday schools among the nobility. Although some of the grand ladies of St. Petersburg contributed to the education of indigent working women,[51] this was the exception rather than the rule. Reports listing the chief supporters of the Sunday schools indicate that aside from prominent industrialists and a few rich merchants, most contributors belonged to special groups such as book dealers (who donated textbooks) and actors (who donated the proceeds of benefit performances); members of the nobility were notably absent.[52]

It is true that many of the university students who taught the workers were of noble origin. Nevertheless they played their role as students rather than as members of the gentry establishment, and in their capacity as Sunday school instructors they were merged indistinguishably with *raznochintsy* students (i.e. students of non-noble background). It is difficult to estimate the proportion of Sunday school instructors with gentry status, but that they were not the dominant element is suggested by a high government official's distress that the schools were in the hands of the "middle stratum" rather than the nobility.[53]

It was the students of St. Petersburg, along with a number of young army officers and petty officials, who were the moving force in the Sunday school movement and composed the overwhelming body of teachers. In the beginning their enthusiasm and idealism were extremely high, and foreshadowed in many ways the mood of the students who were to launch the "movement to the people" of the following decade. K. Ushinskii, editor of the *Journal of the Ministry of Education*, was favorably impressed by the young student-teachers he encountered when he visited two St. Petersburg schools in late 1860, and commented on their "strong and open-hearted striving to be helpful to their pupils."[54] So numerous were the students in the capital who desired to teach in the schools that one school was obliged to limit its teaching personnel to people recommended by students already on the staff.[55]

But by 1861 there were signs that the original enthusiasm of the student-teachers was already on the wane. In September an extreme shortage of Sunday school teachers was reported in several provincial cities. Although the situation in St. Petersburg was less critical, difficulties in recruiting teachers were beginning to appear there as well.[56] Those who did become Sunday school teachers in 1861 were described as less idealistic than their predecessors and as lacking the fraternal, democratic attitude toward their worker-pupils that had characterized the first waves of volunteers. The rate of turnover of the teaching staffs increased markedly, contributing to the difficulty in establishing close relations between teachers and pupils, and from this there followed a decline in the schools' popularity and attendance.[57]

The editors of *Sovremennik* sought to explain this decline in the good fortunes of the schools. "Why have the youth begun to abandon the Sunday schools?," they asked. "To this there can be only one answer: dissatisfaction with the direction the Sunday schools have taken has compelled them to abandon their mission as teachers of the people." This new direction was allegedly the work of the Ministry of Education and its associates (tersely referred to as "the pedagogues"), who, it was claimed, had destroyed the spirit of the student-teachers by limiting their freedom of action, assigning priests to their schools, and narrowly restricting the curricula.[58]

The view expressed in *Sovremennik* had some merit. It will be seen that the originally friendly attitude of the government toward the schools had indeed given way to one favoring restriction and surveillance. But much of this surveillance had remained theoretical, without being rigorously applied. When the schools were closed down in 1862, for example, the newly appointed Minister of Education, A. V. Golovnin (1862–66), told the Tsar that the St. Petersburg clergy, which had been ordered to maintain a close watch over the activities of the schools, had actually carried out these instructions in only two cases.[59] Furthermore, the official who was placed in charge of an investigation of the St. Petersburg schools reported that there had been an "absence of vigilant and real surveillance over the activities of the teachers." Surveillance, he claimed, "had existed on paper only; in reality there was none."[60] There may have been a degree of exaggeration in this statement, but the same view was put forth by P. A. Valuev, Minister of Internal Affairs from 1861 to 1868, who emphasized that although official regulations called for a curriculum strictly confined to reading, writing, arithmetic, and religious instruction, there were many schools where workers were taught history, geography, science, and on rare occasions even such forbidden subjects as ethnography and political economy.[61] It is apparent that the infringement of the "pedagogues" and other government officials upon the activities of of Sunday school teachers was, in practice, less than formidable.

The waning of the teachers' enthusiasm cannot be attributed, then, to government measures alone. Part of the explanation must be sought in the student-teachers themselves, who apparently failed to sustain their original interest when faced with only a modicum of surveillance and restriction. Limitations on subject matter were, after all, a purely theoretical consideration in view of the prevailing ignorance of the laboring masses. The real problem to which the

schools had been dedicated was that of basic illiteracy, and until
the workers had been taught to read and write, they were hardly in
a position to study history or political economy. The student youth
could have dedicated itself to the task of introducing basic literacy
to the workers even in the presence of government or clerical surveillance. Although without the government's decision to close
them down the schools might have eventually recovered from their
decline, the fact remains that many young teachers did abandon
them well before the regime's real assault against the schools had
begun.

The workers' initial response to the Petersburg Sunday schools
was generally positive. The editors of the *Journal of the Ministry of
Education* were pleased to report steady increases in the number
of Sunday school pupils in the capital throughout the year 1860.
By midsummer the journal reported that the number of workers at
the recently founded Vladimirskaia school—staffed entirely by students of St. Petersburg University—had reached 355. Shortly thereafter it reported a constant rise in the attendance of factory workers
at the Samsonievskaia school, with only one slight dip in attendance
when Sunday classes happened to follow payday (the implication
being that the tavern had taken its toll).[62] After this deviation,
attendance at the school again continued to climb steadily, attendance on the average Sunday in September reaching approximately
180 workers. Both schools grew in the following months, and new
ones were successfully founded.[63] By December 1860, in its final
issue for the year, the journal was able to report optimistically:
"Interest in the Sunday schools is not weakening; their number is
increasing, the number of teachers and pupils in them is growing.
The St. Petersburg Sunday schools are constantly attracting masses
of pupils."[64] All in all, according to the estimates of one historian,
approximately five thousand inhabitants of St. Petersburg were
to receive Sunday school instruction before the final demise of the
movement.[65]

The initial enthusiasm of the St. Petersburg pupils was reflected
not only in their numbers, but also in their attitude and conduct.
There were cases, for example, where workers pressed for more
instruction than was actually available. In the spring of 1860 workers at two leading schools requested that additional instruction be
given on workday evenings—a courageous request in view of the

long workdays that then prevailed. There is evidence that such weekday evening classes were actually introduced in certain schools.[66] At a large school for workers near the Schlüsselburg area, some pupils requested that instruction in technical skills and crafts be added to the curriculum.[67]

No less impressive was the fervor displayed by the worker-pupils in the classroom. The prominent educator and surgeon N. I. Pirogov estimated that the Sunday school pupils learned reading and writing two or three times faster than their counterparts in the regular grammar schools.[68] Ushinskii was equally impressed. He characterized the workers whom he had the opportunity to observe during his visits to St. Petersburg Sunday schools as very serious and attentive—"as if in a church." Like Pirogov, he found that they compared very favorably with the pupils in ordinary grammar schools.[69] These workers, Ushinskii wrote with admiration, with their "black, calloused hands, with tarnished faces, each with an odor and color clearly reflecting his trade, had gathered here not to amuse themselves, not out of empty curiosity, but to get something done . . . which seemed to them to be not only a useful, serious undertaking, but something almost holy, something almost religious."[70]

The year 1861 saw a decline in the enthusiasm of the workers which paralleled that of the student-teachers. Signs of this decline became clear only in the fall, although there were forebodings earlier in the year. At the school near the Schlüsselburg area, attendance fell from about 300 in the spring to 30 or 40 in the summer. It is doubtful whether so sharp a drop can be attributed entirely to the return of peasant-workers to their villages for summer work, especially since attendance had only been restored to 150 by October.[71]

By the fall of 1861 there was a general awareness that Sunday school attendance had fallen off. One newspaper reported rumors from various parts of the country to this effect, and attributed the decline to the aloofness of the newer teachers, who were unwilling to fraternize with their pupils.[72] A contributor to *Sovremennik* noticed the same decline of interest among the workers, and likewise saw it as a reaction to the decreased enthusiasm of the teachers.[73] If these explanations were accurate, then the workers' extreme sensitivity to the changing mood of their instructors—to their detachment and lack of personal warmth—suggests the possible persistence of a deeply rooted patriarchal tradition, a continued spirit of dependency among them. Although the evidence is meager, it would seem that the worker-pupils—like their student-teachers—had not yet developed the type of independent spirit that might have enabled them to carry on this exciting experiment under less than favorable circumstances.

Notwithstanding the internal weaknesses of the Sunday school movement, its failure was in the last analysis the direct result of government policy. The original decision to allow the establishment of the schools as a free private institution bore witness to the relatively open and permissive spirit that characterized the first years of Alexander II's reign. This permissiveness, however, operated within certain definite limits. Hesitation about permitting the schools too great an autonomy had existed almost from the very beginning. At almost no point had they been able to function independently from government authority. Although a few schools operated in complete freedom for a very short period, each was soon compelled to apply for official authorization from the Ministry of Education via the provincial governor and the Ministry of Internal Affairs. Additional authorization was also required from the ministry that had jurisdiction over the building where the school was to be housed (usually the Ministry of Education, but often the Ministry of War and occasionally the Transportation Administration).[74]

At first this dependence upon the government, particularly upon the Ministries of Education and Internal Affairs, was of considerable value to the schools. In a circular issued to the provincial governors on March 22, 1860, Minister of Internal Affairs S. Lanskoi spoke very positively of the schools, and in September of the same year, the Ministry of Education rendered them an important service by designating the Imperial school buildings of St. Petersburg for their use on Sundays. Similar actions were also taken by the ministry's representatives in other cities.[75]

The ministries' sympathetic interest, however, was also accompanied by a certain degree of supervision which, although it was supportive rather than repressive, nevertheless tended to rob the movement of its original spontaneity. In St. Petersburg the opening of almost every new Sunday school was given a semiofficial character by the attendance of a ranking official of the Ministry of Education.[76] Even the location of many of the classrooms in government buildings added to the semiofficial character of the schools and left them more open to the threat of official supervision and control than would have been the case had they been located on private premises.

More important, the Ministry of Education—where the greatest sympathy for the schools was to be found, and which supported them down to the bitter end—conceived of their goals and methods in a manner quite different from that of many of the people initially involved in the movement. Such official sympathizers tended to attribute their own conservative and patriarchal goals to the schools, chiefly the preservation of the loyalty of the urban working people. This attitude was clearly expressed in the writings of Ushinskii, editor of the ministry's official journal and an ardent defender of the schools:

The other important moral significance of the Sunday schools consists in the contact between educated people and working-class people. Everywhere some kind of antagonism between these two classes exists, and people of the working class always view the upper class with a distrust that is not without a certain malice. This not even surprising when these two strata of people meet each other only in their pitiless economic relationships; when not a single open, intimate word is exchanged between them, not a single humanitarian, conciliatory thought. . . .

Here [in the Sunday school] he [the worker] learns that the gentleman in the frock coat also works, and works perhaps no less than he does, only at other things. Here he is compelled to recognize the spiritual superiority of the educated man, and to understand why this man stands above him. Sincere, friendly relations between teacher and pupil in the school are the best antidote for those economic relations that have led to such sad events in Western Europe; and if we regard the significance of Sunday schools from this point of view, there is no doubt that we will look upon their quick start just as gladly as we look upon the establishment of temperance societies in the villages. Yes, the sober judgment of the people, enlightened by religion and education, is the best guarantee for the prosperity of the state, for its peace, strength and wealth.[77]

Ushinskii's defense of the Sunday schools provides us with a capsule summary of the contradictions and confusion inherent in the position of many Russian social reformers at this time. His words were printed exactly a month before the emancipation of the peasantry and during the fifth year of Russia's halting and painful but deliberate movement toward industrialization. Both these changes implied a reorientation of the country's social structure, as many suspected. Yet the existing social structure was the basis of the autocratic system, and that system was expected to remain unchallenged. Confusion about the social structure is revealed in Ushinskii's choice of terms. Just who were the "upper classes" for whom Ushinskii wanted to gain the working man's respect? Within a few brief lines they are variously called the "educated people," which taken literally would include the nascent raznochintsy intelligentsia and exclude poorly educated nobles and manufacturers; the "gentleman in the frock coat," which evokes the image of a nobleman; and that stratum of society which has contact with the workers "only in their pitiless economic relationships," which surely could have meant no one else but the emerging class of manufacturers. The argument that the education of workers would contribute to the wealth and prosperity of the state conformed to the government's new plans for industrialization and paralleled the interest of several Petersburg industrialists in worker education. At the same time, Ushinskii argued that the Sunday schools would serve as security against the European disease of social and political unrest among the working class. Treated properly by their betters in the classroom setting, the Russian workers would maintain the piety he thought he had observed during his visits to St. Petersburg Sunday schools. Russia thus would maintain her immunity to class strife even under the conditions of "pitiless economic relations" that he freely acknowledged.

The patriarchal view of the schools was reflected more specifically in the Ministry of Education's efforts to restrict the curriculum to reading, writing, arithmetic, and religious instruction. The first concrete step in this direction was an order, issued in conjunction with the Ministry of Internal Affairs on May 4, 1860, instructing all local educational authorities to observe the Sunday schools in order to guard against any departure from the assigned subjects.[78] This was followed six months later by a detailed circular, occasioned by reports that history and languages were being taught in some provincial Sunday schools, calling for stricter supervision of curricula.[79]

The schools were now prohibited from using any teaching materials that were not approved by the Ministry of Education. Conditions for opening new schools were made more stringent, and teachers who violated "religious truths, governmental authority, and the laws of morality" were to be excluded from the classrooms. To help enforce these regulations and to invest the schools with a proper atmosphere, orders were issued in January 1861 assigning members of the clergy as overseers. In St. Petersburg, Metropolitan Isidor was specifically instructed to assign a priest to each Sunday school to give religious instruction to the workers and to guard "the truths of the Orthodox faith."[80] This step was taken even though (unlike their English counterparts) the Russian Sunday schools were originally conceived as strictly secular institutions.

The decision to assign priests was not entirely a voluntary action, taken out of concern for the workers' morality. It was also an attempt to appease the opposition of powerful elements within the government which lacked the Education Ministry's confidence that the schools were a basically conservative force. Most notable among these antagonists were Prince Dolgorukov, chief of the Third Section; Count S. G. Stroganov, a member of the Council of State and the Senate; and General Ignat'ev, the ubiquitous military governor of St. Petersburg. Dolgorukov and Stroganov were well-known defenders of autocracy, serfdom, and the old order in general—people whom the mildly liberal censor A. V. Nikitenko referred to in his diary as "obscurantists," who were prepared to condemn the Russian people to live forever in a "stagnant swamp."[81] Ignat'ev, of course, while equally reactionary in most respects, was the same official whose strong support for labor legislation is already familiar. We will have occasion to return to this point at the end of this chapter.

The opening salvo from the "obscurantist" camp was contained in a note from Prince Dolgorukov to the Tsar, dated December 18, 1860, prepared (according to Nikitenko) in collaboration with Count Stroganov.[82] Dolgorukov began with a formal acknowledgment that the schools were of some value. But turning to his real point, he warned of the dangers inherent in permitting such an institution to remain in the hands of "middle-class" persons in no official capacity, whom he ambiguously connected with some secret, "invisible" society:

The government cannot permit half of the population to owe its education not to the state but to itself or to the private philanthropy of any particular class. The middle stratum of society and invisible forces that rely upon its strength have arbitrarily assumed the leadership of this important undertaking. By teaching without payment they have established a solid base of trust and gratitude on the part of the masses for whom they are the benefactors.

This statement contrasted sharply with the views of Ushinskii, who saw the Sunday schools as valuable precisely because they would establish the gratitude of the working classes toward their social "superiors."

Although Dolgorukov was not yet prepared to recommend direct and thus obvious measures against the schools, his memorandum outlined a cautious plan that had as its final goal their complete removal from unofficial control. Management of the schools was to be gradually assumed by the one trustworthy class he identified with the state—the nobility. Subsequently the schools would be transformed into official state institutions. In the meantime, the government should give the impression (*dat' vid*) of encouraging the growth of the schools, while waiting for them to weaken from lack of funds, discouragement, and inertia.

The Ministry of Education, cautious and conservative though it was, never proposed exclusive reliance on the nobility or complete removal of the schools from private hands. To do so would have been inconsistent with its vision of the schools' goal, as formulated by Ushinskii: the improvement of relations between conflicting social classes, specifically between the workers and their exploiters.

This difference in attitude soon resulted in a clash between the Education Ministry and the powerful Third Section. Between January 1 and 6, 1861, Minister of Education E. P. Kovalevskii presented the Council of Ministers with his sharp response to Dolgorukov's memorandum. He argued that there was no need to alter the status of the schools and insisted defensively that the recently established regulations and surveillance were quite sufficient. Interpreting Dolgorukov's note as an attack on his ministry, Kovalevskii challenged him to produce specific evidence about any schools where dangerous activities had taken place. Ignat'ev and others had called for repressive measures, but since the Third Section was unable to meet Kovalevskii's challenge, the Tsar—who had listened to Kovalevskii's pleas for several days—accepted his point of view, and no drastic steps were taken against the schools. Nevertheless the order assigning priests to the classrooms was now accepted as a sort of compromise, with even such "liberals" as Grand Duke Konstantin concurring.[83]

Over a year was to expire before the enemies of the schools were able to find a suitable pretext for launching a head-on assault against them. The events that provided this pretext took place in May 1862, but there were signs of renewed danger to the schools two months earlier, when Pavlov, the leading organizer of Sunday schools in St. Petersburg, was arrested. Ostensibly, Pavlov's arrest was the result of an allegedly seditious speech he delivered at a famous literary soirée in honor of the thousandth anniversary of the founding of the Russian state. This speech drew considerable attention in the capital. It was attended by a very large audience that included Nikolai Chernyshevskii and other important members of the radical intelligentsia.[84]

Although no exact text of the speech is available, there is ample reason to doubt the charge that its content was seditious. The text originally submitted by Pavlov to the censor for review (which has been published) contained no criticism of the existing government, but rather a criticism of the preceding era, when only a privileged few knew freedom while the masses suffered and had no rights. By way of contrast, Pavlov praised the present government for having taken the steps necessary to alter these conditions, particularly for having emancipated the peasantry. In concluding, in words that most certainly would have met with the approval of Ushinskii, Pavlov called for the salvation of Russia through the merging of the interests of all classes, from the highest to the lowest. Nothing in the prepared version of the talk even remotely suggested a call to class conflict or antigovernment activity.[85]

A firsthand account of Pavlov's speech, in the memoirs of a St. Petersburg student who attended the soirée, indicates that he barely departed from the original text. Nor did Pavlov himself believe that his talk had contained any remarks that would place him in jeopardy with the government.[86] Yet approximately two days after the speech was delivered, Pavlov was arrested and exiled to Vetluga, in Central Russia, without any formal charges. Those who tried to intervene in his behalf were flatly rebuffed.[87]

Taken alone—and even allowing that Pavlov had spiced his

talk with a few anti-government allusions, as Valuev and other officials believed—Pavlov's speech does not suffice to explain his severe treatment. There is, however, evidence in the archives of the Third Section that points to a clear connection between Pavlov's arrest and the original opposition to the Sunday schools within the government. In August 1862, after the suppression of the schools, Privy Councilor S. R. Zhdanov, the chairman of the commission which had investigated the schools and recommended that they be closed, emphasized in his report to his superior, Valuev (Minister of Internal Affairs since April 1861), that it was Pavlov who bore the responsibility for the formation of the St. Petersburg Sunday schools.[88] Technically, this was not even accurate, since the Sunday school movement in St. Petersburg antedated Pavlov's arrival by some months, although it was, of course, true that he had become its dominant figure. Be that as it may, the important point is that Zhdanov (and other officials, as will be illustrated below) was anxious to link the activities of Pavlov with the supposed dangers inherent in the schools and to link both Pavlov and the schools with the potential dangers of revolutionary plots and seditious ideas.

Since no one had been able to produce any evidence implicating Pavlov in the alleged dissemination of propaganda to factory workers in St. Petersburg Sunday schools, the case against him was based on some flimsy circumstantial evidence connected with his period of activity in Kiev. These accusations have been accepted at face value by historians attempting to adduce the existence of a "revolutionary situation" during these years. Most of their evidence is based on an uncritical evaluation of a report on the Sunday schools, dated September 11, 1862, by Valuev, who by this time shared the views of Dolgorukov concerning the dangers of the schools.[89]

Valuev's allegations against Pavlov may be reduced to three points: (1) four or five students who had cooperated with Pavlov in founding the original Kiev Sunday schools had previously been involved in a conspiratorial society in Kharkov; (2) a secret meeting took place between Pavlov and Alexander Herzen in London in 1858, during which the Sunday school program was allegedly conceived; (3) Pavlov proposed a cryptic toast in Herzen's honor at a dinner in Kiev in 1859, before departing for St. Petersburg. Beyond this, Valuev's report had little to offer in the way of concrete evidence, but he claimed to believe that such evidence existed in the secret archives of the Third Section. This evidence, if such there was, has yet to be uncovered.

Among the allegations, only the charge that Pavlov cooperated with some revolutionary students in setting up the Sunday schools was truly damaging, and even it was of a highly dubious nature. Pirogov—who then held the post of supervisor of the Kiev school district, and who was in close and sympathetic contact with the Sunday schools—pointed out that the involvement of the students in question in a secret society in Kharkov had taken place about four years before the founding of the Sunday schools, and that their conduct since that time had been irreproachable. Moreover, the alleged conspirators had actually been among the least influential of the students involved with the Kiev schools. Finally, in Pirogov's words, "Despite the varied types of teachers and pupils, the complete openness of the schools, and the surveillance both by school and civil (secret) authorities, not once during the time I was in office was anything discovered in the Kiev Sunday schools that could even remotely suggest the existence of political propaganda of a criminal or dangerous nature."[90]

Still more damaging to Valuev's case was Pavlov's earlier exoneration by the official commission that conducted the inquiry into the alleged conspiracy of Kiev-Kharkov students. The commission had found that although Pavlov did speak negatively about conditions in Russia (before the emancipation) during his lectures at Kiev University, he had not been connected with any conspiratorial society.[91] All these considerations, combined with Dolgorukov's attempt, at the time of his original assault on the schools,[92] to link Pavlov to Herzen, point to the conclusion that the arrest of the figure who symbolized the Sunday school movement in St. Petersburg was an important step in Dolgorukov's original plan to undermine the movement.

The next and final step, the total suppression of the schools, came about two months after Pavlov's arrest. Two situations set the stage for this event. The first was the general mood of reaction that interrupted the initial "liberalism" of Alexander's reign around the time of the emancipation. This reaction was stimulated by demonstrations of public disappointment at the terms of the emancipation, the Tsar's wish to appease gentry who opposed the emancipation, the growing unruliness of the students of St. Petersburg University (which led to the temporary closing of that institution), the threatening situation in Poland, and the appearance of revolutionary proclamations. These events are well known, and are not directly related to the Petersburg workers. For us the important thing is that the reaction reached a high point in May of 1862, when a series of devastating fires, alleged but never proven to have been the work of revolutionary plotters, swept the capital.

The second situation was the discovery at last of some concrete evidence of subversive propaganda among the factory workers studying at the Petersburg schools. Since this evidence came to light almost immediately after the fires, an atmosphere existed that made it easy for the enemies of the schools in particular and of private social activity in general to win the day. According to Valuev's own account, the subversive propaganda was uncovered in May 1862, when a Petersburg manufacturer, Glints, informed Valuev that two workers who were enrolled at Sunday schools had made some seditious political remarks to other members of their artel' at the time of the fires. The manufacturer also recounted that some workers had complained to him that socialistic and anti-religious doctrines were being taught at the Sunday schools they attended. On the basis of this information, Valuev arranged for the new military governor, A. A. Suvorov, to arrest the two workers. An unsigned memorandum in the files of the Third Section, probably emanating from the same manufacturer, accused the two workers, Mikhail Fedorov and Vasilii Trifonov, of having advocated the overthrow of the government, the liberation of Poland, and the burning of the entire city of St. Petersburg. The enemies of the schools were thus able to link the frightening fires of recent days to charges of subversive propaganda among the worker-pupils.[93]

The accusations against Fedorov and Trifonov, together with the testimony of another worker that atheistic and socialistic doctrines were being taught at the Samsonievskaia school in the city's Vyborg district, represented the only evidence available to Valuev when, within only two or three days, he made his decision to suppress the Sunday schools altogether. Although Valuev was not without sympathy for the schools in early 1861,* his correspondence with the

* P. A. Valuev, *Dnevnik P. A. Valueva Ministra Vnutrennikh Del v dvukh tomakh* (Moscow, 1961; ed. P. A. Zaionchkovskii), I, 57 (entry of January 5, 1861). Somewhat

head of the Third Section reveals the extent to which he now shared Dolgorukov's antipathy for the schools and his willingness to eliminate them, however meager the pretext. Making no attempt to conceal the paucity of his evidence, he disclosed his three-step plan to Dolgorukov: he would close down the Samsonievskaia school immediately, then launch an investigation of the Sunday school movement, and, in the course of the investigation, close down the rest of the schools in St. Petersburg and throughout the country.[94] It is obvious that Valuev was determined to use the occasion of the recent disclosures to complete the destruction of the Sunday schools irrespective of the outcome of the forthcoming investigation.

On June 1, Valuev's plans were approved by the Committee of Ministers and the Tsar, with Minister of Education Golovnin expressing some reservations.[95] By the next day Valuev was able to inform the Third Section that the first two steps had been completed: the Samsonievskaia school had been closed down along with the Vvedenskaia school (in the Petersburg district), which had been attended by the two accused workers; and a special investigating committee had been formed under the chairmanship of Privy Councilor Zhdanov. To use Valuev's own euphemism, it was anticipated that the investigation would result in the "radical reorganization of the Sunday schools."[96]

When the commission completed its work, the chairman reported to Valuev that the investigation had revealed the "important political significance" of revolutionary propaganda among the workers at the St. Petersburg schools.[97] Similarly, some historians have used such terms as the "wide dissemination" of revolutionary propaganda in the St. Petersburg Sunday schools when discussing this situation.[98] A rapid look at the information actually uncovered by the commission, however, will demonstrate how exaggerated these conclusions are.

To begin with, the number of St. Petersburg's 450 Sunday school teachers actually found to have spread seditious propaganda among the workers was a paltry three.[99] A fourth teacher, a former univer-

---

embarrassed by the sentiment expressed in this entry, Valuev commented in 1868: "At that time information about the Sunday schools was very incomplete, and the affair was looked at superficially. The police knew little about what was happening, which, by the way, is often the case nowadays. In 1862 it turned out that General Ignat'ev was right [about the danger of Sunday schools]." *Ibid.*, p. 310.

sity student, was accused by six workers of having made defamatory remarks about the Tsar in class; and a young officer who was not even a teacher in the schools was indicted by a military tribunal for disseminating propaganda among workers who happened also to be Sunday school pupils.[100] No other person was even accused of engaging in subversive activities in connection with the schools.*

As insignificant as the number of teachers involved in the dissemination of propaganda was the number of schools to which it spread. According to Zhdanov, the total number of Sunday schools in St. Petersburg in 1862 was twenty-eight.[101] Yet the investigation brought to light convincing evidence of seditious propaganda in connection with only two schools, the Samsonievskaia and the Vvedenskaia. There was also the minor case of alleged defamation of the Tsar at a third school, already mentioned. The remaining twenty-five schools were in no way involved in the "widespread" conspiracy that served as the pretext for the suppression of all Sunday schools in Russia. Even Zhdanov was forced to admit the total absence of evidence against the other schools.[102]

As to the number of workers affected by or active in the dissemination of revolutionary propaganda, it turned out that of the five thousand or more workers of various types enrolled in St. Petersburg Sunday schools,[103] a total of only five workers, representing only three of the city's officially listed 374 factories (the Meniaev cotton factory, the Shaw weaving mill, and the tulle factory of the Tiulevoe Tovarishchestvo), were actually brought to trial and convicted as a result of the Zhdanov investigation.[104]

It is of some historical interest to identify these workers by name, as they were the first industrial workers in the history of the city to be indicted on charges connected with revolutionary activity. They were Fedorov, age 17, Trifonov, 18, Egor Kochenkov, 23, and Ivan Antonov, 21—all of whom were peasants—and Mikhail Mitrofanov, 21, a *meshchanin*. (Another peasant, Karp Andreev, died in prison before he could be tried.) All five workers were convicted, but only three—Mitrofanov, Fedorov, and Trifonov—were found

---

* Zhdanov implied that more subversive teachers were not uncovered simply because news of the impending investigation had given them time to cover up their activities (TsGAOR, *f.* 109, *eksp.* 1, *d.* 263, p. 72). Although Ionova claims that the chief administrator of the Samsonievskaia school was also involved in revolutionary propaganda, he did not appear as a defendant in the trial. See *Istoricheskie zapiski* (No. 57, 1956), pp. 197, 199.

guilty of possessing or disseminating seditious literature. Kochenkov and Antonov were convicted only of having failed to report the others. Mitrofanov, who was found guilty of the most serious offenses, received three weeks' confinement and three years' surveillance; Fedorov, Trifonov, and Kochenkov each received a whipping and a year's surveillance; Antonov got off with a strong reprimand.[105] These were the sentences meted out to the first Russian workers accused of participating in a major revolutionary conspiracy. They were the only five—out of thousands of factory workers in the capital—who were even brought to trial.[106]

The Zhdanov commission's efforts to uncover evidence of propaganda or conspiracy in other Petersburg factories came to nothing. Zhdanov and his associates paid personal visits to several factories in search of clues. At least four hundred workers, most of whom had presumably attended Sunday schools, were interrogated, but not one had anything to say that suggested revolutionary propagandizing by the teachers. The only questionable literature unearthed was a brochure advocating workers' associations, which of course had recently found support in perfectly respectable St. Petersburg circles. Of the thirty copies found at the Samsonievskaia school, twenty-eight were unread and uncut. The commission itself was convinced that the brochures were not aimed at inciting workers against their employers. As for the factory owners, they assured Zhdanov that no unrest existed among their employees.[107]

Having established the quantitative insignificance of revolutionary propaganda among the factory workers, it is now possible to briefly summarize what actually transpired.[108] Early in the spring of 1862 a young medical student teaching at the Samsonievskaia school, Khokhriakov by name, read a revolutionary leaflet to his worker pupils. According to the testimony of the workers, he did this two or three times and on the same occasions made some remarks in favor of the cause of Polish freedom. The activities of Khokhriakov apparently remained unknown to the rest of the school's staff. This was the only case uncovered of a Sunday school instructor reading seditious literature to his class.

At approximately the same time, a young army lieutenant named Ushakov was engaged in giving private lessons to workers in his apartment. The circumstances surrounding these lessons are obscure, but it was definitely established that Ushakov had distributed illegal literature to his pupils, including "Molodaia Rossiia" (Young Russia), a violent revolutionary leaflet that had just appeared in the capital. All that could be adduced connecting Ushakov with the Sunday schools was that he became acquainted with the student Khokhriakov around this time and that they probably met through the peasant-worker Karp Andreev, who was both a pupil at the Samsonievskaia school and a frequent guest at Ushakov's home. Andreev soon began to receive illegal literature from both Ushakov and Khokhriakov, and from another student, Krapivin, whom he met through Ushakov. Krapivin was one of the "Sunday school teachers" later arrested, but in fact his entire contact with the movement consisted of three Sundays of teaching at the Samsonievskaia school.

Some of the illegal literature that Karp Andreev received he turned over to another worker, Mitrofanov, who in turn passed it on to the worker Fedorov. Fedorov, who had already been introduced to such literature at the apartment of a teacher from the Vvedenskaia Sunday school, then brought one of the illegal leaflets to his factory, the Meniaev works. There he read it aloud to the peasant-workers in his artel', adding some anti-government remarks of his own. It was at this point that two of the workers reported what they had heard to the owner of the factory, who then informed the Minister of Internal Affairs that he had evidence of seditious activities at the Sunday schools. On the basis of these events alone, Valuev then launched the attack that led to the closing of over three hundred Sunday schools throughout the country.

Conclusions

The closing of the Sunday schools represented a victory for those elements within the government who feared the participation not only of the masses but of any independent social group, above all the so-called middle stratum (roughly defined as educated non-nobles, or educated nobles who did not serve in an official capacity), in the solution of Russia's social problems. These elements found their chief spokesmen in the branches of government that were most concerned with maintaining internal security, that is, in the Third Section and, as time went on, in the Ministry of Internal Affairs. On the other hand, the closing of the schools represented a serious setback to officials, particularly in the Ministry of Education, who—with varying degrees of confidence—believed that some freedom of initiative and increased contacts among diverse social groups might moderate the intensity of social conflict while helping to meet the country's need for an educated working-class population. Since both these groups placed a high premium on social stability, the three years in which the schools were permitted to exist were marked by tense scrutiny of the activities of their participants, with one side endeavoring to demonstrate, the other to deny that the schools were apt to undermine the relative docility of urban workers. Under these circumstances, the existence of the schools had been precarious at best. The slightest evidence that they might encourage the disaffection of workers could be used to arouse the thirty-year-old specter of an alienated, disloyal proletariat, and thus undermine the already shaky position of those who argued that flexibility and experimentation were compatible with conservative goals. And in a situation so delicately poised, any additional elements of crisis—student unrest, revolutionary manifestos, unexplained mysterious fires—contributed to the credibility of alarmists and tipped the scales in their favor.

Having seen the way in which this process operated with respect to the Sunday schools, we are now in a position to formulate some tentative conclusions concerning the collapse of efforts to introduce labor legislation, an episode that encompassed roughly the same years. On the surface the two cases appear to be somewhat different, in that one involved the suppression of an experiment that had actually been launched, whereas the other involved the interment of plans that had never left the drawing board. But substantively, the two situations were analogous in several ways. Industrial courts whose members were both workers and employers, and an inspection system open to formal complaints by organized groups of workers provided the backbone for the implementation of the proposed legislation. In other words, this program could have offered another opportunity for initiative from below in dealing with a fundamental social problem, the difference being that the initiative would have come not from the "middle stratum" that staffed the schools, but from the workers themselves. In the past, during the reign of Nicholas I, proposals of this nature had been undermined whenever events such as the 1848 revolutions or the Crimean War nourished the fears and strengthened the arguments of those who maintained that the formalization of workers' rights vis-à-vis their employers would increase their "pretensions." Similar apprehensions persisted into the reign of Alexander II, as was illustrated by the strong official reaction to even the most peaceful efforts of workers to organize for the redress of their grievances, as well as by the government's precautionary preparations for promulgating the Emancipation Act in the capital. The new proposals that were studied between 1859 and 1864 went considerably further than any previous plans in preparing the way for the formation of permanent, autonomous class institutions that would weld not merely the "middle stratum," but the even more dangerous stratum of urban workers into a cohesive group. With these considerations in mind, it seems reasonable to infer that officials charged with the security of the state would have at least as many reservations about the Shtakel'berg proposals as they had about the Sunday schools.

Obviously the commissions of 1859, like the Sunday schools, would never have been established had the officials who feared these developments been able to exert their influence at that time. By 1862, for reasons that have been indicated, the scales had tipped far enough in their direction to provide for the termination of the Sunday schools; and it is highly unlikely that having abolished those schools the regime was now prepared to introduce new institutions, including workers' associations, that would place factory laborers in an even stonger position to organize themselves as an independent force. That the Shtakel'berg Commission should have been allowed an additional year and a half beyond the death of the schools to play out its mandate by completing its final draft is not particularly surprising,[109] but the actual implementation of its proposals, in an atmosphere that was heated still further by the events of 1863 in Poland, was an entirely different matter. This conjecture is corroborated by the marked reduction of discussions of the labor question in the periodical press beginning in the same year. In short, the abandonment of plans for labor legislation, the suppression of the schools, and the abrupt attenuation of the labor question in the press appear as parts of a single process in which initiatives favorable to the organization of labor were terminated on essentially political grounds; the alleged influence of remote provincial manufacturers (who stood to benefit from some provisions of the Shtakel'berg draft) was at most an extraneous factor.

Yet the context in which the Shtakel'berg proposals were defeated was significantly different from the one in which earlier efforts had been frustrated. Since the Crimean War, although the initial steps were awkward and confused, industrial development had been endowed with a new priority, in some circles even with sanctity. In the prewar years, when the very wisdom of allowing the development of urban industrial complexes could be called into question by the pessimists, and when optimists argued that such complexes were only tolerable because of Russia's good fortune in enjoying an industrial labor force made up of rural serfs, it was not farfetched to view the encouragement of a permanent working class as a dangerous luxury that Russian autocracy could ill afford. Now, a tentative decision to industrialize having been made, this was no longer the case. This is why there were growing forces, both within and without the government, who were determined to extricate the peasant-workers from the no-man's-land that had previously been equated with security and to forge them into a new industrial class that would shed the skin of peasant or artisan and acquire the consistent and reliable work habits that were believed to inhere in the free workers of England and other parts of Europe. Having come to recognize (mainly through their knowledge of Western Europe, but to some degree through their growing awareness of conditions in St. Petersburg) the devastating social consequences of this kind of transformation, the partisans of industrialization were determined to create institutions that would generate a painless resolution to the labor question in Russia.

So convincing was this approach in the postwar climate that even a General Ignat'ev, a colorless police official who was identified by some of his contemporaries as an "obscurantist," saw the need for breaking down traditional impediments to industrial freedom and for filling the vacuum with a new system of industrial courts, factory inspections, and other measures that recognized and legitimized the existence of a working class. Yet the same Ignat'ev, when compelled to deal with situations where workers actually began to organize themselves on a minor scale in a struggle for improved conditions, was quick to deny their efforts any legitimacy, irrespective of the justice of their demands; and when it came to an endeavor by "enlightened" members of St. Petersburg society to assist in organizing workers' schools, a goal endorsed in the report of his own commission (the St. Petersburg commission of inquiry), he joined with those who from the start sought their suppression. Perhaps these contradictions represented nothing more than the hypocrisy of the man, but a more generous and, I would argue, more plausible explanation would point to the fact that Ignat'ev, like the Shtakel'berg Commission, was confronted with a paradoxical situation that stemmed from the circumstances of the workers themselves: on the one hand, profound institutional changes were required before a well-organized, "mature," and stable working class could be formed, but on the other hand, the existence of such a class was a prerequisite for the safe and successful undertaking of those institutional changes. Even the Shtakel'berg Commission displayed little real confidence in the peasant-workers whose transformation was its goal; but the commissioners managed to avoid a direct confrontation with this issue by relying on sanguine predictions based on the alleged advantages of the lag between Russia and Western Europe. Ignat'ev, whose immediate responsibilities as a police official could not be so readily wished away, resolved the conflict by backing down from his theoretical openness to independent labor activity when faced with its direct implications in practice. Despite the increased value that the government as a whole now placed on the development of modern industry, the path of least resistance was the freezing of the traditionally passive position of the peasant-worker, reinforced by police surveillance and occasional intervention on the side of the workers when their situation grew serious enough.

The passivity of the factory workers themselves reinforced the assumption that the risks involved in encouraging the self-activation of workers were greater than the risks of continuing to rely on methods that carried over from the days of official optimism. A more active, sustained, and threatening movement on the part of the workers might well have imparted a sense of urgency to the position of advocates of change by creating the impression that the risks of inertia outweighed those of experimentation. But the workers of St. Petersburg, to whose circumstances the government was most highly sensitized, did not—despite a temporary rise in the frequency and intensity of unrest—apply sufficient pressure to transform this situation. Just as their initial surge of enthusiasm for the Sunday schools subsided when circumstances began to deteriorate, and workers implicated in the Sunday school "conspiracy" testified freely against the other defendants, providing the government with almost its entire case,[110] so too did the workers involved in the incidents of unrest related here quickly collapse in the face of strong official opposition, in some cases supplying information that assisted the government in the isolation of "instigators."

Notwithstanding the changed atmosphere of industrial St. Petersburg in the postwar years, the advocates of industrial reform were still, in large part, basing their case on abstract considerations and drawing their formulas from the experiences of other countries. Consciousness of the dismal conditions in the factories and shops of the capital now was relatively high, but real social conflict in those factories was not an important force behind the urge for a new approach to the labor question.

In this respect it is noteworthy that while the recommendations of the Shtakel'berg and Petersburg commissions remained in limbo, similar but less far-reaching proposals were quickly implemented, apparently with Dolgorukov's approval, in areas of production where the incidence of labor unrest was high. Thus new regulations governing the relations between contractors and laborers in public and semipublic works, particularly railroad construction (1861), and protecting the rights of mining and metallurgical workers in the Ural region (1862), although falling far short of the comprehensive proposals of the Shtakel'berg Commission, nevertheless gave the workers in these two highly volatile areas significant advantages not enjoyed by their fellows in other branches of industry.[111] This would suggest the existence of an elusive but nonetheless functional threshold between the modest degree of labor unrest that merely reinforced traditional official reactions while embarrassing reformers, and a higher level of unrest and conflict that created sufficient apprehension to unlock the door to innovation.

It was not until the end of the decade that some of the workers of St. Petersburg would begin to show signs of providing such an impetus. In the interim, the situation of the laboring population of the city was slowly and undramatically deteriorating.

SIX

The Laboring Population
in the 1860's

IN THE CITY of St. Petersburg, the decade after the emancipation was characterized by significant although uneven industrial growth, and by the expansion of both the industrial labor force and the broader pool of peasant-workers from which most factory workers were recruited. In this chapter I shall examine these developments with the aid of contemporary statistical materials.* Some of the materials are difficult to evaluate, due to the relative inexperience of Russian officials in collecting and analyzing quantitative data pertaining to urban industrial matters.[1] Although methodological improvements began to be introduced around the time of the emancipation,† the legacy of inexperience weighed heavily, and was reflected in the inconsistency and even slovenliness of the work of agencies concerned with the collection of statistics in the 1860's and beyond.

There seems, for example, to have been no generally accepted nomenclature for the categories examined from year to year, no uniform standards for defining "factory," "worker," or "child," and no consistent usage of the name "St. Petersburg," which could mean the province, the district (*uezd*), the city, or the city plus the immediately adjacent suburbs. One year a report would divide

---

* These data were originally gathered by the St. Petersburg municipal police, the office of the provincial governor, the provincial Statistical Committee, the Central Statistical Committee of the Ministry of Internal Affairs, and the Department of Manufactures. (In October 1864 the name of this section of the Ministry of Finance was changed from Departament manufaktur i vnutrennei torgovli to Departament torgovli i manufaktur; for the sake of brevity and consistency, I shall refer to it as the Department of Manufactures throughout.)

† A significant attempt to rationalize the collection of statistics under the newly organized Central Statistical Committee was undertaken in 1858, but the preoccupation of that committee with preparations for the peasant reforms postponed real progress in the area of urban statistics for several years. See A. I. Gozulov, *Istoriia otechestvennoi statistiki* (Moscow, 1957), p. 22; E. Amburger, *Geschichte der Behördenorganisation Russlands von Peter dem Grossen bis 1917* (Leiden, 1966), p. 138.

workers according to age and sex, while the following year one or both of these divisions would be omitted. The definition of factory continued to be subject to the same confusion described in Chapter 2.[2] When, toward the end of 1861, the French consul in St. Petersburg asked the Department of Manufactures for statistical information on the number of factories, the amount and value of their output, the extent of mechanization, and the number and wages of workers in the city,[3] the head of the department, A. I. Butovskii, found himself in the embarrassing situation of being unable to supply much of this information—virtually none regarding wages and the number of machines. "I regret very much," he was forced to reply, "being unable to fill out completely the form attached to your letter, for want of the necessary accurate details."[4]

One aspect of the problem was the difficulty of obtaining reliable information from factory owners. In preparing its second annual report (for 1863) on factories in St. Petersburg, the St. Petersburg Statistical Committee found that many manufacturers had failed to supply some of the required information. It was therefore forced to send representatives to individual factories to obtain the missing information; and even then much of the data it received was too carelessly prepared to be included in the printed report. According to the report, this lack of reliability was a characteristic of manufacturers that dated back many years.[5]

Although the St. Petersburg Statistical Committee acknowledged some signs of improvement in the cooperation of manufacturers, the Central Statistical Committee was still reporting eight years later on its difficulties in obtaining satisfactory information from them.[6] Similarly, a report issued by the Department of manufactures regretted the frequent inaccuracies that entered official documents owing to the manufacturers' "incomprehensible fear . . . of submitting accurate information about their establishments."[7] These citations testify to the limited reliability of data collected from manufacturers, but they also show that responsible officials knew the data they were gathering had to be evaluated with caution.[8]

Indeed, under the stimulus of a growing demand by governmental authorities, especially the War and Naval Ministries, for more precise information concerning St. Petersburg industry,[9] the Department of Manufactures and the provincial Statistical Committee of St. Petersburg began to work together in 1863 to stream-line their methods and to broaden their areas of inquiry, particularly with respect to factory workers.[10] The St. Petersburg Statistical Committee, critical of the old system whereby local police collected information three times a year for diverse purposes, and dubious about the accuracy of the information provided by manufacturers, recommended, among other reforms, that the Department of Manufactures obtain its information on St. Petersburg industry once a year through the committee itself.[11] The committee's proposals were quickly accepted and put into practice, with February 15, 1864, set as the target date for the first report. The report was delayed for another month, however, owing both to the novelty of the new procedures and to the fact that some manufacturers found it "difficult to give an answer right at the end of the year."[12] Although difficulties of this nature would continue to interfere, it is clear that serious efforts were made to improve procedures, and one may safely assume that the data collected became more reliable as the decade progressed.

Broadly speaking, two general features of the 1860's compose the background against which any detailed discussion of these data must take place. The first was the government's continued commitment to a policy of industrial progress. In certain respects, it is true, a period of "reaction" may be said to have set in around 1862 or even earlier:[13] witness especially the suppression of the Sunday schools and the failure of the government to adopt the proposals of its commissions on factory legislation, as well as the general retreat from the relative freedom of expression of the late 1850's. But these events did not signify the government's retreat from its commitment to industrial and financial progress. Indeed, even while personnel changes in the Ministry of Internal Affairs were signaling a partial closing of the gap that had recently opened between the regime and the conservative gentry,[14] some important new government appointments in other branches were given to men with a strong inclination toward industrialization and related social reforms—and even with pro-labor sentiments. These included M. Kh. Reutern, whose appointment as Finance Minister in 1862 was later described by Terner as the beginning of a "new era,"[15] Terner himself, Lamanskii, Tatarinov, and others.[16] The main goal of Reutern's "liberal" administration*—as stated in his proposed program and approved by the Tsar in 1866—was to stimulate and invigorate the nation's industrial forces.[17] But a "reactionary" minister like Valuev could also write (in 1862, even while tightening his vise on the workers' schools) that economic modernization, including private enterprise, banking, and railroads, was desirable for Russia.[18]

The second general feature of the period to be kept in mind is too well known to be belabored. It is the simple but crucial fact that the emancipation, far from ushering in a new age of free labor, replaced the former bondage of the peasants to their landlords with an almost equally restrictive, legally binding, and virtually inescapable attachment to the village commune, based on a complex system of collective fiscal responsibility (*krugovaia poruka*). Disappointing the hopes of the liberal economists, but inadvertently allaying one of the worst fears of the left intelligentsia, the government, for both social and fiscal reasons, chose to avert the creation of a landless, and hence rootless, rural proletariat by preserving through law the traditional institutional ties to the countryside of the vast majority of peasants. In theory, of course, these ties could be severed, and the individual peasant or peasant household could break with the commune; but this freedom was severely limited by a complex set of customary, economic, and legal obstacles.[19]

The overall logic of this situation could be defended with consistency were it not for the regime's concurrent commitment to industrial progress. As it was, the government was attempting to preserve the rural system of communal ties (as well as the urban tsekhi) even while it moved ahead with its policy of encouraging private, large-scale, mechanized industry—a policy that demanded a permanent, stable labor force which had cut its ancient ties and was prepared to assimilate to a new urban industrial environment. The government was still relying on the idea that had nourished the optimism of the 1830's and 1840's: a unique rural institution, the commune, would allow Russia to industrialize while avoiding the

---

* According to Terner (*Vospominaniia zhizni F. G. Ternera*, I [St. Petersburg, 1910], 245-46), Reutern's ministry was distrusted in "ultra-conservative circles," which included the Tsarevich Alexander, because of the extreme liberalism of its personnel. Yet despite opposition, Reutern remained at his post for sixteen years.

hazards of proletarianization. The results, as shall be seen, proved less than satisfactory on both counts.

Industrial Growth

For Russia as a whole, it will be recalled from Chapter 3, the immediate post-emancipation years were marked by a continuation of the industrial contraction that had begun shortly after the end of the Crimean War.[20] While it is sometimes maintained that this situation occurred because many factory peasants returned to their villages to be present at the impending turnover of land,[21] this type of industrial dislocation—if it played any significant role at all—was secondary to the impact of the financial difficulties that had plagued Russian industry for several years before the emancipation and were reinforced by foreign reaction to events in Poland in 1863. Another important factor contributing to temporary industrial stagnation was the outbreak of the Civil War in the United States, which led to a significant reduction in Russia's raw cotton imports from 1861 to 1865 and hence to a decline in the activities of factories engaged in the spinning and weaving of cotton. The withdrawal of peasant-workers from factory work during these years is more reasonably viewed as a result of this decline than as its cause. The Department of Manufactures emphasized the cotton problem when it endeavored to interpret the return of peasant-workers to the land.[22] The fact that the number of employed factory workers reached its lowest point in 1865 (359,679), the last year of the Civil War, and then, began to rise, together with the number of factories and the value of industrial output, would seem to bear out this view.[23]

While Russian industry as a whole was experiencing this difficult period, St. Petersburg industry was already beginning to show some signs of recovery. As the figures in Table 1 show, there was a steady increase in the number of employed factory workers in St. Petersburg during the first half of the 1860's; and the increase was accompanied by a steady rise in the value of output and an almost equally steady decline in the number of factories. The increase in value of output—nearly 60 per cent over a four-year period—was almost twice the rate of growth of the labor force, which was slightly over 30 per cent for the same period. It evidently represented a real increase in industrial production (as opposed to increased prices)

TABLE 1

St. Petersburg Industry, 1861–65

Year	Number of Workers	Number of Factories	Ruble Output	Average Ruble Output per Factory
1861	18,851	410	35,772,805	87,251
1862	20,418*	380*	37,168,392*	97,812
1863	22,566	380*	46,480,587*	122,317
1864	22,461*	364*	48,394,084*	132,951
1865	24,685	361	57,162,266	158,344

SOURCE: Based on TsGIAL, f. 1263, Komitet ministrov, op. 1, d. 2975, "Otchet S. Peterburgskoi politsii" (1861), pp. 29–87; d. 3046 (1862), p. 41; d. 3143 (1863), p. 35; d. 3164 (1864), p. 9; d. 3263 (1865), p. 10; S-PSK, Statisticheskie svedeniia o fabrikakh i zavodakh v S. Peterburge za 1862 god (St. Petersburg, 1863), p. 59; S-PSK, Pamiatnaia knizhka S.-Peterburgskoi gubernii na 1863 god, part ii, p. 106; Zhurnal manufaktur i torgovli, Vol. I (April 1864), sec. iv, pp. 138–42; S-PSK, Fabriki i zavody v S.-Peterburge v 1863 godu (St. Petersburg, 1864), pp. 6–7; S-PSK, Fabriki i zavody v S.-Peterburge i S.-Peterburgskoi gubernii v 1864 godu (St. Petersburg, 1865), pp. 3, 6, 55.
NOTE: Asterisks indicate that a mean has been taken between two divergent figures. This has been done only when the alternatives were close enough so as not to affect the general trend.

and even an increase in the productivity of labor as well. This view must be tested against a more detailed examination of the individual branches of St. Petersburg industry.

The cotton-spinning industry in St. Petersburg, as in other areas, suffered from the curtailment of raw cotton shipments from America during the early 1860's: both the number of factories and, though to a much lesser extent, the number of workers employed in them declined (see Table 2), as did the quantity of steam-driven ma-

TABLE 2

Workers Employed in St. Petersburg
Cotton-Spinning Factories

Year	Cotton-Spinning Factories	Workers
1861	11	—
1862	12 or 13	5,349
1863	6 or 7	4,279
1864	6 or 7	4,426[a]
1865	7	4,561

SOURCE: Based on TsGIAL, f. 1263, op. 1, d. 2975, p. 86; d. 3046, p. 94; d. 3143, p. 86; GIALO, f. 260, Petrogradskii (S.P.B.) Gubernskii Statisticheskii Komitet, op. 1, d. 5, "O chisle zhitelei po sosloviiam (1864)," p. 16; TsGIAL, f. 1263, op. 1, d. 3164, p. 71; d. 3263, pp. 93–100; S-PSK Statisticheskie svedeniia, 1862, p. 55; S-PSK, Fabriki i zavody, 1863, p. 43; S-PSK, Fabriki i zavody, 1864, p. 17.
[a] This figure is somewhat overestimated, since it includes workers in two or three wool-spinning factories (the two categories were not separated in the police report for 1864). The number of workers in cotton spinning probably continued to decline from 1863 to 1864, while rising more sharply from 1864 to 1865 than the table indicates.

TABLE 3
*St. Petersburg Metallurgical and
Machine Works, 1861–65*

Year	Number of Iron Foundries	Number of Related Industries	Total	Total Number of Workers
1861	14	10	24	—
1862	13/14	5	18/19	4,736[a]
1863	10	6/7	16/17	4,669[b]
1864	—	—	18/19	5,396[c]
1865	12	4	16	5,013

SOURCE: E. Karnovich, *Sanktpeterburg v statisticheskom otnoshenii* (St. Petersburg, 1860), p. 109; TsGIAL, f. 1263, op. 1: d. 2975, p. 87; d. 3046, pp. 41, 95; d. 3143, pp. 87–88; d. 3164, pp. 71–72; d. 3263, pp. 93–100; S-PSK, *Fabriki i zavody, 1863*, p. 26; *Fabriki i zavody, 1864*, pp. 10–11; S-PSK, *Statisticheskie svedeniia, 1862*, pp. 42–43, 55.
NOTE: "13/14" means "13 or 14," etc.
[a] Based on 19 factories.   [b] Based on 16.   [c] Based on 18.

chinery.[24] As in other St. Petersburg industries this decline was accompanied by a rise in the total value of output, in this case a rise of about one and a half million rubles from 1861 to 1865.[25] The rise in the case of the cotton industry, unlike the general rise, is clearly attributable to the higher cotton prices that were precipitated by the shortage of raw cotton. For example, from 1862 to 1863 the ruble value of cotton goods produced in St. Petersburg factories rose by nearly half a million, while production fell from 412,000 puds* to 303,000.[26] The reduction in the number of employed workers in the St. Petersburg cotton-spinning industry, a net loss of some eight hundred workers over a four-year period (or about 15 per cent) fell far short of the 34.5 per cent reduction in the number of employed workers experienced by Russian industry as a whole over the same period. The difficulties of the St. Petersburg cotton mills were thus relatively moderate. Nevertheless, it is clear that one must look elsewhere for positive evidence of industrial progress.

St. Petersburg's metal-processing and machine industry, after a period of stagnation brought about by the reduced demand for military products after the war as well as by the money shortage of the late 1850's,[27] began to show new signs of the energy it had exhibited during the war years. Tables 3 and 4 reveal that whereas the

---

* A pud is equivalent to 36 pounds.

TABLE 4

Ruble Output of St. Petersburg Iron Foundries, 1861–65

Year	Number of Iron Foundries	Ruble Output	Average Output per Factory
1861	14	1,194,292	85,307
1862	13/14	1,108,278	85,252[a]
1863	10	1,680,128	168,013
1864	—	—	—
1865	12	2,151,525	179,293

SOURCE: TsGIAL, *f.* 1263, *op.* 1: *d.* 2975, p. 87; *d.* 3046, p. 95; *d.* 3143, p. 88; *d.* 3263, pp. 93–100.
   [a] Based on 13 factories.

number of workers employed in this branch of production increased but slightly, the output of St. Petersburg's iron foundries alone came close to doubling in value between 1862 and 1865.

The nature of the market for which these factories produced, primarily the military branches of the government, leaves no doubt that the ruble figures in Table 4 represent a real increase in production. Despite its severe financial difficulties, the government had been unwilling to neglect its military needs for very long. By January 1862, War Minister Dmitri Miliutin was pressing for a crash program in domestic armaments production, and the tense international situation of 1863 further increased his (and the Naval Minister's) desire to reduce Russia's dependency on purchases of armaments from abroad.* In particular Miliutin stressed the need to produce cast iron and steel domestically, since these items were prerequisites for weapons production.[28] The result was the stepped-up production of new bronze and iron weapons (e.g., rifled cannons in lieu of the old smoothbore artillery) in already existing factories of moderate or large size, and the expansion of relatively small machine factories into much larger, virtually new enterprises. The most notable of these were the Nevskii works on the Schlüsselburg Road, which began to receive large orders for the construction of warships in 1863, and the Ludwig Nobel iron, copper, and steel works in St. Petersburg's Vyborg district.[29] In addition, the construction of an entirely new steelworks, the Obukhov company, was

---

* The requests from the War and Naval Ministries to the Department of Manufactures for statistical information, noted earlier in this chapter, were related to this concern.

launched with government support in 1863. In January 1864 it received a three-year contract for the preparation of 240 pieces of field artillery, an order it managed to fulfill successfully despite severe financial difficulties.[30]

While output and, to a limited extent, the size of the employed labor force were increasing, the number of machine and metallurgical factories fell. Thus the average number of workers per factory increased, along with the average output. The average number of workers per factory in the iron foundries and related industries of St. Petersburg in 1862 was 249 (see Table 3).[31] By 1865 the corresponding figure was 313 (289 for the iron foundries alone). Among the leading branches of St. Petersburg industry, only cotton-spinning factories, where the average number of workers per factory reached 652 in the same year (Table 2), surpassed metallurgical and machine works in this respect.

About the same time, factories became more mechanized, accounting at least in part for the rise in the productivity of labor that accompanied the concentration of workers. In 1859 the total capacity of the steam engines in the city's machine and metal works was 932 H.P.[32] By 1863 it had reached 1,125 H.P. at the very least, to which was added power of unknown magnitudes generated by steam engines in the factory of the Chief Society of Russian Railroads. (That factory boasted the highest output per worker of all the machine works in St. Petersburg: an annual value of 1,790 rubles per worker.)[33] Although mechanization in the years immediately following 1863 cannot be documented directly, the degree to which the rise in value of output outstripped the expansion of the labor force suggests that the process was continuing to accelerate.

In almost every respect, then, although one industry was experiencing a trying period while the other was beginning to expand, cotton spinning and heavy metallurgical production dominated St. Petersburg industry in the early and middle 1860's. Together in 1865 they accounted for nearly 40 per cent of the city's factory workers (ninety-five hundred out of 24,685) and more than 40 per cent of the factories with two hundred or more workers (12 out of 28). In steam power, in 1862, they accounted for 65 per cent of total capacity (2,541 H.P. out of 3,872). Finally, their combined share of the total value of output, although less impressive, was high in relation to the number of factories involved: in 1865 it amounted to 12,445,810 rubles out of a total of 57,162,266, or nearly 22 per cent.[34]

The other important branches of St. Petersburg industry, measured in terms of the value of output, were sugar refineries, tobacco factories, the weaving branch of the textile industry, and tanneries (see Table 5). Notwithstanding the high output figures quoted for sugar refineries, in 1866 there were only five such factories, with a total of 729 workers, and these figures varied little throughout the early 1860's.[35] The tobacco industry, although less important from the point of view of monetary value, was the largest single industry in St. Petersburg in terms of the number of factories operating, and ranked high in the size of its labor force. The number of cigarette, cigar, and tobacco-processing factories in operation from year to year fluctuated between a low of 30 and a high of 40, while the labor force generally fluctuated between two and three thousand. Several of these "factories" were so tiny that they would have been more properly classified as artisan shops. The Miller tobacco factory, by contrast, though totally unmechanized and primitive, ranked among the very largest factories in the city, with a total of 738 workers in 1863.[36]

Among the six most important branches of St. Petersburg industry, weaving mills and tanneries ranked lowest both in the total number of workers and in the average number of workers per factory. During the period 1864–66 there were 21 or 22 weaving mills in St. Petersburg, and the number of workers fluctuated between 863 and 1,434. The number of tanneries was 21 in 1864, 14 in 1865, and 15 in 1866; the total number of tannery workers remained con-

TABLE 5

Ruble Output of St. Petersburg Sugar, Tobacco, and Weaving Industries, and Tanneries, 1861–66

Year	Sugar	Tobacco	Weaving	Tanneries
1861	7,250,819	3,058,015	765,534	2,290,869
1862	7,772,177	2,374,260	1,234,971	1,800,850
1863	11,470,080	1,768,086	2,564,955	2,813,204
1864	10,769,420	3,900,040	991,695	2,753,094
1865	7,649,298	3,640,154	1,440,432	2,195,926
1866	10,323,845	3,716,023	2,075,537	1,976,085

SOURCE: TsGIAL, *f.* 1263, *op.* 1: *d.* 2975, pp. 86–87; *d.* 3046, pp. 94–95; *d.* 3143, pp. 86–88; *d.* 3164, p. 71; *d.* 3263, pp. 93–100; *d.* 3332, p. 209.

sistently in the 700's. Many of the so-called factories in these two branches (tanneries were classified as *zavody*, weaving mills as *fabriki*) were small enough so as to be indistinguishable—except for administrative purposes—from artisan shops. Only the Golenishchevskaia mechanized weaving factory (mentioned earlier in connection with the labor unrest of the late 1850's), which had 384 workers in 1865,[37] could be classified as large.

To summarize, the most significant branches of St. Petersburg industry in the early and middle 1860's were metal processing and machine production (primarily for the production of war materials); cotton spinning; weaving; sugar refining; tobacco processing and the manufacture of cigarettes; and tanning. Together in 1865 they made up 26 per cent of St. Petersburg's factories (95 out of 361; this proportion was fairly stable throughout the 1860's), accounted for 48 per cent of industrial output (27,373,620 rubles out of 57,162,266), and hired some 40 per cent of the employed industrial workers (10,028 out of 24,685). Most of the remaining 74 per cent of St. Petersburg's factories—the exception being print works and breweries, which averaged over a hundred workers per factory—were medium- or small-scale operations, wholly unmechanized, and in many cases hardly different in character from artisan shops.* It was only the metal and machine works, among the various branches of St. Petersburg industry, that showed any serious signs of steady growth during these years. But their dynamism offset the stagnation or wavering of other branches to such an extent that the overall decline of Russian industry in the early 1860's was not experienced in the capital.

Available evidence suggests that general industrial trends in St. Petersburg did not change significantly between 1865 and the end of 1868, the last year of the decade for which the data are comparable (see Table 6). As indicated, the number of factories continued to drop, the number of workers continued to increase through 1866, though it then dropped during 1867–68, and the

* In 1863 they included the following industries, grouped according to the average number of workers per factory. Fifty to one hundred workers: gas works, rope factroies, carpentry shops. Sixteen to fifty workers: dye and bleach works, carriage factories, hat factories, factories manufacturing bronze and silver articles, tapestry works, sawmills, copper works, vodka factories, button factories, sculpture works, quilt works. Fifteen workers or fewer: manufacturers of approximately twenty other items, ranging from pianos to macaroni. S-PSK, *Fabriki i zavody, 1863*, p. 40.

TABLE 6

St. Petersburg Industry, 1865–68

Year	Number of Workers	Number of Factories	Value of Output (in rubles)	Average Output per Factory (in rubles)
1865	20,448	315	42,867,618	136,405
1866	21,606	309	36,794,793	119,077
1867	—	—	—	—
1868	20,600	285	34,010,677	119,336

SOURCE: TsGIAL, *f.* 1263, *op.* 1: *d.* 3263, pp. 93–100; *d.* 3332, pp. 209–10; TsSKMVD, *Statisticheskii vremennik*, series II, issue 6, pp. 1, 128–29.

NOTE: *Statisticheskii vremennik* does not include breweries, sugar refineries, or tobacco factories, that is, industries subject to special excise taxes. Since these industries are omitted for 1868, I have also eliminated them from the figures given for 1865 (which accounts for the discrepancy between these figures and those in Table 1) and 1866. No data at all are available for 1867. Had these industries been included, the figures for value of output and average output per factory would, of course, be considerably higher, since St. Petersburg's five sugar refineries produced well over ten million rubles worth of sugar. A very rough estimate, computed by projecting the 1866 figures for breweries, refineries, and tobacco factories to 1868 (admittedly a dubious procedure), would result in approximately 25,000 workers, 330 factories, and a fifty million ruble output for that year, indicating an average output per factory of somewhat over 150,000 rubles. By comparing these figures with the figures for 1861 given in Table 1, one finds that from 1861 to 1868 the number of factory workers employed in St. Petersburg would have increased by more than 6,000 (over 30 per cent), the number of factories would have declined by about 90 (22 per cent), the output would have risen by over fourteen million rubles (40 per cent), and the average output per factory would have risen by 63,000 rubles (72 per cent).

average number of workers per factory continued to rise. The only notable changes in the industrial trend after 1865 were a decline in the value of output back to a level below that of 1865, and an initial drop, followed by a leveling off, in the average annual value of output per factory. And even these changes were not of general significance, no doubt reflecting little more than the normalization (i.e. lowering) of the price of cotton after 1865.* The fall in value of output in the cotton-spinning industry exceeded the total decline by well over a million rubles; so, with the exception of that one important branch, the overall and average value of industrial output in St. Petersburg were actually rising. Since there is good reason to believe that the fall in the value of cotton thread produced after 1865 reflected the downward shift in cotton prices after the American Civil War rather than a real fall in the volume of production,

---

* Evidence for the fall in prices of spun cotton beginning in 1865 is indirect, that is, it is derived from figures showing a steady drop in the average value of spun cotton produced by one worker in a year: 2,614 rubles in 1864, 2,010 rubles in 1865, 1,810 rubles in 1866, and 1,733 rubles in 1868. It is highly unlikely that such a drop represented a real decline in the productivity of labor in an age of increasing mechanization.

it is safe to conclude that the total volume of industrial production and the average output per factory in St. Petersburg actually rose somewhat between 1866 and 1868.[38] Thus the general trends of the first half of the decade seem to have been sustained for the next few years as well: fewer factories, larger concentrations of workers, greater output per factory, and a somewhat higher volume of production.

No figures are available for the year 1870, but there are strong indications that the years 1868–70 marked an important, almost qualitative change in the industrial life of the St. Petersburg area. E. I. Lamanskii, who was then serving as director of the State Bank, was to look back on them as constituting an "epoch," a "turning point" in the entire Russian economy that "revealed the fruits of all the changes that had ensued since the beginning of the 1860's."[39] Lamanskii was referring, obviously with self-serving exaggeration, to the improvements that had been introduced in the field of banking and credit, and to the rapid development of Russia's railroad network, in part attributable to the improved financial situation, that took place during the years he mentioned.* What this meant for St. Petersburg was a notable increase in the importance of railroad equipment—both rolling stock and track—to the heavy industry of the region.

No real progress had been made in the area of the production of railroad equipment between the end of the Crimean War and Austro-Prussian War of 1866. Indeed, the few experiments at domestic production of rolling stock—mainly in St. Petersburg—had proved unsuccessful. Even the Aleksandrovsk factory, in the late 1850's and early 1860's, was devoted more to the repair of existing equipment than to the production of new stock. The Crimean campaign had intensified official interest in the expansion of Russia's embryonic railroads, but the government continued to choose the cheaper though politically hazardous route of encouraging private

---

* In 1861 Russia had had only 1,422 versts of railroad line (one verst is approximately equal to two-thirds of a mile). Of this, 818 versts were privately owned, 604 versts were government owned. An additional 1,321 versts were under construction. Ten years later 10,959 versts of track had been completed (almost all of it owned by private concessionaires) and an additional 1,685 versts were under construction. Of the 10,959 versts of track, over 3,800 were completed and 2,600 put into actual use in the course of the year 1870 alone. A. I. Del'vig, *Moi vospominaniia*, IV (Moscow 1913), 101, 164, 202–3, 206. Del'vig [Baron von Delwig] was the chief inspector of railroads in the 1860's.

companies to import equipment, duty free, from abroad, rather than the financially hazardous course of heavily subsidizing domestic production.[40]

After the Austro-Prussian War, in which Prussia's military capacity awed Europe, the government's interest in military self-sufficiency was revitalized, and the domestic production of railroad equipment acquired a new priority. It occupied a key position in the Finance Minister's newest plans for industrial development, approved by the tsar in 1866.[41] At the end of that year, the Ministry of Transportation (the Transportation Administration had acquired full ministerial status in 1865) designated a special commission to recommend specific steps for the development of a domestic railroad industry. A second commission followed in 1867. Among the results of their deliberations was the introduction of a new policy whereby the government would guarantee large orders for railroad equipment at several private machine works for six years.[42] In addition, in 1868 the government placed a small but symbolically significant duty on imported foreign machinery, including locomotives.[43]

For the St. Petersburg region, the immediate results of the new policy, while not spectacular, were impressive. Established machine works received substantially increased orders for rolling stock. The output of the old Aleksandrovsk factory (now owned by a private company),[44] reached the enormous value of 1,750,000 rubles in 1869.[45] In 1868 a huge new plant, the famous Putilov works, was opened on the location of an older factory that had recently been closed down. The Putilov works received the government's largest order for rails that year (2,800,000 puds), and was soon producing two million puds of steel-capped iron rails per annum. By the middle of 1870 it had completed its four millionth pud of rail and was employing by far the largest labor force in the entire region—2,500 workers.[46]

Moreover, the growth of St. Petersburg's heavy industry stimulated by railroad construction was paralleled by an upsurge in armaments production that was strongly encouraged by the War Ministry, still pressing for military self-sufficiency.[47] The Obukhov works, for example, raised the ruble value of its ouput from only 10,316 in 1865 to 77,889 in 1867, to 273,007 in 1870, to 784,838 in 1871.[48] By 1869 the Nevskii works was employing some 1,200 workers, using steam-driven machinery with a total capacity of 400 H.P., and producing 575,000 rubles worth of warships and other armaments.[49] In addition, a new munitions factory was established in St. Petersburg in 1866, another was established in 1869, and the St. Petersburg Arsenal was reconstructed and modernized in 1870. The last two were equipped with steam engines and locomobiles with a combined total of at least 440 H.P.[50]

Finally, in 1869, for the first time in the entire decade, the number of factories in St. Petersburg actually rose. The census of 1869 listed a total of 387 factories in the city.[51] If, for purposes of comparison with Table 6, we subtract those factories that were subject to special excise taxes, the total for 1869 was 340, a rise of 55 over the total for the previous year.* Thus in one year the number of factories had jumped from the lowest total in the decade to the highest figure it had reached since the emancipation. This was a significant reversal of the previous pattern, as for the first time St. Petersburg industry was expanding in every respect.

By the end of the decade, St. Petersburg was without doubt Russia's single most important and dynamic center of heavy industry, much of it mechanized. Its progress, of course, was only relative. The Russian economy was still heavily dependent on imports for both armaments and railroad equipment. But to the extent that this picture was beginning to change, it was the St. Petersburg region that was leading the way.

To summarize the industrial situation of St. Petersburg in the 1860's: In general the city had been able to weather the storm of industrial difficulties that beset the country as a whole immediately after the emancipation and during the American Civil War. Industry was growing, although modestly in most branches. In some industries new jobs were gradually being created even while the number of factories declined. Two leading branches of industry in particular, cotton spinning and the production of heavy metal products and machines, were characterized by both larger concentrations of workers and increased mechanization. In both these respects they had clearly come to dominate the city's industrial life, with heavy industry the more dynamic of the two branches. An intermediate group of factories was important from the point of view

---

* One might also compare the 387 figure with the total of 353 for 1866, when factories subject to excise taxes were included. TsGIAL, f. 1263, op. 1, d. 3332, p. 15.

of value of output and the concentration of labor, but generally these industries were not mechanized. Finally, in sheer numbers, the smaller, rather primitive workshops continued to prevail; for side by side with the most modern mechanized metalworks there existed scores of tiny workshops, many of them classified as "factories," but in some cases having as few as four or five employees. There were shelters in the city where the intimacies of village life could be reproduced and there were impersonal conglomerations of human labor that foreshadowed the twentieth century.

Location of Factories

In the early 1860's the province (*guberniia*) of St. Petersburg occupied 39,140 square versts, or approximately 26,000 square miles. It was divided administratively into eight districts (*uezdy*) and thirteen cities. St. Petersburg uezd, though small in size (1,583 square versts or approximately 1,000 square miles), was the most important district, because the Imperial capital, though administratively separate, was located there.[52] The city of St. Petersburg, which had its own government, contained some 46 per cent of the population of the province[53] and had far greater industrial capacity than the eight uezdy and the twelve other cities taken together. (Table 7 compares the number of factories and the ruble value of their out-

TABLE 7

*Factories and Industrial Output in St. Petersburg City
and St. Petersburg Province, 1861–66*

	St. Petersburg City		St. Petersburg Province (less the city)	
Year	Factories	Output (in millions of rubles)	Factories	Output (in millions of rubles)
1861	405	35.8	282	19.4
1862	380*	37.2	300	14.4
1863	380*	46.5*	251	15.0
1864	364*	48.4*	230	20.6
1865	361	57.2	246	19.4
1866	354	55.6	243	19.4

SOURCE: TsGIAL, *f.* 1281, Sovet Ministra Vnutrennikh Del, *op.* 6: *d.* 45, "Po otchetu o sosto-ianii S. Peterburgskoi gub." (1861), pp. 58–64; *d.* 69 (1862), pp. 65–71; *d.* 52 (1863), pp. 74–76; *op.* 7: *d.* 48 (1864), pp. 69–75; *d.* 49 (1865), pp. 6–7, 90–99; *d.* 70 (1866), pp. 5–6, 91; see also TsGIAL, *f.* 1263, *op.* 1, *d.* 3332, p. 14, and Table 1 above. Dates in parentheses indicate the years covered in the reports. The reports on St. Petersburg province are the annual reports of the provincial governor. The reports for 1863 and 1864 are copies.

NOTE: Asterisks indicate a mean between two divergent figures.

put in St. Petersburg city with the corresponding figures for the rest of the province.)

The combined industrial importance of the city and uezd of St. Petersburg becomes obvious when one considers that the most important factories in St. Petersburg province, apart from those in the city, were located in St. Petersburg uezd,* mainly in the outlying areas that surrounded the city. These areas, together with the city proper, formed a single great industrial complex. Outside it there were no really large-scale industrial enterprises to be found in St. Petersburg province except in the city of Schlüsselburg,[54] which was situated on Lake Ladoga at the mouth of the Neva River. And even Schlüsselburg, since it was the terminus of the highway that stretched between it and the capital at a distance of some twenty-five miles (the river connection was somewhat longer), was closely tied to the industry of St. Petersburg city and its suburbs.

The city and its suburbs, then, constituted an island of industry and population in a province that was only moderately industrial and lightly populated. Within the city itself, however, the industrial picture was far from homogeneous; for the most part it resembled the picture sketched earlier for the second quarter of the century.[55] Tables 8 and 9 show the precise distribution of factories and workers within the respective districts of the capital at various times during the 1860's.

By the 1860's the number of administrative districts (*chasti*) in St. Petersburg had grown from ten to twelve, with each one containing from three to six wards (*kvartaly*), making a total of 53.[56] The Narvskaia district now constituted the southwestern extreme and the Karetnaia, or Aleksandro-Nevskaia, district the southeastern extreme of the city; the Obvodnyi Canal, no longer the city's southern border, cut across the two districts.†

As may be seen in Table 8, Moscow, Spasskaia, Kazanskaia, Admiralty, and Liteinaia—the five innermost districts—all had fewer

* In 1865, for example, the 76 factories located in St. Petersburg uezd, outside the city, accounted for over 60 per cent of the industrial output of the province (excluding St. Petersburg city), or nearly 12 million out of 19.4 million rubles. TsGIAL, f. 18, *op.* 2, d. 1770, p. 426.

† The following changes in nomenclature were introduced on February 25, 1865: 1st Admiralty district became simply Admiralty, 2d Admiralty became "Kazanskaia"; 3d Admiralty became "Spasskaia"; 4th Admiralty became "Kolomenskaia"; and Karetnaia became "Aleksandro-Nevskaia." *PSZ*, XL, Part I, No. 41846. Henceforth the new designations will be used regardless of the year under discussion.

TABLE 8

Distribution of St. Petersburg Factories
by District, 1863–65

District	No. of Factories			District	No. of Factories		
	1863	1864	1865		1863	1864	1865
Aleksandro-				Spasskaia	29	25	22
Nevskaia	78	72	73	Kazanskaia	25	24	24
Vasil'evskaia	61	59	58	Rozhdestvenskaia	14	14	13
Narvskaia	49	48	50	Admiralty	8	10	10
Petersburg	36	38	38	Liteinaia	8	6	7
Vyborg	31	33	29	Kolomenskaia	6	6	6
Moscow	31	32	31				

SOURCE: Based on S-PSK: *Fabriki i zavody, 1863,* p. 6; *Fabriki i zavody, 1864,* pp. 3–4; TsGIAL, *f.* 1263, *op.* 1, *d.* 3263, pp. 93–100.

NOTE: The totals listed for 1863 and 1864 differ slightly from those in Table 1, which represent a mean between somewhat varying figures in different sources. This accounting includes "factories" employing fewer than sixteen workers and producing less than ten thousand rubles worth of goods per year.

than thirty-two factories, and two of them, Admiralty and Liteinaia, had ten factories or fewer. The district with the greatest number of factories, Aleksandro-Nevskaia, was one of the outer districts, located mainly to the south of the Obvodnyi Canal and bordering the Neva River near the beginning of the Schlüsselburg Road. Taken together, the Aleksandro-Nevskaia, Vasil'evskaia, and Narvskaia districts contained half of the factories in the city. The two northernmost districts, Vyborg and Petersburg, each had a moderate number of factories. Kolomenskaia, the district with the fewest factories, was also the smallest district in area. The only border district with an insignificant number of factories for its size was Rozhdestvenskaia, to the east of the Moscow district.

The border districts of St. Petersburg thus appear to be of greater industrial importance than the inner districts, although the picture is uneven. If, however, we remove from our calculations those "factories" that by virtue of their small labor force or low output might better be classified as small workshops (i.e., establishments having fewer than sixteen workers or an annual product lower in value than ten thousand rubles), and if, then, after subdividing the remaining factories on the basis of the number of workers employed, we show the distribution of these subdivisions by district, a clearer picture emerges (see Table 9).

It now becomes evident that the number of factories in four of

TABLE 9
Distribution of St. Petersburg Factories and Workers by District, 1862 and 1865

Year and District	Number of Employed Workers	Factories with 16–50 Workers	50–100	100–200	200–500	500–1,000	1,000 or More	Total Number of Factories
1862								
Vyborg	4,429	6	1	6	3	—	2	18
Narvskaia	2,970	13	5	6	4	—	—	28
Vasil'evskaia	2,855	15	12	6	2	—	—	35
Aleksandro-Nevskaia	2,334	14	3	4	2	1	—	24
Rozhdestvenskaia	2,304	3	2	1	—	—	1	7
Petersburg	1,458	14	6	1	2	—	—	23
Moscow	1,361	9	1	2	—	1	—	13
Kolomenskaia	951	1	1	—	—	1	—	3
Liteinaia	313	4	3	—	—	—	—	7
Spasskaia	311	10	1	—	—	—	—	11
Kazanskaia	156	1	2	—	—	—	—	3
Admiralty	101	4	—	—	—	—	—	4
Total	19,543	94	37	26	13	3	3	176
1865								
Narvskaia	4,192	15	5	1	9	1	—	31
Vyborg	4,040	5	3	3	3	3	—	17
Vasil'evskaia	3,422	13	12	10	1	1	—	37
Aleksandro-Nevskaia	2,843	9	8	6	3	—	—	26
Rozhdestvenskaia	2,316	—	—	2	1	—	1	4
Petersburg	2,117	13	4	2	3	1	—	23
Moscow	1,530	5	2	12	—	—	—	19
Kolomenskaia	999	3	—	—	—	1	—	4
Spasskaia	579	4	5	—	—	—	—	9
Liteinaia	301	—	4	—	—	—	—	4
Kazanskaia	255	5	1	—	—	—	—	6
Admiralty	110	3	1	—	—	—	—	4
Total	22,704	75	45	36	20	7	1	184

Summary (1865)

4,000 or more workers	Narvskaia (11),[a] Vyborg (9)
3,000–4,000	Vasil'evskaia (12)
2,000–3,000	Aleksandro-Nevskaia (9), Rozhdestvenskaia (4), Petersburg (6)
1,000–2,000	Moscow (12), Kolomenskaia (1)
500–1,000	Spasskaia (0)
Fewer than 500	Liteinaia (0), Kazanskaia (0), Admiralty (0)

SOURCE: Based on S-PSK, *Statisticheskie svedeniia, 1862*, pp. 2–38, and TsGIAL, *f.* 1263, *op.* 1, *d.* 3263, pp. 93–100. The years 1862 and 1865 are the only ones for which sufficient data are available to make the necessary breakdowns. The figures for 1865 include some rough estimates in cases where figures for a number of factories of one type are combined in the original source.

a Figures in parentheses indicate the number of factories with 100 or more workers.

NOTE: Data here are for factories employing sixteen or more workers and having an annual product higher in value than ten thousand rubles.

the five inner districts was barely a handful. The three most highly industrialized areas (i.e. areas with the most factories) remain the same, but the Aleksandro-Nevskaia district drops from first to third position. The remaining districts continue to occupy more or less the same relative positions as before. If the districts are now considered with regard to the number of employed workers, we find that four of the five inner districts had not a single factory with 100 workers or more, and the total number of workers in these four districts came to fewer than there were in any other single district (except for tiny Kolomenskaia, in 1865). Three border districts—Narvskaia, Vyborg, and Aleksandro-Nevskaia—together with Vasil'-evskii Island accounted for nearly two-thirds of all the factory hands in St. Petersburg in 1865 (14,497 out of 22,704) and contained 41 of the 64 factories with one hundred or more workers, 21 of the 28 factories with two hundred or more workers, and 5 of the 8 factories with five hundred or more workers. In 1862, two of the three factories in St. Petersburg that employed a thousand or more workers were located in the Vyborg district (both had fallen below a thousand by 1865).

The presence of a single enormous cotton-spinning factory, the Nevskii factory (1,957 workers in 1862; 1,718 workers in 1865) accounts for the high number of employed factory hands in the Rozhdestvenskaia district. The largest factory in the city and one of the most highly mechanized, it was located in the southeasternmost sector of the district, on the bank of the Neva, just to the north of the Aleksandro-Nevskaia district, forming, in effect, an extension of the industrial complex of that area. In the tiny Kolomenskaia district on the west edge of the city, the large, steam-powered Baird machine works (862 workers in 1862; 900 workers in 1865) was, in effect, the only industry worthy of the name. Finally, in the Moscow district, almost all the industry of any importance was located in the southernmost areas near the Obvodnyi Canal. It, too, constituted part of the outlying industrial belt.

A fairly short distance beyond the administrative borders of the city were many important and large-scale industrial works, which shared the industrial history of St. Petersburg and formed a continuum with the peripheral industrial complex of the capital. Most of them were located either directly opposite the Aleksandro-Nevskaia district on the opposite bank of the Neva, or further southward along the Neva and the Schlüsselburg Road. Of the 76 factories in St. Petersburg uezd that accounted for over 60 per cent of the industrial output of provincial St. Petersburg in 1865,[57] most were located in these areas. There is perhaps nothing more symbolic of the growing unity of the merging concentrations of industry on the two sides of the city's southern boundary than the decision of the Putilov company, in 1870, to construct a small railroad network uniting docks at the southwestern edge of the city with the southeastern section of the Neva, linking both extremes with the Warsaw and Moscow railroad lines, and connecting the entire complex with the Putilov works in the Narvskaia district, the Nevskii machine works a few miles down the Schlüsselburg Road, and other outlying factories.[58] Later it will be seen that police officials as well as industrialists were beginning to recognize the significance of the interdependence between the outlying industrial areas and the industrial areas of St. Petersburg city.[59]

Composition and Movement of the Population

On December 10, 1869, the first thorough and relatively efficient census of the population of urban St. Petersburg was taken. The St. Petersburg Statistical Committee, under whose supervision it was conducted, had been well aware of the deficiencies of earlier attempts to ascertain the size and composition of the population of the city. The most serious attempt to date, that of December 1864, was the first to have collected names. But that census, though it was probably fairly accurate in its grand totals, failed to yield a detailed classification of occupations and professions, and to distinguish between the settled, more or less permanent population of the city and the otkhodniki, who wandered in and out, seeking and abandoning jobs.[60]

The census of 1869 was meticulously designed to obtain a comprehensive picture of the social composition of the capital. A special subcommittee of the St. Petersburg Statistical Committee, under the chairmanship of General F. F. Trepov, the municipal chief of police, drew up a series of highly refined and detailed questionnaires in which it attempted, somewhat in the spirit of the old Shtakel'berg Commission, to distinguish between juridical class (soslovie) and occupation (zaniatie). These two concepts having long since failed to correspond in St. Petersburg, the committee was doing nothing more than beginning to catch up with the facts of the city's economic life.

For the sake of accuracy, arrangements were made to complete the entire census in one day, December 10. On December 5 the census takers and their assistants began to station themselves in all the districts of the city. On the fringes, where, according to the authors of the census report, "mainly the poor working people—who are, for the most part, illiterate—live," the census takers personally visited living quarters to instruct the workers on how to answer the questions. Except in these difficult areas, all the completed forms were collected on December 10 and 11. In the working-class areas, where the census takers were sometimes compelled to fill in the answers themselves, the process was completed somewhat later. By December 17 the results had been verified and the basis for a serious study of the population was at last available. The Statistical Committee bragged: "The success of the census not only fulfilled [our] expectations, it even surpassed them."[61]

In order to see what changes occurred during the decade, let us briefly examine the available scattered information on St. Petersburg's population before 1869. As indicated in Table 10, the population of the city decreased significantly between 1861 and the end of 1862 (for the first time during peacetime in several decades),[62] but it was not the beginning of a trend. Between 1862 and the end of 1866 it rose or fell only slightly from year to year, while remaining below the level of 1861. With the important exception

TABLE 10
Movement of Population in St. Petersburg, 1860–66

Year	Total Population	Annual Shift	Births	Deaths	Net Migration
1860	565,421				
1861	586,293	+20,872	21,376	18,280	+17,776
1862	535,594	−50,699	19,287	18,055	−51,931
1863	539,481	+ 3,887	20,391	19,965	+ 3,461
1864	537,824	− 1,657	20,809	21,881	− 585
1865	539,122	+ 1,298	19,031	30,764	+13,031
1866	539,475	+ 353	18,012	28,070	+10,411

SOURCE: Based on TsGIAL, f. 1263, op. 1: d. 2975, pp. 30–31; d. 3046, p. 43; d. 3143, p. 37; d. 3164, p. 6; d. 3263, pp. 5–6; d. 3332 (1866), p. 8.
    NOTE: As far as I am able to determine, population was usually computed from year to year by combining the previous year's figure with the registered births and deaths and the number of passports received and returned during the year reported on.

of 1862 and the minor exception of 1864 (when the net loss was very slight), considerably more people entered St. Petersburg than departed each year.[63] The decline in population in 1862, as was pointed out in the annual report of the St. Petersburg police for that year, was caused by the uncertainty over the new situation on the land, precipitated—apparently after several months' delay —by the emancipation proclamation: "The reason for the inordinate decrease in population is the departure of nobles and temporarily obligated peasants* from the capital to make arrangements regarding their landed property."[64] Despite the reference to nobles, the overwhelming majority were, of course, manorial peasants, of which the total number in St. Petersburg dropped from 209,698 in 1861 to 140,994 in 1862.[65]

The statement in the police report is in one respect misleading. The significant decline of the peasant population of the city evident in 1862 was less a reflection of an unusually large exodus than of the failure of the usual large number of otkhodniki to arrive. If we consider the number of peasants working in St. Petersburg who reclaimed their passports from the local authorities in order to return to their villages in 1862, we find that despite the enormous decrease in population that year the number of applicants, 73,702, hardly varied from other years. In 1865, when there was a sizable net increase in migration to the city, the number of peasant passports reclaimed was almost as great—71,324. From 1861 through 1865 the number of passports reclaimed annually was never greater than 76,125 (1861) and never fewer than 70,130 (1863).[66] The great decrease of 1862 should therefore be understood not so much in terms of the large number of peasants who departed, as in terms of the unusually small number of peasants who—for the reason stated in the police report—entered or re-entered St. Petersburg that year.

The regular annual flow of peasants into the city seems to have adjusted itself rather neatly to the maintenance of a population of close to 540,000. In 1863 and 1864, when the number of births and deaths more or less canceled each other out, the number of peasants in St. Petersburg remained almost constant (about 160,900 in 1863; 161,300 in 1864).[67] A much higher death rate in 1865 and 1866

* "Temporarily obligated [vremenno obiazannye] peasants" refers to manorial peasants who were covered by the terms of the emancipation and whose obligations to their former lords were to continue for the period preceding redemption, i.e., until their share of the price of the land given up by their lords had been paid.

failed to reduce the size of the total population.* This indicates that the yearly increase in the number of arrivals compensated for the net natural decrease in population. The growth of demand for factory labor during these years—from 22,500 employed workers in 1863 to 26,100 in 1866[68]—may have been one of the factors sustaining peasant immigration, but only to a small degree, which more or less compensated for the excess of deaths over births.

Now let us turn to the findings of the census of 1869. At first glance, the most striking figure is that for total population: 667,207. Not only had the post-emancipation losses apparently been made up, but the population had risen by nearly 14 per cent over the figure for 1861 and by approximately 24 per cent over the figures for 1863, 1864, 1865, and 1866. This growth was not taken very seriously by the Statistical Committee, however, which proudly attributed the disparity to methodological progress: "This rise is mainly the result of the greater accuracy of the last census rather than a real growth in population, although there can be no doubt that the flow of population into our capital is becoming greater from year to year."[69]

One must question the judgment of the Statistical Committee in dismissing a 24 per cent rise over a three-year period (1866–69) as mainly a matter of statistical accuracy. Whatever the shortcomings of earlier counts, it is more plausible that the flow of peasant population into St. Petersburg was a principal factor accounting for the rise in population than that it was a minor one, especially since there were several different years with which to compare 1869. Moreover, even without the advantages of the Statistical Committee's techniques, the St. Petersburg police gathered data that enable one to estimate the total population at 679,257†—a figure amazingly close to the official one, which suggests that earlier fig-

---

* Although population figures for 1865 show considerably fewer registered peasants than do the figures for the previous year, it is more likely that this was due to some peasants having changed their legal status to that of meshchane or tsekhovye than that it was due to a fall in immigration; the number of persons listed as meshchane and tsekhovye increased from 1864 to 1865, and the number of passports reclaimed fell slightly. TsGIAL, f. 1263, op. 1, d. 3263, pp. 6, 48, 84–85. The transfer of peasants to urban legal status is discussed further below, pp. 229–30.

† The figure 679,257 was not actually mentioned in the police report for 1869, which may serve to explain why the Statistical Committee failed to note the close correspondence between its calculations and those of the police. I derived the figure by dividing the number of deaths reported by the police by the death rate given in the report. It is highly unlikely that the Statistical Committee's figure was available to the police at the time they made their report, which makes no mention of it whatever. See TsGIAL, f. 1263, op. 1, d. 3526, p. 199.

TABLE 11
Social Classes in St. Petersburg, 1869

Class	Population	Percentage of Total Population (rounded)	Males	Females
Nobles	94,584	14%	45,946	48,638
Clergy	6,113	1	3,249	2,864
Honored citizens	6,990	1	3,848	3,142
Merchants	22,333	3	11,851	10,482
Meshchane	123,267	18	54,415	68,852
Artisans	17,678	3	8,725	8,953
Peasants	207,007	31	142,819	64,188
Soldiers[a]	132,126	20	79,256	52,870
Foreigners[b]	38,540	6	19,125	19,415
Raznochintsy[c]	18,569	3	8,146	10,423
Total	667,207	100%	377,380	289,827

SOURCE: Based on *Sanktpeterburg po perepisi 1869 goda*, I (St. Petersburg, 1872), 110.

[a] Includes those on active or inactive duty, retired, and on leave, as well as their wives and children. According to a contemporary source, St. Petersburg had the highest proportion of military population of all European capitals. See Iu. Ianson, "Naselenie Peterburga, ego ekonomicheskii i sotsial'nyi sostav po perepisi 1869 g.," *Vestnik Evropy*, V (No. 10, 1875), 617.

[b] Includes subjects of the Grand Duchy of Finland.

[c] Includes other inhabitants without special designations.

ures arrived at by the police may not have been very far off the mark.

That a significant rise in the city's peasant population had taken place since the emancipation is corroborated by census figures on the class groupings of the city's inhabitants, as presented in Table 11. By 1869 the peasant population of St. Petersburg was over 207,000 and constituted over 31 per cent of the city's population, while the honored citizens, merchants, meshchane, and artisans— i.e. the classes designated as "urban" — came to little more than 170,000 inhabitants, or some 25 per cent of the population. Only six years earlier, in 1863, the peasant population had been estimated at 160,856 (then, too, about 30 per cent of the total population).[70] In other words, the peasant population had risen by over forty-six thousand, or nearly 29 per cent, in six years, and was growing at a slightly higher rate than the city's population as a whole (even without taking into account those peasants who had entered the ranks of the urban classes). Furthermore, since the total population of the city remained more or less at the 1863 level through 1866, the significant increase in peasant population probably took place during the three-year period between 1866 and the end of 1869.

From 1866 to 1868, as we know, the opportunities for industrial employment in St. Petersburg were contracting slightly, or at best, granting the possibility that the three branches of industry for which no information is available may have expanded their labor force somewhat, holding steady (see Table 6). It is therefore impossible to attribute whatever rise in peasant immigration took place in those years to the expansion of urban industry. From 1868 to 1869, by contrast, the evidence suggests that many more factory jobs were available, which may well have been a factor in attracting increased numbers of peasant-*otkhodniki*. Nevertheless, the job market could not have expanded at a rate that was commensurate with the growth in population, which in any case is unlikely to have taken place in the course of only a single year. If, then, it was not primarily a significant rise in employment opportunities that drew so many peasants to the capital in the late 1860's, an explanation must be sought elsewhere.

Any peasant migration to an urban area will, of course, reflect both some dissatisfaction with rural conditions and the expectation of urban employment. The question is one of degree and of relative importance. If an unusually large peasant migration takes place at a time when opportunities in the city are not especially promising, there is a strong indication that problems on the land are paramount. It is not my intention to undertake a study of Russia's agrarian problems here, but a brief look at the situation of the rural regions of St. Petersburg province, the villages of which provided the capital with a substantial number of its peasant inhabitants and industrial workers, will suggest the extent to which deteriorating conditions in the countryside encouraged otkhodniki to move to the capital.*

St. Petersburg province—one of the least fertile and most densely populated provinces in the country[71]—had experienced serious agrarian difficulties throughout the decade. In his annual report for 1860, the governor of the province had commented unhappily

---

* In 1869, most (71 per cent) of the peasants in the city came, as might be expected, from the three adjoining provinces of the Lake Region, St. Petersburg (13 per cent), Novgorod (9 per cent), and Pskov (4 per cent), and the northernmost provinces of the neighboring Central Industrial Region, Iaroslavl (22 per cent), Tver (14 per cent), and Kostroma (6 per cent). (For precise figures see Table 13, p. 237.) On the basis of the limited information available, it seems likely that agricultural conditions in St. Petersburg province were fairly typical of conditions in all these provinces. All were agriculturally weak. On the provincial origins of peasants employed as industrial workers in the capital, see Table 14, p. 238.

that agriculture was "far from that degree of development which should be expected in the vicinity of a highly populated capital city." The harsh climate, the poor soil, and the peasants' neglect of agricultural work in favor of lucrative industrial jobs in and near the capital were cited as causes.[72] The complex and distracting terms of the emancipation settlement threw the rural economy into even worse disorder, causing the size of the harvest to diminish from year to year.[73] The situation was reviewed in the annual report for 1863. It noted that with the emancipation of the peasants the pomeshchiki were less and less able to carry on as before. Although hired labor was readily available, a great many landowners—all but a tiny minority—suffered financial losses and significantly reduced or altogether gave up the tillage of their estates. The report stressed that the high cost of labor presented a great threat to the survival of the manorial economy, especially on estates near the capital, which lured peasants with the promise of easier work and higher wages.[74] The burden of the 1864 report was essentially the same, the only significant differences being that a new field of employment, railroad construction, was added to those already drawing peasants away from farming, and the scarcity of credit was presented as a further explanation of the landlords' deteriorating position.[75]

Over the next four years the reports showed few changes, except that by 1868 the situation had become sufficiently grave to justify the use of the term "famine" to describe the results of the crop failure of the previous year.[76] Early in 1868 one could read in the press that "working people, impelled by hunger, are heading for St. Petersburg in huge crowds; with the news of the opening of operations at the Putilov iron-rolling mill, there was simply no turning back the workers who gushed in, and the factory administration was obliged to drive them away with water."[77]

This description, viewed in the context of what we already know about the pace of St. Petersburg's industrial growth, suggests that the governor's reports highly exaggerated the importance of urban employment opportunities as a factor in the decline of agriculture. That claim certainly makes no sense for the middle of the decade, when the small gains in industrial employment were more than offset by a decline in employment opportunities in handicrafts.* Nor

* The number of journeymen and apprentices employed in St. Petersburg artisan shops rose slightly from 1861 to 1863, declined slightly in 1864, and then fell sharply,

is it plausible for the years 1866–68, when the level of factory employment was constant at best and the level of real wages in the city, at least among the mass of unskilled "black" workers, fell by over 10 per cent.[78] Even for the last two years of the decade—when industrial employment opportunities were indeed on the upswing—its plausibility is marred by the description of the large, new Putilov factory turning away large numbers of job seekers. News of the opening of this mammoth enterprise merely attracted a surplus peasant population that was already being driven from the land by the provincial landlords' difficulties in shifting to hired labor and by natural conditions that were generally unfavorable to agriculture. What existed in and around St. Petersburg were not opportunities for lucrative employment, but rather sufficient opportunity for some kind of employment to induce thousands of peasants to take their chances there rather than continue to face the hopelessness of the struggle for existence in the countryside.

The peasants who came to the city in the 1860's entered a highly overcrowded and rather unstable job market, one in which just enough temporary and semipermanent employment was available, for those who were willing to spend some time looking, to justify the decision to leave the countryside. The fact that the job market was unstable, it should be noted, was not necessarily a discouragement to peasant immigration. For the simultaneous rise in factory jobs and decline in artisan work, the liquidation of smaller factories in favor of larger ones as the industrial labor market gradually expanded, the displacement of men by machines under the same circumstances—all served to keep the employment situation fluid, to encourage a large turnover, and thus to increase the possibilities for obtaining temporary employment at any given moment.

This picture is confirmed by the only existing literary portrayal of industrial life in St. Petersburg: F. M. Reshetnikov's lengthy novel, *Gde luchshe?* (Where Is It Better?),[79] which was published in installments in *Otechestvennye zapiski* beginning in June 1868 (Vol. CLXXVIII). In the first half of the novel, a group of unemployed emancipated factory peasants from the Ural mining region wanders westward from the Urals in a fruitless and dreary search for

---

from 35,651 in 1864 to 28,621 in 1865. TsGIAL, *f.* 1263, *op.* 1: *d.* 2975, pp. 28–29; *d.* 3046, pp. 39–40; *d.* 3143, pp. 33–36; *d.* 3164, p. 9; *d.* 3263, p. 9. I have been unable to locate data for later years.

work. One of the most common responses to their inquiries among the peasants and workers they encounter is that "Piter" (popular colloquial term for St. Petersburg) is their best hope. Pelageia Prokhorovna, the heroine, after hearing from impoverished peasants in Kostroma and Iaroslavl that they are heading toward the capital, "where it's better," decides to go to Tver by riverboat and thence to St. Petersburg by rail (on the first train she has ever seen).[80] The situation she encounters in St. Petersburg, sometime in the mid-1860's, is confusing. When the train passes through the Tver station, she hears conflicting reports from peasants returning from St. Petersburg to their villages, but notes that even those who dislike conditions in the city intend to return there. Once in the city, she sees the many large, impressive, noisy factories, but also hears from *otkhodnik*-villagers from Tver and elsewhere that jobs are difficult to come by and life is hard.[81] Not only Pelageia, but many strong young men whom she encounters in the city have difficulty finding permanent employment. Opportunities are just sufficient to cause them to be indecisive about staying or leaving. Those with industrial skills, like Petrov, an experienced joiner whom Pelageia befriends, are in a better position; but even for them the market is tight, and they too need to have friends among the employed workers in order to be recommended for a job. The pattern for almost everyone, skilled or unskilled, is to move from job to job, sometimes with weeks of unemployment in between.[82]

Literary evidence must, of course, be used with caution, but Reshetnikov knew the milieu he depicted firsthand,[83] and the picture he presents corresponds to the situation we have already seen in documentary form. Growing poverty in the depressed provinces of northern Russia pushes peasants out in search of new sources of income. Industrial and other employment opportunities in St. Petersburg make the city a popular destination, but are not of a sufficient magnitude to absorb the peasants into a permanent urban labor force.

It may be that the expansion of heavy industry in 1868–1870 (after Reshetnikov's novel had been written) altered this situation somewhat—a possibility suggested by a slight upward turn in real wages in 1869[84]—but by that time crop failures and related agrarian problems had further reduced the likelihood that St. Petersburg industry could absorb the surplus rural population of the region.

In short, it was mainly stagnation in the provinces that stimulated the rise in St. Petersburg's urban population, and it is meaningless to posit any significant destructive influence of urbanization and industrialization on the stability of the rural life of the region, however valid such a proposition may be with regard to the history of industrialization in other countries. The peasant population of St. Petersburg may have been attracted there by news of industrial employment, but only because it was being pushed there by rural poverty. In both areas, it constituted a labor surplus. Chevalier contends in his discussion of population growth in Paris that rural economic stagnation tends to encourage migration to large cities even when the cities are themselves suffering from economic difficulties. Both at times of crisis and at times of prosperity, "the city always exerts a drawing force, even beyond its capacities."[85] For St. Petersburg, these were neither times of crisis nor times of prosperity, but times of just enough development to give the city the appearance of a crude shelter when life on the land became intolerable.

Before turning to other aspects of the composition of St. Petersburg's population, I shall make a brief attempt to shed some light on the difficult question of peasant transfers to legal urban status. No direct information is provided in the sources I have consulted. As was seen earlier, the official data on peasant movement to and from the city yield only net migration figures. They do not tell us, for example, how many St. Petersburg peasants, instead of returning to their villages, entered the local meshchanstvo, and how many otkhodniki in excess of the net gain in peasant population balanced the loss that resulted from this process. Given what is known about the manifold and complex obstacles to permanent severance from the village commune after emancipation, the likelihood that peasants moved into the meshchanstvo on a massive scale is rather small.* Nevertheless, some scattered evidence of a possible limited flow of peasants into the St. Petersburg urban societies in the 1860's exists, and will be presented here and briefly assessed.

To begin with, the two years immediately following the promulgation of emancipation saw a remarkable increase in St. Petersburg's

* The largest pool of former serfs who did not face those obstacles, former possessional serfs from the Ural region and the recipients of the "beggarly" land allotments (to which no conditions were attached), mainly in the black-soil provinces of the South, came from regions that were scantily represented in St. Petersburg. See below, p. 237.

meshchane population, by well over fourteen thousand persons. In the absence of any other plausible explanation, one must recognize the possibility that this phenomenon represented, in part, the inscription of former serfs. The difficulty with this explanation, however, is that no change in the status of former serfs was supposed to take place until 1863. But from 1863 to 1864, when the peasant population of the capital held steady, the meshchane population did likewise. Then from 1864 to 1865, with the figure for peasant population falling and the overall population holding steady, the number of meshchane and tsekhovye increased by an amount in excess of the peasant decrease. This is the first fairly convincing, albeit indirect, evidence of a definite trend among the peasants toward adopting permanent urban social classifications.[86]

From 1865 to 1869 there was little change in the number of tsekhovye, but the number of meshchane rose by some twenty-six thousand, from 97,198 to 123,267 (Table 11). Given the unfavorable ratio of births to deaths in St. Petersburg at that time, and the smaller number of peasants who were returning to the villages (as shown by the number of passports reclaimed in 1866), it again follows that at least a substantial part of the increase is attributable to transformations in the status of peasants.* Primarily, the reduction in the number of peasants leaving the city should be seen as marking the beginning of the rise in St. Petersburg's peasant population noted earlier, but it may have signified a number of transfers to urban status as well. If it did, this was barely more than a modest beginning. Whatever progress a small number of peasants were making toward assimilation to urban status by the late 1860's was overshadowed by the very obvious growth in the ranks of otkhodniki, of which there were more than fifty thousand new recruits from 1865 to the end of 1869.†

---

* For birth and death figures for 1865 and 1866, see Table 10, above. The corresponding figures for 1868 are 23,722 deaths and 18,203 births; for 1869, 22,770 deaths and 18,716 births. (TsSKMVD, *Statisticheskii vremennik Rossiiskoi Imperii*, series II, issue 12, pp. 20–23, 114–17; issue 13, pp. 20–23, 114–17.) The number of peasants who applied to reclaim their passports in 1866 was only 37,768 (TsGIAL, *f.* 1263, *op.* 1, *d.* 3332, p. 43), as compared to 70,000 or more in each of the five previous years. Unfortunately, corresponding figures are not available for the rest of the decade.

† The fifty thousand is, of course, a net increase. The actual or gross number of peasant arrivals is indeterminable, but would be much greater than fifty thousand if one took into account transfers of legal status, the permanent departure from the city by some, and the excess of deaths over births.

Other Demographic Patterns

The census of 1869 attempted to classify the population of the capital on the basis of occupation as well as juridical status. Furthermore, it attempted, with varying degrees of success, to pin down occupational areas within the different juridical categories. These efforts were in themselves a form of recognition of the archaic character of St. Petersburg's corporate structure.

It is necessary to be cautious in dealing with the results of the census, for even the smoothly functioning Trepov committee was sometimes lacking in precision. Two points must be kept in mind from the outset. First, one should not be misled into thinking that an occupation listed necessarily implied that the respondent was actually employed in that area at the time of the census. The respondents simply recorded that urban occupational area to which they felt they belonged, regardless of their employment situation at the moment. Hence the fact that virtually all adult males were identified with an occupational area in no way implies that full employment existed in the city; nor is there any way to determine the level of unemployment from the data of the census. Second, intentions aside, the committee composed the questionnaires in such a way as to make the precise determination of occupations difficult in most cases, and virtually impossible in the cases that are relevant to this study. Instead of attempting to pinpoint particular types of jobs, the committee generally confined itself to determining what I have called occupational areas, for example, manufacturing, commerce, transportation, and so forth. Thus the manager of a factory, a factory worker, an artisan, and a janitor employed in a sawmill, all fell under the rubric of "manufacturing" as defined by the census takers. The difficulties this procedure creates for those who attempt to analyze the data, the need it arouses to make some not fully corroborated assumptions about the material in order to make it workable, will soon be apparent.

The bulk of the peasants in the capital were classified under four main occupational areas: manufacturing, 93,000; domestic service, 46,000; trade and commerce, 25,000; and land transportation, 16,000.[87] Our main concern, of course, is with those involved in manufacturing, and we are immediately faced with the problem of interpreting the figure 93,000. The existence of factory owners,

administrative personnel, or proprietors of artisan shops with peasant juridical status is out of the question. Such persons, regardless
of their origins, would have been required to obtain urban status
by inscribing in an appropriate urban society or guild. Skilled
peasant craftsmen who worked alone in their quarters, producing
directly for the consumer—they were known as *odinochki* (literally,
"loners") and were mainly tailors—appear to have been too few in
number to have had a significant effect on the figures. On the other
hand, we know, because the census gives precise figures, that in certain branches of industry — textiles (spinning, weaving, dyeing,
etc.), machines and metallurgy, food, beverages, and tobacco products—almost all the peasants listed were actually operatives, either
in factories or in artisan shops.[88] We may assume, therefore, that
almost all of the 93,000 peasants listed under "manufacturing" were
actually workers broadly defined. Although there is no way to sort
out those who worked as non-*tsekh* craftsmen in artisan shops and
those who performed auxiliary functions from those who worked
in factories,* the industrial expansion that took place in St. Petersburg from 1868 through 1869, combined with a fall in the number
of artisan shops by more than four hundred over the previous four
years,[89] suggests that a fairly high proportion of the 93,000—perhaps
as many as 30,000—were factory workers.

From this point on our analysis of the results of the 1869 census
will be confined to the districts we know to have been the most industrial. As may be seen in Table 12, the industrial physiognomy
of the city in 1869 was only slightly different from what it had been
in the middle of the decade. Aleksandro-Nevskaia continued to be
the district with the greatest number of factories, and three districts—Aleksandro-Nevskaia, Narvskaia, and Vasil'evskaia—continued to harbor over half the factories in the city, the proportion
being even higher than before (181 out of 361 factories in 1865; 200
out of 387 in 1869). The most significant rise was in the rapidly developing Narvskaia district, where the number of factories had increased by 23. This figure is especially impressive when one considers that even in 1865, the Narvskaia district had the greatest num-

* The respondents were not asked to specify their place of employment. For some
branches of production, however, it is clear that artisan shops played only a minor
role, since the ratio of workers to employers was high (e.g. 88:1 in the textile industry).
See Iu. Ianson, "Naselenie Peterburga, ego ekonomicheskii i sotsial'nyi sostav po
perepisi 1869 g.," *Vestnik Evropy*, V (No. 10, 1875), 636.

TABLE 12

Distribution of St. Petersburg Factories
by District, 1865 and 1869

District	Number of Factories		District	Number of Factories	
	1865	1869		1865	1869
Aleksandro-Nevskaia	73	77	Kazanskaia	24	15
Vasil'evskaia	58	50	Spasskaia	22	23
Narvskaia	50	73	Rozhdestvenskaia	13	13
Petersburg	38	39	Admiralty	10	5
Moscow	31	41	Liteinaia	7	15
Vyborg	29	26	Kolomenskaia	6	10

SOURCE: Based on TsGIAL, *f.* 1263, *op.* 1, *d.* 3263, pp. 93–100, and *Sanktpeterburg po perepisi 1869 goda*, II (St. Petersburg, 1872), sec. ii, pp. 121–23.

ber of factory workers and some of the largest factories in the city (see Table 9).

The Narvskaia and Aleksandro-Nevskaia districts now accounted for 150 of the 387 factories in the capital, or 39 per cent. The following paragraphs will be devoted to these two southern border districts alone, the assumption being that given the failure of the 1869 census to distinguish between artisans, factory workers, and other laborers, generalizations concerning "workers" in the two most highly industrialized districts will more nearly be a true picture of the industrial labor force in St. Petersburg than an analysis based on the "workers" of the entire city.

The combined population of the two districts in 1869 was 84,140.[90] Of these, 20,775 belonged to the "urban" classes, a proportion of the total that corresponded exactly to the proportion of urban-class residents in the city as a whole (25 per cent). The number of peasants was 34,176, or more than 40 per cent of the population of the two districts. Since the proportion of peasants throughout the city was considerably lower (31 per cent), it would appear, as might be expected, that heavily industrial areas drew an inordinately large share of the peasantry. The same was true in some of the areas where a large share of the city's handicrafts was located.[91]

By occupational area, 20,009 inhabitants of the two districts were listed under manufacturing—24 per cent of the total population of the districts. (They included 3,612 in the metallurgical and machine industries, 3,542 in the textile industries, and 1,864 in industries manufacturing or processing foods, beverages, tobacco, and other provisions.) An additional 3,098 were listed under rail-road transportation, a category that included workers employed in plants manufacturing railroad equipment.[92] Combining these categories, we find that 27 per cent of the population of the two districts belonged to occupational areas related to manufacturing, as compared with 23 per cent of the population of the city as a whole. Since the number of artisan shops in the two districts was relatively small,[93] a large number of these persons, perhaps the majority, must have been employed by factories (some, of course, in other capacities than that of laborer).

Among those inhabitants of the two districts who were employed in manufacturing, the proportion of males to females was extremely high, about 4:1. Among persons in manufacturing in all districts, the proportion of males to females was about 3:1, which, in turn, was higher than the proportion of males to females among the entire population of the city, 1.2:1.[94] Thus not only was the number of men living in St. Petersburg without families extremely high among workers in general, but there were proportionally even more of them in the industrial districts. The male to female ratio among the peasants in the two districts, irrespective of occupational area, was also quite high (2.9:1), but was considerably lower than the corresponding figure for persons specifically in manufacturing.

In sum, one begins with a city where males outnumber females by a relatively small margin (1.2:1), but where the margin increases among peasant inhabitants (2.2:1), grows even higher among peasants in the most industrialized areas (2.9:1), and reaches its peak among those inhabitants, primarily peasants, who are engaged in industrial pursuits in the same areas (4:1). Moreover, if one compares the Narvskaia and Aleksandro-Nevskaia figures with those of St. Petersburg's main artisan district, Spasskaia, one finds that although the ratios in Spasskaia were also very high (2.5:1 among peasants in general and 3.6:1 among persons engaged in industrial pursuits), they were definitely lower than the corresponding figures in the two factory districts, suggesting that peasants who worked in factories were more likely to be living in St. Petersburg without families than were those who worked in handicrafts.[95]

In the Narvskaia and Aleksandro-Nevskaia districts, as in the city as a whole, it was between the ages of fifteen and twenty that the numerical gap between men and women widened significantly, while from the age of twenty to a small degree, and particularly from the age of thirty, the gap began to close.[96] The closing of the gap is attributable in part to the greater longevity of the female population, but given the early age at which it began, one may infer a tendency on the part of single male peasants to return to their villages after they had passed their prime, to be replaced by younger peasant arrivals. However, whereas in most districts the number of males and females converged during the age range fifty-sixty, in the two main industrial districts the number of women did not equal or surpass the number of men until the sixty-seventy range. Thus it may be that industrial workers were less likely to return to their villages than were other migrant male peasants, although the difference is slight.

The male to female ratio in St. Petersburg as a whole was highest for the ages of early adolescence and youth and the prime of early adulthood (i.e., 1.8:1 for the age range fifteen to twenty, and 1.7:1 for the age range 20–30 as compared to 1.2:1 for all ages). The same pattern was followed in the two industrial districts, except that in each case the ratio was even higher: all ages, 1.5:1; ages fifteen-twenty, 2.3:1, ages twenty to thirty, 1.8:1. Unfortunately, the census did not give a breakdown of age groups by occupational area or by juridical class, but since—as has already been noted—the ratio of men to women in the two districts was highest among peasants in general and among those employed in manufacturing in particular, it follows that the age group fifteen-thirty must have contained an even higher proportion of males within those categories.

Iu. E. Ianson, a famous contemporary statistician with broad humanitarian sympathies, remarked in commenting on the 1869 census: "In St. Petersburg, many persons who are engaged in production or who live off wages live without families; this homeless population constitutes no less than a third of the inhabitants of the capital."[97] It has been established that this "homeless population" consisted for the most part of young men in the prime of life.* While many of these men were simply unmarried, a substantial number were married men who lived in the city without their families. Thus of 237,844 married persons in St. Petersburg at the time of the census, only 89,750 were women while 148,094 were men.

* In *Gde luchshe?* (p. 544) Pelageia, fearful for her reputation, refuses the request of a group of young workers to move into their artel' as their cook.

It follows that at least 58,000 married men, presumably peasants, had left their families behind to come to St. Petersburg.* Although it cannot be stated with any degree of certainty how many among them were industrial workers, we do know that at least ten thousand of them lived in the two industrial districts under discussion, and that the ratio of married men to married women in those districts was even higher than in the city as a whole (1.8:1 as compared to 1.65:1; there were 22,626 married men and 12,464 married women in the two districts). As to the unmarried men in St. Petersburg (excluding widowers, divorcees, and children under fifteen), they outnumbered unmarried women by approximately the same differential (55,765) as that by which married men outnumbered married women.[98]

If the absence of family life was an important characteristic of the lower-class population of the capital, so too was the high degree of illiteracy.[99] Of 560,683 persons of all classes for whom information on literacy is available, 218,638, or about 39 per cent, were wholly incapable of reading or writing (about 32 per cent among males, 48 per cent among females). Not unexpectedly, the rate was higher, the highest in the city, among the peasant population—approximately 58 per cent (48 per cent among males, 82 per cent among females).

Illiteracy was especially prevalent in the two industrial districts (49 per cent overall; 45 per cent among males, 56 per cent among females). In sharp contrast was the heavily artisan-populated Spasskaia district, which, while it had roughly the same proportion of peasants as the two industrial districts, had the same rate of illiteracy as the city as a whole. It follows that the peasant-workers of the industrial areas figured among the least educated of the populace (a deduction that will receive confirmation from non-statistical sources in subsequent chapters). St. Petersburg had made little progress since the closing of the Sunday schools in 1862 in providing the rudiments of education for its nascent industrial working class, although the rate of literacy in the Narvskaia and Aleksandro-Nevskaia districts may have been slightly higher in 1869 than in 1865.[100] Ironically, this failure in the field of lower-class education

---

* It is clear from Table 11 that most married soldiers stationed in the capital were accompanied by their wives.

persisted despite a considerably higher ratio of teachers to children in St. Petersburg than in London or Berlin.[101]

We can indirectly confirm the extent of illiteracy among workers in St. Petersburg industries by comparing data on the literacy of peasants by province of origin with data on the provincial origins of peasants in some important branches of factory industry. The statistics in Tables 13 and 14 are only for the ten provinces from which most of the city's peasant population came and for three leading branches of industry. According to Table 13, the illiteracy rate among peasants from Tver, the province most prominently represented in the city's most important branches of industry, was 64 per cent, the sixth highest illiteracy rate among the peasants of the ten provinces. It is noteworthy that the rate was 6 per cent higher than the overall rate of illiteracy for peasants in the city. The rates for peasants from Vitebsk, Novgorod, St. Petersburg, and Smolensk provinces, who together played a leading role in St. Petersburg industry, were even worse.

Thus the impression of a backward and barely literate industrial labor force in St. Petersburg seems to be confirmed. These characteristics do not, however, fundamentally distinguish the factory workers from other segments of the urban poor; they only seem to have been intensified in the case of the workers. At this crucial

TABLE 13

*Illiteracy of Peasants in St. Petersburg
by Provincial Origin, 1869*

Province	Number of Peasants	Number of Illiterates	Percentage of Illiterates
Iaroslavl	45,180	16,056	37.5%
Tver	34,402	21,133	64
St. Petersburg	27,012	18,983	72.5
Novgorod	18,254	13,388	76
Kostroma	12,530	5,960	50
Pskov	8,168	6,164	79.5
Riazan	7,361	4,209	60.5
Moscow	6,925	3,106	49.5
Smolensk	6,314	4,254	71.5
Vitebsk	5,476	4,124	81.5

SOURCE: Based on *Sanktpeterburg po perepisi 1869 goda*, I, 118, on the basis of information from 204,347 peasants (99 per cent of the peasants in the city).

NOTE: Children under seven years old are excluded from the second column, and percentages are rounded off to the nearest .5 per cent.

TABLE 14
Provincial Origins of Peasants in
St. Petersburg Industry, 1869

Branch of Industry	Number of Peasants	Number of Peasants from Leading Provinces			
		(1)	(2)	(3)	(4)
Metallurgy[a]	7,610	Tver, 1,897	Novg., 923	Iaros., 855	St. P., 798
Textiles	7,060	Tver, 1,608	Smol., 969	Viteb., 708	Novg., 665
Tobacco	2,023	Tver, 584	St. P., 565	Iaros., 255	Novg., 171

SOURCE: Based on *Sanktpeterburg po perepisi 1869 goda*, III (St. Petersburg, 1875), 90–139.
  [a] Includes production of iron, steel, copper, and bronze products, machines, and railroad equipment.

stage of urban industrial development, not only was St. Petersburg drawing heavily on a backward peasantry for its labor supply, it seemed to be attracting an even less advanced type of worker than were other fields of employment. At the same time, it was failing to make any significant headway in the peasant-workers' education and training.

This completes our picture of the working class population of St. Petersburg in the 1860's insofar as such a picture may be drawn with statistical materials. The development of St. Petersburg industry in the course of the decade was uneven and to some extent chaotic. In the first years after the emancipation the city had managed to emerge from a fairly serious economic crisis, steel itself against a temporary industrial decline that was affecting other parts of the country, and modestly expand its industrial employment opportunities. The steadiness of this advance conceals, however, the chaotic aspect it presented to the peasant-worker. Some branches of industry thrived, and created more and more jobs, but others declined; and in almost all branches some of the smaller factories disappeared altogether. Thus while employment opportunities grew, the opportunities for steady and settled employment were uncertain. Peasants came and peasants left, and the turnover of factory workers must have been heavy. Sometime around 1866 even the modest growth in industrial jobs was temporarily curtailed, and not until 1868–70 was the expansion resumed.

Yet into this less than promising environment there streamed thousands of anxious peasants, spurred more by discontent with conditions on the land than by confidence in conditions in the city. By the last years of the decade the influx of peasants reached mammoth proportions, renewing the semi-rural character of the city's population and overshadowing the conversions from peasant to urban status. Many of the newcomers settled in the industrial border areas of the city, where they lived without families. Their incorporation into the city was only nominal, and for all practical purposes they belonged more to the industrial suburbs that stood beyond the city limits than to an urban community.

SEVEN

The Problem of Disease
and Depravity

THE SOCIAL environment of St. Petersburg in the 1860's was like that of pre-emancipation years in most respects. The expansion and growth of the industrial belt was not accompanied by any corresponding changes in municipal institutions to accommodate to the new era of "free labor." As a result, the only significant change was the deterioration and decay in the material and spiritual conditions of lower-class life during the years of industrial expansion and rapid population growth.

In the first two sections of this chapter, I will explore some specific manifestations of this deterioration and their effects on the city's laboring population—in particular the factory workers, where information is available. In the last two sections I will examine the attitudes toward these developments of two of the elements of St. Petersburg society that had most contact with them: local officials (mainly police), and members of the medical profession who were concerned with questions of public health.

These tasks are complicated by the limited and sometimes questionable sources of information. In the absence of any system of factory inspection (until the 1880's) or any recorded observations of working-class life by members of the St. Petersburg intelligentsia (until the 1870's; Reshetnikov's novel constitutes the sole exception), reports by police officials and medical doctors constitute the only available primary sources of information about the laboring population of the city. To some extent these same documents also betray the attitudes and assumptions of their authors. Any strict dividing line between the "objective" information contained in them and the "subjective" views of their authors would, of course, be artificial. Fortunately, there is sufficient consistency in the data of the police and the observations of the medical doctors to reinforce our confidence in their basic authenticity. Where the observers tended to deviate was in their evaluation of the data.

Health and Sanitation

All available evidence indicates that during the 1860's, particularly during the second half of the decade, health and sanitation levels in St. Petersburg declined. The death rate in the city had been rising fairly steadily over the last hundred years. During the decade 1771–80, the average annual rate had been 27.9 deaths per 1,000 people; by the decade 1851–60 it had risen to 42.2 per 1,000, and it was even higher (42.4 per 1,000) for the years 1856–65.[1] In the early 1860's the death rate temporarily fell,[2] leading the municipal police to boast in their report for 1861 that "many of the causes that once made the death rate so high have been removed."[3] But this trend for the better was sharply reversed in 1865, when a devastating typhus epidemic struck.[4] The death rate in St. Petersburg leaped to 57 per 1,000, and it declined only slightly in the cholera year that followed (see Table 10, p. 221).

By 1869 the death rate had again receded, to 34 per 1,000,[5] owing to a reduction in the incidence of disease (mainly cholera and recurrent fever) after 1866; but this too was only a temporary respite. Although exact mortality figures for 1870 are not available, that year saw the beginning of a resurgence of cholera and the appearance of a grave new danger, smallpox. Both diseases claimed thousands of victims over the next two years.[6]

The high susceptibility of the St. Petersburg population to disease, making it the most deadly of all major European cities,[7] reflected both the extremely crowded living conditions and the massive accumulation of filth in the lower-class areas of the city. Housing conditions were already very crowded during the reign of Nicholas I, as had been noted by investigators in the 1840's.[8] That these conditions were at least equally wretched at the beginning of the succeeding reign was freely acknowledged by Minister of Internal Affairs Lanskoi, who described the housing situation in the capital as an "evil," and encouraged the formation of a Society for the Improvement of the Lodgings of the Laboring Population by a group of prominent aristocrats and businessmen.[9] At that time—1857—there were no more than sixty-six buildings in the entire city where lodgings could be had for less than ten rubles a year, and fewer than two thousand buildings that rented lodgings for thirty rubles or less. To alleviate this situation the new society planned to build apartment houses and other types of living quar-

ters, which would be financed by the sale of stock shares, with annual profits limited to four per cent. The apartments were then
to be rented to workers at moderate prices. It was hoped that the
availability of cheap new housing would also serve to depress the
high prices of existing units.[10]

At first everything seemed to go well for the new project. In 1859
one journal wrote optimistically of the positive influence the Lodgings Society would soon be exerting on the health and strength of
St. Petersburg workers by freeing them from the necessity of living
in "crowded, filthy, dark, damp, and cold cellars and corners."[11]
But the actual results of the Society's activities were much less impressive. By 1860 it had accomplished nothing beyond the completion of the third story of a planned five- or six-story building, and
was still not renting any apartments.[12]

Whatever the successes the Society may have had in the next
few years (I have found no information on its activities after 1861),
they were modest at best, judging by the sad situation of St. Petersburg housing at the end of the decade. What appeared to be a very
favorable ratio of space to population in the city as a whole did not
hold true for most lower-class areas. According to the figures of the
1869 census, the city contained 19,432 dwellings (subdivided into
some 92,000 apartments), with an average of 27.7 persons per house.
But in reality the situation in the poorer parts of the city was much
worse: there was as high an average as 247 people per house in the
miserable neighborhood of shop workers and lumpenproletariat
surrounding the Sennaia Ploshchad', and conditions in some of the
industrial border areas were equally bad.[13]

The most characteristic form of poor and unsanitary housing in
St. Petersburg, especially after the population growth of the late
1860's, was the cellar apartment. Originally, the cellars had not
been intended to serve as living quarters, but as population growth
increased the demand for housing, they began to develop into a
new and profitable source of rent. In 1870 or 1871 Dr. F. Erisman
conducted an investigation of cellar lodgings with the assistance
of the municipal police. The investigation was limited to those
parts of the city where conditions were known to be critical, most
notably the lower-class areas of the inner city (parts of the Spasskaia
and Moscow districts) and the industrial areas of the periphery
(parts of the Narvskaia, Aleksandro-Nevskaia, Rozhdestvenskaia,

and Petersburg districts). All in all, the investigation covered about one-sixth of the cellar dwellings in St. Petersburg, which were inhabited by some five thousand persons—from which it was estimated that about thiry thousand people lived in such dwellings.[14]

Approximately 40 per cent of the cellar dwellings were flooded at the time of inspection. Almost all of them had little or no ventilation; few had adequate lighting (if any), most were cold and damp, and many were located in proximity to accumulated excrement and refuse.* These conditions, according to Dr. Erisman, were the underlying cause of frequent and widespread diseases. The darkness and dampness of the cellars produced fatigue, apathy, and susceptibility to infection from polluted air and water. The entry of polluted water into the cellars and the lack of adequate plumbing and consequent accumulation of excrement made the inhabitants of the cellars particularly susceptible to typhus and cholera, as had been noted during the cholera epidemic of the previous spring and summer. So direct was the impact of the impurities of soil and atmosphere upon the cellar apartments, that to a certain extent the cellars were acting as a buffer, protecting the upper apartments from impurities by absorbing them.[15]

The accumulation of excrement and other refuse noted by Dr. Erisman was a crucial element in the spread of disease. According to an estimate made in 1869, some 1.8 million puds (over thirty thousand tons) of filth were piled in the courtyards of the city, poisoning the atmosphere and thus opening the door to deadly epidemics. Removal procedures simply could not keep pace with the day-to-day accumulation, and impurities from courtyard latrines and outhouses easily penetrated the cheap dwellings that were most likely to be occupied by lower-class people.[16]

* Yet the inhabitants had no choice but to pay dearly for these miserable quarters. One very poor old man, for example, paid two rubles a month, in 1871 the equivalent of over three days labor for healthy young *chernorabochie* (Rykachev, *Vestnik finansov*, No. 31 [1911], p. 201), just for a corner (*ugol*) of one of the worst cellars in St. Petersburg. The entire cellar rented for ten rubles. So great was the housing shortage that the worst cellar dwellings imaginable rarely remained vacant very long, and people were even willing to pay relatively dearly to share such apartments with strangers. In at least one house that was visited, several small cellar apartments occupied by factory workers from Vitebsk province were shared by bachelors and families. Others were occupied by artisan-workers who lived and worked in the same miserable room. Worst of all were those apartments where, in order to make ends meet, the tenants rented out corners to strangers by the night. See F. Erisman, "Podval'nye zhilishcha v Peterburge," *Arkhiv*, No. 3 (1871), sec. iii, pp. 60–61, 78; No. 4 (1871), sec. iii, pp. 1, 7, 14–15.

If the lower-class or laboring population in general provided the epidemic diseases with their chief victims, how susceptible were factory workers in particular? Although no precise answer is possible, there is some evidence indicating that factory workers were especially vulnerable.

At the end of the 1850's the organizers of the newly formed Lodgings Society had deliberately chosen to reject proposals for the construction of special housing for factory workers, modeled on Louis-Napoleon's *cités ouvrières* (one of Terner's pet schemes), on the grounds that the outlying industrial areas where such settlements might be appropriate were already relatively well provided with working-class housing by local industrialists.[17] This assumption, however, proved to be oversanguine. We have already noted that along with the slum areas of the city's interior, the industrial border areas had the highest ratios of people to housing units and the least adequate, most crowded dwellings. In the novel *Gde luchshe?* the joiner Petrov, who shares two rooms near his factory with seventeen of his fellow workers, explains that it is almost impossible for a new arrival to find a place to live in the area unless he is taken in by workers from his own factory. Workers with families commonly rented a room and then sublet parts of it to relatives and friends in order to be able to pay the eight or nine rubles monthly rent (plus three rubles monthly for winter firewood).[18] In other words, living conditions among industrial workers were at least as bad as they were among the lower-class populace in general.

Information provided both by the city police and by medical doctors suggests that factory workers were heavily victimized by ill health and disease. Shortly after the typhus epidemic of 1865, the pro-industrial newspaper *Birzhevye vedomosti*, noting with consternation the high death rate in St. Petersburg, concluded that "it is mainly labor in factories and plants that hastens the death of the young people flowing into the capital from the provinces."[19] This judgment was confirmed by the local police, who sought out the reasons for the spread of cholera among factory workers in foundries and cotton mills during the epidemic of 1866. It was found that because of the extreme heat in some of the factories, workers were drinking large quantities of ice water, a habit believed to be conducive to the contraction of cholera. To counteract this danger the police encouraged factory owners to supply their workers with ordinary water, without ice, and an admixture of vodka (a rather curious recommendation in view of a recently launched campaign against lower-class drunkenness).[20]

The observations of *Birzhevye vedomosti* and of the police were generally substantiated by the investigations of medical experts. Dr. Iu. Giubner, for example, posited a close relationship between disease and industrial life on the basis of his experiences as a physician in one of the industrial sections of the Petersburg district (chast') during the cholera epidemic of 1866. According to his account, the first case of cholera in that section was a mild infection contracted by a skilled factory worker of English origin. Further investigation demonstrated that the chief centers of cholera in the area were factories and plants, including the important Nobel ironworks and the only tulle factory in the city. Together with the workers in the mint, the employees of these two factories accounted for one-fifth of all the cholera cases in that small section of the city (74 out of some 370 cases), 45 cases having occurred in the Nobel factory alone. All the workers from the two factories lived apart, in different neighborhoods, a strong indication that they had contracted the disease in their respective factories, and not in their living quarters. Moreover, in most of the houses where the disease was discovered, 99 in all, the first case was found to be one of these workers. After interviewing many of the workers, Giubner arrived at the conclusion that the source of infection was the unsanitary toilet facilities at the factories.[21]

Giubner also concluded that apart from the factory workers, the workers most susceptible to cholera were the *chernorabochie*, who were usually day laborers (*poden'shchiki*) and who almost always lived alone. By contrast the *artel'* workers were rarely afflicted with cholera, because, Giubner explained, they rarely lived in extreme poverty or hunger.* The poden'shchiki, many of whom were former members of arteli who had been expelled because of bad working habits, excessive drinking, and the like, were isolated from one another. Lacking the advantages of mutual support that the members of arteli enjoyed in times of stress, they often suffered from extreme poverty and hunger, which accounted for their low resistance and the high frequency of cholera among them.[22]

---

* On the question of the relative immunity of artel' members, there was substantial disparity between the observations of Giubner and those of the police, who singled out arteli as groups in which both typhus and cholera infections were especially frequent. See TsGIAL, *f.* 1263, *op.* 1: *d.* 3263, pp. 40–41; *d.* 3332, p. 55.

Other concerned physicians tended to be less specific than Giubner in identifying the lower-class groups whose health was affected most adversely by the conditions they described. Like the police, they used varied terms — "the working class," or "the poor class," or "the proletariat" — without differentiating among them. Dr. Erisman spoke of "the rapidly growing proletariat," "the large mass of poor," and "the poor class," using these and other terms more or less interchangeably.[23] Arkhangel'skii was particularly free in his use of the term "proletariat":

We have already seen the terrible influence of poverty on the death rate; it affects the proletariat seven times more than other classes of the population. But even among the classes that have the good fortune not to belong to the proletariat, the degrees of wealth, the degrees of ease are not equal, and a series of levels are formed from the very lowest condition, bordering on pauperism, to the wealth of a millionaire, sufficient for oriental luxury.[24]

The words "proletariat" and "working class" were often used to refer to the poor and the lowly, and neither necessarily connoted industrial workers specifically. Nevertheless, apart from Giubner, the editors of the medical journal in which the doctors published their findings emphasized the "extremely bad, antihygienic situation of the workers at our factories" over the past several years. A detailed study or description of that situation had not been undertaken, they explained, only because the factories were generally closed institutions, inaccessible even to doctors.[25] In the absence of any system of factory inspection and without direct access to up-to-date information on factory conditions, the doctors had little choice but to confine themselves to discussing the problems of the lower classes in general. When incidents revolving around the unsatisfactory feeding and housing of workers at a St. Petersburg tannery culminated in widely publicized civil court proceedings, however, the journal was quick to use the occasion to expose the problems of health and sanitation that specifically related to factory workers.[26]

Finally, a cursory examination of available information concerning which sections of the city were most badly hit in the typhus epidemic of 1865 and the cholera epidemic of 1871 reveals that although the people living in Spasskaia suffered most, those in the two most industrialized border districts, Narvskaia and Aleksandro-Nevskaia, were consistently among the most vulnerable. During the typhus epidemic Narvskaia and Aleksandro-Nevskaia ranked second and fourth, respectively, in number of persons infected per 1,000 population, and during the cholera period they had the first and third highest mortality rates. Of the five uchastki where the mortality rate climbed above 50 per 1,000 during the latter period, two were in the Aleksandro-Nevskaia district and one was in the Narvskaia district.[27] This, like the other evidence presented here, suggests that factory workers were among those who suffered most acutely from the deterioration of sanitary conditions in the late 1860's.

Moral Conduct

It is well known, if not proverbial, that excessive drinking was a perennial problem among the Russian lower classes—the peasants in particular. Past attempts by the government and by private groups to curtail the consumption of alcoholic beverages had consistently floundered. Not only was there stubborn popular resistance to all efforts to encourage temperance, but the government itself was in the difficult position of attempting to discourage a habit on which it depended for a third or more of its revenue.[28]

After the emancipation, drunkenness became even more widespread, to the extent that a prominent St. Petersburg newspaper considered it one of the first problems Russia had to face if the "moral transformation of the people" was ever to be achieved.[29] Drinking was especially heavy in the capital, where in 1859, before the emancipation, the average man spent about 16½ rubles per year on vodka—roughly the equivalent of an unskilled worker's monthly wage. In part this reflected the extremely high price of vodka in St. Petersburg, but it also reflected the quantity consumed, the average *per capita* consumption of vodka being higher in St. Petersburg than in any other part of the Empire (1.68 vedros, or about 4.62 gallons in 1859).[30]

By 1865, St. Petersburg city had as many as 1,840 taverns or public houses (*kabaki*), 562 inns, 399 alcoholic beverage stores, 229 wine cellars, and several other miscellaneous places where vodka was sold. Counting only the taverns, there was approximately one drinking place for every 293 inhabitants. An additional 163 *kabaki* were located in St. Petersburg uezd, which included the adjacent industrial suburbs. The ratio of population to taverns was clearly a function of the social and economic situation of the inhabitants of particular neighborhoods. The Admiralty district, where the upper classes tended to congregate, contained one tavern for every 639 inhabitants, the smallest proportion in the city, and in the first uchastok of that district, which was inhabited by the most prosperous persons, the proportion was even lower—one tavern for every 715 people. In the outlying industrial districts the situation was reversed: the Vyborg, Petersburg, and Aleksandro-Nevskaia districts each had approximately one tavern for every two hundred people. This does not, however, mean that the presence of factories was the main determinant of the proportion of taverns in a given area. The Narvskaia district, considerably more industrialized than the Vyborg and Petersburg districts, had significantly fewer drinking establishments in proportion to its population (1:267). Not the presence of factories alone, but any large congregation of lower-class people, whether owing to the proximity of barracks, large markets, artisan shops, or factories, brought in its wake an abundance of taverns and other sources of alcoholic beverages.[31]

Heavy drinking among the lower classes resulted in more and more cases of extreme intoxication, which sometimes culminated in dipsomania and death. According to Dr. Gorman, a physician who treated alcoholics in a local hospital, the number of persons treated in St. Petersburg hospitals for temporary insanity from excessive drinking rose steadily from 1861 to 1866 (that is, before the onset of the new phase in the city's population growth), as did the percentage of fatal cases among them. Another doctor, Val'kh, reported a high incidence of treatment and hospitalization for extreme intoxication, delirium tremens, and so forth, from 1867 to 1870, with an extremely high number of patients during 1870 (1,579 from January through August alone).[32]

Dr. Gorman, on the basis of his professional experience, observed that with very few exceptions the persons who suffered from alcoholism were common people and "proletarians."[33] Once again, the use of the term "proletarian" should not be interpreted too narrowly; it was used to denote any poor urban working person, whether employed in a factory or not, whether landless meshchanin or immigrant peasant. Dr. Val'kh was somewhat more specific. He reported that the patients in question were almost exclusively from the "non-privileged," "unpropertied" (neimushchii) classes, specifically peasant-otkhodniki, artisans, and meshchane, all of whom labored in a wide variety of trades. Among them, chernorabochie were the most highly represented.[34] Although neither doctor specified the extent to which factory hands counted among their alcoholic patients, *Birzhevye vedomosti* offered the observation in 1864 that drunkenness among industrial workers had reached "terrifying proportions."[35] The indications are, then, that heavy drinking was endemic among the lower classes of St. Petersburg in the 1860's— probably affecting factory workers and others with comparable force.

The importance of the tavern and drink in the lives of St. Petersburg's industrial workers is heavily stressed in Reshetnikov's novel, *Gde luchshe?* There one encounters workers drinking in taverns as early as 5:30 A.M. as they await the sound of the factory whistle. Scenes of extreme intoxication are not uncommon, and the problem of excessive drinking is a frequent conversational preoccupation among the protagonists.[36] Reshetnikov describes the drinking habits of workers in the industrial neighborhoods of the Vyborg and Petersburg districts in considerable detail. There are some twenty-five working-class taverns in the immediate area. Workers from particular factories tend to become attached to particular taverns, which they abandon only when the innkeeper loses confidence in their credit reliability. The particular tavern frequented by the joiner Petrov and his comrades has about 150 steady customers from five local factories. The heavy drinking takes place on Saturday evenings (Saturday was the usual payday) after the factories have closed and the workers have gone to the public bathhouses for their weekly baths. Drinking begins at a slow pace, then builds up rapidly as the workers grow increasingly heedless of the cost. At first, joyous carousing and song characterize the workers' intoxication,* but sometimes the drinking culminates in rowdy squabbles and minor brawls.[37]

This pattern of several days or more of abstention followed by intense drunken sprees is generally confirmed by the observations of Dr. Gorman,[38] and corresponds in most details with the picture painted by another doctor, "R," who preferred to remain anonymous: harried factory workers finished their week's work on Satur-

---

* Reshetnikov's description closely corresponds to the observation of a contemporary St. Petersburg journalist that the most characteristic traits of intoxicated Russians were exuberance, noisy chatter, light-hearted dissipation, and expressions of affection. *Birzhevye vedomosti*, September 18, 1864.

day evening, took their traditional weekly baths, attended the local church on Sunday morning, and immediately began their daylong visits to nearby taverns. The period of continuous dissipation often extended throughout the following day as well, despite the start of a new work week (hence the special St. Petersburg term—*ponedel'-nichan'e*—for what is called "blue Monday" in the English-speaking world).[39] The only conflict between this description and Reshetnikov's is that the drinking begins on Saturday night in *Gde luchshe?* It is likely that both practices were common.

The rise in drunkenness in St. Petersburg was accompanied by a corresponding rise in crime, "vice," and disorder. A survey of the annual reports of the St. Petersburg city police covering the years 1861 through 1866 reveals that even while the population remained more or less constant, a large and rapidly increasing number of incidents leading to arrest and confinement took place each year: 69,000 in 1861, 73,000 in 1862, 124,000 in 1863, 121,000 in 1864, and 130,000 in 1866.[40] Thus by 1866 something on the order of one out of every four inhabitants of St. Petersburg was arrested annually, although, allowing for recurrent offenders, this estimate is probably too high.

For the most part the offenses were minor, and judging by the number of persons actually under confinement or arrest on January 1 of each year, it was rare that more than two thousand persons were under detention at any given time. Serious crimes such as murder and major robbery were few, considering the size of the population; together with "sacrilege" (the three categories were lumped together in police reports), they generally numbered from four hundred to six hundred incidents a year. The vast majority of arrests involved cases of disturbing the peace, rowdiness, begging, vagrancy, prostitution, resisting or insulting the police and, above all, drunkenness, for which more than twenty-six thousand persons were detained in 1864 and in 1867.[41] Intoxication is likely also to have been a factor in many of the offenses not officially listed as "drunkenness"; but even apart from this consideration it is clear that excessive drinking, although it did not give rise to many major crimes, did indeed represent a serious social problem in the capital.*

* Even in 1864, Nikitenko was writing in his diary (with what was evidently undue alarm): "Never, it seems, have such abominations been committed in St. Petersburg

There are strong indications that the problems of drunkenness and petty crime became especially acute during the population rise at the end of the decade (years for which total arrest figures were not available to me). The number of arrests for drunkenness reached an all-time high of 34,622 in 1869; and the number of taverns showed a significant annual increase in 1868, 1869, and 1870.[42] The problem of prostitution—closely related to drink, crime, and the presence of a large surplus male population—also intensified during these years. The number of brothels and registered prostitutes remained nearly constant in the early and middle 1860's (fluctuating between 134 and 153 brothels, eighteen hundred and two thousand prostitutes).[43] Then, in early 1868 the number of registered prostitutes surpassed two thousand for the first time; by the beginning of 1870 it had jumped to thirty-six hundred, and by the end of that year to forty-four hundred.[44] And these figures did not even take into account the growing number of unregistered prostitutes, whose increase was reflected in the rising frequency of syphilis cases (6,353 known cases in 1861; 14,895 in 1868).[45]

To summarize the conditions described thus far: the 1860's saw a general trend in the direction of crowded living conditions, poor sanitation, ill health and disease, petty crime, and depravity among the lower classes of the capital. Conditions worsened during the last few years of the decade, in part because of a rapidly growing immigrant population. Though the degree to which these deteriorating conditions affected factory workers in particular cannot be determined exactly, most of the evidence suggests that at best their experience was the same as that of the laboring population in general, and in some respects—most notably in the area of health—it may have been worse.

Attitudes and Actions of Local Officials

As was commonly the practice in European cities at the time, responsibility for keeping close watch over the health and welfare of the St. Petersburg population and for maintaining a sanitary

---

as nowadays. . . . Thievery, by day and by night, huge numbers of robberies every day and every night, drunkenness unparalleled even in Russia—to the point that drunks wander along the streets in crowds and lie about and pant like cattle wherever they fall. . . . All kinds of disorder on the streets." Nikitenko, *Dnevnik*, II, 393–94 (entry of January 6, 1864). Nikitenko was venting his fury against what he considered to be the excessive leniency of the "blockheaded" military governor, Suvorov. See also *Dnevnik*, II, 454 (entry of August 1, 1864).

environment was vested mainly in the local police. Since St. Petersburg was the Imperial capital, however, conditions there could not be viewed as simply a local problem; they had long been the subject of governmental scrutiny. As early as the 1840's, it will be recalled, the Buksgevden commission—established because of the Imperial government's alarm over the extent to which the unsanitary living conditions of the lower-classes were contributing to the spread of disease in the capital—was headed by a ranking representative of the Third Section.[46] Not surprisingly, the same problems were given high priority early in the reign of Alexander II.

In 1857, the government acknowledged the need for a systematic health and sanitation program in the capital by establishing (and reorganizing in 1860) a so-called Committee of Public Health (Komitet obshchestvennogo zdraviia) under the chairmanship of Military Governor Ignat'ev.[47] In 1864 Ignat'ev's successor, Prince Suvorov, took the further initiative of organizing a special commission, consisting of doctors and police officers, to set standards for and investigate the cleanliness of workers' housing, particularly the housing of workers who lived in arteli.[48] Although the Committee of Public Health ceased functioning in 1866, when the office of military governor was abolished,[49] it was succeeded in 1867 by a new commission on sanitation headed by the municipal chief of police, General F. F. Trepov.[50] In addition to these special bodies, the regular municipal police continued to carry out traditional routine health measures, such as the daily inspection of food sold in the city, the periodic inspection of foods consumed by *cherno-rabochie*, and of their living quarters, the medical examination of chernorabochie for possible signs of syphilis, and surveillance over houses of prostitution.[51]

It is clear from the data already examined that none of the police measures, including the sanitary commission, proved adequate during a period of growing population and widespread disease. In 1867 the police authorities candidly admitted that owing to the small number of doctors at their disposal, relative to the size of the working class,* their program of sanitary inspections and re-

---

* In 1865 there were only 623 medical doctors in the city of St. Petersburg, of whom 32 were employed by the police administration. A large majority of the 623 resided in the interior districts of the city. None of the border districts had more than forty doctors, and the highly industrialized Aleksandro-Nevskaia district had only four. TsGIAL, f. 1263, op. 1, d. 3263, p. 32.

lated measures was being carried out "very superficially."[52] And even had there been an adequate supply of medical personnel, there would not have been enough hospital space: according to one official estimate, the city was short five thousand hospital places between 1868 and 1870 (that is, *before* the new epidemics began to build up).[53] Yet, despite the inadequacy of the measures undertaken, the fact remains that health and sanitation was the one aspect of lower-class existence in St. Petersburg to which local officials attended most consistently during the second half of the 1860's.

Whether or not, in carrying out their various programs, these officials conceived of the worsening health situation in St. Petersburg as in any sense a new kind of social problem, distinct from their routine concern with the health of the St. Petersburg poor in the past decades, is a moot point. The expressions "working class" and "working classes" were frequently used in police reports to identify the major victims of disease. Thus in analyzing the typhus epidemic of 1865, the police noted that infection was most prevalent among "working-class men"; and the annual police report for 1866, in commenting on the cholera epidemic, observed that neighborhoods with the greatest accumulation of filth had been particularly susceptible to the disease and offered as its main example the living quarters of "working-class people."[54] In neither case, however, was "working class" intended to refer specifically to factory workers, as distinct from the mass of laboring poor.

This lack of terminological differentiation, which we have already encountered among the physicians, in part reflected real conditions, namely the fact that labor itself was still relatively undifferentiated. Nevertheless the actions of local officials concerned with health and sanitation reveal a growing consciousness of the special problems of industrial neighborhoods. The same police report on the cholera epidemic that was just cited mentioned that the police were attempting to stop the spread of the disease in textile and metallurgical factories. Indeed, the only national legislation promulgated in the 1860's (or 1870's) that was aimed at improving the lot of factory workers—an 1866 statute that obligated factory owners to provide hospital facilities for their workers—was a direct outcome of the cholera situation.[55]

The formation of the police commission on sanitation in 1867 did not represent any kind of sharp break from the municipal police department's traditional focus on workers in general. Individual acts of the commission—such as the continued pressuring of factory owners to conform with requirements to erect hospital facilities—do, however, suggest that the commissioners were discovering connections between new health problems and industrialization. So too does the inclusion of surveillance over hygienic conditions in factories as one of the sanitation commission's official duties.[56] Furthermore, recognition of the special vulnerability of the industrial population to diseases can be discerned in a police department analysis of health problems in the industrial suburbs. During rather serious outbreaks of smallpox, typhus, and scarlatina in St. Petersburg and the surrounding areas in 1869, the police explicitly attributed the fact that hospitals were overflowing with victims from the industrial suburbs to the "harmful conditions" of factory life to which most of the suburban population was exposed.[57] In 1872, when epidemic diseases (smallpox, cholera) were again on the rise, the municipal authorities considered it noteworthy that the epidemics seemed to spread from the outlying suburbs to the city. The police were quick to focus their attention on what Trepov called "the working classes" and to intensify inspections of places where working people gathered, among which Trepov included factories, workshops, and arteli.[58] Eventually a pattern was discerned (which had also been noted by Dr. Giubner): factory workers were the first to become infected and then became the source of infection among the working classes in general.

Despite their de facto recognition that the industrial population, together with the chernorabochie of the central city, was increasingly a breeding ground for epidemics, the police authorities were loath to develop a basic social analysis of the situation they encountered. To recognize that disease took its highest toll among the lower classes, that epidemics chose particular social groups as their primary victims, was commonplace. It was quite another thing to relate the spread of disease to the growth of industry and population in a systematic way, and to derive far-reaching and imaginative policy innovations from such an analysis. St. Petersburg officials confined themselves for the most part to making casual allusions to social conditions as a factor in the deterioration of public health, in a context that emphasized the roles of climate, soil, topography, and other impersonal forces. Thus Trepov's annual report for 1869 stressed the harmful effects of "atmospheric" conditions in St. Petersburg as an explanation for the spread of diseases, while another report emphasized the conduciveness of the spring climate to cholera.[59] Although specific pressures were brought to bear on factory owners, usually on an ad hoc basis, in no case was fundamental criticism of factory owners and other employers involved in official explanations of the prevalence of disease among the working classes of St. Petersburg. To this extent, at least, it is correct to say the police had failed to conceive of the deterioration of health as a new kind of challenge, as a part, in other words, of a "labor question" or "social question." This was equally true, as will now be shown, of police approaches toward lower-class moral conduct.

The 1860's witnessed a growing concern on the part of the St. Petersburg police with the "moral life of the people" (*narodnaia nravstvennost'*). Beginning with the formation of a special "department for the preservation of social order and calm in the capital" late in 1866,[60] the police went considerably beyond traditional modes of surveillance over the behavior of the local population and began to introduce positive programs intended to prevent any further decline in the morals of the lower classes. The initiative for these actions came from Tsar Alexander II himself, who claimed to have noticed a significant increase in "debauchery, depravity, and especially drunkenness" among the inhabitants of the capital in recent years, and in June 1866 ordered the local police to take vigorous measures to assure the maintenance of proper decorum and morality.[61]

The following year, in compliance with the Tsar's command, the police began to institute measures aimed at restricting the public consumption of alcohol, particularly on holidays, when the "common people" tended to "spend their time in the most degrading debauchery and intoxication." A complete prohibition was placed on the sale of alcohol during "people's promenades" (*narodnye gulian'ia*),* the customary holiday excursions of thousands of people, during which there was usually heavy drinking and rowdiness; henceforth only tea was to be sold at such events. Beyond this,

---

* *Gde luchshe?* describes a people's promenade: "The Thursday of Shrovetide had come, the day when workers in St. Petersburg got paid and began to promenade. Beginning on Friday everyone was on a spree [*zaguliali*]. Crowds of people dressed in their finest headed toward Admiralty Square." Reshetnikov, p. 643; see also p. 617.

the police attempted to play a more constructive role by arranging special activities during the promenades, aimed at distracting the participants from intoxication and vice. Thus on August 30, 1867, when a large promenade was scheduled for Mars Field, the police arranged for games and contests, singers and military bands, carousels, and other forms of entertainment. If the official report is to be believed, the results were excellent. By evening, a hundred thousand people had participated in the festivities without a case of drunkenness or any untoward incident. The event broke up at midnight without a single arrest having been recorded.[62]

The new police measures did not stop, however, with such attempts to divert the populace from the attractions of drink and debauchery. As part of a long-range attack on the same problems, an effort was made to enlist the support of the Orthodox clergy in strengthening the character of the lower classes (an attempt reminiscent of the approach of some government officials at the time of the Sunday school movement). As first steps, local police officers were simply ordered by their superiors to see to it that proper decorum was observed by the people when they attended church—especially during holidays when attendance was high—and to enforce local regulations prohibiting the location of drinking establishments within 280 feet of churches, monasteries, and cemeteries. These measures were taken with the aim of establishing greater respect toward religion. Further, the clergy itself was called upon by the police to accomplish the tasks that the police, by their own admission, were unable to perform. The police authorities frankly admitted that all their efforts notwithstanding, they were incapable of coping with the "decline of popular morality" which they identified as the real cause of the evils of debauchery and intoxication. The clergy, on the other hand, was equipped to handle this problem through edifying sermons. Working through the office of the bishop of St. Petersburg, the police summoned the clergy to direct its sermons as often as possible against the "pernicious tendencies that were drawing the people toward poverty, illness, and vice."[63]

In general, the police regarded a combination of repression and superficial religious edification as the basic solution to drunkenness, disorder, and vice. No attempt was made to seek out the social origin of these problems or to distinguish between symptoms and causes. This response was in keeping with traditional attitudes and practices and is not at all surprising. What demands explanation, however, is the Tsar's intervention in what was essentially a routine local administrative problem.

It was only natural that the spectacle of repeated drunken rowdiness in the capital city, in fair proximity to the Imperial residence, should arouse the concern of the Tsar. Nevertheless, the timing of the Imperial order to the Petersburg police, which—if my reconstruction of events is correct—was issued before the most serious decline in the hygienic and "moral" condition of the St. Petersburg population, suggests that other considerations may well have been preeminent.

On April 4, 1866, exactly two months before the issuing of the order, D. V. Karakozov made his notorious attempt on the life of Alexander II, thus providing the occasion for a new wave of official reaction.[64] Taken by itself, this act by a former university student of noble origin cannot explain the sudden renewal of official interest in the moral character of the lower classes of St. Petersburg. Indirectly, however, the incident was linked with other events that could not have escaped the Tsar's attention, or failed to arouse his apprehensions concerning the potential disloyalty of workers.

Late in the summer of 1865, a unique conflict had developed at a mining works in the factory village of Liudinovo, in Kaluga province (just south of Moscow).[65] The main issue was the right of the Liudinovo workers, who were recently emancipated serfs, to choose their own village elder (*starosta*) without interference by local officials. From the summer of 1865 to the summer of 1866, the villagers —through passive resistance—defended their rights so stubbornly that the Third Section and even the Tsar became highly concerned. Only a show of military force and the punishment of "instigators" finally succeeded in restoring order and obedience.

Apart from the exceptional obstinacy of the villagers, what imparted an unusual quality to these events were first, the involvement of radical intellectuals, and second, an attempt by some of the peasant-workers to establish a metallurgical factory based on principles of association, to compete with the private works in the area. At one point, two of the villagers went to St. Petersburg along with some local luminaries, including a former "peace arbitrator"* who was already under suspicion for harboring "dangerous liberal

* *Mirovoi posrednik*: a local official chosen by the gentry to assist nobles and their former serfs in arriving at detailed settlements in connection with the emancipation.

ideas." There they were introduced to some prominent radical publicists; among the latter was the well-known member of the *Sovre-*
mennik editorial board, G. Z. Eliseev, whose support was solicited
for the plan to launch a worker-run factory. In addition, they became involved (through the intellectuals who had initiated the
factory plan) in the early stages of a plot to liberate the exiled Chernyshevskii. These and related activities, the Third Section later revealed, had taken place in collaboration with a secret revolutionary
society, "Organization," members of which were consulted by the
workers while in the capital. Karakozov, the would-be assassin of
the Tsar, was known to be a relative and close associate of Nikolai
Ishutin, who headed the secret society. Thus, however naively the
Liudinovo workers had approached the problem of setting up their
own factory—they had actually petitioned the government for financial aid in subsidizing the enterprise—it was possible for the
Third Section not only to raise the specter of "communism," but,
for what was probably the first time in Russian history, to link the
activities of radical intellectuals and factory workers without departing too far from the facts (as had happened during the Sunday
school controversy).*

Although the Liudinovo workers were not urban workers, it was
not illogical for the government to conceive of the potential danger
of these events as transferable to conditions in the capital. The episode may have reinforced the already existing official suspicion of
the "working classes," leading the Tsar to order special precautions
with respect to the behavior of the St. Petersburg population, and
the police to fall back on religious indoctrination in trying to exe-
cute the order. It is noteworthy in this regard that drunkenness
and disorder, stressed by the Tsar in 1866 and the police in 1867,
had been mentioned in the official correspondence of 1865–66 concerning the incidents at Liudinovo.

Two other sets of circumstances may also have contributed to the
timing and content of the Tsar's command and the subsequent activities of the police. First, a cholera epidemic, which had been anticipated since November 1865, struck the St. Petersburg area in
June 1866, just when the order was issued.[66] It will be recalled that

* The fact that Karakozov placed a copy of his proclamation "Druz'iam rabochim"
(To Our Worker Friends), in which he justified his intention to assassinate the Tsar,
at the gates of a large St. Petersburg factory (the future Putilov factory), no doubt
added to the alarm of officials. See E. S. Vilenskaia, *Revoliutsionnoe podpol'e v Rossii*
(*60-e gody XIX v.*) (Moscow, 1965), p. 421.

the previous cholera epidemic, in 1848, had provided one of the rare occasions for relatively sustained popular unrest in the capital, and that one focus of attention of the Third Section had been the industrial areas.[67] It seems likely that memories of 1848 were revived in official circles by the coming of the new epidemic: witness the special attention that the police devoted to factory workers throughout the summer.[68]

Second, the Tsar's order came on the eve of the emancipation of state peasants, many of whom, as workers in government-owned factories, represented the last vestige of forced industrial labor. For the first time since the beginnings of Russian industrialization, all industrial labor (except for certain criminals and soldiers in a number of munitions factories) was about to become free, or, more accurately, noncompulsory. This was a particularly important development in suburban St. Petersburg, since some of the most prominent industrial enterprises there—including the Okhta gunpowder factory, the Sestroretskii armaments factory, and the Aleksandrovsk machine works — were government-owned factories, where discipline over state peasants was enforced by official factory police holding military rank. Now that these peasant-workers were to be released from direct government control, a new potential for disorder existed on the fringes of the capital.[69] Whether the Tsar or his advisers actually anticipated disorders in the summer of 1866 cannot be ascertained. What is clear, however, is that the St. Petersburg police, in carrying out their orders in 1867 and later, were remarkably conscious of the difficulties that the transformation from serf to free laborer was creating among the former state workers of the industrial suburbs.

The problems of disease and immorality, and the alleged danger of "subversive" influences on workers, all converged in the course of a jurisdictional dispute among administrative authorities that began largely as a by-product of this transformation. The most complicated situation was the one that arose at the Aleksandrovsk machine works, one of the scenes of labor unrest in 1860. Although the workers there were state peasants, the government had decided to begin their emancipation in 1861, five years before the emancipation of most categories of state peasants.* The logical corollary

* The liberation of the Aleksandrovsk workers was proclaimed in a special decree issued by the Tsar on June 13, 1861. It provided that workers who had completed twenty years of service at the factory were to be liberated immediately, those with

to the workers' liberation from servitude to the government was the abolition of the factory police, that is, the small military garrison that, under the Transportation Administration, had been responsible for overseeing their conduct. This measure was originally scheduled for the summer of 1863, but in practice the office was maintained until 1866. Thus instead of being transferred to the jurisdiction of local police authorities, as had originally been intended, the Aleksandrovsk workers continued to be held in semi-bondage for several years beyond their official liberation, in the sense that unlike other freely hired workers, they were still subordinated to extra-civil, military authorities for disciplinary purposes.[70]

This arrangement, however, was not without its advantages for the workers. Since 1861 the factory police office had been under orders from the government to provide the workers with certain services that were not to be found in most private enterprises. These included a factory school, which provided instruction in reading, writing, arithmetic, and, of course, religion to the workers' children, and a twenty-five-bed hospital with a seven-man medical staff. Indeed, it was, in part, because the police office performed these services that the Transportation Administration's Department of Railroads wished to retain it, even while acknowledging the contradiction involved in maintaining such a force after compulsory labor had been abolished.[71] Although the school had been anything but a success,* the hospital had proved indispensable to the workers during the outbreak of typhus in 1865.

Ironically, the final transition of the Aleksandrovsk workers to a free labor status in 1866 entailed the loss of this asset. By the spring of that year, only a few months before the factory police office was abolished, the hospital had become so crowded with victims of the typhus epidemic that the police chief—who had come to take

---

fifteen years of service were to be liberated in one year, and all the rest were to be liberated within two years. Subsequent to the decree, the Director of Transportation decided, in view of the labor surplus in the St. Petersburg area, to free any workers who so desired as of July 1862. TsGIAL, *f.* 446, *op.* 26 (1862), *d.* 9 (1–73), pp. 138–41. For the full text of the decree, see PSZ, XXXVI, Part I, No. 37101.

* Among the defects from which the school program suffered were the conflict between the schedule of classes and the working hours of some two hundred of the children, and the absence of an adequate school building. In 1867 all classes had to be terminated until an adequate schoolhouse was constructed *not* by the government, but by the American contractors who still administered the factory for the government. TsGIAL, *f.* 219, *op.* 1/1, *d.* 356, pp. 25, 51, 56, 57, 64, 209–12.

this aspect of his responsibilities quite seriously—requested the Department of Railroads to provide additional funds and medical personnel in anticipation of the growing threat of cholera.[72] Instead, after some hesitation, the Department ruled that although the hospital itself could be maintained, after the abolition of the factory police its staff would be reduced to a bare minimum (one doctor and one medical assistant), and there would be no expansion of funds or facilities.[73] When the transition from state to private enterprise was completed three years later, the new owners, the Glavnoe Obshchestvo Rossiiskikh Zheleznykh Dorog, found so near a total wreck where once had stood a functioning hospital that the hospital building had to be knocked down and a new structure—paid for by involuntary contributions from the workers—erected on the old foundation.[74] Thus the net effect of emancipation for the Aleksandrovsk workers was to be left helpless during a period of mounting epidemics.

Luckily for the local authorities, the painful transition to free labor at the Aleksandrovsk works passed without any active protest on the part of the workers. This was not the case at the Sestroretskii armaments factory, run by the Ministry of War, where, in 1867, the liberation of state peasants and the concomitant shift to a quasicommercial system of accounting and administration provided the occasion for the most serious disorders in the St. Petersburg region between 1860 and 1870.

The Sestroretskii workers were transformed into free peasants (organized, of course, on a tight communal basis) by an Imperial decree dated February 7, 1867.[75] Reluctant to act as the employer in a free labor market, the government now continued its pattern, dating from the Crimean War, of abandoning state-run enterprises in favor of private commercial ones. Accordingly, the factory was leased to its commanding officer, Colonel Lilienfeld, to be run on a competitive commercial basis in partnership with a local merchant-entrepreneur.[76] Almost immediately, the emancipated workers were dealt a terrible blow as a result of these changes. On March 25, 1867, when the workers assembled to collect their monthly wages, a shocking announcement was made by the factory administration. In accordance with the Imperial decree, they would henceforth be released from all obligatory labor; but together with this liberation would come a number of changes reflecting the new commercial basis on which the factory was to be run. The work force of eight hundred men was to be reduced to two hundred, and the distribution of free food and provisions, a long-standing custom at the factory, was to be terminated.[77]

The termination of food distribution was particularly grave. For some undisclosed reason probably connected with the problems of transition, the workers had not received their piece wages for eight months, and had been living from month to month, wholly dependent on these distributions. Their families faced with the prospect of starvation, the workers soon began to mill around in large crowds outside the factory, demanding that their legitimate claims be met by the unyielding factory administration. Only the intervention of the district police inspector procured temporary food supplies for workers who had been laid off, and brought about the payment of the wages due. Whether the two hundred workers who remained at the factory would continue to receive provisions in addition to their piece wages (they claimed that their wages should be raised if food distribution were abolished, since only the free provisions had enabled them to support their families at such low pay) was left to a delegation of "experts" requested by the police inspector.[78] Thus calm was restored and disorder kept at a minimum on the basis of provisional concessions obtained through the intervention of regional police authorities.

The transition to free labor at the War Ministry's Okhta gunpowder factory, decreed on December 24, 1866,[79] seems to have precipitated no notable unrest, possibly because the workers displaced there were regular soldiers rather than state peasants.[80] But when work was temporarily curtailed and many workmen were discharged at the Naval Ministry's Izhorsk Admiralty factory in December 1866, some of the workers went on a spree of theft and looting near the village of Kolpino, where the factory was located. A detachment of police was sent to investigate the disorders, leading to the arrest and punishment of some of the workers. The rest were able to return to their old jobs at the beginning of the new year.[81] In the absence of further information about this incident, it is unclear whether the shift to hired labor was involved in its origins. But occurring as it did at about the same time as the Aleksandrovsk and Sestroretskii difficulties, it fit perfectly into what appeared as an ominous pattern of turmoil in St. Petersburg's industrial suburbs, one that police officials could readily identify with the degeneration of lower-class morality.

In 1867, while the municipal police were taking steps to raise the level of morality of the working classes living in the capital, the provincial administration began to pay special attention to the problems of the industrial areas surrounding the city. Before 1867 these areas, lying outside the jurisdiction of the municipal authorities, had been administered by the police of St. Petersburg uezd, who in turn were responsible to the governor of the province. Because of the growing concentration of industry and industrial workers in this area, the feeling had arisen in the 1860's—not only within the provincial government but even among the members of the regional *zemstvo*—that a special police authority with exclusive jurisdiction over the industrial suburbs (*prigorodnaia politsiia*) was needed. As the provincial governor, Count N. V. Levashev, explained in his annual report for 1867, the ordinary uezd police had insufficient means at its command to "keep a successful watch over a mass of workers who, because of their moral condition, are in need of special surveillance."[82]

The specific plan and much of the pressure for the creation of a special suburban police authority had originated in November 1866 with Count Peter A. Shuvalov, the newly appointed chief of the Third Section. Shuvalov, a former St. Petersburg chief of police (1857–60) under Military Governor Ignat'ev, had replaced Dolgorukov when the latter resigned in the aftermath of Karakozov's attempt on the Tsar. The circumstances of his assumption of office are enough to explain both his avowed desire to fortify "moral-political surveillance" in the St. Petersburg and Moscow regions and the ease with which he was able to obtain approval for his plan.[83] As has already been suggested, the governor of the province —who specifically mentioned the difficulty he would have in coping with problems that might arise because of the abolition of factory police at the Aleksandrovsk, Okhta, and Sestroretskii factories[84]—more than welcomed the introduction of a new police administration within his jurisdiction.

The duties of the new suburban police, of course, took them well beyond the factory gates. By the end of the year 1867, their authority extended to all the suburban uchastki in the neighborhood of the capital where large numbers of workers lived: Schlüsselburg, Poliustrov, Petergof, Lesnoi, and Novoderevnia. Their activities in these areas, according to the governor's report, had immediate success, including the uncovering of a large number of crimes, the introduction of order to the streets of the more populated areas, and the return to their villages of many passportless persons who were congregating near St. Petersburg illegally (apparently refugees from the rural crisis that had recently begun).[85]

Originally the new police force was placed under the jurisdiction of the provincial governor because the areas where it operated lay outside the administrative boundaries of the capital. However, as we have noted, the industrial suburbs and the industrial border districts within the capital actually formed a single vast industrial complex ringing the administrative, commercial, and cultural inner city, from which it was essentially separate. Since the portion of this industrial region that was located within the city limits was under the authority of the municipal police, and since the municipal police was responsible not to the governor of the province but directly to the Minister of Internal Affairs (via the military governor before the abolition of that office in 1866), a rational approach to the reorganization of police authority was to recognize the unity of the industrial complex and subject the entire area, on both sides of the municipal boundaries, to the authority of the municipal police. Such a plan was put forth in 1868 by the Committee of Ministers, which recommended to the Tsar that in view of the unity of their work, the recently formed suburban police and the police of the capital should be merged. This recommendation was tentatively approved by the Tsar on September 10, 1868, without (if Governor Levashev is to be believed) prior consultation with provincial authorities.[86]

Ironically, the impulse to remove the suburban police from the jurisdiction of the governor stemmed from the same considerations of security and order that had led the governor, and others, to see the need for such a force in the first place. It was now deemed necessary to take decisive steps to strengthen the police authority in the capital as well, by elevating its status and power. The removal from office of the "soft" military governor, Suvorov, and his highest ranking subordinate, Chief of Police I. V. Annenkov (1862–66), the replacement of Annenkov by the hard-nosed General Trepov, and finally the abolition of the office of military governor itself—

all within three or four weeks of the attempted assassination—were greeted as signs that a tough, new police regime was being established in the city.[87] The elimination of the office of military governor made Trepov the highest ranking municipal official—in effect, the municipal governor (a post that was actually created for him in 1871)—while his personal stature gave him direct access to the Tsar, with whom he sometimes dealt without going through his statutory superior, Minister of Internal Affairs Valuev. Within a few months of taking office, Trepov had succeeded in obtaining large sums of money for the reorganization and strengthening of his police force, despite the reluctance of Finance Minister Reutern.[88] Little wonder, then, that when the Committee of Ministers recommended extending Trepov's awesome authority to guarding the security of the outlying suburbs, the Tsar was quick to give his approval.

Count Levashev, however, was not prepared to relinquish his authority in that area without a fight. Responding in kind, he attacked the proposed merger mainly on the grounds that retention of the suburban police under his authority was essential in order to combat subversion. A special police force for suburban areas had been organized in the first place, he argued, not only because of the dangers posed by the "density and character of their population," but also because of the need to concentrate direct responsibility for the gathering of secret information in his own office if adequate surveillance over "suspicious persons" who inhabited the areas bordering the capital were to be maintained. These "suspicious," "dangerous," and "criminal" elements, he claimed, took advantage of the confusion caused by the fact that while responsibility for surveillance over them was invested in his office, the city of St. Petersburg was completely outside his jurisdiction. Thus it was easy for them to move rapidly and stealthily back and forth between the city and the suburbs to escape arrest. Ultimately, Levashev argued, shifting to the offensive, the only real solution lay in the subordination of all municipalities in the province, including the capital, to a single authority—his own. Placing the suburban police under the authority of the St. Petersburg municipal chief of police, Trepov, was a retrogression, the results of which could only be a weakening of security in a critical region close to the Imperial family's residence.[89]

Levashev's arguments, calculated to play on what was by now a heightened sensitivity to the danger of regicide, were not sufficiently convincing to prevent some encroachment of Trepov's authority into his jurisdiction, as approved by the Tsar. The statute of July 17, 1871, that united the police and civil administrations of the capital (in the person of Trepov) into the new and exalted office of municipal governor or commandant (*gradonachal'nik*) confirmed this situation by authorizing the extension of the municipal governor's police powers to the outlying suburban area.[90] On the other hand, the jurisdiction of the provincial governor over that area was not removed; the suburban police remained formally under his command. A proposal by the new Minister of Internal Affairs, A. E. Timashev (1868–78), to turn the suburban police wholly over to the supervision of Trepov was rejected by the Council of State, which repeated certain of Levashev's arguments regarding security needs. While recognizing the practicality of eventually extending the boundaries of the capital to include some of the quasi-urban border villages, the Council of State was unwilling to divide police activities from general administrative authority. On the basis of these and other, more technical, considerations, the life of the suburban police was therefore renewed on January 1, 1871, for a three-year period, during which time it was to remain as a branch of the provincial administration.[91]

Viewed from the standpoint of the effective policing of the "morality" of the working-class population, there is some evidence which suggests that those who favored the unification of the two police administrations were probably correct. If Trepov is to be believed, the continued growth in the frequency of drunkenness in St. Petersburg at the end of the 1860's and beginning of the 1870's—that is, the failure of his much-vaunted campaign against intoxication—was attributable to the fact that the police administrations of the city and the suburbs had not yet been effectively unified. Specifically this meant that his tightened rules for the opening and management of drinking establishments were not enforced in the industrial suburbs—although he pressed the Ministry of Internal Affairs to allow him to apply them there—and the outlying areas were used by working people as "gathering places" for "limitless debauchery and drunkenness," safely beyond the reach of his police.[92] In effect, just as the provincial governor had claimed to need total police control over the city as well as the suburbs in order to provide effective security, Trepov insisted that he needed control over the suburbs as well as the city in order to supervise the morals and behavior of the working classes there. From either standpoint the unity of the industrial suburbs and the industrial border districts within the city was perforce recognized. From the point of view of health considerations, it will be recalled, the police saw the suburbs as a source of infection for the workers within the city and of the excessive influx of infected workers into city hospitals during epidemics. Now, from the point of view of considerations of security, morality, and "order," they were seen as a temporary haven for dissolute city workers and for "dangerous" persons entering the city from elsewhere—in short, as a sort of suburban conveyor belt of vice, sedition, and disease.

Conceived in a context of political fear, the approach of local officials to welfare and morality in the late 1860's represented nothing more than a strengthening of the traditional tendency to regard the problems presented by the presence of a large working-class population as essentially police problems rather than as social problems with police ramifications. In the field of sanitation, one could at least point to the inadequate but nonetheless serious efforts of the police, particularly of Trepov's commission on sanitation, with its inspections of housing and food and its sporadic attempts to improve hospital facilities at factories. But in the more intangible area of moral life, Trepov could come up with nothing more imaginative to help integrate the city's peasant-workers into urban life than arranging sober entertainment during holiday promenades, while encouraging the local clergy to preach morality and loyalty to its lower-class flock. Flickers of industrial disturbance in the suburbs stimulated not an effort to contrive new institutions for the benefit of the recently liberated workers, but a narrowly conceived jurisdictional quarrel over who would apply the old administrative methods in new regions. Whatever traces may have been left of the old official optimism could hardly have survived the last three years of the decade, when the internal deterioration of city life, far from precipitating a return of the otkhodnik population to the security of the land, was accompanied by the largest influx of hungry peasant job-seekers to date. St. Petersburg clearly had a proletariat in the worst sense (as the physicians explicitly noted, and the police repeatedly recognized with their deeds if not their words), but as yet it had neither a permanent, well-defined industrial working class, nor the institutional mechanisms—such as had been proposed by the Shtakel'berg Commission—to facilitate the development of such a class in a relatively humane atmosphere. The seriousness of this situation—far from being clear only in retrospect—was understood by a number of contemporary, apolitical physicians, men who had little influence but much experience with the problems we have been describing.

The "Arkhiv" Doctors

The measures taken by the police in the 1860's to improve health and sanitation among the St. Petersburg working classes, though unsatisfactory, as even the police admitted, nevertheless represented a small step in the direction of a public health program. There was scarcely any other group in St. Petersburg, after the Shtakel'berg Commission was dissolved in 1864, that paid as much attention as the police to the welfare of the lower classes. Even the St. Petersburg municipal duma failed to take a serious interest in overseeing hygienic conditions until 1868. In that year it offered to sponsor an organization, the "St. Petersburg Society for the Protection of Public Health," that would supervise the cleanliness of the city, procure medical aid for the sick, and disseminate information about hygiene among the masses; but even this plan had not been implemented by the end of the decade.[93]

There was, however, one group of people in St. Petersburg with an outstanding record of promoting the health and welfare of the lower-class population; this group, protected by its professional status, was able, as well as willing, to boldly criticize the inadequacies of the measures taken by the police and other government officials and to search for the underlying causes of drinking, disease, and debauchery among the laboring population. It consisted of a number of medical doctors who comprised the editorial board and contributing staff of the journal *Arkhiv sudebnoi meditsiny i obshchestvennoi gigieny* (Archive of Legal Medicine and Social Hygiene).

These doctors shared the implicit assumption of most educated Russians in the 1860's that a distinct industrial working class in the Western European sense still did not exist in Russia. They be-

gan with the commonplace but accurate premise that poor sanitation, disease, and depravity were problems of the poor in general.
Yet their research and personal investigation of the poorer neighborhoods in St. Petersburg led them to at least a limited awareness of the peculiar problems of an industrializing city, heavily
populated by a transient class of peasant-workers. Although other
people on occasion made observations similar to those of the doctors, no one did so with equal forcefulness and consistency; above
all, no one else was willing or able to transform observations and
insights into a comprehensive and far-reaching program.

The journal *Arkhiv* was founded in St. Petersburg in 1865 as a
quarterly publication. Many of its pages were devoted to specialized medical problems that are unrelated to our interests. But the
subject most consistently discussed was the health problems of the
Russian masses—most notably the misery of the St. Petersburg
lower classes, the deplorable sanitary conditions in which they
lived, and the epidemic diseases to which they were repeatedly exposed, beginning with the typhus epidemic that coincided with the
founding of the journal. It was while experiencing the devastation
of the epidemics and near-epidemics that struck the St. Petersburg
population between 1865 and the early 1870's that the contributors
to *Arkhiv*, some of whom served as medical adjuncts to the municipal authorities, came to formulate their own analysis and program.*

In certain specific respects, the reactions of the *Arkhiv* doctors to
what they observed were similar to the views expressed by the St.
Petersburg police. For instance, the police, as was noted earlier,
were well aware that the epidemics struck most lethally in overcrowded lower-class areas, that the cholera had taken a heavy toll
among overworked and exhausted industrial laborers. These and
similar observations were completely in line with the views that
were simultaneously being expounded in the pages of *Arkhiv*. But
there were also important differences. Whereas local officials looked
at social conditions only in passing, and looked to climatological
and other impersonal factors for their basic explanation of ill

* The young Russian medical profession, which dated back only to the beginning of
the nineteenth century, had displayed an acute social conscience and active interest
in the problems of the lower classes early in its existence. See Roderick E. McGrew,
Russia and the Cholera, 1823–1832 (Madison: University of Wisconsin Press, 1965),
esp. Ch. 2 and 6.

health in St. Petersburg, the doctors came to see social conditions as fundamental, and followed their observations to more radical conclusions, thus transforming themselves into at least occasional critics of the police (with whom they at times cooperated).

The first serious attempt by an *Arkhiv* doctor to link the spread of disease in St. Petersburg to social conditions was Dr. Giubner's partially firsthand account of the 1866 cholera epidemic.[94] It said nothing that could not have been found in a police report. The role of factories and the particular susceptibility of the chernora-bochie were, after all, points that local officials had already touched on. But the *Arkhiv* doctors soon went beyond such casual observations and developed Giubner's quasi-sociological approach into a more thorough and basic position (while not necessarily agreeing with him on all specifics) that eventually turned some of them into rather severe critics of official policy. Although Giubner did not indulge in any criticisms of the police in his 1868 report, this line of development was anticipated in an editorial footnote to his article.* The editors of *Arkhiv* drew attention to the freedom with which independent doctors like Giubner could attack the particular problems of the working class, and expressed regret that doctors who worked for the local police, what with their multitude of official duties, were unable to play the same kind of role. The argument was carefully worded and uninflammatory, but it did call for the use of special public health doctors to fill the critical gap that police doctors evidently could not fill.[95]

The first open attack on St. Petersburg officials for their approach toward the health problems of the poor came from the pen of Dr. G. I. Arkhangel'skii.[96] Basing his analysis on statistical data collected by the Central Statistical Committee of the Ministry of Internal Affairs, Arkhangel'skii examined the problem of death and disease in St. Petersburg not merely in connection with the recent epidemics but also in terms of the generally unhealthy and continually deteriorating conditions that had prevailed in the city for many decades. Presenting his data in a comparative framework, he reiterated the familiar view that pauperism had developed to terrible proportions in the major European capitals, that chil-

---

* The chief editor at the time was Dr. S. P. Lovtsov, who retained the position until 1871. He was then succeeded by Dr. G. I. Arkhangel'skii, of whom more will be said below.

dren in those cities had been dying in huge numbers, and that poor adults were rarely reaching old age. He then went on to show that conditions in the Russian capital were even worse, that whereas one person out of forty died each year in London, one person out of 23.6 died in St. Petersburg, with the figures for other major European cities ranging between these two extremes. Moreover, among the cities he listed, only St. Petersburg had a higher death rate than birthrate. Whereas the recent trend in the well-established capitals of Western Europe had been for the death rate to decline as population grew and the accoutrements of civilization developed, the trend in St. Petersburg had been the exact opposite. Ironically, what the natural decline of population in St. Petersburg meant was that the city in effect owed its very existence to the immigrant peasant population, the very segment of the population that was most subject to the miserable conditions of the city. The city, in other words, was absorbing but not integrating the people whose presence made possible its continued growth, even its survival.[97]

Neither Arkhangel'skii nor the Central Statistical Committee doubted that there were special features of the capital which accounted for the high mortality rate. But whereas the committee, even more than the municipal police, emphasized climatological and topographical conditions that were basically beyond human control, Arkhangel'skii (and other *Arkhiv* contributors as well) disputed this view and emphasized instead those conditions that could be eliminated through social policy. Pointing out that the deadliness of the St. Petersburg climate had yet to be established on the basis of positive climatological data, Arkhangel'skii strongly criticized "society" (a cautious euphemism for "government," in the context) for attributing "the harmful results of its own failings . . . , of its own errors and ignorance, to the influence of climate." What *could* be established on the basis of scientific data was that the extremely high death rate was primarily a function of wretched hygienic conditions, established or tolerated by the inhabitants of the city themselves. Climate, according to Arkhangel'skii, was a secondary factor that served to compound the harmful effects of these conditions. For if climate were the crucial factor, there would have to have been a natural deterioration of climatic conditions in order to account for the steady rise in the death rate over the past century, but in fact no significant changes in the local climate had taken place.[98]

Foremost among the special circumstances in St. Petersburg to which Arkhangel'skii attributed high mortality was the predominance of extremely crowded living conditions. This phenomenon was, of course, typical of most large urban centers where the population was growing, but in St. Petersburg improvements in policies of public health on a scale that corresponded to the growth in population were lacking, and the problem was compounded by the peculiar composition of the population. St. Petersburg was a city where the native population comprised something on the order of one-third of the total, while an enormous proportion, at least one-half, consisted of settlers from other parts of the province and the country who came to St. Petersburg without their families. Arkhangel'skii and the officials of the Central Statistical Committee agreed that this family-less immigrant population (sometimes referred to by Arkhangel'skii as *prishel'tsy*, roughly the equivalent of what I have been calling *otkhodniki*) provided the greatest proportion of the city's victims of disease and premature death.* But the officials whose views Arkhangel'skii was questioning then reverted to a climatological explanation of the non-native population's susceptibility to disease, namely that unlike the native population, these people were not conditioned to adjust to the harshness of the local climate. The importance of the poor and crowded conditions under which the otkhodniki lived once they settled in the capital was admitted, and there was no denying that large masses of these people were repeatedly contracting dangerous diseases in the same crowded neighborhoods and buildings. But these conditions were considered secondary in importance to the effects of climate.

In order to destroy this argument, Arkhangel'skii pointed to the simple fact that a huge proportion of the non-native population of St. Petersburg actually came from neighboring areas where climatic conditions were fairly similar to those of the capital, or where they were scarcely better: St. Petersburg province, Iaroslavl, Tver, Novgorod, and Finland. Not the impact of climate, in Arkhangel'skii's view, but the living conditions to which such persons were

---

* Similarly, the municipal police reported that during the typhus epidemic of 1865, resistance to infection was extremely low among the temporary inhabitants of the city. TsGIAL, *f.* 1263, *op.* 1, *d.* 3263, pp. 40–41.

suddenly exposed when they settled in the city provided the most convincing explanation of their special susceptibility to disease.[99]

Upon first arriving in St. Petersburg, the immigrants were no weaker or more prone to illness than the native population. On the contrary, Arkhangel'skii argued, these people, mostly poor peasants in search of a livelihood, arrived with only one solid asset: their "iron health and strong muscles."[100] It was true, of course, that the immigrant peasants were not only very poor but also very ignorant people, with little inclination to pay serious attention to their hygienic situation.* This state of ignorance was recognized by Arkhangel'skii as a serious obstacle to curtailing the spread of disease and death among them, but he refused to blame them for it; their passive approach to their own plight was inevitable in a city they could hardly think of as their own. Responsibility lay with those who had it in their power to improve the living quarters into which the immigrant population was crowded. This meant, in particular, the approximately nine thousand owners of multiple dwellings on whom almost the entire urban population was dependent for housing, as well as the local officials who, despite certain praiseworthy accomplishments, had failed to apply the necessary pressure on the landlords. A century of experience had demonstrated, Arkhangel'skii charged, that the landlords had little concern about hygienic conditions in the city, that the shortage in housing made it possible for them to rent inferior quarters without having to introduce competitive improvements, and that only official compulsion could bring about the kind of progress that was needed.[101]

Both landlords and the local authorities were held accountable by Arkhangel'skii for the tremendous heaps of refuse that had been allowed to accumulate in the courtyards of the city, a situation that had far more to do with disease, he argued, than did the general climatic conditions. The poisoned atmosphere, in turn, reinforced the apathy of the laboring population. The worker, after sixteen hours or more of physical labor in a hot workshop, would return to a cold apartment that was permeated with the toxic odors of nearby toilets and disposal areas. Faced with such conditions, Arkhangel'skii asked rhetorically, were the working people guilty if

---

* Dr. Giubner had already described the resistance of artel' workers to medical treatment and their suspicious attitude toward doctors. He claimed, however, the workers' suspicions would rapidly break down once it was seen that a few of their number had been cured. *Arkhiv*, No. 1 (1868), sec. vi, p. 12.

their sensitivities atrophied, if their thought processes disintegrated? Little wonder that they were unable to adopt a rational attitude toward the problem of improving hygienic conditions; little wonder that they turned to wine, vodka, and tobacco.[102]

It was first and foremost the landlords, the people who profited by renting substandard housing to the lower classes, that Arkhangel'skii held accountable for these conditions: "Every city is in the hands of a certain number of people on whom the cleanliness of the city depends: the landlords. They are the masters of the city, and in big cities they have at times saved the rabble from epidemics, by undertaking sanitation measures with warm compassion; but they have at times been abettors of death, by remaining oblivious to sanitary needs and, in their own properties, preparing the soil for epidemics." The doctor left no doubt that the landlords of the Russian capital belonged to the second category, the "abettors of death." Their failure to deal with the enormous accumulation of excrement and garbage was murderous for the inhabitants of the city and even for society in general, since society, as Arkhangel'skii put it, was losing many of its most productive working-class members, especially in the important age group 16–20, which experienced the greatest death toll during the typhus epidemic of 1865.[103]

As for city officials, by continuing to perpetuate the myth that climate was the main cause of diseases and epidemics, they shared in the responsibility of the landlords. Arkhangel'skii proposed that the city administration take coercive measures to force landlords to remove the accumulated filth, introduce an obligatory system of daily removals, channel pure water from the Neva River into the interior of the city through a system of water pipes, prohibit the commercial use of polluted canal water, and enforce existing prohibitions against the sale of rotten and dangerous foodstuffs. With such a program, he maintained, the migrant population could be relieved of the prevailing "unbearably wretched hygienic conditions," and the death rate in St. Petersburg could at least be reduced to the level that existed in other European capitals.[104]

Arkhangel'skii did believe that he saw some signs of movement in the direction that he prescribed. Trepov's police sanitation commission had begun to take a serious interest in the problems of the migrant population. It had already saved the lives of thousands of workers and had been willing to extend a helpful hand to the "forgotten classes." There was even hope that effective steps might be taken toward the removal of disease-producing filth.[105] But this optimistic note was almost parenthetical in the context of the bleak picture painted by Arkhangel'skii throughout most of his discussion. And the failure of the sanitation commission to embark on the kind of systematic program he envisaged was to call forth even more vigorous pronouncements by his *Arkhiv* colleagues in the ensuing years.

Other contributors to *Arkhiv* developed the same basic themes with only minor variations. The recurrence of epidemic and near-epidemic diseases in the capital over the next two years and the inability of local officials to counteract them effectively moved other *Arkhiv* doctors to follow Arkhangel'skii's example. New discoveries were made by the doctors through their work in the field, but most of the information they uncovered simply corroborated his views. Dr. Erisman, for example, while he considered Arkhangel'skii's judgments to be somewhat one-sided, invoked almost identical arguments against those who would blame the terrible results of an unsatisfactory social situation on climatic conditions, an attitude which he feared would encourage a fatalistic approach. If, on the other hand, it could be demonstrated that working conditions, housing, and eating habits were the chief factors influencing the death rate, then hopefully the public would begin to be less apathetic.[106] All the other *Arkhiv* doctors whom I have drawn on for information on disease and death in the capital—including the chief physician of the city's largest medical center (the Obukhov hospital)—shared this view of the primacy of social conditions, most of them stressing the inadequacy and filth of lower-class housing.

It is evident that Arkhangel'skii's program was not directed toward improving the lot of factory workers in particular, but the plight of the lower-class urban population in general. Like other *Arkhiv* contributors in the late 1860's, he at times took special note of the situation of factory workers (for example, he noted that although St. Petersburg women resisted infection better than men, disease was reaching epidemic proportions among women factory workers),[107] but his stress was on a generalized immigrant "working class," plying a wide variety of trades. As evidence began to mount that factory workers were being heavily victimized, however, attention began to be concentrated on them. In 1870 a widely publicized incident at a St. Petersburg tannery, mentioned earlier, provided

Arkhiv with the occasion to present its readers with a comprehensive exposition of St. Petersburg's health and sanitation problems as they related to conditions in factories. Indeed, the *Arkhiv* presentation—which appeared over the initial of the mysterious Dr. "R"[108]—contained all the elements of an analysis, a comparative study, and a program for the future.

In November 1870 a number of police officers, accompanied by a private doctor, conducted an inspection of a tannery on Vasil'evskii Island, owned by the St. Petersburg merchant Feodor Egorov. In making the rounds of the factory, the inspection team discovered not only that the living quarters provided for workers at the factory were extremely filthy, damp, and cold, but also that an *artel'* of Finnish workers employed there had been regularly using leather shavings as food with the knowledge of the factory owner.

It was quickly decided that Egorov should be prosecuted. In the absence of factory legislation, however, the presentation of a legal case against him proved to be very difficult. All that the prosecuting authorities could fall back on was a section of an obscure medical statute of 1857, which amounted to nothing more than an authorization for police doctors to maintain surveillance over the cleanliness and quality of the housing of workers (factory workers were not even specified). After ten years of virtual noncompliance and nonenforcement, precedents were lacking for dealing with delinquent employers by other than arbitrary means. The problem was further compounded by the fact that the statute contained no provision for punishment. The authorities could only present a case by arguing that the obligation of manufacturers to provide satisfactory food and housing at their establishments was implicit in the statute, and that failure to comply was therefore a punishable offense. It was eventually conceded that Egorov had a superficially tenable defense regarding the workers' consumption of leather shavings, namely that the workers had been hired with the understanding that they would be responsible for their own nourishment. But Egorov was unable to defend the damp and cold living quarters to the satisfaction of the court. Notwithstanding the vagueness of the statute, he was found guilty and sentenced to a 50 ruble fine.[109]

The Egorov incident provided *Arkhiv* with an occasion for presenting its own program for improving the situation of factory

workers. The haphazard way in which the police had handled
that case was obviously inadequate to cope with the general problems which the incident reflected. *Arkhiv* therefore called for basic
institutional changes to deal with such problems: "If we had proper
sanitary surveillance of industrial establishments," it said, "then the
workers' food would of course be one of the objects of that surveillance, and one may readily state that incidents like the one discovered at the Egorov factory would be impossible." Implicit in
this statement, and openly argued as well, was the contention that
the sanitation commission that had been operating over the past
few years had failed as an institution for maintaining the life and
health of St. Petersburg's workers. Most specifically, two basic in-
gredients had been lacking: an effective body of legislation to provide the persons conducting sanitary surveillance with a strong
basis for their actions, and a corpus of personnel to assume the special responsibility of surveillance over industrial establishments
and the sanitary conditions of the workers.[110]

Neither of these desiderata were radically new ideas in St. Petersburg. As we know, the need for factory legislation and factory inspectors (which is what the second proposal essentially boiled
down to) had been widely discussed at the beginning of the 1860's
both in the press and among various official commissions. Now,
after several years had elapsed, after urban and suburban industry
had modestly but definitively begun to enter a new stage of development, after a rapid growth of migrant population had further
stimulated the spread of disease, and after a number of *Arkhiv* doctors had begun to question the adequacy of existing institutions,
one of their number went one step further by returning, in effect,
to the abortive proposals of the past. Like his predecessors, Dr. "R"
found it necessary to approach the problem through the circuitous
route of Western European experience; unlike his predecessors, he
had at his command sufficient empirical data concerning local conditions to make comparisons vivid and meaningful.

The chief Western example used by Dr. "R" was England. The
details of his discussion of England need not concern us. I shall
dwell briefly only on the main points that he considered relevant
to Russia in general and St. Petersburg in particular.

"R" was favorably impressed by the labor and factory legislation
that had been introduced in England over the years since the Fac-

tory Act of 1833 established the factory inspectors and the nine-hour day for minors.* In his view, at the time the first of these laws was enacted in the 1830's, the situation of English workers had been similar to the "horrible" situation of Russian workers at the time he was writing. Since that time, English workers had attained a considerably higher level of health, education, and well-being, and although he warned his readers against excessive optimism by drawing their attention to the works of Karl Marx (whom he seemed to view mainly as an expert on labor conditions in England), "R" had no doubt that the significant improvement in the situation of English labor which had taken place over the past thirty-five years was attributable to the influence of factory legislation.[111]

By far the most important single aspect of English factory legislation, as "R" saw it, was the use of special factory inspectors to defend the workers from exploitation by their employers: "The establishment of government factory inspectors seems to us to be the best, the most reliable preventive measure against abuses in factories, plants, and similar establishments." Legislation alone would always remain a dead letter, unless it was reinforced by inspectors with expert knowledge. Declaring the medical police to be too overburdened with other responsibilities to be capable of doing their job properly (a view shared by his colleagues), "R" called for the enactment of factory legislation in Russia and its enforcement by a special inspectorate. Only with the introduction of this system would incidents such as the one at the Egorov factory become the exception rather than the rule; in its absence, there was no possibility of "eradicating the abuses of employers and their exploitation of the workers." He welcomed recent signs that the government, because of the "crying abuses" of employers, might be reviving its interest in introducing factory legislation; but he was fearful that such legislation would not go far enough. He insisted on legislation that would cover the areas of health, sanitation, safety, education, housing, and the length of the workday. Most important, he feared that there would be no system of government factory inspection to give the new legislation teeth. In short, the cry was being raised for a pro-

---

* Acts of 1844 and 1847, reorganizing the factory inspection system and placing further limitations on child and female labor; Enabling Acts of 1851 and 1855, establishing sanitary standards for workers' housing; Industrial Schools Act of 1861; and several other pieces of legislation, including a series of laws on health and sanitation aimed at the public in general, but particularly helpful to the working class.

gram similar to, but stronger than, the proposals made by the commissions and others between 1859 and 1864, proposals that the government had thus far failed to implement.[112]

Taken as a whole, "R's" ideas were similar in spirit to those of his *Arkhiv* colleagues, transcending them only in their programmatic detail. All of them represented attempts to apply an enlightened socio-scientific approach to the problems of the St. Petersburg working classes. These problems had become increasingly manifest since the mid-1860's, that is, since the rapid rise of rural migration to St. Petersburg had crossed paths with the development of industry. The confluence of these two streams had produced serious problems of urban dislocation, expressed most vividly in the deterioration of sanitary conditions and health. The *Arkhiv* doctors were aroused by their firsthand professional experience of these conditions, and some of them recognized, at least implicitly, the connection between the agrarian and urban situations. "R" was very explicit on this point. He saw that poor conditions on the land were creating an excessively large surplus of peasant-workers who were prepared to accept low industrial wages and terrible working conditions in the city in order to meet their financial obligations to their villages and to the state.[113] None of the doctors, however, attempted to suggest specific solutions to the agrarian side of the problem. Their only goal was the transformation of the immediate situation in the city.

The degeneration of the condition of the St. Petersburg working classes seen and foreseen by the *Arkhiv* doctors was not limited to questions of physical health and well-being. Questions of moral behavior, conduct, and character were of at least as much concern to the doctors as they were to the Tsar and the police. But whereas officials tended to view such questions in terms of the need for repression, abstinence, and superficial religious indoctrination, the doctors considered them to be as intimately related to social conditions as were problems of health. Thus to Dr. Erisman, the cellar apartments were the cause of vice as well as disease: "Doesn't our scientific, civilized society see that precisely that economic situation which forces people to spend their lives in disgusting cellars must inevitably bring in its wake every kind of crime? If society sees this, then why does it remain an indifferent witness to an evil against which active measures are needed?"[114]

Similarly, to "R," the debauchery and depravity of the Petersburg workers, so heavily reviled by the police, were not signs of low moral character so much as symptoms of societal ills. Rather than condemning what, to the officials, were disgusting or evil habits, "R" chose to interpret them as the physical symptoms of recent developments in economic life. Specifically, he postulated that the strenuousness of labor under modern economic and technological conditions created a greater demand among workers for various forms of sensual stimulation (*Genussmittel*) in order to keep their nervous systems attuned to their work, suppress their bodily pains, and provide psychic relief from the agonies of everyday life.* The problem was not so much to eradicate this unavoidable craving for sensual gratification as to channel it in a more constructive direction, to create in the people "a demand for more civilized and civilizing pleasures." What was needed to produce this demand were education, beginning in early childhood; work that taxed the intelligence, and not just the body; and leisure hours, which the laborer could devote to his moral and intellectual development.[115] Clearly this view paralleled "R's" position regarding the workers' physical health. In both cases he accepted the fact of economic transformation and progress, and in both cases he sought new means to reduce the dire consequences of this transformation to the working class.

Whereas the two authors just cited raised the question of immorality among the working classes only in passing, other contributors to *Arkhiv*—as was seen in our earlier discussion of "morality"—chose to deal with the problem more thoroughly, especially with regard to drunkenness and sexual depravity. Dr. Val'kh was particularly clear in presenting the problem of intoxication in St. Petersburg as essentially one of class.[116] *Arkhiv* doctors who dealt with the questions of prostitution and venereal disease were critical of the St. Petersburg police for underestimating the extent of prostitution and syphilis in the city.[117] More importantly, they persistently placed the spotlight on the question of causation and focused it on the social problems of the working classes.

---

* In the novel *Gde luchshe?* a conversation takes place among the workers in which some extol the virtues of the tavern and intoxication as relief from the pressures of their daily life in the capital. "In my opinion," says one worker, "things are best when you don't feel anything." Reshetnikov, pp. 610–11.

Neither police methods nor moralistic preaching, one author contended, was an adequate approach to the problem of prostitution. Rather, society must eliminate the conditions that encouraged it.[118] These conditions, as was explained in another article, stemmed from a familiar situation: the large numbers of men who came to the city alone in search of temporary employment.[119]

Another *Arkhiv* contributor, M. Kuznetsov, attempted to deal with the other side of the question. Why did women in St. Petersburg turn to prostitution? The answer, he thought, lay in their extreme poverty. It followed that "measures against prostitution are synonymous with measures against pauperism, against the exploitation of the workers' strength and labor."[120] To some extent this argument was gratuitous. Kuznetsov never really analyzed the connection between the two evils; but this only serves to underscore the ease with which, by 1870, the *Arkhiv* doctors accepted the misery of the working classes as an automatic explanation for the existence of disease and vice.

Kuznetsov was very critical of local officials. He pointed out that the municipal administration, while well aware of the extent of prostitution and of widespread venereal diseases among the working classes, had done nothing effective to deal with the problem. In 1865 the medical police committee had demanded that employers fulfill the responsibility of having their workers examined for syphilis, but Kuznetsov was unimpressed with this gesture, and spoke of the "bankruptcy of the measures taken by the government for the eradication of syphilis among the chernorabochie."[121]

Dr. "R" made a similar point by describing an incident that took place when Chief of Police Trepov requested a local physician to examine the workers of a certain unnamed factory. Before he arrived at the factory, the doctor was told by the factory clerk that such inspections were nothing more than a formality. The doctor, however, took his assignment seriously, and was surprised to find, upon arriving at the factory, that the factory administration was deliberately placing various obstacles before him. Only by doggedly persisting until he finally gained compliance was the doctor able to discover that several workers at the factory were syphilitic, a situation that the factory administration had undoubtedly been endeavoring to conceal. "R" pointed out that another, less persistent doctor would probably have ended by making a report that there were no syphilitics among the workers, not to mention the clean bill of health that was virtually guaranteed to manufacturers who hired their own factory doctors to cover up for them.[122]

The above incident was recounted in *Arkhiv* in order to buttress the case for the introduction of a factory inspection system and, more generally, to support the argument for a comprehensive system of social legislation. Either directly or indirectly, virtually all of the *Arkhiv* doctors who were concerned with the problems of St. Petersburg took this approach. The direction of development, or deterioration, that the city had been taking throughout the 1860's, and particularly during the last years of the decade, had provided them with ample evidence that a period of social dislocation and confusion had begun, and that the physical and spiritual degeneration of the barely urbanized working masses was certain to be one of its outstanding characteristics. As a small group of doctors in a city of over six hundred thousand people, they were well aware that they were unequal to the task of providing remedies without the direct assistance of the coercive power of the state. Only the state was capable of forcing those with vested interests, above all the landlords and the manufacturers, to face up to their social responsibilities. The doctors were, in effect, asking the autocracy, or at least its local representatives, to assume the burden of providing drastic improvements in the social situation of the urban poor, a burden that had been imposed on the government by its encouragement of industrialization as well as by its post-emancipation failures in the countryside.

EIGHT

The Labor Question, 1867–1870

DURING THE EARLY YEARS of Alexander II's reign, a number of loosely associated pro-industrial economists, publicists, and academicians—many of them with connections in the Finance Ministry—had become the first to manifest a serious concern with the plight and fate of industrial workers in Russia. Drawing on both practical and humanitarian arguments, these professionals had called for the development of a free, independent, and educated post-emancipation working class, guarded from the vicissitudes of free enterprise by a network of protective institutions ranging from Terner's "associations" to a comprehensive body of factory legislation. Although the termination of the Shtakel'berg Commission—whose draft legislation had embodied most of these proposals—did not end all hope for their implementation, it did mark the beginning of a hiatus in public discussion of the labor question.

Toward the end of the decade, as was just seen, the silence was broken by a number of medical doctors, whose narrow professional interest in public health eventually brought them around to a thoroughgoing discussion of the labor question. Similarly, it was their expertise and professionalism that permitted economic and technological specialists to revive their public discussion of the labor question during roughly the same years, 1867–70. Though general discussions of the labor question as it affected Russia were notably absent from the periodical press after 1863,* the government's

---

* Occasional references to "the labor question" by populist-oriented writers of the Left (especially in the journal *Otechestvennye zapiski*, beginning in 1868) were not really discussions of the labor question as defined in this study, but variations on the theme of the peasant question. Nor were they of any particular significance to developments in Russia during the period treated here. They are, however, important to an understanding of the Populist attitude toward industrial workers in the 1870's, a topic that I intend to treat in a sequel to the present study. Despite its title, V. Bervi-Flerovskii's study "The Situation of the Working Class in Russia" (*Polozhenie rabochego klassa v Rossii*), published in 1869, does not, in my view, qualify as an exception to the above statement. See below, p. 382n.

continued interest in industrial progress, especially after the Austro-Prussian War of 1866, precluded the continued silence of those persons responsible for the technical side of industrialization—economists, engineers, professors, and some manufacturers.

The mid-1860's marked the beginning of a new professionalism in Russia, which is most commonly discussed in terms of the legal and medical professions but was equally important in the areas of industrial technology, economic statistics, and other specialized endeavors related to industrial activity. In 1866 official permission was granted for people in these professions to establish in St. Petersburg, with the sponsorship and collaboration of the government, the so-called Imperial Russian Technical Society (Imperatorskoe Russkoe Tekhnicheskoe Obshchestvo), which was followed in 1867 by the somewhat less professional Society for the Encouragement of the Development of Industry and Commerce* (Obshchestvo dlia sodeistviia razvitiiu promyshlennosti i torgovli).[1] These organizations quickly replaced the Imperial Geographic Society as the natural forum or semipublic arena in which those in the forefront of Russia's economic modernization could discuss and debate such matters as tariff policy, railroads, inventions and patents, government subsidization of industry, and, inevitably, the labor question. The composition of these organizations—which in addition to professional experts included a number of prominent St. Petersburg industrialists—dictated that the emphasis in their discussions would fall more on the practical and instrumental than on the abstract or theoretical side of things. What this meant with respect to the labor question was that the concrete experience of the last several years of postemancipation industrial life would be brought to bear on their deliberations, thus providing us, in effect, with a practical test of the government's failure to encourage the development of an independent and permanent urban labor force buttressed by an up-to-date industrial code. If the practical interests of persons involved in bringing about economic modernization differ substantially from the narrower police interests of an autocratic regime, those persons may find themselves moving inadvertently in a different direction from the very government that first had promoted their activities. This was the case in St. Petersburg in the late 1860's.

* Hereafter called Technical Society and Industrial Society, respectively.

The Imperial Russian Technical Society

The Technical Society, at first the more active and outspoken of the two new organizations, was officially chartered in April 1866 and began functioning in November of that year. Its secretary and guiding spirit at that time, E. N. Andreev, was an official of the Ministry of Finance and a professor at the St. Petersburg Forestry Institute. He was also one of the liberal economists who had been consulted by Ignat'ev's commission on the labor question.[2] The Technical Society's first chairman, Baron A. I. Del'vig, was chief inspector of railroads; and its honorary chairman, whose appointment was evidently intended to symbolize the close ties between the Society and the regime, was Duke Nikolai Maksimilianovich Leikhtenbergskii (Leuchtenberg), grandson of Nicholas I, president of the Mineralogical Society since 1865, and an active St. Petersburg industrialist.[3] The Grand Duke Konstantin Nikolaevich (whose close relations with members of the circle of liberal economists were noted in Chapter 3) was considered too controversial for the position of honorary chairman, but he did become the patron of one of the Technical Society's departments.[4]

With this kind of prestigious support behind it, the Technical Society soon became an active and flourishing organization. Its charter membership of two hundred dues-paying members quickly rose to five hundred (at ten rubles each per annum). Free office space was given to it by the Ministry of State Property. More important, the Society received large contributions from individual backers, most notably from prominent railroad entrepreneurs who were anxious to curry Del'vig's favor.[5] These resources enabled the Society to begin publishing its own journal, *Notes of the Imperial Russian Technical Society*,[6] in 1867.

The participation of a number of prominent manufacturers in the activities of the Technical and Industrial Societies represented a new phase in the development of Russian industrialists as a self-conscious social group. A break from their docile past had already begun in the wake of the Crimean defeat, when the growing recognition of the importance of industry encouraged a small number of articulate industrialists to speak out on the positive effects emancipation would have on manufacturing, the need for protective tariffs, and other controversial issues. A few, we know, had even gone so far as to cautiously criticize some aspects of proposed legislation on the labor question. But these early flashes of class assertiveness had been feeble and largely ineffectual. More importantly, they had aroused hostility toward manufacturers even from those economists, officials, and publicists who were most well-disposed toward the goal of industrialization.[7]

This gap between the active industrialists and the spokesmen for industrialization was bound to close somewhat as industry rose in the order of government priorities. The healing process was facilitated because, almost from the very beginning of the postwar debate over economic issues, critics of Russian manufacturers tended to exempt the more prominent industrialists in St. Petersburg from their general attacks, even while condemning some of them for the intolerable conditions in their factories.[8]

Taken as a group, St. Petersburg industrialists could be described with fair accuracy as more advanced, sophisticated, and—at least in their public postures—more enlightened and conscientious than most of their provincial counterparts. Several of the most prominent among them had distinguished themselves by supporting Sunday schools for workers in the early 1860's. Many others had made it a point to commend labor legislation proposed by the St. Petersburg commission in 1859–60.[9] Besides taking these specific positions, a number of St. Petersburg industrialists were beginning to develop an ingratiating style of discourse that helped bridge the gap between them and their critics. As they exposed their views to the public, these few vocal, active entrepreneurs became increasingly adept at formulating sophisticated arguments, some of them already familiar in the more industrialized countries of Europe, through which they attempted to link their own needs and desires with the alleged needs of the state and of society, and to demonstrate that the policies they advocated were in the national interest.

Typically, these advanced entrepreneurs were industrialists who had recently achieved prominence in the machine and metal-processing industries by virtue of their government-sponsored efforts to develop the private manufacture of war-related products. Most were either of close foreign background[10] or, more commonly, were Russian nobles with advanced technical educations who had served in the government and still retained close ties in one or another ministry.

An outstanding industrialist of this type, one who became a leading member of the Technical Society, was Vasilii Poletika,[11] owner of the widely known Nevskii or Semiannikovskii foundry, whom we encountered earlier as an unsuccessful advocate of protectionism in St. Petersburg's economic press and an organizer of an awkward attempt to demonstrate to the Tsar the gratitude of St. Petersburg workers for their emancipation. Poletika came from an ancient line of Ukrainian nobility, a fact that may explain his self-confidence, his readiness, rare among manufacturers, to express himself openly on public issues. In 1856 he retired from military service with the rank of colonel and settled in St. Petersburg, where, together with Semiannikov, a colleague from his army days, he soon purchased a small foundry on the Schlüsselburg Road by the Nevskii gate. Under the protective wing of the Naval Ministry, the foundry was able to survive the postwar economic crisis. By 1864, when Poletika and his partner acquired the adjacent Thomson foundry, the Nevskii foundry was well on its way to becoming one of the largest mechanized industrial plants in the capital. Toward the end of the decade, it was further enlarged through the purchase of a neighboring textile factory. All this expansion was made possible by large orders from the Naval Ministry for the construction of warships and nautical equipment and, in the latter part of the decade, from the Transportation Ministry for locomotives and railroad equipment.[12]

Not satisfied with pursuing purely entrepreneurial activities, Poletika, who held an advanced degree in mining engineering, began to publish articles and deliver public lectures on controversial economic questions. By the early 1860's, he had already established himself as the most articulate and colorful figure among the industrialists of the capital, and in particular as their leading spokesman for protectionism. His name was fast becoming a St. Petersburg institution, and he himself the prototype of a new kind of urban entrepreneur—of noble birth, educated, connected with government officials, self-assured, at ease in an official milieu and in his relations with fellow industrialists of foreign extraction.*

* According to the annual report of the St. Petersburg Statistical Committee for 1863, almost half of the St. Petersburg enterprises classified as *fabriki* and *zavody* belonged to foreigners. SPSK, *Fabriki i zavody v S.-Peterburge v 1863 godu*, p. 8. Most Soviet historians have been reluctant to acknowledge the relatively large role of foreign entrepreneurs (as distinct from foreign capital) in the early development of Russian industry. Gindin, however, in his recent article, faces the issue squarely and points to the

As a leading public spokesman for the development of machine and metal industries, railroad construction, and the lessening of reliance on foreign imports, Poletika consistently attempted to relate the aspirations of specific industrial interests to the more general interests of the government and nation. In 1863, for example, speaking against the background of international tension precipitated by events in Poland, he argued that "the independent and broad development of our iron industry has become positively necessary for us, both for the sake of retaining our political independence and for the construction and development of our economic life."[13] The following year, in a series of public lectures, he used the Crimean War to illustrate the military disadvantages Russia suffered in conflict with industrially more advanced countries (a lesson the government had already assimilated), and maintained that the same lesson was to be learned from the situation of 1863, which had brought Russia to the brink of war with European powers whose armored ships and steel cannons guaranteed them military superiority. "In the course of a single decade," he said, "we have twice risked our political independence, and both times we have been unprepared to deal with an enemy invasion *only because the situation of our iron industry does not correspond to the more modern development of the industry in Europe.*"[14] Stressing the importance of the rapid construction of railroads for the economic and political development of the nation, Poletika went on to argue that not railroad construction alone, but the production within the country of all items connected with railroads was urgent if Russia were to maintain her status as an independent power.

The industrialist who played the second most active role in the Technical Society was Ludwig Nobel, owner (since 1862) of the Nobel metalworks, whose situation differed from Poletika's only in that his background was foreign and his main official patron was the War Ministry rather than the Naval Ministry.* The other, less

---

importance of foreign capitalists in the metal-processing industries of the Moscow Region (notably Bromly and Lessing) and in the industries of St. Petersburg in general (Baird, Carr, Nobel, Thornton, and others). See Gindin, "Russkaia burzhuaziia," *Istoriia SSSR*, No. 2 (1963), pp. 64, 70–71.

* Nobel was a cousin of Alfred Nobel, the Swedish inventor of dynamite. His father, himself a specialist in the manufacture of explosives, had been commissioned by the Russian government in 1846 to start a plant in St. Petersburg for the manufacture of underwater mines and firing mechanisms for naval ordnance. During the extreme financial difficulties of the years following the Crimean War, the government had tem-

aggressive, less outspoken industrialists who participated in the work of the Technical Society—such as R. K. San-Galli, V. I. Butz, M. L. MacPherson, and N. I. Putilov, all leading figures in the metal-processing and machine industries of St. Petersburg and producers for a government or government-subsidized market—shared the orientation of Poletika and Nobel on most important questions. Indeed, in reading the minutes of the Technical Society's first plenary meeting, held in St. Petersburg in the spring of 1867, one is immediately struck by the near unanimity of the viewpoints and assumptions expressed by most speakers, whether industrialists, technical experts, or professional economists.[15] On the subject of the development of heavy industry, it can safely be said that with very few exceptions, the speech of any single participant stated the essential opinions of all. In short, a nearly uniform outlook had begun to develop among leading St. Petersburg industrialists, economists, and technologists; and it had found an organizational expression. Thus in this new phase in the history of Russia's industrial class, the socially and politically active industrialists separated themselves from the vast bulk of Russia's native, non-noble, "backward" manufacturers, and began to adopt the more "advanced" attitudes and public styles of the experts.

The labor question as such received little direct attention at the Technical Society's plenary meeting of 1867 (our main source of information on the views of the Society's members before 1870). Indirectly, however, the labor question gradually emerged as a corollary of the main question that held the attention of the participants: how to stimulate the development of Russia's machine industry and create the conditions in which it would thrive. This issue was pressing, in view of the pending tariff revision and the government's intention to embark on a new and stepped-up phase of railroad construction. In October of the previous year the government had announced that the Naval, War, and Transportation Ministries would soon be curtailing their orders from foreign factories. Although the announced goal of this measure was primarily fiscal, it clearly amounted to a form of subsidization and protection for domestic

porarily curtailed its orders, and Ludwig's father, finding himself bankrupt, closed the factory and returned to Sweden. Ludwig, however, remained in St. Petersburg, where, in 1862, he purchased a small factory in the Vyborg district from an Englishman and converted it into a major machine and armament works, which was soon doing important pioneer work for the Russian army. Stolpianskii, *Zhizn' i byt*, pp. 169–72.

producers of armaments and railroad equipment.[16] With this situation in the background, it is not surprising that the future of Russia's machine industry became the focus of discussion at the conference.

The opening session on machine industry was chaired by Professor I. A. Vyshnegradskii of the St. Petersburg Technological Institute (the future Minister of Finance, 1887–92); the keynote address was delivered by Nobel; and the lengthiest, boldest statement on the question at hand was made by Poletika, the most vociferous participant throughout the sessions. Poletika's speech proceeded from the easily demonstrated premise that under existing conditions Russia's machine industry was incapable of competing with that of Western Europe. His more controversial conclusion was that with the introduction of specified changes in government policy, successful competition would be relatively simple to achieve. Very little was needed, he proclaimed, for Russian industrialists not only to compete with Western Europeans, but even to surpass them. But this could not come to pass as long as the survival of Russia's machine industry (including his own factory, which had been well served by government orders over the past few years) depended on government subsidies in the form of orders from the various ministries.[17] The same point was made even more directly by Ludwig Nobel, who acknowledged that the machine works of St. Petersburg simply could not survive without government orders. Clearly such orders were a form of protection, since the same products could be obtained abroad at lower prices.[18]

The point, of course, was not that government subsidization was objectionable on principle, but that the existing form of subsidization was inadequate. In the first place, in the expanding area of railroad construction, even government orders placed with home industries tended to favor factories belonging to companies with a high investment of foreign capital, such as the Glavnoe Obshchestvo (this complaint was made by the foreigner Nobel). More important, the current system of subsidization failed to provide the manufacturers with long-term security. A manufacturer could never be sure when he would get orders from a certain ministry, when the orders would cease, when the government would transfer its orders to foreign companies. The only government policy that could overcome the insecurity of the Russian manufacturer would be one that imposed stringent protective tariffs on foreign machines and related products (railroad cars and locomotives, steam engines, nautical equipment, armaments, etc.)—tariffs that were high enough and stable enough to enable manufacturers to plan long-range capital investments in equipment and machinery without fear of incurring major losses. It was the consensus of the meeting, expressed most vigorously by Poletika, that only measures of this kind could make a serious contribution to the development of Russian machine works, a precondition for Russia's economic and political autonomy in the years to come.[19]

That a native machine industry would serve the best interests of the Russian people as well as the state was a view expressed by several participants. Most speakers saw machine production as the hallmark of advanced civilization and culture. Dependence on the import of foreign machines, one speaker argued, hurt Russia economically not only directly but indirectly, by retarding the development of the creative abilities of workers, robbing them of the opportunity to make use of their technical knowledge, thus allowing the country to fall even further behind.[20] In sum, the conference was agreed that a highly developed metallurgical and machine industry was essential to the country from political, economic, and cultural points of view. By introducing protective tariffs, provided they did not conflict with "higher governmental considerations,"[21] the government would only be doing its duty toward the country.

How did industrial workers fit into this discussion? First, they were cited by several speakers as one of the groups that would benefit materially and intellectually from a change in government policy. Nobel made this point directly: "No enterprise is as conducive to the general development of industry and the intellectual development of the working people as are metallurgical and especially machine-building works." Moreover, experience in the complex area of machine production, he argued, would increase the capacity of the Russian worker for mental work and mechanical application in other branches of industry—even agriculture.[22] Poletika, too, felt compelled to demonstrate that workers would benefit substantially from the protection of machine industry. Using somewhat more circuitous arguments than Nobel, he posited a sharp contrast between the effects of a free trade policy in Western Europe (presumably England) and in Russia. In the West the working class had borne the burden of high tariffs by having to pay high prices for bread. Those Europeans who favored free trade had therefore been acting in the interests of the working class and to the detriment of the agrarians. In other words, Poletika said, "the question of free trade in Europe is the question of the proletariat, the question of the working class." In Russia, on the other hand, since high tariffs would place a burden only on the well-to-do, their introduction would in no way be detrimental to labor.[23]

A second way in which the working class was brought into the discussion of the Technical Society was more complex. Implicit in Nobel's contention that the flourishing of machine industry would bring about a higher level of achievement among the working class was the recognition that as matters then stood, Russian workers were backward and uneducated. Indeed he stated quite explicitly— apparently on the basis of experience at his St. Petersburg machine works—that the scarcity of skilled, educated workers had raised the cost of what "intelligent" labor there was, thus adding to the difficulty of competing with the machine industries of Western Europe, which enjoyed the advantages of a complex division of labor and a specialized and efficient labor force. Most Russian workers, he conceded, were not receiving as high a nominal wage as their counterparts in Western Europe; but, on the other hand, their primitive habits and attitudes reduced the real value of Russian workers to their employers. Specifically, Nobel complained of the large number of holidays that Russian workers were accustomed to observing, holidays "that do not serve the needs of religious sentiment so much as they contribute to the debauchery of the workers, and thus damage production, diminishing the quantity of manufactured items and raising the cost of labor."[24] In a similar vein, but without Nobel's derisive overtones, the St. Petersburg industrialist R. K. San-Galli maintained that although nominal wages in Russia were the same as they were abroad (he gave no indication of how he had arrived at this conclusion), insufficient specialization among Russian workers meant that less real value was being derived from their labor.[25]

Nobel and San-Galli—both experienced industrialists in Russia's most advanced industrial region—were arguing, in effect, that Russian industry was suffering from the fact that the workers still lacked the specialized skills and routinized work habits of Western

European labor. Nobel emphasized the workers' archaic, preindustrial habits, which led to low productivity. San-Galli emphasized the amorphous, undifferentiated quality of the mass of peasant-workers, a point also implied by Nobel when he envied Western European factories their complex division of labor. In both cases the primitive ways of the peasant-workers were seen as a major obstacle to the development of a modern industry. In the context in which this problem was raised, however, the speakers were unable or unwilling to suggest solutions that went beyond their most immediate and pressing demand—the erection of tariff barriers. According to this approach, the government, through a policy of protectionism that would encourage the activities of wary manufacturers, would contribute to raising the cultural level and improving the skills of workers simply by providing new job opportunities.

This approach led to certain contradictions in the position of the advocates of protectionism. If the absence of protection was the only serious obstacle to the development of machine industry, then it followed that in other respects Russia was in a position to make rapid progress in that area. Since one of the main arguments of the few opponents of protectionism at the conference (whose spokesman was I. V. Vernadskii, an economist, journalist, and advocate of free trade) was the harmfulness of protecting a fledgling branch of industry from the stimulating effects of international competition,[26] the advocates of protectionism were compelled to depict the resources already available to Russia's machine industry in the most positive light, and one of the most important of those resources was labor. Thus a speaker whose intent was to support Nobel's basic position inadvertently contradicted his unflattering description of Russian workers by lauding their virtues, claiming that they *were* capable of the complex and specialized labor demanded by mechanized industry, and arguing that anyone familiar with Russian workers could vouch for the ease with which they were transformed into excellent skilled workers. Similarly, the chairman of the meeting, in his closing remarks, stated without any challenge from the floor that there could be no question but that technical skills were already widespread among the Russian people.[27]

This vacillation between positive and negative assessments of the qualifications of Russian workers reflected the conflict between the St. Petersburg industrialists' actual experience over the preceding years and their desire to convince the government that its tariff policy was the sole remaining obstacle to a flourishing machine industry. The more negative picture conforms in general with the information on population, literacy, and "moral life" examined in the last two chapters, as well as with the earlier evaluations of the Shtakel'berg Commission. Furthermore, Nobel's disparaging remarks seem much more genuine than the eulogies to Russian workers made by other speakers. But perhaps most telling was the increasing outspokenness of the experts, their industrialist colleagues, and other observers on the subject of the backwardness of workers over the next three years, as heavy industry continued to expand. Whatever may have been said in praise of Russian workers, the thrust of the opinions expressed at the 1867 meeting was that the workers were generally undisciplined and poorly trained, that their lack of development was an obstacle to industrial progress, and that a change in tariff policy was needed if they were to advance to the stage of development of their counterparts in Western Europe— an accomplishment that would serve both their own interests and the goal of industrial modernization.

Protective tariffs were not the only supposedly pro-labor measure advocated at the meeting of the Technical Society. A brief session was devoted exclusively to labor problems, mainly the problem of improving sanitation in working-class areas.[28] Here again participants argued for the desirability of Russia's achieving the higher standards of the more advanced European countries where, to quote the opening speaker, "well-meaning people who are sympathetic to the development of national industry have long since devoted attention to the dark sides of factory and plant life, and the result has been a whole series of sanitary regulations, inspections, and protective technical structures."[29] Not one voice was raised in opposition to the view that such measures should be introduced in Russia.* The only conflict arose over the specific suggestion that a force of "technical police"—by which was meant something roughly like an organization of factory inspectors—be organized in order to protect

---

* The absence of fundamental dissent may be somewhat misleading, however, since the most important St. Petersburg industrialists, if they attended this session, failed to express themselves on the subject in any way. But even the absence of critical comments may be taken as evidence that hostility to sanitary regulations was at least not sufficiently strong among participating industrialists for them to risk the embarrassment of breaking the consensus of the conference.

the workers (child laborers in particular) from abuses on the part of their employers. The issue was joined over the relative merits of "preventive" and "punitive" measures. The "punitive" position held that once ample factory legislation existed, it was sufficient to prosecute violators in the courts, whereas the "preventive" position maintained that it was also necessary to introduce a regular system of surveillance over factory conditions. Even advocates of the "preventive" approach, however, displayed their sensitivity to the feelings of factory owners by adopting the position that the inspectors should be chosen from among the manufacturers themselves.[30] Thus even the strongest pro-labor position taken at the conference failed to achieve the clarity and forcefulness of the views expressed by the Shtakel'berg Commission and others a few years earlier, or that were soon to be expressed in the journal *Arkhiv*.

In reading the speeches favoring factory legislation, one is struck by the absence of the slightest note of criticism directed toward the government. Indeed, the prevailing tone was one of confidence that the Technical Society's support of factory legislation was in accord with official goals. This confidence seems to have been based on the belief that official approval of the earlier proposals of the various commissions was still pending and that their implementation was only a matter of time.[31] Be that as it may, the absence of any defiance fit well with the overall tone of the meeting. Even most of the speeches on tariff policy were characterized by extreme cautiousness, sometimes bordering on obsequiousness. It was necessary to abide by whatever decisions the government might make on the basis of "higher considerations," the duty of experts and experienced industrialists being merely to offer the government such specialized information as would best further the national interest, and to do so in a manner, as one officer of the Technical Society put it, that would impress the government with "our practical way of thinking, our competence: in a word—enhance rather than diminish the dignity of our Society."[32] In this case the national interest would benefit from factory legislation because at present industrial accidents and deficient hygienic conditions damaged the workers physically and morally, spreading fear and aversion to factory life and thus depriving Russian industry of an adequate labor supply.[33]

In effect, then, on the basis of "hard," practical considerations, the members of the Technical Society favored bringing the status

of factory workers into line with the requirements of modern industry. Having made their point, they adjourned to await the decisions of the government.

Although some industrialists participated in a preliminary review of the tariff of 1868 (the first tariff ever so reviewed), the new
law failed to meet the expectations of the manufacturers and experts who had assembled in St. Petersburg the previous year.
Despite the government's gesture of placing a token duty on imported machinery, it proved to be even more liberal and less protective in some respects than the 1857 tariff it replaced.[34] This was
a major victory for free traders and a serious rebuff to the leading
representatives of St. Petersburg's machine and armaments industries. Nevertheless, as was seen in Chapter 6, the years 1868–70 were
marked by considerable successes in those industries, mainly because the government intensified its subsidization programs and
placed them on a more reliable, longer-term basis.

Expanded production, however, did not entail the increased productivity of labor. The Technical Society's less-than-enthusiastic
request for factory legislation fared no better than its more impas-
sioned request for protectionism, while in the absence of protectionism, the impact of high tariffs on the skills of the working class remained a moot point. No concerted efforts were undertaken by the
government to close the gap—pointed out by Nobel, San-Galli, and
others—between a culturally backward and uprooted labor force
and an expanding and modernizing industry.

Only in one respect did the regime begin to show a willingness
to adjust to the need for a better qualified industrial labor force.
Without itself taking an active role, the government in 1867 authorized the Technical Society to do what it had prohibited private individuals from doing five years earlier: conduct Sunday and evening schools for workers and their children in St. Petersburg. By
1870 two such schools were functioning in the capital, and plans for
establishing at least two more were in progress. Unlike the original
Sunday schools—a grass-roots undertaking initiated by educated
well-wishers of the lower classes—these schools bore the semiofficial
character of the organization that founded them. In keeping with
the orientation of the Technical Society, they also emphasized practical vocational training, in contrast to most of the earlier Sunday

schools, which had confined themselves to reading, writing, arithmetic, and religious instruction. The traditional subjects were not neglected in the new schools (religion, of course, was stressed), but the ultimate goal was the training of badly needed skilled workers.[35]

The new schools represented only a small inroad; in general the problem of training and acculturating the bulk of peasant-workers remained unresolved. The shortage of skilled and educated workers alluded to at the 1867 meeting had been plaguing the Russian machine and armaments industries since the end of the Crimean War, and was one of the reasons the government had reluctantly turned to foreign companies.[36] In 1862 War Minister Miliutin had attributed the unsatisfactory condition of Russia's military industries to the low productivity of labor, but sanguinely foresaw the solution to this problem in the elimination of the last remnants of forced labor.[37] As forced labor was gradually abolished in the following years, however, it became increasingly clear that although costs were sometimes reduced and skilled free workers were hired in some military factories the mere transition to free labor provided no panacea.* Nor did private factories fare significantly better. Nobel, for example, while benefiting from large government orders for rifles in 1868, was able to complete only a small fraction of them, and those that he completed were of less than satisfactory quality. This was due, at least in part, to the extensive use in this "advanced" factory of child labor.[38] So serious was the scarcity of skilled labor in St. Petersburg that a few years later the industrialist Putilov, having been forced to limit production because of new financial difficulties, feared to lay off his skilled workers lest he be unable to rehire them in the future.[39] In 1870 *Birzhevye vedomosti* reported that most of the highly skilled positions in Russian industry were still held by foreign workers, while the typical Russian peasant-worker, lacking the requisite industrial skills, was relegated to poorly paid, physically debilitating "black" manual labor.[40]

* Shortly after the shift to hired labor at the Tula armaments factory in 1864, the Artillery section of the War Ministry concluded that the use of free labor at factories administered by the state was an "almost inconceivable" approach, "more harmful to the state than compulsory labor" (quoted in Zaionchkovskii, *Voennye reformy*, p. 141). We have already noted some of the problems encountered during the transition to free labor and private, commercial administration at state factories in the St. Petersburg area in 1866–67. For evidence that the transition did cut costs at some military factories, see Zaionchkovskii, pp. 144–45.

The constricting effects of the character of the industrial labor force were confirmed by an astute German writer, Friedrich Matthäi, who visited St. Petersburg in 1870. On the basis of personal observations and extensive materials collected in St. Petersburg during the All-Russian Industrial Exposition of that year, Matthäi wrote and published a very thorough study of Russian industry.[41] In it he raised the question of why it was that real labor costs were considerably higher in Russia than they were in England, France, and parts of Germany. The answer, he believed, was to be found in the greater "moral purposefulness" of the European workers, who, unlike the Russians, were not in the habit of frequently interrupting their work. The lack of self-discipline among Russian workers was, in turn, a reflection of their cultural backwardness, their semi-peasant existence:

The reason for the work interruptions that frequently occur in Russia [in contrast to the causes of industrial strikes in Western Europe] . . . lies in the customs and the institutions of the country, in the lack of popular education, in the drunkenness of the Russian people, in the large number of holidays, [and] in the constraining influence of landed property, specifically in the circumstance of communal ownership of peasant lands, which forces factory workers to stop their work in the factories for months at a time so as to look after their affairs in their communes, and which compels the factory workers to lead a separate life from their families, since the latter usually have the obligation of looking after the land. A worker who—as in the case of other countries—remains at his work year after year, six days a week, will always produce more than the Russian worker, who not only conscientiously celebrates every royal and church holiday, but the various local holidays as well, and who for weeks if not months at a time stops his factory work in order to perform his farm work. The result of this dual existence [Zwitterstellung] of the Russian working class, or, more accurately, peasant class, is that Russia has neither true workers nor true peasants, that the latter are partially both but wholly neither. This is a necessary consequence of communal tenure of the communal land, and as long as [communal land] is not eliminated, an improvement of these relations will be impossible.[42]

Strongly emphasizing the detrimental influence of holidays, Matthäi went on to describe a situation with which we are already familiar: not only did the worker spend his holiday drinking away his wages, he drank himself into a condition that incapacitated him for work for several days thereafter. "Herein lies the weakness of Russian industry," said Matthäi, "indeed, of the entire economic life of

Russia." So long as these habits continued, Russian industry, even with all the protective tariff systems, would always be on weak legs.*

Matthäi outlined a multifarious program with which to attack these problems. It included education, moral instruction by the clergy, and rational, regulated labor relations that would constrain the workers to consistently meet their obligations to their employers. "Labor must be organized, labor relations must be regulated," Matthäi stressed in bold print. "The interests of industry, of absolutely all industrial pursuits, must be guaranteed through national legislation." His specific program included the prohibition of night labor, the shortening of working hours, and the elimination of arteli and other forms of non-familial, collective living. The reduction of the workday would allow time for education; the elimination of arteli and communal housing would enable the urban worker to reap the moral benefits of family life, to assume responsibility for his own needs and those of his immediate family, and would thus help him to realize the harmfulness of squandering his money on alcohol. He would soon grow accustomed to independence, frugality, and self-esteem. In short, Russia must take the steps required for the creation of a distinct and independent working class (*Arbeiterstand*) unfettered by the peasant commune and other vestigial institutions. A real working class would finally be able to achieve a sufficiently high level of education and technical competence to lessen production costs for industrialists, enabling them to compete on a reasonable footing with Western Europe.[48]

Thus, what had once been the source of optimism and pride to Russian officials (and to an earlier German observer of Russian economic life, Haxthausen)—the semi-peasant character of the Russian factory worker, his ties to the village community and the artel', in short, his incomplete proletarianization—was, by the end of the first decade after emancipation, the greatest source of the weakness of Russian industry in the eyes of a knowledgeable foreign observer. Matthäi's analysis appeared to vindicate the views held by liberal economists and government commissions in the early 1860's, their forewarning that a separate class of free industrial workers, protected in their new status by industrial legislation, was a prerequi-

---

* The ruinous effect of drink—which "sucks the juice out of the people"—on the productivity of labor was also observed by Dr. Gorman in 1868. *Arkhiv sudebnoi meditsiny*, No. 1 (1868), sec. iii, p. 54. See also *Birzhevye vedomosti*, Sept. 18, 1864.

site to significant industrial progress. At the same time, the observations of the *Arkhiv* doctors and others underscored the fact that the preservation of communal ties and arteli had not prevented the evolution and growth of a destitute urban surplus population with all the worst characteristics of a proletariat. Hence by 1870 a favorable case had begun to be made for reexamining old approaches to the labor question, the official approach having proved less than adequate to either task—the avoidance of pauperism or the creation of an adequately skilled and reliable labor force.

The First Industrial Exhibition

Viewed superficially, St. Petersburg in 1870 showed little sign of being a city that was undergoing any difficulties in its industrial life. In the spring of that year, the capital was abounding with activity, filled with a spirit of pride in the city's recent industrial achievements and confidence in its and the country's industrial future. The activity in St. Petersburg centered around two major coincident events: the first All-Russian Industrial Exhibition and the first All-Russian Congress of Manufacturers and People Interested in Native Industry. The two events neatly complemented each other. The first exhibited the achievements of Russian industry, and therefore symbolized the importance of the new industrialists and experts to Russian society, while the second provided members of these groups with a national forum in which to voice their aspirations.

The exhibition was scheduled to open in mid-May. By April *Birzhevye vedomosti* was reporting regularly and enthusiastically on the preparations that were taking place. Visitors to the exhibition grounds could see, one reporter proudly claimed, that "in many branches of manufacturing we can bravely compete with the West."[44] The newspaper was especially impressed by the display of products of Russia's machine industry, including military weapons, locomotives, and a large and costly exhibit of railroad cars manufactured by the Glavnoe Obshchestvo in St. Petersburg.[45] The preparations placed great emphasis on what we would now call "public relations." The Technical Society, as a leading promoter of the exhibition, arranged for a free series of easily comprehensible public lectures by industrial specialists, with each lecture to be followed by a guided tour of the appropriate St. Petersburg factories.[46]

In order to ensure the broadest possible attendance at the exhibition, a descending scale of entry fees was designed by the commission in charge of preparations. Admission on the opening day was by invitation only, and for the next three days a prohibitive price of two rubles was charged, but thereafter the fee was gradually scaled down to ten kopecks. In recognition of the contribution made by factory workers to the production of the objects on display, the commission also set aside special days when admission would be free for workers who had special notes from their employers (an approach that was typical of the efforts of industrialists to project a paternalistic concern for their employees during the exhibition and the congress). This gesture was lauded by *Birzhevye vedomosti*, which also lavished praise on the Russian working class for its contributions to industrial progress. One of its editorials said, "The main host of the exhibition should be recognized as the simple worker, for only the entire sum of labor completed by the individual workers has made such an exhibition possible."[47]

The exhibition opened with great ceremony. High dignitaries of the Orthodox Church—the metropolitans of St. Petersburg and Kiev—delivered the opening prayers and blessed the site with holy water. High government officials—including Reutern and the directors and vice-directors of the Finance Ministry's various departments—were present at the opening ceremonies and at the sumptuous luncheon that followed. At the luncheon, toasts were proposed to the Tsar, the Minister of Finance, and other officials, one of whom responded in kind by proposing a toast to "the blossoming of commerce and industry in Russia." Sentiments of patriotism and of confidence in Russia's industrial future abounded.* A poem was read, especially written for the occasion, praising science, labor, the fatherland, native enterprise, and the exhibition site in five short stanzas.[48]

In general, the exhibition seems to have been effective. *Birzhevye vedomosti* expressed the view that it clearly demonstrated the ex-

---

* At one dinner held in connection with the 1870 congress overzealous patriotism proved a source of embarrassment. The dinner speaker, Poletika, complained—in the presence of Del'vig, who chaired the evening—that there were more German than Russian names among industrialists in Russia's machine industry, and even cited "Baron von Delwig's" presence as chairman as a symptom of the problem. Del'vig replied with injured pride that his name had been regarded as Russian for over fifty years, at which point the audience burst into applause. Del'vig, III, 385–87.

tent to which certain branches of Russian industry had been progressing, and regretted only that many manufacturers, still oblivious to the importance of events of this sort, had refrained from displaying their products.[49] The German observer Matthäi voiced his somewhat patronizing amazement at the progress the exhibition revealed:

One was justly astonished at the development which Russian industry has undergone in the past years, a development . . . of which one would hardly have considered Russia capable. All branches of an independently developed industrial life were represented at the exhibition, and the impartial critic had to ask himself with astonishment whether all these industrial products had really originated in the agricultural state of Russia.[50]

The exhibition was still more impressive when compared to the rather poor showing that the Russian displays had made at the Paris exhibition of 1867, where only three years earlier (according to Matthäi) people had laughed at the poor quality of Russian products.[51] Even without the aid of the tariff protection that the Technical Society had requested in 1867, Russian industry had made considerable progress, as a person as skeptical about the nature of that progress as the old censor Nikitenko was constrained to admit.*

The First Industrial Congress: Backwardness of Manufacturers

With the exhibition in the background, the industrial congress prepared to open its sessions, in the hall of the St. Petersburg municipal duma, on May 18, four days after the opening of the exhibition. Its initiators and sponsors, the Technical and Industrial Societies, had been permitted and even encouraged to hold the congress by the responsible authorities, the ministries of Finance and Internal Affairs. The sessions were to be open to the public without charge.[52] Like the organizers of the exhibition, the officers of the congress arranged impressive luncheons and special events for industrialists, officials, and technical specialists from all over the country. The avowed support of the government for the purposes of the congress

* On May 24, 1870, Nikitenko wrote in his diary: "Attended industrial exhibition. The general appearance is majestic and elegant. Russian industry, it seems, has really made significant progress, that is, it has demonstrated that we are capable of producing good things. But what of it? Do they constitute an item for foreign trade and general internal consumption? Isn't it true that only in that case does industry have an enriching and civilizing force?" Nikitenko, Dnevnik, III, 175–76.

was symbolized by the prominent role at one gala luncheon of the Duke of Leuchtenberg,[53] who, despite indications that his relationship with the Technical Society may have cooled since 1867,[54] served as the honorary chairman of the congress.

Yet these effusive celebrations of the new industrial age concealed some of the serious difficulties that beset the congress from the outset—not the least of them being poor participation by manufacturers in a meeting that purported to be Russia's first national gathering of industrialists and supporters of industrialization. Although no precise breakdown of participants has been preserved, the poor attendance of manufacturers was remarked on several times. "In the sessions of the congress that have taken place thus far," one reporter lamented, "the majority of our industrialists have been conspicuous by their absence."[55] Similar complaints were voiced by some of the participants.[56] Perhaps the most pungent remarks were made by the industrialist Poletika, who, at the final plenary session, took his fellow manufacturers to task. After praising the government, the press, and the public at large for their support of the activities of the congress, Poletika had this to say about the role of the industrialists:

The manufacturers and industrialists themselves have continued to be the most indifferent. To our general surprise and regret, they were conspicuous by their absence. And I absolutely do not know how to interpret this and how to explain it. Was it the result of some kind of dissatisfaction with the affair, and a demonstration against it; or the result of our usual indifference and apathy; or does the fault lie in our everlasting slumber?

It was true, he continued, that manufacturers had been unjustly vilified at the sessions on factory labor (discussed below), but this neither justified nor excused their absence. If society were treating manufacturers unsympathetically and unfairly, all the more reason for them to come to such events and let their voices be heard. Poletika also speculated that the complex theoretical aspect of some of the debate at the congress may have taken the manufacturers unawares, for they were not really equipped for this sort of discussion. He concluded,

We hope that all this will change with time. The more confidence the government places in them, the more they will be compelled to work for their own well-being. It is time for manufacturers to stop counting on others and to get busy working out and elucidating their needs by themselves. Let us hope that this congress will mark the beginning of a permanent organization of congresses. Then the Russian [manufacturer] will free himself from his oppressive self-consciousness and the feeling of his own backwardness.[57]

Thus even while chastising his fellow industrialists, Poletika managed to introduce certain points that were clearly aimed at evoking his audience's sympathy for them: manufacturers were being judged too harshly and unfairly; they were not trusted by the government; they lacked a permanent class organization through which they might act assertively and rid themselves of their sense of inferiority. By weaving these remarks into his criticism, Poletika managed to soften it considerably and to speak as an enlightened defender of his class as well as a critic.

The presence at the congress of men like Poletika helps us to account for what appears to have been an anomaly: a congress that insisted on representative institutions for manufacturers, and yet was barely attended by members of the class whose interests it purported to represent. Here was a phenomenon not unfamiliar to students of Russian history: a group of educated people, under the influence of advanced ideas from "highly developed" countries, presuming to speak in behalf of the alleged interests of an economically important but socially backward class. If, between the Crimean War and the emancipation, the interests of manufacturers had begun to be expressed more forcefully and openly than in the past, particularly in connection with the tariff question, this change was largely the work of a small group of unusually articulate men, either new industrialists of noble origin and a background of government service or publicists who spoke in the manufacturers' name. Most manufacturers, still unsure of their place in a society that continued to be dominated by the nobility, and reluctant to display in public their lack of education and manners, had preferred to remain in the background. The 1870 congress offered numerous examples of this situation.

An incident that took place during a discussion of the labor question is illustrative. To the extent that it has been possible to identify the various orators, this session provides the only certain case of a manufacturer taking the floor who did not belong to the industrial elite; that is to say, it was the only speech by a typical Russian merchant-manufacturer.* The circumstances under which he took the floor reveal the incongruous situation such manufacturers found themselves in at the congress.

In the middle of a lively discussion about industrial workers, F. N. L'vov, a chemistry professor at the Artillery School who was serving as secretary of the congress and of the session, interrupted the proceedings to make the following appeal:

> Some people are embarrassed because they do not speak eloquently, and yet they are capable of presenting facts from actual life. I submit that under such circumstances the lack of oratorical talent or being unaccustomed to speaking before a large meeting should not serve as an obstacle, and that every word of a practical man will be accepted by you, gentlemen, with special acclamation.[58]

These remarks (which were greeted with a round of applause and shouts of "Yes, yes, of course!") represented a rather condescending effort to bring the few uneducated manufacturers who were present into the foreground.

Only one, M. P. Syromiatnikov, responded. He began his first foray into public speaking with an expression of pride in being a "practical man," couched in the form of an apology: "I should first of all ask your forgiveness for not being an orator, for not being able to speak eloquently; I can only present facts."[59] Not unexpectedly, this apology only served to elicit shouts of "Bravo!" from the delighted audience, which rallied to his defense when he began to speak about a problem that was not on the agenda—the lack of education not among workers, but among the members of his own class. Syromiatnikov bemoaned the fact that so many manufacturers, whose activities were so important to the wealth of the nation, were, like himself, uneducated persons, many of whom could not even sign their names. But he was quick to add that this was not the fault of the merchant-manufacturers themselves, so much as the reflection of an inadequately developed system of provincial schools.[60]

L'vov's original plea, the positive response of the audience, and Syromiatnikov's mixture of class self-deprecation and defensiveness all illustrate the paradoxical position of Russia's manufacturers. By 1870 their importance to the nation had come to be recognized

---

* Some thirty-one persons actually participated in the discussions at the sessions of the congress that most concern us; I have been able to identify seventeen positively and four tentatively.

widely. Yet their social and intellectual status remained inferior, not only in relation to the nobility and the bureaucracy, but even in relation to the technical experts and the few advanced industrialists who were attempting to resolve problems that directly affected them.

The warm reception accorded Syromiatnikov scarcely compensated for the explicitly or implicitly derogatory comments about manufacturers that cropped up repeatedly during the proceedings. As Poletika indicated, they were especially frequent during the sessions on the labor question, but even at other sessions manufacturers were subjected to ridicule. Their continued unwillingness to provide accurate statistical data, for example, was emphasized by speakers at the session on industrial statistics. The Russian manufacturers, declared T. S. Morozov (himself a prominent industrialist), were so frightened of possible taxation that it was "impossible to look to them for accuracy."[61] So pervasive was this view, that R. K. San-Galli felt obliged to affirm that although he was a manufacturer, he was well disposed toward statistics.[62] Still other speakers took note of the cultural backwardness of manufacturers, particularly their extreme illiteracy.[63]

Despite the less than flattering opinion of the majority of Russian manufacturers that prevailed at the congress, most members strongly favored the establishment of new and more direct channels through which the needs of manufacturers could be placed before the government. The congress itself, of course, was one such channel, but it lacked permanence, and events had shown that it failed to elicit the participation of most of the manufacturing class. The congress therefore took it upon itself to further the cause of establishing permanent institutions "to represent the views of our manufacturers, industrialists, and business people." Much of the discussion of this problem centered around proposals to reorganize and democratize the Manufacturing Council and its affiliated organizations (a need that had been recognized by the Shtakel'berg Commission several years before).[64] The agricultural economist V. I. Veshniakov, chairman of the session that dealt with this question, stressed that the rights of the Manufacturing Council existed "only on paper," that the council was completely dependent on the government, and that it was in no sense a truly representative institution, since its members were appointed by the Ministry of Finance.* As was by this time the common practice in these circles, Veshniakov and other speakers turned toward Western Europe for examples of more independent institutions that truly represented manufacturers, specifically the chambers of commerce and industry in Prussia, Belgium, France, and especially England.[65] K. A. Skal'kovskii, an influential young mining engineer with close ties to the government and the business world, and an officer of the Industrial Society, came out strongly for an autonomous Manufacturing Council, the members of which would be elected by the manufacturers and business people from among elite industrialists of the type participating in the meeting; he was quite certain that such industrialists were sufficiently knowledgeable in technology, but if necessary they could collaborate with the type of technical experts who composed the majority of the congress.[66] A version of this plan was adopted by the plenary session. In keeping with Poletika's suggestion that the present congress regularize the future organization of industrial congresses, the plenary session also expressed its hope that "congresses of manufacturers, industrialists and people interested in the progress of native industry, both all-Russian and local, be repeated as often as possible."[67] By these means the experts and the industrial elite endeavored to obtain greater representation before the government for a class that many of them held in contempt, but that the congress purported to represent; at the same time, they attempted to ensure that they themselves would continue to be the chief public spokesmen for that class. This program appeared to be a reasonable resolution to the problem of granting a still culturally backward entrepreneurial class a voice in decision-making commensurate with Russia's present and future industrial modernization.

The case for increasing the influence of industrial interests on the government, at least as it was cautiously presented by the speakers, did not derive from an abstract commitment to representative institutions. The right to class representation was never advocated as a

---

* Veshniakov's comments may be taken as further evidence of the weakness of the view, held by Tugan-Baranovskii and others, that the Manufacturing Council was the powerful organ of the industrial bourgeoisie, capable of thwarting the plans of the St. Petersburg and Shtakel'berg Commissions.

general principle (except by implication, when British institutions were cited as a model). The main general argument for more representative industrial institutions than the Manufacturing Council was a practical one, namely, that the failure of existing institutions to generate publicity and influence for the views of manufacturers had been detrimental to industrial development. Behind this argument stood the conviction that the need for certain concrete measures that would benefit both manufacturers and the national economy was being ignored by the government. It is noteworthy that Skal'kovskii, the dominant figure at the session that dealt with these matters, specifically raised the sensitive tariff question as an important example, indeed the only concrete example offered, of the failure of existing institutions to make known the needs of the business classes.[68] And the extreme vigor with which the tariff question was resumed at other sessions of the congress lends weight to the notion that the government's failure to answer to the Technical Society's earlier plea for protectionism provided the context for the congress's efforts to establish more influential institutions for manufacturers.*

Industrial Congress: On the Machine Industry

The deliberations of the industrial congress over the tariff question, and the renewed discussions of the broader problem of encouraging the development of Russia's machine industry, reveal yet another area in which a veneer of effusive optimism thinly concealed some major deficiencies. Despite the evident expansion of government-subsidized machine industry since 1867, that industry, as Poletika was the first to affirm, had been experiencing serious difficulties.[69] Over the previous four years government assistance had enabled the machine industry to manifest "a very significant movement forward," in the words of P. V. Vol', an official of the congress, yet it was still incapable of competing on its own with foreign factories.[70]

While Poletika, Vol', and other speakers pointed to the difficulties experienced by the Russian machine industry as evidence for the necessity of protectionism, others used the same evidence to argue

* This interpretation is also supported indirectly by the fact that the question of reorganizing the Manufacturing Council had not even been broached at the 1867 meeting, when there was still hope that the government would revise its tariff policy along the lines suggested. It was only after the disappointing tariff law of 1868 that this question was seen as germane.

that machine production was overprotected. In general, the congress incorporated a broader spectrum of opinion than did the 1867 meeting, and the free trade position, although still in a minority, was more strongly represented. Free traders such as Iu. O. Shreier, an expert on military affairs, echoed Vernadskii's view that tariffs would only serve to discourage manufacturers from introducing the qualitative advances that were needed if Russia were ever to become industrially competitive. "The development of machine industry," he asserted, "is brought about not by artificial measures, but by actual supply and demand."[71]

The advocates of both positions, protectionists and free traders,* were clearly agreed on one point: that whether because of excessive or inadequate government support, the state of Russia's machine and metal industry was disappointingly weak, reflecting what one protectionist speaker called the "disgrace" of Russia's backwardness. To illustrate this weakness, A. T. Velikhov, a leading advocate of protective tariffs, cited the uncompetitiveness of the largest and most important new factory in St. Petersburg—indeed, the most favored rail factory in Russia and a source of great public pride at the industrial exhibition—the Putilov metal and machine works. The so-called success of the Putilov factory, he emphasized, was based entirely on government favors, such as the sale of five million puds of used rail to the factory at an extremely low price, and the purchase of the finished product from the factory at a price considerably higher than its real value or than the cost of foreign rails.[72] Even the Putilov factory, he concluded, was incapable of maintaining itself independently as a basic producer of rails for Russian lines; at best it could exist only as a major repair facility. Similarly, the recent expansion in the domestic production of locomotives and railroad cars had occurred only because the government had forced private railroad companies to purchase rolling stock in Russia as a condition for acquiring public concessions. Echoing the arguments of 1867, Velikhov contended that (in the absence of high pro-

---

* I am oversimplifying somewhat by reducing the debate to only two opposing positions, pro- and anti-protection. Although these were the choices to which the congress was finally reduced, various compromises and combinations were proposed in the course of the debate, in part because even some staunch advocates of protection considered it unrealistic to ask for a reversal so soon after the 1868 tariff was implemented. Poletika, for example, considered that pressing for a revision would be "unpolitic," but ultimately made one of the most spirited arguments for protection at the congress.

tective tariffs) if the government terminated this practice even for a year or two, these companies would immediately start buying abroad and domestic machine works would be forced to close down.[73]

After a spirited debate over the relative advantages of protection and free competition as means for stimulating and strengthening heavy industry, the congress approved a resolution calling for the upward revision of the 1868 tariffs on products made of iron, steel, and copper "to the level of the tariffs that exist on these items in countries that have long since surpassed us in machine industry: France, Prussia, and the United States." In addition, the congress passed resolutions calling for the transfer of government-owned metallurgical factories to private hands, furthering the shift toward private enterprise that had been going on since the Crimean War, and the continued government support of Russia's railroad car and locomotive construction "until such time as that industry will have acquired a completely independent existence" (which meant, in the given context, until such time as high protective tariffs were established).[74]

All in all, except for a greater note of pessimism about the possibility of obtaining higher tariffs in the near future, the views expressed on the development of the machine industry by the majority of participants barely differed from those expressed three years earlier. As in 1867 the interests of heavy industry were claimed to coincide with the interests of the nation, although now this point could be taken more for granted. At the same time, it was rather embarrassing to imply that the government's latest tariff policy might be contrary to the national interest, so the congress emphasized the progress achieved by protectionism in other countries, rather than the retrogressive aspects of current policies. But this was only a shift of emphasis; the basic point of view remained the same. Also unchanged was the majority posture of unquestioned acceptance of the idea that whatever benefits might accrue to the machine industry had to be derived from the government, whether in the form of protective tariffs or other kinds of assistance and subsidization.

Industrial Congress: On the Backwardness of the Workers

The third important problem area that was obscured by the external aura of success surrounding the exhibition and congress was the continued backwardness and unhealthiness of the industrial labor force. Because of the recent growth of heavy industry the inadequate skills and disorganized way of life of Russian workers, which were superficially noted by the Technical Society in 1867, had become by 1870 a much more pressing problem. Not only the observations of outsiders such as Matthäi, but the remarks of leading Russian industrialists and experienced industrial specialists at the congress strongly suggest that the discrepancy between the needs of industry and the capacities of workers was even greater by 1870 than before.

At the Technical Society meeting of 1867, it will be recalled, the narrow problem of sanitation had provided the framework for the only systematic discussion of factory workers that took place. At the 1870 congress, by contrast, several sessions were scheduled for examining the whole question of working-class culture and patterns of behavior and assessing the respective roles of government and industry, coercion and encouragement, in raising the laboring classes to a cultural and intellectual level that was adequate to the needs of modern production.

The problem was posed very simply and succinctly: "What measures can be taken to encourage the intellectual and moral development of our working class?"[75] The sessions in which this question was debated were the most exciting and controversial of the congress, had the largest enrollment and attendance and the longest list of speakers, and were accorded the special attention of the press. One session continued without interruption from the early evening until two o'clock in the morning. No other sessions elicited as much acrimonious debate, applause, booing, catcalling, and general disorder among the audience.[76]

The prominent, university-educated St. Petersburg industrialist V. P. Vargunin,[77] an active supporter of the Sunday school movement a decade earlier, was supposed to have presided over these sessions, but because of his unexplained absence, most of the meetings were chaired by Viktor Delavoss, director of the recently established Imperial Technical School in Moscow.* Delavoss attempted to set the tone for the discussion in his opening address by acknowledging the "enormous significance" of the question at hand and en-

---

* Delavoss was a pioneer in the field of technical and vocational education whose ideas were to have an important impact in the United States beginning in the 1870's. His name was spelled Della Vos or Della-Vos in the United States. See Lawrence A. Cremin, *The Transformation of the School: Progressivism in American Education, 1876–1957* (New York: Alfred A. Knopf, Inc., 1961), pp. 24–27.

deavored to create a mood of harmony and optimism by emphasizing his belief that solutions were in sight. The ignorance of the working class was detrimental both to industry and to society, he argued, and except for a few isolated incidents, nothing substantial had been done about it. Delavoss attributed society's failure to act to the still small size of the working-class population and to the low stage of development of Russian industry, which put a premium on strictly physical labor, thus maintaining the laborer as nothing more than a "unit of mechanical work." But he expressed his confidence that this attitude toward the worker would soon be altered in Russia as it had been in Western Europe.

The decisive factor that was bound to improve the situation, Delavoss argued, was the scientific and industrial revolution that had taken place in Western Europe and was now in progress in Russia. As machines began to replace purely physical labor, the mental development of the worker would become increasingly important; as the multiplication of complex tasks raised the demand for skilled and educated workers, the position of the worker was bound to improve. The responsibility of the congress, therefore, was to find ways to facilitate the worker's intellectual progress so as to assist him in meeting the demands of modern industry. "Practical and rational measures" would surely be found to achieve this goal, since it was certain that the manufacturers on whom their implementation depended were equal to the task: "It may be stated without doubt," Delavoss said, "that the entire matter is in the hands of our industrial managers. This circumstance, however, gives us the right to assume that the question under discussion will be satisfactorily resolved in the very near future." For over and beyond the material interest of manufacturers in having an intelligent, reliable working class, an unusual characteristic distinguished the Russian from the Western European industrialist: his "readiness to allocate the surplus from his accumulated wealth to his younger brothers," that is, his workers. On this note of optimism, and having admonished the participants to steer clear of the abstract and theoretical, and to confine their remarks to points that could be discussed strictly in terms of their "practicality and applicability," Delavoss opened the floor to discussion.[78]

The heated debate that followed gave short shrift to Delavoss's hope that the subject could be discussed without discord. It is more than likely that he knew serious difficulties lay ahead, and had merely been attempting to defuse the atmosphere. Had Russian industrialists really been prepared to come to the assistance of their "younger brothers," much of the ensuing discussion would have been superfluous. But participants in the sessions on labor were much too aware of the hardships of Russian workers to be taken in by Delavoss's optimism. The recent writings of the *Arkhiv* doctors, for example, were quite well known to them.[79] Delavoss (and others) managed to cling to the assumption that the more enlightened views expressed at the congress were somehow representative of industrialists in general, despite the general disappointment in their poor participation. He preferred not to admit that they only represented the views of educated specialists and a few advanced St. Petersburg manufacturers, whose education and experience led them to share the attitudes of the experts with whom they mingled, or at least to express themselves in a manner appropriate to that milieu. Even *Birzhevye vedomosti* added to the confusion by at times alluding to the congress as if it were truly representative of the manufacturing class, and then using the congress's support of measures such as technical education as evidence of the enlightened self-interest of "our industrialists."[80]

When discussion of "workers' education" opened on the floor it soon became clear that this subject could not be treated separately from other thorny problems. Had debate been limited to education and technical training, the sessions might well have proceeded without serious controversy, for almost everyone agreed that a more highly educated working class was essential. The educational program proposed at the congress in the name of the Technical Society—essentially an expanded version of the program the Society had been pursuing since 1867—was virtually unopposed in its substance.* Some fairly substantial disagreements did arise, however, when the discussion turned to questions of implementation and detail. How, for example, was the new educational program to be financed: by the manufacturers, by government agencies, by the workers themselves, or by some combination of these?

* The Technical Society's proposals, presented by L'vov, included the establishment of elementary technical schools for workers by the industrialists as part of the training program in their factories, and the establishment of regular Sunday and evening courses for adult workers by the municipal and rural administrations of industrial regions. *Zapiski*, No. 1 (1871), pp. 47–50.

According to the Technical Society's original proposal, the basic financing was to be carried out by combining the resources of municipal administrations, zemstva, and the industrialists themselves. But in order to provide psychological incentives to the workers, to encourage them to look upon education as something of value rather than as "the whim of philanthropists," L'vov had proposed that nominal fees be charged for enrollment in Sunday and evening courses.[81] The liberal economist E. R. Vreden,[82] who emerged as one of the leading proponents of a pro-labor position at the congress, was even more adamant than L'vov about placing legal responsibility for the education of workers on the manufacturers: since the employer drew his workers into an exhausting and dangerous situation, one that tended to undermine normal family life, he had a "civic responsibility" to compensate for these evils by making financial sacrifices in the workers' behalf, all the more so because he himself stood to benefit by investing in their education. On the other hand, Vreden went far beyond L'vov with respect to the share of the costs of education to be borne by the workers. Whereas L'vov favored only a nominal fee, Vreden proposed that the cost be divided equally between the workers and employers, thus transforming the basis of the program from charity to mutual self-interest. He argued that in general the relation of the worker to the entrepreneur could not be determined by sympathy or by charitable impulses. "For the most part," he said, "one cannot appeal to general sympathetic feelings in guaranteeing the economic position of hired laborers; on the contrary, no other ties but economic ones should exist here. The only safe and reliable bond is one that is based on mutual advantages and on the incentive of higher profits for all who participate in production." Equal financial participation would underline the reciprocity of the advantages entailed in the education of workers, while providing the only guarantee of the workers' serious commitment to self-help.[83]

Alternative proposals for financing the education of workers ranged from placing the burden almost entirely on the workers (by deducting the costs from their wages) to placing it entirely on the state. As one speaker pointed out, small manufacturers were not able to set up schools; nor were workers capable of planning their own education. Since Russians were already accustomed to relying on the initiative of the government in all important matters, the government should assume the primary burden in this case as well.[84]

No clear decision was reached about which of the various alternatives should be endorsed by the congress. The final resolution on the matter simply expressed the judgment that the "intellectual and moral education of the working class" could be furthered by the establishment of elementary schools by industrialists, the organization of Sunday, holiday, and evening classes at large factories and in industrial centers, and the establishment of elementary technical schools by zemstva and municipalities. No mention was made of just how the various programs would be financed or of how the participation of manufacturers was to be assured.[85]

A second, more dramatic dispute arose in connection with determining the subject matter for the projected educational program. The discussion of this question gives us a sense of the overall view of the working class that was held by participants in the congress. The basic topic of these sessions, it will be recalled, included the "moral" as well as the "intellectual" development of the working class. In introducing his original proposal, L'vov, while recognizing the prime importance of technical knowledge and on-the-job training, had emphasized the Technical Society's concern with moral and religious instruction, which was being given high priority at the two schools recently established by the Society. The proposal before the meeting affirmed "that the moral education of the working class constitutes the necessary basis for the conscientious execution of work, and that it is achieved through the teaching of religious truths, good counsel, and good example." Specifically, it provided for instruction in Christian morality and periodical classroom discussions on the "practical utility" of good behavior, frugality, and integrity in relations with other people. Further, the owners of big factories were to honor exceptionally able and well-behaved workers by receiving them as their guests. The drinking and rowdiness that usually accompanied the entertainment of workers by their employers, however, was to be avoided. According to L'vov, such receptions were certain to edify the working class with respect to proper social relations and would thereby "raise morality and preserve peace and agreement among people."[86]

This approach to the moral edification of workers recalls some of the views expressed a decade earlier by certain supporters of the Sunday school movement, particularly K. Ushinskii, then the editor of the *Journal of the Ministry of Education*. Like Ushinskii, L'vov (and presumably the Technical Society as a whole) was sensitive to the existence among the workers of what, from the standpoint of industrial needs, might be described as anti-social attitudes conducive to inefficiency and strife. L'vov's concern with the danger of conflict was made quite explicit by his reference to the need to "preserve peace and agreement among people." The program he offered in the name of the Technical Society duplicated the old approach of the Ministry of Education to the Sunday schools, in that it stressed religious instruction as a vehicle for the workers' moral development. It differed from St. Petersburg officials' use of the clergy to instill proper ideas in the minds of the working-class population only insofar as it tied religious instruction to a program of technical education, which was inspired by the needs of industry and aimed at the creation of a more skilled and advanced working class resembling that of Western European countries (a goal to which the government had not yet committed itself). Ushinskii, the St. Petersburg police, and the Technical Society all hoped to employ moralistic religious instruction to forestall the estrangement of peasant-workers from values conducive to social harmony.

There were those at the congress, however, who took a considerably broader view of working-class education. One participant, Kaigorodov by name,* proposed that factory schools effect the moral and intellectual development of workers through a program that went far beyond the sermonizing and moralizing approach suggested above. His program included all the subjects that the government had been anxious to avoid in the earlier Sunday schools—natural sciences, Russian history, geography, etc.—as well as a new and original suggestion that factory schools be used to acquaint the workers with "the main legal statutes relating to the working class and industry." In essence, he was asking for the introduction of a program that would eventually carry to its logical conclusion the congress's vague recognition of the need to transform Russia's semi-proletariat into a genuine urban industrial class. Positing the evolution of a complex industrial order governed by a system of legislative norms, Kaigorodov projected a vision of the working class not as just a trained but intellectually limited and dependent semi-proletarian mass, conditioned to its place in industrial society by religious indoctrination, but as an educated and distinctive stratum of

---

* Kaigorodov was a technical specialist connected with a gunpowder factory in St. Petersburg, but in precisely what capacity is not clear.

the population, whose acquisition of technological skills would be accompanied by advancement in general education. At the same time, he shared the common assumption at the congress that without the counterweight of moral edification there was a serious risk that the working classes, especially the youth, would evolve in a dangerous direction.[87]

Shreier, the military expert and proponent of free trade, went even further in defining the scope of the education that workers should receive. He wanted them to become capable of understanding economic and even political questions. If they are to lay the foundation for their future well-being, as he put it, workers must be taught to master "basic economic truths" and be instructed in matters that concern their own economic position, such as the problems of capital, savings, and the division of labor. Shreier let it be known that his goal was nothing less than the transformation of Russian workers into "fully competent citizens" (vpolne polnopravnye grazhdane). Like Kaigorodov, he used the example of Western European countries to reinforce his proposals, claiming that the kind of program he was suggesting had been realized in practice abroad. A useful strategy for the moral edification of workers, he insisted, must be utilitarian in content rather than moralistic. As an initial step, he proposed the organization of public discussions for St. Petersburg workers on matters relating to political economy.[88]

Shreier's talk was almost revolutionary in its implications. At a time when the very concept of citizenship was at odds with the assumption that society is properly divided into ruler and subjects, privileged and non-privileged estates, Shreier was proposing not only that Russia's amorphous mass of peasant-workers be forged into a permanent working class—which almost everyone at the congress seemed to desire to one degree or another—but that they be trained to become politically competent citizens. Yet despite its highly controversial character, Shreier's proposal was brought to a vote and passed by a 39-vote majority without further discussion.*

Toward the end of the sessions on the labor question, L'vov, in summarizing the proceedings, stated that everyone present had been

* Zapiski, No. 1 (1871), p. 73. The 39-vote majority meant that if all participants were present and voted, 68 members favored the proposal and 29 opposed it. It is difficult to believe that none of the dissenters had anything to say in rebuttal to Shreier, which leads one to suspect that some of the discussion of this controversial question may have been censored from the published version of the protocols.

in favor of establishing schools for workers, but that the meeting had been divided between those who favored instruction in reading, writing, and arithmetic only, and those who favored the teaching of science, technology, and the rights of citizens as well.[89] Although this statement gave only a rough approximation of the divisions actually reflected in the various speeches (in point of fact no one had spoken in opposition to technical education), L'vov was correct in suggesting that differences over whether efficiency or citizenship was the proper goal of worker education accounted for an important, albeit shadowy line of division among the participants.

Sharper divisions developed over the question of the workers' material well-being. Shreier had suggested at one point that the material situation of Russian workers was integral to any consideration of their intellectual and moral uplifting. Indeed, almost from the very beginning the unity of these two problems had been so clear that the session voted unanimously to consider the educational and material questions together,[90] thus moving the congress considerably closer to the position of the *Arkhiv* doctors.

The question of child labor provided the point of departure. Kaigorodov was the first to point out the extent to which child labor impeded intellectual and moral development. Restricted to evening classes, working children could obtain little moral or educational benefit after a day of exhausting work. Kaigorodov condemned existing child labor practices in St. Petersburg and elsewhere, and called for the prohibition of all factory work for children under fourteen as a necessary precondition to the improvement of their intellectual and moral well-being.[91]

The opposite point of view was most vigorously represented by Skal'kovskii, whom we have already encountered as an ardent proponent of representative bodies for manufacturers. In principle he agreed—indeed, no one at the congress disagreed—that legislation of the sort suggested by Kaigorodov would be "one of the most humanitarian" measures the congress could propose for improving the life of factory workers, and he applauded recent efforts in Western European countries to place limitations on child labor. But in Russia, he maintained, the situation was different. Whereas Western European countries had an excess labor supply and were therefore in a favorable position to stipulate who might or might not be hired, the labor shortage in Russia precluded any restrictions on the hiring

of children or even on the factory work of pregnant women. Moreover, he said, restrictions would have "a burdensome effect on our
working class, which is extremely poor."

In my opinion it is necessary not to curtail but to expand as much as possible the means for increasing earnings, since moral improvement depends on material welfare. Manufacturers are completely justified when
they argue that children perform only easy labor in the factories, and if
indeed the factory atmosphere cannot be considered healthy compared
with that which they enjoy in the country, on the other hand the children eat much better at factories than in the country.[92]

Thus Skal'kovskii—who was also working from the premise that
material well-being was a prerequisite for moral and intellectual development—shifted the emphasis from the working conditions of
children to the financial resources of working-class families, reverting to the stock argument of early English industrialists that the
right of women and children to accept any form of industrial employment served the interests of the working classes by supplement-
ing family incomes. But he tied this argument to the specific assumption that Russia was suffering from a severely restricted labor
supply, thus obscuring the point, generally acknowledged at the
congress, that it was not a labor shortage as such that impeded Russian industry, but rather an extremely large labor pool that was too
unstable, unskilled, and undisciplined in its habits to serve the
needs of modern production.

The clash of views between Skal'kovskii and Kaigorodov set the
stage for a general debate on how to improve the material situation
of the working class. Skal'kovskii evolved as the spokesman against
various forms of government intervention on labor's behalf, while
the initiative in defending what may be loosely called the pro-labor
point of view soon passed from Kaigorodov to Professor Vreden, the
political economist. Using arguments similar to those he had used
to demonstrate the obligation of manufacturers to educate their
workers, Vreden appealed to both economic self-interest and civic
responsibility in making his case for restrictions on the working
hours of childen. It was up to society in general and the government
in particular to act as "the guardians of all those who, by themselves,
by their own means and powers, are incapable of defending their
own rights." Specifically, Vreden favored an absolute legal prohibition on the labor of children under the age of twelve, and restric-

tions on the labor of minors between the ages of twelve and seventeen. This legislation was to be binding regardless of the views of the parents (a point that was greeted with shouts of "Bravo! Bravo!" from the audience). Rejecting Skal'kovskii's argument that these restrictions would reduce the size of family incomes, Vreden demonstrated in simple terms that competition with child labor eventually drove down the wages of adults.[93]

But Vreden was not content to discuss child labor only. He was the first at the congress to attack the general problem of the standard of living of working-class adults. Since the entrepreneur depended on the efforts of his laborers for his profits, it was his obligation, Vreden maintained, to assure that "life is possible . . . and poverty is never a threat." It was the duty of the manufacturer, for example, to provide for such contingencies as illness and death in the working-class family, through a jointly financed insurance system. By contributing in this way to the workers' economic security, by protecting them and their families from poverty, employers would be making the soundest contribution to the workers' moral development.[94]

To these suggestions Kaigorodov added a series of propositions based on the assumption that "the intellectual and moral development" of the working people *is possible mainly through the improvement of their material and physical well-being.* So long as Russian workers eat badly and inhabit unhealthy quarters, he said, "all measures directed *exclusively* to raising the level of their moral and intellectual development will bring about only small and passive benefits. Our industrialists and manufacturers must therefore pay special attention to and not begrudge spending money on improving the food and living quarters of the workers."[95] On the question of food, he cited the example of English industrialists, who had understood the relation between nourishment and labor productivity. On the question of housing, he cited the example of little garden houses for workers and their families that had recently been constructed by French and Swiss manufacturers and sold to the workers on reasonable terms. Similar measures in Russia, he argued, would have a positive influence on the workers' stability, sobriety, and moral life generally. Finally, Kaigorodov advocated establishing savings and loan funds for workers and encouraging workers to establish their own consumer and industrial associations and arteli.[96]

The last proposal was picked up and developed by several other speakers, notably by Shreier, who agreed that material security was an absolute prerequisite to a worker's becoming "a participant in the progress of civilization." It alone guaranteed him sufficient independence to become "a full citizen of the state." Like Terner and the Shtakel'berg Commission before him, Shreier cited the example of work undertaken in Prussia by the social reformer Schulze-Delitzsch in the field of workers' cooperation. Having seen the work of Schulze-Delitzsch at first hand several years earlier, Shreier now presented it as a viable model for the Russian working class; and with this model in mind he called on the congress to endorse the establishment of various kinds of workers' societies.[97]

P. A. Miasoedov of the Industrial Society also praised Schulze-Delitzsch, whom he had met while traveling in Germany the previous summer. According to Miasoedov, Schulze-Delitzsch regarded France and England as demoralized nations that had "outlived their era," and argued, "if there are two nations who have some kind of future in the politico-economic sense, they are the Germans and the Slavs." The point seemed to be that whereas France and England had entered a period of unmitigated struggle between capital and labor, the introduction of legislation favorable to the formation of workers' associations in northern Germany in 1867 had staved off similar developments there, and it was not too late to produce the same results in Russia through comparable legislation. Because the Russian working class still remained at an earlier stage of development than its Western European (presumably French and English, rather than German) counterparts, Miasoedov believed that class antagonisms might still be arrested:

Although in the West, where there is a special class of workers, one may speak about workers in general, this is completely inconceivable in Russia, where workers are in a totally different position than in the Western states. In our country there are workers in factories, there are workers who labor in certain trades during the time that is not taken up by agriculture. This is the entire contingent of our working class. The main reason that the working class cannot be viewed here in the same way as in the West is that in our country there is no proletariat. . . . The stratum that comprises the working class in our country works almost exclusively at agriculture. It follows that here there are not two classes, but simply two ranks of [non-agricultural] workers, one working in factories and the other [those engaged in *kustar'* or home production] in its own villages, primarily in regions where agriculture does not guarantee an adequate livelihood, and where, consequently, the inhabitants must turn to trades and handicrafts in order to increase their earnings.

Reverting to a modified version of the old official optimism, Miasoedov claimed that this relative absence of differentiation gave special advantages to the Russian workers; in particular, their housing problem was mitigated by their connections with the villages. But more realistically, Miasoedov recognized that workers had serious outstanding problems, foremost among them the need to meet the relatively high cost of food and clothing and to overcome the problems of drunkenness and indolence, which he saw as manifestations of the demoralization that resulted from low earnings. These were problems that could only be resolved through wholesale purchases of consumer goods and the establishment of savings and loan funds by workers' associations. Echoing Terner, Miasoedov maintained that since Russia already had the basis for associations, namely the artel', such experiments were more likely to succeed in Russia than they had in the West. He therefore proposed, using as a model the legislation passed in northern Germany in 1867, that the government extend juridical recognition to the industrial artel' and define its rights in a manner comparable to existing legislation governing the operations of stock companies or municipal banks. Though he frankly described these measures as merely "palliative," that is, as measures that could only slightly improve the lot of workers given the continued "exploitation of labor by capitalists," Miasoedov was nonetheless hopeful that benefits might accrue to the workers from his proposals and contribute to the eradication of Russia's "general disease": intoxication. The citation of Schulze-Delitzsch's words on the promising future of Germany and Russia provided the closing note for his remarks.[98]

Kaigorodov, Shreier, Vreden, Miasoedov, and other experts who favored concrete measures to improve the lot of the working classes, whatever their differences in emphasis, were all attempting to find imaginative but practical ways to bring the situation of the workers into line with the demands of modern industry. For them, material security was the necessary foundation for moral and intellectual development, which in turn was the prerequisite for a working class that was both technically competent and socially stable. Less sweeping in their approach than Terner, who a decade earlier had looked to the principle of association to provide a basis for the partial re-structuring of Russia's industrial life, they treated the private ownership of industry as a given, and looked to association as a principle that would eventually contribute to the greater effectiveness and rationality of industry, which was, after all, the basic goal of the congress and its organizers.

Although some of the measures they proposed had far-reaching, perhaps even radical implications when examined in the context of Russian society as it was then ordered, there are no grounds for inferring that any of the speakers considered themselves to be throwing a direct challenge before the government. On the contrary, their attitude toward the government was both deferential and hopeful. Like the earlier commissioners, they said nothing to suggest that proposals such as the introduction of protective legislation, the establishment of independent workers' associations, or the reintroduction of Sunday and evening education with substantial content—in short, the encouragement of a self-reliant urban working class— might be viewed by the government as conflicting with basic state interests. The single oblique reference at the congress to the old Sunday school episode repeated the myth that the government had acted only against subversive political tendencies within the schools, and not against their independent character.[99] Even Shreier, whose comments on workers' citizenship came closest to a political challenge, assumed that the government was on the verge of implementing its earlier draft legislation on labor.[100] Moreover, as shall be seen shortly, even the most fervent advocates of labor reforms were to agree, in the end, that the wisest course for the congress was to throw the entire problem back into the lap of the government.

The attitude of the pro-labor speakers toward the manufacturers, though sanguine, was more ambiguous. They stressed the theme that the proposed measures would ultimately benefit the industrialists themselves. It seems to have occurred to no one that the congress, by advocating increased influence for a broader spectrum of the manufacturers, might be placing an obstacle in the path of labor reforms. Just as many Russian radicals were to assume that their own view of what would serve the interests of the peasantry or working class must some day become that of the peasantry or working class itself, so members of the "avant-garde" of Russian industrialization assumed, or spoke as if they assumed, that their own version of what labor policies would serve the long-range interests of manufacturers must perforce be shared by manufacturers. On several occasions optimistic statements were made to this effect, including one by Shreier, who, while deploring the poor attendance of manufacturers at the congress, surmised that they were in sympathy with what was happening and would be willing to exert some constructive influence to further the cause of workers' associations.[101] But such optimism was neither pervasive nor consistent, for almost all the advocates of pro-labor measures, convinced that the force of persuasion was inadequate, favored coercive moves on the part of the government. Shreier's optimism regarding manufacturers was tempered by his sober proposal that legislative measures be introduced with all possible speed.[102] More to the point, the insistence with which certain speakers proclaimed what the obligations of manufacturers *should* be belied any genuine conviction on their part that most manufacturers actually accepted those obligations.

Somewhere among these positive and negative appraisals, and more or less resolving the apparent contradiction between them, stood an unarticulated attitude that disparaged the current behavior of manufacturers but expected a combination of persuasion, education, and coercion to alter it in the not too distant future. Secretary L'vov, in attempting to synthesize the various views expressed at the sessions, came closest to expressing this position, although without alluding to the role of government coercion. He suggested that the labor question had taken the manufacturers unawares.

Perhaps many did not even think that these questions exist for Russia, that they already stand before us, and . . . it may well be that one of the reasons why they seem to regard this question with indifference is that the representatives of industry are themselves still not sufficiently advanced to understand that these questions are actually connected with their own interests, with their own well-being.[103]

The apparent acquiescence of the manufacturers in attendance undoubtedly contributed to the hopeful atmosphere. Whether on the basis of conviction or conformity, not one of the educated St. Petersburg industrialists—not Poletika, or Nobel, or Vargunin, or Putilov—would risk his reputation for enlightenment among his colleagues by taking the floor against any of the worker-oriented proposals. Among the speakers who did, however, was one of the "not sufficiently advanced" manufacturers referred to by L'vov.

We have already encountered M. P. Syromiatnikov as the modest, poorly educated provincial industrialist who hesitated to speak because of his lack of eloquence, who could "only present the facts." In the discussion of the labor question, Syromiatnikov emerged as a leading supporter of the laissez-faire position. On the practical level he echoed Skal'kovskii's view that the abolition of child labor would cause greater deprivations for working-class families, denied that child labor was exhausting or dangerous, and argued against individual cottages for workers because of the expense to manufacturers. He even found technical schools to be superfluous—the closest thing to a heresy at the congress—inasmuch as actual work was an adequate way for children to develop skills, and he favored factory schools only with the proviso that they be limited to accommodate no more than 10 per cent of the workers of each factory. Finally, he opposed any reduction in the workday on the grounds that Russian workers already observed so many holidays that there were only 265 effective workdays per year (in contrast to 313 in England).[104]

On a somewhat more theoretical level, Syromiatnikov reinforced his case against prohibitions on child labor by arguing that workers had the right to seek employment as they wished. "I do not know on the basis of which theory the professor [Vreden] reached his conclusions," he said, "but I submit that he transgressed against the theory of free labor when he said that children should be barred from work."[105] Skal'kovskii had made the same point in more general terms: "Nowadays people speak a good deal about freedom of trade and freedom of industry; but freedom of industry also consists in the least possible number of restrictions, prohibitions, and supervisions."[106]

When the draft labor legislation of the early 1860's had been presented to provincial manufacturers for their comments and criticism, only one manufacturer, it will be recalled, had invoked the classic concept of "the freedom of labor" to justify dissent from certain aspects of the proposals. There was precious little in Russian tradition to lend popularity to this type of argument, and its use at the 1870 congress was certainly exceptional. It appealed to almost no one, not even participants such as A. M. Loranskoi, who wholeheartedly endorsed the so-called practical arguments against the prohibition of child labor. (Loranskoi refrained from using the theoretical argument in part, perhaps, because he did favor limitations on the length of the workday.)[107] The only person at the congress other than Syromiatnikov and Skal'kovskii to use theoretical arguments against a pro-labor measure was Miasoedov, the advocate of workers' associations, who spoke against government intervention in the fixing of wages as a violation of the basic rights of the entrepreneur.[108] It is significant that chairman Delavoss, who (except in the area of education) strongly opposed almost all of the pro-labor proposals, belittled their supporters for being excessively theoretical and scholarly, and praised their critics, whom he inaccurately identified as manufacturers (only Syromiatnikov clearly fitted this description), for using practical arguments against association and other untested theories that threatened to overturn the traditional order.

Sensing the pro-labor sentiment of the meeting, Delavoss urged the congress not to come out for specific positions that called for "energetic, repressive action on the part of autocratic power with respect to the affairs of the very faction of participants [i.e. the manufacturers] with which we have now been attempting to conclude an alliance for the pursuit of common goals."[109] The common goals, of course, were related to industrial development, which was not even a controversial question among the "factions."[110] Those who argued most vigorously for measures to improve the situation of the working class—presumably the aim of the sessions conducted by Delavoss —were acting, at least in part, in pursuit of this goal. This being true, the congress was in the strange position of having been asked by one of its leading officials to avoid recommending measures that most members considered to be necessary precisely in order to further the purposes of the congress, and this to appease a "backward" group that was barely represented at the meetings.

But the opposing forces at the congress never really joined combat on this level. There was as yet no need for the advocates of pro-labor measures to concede that their position might prove to be in conflict with the sentiments of the manufacturers whose ultimate interests they purported to represent. Delavoss's plea and Syromiatnikov's remarks reflected a widening gulf between the experts and elite industrialists on the one hand, and the typical manufacturers on the other. But the latter were still passive, with only a single forthright representative of their class and a handful of dissenting experts willing to argue their case in a public forum. Given their

conspicuous absence, and the presence of a number of the more enlightened St. Petersburg industrialists, a Syromiatnikov could easily be disregarded.

Perhaps in deference to Delavoss's plea, the congress chose to
avoid specific recommendations on most of the proposals debated.
It was decided instead to defer the framing of concrete proposals
to a special study commission. Modesty about the state of their
knowledge of existing labor conditions in Russia provided the
participants with a rationale for adopting this solution, which was
supported by secretary L'vov on the grounds that the measures proposed at the sessions had been based on the experiences of other
countries and might therefore turn out to be "inappropriate to the
character, customs, and conditions of our social and economic life."
What was needed first and foremost was a systematic and thorough
investigation of actual conditions in the factories.[111]

The original proposal for such an investigation came from the
pro-labor camp, and contained the dramatic and novel idea of including representatives of both manufacturers and workers on the
investigatory commission. Moreover, the hearings of the commission were to be open, with representatives of the press present in
order to awaken public concern and thereby avoid the pitfalls encountered by most government commissions: procrastination, a
"halfhearted" and narrow approach, apathy, abstractness, and
"petty-bureaucratic dispassionateness" on the part of the members.[112]

Couched in these terms, and particularly with the suggestion of
open working-class participation, the proposal for such a commission was obviously not a pretext for delay, but a radical step toward
public discussion of the labor question and a new and unprecedented role for factory workers in public life. As reconstituted by
L'vov, however, the proposal took on a more conservative, much less
daring character. The L'vov version reverted to a more traditional
model of official investigatory commissions, membership being
limited to official representatives of various ministries plus delegates chosen by organizations such as the two societies that sponsored
the congress; there was to be no place on the commission for representatives of labor or even of capital as such, although workers and
manufacturers were to be interrogated by its members. Representatives of the press would be permitted to attend only with the stipu-

lation that they refrain from publishing the names of individuals, which meant that public opinion could not be brought to bear against the abuses of particular manufacturers.[113] Clearly this program fell significantly short of both the letter and spirit of the original plan.

No speaker rose to challenge the modified version. Indeed, the resolution that was finally formulated and passed was even weaker. It simply called for an investigation—to be conducted by the government in cooperation with scholarly societies and specialists—into "the present situation of the working class in its moral, intellectual, and material aspects." No mention was made of the participation of workers or manufacturers, and the role of the press and publicity was completely ignored.[114]

Despite this generally inconclusive outcome, two important points were won for the pro-labor position. In defiance of Delavoss's warning, a resolution was passed in support of various forms of workers' associations such as savings and loan funds, consumers' societies, mutual credit organizations, and even producers' societies. The resolution was phrased in a manner that left unclear just what immediate steps the congress wished to see implemented and by whom, but in addition to asking for a government study of the question, it did call for the promulgation of normal statutory law setting forth the rights and the juridical organization of workers' arteli. More seriously out of line with Delavoss's admonition was a second resolution calling for limitations on the labor of both children and adults. Again the resolution lacked specificity, but it did point in a definite direction not only by endorsing the concept of legal limits on working hours, but also by encouraging the government, "in accordance with legislation recently established on this subject in other countries," to inquire whether children should work in factories at all.[115]

In two important areas, then, the congress attempted to put forth some guidelines for the proposed commission to follow. But it scrupulously avoided any more specific proposals, leaving it up to the future commission to find its own answers. The resolution on the less divisive question of the moral and educational development of the working class was considerably more specific, as we have already seen, but it failed to resolve some of the problems that had been debated, including the crucial question of financial responsibility for educating workers.

Despite these limitations, there was much apparent promise in the work accomplished by the congress. Russia's leading advocates of industrial development had recognized publicly the extent to which the depressed and backward condition of the working classes impeded economic modernization—notwithstanding the image of progress projected at the exhibition. They had vindicated the views of the *Arkhiv* doctors by agreeing to stress material conditions as a primary problem area. Although the wording of their final resolutions lacked decisiveness, they had nevertheless called for concerted government action in behalf of the factory workers even at the cost of interference with what a very few participants held to be the inherent rights of manufacturers. And by placing a positive emphasis on workers' associations, they had called for a new direction for labor policy that if followed might well have transformed the artel' from a vestigial peasant institution, embodying the otkhodniki's continued rural bonds, into the nucleus of a permanent urban institution for self-reliant industrial workers. Finally, it should not be overlooked that not only the relatively insipid resolutions of the congress but its lively and acrid debates were about to be published in St. Petersburg for the benefit of the interested reading public.

When the congress was over there seemed to be ample reason to expect a positive response from the government to the resolutions passed. Enthusiastic endorsement of the congress by important government figures had first suggested that its basic goals coincided with those of the regime. In the weeks that followed, further signs of government support appeared. By August the Ministry of Education, despite its movement to the right since 1866, had responded positively to a request from Leuchtenberg, the chairman of the congress and its main link with the government, to assist in implementing the resolutions. Even the Minister of Foreign Affairs, while recognizing that most of the proposed measures stood outside his field of competence, lent his prestige to the work of the congress by informing its chairman that he was "in complete sympathy" with many of the proposals and considered it his duty to cooperate in their realization with all the means at his disposal.[116]

This sense of promise was reflected in the optimistic words of *Birzhevye vedomosti*, which had followed the work of the congress closely and had sung its praises throughout. Just prior to the final plenary meeting, with all the draft resolutions of the various sessions already available, the paper noted the practical value of the resolutions about to be passed, and unprophetically referred to the work of the two sponsoring organizations as a contribution that "will be noted in the history of our industrial development."[117] The editors assumed that the congress had spoken both for the manufacturing class and for the government, and that therefore no serious obstacles to the realization of its program existed. The absence of manufacturers was written off as inconsequential, since the participants in the congress were for all practical purposes their authentic representatives: "Not many of our manufacturers and industrialists were to be seen at the sessions . . . , but almost all of the draft resolutions were such that they may be acknowledged to be a direct expression of the needs of the industrialist class." And with respect to the government, the paper's final summary of the situation bears witness to its supreme optimism:

Our first all-Russian industrial assembly . . . testifies eloquently to the ripeness of our society for calm consideration of the economic needs of our country. And since the majority of the resolutions completely coincide with the liberal aspirations of our supreme government, there is no doubt that many of these resolutions will not remain a mere wish, but will be applied in practice.[118]

Was Russian society really ripe for the "calm consideration" of the economic needs of the country as they pertained to the labor question? Clearly a large number of experts in industrial technology, technical education, political economy, and related fields, as well as at least a handful of St. Petersburg industrialists, were willing and in some cases even anxious to consider adopting innovations in the realm of labor policy in order to meet the needs of a modernizing industry. Some were even prepared to take such steps out of purely humanitarian motives. But even while the experts were gathered to discuss the future of the labor question, the decade of peace that with minor exceptions had prevailed in St. Petersburg factories was drawing to a close. The first prolonged strike in the history of the city was ushering in a new decade of unrest, forcing immediate decisions upon the complacent government and making the call for "calm consideration" obsolete.

NINE

The Nevskii Strike of 1870

THE END of the 1860's saw the disintegration of most of the remaining traces of the old official optimism about Russia's immunity from the labor question. Most of the warnings sounded earlier in the decade had been vindicated by 1870. Even before the 1861 emancipation St. Petersburg officials and other observers had been aware of horrible conditions in the factories, workshops, and lower-class neighborhoods of the capital. With the growth of the urban population, the proliferation of slums and the outbreak of epidemics during the last years of the decade, it became impossible to contend in earnest that workers' legal and customary rural ties protected Russian cities from the scourge of pauperism, proletarianization, and their accompanying vices. The change was implicitly acknowledged in the serious though inadequate behind-the-scenes efforts of Trepov's police. Publicly, the myth of immunity was exploded by the *Arkhiv* doctors, who exposed the accumulating evidence of degenerating urban conditions.

Nor was it easy by 1870 to argue convincingly that the semi-rural character of urban workers could be preserved without impeding industrial progress. The conviction of the Shtakel'berg Commission and leading liberal economists that the future needs of industrialization required a clear division of labor and the development of a class of highly skilled, completely urbanized industrial workers was no longer a matter for conjecture, but the opinion, grounded in practical experience, of many industrial experts, Russian and non-Russian. Thus the government's earlier decision to ignore the suggestion of its own commission that it encourage the evolution of a distinct class of factory workers seemed to have been self-defeating on two counts: it had allowed the growth of a class of urban paupers, that is, of a proletariat in the strictly negative sense, and it was responsible for the lack of skilled and stable manpower on a scale commensurate with the rate of industrial growth that the government itself desired.

One important aspect of the old mythology, however, had remained intact. Throughout the 1860's the idealized docility of the Russian working class continued to have a basis in reality. True, there were those in government circles, officials of the Third Section in particular, who were apprehensive, as is shown by the suppression of the Sunday schools in 1862, and by the zealous efforts of local officials to instill religious morality into the lower classes of St. Petersburg and to gain administrative control of the industrial suburbs later on. True, there had been warnings—sounded by the press and the government commissions—that social unrest might ensue if improvements for the workers were not introduced, and the warnings were occasionally echoed at the 1870 congress. But all in all, in 1870 there was still little sense among government officials, industrialists, experts, and the press that steps toward giving workers a more dignified personal status and a more vital role in national life should be taken today and not tomorrow.

This complacency was not unjustified. Labor unrest in urban factories had been so slight as to escape public notice. Almost all of the known incidents in the St. Petersburg area in 1857–60 and 1866–67 had occurred outside the city limits and were easily and quickly arrested. None had attracted any public attention. The most recent incident of any import, the Aleksandrovsk unrest, was ten years in the past, and the more recent difficulties of 1866–67 were temporary, transitional affairs related to dislocations caused by the shift from compulsory to freely hired labor in state-owned factories. Drink, debauchery, petty crime, and vice—these were problems the most sanguine observer in St. Petersburg was forced to recognize. But open, "European" strife between workers and owners, between labor and management, in other words, a full-fledged strike in the Russian capital, was unimaginable.*

* The infrequency of the kind of labor unrest likely to draw public and official attention does not, of course, signify the absence of tension and conflict in St. Petersburg factories in the 1860's. For a description of the kind of conflict that would never have produced a public documentary record, since it was contained within the confines of the factory, see Reshetnikov, Gde luchshe?, pp. 614–17. Reshetnikov describes the workers' reaction to an arbitrary wage cut at a St. Petersburg foundry. Their anger leads them to a heated discussion about the possibility of walking out, but they reject this option as too risky. See also the footnotes on pp. 347 and 357 below.

Early in 1870 a recent upsurge of labor unrest in Western and Central Europe, ranging from Le Creusot and Lille as far east as Budapest and Galicia, attracted the attention of the editors of *Birzhevye vedomosti*. At almost the same time, some of these events also attracted the attention of the editors of a newspaper as remote from St. Petersburg as the *New York Times*. This interesting coincidence resulted in a front-page editorial in the St. Petersburg paper on February 2, 1870.[1] In addition to illustrating the persistence of the claim that Russia was immune to serious labor strife, even by a publication that had no illusions about the problems of Russian industry, the editorial provides a curious footnote to the Tocqueville thesis concerning the parallel destinies of Russia and America.

The main theme of the St. Petersburg editorial was the contrast between European social conditions, which were producing labor unrest, and Russian conditions, which were not. The main theme of the New York editorial (which was reproduced in translation in the Russian paper)[2] was almost precisely the same, except, of course, that Europe was contrasted with the United States instead of Russia. The underlying assumption of the Russian article was that strikes were endemic to Western Europe, and not Russia, precisely because industrial development had produced an authentic urban proletariat, uprooted from the land and prone to disorder. In Russia, it said, the problem of "the relation of capital to labor . . . has no immediate significance," but in Western Europe, with its

mass of landless proletarians, who live only by their personal labor, it has a tremendous significance, and threatens terrible upheavals. Government and society in Western Europe apparently either fail to understand the full significance of this question, or find it impossible to undertake any active measures to resolve it, for up to this time they have been content with merely palliative, soothing measures. Two young nations— Russia and America—find themselves in somewhat different circumstances than the old European countries in this regard, and are able to judge this question and its significance more dispassionately.

The editorial in the *New York Times*, as presented in the Russian paper, argued that a new war was developing in Western Europe, "more dangerous and deadly" than the dynastic struggles of the past.

This war, which holds back the march of progress and paralyzes the development of industry, is the war between the laborer and the employer. No sooner has the industry of a country achieved a certain level of development than a test of strength between these two rival forces occurs. . . . Intervals of peace between them conceal a hidden enmity. This is one of the most important issues the future solution of which stands before Europe. . . . The struggle becomes a conflict between two classes of society, and it will be fought to the death unless a force is discovered that can reconcile them, as powerful as that which now divides them.

Under the present conditions, we see in the future only perpetually recurring strife, allayed in one country only to break out more strongly in another. . . . Our country [the United States], presenting a much wider arena for individual activity and an unlimited wealth of productive power, is less subject to the dangers that menace the older civilizations at present. For them this question is of the most pressing importance, though it may require several warnings such as the events in Le Creusot to force society to give it serious attention.

In the minds of the editors of *Birzhevye vedomosti*, if America, as the *Times* maintained, had less reason to be concerned about future labor unrest than did Western Europe, Russia was in a more favorable situation still:

We have perhaps even a greater right to say of our own motherland that she is not subject to the dangers currently threatening the older civilizations of Western Europe from the side of the workers and, more generally, from so-called socialism. The mass of our people are not landless proletarians who live from day to day by their personal labor at strange factories or plants, dependent on the will of their employers and on frequently changing commercial conditions.

There is obviously a great deal of vagueness and confusion in both the *Times* and the *Birzhevye vedomosti* editorials. In the *Times*, the powerful force that hopefully would mitigate the existing struggle between capital and labor was left undefined. The St. Petersburg editorial is even less clear. It accused Western European societies of confining themselves to palliative measures in the area of labor relations; yet these palliatives, in most cases, had already gone well beyond any measures introduced in Russia. It correctly pointed out that Russian workers still had closer ties to the land than their Western counterparts, but from this fact it derived a conclusion that was no longer accurate as far as St. Petersburg factory workers were concerned. For landless or not, St. Petersburg workers *did* "live from day to day by their personal labor at strange factories or plants, dependent on the will of their employers and on frequently changing commercial conditions." It was true, however, that this situation had not yet led to serious labor unrest.

Unlike some past purveyors of the optimistic message about Russian workers, the editors of *Birzhevye vedomosti*—despite appearances to the contrary—were not arguing for inaction. Indeed, probably anticipating important positive results from the forthcoming industrial congress, the editors seemed to have had little doubt that important labor reforms, which they viewed with favor, were soon to be recommended, accepted, and implemented. They could therefore take pride in the thought that these accomplishments would be brought about in Russia without their having been provoked by the class conflict that elicited reforms in other parts of Europe. Peace and prosperity in Western Europe, they predicted, concurring with the *New York Times,* would not be durable as long as "the question of the relation of capital to labor" was not resolved.[3] They seemed to have little doubt, however, that owing at least in part to the semi-peasant character of the labor force, this question would be peaceably resolved in Russia.

Two months later, in an article entitled "The Labor Question in the Nineteenth Century,"[4] the paper made the same point. Having cited the notorious example of France to illustrate the violence that was spreading in Western Europe* because of the failure to resolve the "labor question," the authors proceeded to gloat over the situation in Russia:

There is of course no reason for us Russians to worry about what is happening abroad; in our country, thank God, everything is still going well. Our factories have still not been deserted and are operating; our workers, too, are not in a state of agitation, but go about their business peacefully; if they make a little noise at times and quarrel when drunk, they do so among themselves, without any kind of definite goal.

This time it was pointed out that the present situation in Russia might not last indefinitely. Assuming that it was the primitiveness of Russian economic and social development that was staving off industrial unrest, the authors emphasized the importance of furthering the workers' accommodation to industrial life before Russian industry achieved the level of development of industry in the

* The massive strike at Le Creusot had just resumed after several weeks of relative calm.

West. "It is better," they wrote, echoing Terner's treatise of 1860, "to prevent the appearance of an evil when one has the requisite means, than to treat it when it has already succeeded in manifesting its symptoms." Clearly then, it was not a stand-pat optimism that the editors wished to convey, but rather a sense of hope that Russia might profit from the sad lessons of European experience while time was still available. This prophetic warning, however, was advanced—like those at the forthcoming congress—without a sense of urgency, referring, it appeared, to the still fairly distant future.

The Putilov Banquet

The era of labor docility that was drawing to a close found its last symbolic expression in a public display of paternalism by the industrialist N. I. Putilov. Putilov, far from being a barely educated provincial manufacturer of the Syromiatnikov variety, was an advanced, sophisticated St. Petersburg industrialist, very well educated and close to government circles—in the words of Del'vig, a "remarkable person."[5] Like Poletika, he belonged to the nobility (of Novgorod), began his government career in the military (Naval Ministry), and obtained a highly specialized technical education (in naval mathematics). In the 1840's and early 1850's Putilov served as an instructor at the Naval Academy. During the Crimean War, when Russia was in dire need of steam-powered gunboats, Putilov was chosen, among others, at the request of the government, to develop St. Petersburg's shipbuilding and munitions industries. His success in these endeavors soon brought Putilov fortune, fame, and the patronage of Grand Duke Konstantin. By the mid-1860's he had acquired several factories in St. Petersburg, including the Samsonievskii machine works (formerly the property of Nobel) and the Duke of Leuchtenberg's foundry, both of them leased with government backing in 1863 in order to expedite munitions production in the event of a European war over the Polish rebellion.

Putilov's successes, however, were not unqualified. Foreign competition and, until the late 1860's, the irregularity of even the government market under conditions of financial strain, began to place him in considerable debt. The government's renewal of subsidization for war-related industry and railroad construction, beginning around 1867, therefore came as a windfall to him, for it enabled him to acquire the old bankrupt Ogarev factory, along with enormous government contracts (paid in advance to facilitate the purchase) for the production of rails. His other factories, which included a number of metallurgical works in Finland, soon began to prepare metals for use in the new enterprise, which came to be known as the Putilov works. By 1870, as the owner of several factories and the employer of some sixty engineers and twelve thousand workers (twenty-five hundred in the new factory alone), he had established himself as one of the leading entrepreneurs of the Empire, the man some looked to as the one who would bring Russian railroad and artillery production to a point where it could compete successfully with the industries of Western Europe.[6]

Putilov, ever conscious of his public image, had inaugurated the custom of marking the completion of each million puds of rail by his factory with a gala celebration. Whether by coincidence or by design, Putilov managed to complete his four millionth pud of rail while the congress and exhibition of 1870 were still in progress, thus providing himself with a supremely suitable occasion for an enormous celebration. On June 13, shortly before the termination of the congress, Putilov invited 250 guests to what were to be the biggest and liveliest festivities he had ever orchestrated, an event triumphantly described in the press as a "Russian people's industrial celebration." The guests arrived promptly at 2 P.M. and gathered at the factory entrance, where they were met and greeted by Putilov. After inscribing their names in the guest book, they then commenced a guided tour of the factory premises, conducted by specialists in the various aspects of rail production. At the end of the tour the guests were seated at tables in one of the factory's enormous workshops, which had been rearranged as a banquet hall and strewn with flowers.[7]

There followed a vast and sumptuous feast, complete with the usual array of toasts to the health of the Tsar and members of the Imperial family, and of course to Putilov himself and his enormous achievements. But the main attraction of the afternoon's festivities was neither the food, nor the drink, nor the high-ranking guests. The featured attraction presented by the exuberant host was none other than his labor force, twenty-five hundred strong, ranged at tables on either side of the two hundred fifty invited guests. The message that Putilov intended to convey through the presence of these workers was summarized succinctly by *Birzhevye vedomosti*: "The concept of productive labor united everybody into one common family. The workers had evidently risen to the recognition of this truth. With a sensitivity not always encountered in more developed circles, they conducted themselves with dignity."

The first toast to the health of the Tsar was greeted by the workers with enthusiastic hurrahs lasting for several minutes while they tossed their caps in the air. Toasts to other members of the Imperial family produced similar reactions. When one dignitary went among the workers to propose a toast to their employer, Putilov, the response was overwhelming. Before a series of speeches by Putilov, Poletika, and others began, free Bibles were distributed to the workers by the ladies among the guests.

Putilov's speech provided the crowning touch to the occasion.[8] It took the form of a panegyric to the abilities and character of the Russian people, especially the working-class people, built around the presentation of four "facts" intended to illustrate the "amazing capacity of the Russian people for mechanical and in general for industrial work." Three of the facts, not surprisingly, were related to the successes of the factory over the preceding three years and the role of the workers in bringing them about. Following his presentation of each fact, Putilov asked his guests rhetorically: "Doesn't this demonstrate the Russian's capacity for mechanical and industrial work in general, and shouldn't this fact be inscribed in the pages of the history of the development of Russian industrial activity?" Putilov concluded, as he had begun, on a note of modesty: "And if I have been deserving of anything, it is only because of the capacity of the Russian people for mechanical work." The guests responded with heavy applause and cries of "bravo." Not content with this effect, Putilov attempted to underscore the goodwill and affection that existed between him and his workers by circulating among the tables, shaking hands with the workers, addressing them familiarly by first name and patronymic, and asking them about their personal affairs.[9]

The Putilov celebration presented an idyllic picture of relations between workers and manufacturers in St. Petersburg: a kind and paternalistic industrialist gave his workers the credit due them, looked out for their interests, both moral and material, and managed in the course of only three years (as Putilov spared no pains in reminding his listeners) to transform raw provincial recruits into skilled industrial workers; a grateful and acquiescent labor force was obedient and eager to learn, receptive to the Gospel, and anxious to praise the Tsar. This excellent relationship seemed to have been forged single-handedly by the will and skill of Putilov, without the assistance of factory legislation or government intervention, without recourse to dubious principles of association or any other of the innovations that were under discussion at the concurrent congress. Indeed, if Putilov's alleged accomplishments were indicative of the pattern being followed by urban industry in general, one would be tempted to ask just what the discussions at the congress were really all about.

The congress, we should recall, reflected a consensus opinion that the industrial labor force was badly in need of technical training and moral uplifting. The line of division had fallen, roughly, between those who conceived of moral uplift in terms of narrow religious instruction aimed at forming pliant habits of obedience among undisciplined semi-peasants, and those who hoped for the evolution of a self-reliant, culturally advanced, and socially aware working class. It is highly questionable whether Putilov's work force met even the narrowly conceived standards of which he bragged. Speakers at the congress had used his plant as an illustration of Russia's *inability* to produce rails at competitive costs. That the difficulties and the "enormous" expenditures of training completely unskilled workers had plagued Putilov's factories was confirmed by the well-informed Del'vig, who, in addition to questioning the quality of Putilov's rails, also noted the daily record of damage inadvertently inflicted by his workers when factory administrators were not present to supervise them.[10] Perhaps the most revealing indication of the true situation was Putilov's extreme reluctance, even when forced by financial difficulties to decrease production (in 1871–72), to release those almost irreplaceable workers in whose training he had invested heavily.[11] Less open to question, however, was the general picture of the workers' docility projected

by Putilov at the banquet, a picture that seemed to lend credence
to the arguments of those at the congress and elsewhere who believed that paternalistic authority was the safest path to continued
social peace in the Russian factory. Putilov, one of the most enlightened of the St. Petersburg elite who took part in the congress, kept
silent during the sessions on the labor question, but clearly believed
that a meek and pliant labor force could still be taken for granted.
Even while his celebration was in progress and the congress still in
session, the basis for this belief was in the process of being shattered.

The Strike

Sometime in May, the date is uncertain, a rather minor incident
took place in the St. Petersburg clothing industry.[12] The employees
in a number of workshops, including a large tailor shop where only
women were employed, announced their refusal to continue work
unless they received a wage raise. The women also demanded two
days off per week rather than the traditional one. No further details about what transpired are available, other than that the employers adopted an adamant position and refused to meet the demands.[13] Since nothing more was heard of the incident, one may
assume that the workers dropped their demands, or at least that a
settlement was reached without much difficulty.

More significant than the incident itself was the reaction of
Birzhevye vedomosti, which commented, "If we are not mistaken,
this is the first example of strikes by workers [*stachki rabochikh*] in
Russia, and it should be assumed that for the moment they will not
give rise to the same kind of difficulties here as in Western European countries."[14] Note first of all that by implication the paper rejected the notion that the cases of labor unrest that had arisen in St.
Petersburg a decade earlier partook of the character of "strikes."*
In this case, the fact that a group of workers had announced their
refusal to work pending the introduction of certain improvements
in their situation was sufficient cause for the paper to use the word
"strike" and to point to the incident as a unique historical event.
Note secondly that the incident was nevertheless minor enough in

---

* It shall shortly be seen in connection with the Nevskii episode that the definition of
"strike" presented some special complications in Russia, but these complications were
not pertinent to the case under discussion.

scope and sufficiently episodic in character to leave intact the paper's confidence that Russia's immunity to serious labor unrest would remain unaltered in the foreseeable future. But on the very day that *Birzhevye vedomosti* reported the incident to its readers, events were unfolding at the Nevskii cotton-spinning factory* that marked the beginning of a new pattern in the history of St. Petersburg factory labor.[15]

On May 22, 1870, sixty-two or sixty-three spinners at the Nevskii factory (located in Rozhdestvenskaia district, near the point where the Neva turns from its northerly to its westerly course across the city) approached the plant's head foreman, an Englishman named John Beck, and demanded an increase in their piece wages. When Beck refused to consider their demand, a chain of events began that led in a matter of days to the cessation of production in one of the largest sections of the factory, employing some eight hundred men. The shock with which the St. Petersburg public received the news of this unprecedented situation was reflected in the opening line of a lead article in the newspaper *Novoe vremia* (New Times): "And a strike has befallen us, and God has not spared us!"[16]

Just what happened between the spinners' original approach to Beck and the outbreak of the strike was a matter of controversy. Two differing versions of the intervening events were given at the ensuing trial, each presenting the attitudes and actions of the workers involved in a substantially different light. One version was essentially that of Beck, the factory administration, and the prosecution. The other version was that of the worker-defendants and their attorneys. (For purposes of simplicity, I shall refer to them as the prosecution and the defense versions respectively.) Before turning to this aspect of the controversy, however, it is necessary to establish the circumstances leading to the original demand upon Beck.

The Nevskii factory had been founded in 1843, one of the first of the mechanized cotton mills to spring up in St. Petersburg after the British lifted their ban on the export of spinning machinery. In 1859 it joined the ranks of the St. Petersburg factories that were transformed into joint-stock companies after the Crimean War. During the early 1860's, despite the strain placed on the St. Petersburg cotton-spinning industry by the civil war in the United States,

* Not to be confused with the Nevskii machine works, owned by Poletika.

the Nevskii factory fared relatively well; it employed some 1,700 "adult" workers (i.e. persons above the age of fourteen) and 250 children, maintained three steam engines (which together generated 550 H.P.), and produced an output valued at from 3.6 to 4.6 million rubles annually. In all these respects—size of work force, degree of mechanization, and value of output—it was far and away the leading textile plant in the capital, with an output and labor force nearly equaling those of all other St. Petersburg cotton-spinning factories combined. Its labor productivity was relatively high, the average annual output per worker exceeding the average for the St. Petersburg cotton industry as a whole, a reflection not only of the degree of mechanization of the factory, but also of the relatively high level of skills and education of its workers. Over 1,200 out of 1,700 Nevskii workers were at least nominally literate as early as 1862.[17]

Between 1865 and 1867 the factory experienced certain difficulties that led to a slight decrease in production and the size of its labor force,[18] but the setback proved temporary and the factory took part in the general revival of the cotton industry between 1867 and 1870. Its output again began to rise, as did the value of the company's stocks, while the labor force—according to figures presented by the factory administration at the 1870 exhibition—expanded to two thousand.[19]

We are dealing, then, with one of St. Petersburg's most successful mechanized factories and with a relatively advanced segment of the St. Petersburg working class. Although most of the Nevskii workers, as was typical, were peasants from neighboring provinces, a large proportion had been with the factory for as long as a decade, which meant they were now among the workers most prepared for assimilation into urban industrial life.* Or to put it somewhat differently, they were the workers who might well have been the most receptive to the kind of reforms then under discussion at the industrial congress. Other characteristics of the Nevskii workers will be brought out further on, but I mention this factor now in anticipation of one of my conclusions regarding the significance of the strike: that the Nevskii workers in 1870 were better prepared for

---

* In *Gde luchshe?* (p. 618), where the action takes place around 1867, Reshetnikov speaks of *five* years as a notably long period for workers to be employed regularly in a St. Petersburg factory.

an efficient and rationalized industrial system than were either their employers or the regime.

What circumstances brought a significant number of these workers to the factory foreman with a request for a wage raise? As revealed in testimony taken at the trial,[20] all the workers originally involved were skilled spinners who worked in the same shop in the same section of the factory. In their work they were assisted by young helpers or "boys" (*mal'chiki*) who held the cotton thread for them and performed other unskilled chores such as washing the workshop windows. (There were also some slightly older, slightly more skilled helpers known as *podruchnye*.) In theory, the division of labor that existed within the shop called for the spinners to operate, clean, and maintain their machines, while other more menial tasks were left to the helpers. In practice, however, there had apparently been minor conflicts from time to time, precipitated by the shop foreman's habit of calling upon spinners to perform some of the menial tasks as well.* This practice—which was symptomatic of a more general pattern of inefficiency in the administration of the factory—was resented by the spinners, who not only found it humiliating, but also viewed it as a form of unpaid labor, since unlike the helpers they received a piece wage rather than a fixed monthly salary. Nevertheless, they would generally perform the additional tasks when called upon, and at times would receive extra money for so doing.

This discrepancy in the factory's wage system was at the root of the conflict that developed. The Nevskii spinners were among the highest paid workers in St. Petersburg industry. They generally managed to earn well over 40 rubles per month in piece wages, though only by working long hours (five and three-quarters days a week, thirteen hours a day, with one hour off for lunch and for cleaning their machines). The 40-ruble figure was deceptive, however, since the fixed wages of the helpers were deducted at the end of the month from the total earnings of the particular spinners whom they assisted. In general the monthly wages of the mal'chiki

---

* Curiously, when the Nevskii factory was visited by members of the St. Petersburg commission in 1859, it was found that injuries among the mal'chiki were very frequent, in part because they were required to clean the machines without proper instruction. The commission recommended certain procedural changes at the factory. Kazantsev, "Istochniki," p. 107. These recommendations may account for the fact that by the late 1860's the situation had apparently been reversed, that is, adult workers were being asked to perform tasks supposedly reserved for children.

and podruchnye were in the range of 5 to 14 rubles, and in the spring of 1870 their wages averaged 8 and 12 rubles respectively. Hence a spinner's monthly earnings actually came to his total piece wages *minus* approximately 20 rubles.

It had long been tradition at the Nevskii factory to close down for the annual Easter holidays, the last four or five days of Passion Week, thus giving the workers at least an additional two and three-quarters days off (Saturday being a three-quarters workday and Sunday a regular day off). For the mal'chiki and podruchnye these days represented a paid vacation, since their monthly salaries were not affected. The spinners, on the other hand, suffered a definite loss in their monthly earnings. Thus a serious discrepancy in the wage system contained the seeds of potential conflict between the skilled workers and their unskilled young helpers. Although the spinners' resentment over this incongruous situation had been voiced in previous years, their complaints had gone unheeded. How it came about that this particular April some of the spinners devised what seemed to be a just and obvious plan for redressing the balance will never be known. The idea was simply to deduct a proportional amount from their helpers' wages for the time missed, in order to compensate for their own losses, which in some cases were considerable.

There had long been some confusion at the factory about whether the spinners were to receive their entire monthly piece wages and then pay their helpers themselves, or whether the factory paymaster was to pay the helpers, having withheld the appropriate sum from the wages of the spinners. Both systems seem to have been used from time to time, but apparently the former—the only system actually permitted by the much-abused factory rules—was the more common.*

Because this system had led to conflicts between the spinners and their helpers (particularly the mal'chiki) in the past, the factory

---

* Judging by some of the comments of the Shtakel'berg Commission, the direct hiring of minors by adult workers was a widespread practice in Russia, and often led to the mistreatment of the children. The Commission therefore proposed that employers be required to keep themselves informed of the conditions under which the employment of child workers by adults was carried out. However, it rejected the idea that minors should be hired by the employer, on the grounds that such a change would cause dissatisfaction among the adults whom the minors assisted (a judgment borne out, in a sense, by the events at the Nevskii factory). See *Trudy*, I, 293–94; III, 30, 98–99. The St. Petersburg commission was sufficiently concerned with this problem to include it as an item on its 1859 questionnaire. GIALO, *f.* 253, *op.* 2, *d.* 205, p. 8.

administration had made it a habit to instruct the factory watchman not to allow the spinners out of the factory on paydays until
they had settled accounts with their mal'chiki, although this instruction does not seem to have been widely followed in practice.
On May 16, the payday following the Easter holidays in 1870, some
of the spinners, finding that their actual take-home pay after paying
off their helpers would in many cases be barely higher than that of
the mal'chiki, simply refused to turn over the full amount of the
wages due. (They withheld about 3 rubles each). The mal'chiki
immediately complained to the shop foreman, an Englishman
named March, who thereupon instructed the spinners to pay the
full amounts. When some of them refused to do so, the paymaster
began to deduct the appropriate sums from the earnings of the remaining spinners and distribute them directly to the mal'chiki.
Thus the factory administration placed itself squarely on the
mal'chiki's side of the controversy. In so doing, it transformed
the situation into a conflict between the administration and the
spinners.

During the trial some of the workers testified that the paymaster's
deductions had left them with barely enough money for food. This
complaint was probably exaggerated. Many of the spinners had
managed to earn as much as 36 rubles in piece wages that month
despite the holidays, which still left them with 16 to 18 rubles after
the deductions. Some fared less well, however, and at least one spinner, one of the defendants, as it turned out, had netted as little as
10 rubles for the month. In any case, resentment began to spread
among the spinners, compounding their general dissatisfaction
with having to perform some of the menial, unskilled tasks that
they considered to be the obligations of the mal'chiki. Some of the
spinners were particularly distressed at foreman March's threats to
fire them if they refused to pay the mal'chiki in full.* The spinners
soon began to discuss the problem among themselves.

---

* At the pre-trial investigation, March admitted to having made such threats. At the
trial itself he began by denying having made them, but he reversed his position again
when confronted with his earlier testimony.

There is no evidence indicating that the fact that March and Beck were foreigners
played any role in forming the attitudes of the workers, increasing their resentment,
and so forth, although such considerations were to be an important element in some
of the incidents of labor unrest in the years ahead. The foreign foreman was so common a phenomenon in Russian industrial life that he began to appear as a sort of stock
figure in literature. See Glickman, "Literary Raznochintsy," Chapter 3. In *Gde
luchshe?* he appears as the cigar-smoking German, Karl (p. 615).

Sometime between May 16 and May 22, under exactly what circumstances is not clear, some of the workers decided to approach the head foreman, Beck, with a request that the factory reimburse them the approximately 3 rubles each deducted for the mal'chiki *and* raise their wages. It must be stressed, however, that at the time the spinners approached Beck, and in fact throughout the events that followed, it was the question of reimbursement that was vital to the workers and not the additional request for a pay raise. It is clear from the trial testimony that a decision on the part of the factory administration to make good the money deducted would have terminated the conflict at any stage. This point is pertinent to any assessment of whether what developed was an "offensive" or a "defensive" strike.

References to the Nevskii episode by historians invariably stress the demand for higher wages as the origin of the strike. The historian Balabanov, writing in the relative freedom of the 1920's, referred to the reimbursement issue only in passing.[21] More recent Soviet writers have ignored the spinners' conflict with the mal'chiki altogether, relating the Nevskii events as if the entire matter began with a demand for higher wages on May 22.[22] The impression left by these accounts is that the Nevskii workers simply took the initiative of demanding a pay raise, and then called a strike when the demand was refused. In point of fact, while it might be reasonable to consider the original plan to hold back wages from the mal'chiki an offensive or aggressive action by the spinners, the main thread that ran through the strike was the workers' resentment at what they felt to be an unjust deduction of wages due them. In this respect it never lost its essentially defensive character, additional demands for a raise notwithstanding.

The approach to Beck was made in a fairly casual manner. On the afternoon of May 22, the sixty-two or sixty-three spinners, having just returned from their lunch hour, accosted him in the corridor near the factory entrance to tell him of their demands. Their manner was peaceful, and no threat to stop working was voiced.

Although all witnesses agree that Beck was furious at the workers' approach, his precise reaction was one of the major points contested at the trial. According to the defense, he immediately ordered the watchman to unlock and open the factory door and angrily commanded the workers to leave. In other words, the defendants claimed, they were "involuntarily driven out" of the factory by the head foreman. This point was crucial to their lawyers' basic argument that no strike had taken place. The version presented by Beck and the prosecution was significantly different. They admitted that Beck had ordered the watchman to open the door but denied that he had commanded the workers to leave. Instead, they claimed he had said, "Whoever is willing to work may go on into the factory, and those who are not willing may go home, since I have no right to hold you back." In short, the workers had been given the choice of returning to their shop or walking out on their own. According to the prosecution, this meant that those who walked out were fully responsible for their actions, that is, for having launched a strike.*

The prosecution version was confirmed by the assistant foreman and the watchman, the only other witnesses to the exchange between Beck and the defendants. The watchman's account differed somewhat from Beck's: he claimed that Beck had simply ordered him to open the door and said nothing else. Even this version, however, supported the prosecution's claim that Beck had not forced the workers to leave the factory. The 55 or 56 defendants, on the other hand, were unanimous in their claim that they had been ordered out of the factory. Charges against several of the spinners were dropped when it was established that they had returned to work voluntarily, immediately after the encounter with Beck. Whichever version may have been more nearly accurate, it is important to note that neither Beck nor his assistant nor the watch-

---

* Some of the similarities between these events and Reshetnikov's fictionalized account of unrest in a St. Petersburg factory are striking. In *Gde luchshe?* (pp. 614–17) the cause of dissatisfaction is a threatened cut in pay, arbitrarily announced by the factory administration. When the worker Petrov approaches a factory official to verify the news, the official shouts, "Get out of here!" The very idea of approaching him on this matter is considered an act of defiance and an insult. There is some confusion thereafter about whether or not Petrov and several of his comrades have been fired. Petrov urges a walkout, but the others fear they will be replaced. They gather at the factory office, but finally yield when threatened with being laid off (much to Petrov's disgust). Thus they reached much the same point as the Nevskii workers but failed, so to speak, to pass the point of no return, that is, failed to walk out. It was the act of walking out that transformed the Nevskii situation into a public event. Clearly Reshetnikov's story was based on his knowledge of real events. The difference was that the Nevskii workers chose (or were ordered) to transfer the scene of action from the factory premises to the street, as was to happen many times in the years ahead. And this was the difference between a decade of unrecognized industrial tension and a decade of open industrial conflict.

man had felt that the spinners, in walking out the door, were trying to force the factory to halt its operations.

On finding themselves out on the street before the factory gate, the spinners reverted to the traditional approach of dissatisfied workers without a background of independent activism: they turned to the local government authorities for assistance. A decade earlier, as we know, attempts by St. Petersburg workers to seek assistance from government sources had produced some rather disappointing results. These had been isolated incidents, however, and it is not likely that news of them had traveled much beyond the confines of the factories involved. Although many of the Nevskii spinners had been working in St. Petersburg at the time (as mal'-chiki), it is clear from their conduct in 1870 that they had little or no apprehension of the possible consequences of petitioning the authorities for redress of grievances. Their next move, therefore, was to present their case cautiously but confidently to the local police.

Consciously attempting to avoid any impression of disorderliness, the workers decided to send three representatives rather than proceed down the street to the police station en masse. The three were Semen Slezkin[23] (a 21-year-old peasant from Tver province), Boris Potapov (a 30-year-old peasant from Smolensk province), and Vasilii Akulov (a 23-year-old meshchanin from a town in Vitebsk province). Unfortunately, there is no evidence indicating how and on what basis they were chosen or whether they had played any special role in the earlier phases of the dispute. Once having become the spokesmen for the group, however, they continued in that role throughout the ensuing controversy, thus exposing themselves to the traditional charge of having been the "instigators" of the trouble.

Their first "official" act was to walk to the nearest police headquarters to inform the authorities of what had been happening at the factory. There they were received by Major Arbuzov, an assistant inspector, who listened patiently to their story. In relating the circumstances of their departure from the factory, they emphasized the point that Beck had driven them out, which—unless one assumes that this explanation had been concocted as a cover story immediately after the exodus from the factory premises—lends some credence to the defense's version of what had transpired between the workers and Beck. The three spinners then went on to explain their specific financial grievances. Major Arbuzov continued to listen sympathetically, leaving the impression that he would have the matter investigated.*

The evidence for what happened between the visit to the police station and the morning of May 25 is very meager. The day following the initial confrontation was a Sunday, so there was no question of returning to work. By Monday, May 24, the spinners had reached but not yet announced a decision not to return to work unless their demands were met (significantly, no such threat had been made on the first day). Thus, although they were absent on Monday, it is only from the morning of Tuesday, May 25, that something on the order of a strike was taking place.† On that morning, having returned to the factory to pursue their demands, the spinners succeeded in preventing the mal'chiki and the podruchnye from entering the workshops, an action that effectively immobilized their entire section of the factory. Although the prosecution would later accuse the defendants of having compelled some eight hundred workers to lay down their tools involuntarily, it seems unlikely that all of the workers, most of them spinners, would have tolerated the exclusion of their helpers from the shops had they not been in sympathy with the actions of the defendants. Apparently the factory had managed to operate on the previous day despite the absence of the 55 or 56 spinners, but the cessation of operations at a major section soon brought production to a halt throughout most or all of the factory. A work stoppage had now begun, the likes of which had never before been seen in St. Petersburg.

The factory superintendent quickly joined battle with the recalcitrant workers by employing one of the most potent weapons at the disposal of Russian manufacturers, one that directly reflected the "free" peasant-worker's continued semi-bondage to the land after 1861: he removed the spinners' indispensable internal passports from the factory office.‡ News of this action produced the only disorderly scene of the entire controversy. Slezkin and another

---

* Apparently the extent of Major Arbuzov's investigation was to consult with the factory superintendent, Landezen, who informed him that the whole matter was trivial and that the spinners would undoubtedly return to work. Therefore the St. Petersburg police kept out of the controversy until the workers approached the chief of police a few days later.

† It was only on May 26 that the situation began to be reported in the St. Petersburg press. Two days later the Third Section communicated the news to Alexander II.

‡ It is possible that this action was taken the previous day, May 24.

spinner entered Superintendent Landezen's office on the run and sharply demanded the immediate return of the passports. Slezkin threatened to run out to the Nevskii Prospekt to denounce the factory administration. According to Slezkin, the superintendent then told him to put their demands in writing and submit the draft for possible consideration.

As in the case of the Aleksandrovsk unrest ten years earlier, it was at the nearest tavern that the workers sought assistance in drafting their demands. A delegation of nine to twelve spinners, including the three who had originally approached the police, asked the proprietor, a fellow peasant, to transcribe their demands while the rest of the workers waited outside.* According to the defendants this was done with the approval of the entire eight-hundred-man work force of their section. The workers then returned to the factory to present their written demands to Landezen. Rather than confront so large a group of workers, Landezen now asked them to choose five representatives, reverting to a familar pattern whereby "instigators" were created by the practical needs of the authorities (later both the factory director and a police investigator would make similar requests, reinforcing the pattern). In addition to the three workers already mentioned, a Riazan peasant named Fedor Petrov and another peasant, Vasilii Ivanov, were chosen. All five were then permitted to meet with Evrennov, the factory director.

Although the written demands presented by the delegation included the demand for additional wages, according to Evrennov (who testified for the prosecution) it was reimbursement of the *deducted* wages that the delegates insisted upon in return for their agreement to return to the job. Evrennov, however, displayed no interest in discussing the merits of the case. Instead, he insisted on the detrimental effects of their actions on the situation of the rest of the workers and on production, and urged them to return to work unconditionally. The delegation refused, and the meeting terminated.†

Frustrated by the negative reaction of the factory administration,

---

* Their reliance on the innkeeper would suggest that the standards used by the St. Petersburg Statistical Committee for distinguishing between literate and illiterate workers were very low. The ability to sign one's name was probably the minimum standard.

† Since Evrennov had specifically informed the delegation that the spinners' refusal to

the spinners now decided to turn once again to the police. This time, however, instead of returning to the local station, they decided to go straight to the top—to the municipal chief of police, General Trepov. A petition addressed to Trepov was drafted by Slezkin in the name of the eight hundred workers. Whether their approval was actually obtained cannot be established, but the prosecution was unable to offer any evidence to the contrary, despite its desire to minimize the extent of the defendants' support. The unsigned petition, having been transcribed into a smooth copy by the innkeeper who had copied out the original demands, was placed in the mailbox of the chief of police by Slezkin and Fedor Petrov that evening.

The petition produced a rapid response, for the next morning Trepov's deputy chief of police, Colonel A. A. Kozlov, arrived at the factory.* Arrangements were quickly made for Kozlov to meet with the workers. This time it was the police officer who asked that a handful of representatives be designated. The same five delegates were chosen. Kozlov pleaded with them to go back to work, explaining that their actions violated the factory rules, constituted a "strike," and were therefore punishable under law.† Evrennov made the same plea, and argued that if the workers felt they had a legitimate grievance against the factory administration they should bring it before a civil court rather than take matters into their own hands.‡

The five delegates stubbornly stood their ground. Frustrated by their obstinacy, Kozlov decided to appeal to the main body of workers directly. A large crowd of spinners had gathered in the factory courtyard to await the outcome of the meeting inside. Kozlov now went before them, read them the law prohibiting strikes, and urged

---

work was bringing production to a halt throughout the factory, the prosecution was later able to maintain that at least as of this time (probably around midday, May 25) the defendants were conscious of the full consequences of their actions.

* At the time he received the petition, some four days after the original walkout, Trepov had still not received any complaint from the factory administration. It was only the workers' petition (and possibly the first news of the developing situation in the papers that morning) that brought the police to the Nevskii factory.

† The workers' legal accountability for having violated the law against strikes, and the validity of the factory rules became two key questions disputed at the trial.

‡ It is possible that Evrennov used this argument when he met with the workers on the previous day. It was also repeated by Kozlov.

them to return to work. But the crowd in the courtyard proved to be as stubborn as the delegates. Rejecting Kozlov's pleas, they announced their solidarity with the five and informed him that they would not return to work until their demands had been met. The strike was now in full swing.

The Trial

Kozlov's failure soon made it clear to General Trepov that he was dealing with an unusual and serious situation that warranted his reporting to the Tsar.[24] In his report, Trepov gave a brief and cursory summary of what had transpired at the factory, but (like future historians) completely omitted the conflict with the mal'chiki and the wage deductions from his account. He also informed the Tsar that steps had already been taken to bring the strikers to trial.

Trepov's general evaluation of the situation—the most illuminating part of the report—was contained in the following passage:

There is as yet no reason to see any general movement of the working-class population in this situation; it is probably only the result of an insufficient understanding of the legal rights and obligations that exist between manufacturers and workers. Nevertheless, in view of the importance of such incidents from the point of view of industry, and the necessity of stifling illegal and unauthorized [samoupravnye] activities on the part of workers at the very beginning, I quickly took the most urgent measures in this regard. To this end the case has already been turned over to the examining magistrate, and my assistant has been charged with giving him his constant personal cooperation in order that the case may be expedited as much as possible.

Moreover, I have arranged with the judicial authorities that the rapid consideration of this case be guaranteed by special arrangements to remove it from the regular schedule. In this way it may be hoped that the rapid punishment of the guilty parties will produce a salutary impression on the entire mass of the working-class population in the capital.

Independently of this, special police surveillance of all factories has been reinforced.[25]

Trepov's words and actions, followed by the Tsar's emotional reaction to them,* suggest a high degree of uncertainty with respect to the reliability of the city's working-class population. Trepov seemed

---

* In the margin next to the line where Trepov expressed the hope that the rapid punishment of the offenders would have a salutary effect on St. Petersburg's working-class population, Alexander wrote the words: "May God grant it!" (Dai Bog!).

to be considerably less sure of the docility of St. Petersburg workers than were Putilov, the editors of *Birzhevye vedomosti*, and the representatives of industry who were then gathered at the industrial congress. While many of the latter were discussing long- and medium-range plans for improving the material and cultural situation of industrial workers, the St. Petersburg chief of police was taking extraordinary measures to prevent the threat of a "general movement of the working-class population" from materializing.

Given what we already know about the government's handling of labor protest a decade earlier and about the preemptive police measures that had been rather clumsily introduced in the city by Trepov since taking office in 1866, the panicky attitude now adopted by him should come as no surprise. What was novel and most striking, however, was his apparent deviation from traditional police approaches. Instead of approaching the crisis at the Nevskii factory administratively, that is, by isolating and punishing the "instigators" and putting quiet pressure on the factory administration to rectify whatever shortcomings were found to have caused the unrest—the method used for cases considerably less serious than the present one—Trepov spoke of legal rights, judicial investigations, and trials. The explanation lay, of course, in the new judicial system that had been introduced in the intervening years.

The comprehensive and carefully elaborated judicial reforms that were promulgated in 1864, and implemented for the most part by 1866, had provided Russia for the first time in her history with an independent judiciary and the right to public trial by jury; and in theory at least, they virtually eliminated class considerations in the administration of justice (with the very important exception of the villages). Of the various reforms that had been introduced since the emancipation of the peasantry, the judicial reform was the only one that provided the non-privileged classes of the urban population, including the peasant-workers, with an institution in which they might come to function as citizens (in Shreier's sense), on a more or less equal footing with other classes. In light of the government's failure to establish the industrial courts proposed by the Shtakel'berg Commission and by others, the new judicial system, although it was not set up for this purpose, represented the only institution to which urban workers might eventually turn for a resolution of industrial conflicts without the risk of administrative reprisals.*

If the opportunities presented by the judicial reforms are contrasted with the failure of the government to provide legislative-institutional remedies to the problems of factory life during the first decade after emancipation, one readily discerns the existence of an anomalous situation. The adjudication of labor problems in courts of law presupposes the existence of legislative norms on the basis of which rational and consistent decisions may be reached. It was not that Russia had no body of laws and customs in this area with which the courts might work. (Such laws and customs were to be cited by both parties to the Nevskii case.) But for the most part these laws and customs were confused, widely ignored, contradictory, and, given the needs of modern industry, out of date. On the other hand, the absence of a coherent and up-to-date industrial code gave the courts enormous latitude in dealing with a case like the Nevskii conflict. In a sense it gave them a sort of potential legislative power in the area of labor relations. Judicial interpretation might well have established the norms for factory life that had not yet been established by other means, had not the Nevskii case turned out as it did.

It is hardly likely that Trepov was affected by such considerations when he placed the Nevskii case before the courts. When he told the Tsar that there was "an insufficient understanding of the legal rights and obligations that exist between manufacturers and workers," he was perfectly correct, but he also made it clear that he attached little significance to this aspect of the problem. Insofar as it was "only" the result of legal confusion in the area of industrial relations, the Nevskii unrest was not yet a cause for alarm. Trepov's only immediate interest was the "rapid punishment of the guilty parties" so that others would be discouraged from similar acts—in other words, he took the approach of 1860. The important difference was that the law now required a trial. Trepov despised the new courts, and especially the concept that police authority should

---

* The word "eventually" should be stressed, since there is not the slightest evidence that the Nevskii workers were in any way conscious of the opportunities for litigation provided to them by the reforms. They had in fact been totally unresponsive to director Evrennov's and Colonel Kozlov's suggestions that they bring their grievances against the factory before a justice of the peace.

be subordinated to them.[26] But he felt he had resolved the problem by making special arrangements with the judicial authorities to expedite the case. There seems to have been little doubt in his mind that the accused workers would be swiftly convicted or that sentences severe enough to be exemplary would be imposed.

The case of the Nevskii strikers was heard before the third criminal section of the St. Petersburg circuit court on June 13, 1870, shortly after the completion of the pre-trial investigation required under the new judicial procedures, and only three days after the case was officially brought before the court. It was heard without benefit of a jury, before a panel of three professional judges.[*] The defendants consisted of the 62 spinners who had been present at the original confrontation with foreman Beck (charges against six of them were dropped in the course of the trial). They were represented in court by three public defenders appointed by the Ministry of Justice.[†]

Before discussing the interesting lines of argument pursued at the trial, it should be stated that the general conduct of the trial was excellent. The public defenders strove diligently to present the best possible case for the accused. The judges displayed complete impartiality, though one may question the logic of their final decisions. The prosecutors, while of course attempting to present the strongest possible case against the defendants, never resorted to intimidation or other improper tactics. Even the police officers who testified for the prosecution seemed to take pains to present a fair picture of the defendants' behavior. In this respect they differed from some of the representatives of the factory administration, who at times seemed to be as much on the defensive regarding their own conduct as were the accused.

---

[*] The new judicial reforms limited the use of juries to major criminal offenses: see Samuel Kucherov, *Courts, Lawyers, and Trials under the Last Three Tsars* (New York: Frederick A. Praeger, 1953), p. 64. There is nothing in the trial record to indicate that there was any discussion of why the Nevskii case should or should not fall into that category.

[†] One lawyer represented five of the six workers accused of having been the "instigators"; a second lawyer represented the sixth "instigator," Slezkin, who was accused of having played the leading role; the third lawyer represented the remaining fifty-six (later fifty) defendants. For the sake of simplicity I shall refer to all three lawyers as "the defense."

The main charge leveled against the defendants was that they had violated article 1358 of the Criminal Code of 1866. This statute, although a carry-over from the reign of Nicholas I, had never before been invoked in the courts. The pertinent section stated that workers who were guilty of engaging in a strike (*stachka*), "at any plant, factory, or manufactory" for the purpose of "stopping work prior to the expiration of the time contracted . . . in order to compel the owners to raise their wages, are subject to imprisonment: instigators for a period of three weeks to three months, and others seven days to three weeks."[27]

The Russian word *stachka*, usually rendered by the English "strike," is derived from the verb *stachivat'*, meaning "to seam together." As used in the Criminal Code (and in the discussions at the trial), stachka is more accurately rendered by the English word "combination" than by "strike." To put it another way, in the trial of the Nevskii workers stachka did not, strictly speaking, apply to the entire walkout and related actions, but only to the planning of the walkout by the workers involved, to the (alleged) fact that they had come together in advance to plan their actions. In short, it implied an element of conspiracy.

In order to substantiate the charge against the workers the prosecution was required to prove several points: (1) that the defendants conspired in advance; (2) that the goal of their conspiracy was to obtain a wage raise; (3) that they intended to stop work prior to the expiration of their contracts in order to achieve this goal. A derivative point that the prosecution would have to prove, at least if it were contested by the defense, was (4) that a clearly understood contract, requiring the defendants to work until a specified date beyond the date of the walkout, actually existed. Conversely, the defense was in a position to argue along the following lines: (1) that the walkout was not planned in advance; (2) that the goal of the defendants was not a wage raise but the reimbursement of deducted wages; (3) that there was no intention of stopping work in violation of existing agreements; and (4) that there was no contract governing the length of employment at the factory, which meant that the defendants had the right to walk out at any time. These, then, were the four main points contested in the course of the trial.[28]

First, did the defendants conspire in advance to walk off the job?

The prosecution said yes. The defense conceded the existence of a preliminary agreement to approach Beck and present the demands, but denied that the agreement included a plan to walk off the job. The defense claimed that the walkout was a spontaneous act, prompted by Beck's behavior in the factory corridor. Since the prosecution was unable to introduce any direct evidence that the walkout had been part of the original plan, the actions of Beck and the defendants immediately preceding the walkout became the crucial factor. We have already noted the conflicting versions of this episode, neither of which was completely convincing. The only point that emerged clearly from the testimony at the trial was that no one, not even the hostile witnesses, saw the walkout as a conscious attempt to close down the factory. Nevertheless, the court ruled that the prosecution was correct in its claim that the walkout was the result of an earlier decision on the part of the defendants.[29]

Second, was the goal of the defendants simply to be reimbursed the deducted wages or was it also to procure a raise? A literal reading of article 1358 shows the latter goal to be a precondition for conviction. Recognizing this to be the case, the prosecution argued, quite convincingly, that a wage raise had been one of the demands of the defendants from the time of the original meeting with Beck. The defense could not contest this point. It therefore argued, also quite convincingly, that reimbursement had remained the central demand of the spinners throughout, that the conflict could have been terminated at any point if the administration had been willing to return the deducted wages, and that even now, while the trial was in progress, the defendants were prepared to return to work immediately if the administration would meet that one condition.* From the point of view of the historian who wishes to understand the motivation of the workers, the interpretation presented by the defense is of greater significance than that presented

* The Nevskii factory remained wholly or partially inoperative throughout the trial, which meant that the walkout remained effective for some three weeks. The fact that the 56 spinners were not replaced for that long a period may be seen as further evidence of the shortage of skilled labor. In the fictional incident described by Reshetnikov, a worker who is against walking out argues that a walkout would be ineffective since the factory would immediately find replacements. Petrov retorts that new, i.e. untrained, replacements would ruin everything in the factory (Gde luchshe?, p. 616). This exchange is illustrative of the coexistence of a general labor surplus with a shortage of skilled labor.

by the prosecution. From the point of view of the letter of the law, however, the prosecution was clearly in the right on this point, and the court so ruled.

Finally, by leaving the factory and remaining away from work, were the defendants in fact intentionally breaking their contract with the factory administration? And was there indeed such a contract? If so, was it clearly understood by all parties, and was it binding upon the defendants? These questions are obviously closely related, and they represent the most interesting and significant aspect of the litigation, at least from the point of view of this study.

According to the prosecution, by leaving the factory, and above all by refusing to return, the defendants acted in violation of a factory regulation that required thirty days' notice from any worker who wished to leave the job, and that stipulated that a worker who quit without having given such notice was subject to the forfeiture of pay for the previous month. It was this regulation that the prosecution used as evidence that the defendants had stopped working "prior to the expiration of the time contracted with the proprietors." However, early in the trial it became perfectly clear that no contracts or comparable forms of written agreement, such as workers' booklets, were used by the administration of the Nevskii factory in their hiring procedures (testimony of Superintendent Landezen, foreman March, and sub-foreman Tarasov). Workers were hired strictly by verbal agreement with the foremen, who then simply informed the administration that the particular workers had been hired. The only document wherein the conditions of employment were set forth was the list of regulations governing internal order at the factory, copies of which were posted on the walls of each shop. In the absence of a real contract or its equivalent, the prosecution had no alternative but to argue that the factory regulations served the purpose of a contract within the purview of article 1358. For various reasons, this notion proved to be very difficult to maintain. It gave the defense its main opening for a line of argument that not only weakened the position of the prosecution, but also placed the factory administrators so much on the defensive that in the end even the prosecution criticized them with some vigor.

To begin with, the absence of written contracts or workers' booklets was in clear violation of existing law. In principle, such contracts had been required of manufacturers since the legislation of 1835,[30] and the law was still on the books as article 107 of the Industrial Code.[31] The failure of the Nevskii factory to comply with this legally binding requirement, among others, confirms the generally accepted view that whatever protective legislation existed in Russia for the benefit of workers was strictly nominal, and in practice had not been enforced during the interval. Now that the judicial reforms had been introduced, however, the government—having failed to implement the Shtakel'berg proposals for a new and unified industrial code—found itself in the somewhat embarrassing position of seeing its own unenforced and unobserved laws invoked in defense of those persons whom it was attempting to prosecute. Once legal prosecution before duly constituted courts had become the recognized method for dealing with recalcitrant workers, the government could not avoid the logic of a defense that was based on existing statutes, even statutes that had never been put into practice. If a systematic complex of industrial legislation, such as the Shtakel'-berg draft, implied the need for a new kind of judiciary, so too did a modern judicial system imply the need for a real industrial code.

The posting of regulations governing the internal order of the factory was also a requirement of the atrophied law of 1835 (para. 6) and the undigested Industrial Code (article 108), and this requirement had been met. But the prosecution's affirmation that these regulations were the equivalent of a written contract contradicted the wording of the law, which clearly distinguished between the two. Moreover, not only were the posted regulations signed by neither the administration nor the workers (testimony of police officer Putilin and others), but also the defense was able to establish that in practice the foremen never called the regulations to the attention of workers at the time they were hired (testimony of March). Some of the workers—many of whom were unable to read—were not even aware that the regulations existed, and even foreman March, an Englishman who knew very little Russian, was ignorant of their content. Those workers who *were* aware of the regulations claimed to know nothing about the requirement of a month's notice before quitting.

This claim is quite plausible, since, as it turned out, the practice at the factory had generally been to allow workers to quit whenever they liked (testimony of Landezen), that is, the factory administration did not even enforce its own rule. Nor did it comply with a part of its own regulations (based on article 104 of the Code and para. 3 of the law of 1835) that was the converse of the section that called for notice before quitting: workers might be fired only with two weeks' advance notice from the administration. Foremen Beck and March admitted that whenever a worker's performance proved unsatisfactory, he was simply told to leave on the spot.

The defense was thus in a position to argue that the defendants' departure from the factory and their refusal to return did not violate an existing contract, but only violated the internal rules of the factory, which in any case had no validity because they had been generally disregarded by all parties. Moreover, in this particular dispute it had been the factory administration and not the workers who first acted in violation of the rules and thus precipitated the course of events that led to the walkout: specifically, the defense was able to show that the administration's intervention in the financial dealings between the spinners and the mal'chiki not only violated factory custom, but directly contradicted one of the administration's own rules, which explicitly denied the administration any control whatsoever over the relations between workers and their helpers. It followed that even if the contractual validity of the rules were granted, the administration was the first to break the contract, thereby releasing the defendants from any obligation to comply with its other terms. Thus whether or not the walkout was a voluntary act, it was legally justifiable from several points of view. Once having left the factory, the defense argued, the spinners had placed themselves in the position of free agents seeking to negotiate a new contract with their former employers on better terms, rather than in the position of strikers.

Finally, by way of placing the finishing touches on all these arguments, the defense maintained that the entire question of who was right and who was wrong in interpreting the meaning and validity of the factory rules was a question to be decided in civil rather than criminal proceedings. Only after a civil tribunal had ruled that the defendants' actions constituted a violation of an existing contract would it be reasonable to file criminal charges against them under article 1358.[32]

In summary, it would seem that the prosecution succeeded in establishing that the defendants had conspired in advance, and that a wage raise had been one of their goals, albeit a secondary one, but failed to establish their prior intention to stop working in violation of a legally binding contract. The defense, on the other hand, had argued convincingly that even apart from the question of intent, there existed no valid contract that the defendants could have violated, but merely a set of internal regulations lacking the force of law or even custom. Two of the essential elements required for a conviction under article 1358 were therefore lacking.

Nevertheless, all the defendants were found guilty of having participated in a strike as defined in the Criminal Code of 1866. How was the court able to justify its findings in the face of the above arguments? While conceding that the defense had raised questions concerning contractual relations at the factory that could only be settled in a civil suit, the court ruled, in effect, that these questions were irrelevant to the case before it. The court argued along the following lines. Since the law against strikes was located in the section of the Code (sec. VII) that dealt with offenses against the social order (*obshchestvennoe blagoustroistvo i blagochinie*), it was unrelated to offenses against private property. The purpose of the law was therefore the protection of public, not private interests; and strikes, being harmful to the progress of industry and detrimental to the morality of the workers involved, represented a serious threat to the social order. The presence of such a threat could be established by demonstrating the existence of a preliminary agreement to stop work in order to obtain a wage raise and the actual occurrence of an "arbitrary" work stoppage, *irrespective* of whether or not the work stoppage was permissible under civil law. If the defendants had simply left the factory because they were dissatisfied with conditions there and believed that they were not legally required to stay any longer, then criminal prosecution would have been out of order. But since the defendants' intent was to obtain higher wages, terms of contract had no bearing on the case. The role of the court was therefore reduced to findings of fact regarding the prior agreement among the defendants, their intentions, and the circumstances of the walkout. On all these points the court found the prosecution's case convincing.

On one important question, however, the court ruled in favor of the defense. The six defendants who had been subjected to the additional charge of having been the "instigators" of the strike were all found innocent on that count. The prosecution was unable to demonstrate that the strike had been planned, contrived, or directed by the six, and the court ruled that evidence to the effect that they played a more active role than the others (e.g. in drafting the petition, approaching the police, serving as spokesmen for the strikers) was not sufficient to convict them. Accordingly, the alleged instigators were found guilty only of simple participation in a strike. Four of them received somewhat harsher sentences than the other defendants, but well within the maximum prescribed under article 1358.

If the findings of the court served mainly to vindicate the contentions of the prosecution, it was the defense that had its moment of triumph when the sentences were announced. The four principal offenders were sentenced to only seven days confinement and the remaining defendants were sentenced to only three. These sentences were amazingly light considering the maximum sentences available, the avowed intentions of so powerful an official as Trepov, and the sort of punishment that had been meted out administratively for similar but less serious offenses a decade earlier.

In explaining the leniency of the court, the presiding judge cited precisely the evidence of the factory administration's culpability that the defense had presented in upholding the workers' innocence: the administration had acted improperly when it deducted the wages and interfered, in violation of the factory rules, in the spinners' relations with their helpers; it had violated the Industrial Code by using oral agreements in lieu of written contracts or workbooks; it had set a bad precedent by failing at times to observe its own rules. In the opinion of the court, more judicious action on the part of the factory administration might well have averted a strike, or at least have led to its early conclusion. (The court was not explicit on this point, but it could only have had in mind the failure of the administration to recognize its own mistakes and to reimburse the spinners the deducted wages.) Finally, the court noted the peaceful, nonviolent behavior of the defendants throughout the strike and the fact that most of the defendants, being illiterate and uneducated, were unaware that they were acting illegally. For all these reasons, it was the judgment of the court that only minimal sentences should be imposed. Having announced the findings and the sentences, the court instructed the defendants on the procedures for appeal.[33]

The Government's Response

As soon as the trial ended, Colonel Kozlov, Trepov's deputy, reported the results to the Tsar.[34] Apparently disappointed with the mildness of the sentences, which lacked the exemplary quality that had been eagerly anticipated by Trepov, Alexander penned the words "Exceedingly light" (*Ves'ma slabo*) on Kozlov's report. Undoubtedly there was further correspondence on the subject between the Tsar, the Third Section, and Trepov's office over the next two weeks. The details of this correspondence are lost to the historian, but its outcome is perfectly clear. Sometime before July 3 a decision was reached to punish the four principal offenders beyond the terms of their legal sentences. Claiming that the nature of their offense was too dangerous to the social order to allow the men to remain in the capital, Trepov requested permission from the Ministry of Internal Affairs to exile Slezkin, Petrov, Potapov, and Akulov to their native provinces upon the completion of their prison terms, with the further stipulation that the four be placed under special surveillance by the local authorities in their places of exile. This request was granted by the ministry, which then forwarded the relevant information to Chief of the Third Section Shuvalov and the governors of the appropriate provinces.[35] Thus the judicial reforms had failed to prevent the government from returning to its favorite method: administrative exile for the "instigators" of labor unrest.

But this was not all. Having disposed of the Nevskii case, the Ministry of Internal Affairs now proceeded to elevate the method of handling the case to the level of general policy. A confidential circular was forwarded by the ministry to all provincial governors, outlining the way such cases should be handled in the future. This important document, which effectively negated the applicability of the judicial reforms in the area of labor relations, is worth quoting at length:

To the provincial Governor. By Supreme command. At the beginning of this summer, freely hired factory workers who work at one of the largest factories in the vicinity of St. Petersburg organized a strike, in order to compel the factory owners to increase their pay. As a result an investigation was conducted, after which the case was referred to a judicial hearing, whose outcome was later published in the newspapers of the capital.

The strike by the workers of the Nevskii cotton-spinning factory, as a completely new phenomenon that had never before appeared among our working population, attracted the attention of the Supreme authority, and it pleased His Majesty the Emperor to command me to instruct the Governors to keep factory workers [*fabrichnoe i zavodskoe naselenie*], and particularly all those ill-intentioned persons who might have a harmful influence on the multitude, under the most stringent and unremitting surveillance; for the eruption of strikes among workers can without doubt positively be attributed to the influence of persons who are striving to transfer this form of expression of dissatisfaction, which is foreign to the Russian people, to our soil, with the goal of sowing discord and bringing about disorder and agitation. But aside from this general surveillance, it also pleased His Majesty the Emperor to command that . . . [in the event of] strikes by workers at any plant or factory in the province entrusted to you, as soon as the chief instigators among the factory workers have been identified by the police, Your Excellency should banish them to one of the below-mentioned provinces *without allowing the case to go before a judicial hearing* and without requesting prior permission from the Ministry of Internal Affairs: Arkhangelsk, Astrakhan, Vologda, Viatka, Kostroma, Novgorod, Olonets, and Samara.[36]

In the last paragraph, the ministry requested to be informed by telegraph whenever a governor felt called upon to invoke this new authority, the wire to be followed by a detailed report in the first mail. The memorandum was signed by Prince Lobanov-Rostovskii, the Acting Minister of Internal Affairs.

The decision to revert to administrative methods was a severe blow to the integrity of the judicial reforms. It removed an entire area of litigation from the courts, thus guaranteeing that the complicated problems of labor-management relations could not be worked out through a gradual process of judicial ruling. This decision was all the more important in that the Nevskii strike turned out to be only the first episode in a decade of labor unrest in St. Petersburg.

Beyond its damaging effect on the judicial reforms, the government's reaction to the Nevskii episode also resulted in further restrictions on freedom of the press, already in a most precarious position. On June 3, ten days before the trial, the Third Section urged the press department of the Ministry of Internal Affairs to consider suppressing newspaper and journal articles that dealt with conflicts between workers and their employers.[37] Two days later, in response to this request, the ministry instructed the St. Petersburg Censorship Committee to curtail the publication of such articles.[38] The order was not immediately put into effect, however, and the Nevskii case continued to receive heavy coverage in the press over the next few weeks.[39]

During the month of July, officials of the Third Section continued to be troubled by the press's coverage of the Nevskii case and its renewed interest in labor questions in general. A secret intradepartmental memorandum in the files of the Third Section, dated July 13, 1870, attacked an article recently printed in the newspaper *Moskovskie vedomosti* (Moscow News) for having taken the position that in the absence of violence and certain other conditions, the events at the Nevskii factory did not constitute a strike, and that in the absence of a strike, the police had no right to intervene and the court no grounds for convicting the defendants. The article had gone on to predict that if such rulings continued to be made by the courts, they would only serve to intensify the already existing oppression of workers by manufacturers. The author of the secret memorandum was quick to see the potential dangers of this kind of article. If factory workers heard about the article, "it could have a dangerous influence upon them, giving rise to questions about those of their rights which they may [already] be aware of and about abuses that exist in their relationships with the manufacturers but which they still do not understand, and also arousing mistrust toward administrations and courts." In a similar vein, the memorandum called attention to a pro-labor article in the newspaper *Russkie vedomosti* (Russian News).[40]

Although no further documentary evidence relating to official discontent with journalistic treatment of labor conflicts has been located, it is perfectly clear that the summer of 1870 marked an important turning point in the reporting of such conflicts in Russian periodicals. The remaining years of Alexander's reign were frequently disturbed by incidents of labor unrest in St. Petersburg, some of a magnitude that dwarfed the Nevskii strike; but the occasional references to these events in the St. Petersburg press were oblique, constrained, and for the most part not informative. In no case would they resemble the detailed coverage received by the Nevskii strike in 1870. There can be no doubt that coverage of labor unrest was strictly censored in accordance with the views that had been expressed by officials of the Third Section. Thus the first major industrial strike in Russia had the direct effect of eliminating most cases of labor unrest both from the judicial system and from the newspapers, and the indirect effect of depriving future historians of two important sources of information.

The decision to resurrect the practice of imposing exile represented a stubborn refusal to experiment with new institutions, in this case the new judicial system, in the face of an unfamiliar and menacing situation. It is important, however, not to interpret this decision as a sign that the government was adopting a clearly anti-labor and pro-capital position. Following the disposition of the Nevskii case, the government persisted in the two-pronged approach to labor-management relations that we encountered at the turn of the previous decade: it continued to use compulsion against manufacturers as well as workers whenever there was evidence that manufacturers bore the initial responsibility for a situation that resulted in labor unrest. The conduct of the Nevskii factory administration reactivated the government's sensitivity to the need for imposing consistent standards of behavior upon manufacturers. Shortly after the issuance of the circular regarding the summary exile of the instigators of strikes, it occurred to officials within the Third Section that along with this policy there ought to be a program of stricter control over the treatment of workers by their employers, lest the government be accused of favoring only one side in labor-management conflicts. Considerations of this sort had been implicit in the government's handling of earlier cases of labor unrest, but the events of 1870 had the effect of encouraging officials to generalize about problems that they feared could no longer be dealt with on a purely ad hoc basis. An unsigned memorandum was circulated within the Third Section on July 17, inquiring whether it would not be useful, as a supplement to the circular that was recently sent around, to dispatch another one that would instruct the branches of the Third Section

to oversee the relations between workers and employers from the point of view of protecting the former from excessive, unconscionable exploitation by the latter? . . . If the government will always take the side of the employers, in so doing it will dispose the workers to harken to the teachings of the agitators. The exile of two or three so-called instigators will not remove the cause of the evil, which could have very nasty consequences.[41]

No copy of such a supplementary circular has been preserved in the central archives of the Third Section. However, a communication from the head of the Moscow division, dated July 23, suggests that instructions along the lines proposed in the July 17 memorandum may have been received.[42] More important, even a cursory glance at Third Section documents on labor unrest covering the period 1871–81—a period beyond the scope of this study—will reveal a persistent preoccupation with the abuses perpetrated by manufacturers upon their employees. What was missing in government labor policy was not so much the will to deal harshly with the abuses of particular manufacturers, as the capacity to establish a predictable relationship between the abuses of employers and the treatment of workers who attempted, however peaceably, to resist them. The "two-pronged" approach thus excluded the concept of distributive justice which, if the Nevskii case is any indication, would almost certainly have developed within the courts had labor-management conflict been allowed to remain a normal area of litigation.

Conclusions

The St. Petersburg exhibition, the industrial congress, and the trial of the Nevskii workers all ended at approximately the same time, in the month of June. But the relationship of these events to one another was more than coincidental. The industrial exhibition both demonstrated and symbolized Russia's—particularly St. Petersburg's—entry into the industrial age, at least as far as technological achievement was concerned. The congress represented a concerted effort on the part of men to whom the question of industrialization was most pressing to seek and find ways to adjust other aspects of Russian life to the needs of a growing industrial economy. Among the problems it attacked was the backwardness of the labor force, which was a drag on the forward momentum of industry; among the solutions it suggested was labor legislation. The strike at the Nevskii cotton-spinning factory also, in its own way, symbolized St. Petersburg's entry into the industrial age and Russia's susceptibility to the disruptive by-products of industrialism, which some still believed to be unique to Western Europe.

The recognition of a single pervasive need had been embedded in the complicated deliberations on the labor question at the congress: the need to abandon the vestiges of rural life that continued to characterize the situation of most factory workers—the need to rationalize and streamline industrial relations in order to narrow the gap between an advancing industry and an agrarian, essentially premodern society. The Nevskii strike—the omen of an era of labor unrest—was caused by the failure of factory administration to adjust its practices to those of modern industrial life or even, for that matter, to the minimal standards that already existed in Russian law. The absence of written contracts, the failure to comply with regular procedures in the hiring and firing of workers, the habitual violation of the factory's own regulations, the payment of helpers without regard to the normal financial arrangements of the factory, the simultaneous existence of fixed monthly wages and piece wages within a single shop—these were the conditions that led to St. Petersburg's first sustained strike. The specific demand that sparked it was both traditional and modern in its implications, traditional in that the spinners demanded their customary sovereignty in financial dealings with their helpers, modern in that the spinners expected the administration to comply with fixed and regularized procedures. The entire affair was a warning to the government and to society that factory administration was not equipped to cope with the problems of the new decade. The banquet at the Putilov factory was of antiquarian interest, while the failures of the Nevskii factory presaged the future.

The trial of the workers itself did not present a clear response to this situation, but it certainly dramatized the need for fixed procedures in factory administration that would make the consequences of a given set of actions predictable. If the failure of the court to acquit the defendants communicated the regressive message that the labor power of a Russian worker was at the disposal of his employer irrespective of contractual conditions, the light sentences and the court's explanation of its leniency carried the implication that factory owners were under a serious obligation to bring their practices into line with more rational norms and routines. Unconsciously, the magistrates seemed to be fulfilling the demands of the Shtakel'berg Commission and the industrial congress, at least in part.

But by removing industrial strikes from the jurisdiction of the courts and reverting to arbitrary administrative punishments as the normal mode of disposition for such cases, the government effectively negated the potential impact of the court's ruling. Nor was the Third Section's revitalized concern with the plight of severely exploited workers a satisfactory substitute for the creation of an enforceable set of norms for labor-management relations against which the merits of each case could be settled juridically, with the workers acting as equal parties to the litigation. Given the views expressed by some of the country's most prominent industrial experts and leaders, the warning provided by the Nevskii episode, and the implications of the court's decision, the rigid response of the regime appears to have gone well beyond the realm of necessity. Once the choice had been made, however, it was virtually impossible to reverse.

Epilogue

MOST OF THE ELEMENTS that characterized the emergence of the labor question in Europe in the second quarter of the nineteenth century could be found in St. Petersburg by 1870: the concentration of urban industry; the expansion of population and hence of the labor supply; the inability of the new industries, despite their growth, to absorb the surplus population; the resultant emergence of a highly visible, steadily enlarging stratum of urban poor; and the perception of all these developments by diverse elements of society as constituting a new and qualitatively different challenge.

Certain significant aspects of the context in which the labor question evolved, however, lent it unique and typically Russian features. The most important of these were the almost totally agrarian nature of Russian society—in particular the continued ties of the peasantry, and hence of most peasant-workers, to the land—and the experiences of Western European countries on which contemporaries could base their assessments of the labor question in Russia. These two factors combined to encourage a belief in the possibility of a unique, peculiarly Russian solution—the belief that Russia was blessed with ample time to benefit from the lessons of the West before the transition from peasantry to proletariat was completed, and that the evolution of a proletariat without paupers, or, if one prefers, of a working class without proletarians, was possible if the right formula were found. But the very same factors, the peasant character of the labor force and the example of Western Europe, lent themselves to an entirely different interpretation: that *no* new approach was needed to forestall the labor problem in Russia, that traditional autocratic methods, intensified when necessary, were sufficient to the task.

In the first half of the 1860's, the view that the labor problem could still be handled in the traditional manner, with an autocratic and quasi-paternalistic government dealing arbitrarily with the problems of its peasant subjects as they arose, was still easily defended. Those who argued for trade unions, workers' associations, philanthropic societies for workers, the rule of law in industrial relations, and the like, were still essentially idealists who, despite their awareness of the plight of laborers in Russia, drew their formulas from the experience of other countries rather than from their immediate surroundings. With few exceptions, industrial labor was quiescent. Once the minor unrest of 1857–60 had subsided, and the brief Sunday school experiment had been quashed, it was relatively easy to mark time and retreat behind the myth of a contented, complacent working class. The terms of the emancipation, by making use of the village commune to preserve the peasantry's connection with the land, helped sustain the belief that the Russian factory worker would not become a proletarian in any sense. Offering the preservation of the workers' ties to the village commune (qualified only by the tenuous possibility of their enrolling in the ranks of the urban *meshchanstvo*) as a substitute for reform, the regime ignored the better judgment of some of its more outstanding officials.

This system was preserved even while the government moved ahead with its policy of encouraging the development of modern mechanized industry, and the result, not unexpectedly, proved unsatisfactory for both labor and industry. The industrial skills of the peasant-worker developed all too slowly, owing to structural and educational barriers to his assimilation; and industry developed too slowly to absorb the increasing number of peasant-workers who were compelled to leave the land for protracted periods. The already existing tendency of peasant-workers to congregate in large numbers on the outskirts of the city and to work together in increasingly large units, cut off from the smaller workshops, stores, and markets of the inner city was intensified, and because so many workers were temporarily uprooted peasants whose ties with the countryside, however unrewarding, continued to exist, and because the chaotic nature of industrial development in the city also contributed to the impermanence of employment, the workers' roots in the city were shallow and easily severed. By the end of the decade, these peasant-workers were subjected to a factory situation that was untempered by any mitigating influences such as labor legislation, recognized channels for bargaining and protests, or institutional ties to the city. Under these circumstances, rather than the peasant-worker idealized by the government, many became instead the shadow of that ideal—the uprooted quasi-proletarian, potentially as dangerous to the autocracy as the genuine proletarian whom it feared. While St. Petersburg industry was more advanced and St. Petersburg industrialists and experts more conscious of their own importance than ever before, the peasant-workers of St. Petersburg were if anything even more poorly adapted to urban industrial life than in the past.

The congress that assembled in the city in 1870 and the major industrial exhibition that was arranged to coincide with it, celebrated the advancement of industry, and underscored the heightened consciousness of technicians and certain industrialists. The majority of those who met at the congress were determined, within the limits of their powers, to abolish the anachronistic legacy of Russia's working class, to remove potential sources of unrest, and to eliminate other obstacles to industrial progress. The Nevskii strike, which began even while the congress was in session, launched St. Petersburg upon a decade of industrial conflict and thereby represented an important turning point in the history of Russian factory labor. It is significant that the workers involved, in their own barely conscious way, were exposing the very kind of weaknesses and contradictions in industrial relations at their factory that the experts wished to see corrected on a broader scale.

The year 1870 was therefore unique in that for the first time the pressures for change in industrial relations emanated simultaneously from two potential antagonists—workers and employers (and their associates)—and for nearly the last time restive workers acted entirely on their own, without prompting or encouragement from the radical intelligentsia. Within two or three years this situation would alter significantly, and the government could present a genuine case for dealing with labor protest in the context of its political as well as its social ramifications. In 1870 this point had not yet been reached, and there existed instead a sort of pristine moment in which the government could act constructively by lifting the barriers to the development of an independent working class, one that would have effective means of participation in national, or at least municipal life.

Before concluding this study let us move briefly into the decade of the seventies in order to sketch the direction that some of the trends begun in the sixties would take, bearing in mind, of course, that there arose in the seventies a whole range of new problems: war, depression, a strike movement, and an embryonic association between workers and radical students.

The problem of the semi-peasant status of the industrial worker continued to generate confusion in government circles. This was clearly manifested in the activities of a new series of government commissions that were founded in the wake of the Nevskii strike. The very manner in which the first of these—known as the Ignat'ev commission—was founded is illustrative. Originally, the plan had been to establish a commission to review existing procedures for the hiring and release of agricultural laborers. It was only after the Nevskii strike that the Minister of Internal Affairs, though he had recently damaged the chances for rationalizing industrial relations by ordering the summary exile of strikers, concluded that the proposed review should be extended to all categories of hired labor, including factory workers.[1] The labor question having thus been grafted onto the agrarian question, the Ignat'ev commission (which began operating in December 1870) was faced with the virtually impossible task of proposing legislation that would apply both to the skilled urban workers of Russia's most advanced industries and to the most backward peasants engaged in agicultural work for their former masters. Whereas the Shtakel'berg Commission—in the heady days when many still anticipated the clean removal of all shackles on free labor—had been charged with drafting a multi-faceted industrial code, of which factory legislation was to be only one integral component, the new commission was charged with drafting rules for a single dimension of the labor question, the making and breaking of contracts, as it applied to virtually *all* categories of Russian labor.

Within the new commissions, confusion over whether factory labor should be merged with peasant labor or treated as an entirely distinct sphere was expressed in a revival of the old controversy over whether to require workers' booklets, and the related question of whether internal passports should be abolished. The obligatory introduction of workbooks and the abolition of internal passports had been advocated at the 1870 industrial congress.[2] Moreover, the absence of workbooks had been an important aspect of the Nevskii affair. When the same questions were raised in the 1870's, however, they quickly became entangled with the problems of agricultural labor and the interests of the landowning nobility. This entanglement placed the entire question in a different light and thus contributed to the endless difficulties of the new commissions. By the end of the decade, most concerned officials had come to the belated realization that it was in the interests of the government to treat the industrial labor question separately from the peasant question, a point that some industrialists and experts and the foreign observer Matthäi had stressed a decade earlier, Shtakel'berg and others a decade earlier still.[3]

Among the first officials who reached this conclusion in the early 1870's were those whose primary consideration was internal security. Important police officials, having come to recognize that traditional police measures were an insufficient guarantee of tranquility among factory workers, began to criticize the government for failing to approve proposed factory legislation. This new awareness was exemplified by the municipal governor of St. Petersburg, Trepov, whose name had been synonymous with a police approach to labor problems. In 1872, when that approach had obviously failed to curb the spread of industrial conflict, Trepov began to criticize the government for not having insisted on the regularization of contractual relations between management and labor. The greater the unrest, and the more dissatisfaction began to be expressed politically (for example, in the formation of the Northern Union of Russian Workers in St. Petersburg in 1878), the more the government recognized the danger of postponing whatever measures might prevent further alienation of labor from the social and political status quo. Yet the same developments had the effect of preoccupying the government with immediate police measures and paralyzing its will to experiment. Thus it was that toward the end of the 1870's, at the crest of the St. Petersburg strike wave, the government opted for a more sophisticated police approach and tem-

porarily abandoned its reform projects, despite its growing sense of
their urgency.

Although Trepov's rather casual conversion to the cause of labor
legislation should come as no great surprise (we have seen the paradoxical coexistence of this position with the traditional police approach in other local officials, such as Ignat'ev and Zakrevskii, in an
earlier period), it is of special interest that even the Third Section
began to abandon its resistance to institutional change in this area
after 1870. During the 1860's the Third Section had already come
to fear the potential danger of disaffection among urban workers
should they fall under the influence of subversive agitators. Horrified by developments in the West, it had been prepared to dispatch
its agents to industrial centers ("the most fertile soil for agitation,
given the character of the populations") at the slightest alarm.[4] Indeed, even before the Nevskii episode the Third Section regarded
the "proletariat" as the greatest source of potential danger to the
state:

> If this fourth estate still does not exist in our country, or at least has not
> achieved the relative numerical strength and the political significance
> that it has in Western Europe, its organization [nevertheless] comprises
> the main, one might say the only, goal of [radical] propaganda worthy
> of serious attention at the present time. The "fourth estate" includes not
> only idle and lazy people, but working people as well, not only the poor,
> but also the well off; it embraces all those who have left or been excluded
> from the social groups to which they formerly belonged, who consider
> the division of society into classes to be a crime against humanity, who
> declare themselves to be "the people." . . . They strive toward the merger
> of all peoples . . . into a single common mass. . . . Neither class conscious-
> ness nor national consciousness should exist. In short, the fourth estate is
> distinguished by the complete absence of historical and national roots.[5]

This passage, from the Third Section's annual report for 1869, includes in the "proletariat" alienated anti-government elements who
might better be described as non-noble or *raznochintsy* intelligentsia rather than proletarians; but it also includes working people,
both the rootless, irregularly employed, and impoverished urban
poor and the relatively stable, regularly employed industrial laborers. It would follow from this, though the specific conclusion is not
spelled out, that the preservation of the still relatively low numerical strength of the "fourth estate" was a vital goal. If the absence

of roots was a prime characteristic of this potentially dangerous class, and if workers were particularly likely to contract the disease of rootlessness and thus become exposed to propaganda conducive to the breakdown of "class" (i.e. peasant *soslovie*) and national consciousness, then it was the duty of the police to see to it that the native, i.e. rural, roots of the workers held firm.

This aspect of the Third Section's perspective on the labor question remained with it in the 1870's; but the changes in Russian society that were signaled by the events of 1870 were bound to have their effects. Toward the end of 1870 a group of prominent residents of Moscow came up with a proposal that not only embodied the spirit of some of the resolutions passed by the industrial congress, but in its specifications even went considerably beyond them. In brief, it was an attempt to create a new organization that would bring the working class under the wing of forward-looking industrialists and their associates, who would guide the workers' moral and intellectual development. Our interest in this proposal is not in its origins, which in any case remain obscure, or even in the details of its content, but in the nature of the reservations regarding the project raised by ranking officials of the Third Section.[6] Those reservations—which not only were not obscurantist and traditionally reactionary, but were actually highly sophisticated, and in a certain sense even enlightened in their assumptions—provide us with an interesting glimpse at how the enlightened conservatism of Alexander II's regime was able, by virtue of its consistency, to undermine the possibility of urbanizing the industrial labor force.

The proposal in question called for the formation of a Society for the Care of Workers that would establish special schools, libraries stocked with popular literature, low-priced popular theaters and concert halls, gymnastic programs, savings and credit societies, and other institutions particularly suitable for the amusement and the cultural and material improvement of the working class.[7] The project was specifically aimed at counteracting the dangerous influence of drinking and tavern life, increasing the supply of skilled workers (and thereby reducing the costs of labor), and giving the workers opportunities for the kinds of activity that would improve them morally and intellectually, while awakening in them a new sense of their value as human beings. The authors of the project were hopeful that the program they envisioned would have a salutary effect on relations between employers and workers and thereby reduce the likelihood of strikes, demonstrations, and other protests.[8]

In attempting to evaluate this project, Minister of Internal Affairs Timashev asked the chief of the Third Section, Count Shuvalov, for his views as to the advisability of permitting the formation of a special unofficial organization for members of the working class.[9] Both the response of Shuvalov and the report of the Third Section on which it was based leave no doubt about the seriousness with which the Third Section now regarded the labor question. In the words of this report, "the question of the propertyless classes and of the relations between labor and capital" was "the most important of the questions now standing on the agenda in the historical development of civilized societies; [it] has already been troubling Western European states for over twenty years, where it ... presents a persistent threat to social order and tranquility."* The standard statement of Russia's immunity to the proletarian infection, which followed, showed a salient lack of conviction that bespoke the effects of the Nevskii strike and other incidents of unrest that had since taken place.[10] But the authors of the report, having restricted themselves to the cautious formulation, *"if we grant that this question has already been posed in our country,"* proceeded to pinpoint the way in which the Russian situation continued to be unique, and therefore relatively manageable:

In the first place, in our country this question does not touch the basic principle of our governmental system, i.e. autocracy, and does not arouse a struggle for predominance among classes. In other words, in Russia the "labor question" loses its specifically political and social side, and becomes essentially [one of] a series of problems of an economic character, relating almost exclusively to the material life of the masses.[11]

Coming from agents of the Third Section, the claim that the Russian version of the labor question had virtually no serious social and political implications has a false ring. As early as the time of the Sunday school movement, the Third Section had been quick to see

---

* The reference to "over twenty years" undoubtedly referred to the European revolutions of 1848, and indeed the report expressed the fear that in the West the question was heading toward a violent revolutionary solution. Here the report was not far off the mark, for these words were penned either on the very eve of the proclamation of the Paris Commune or shortly thereafter.

'mplications in what was basically a nonpolitical attempt
_ literacy among the working masses, and this at a time
..nen the factory workers of St. Petersburg were dormant and when
docility and ready submission to authority characterized even those
workers who occasionally became involved in mild disturbances;
and the Nevskii strike, a nonviolent if aggressive attempt to reclaim
deducted wages, had led to the overturning of the judicial process
in matters having to do with labor unrest. In short, what had characterized the Third Section's approach to the problems of factory
workers had been a *refusal* to allow them to be treated and resolved
as purely economic or purely educational questions. In the report
of the Third Section it was stated that there already existed in Russia the danger that "deficiencies" in the situation of the working
class, "real or imagined," would be exploited by "antisocial" agitators. It was precisely on the basis of this consideration—notwithstanding its inconsistency with the view that Russia's labor problems were purely economic in character—that the authors of the
Third Section's report welcomed the proposal of the Moscow group,
at least in principle.[12]

But if the Society for the Care of Workers was welcome in principle, it did not follow that it was acceptable in practice. The content of the proposal had first to be examined and evaluated with
respect to its potential danger to the existing order. In its discussion of this question, the report defined the role of autocratic government in Russian society in terms that placed old assumptions in
a context that incorporated some of the changes of recent years. The
main principle invoked was that "in an autocratic state, the power
of the government stands *outside* class interests, and is thus able to
balance the interests and to prevent in good time [those] disagreements and contradictions that are capable of arousing the mutual
enmity of classes." Since relations between the manufacturing and
working classes are often tense and characterized by suspiciousness,
"enemies of the social order" have an opportunity for "dangerous
agitation" whenever "even out of beneficence toward the working
people and solicitude for them, the representatives of capital attempt to unite their forces. Such a merger will always be interpreted as a combination on the part of capital [*stachka kapitala*]
aimed at the exploitation of labor." It was therefore important to

ask whether the proposed society was apt to create the impression among workers that its members had ulterior motives, antagonistic to their interests, an impression that would serve to fan the flames of class antagonisms. Conflict between capital and labor could probably be restrained only so long as all social classes continued to be equally subjected to autocratic power, for it was the predominance of particular classes, the nobility and the clergy in the middle ages, the bourgeoisie since 1789, that had undermined the societies of Western Europe throughout history. So ran the argument of the Third Section* against introducing any institutions that might be suspected of secretly encouraging class subjugation or exploitation. If there was a reasonable possibility that the proposed society might be vulnerable to such suspicions, then it was the role of the government, as the equalizer and balancer of conflicting social interests, to prevent this from occurring.[13]

Turning to the history of the "labor question" in Western Europe for further instruction, the Third Section then pointed to the experience of organizations similar to the one now contemplated for Russia. Like the proposed society, the European organizations had often evoked considerable sympathy from employers. Yet history had shown the results of these endeavors to be "completely negative." They had failed entirely to reduce the distrust and hostility of labor toward capital, as could be seen at the present time in all Western European countries.[14]

Having ruled out the possibility of counteracting the workers' suspicions about the proposed society by including representatives of labor on its governing council,† the report then pointed to the danger that "people-loving" (*narodoliubstvuiushchie*) demagogues would penetrate the membership, thereby obtaining a firm base for their propaganda among the workers: "Such has been the course of events in other countries, and such it would be in ours." Ultimately,

---

* These arguments were repeated in slightly different form in Shuvalov's response to Timashev. Shuvalov insisted that the government must "constantly maintain a balance" between capital and labor, whose interests he considered to be contradictory. TsGAOR, *f.* 109, *eksp.* 3, *d.* 44, *op.* 1871, p. 36.

† The authors of the proposal had allotted half the seats on the council to employers, but none to workers. The Third Section argued that only if the other half went to workers would the plan be equitable, but then itself ruled out this alternative on the highly dubious grounds that the workers would be unable to pay the annual membership dues.

the Third Section concluded, "the very raising of the moral and intellectual level of our workers," which was the intended purpose of the Society, "would only lead them to a more conscious hatred of those who, with sincere generosity, are now offering them help and care."[15] The establishment of an organization to deal with the difficulties of labor, however munificent the motives of its founders, would in the long run be viewed by the working class, guided by dangerous intellectuals, as a concealed form of class hegemony. The government's responsibility for maintaining the existing "balance" between capital and labor thus precluded approval of the proposal in its present form.

This reasoning brings to mind the attitudes toward the Sunday schools that had been expressed a decade earlier by Dolgorukov, Shuvalov's predecessor: "The government cannot permit half of the population to owe its education not to the state but to itself or to the private philanthropy of any particular class."[16] But conditions had changed since Dolgorukov penned these words, and it was no longer sufficient to criticize a proposed solution like the Society merely because benefits for the lower classes were supposed to accrue through the periodic generosity of the government; it now seemed logical to show in some detail the danger that the project might contribute to the spirit of class struggle so recently expressed in the Nevskii strike. It could no longer be maintained that the rural bonds of the urban workers represented an adequate countervailing force to the deterioration of their condition.

With the government committed to strengthening the state by means of industrialization, the labor question had to be regarded as a long-range problem. Ad hoc government interventions—whether to punish "instigators" or to pressure recalcitrant industrialists into easing the plight of their most blatantly exploited employees—may have been consistent with the image of the government as the supreme arbitrator of conflicting class interests, but they did not represent a reliable prophylactic policy for the dawning industrial age. This is why the Third Section could not criticize the actual content of the present project. No less than the participants in the 1870 congress, the Third Section now recognized the need for measures to improve the economic, intellectual, and moral position of Russian labor. The real issue lay not in the programmatic content of the proposed measures, but in the question of how and by whom they would be administered. The authors of the plan placed their hopes in public-spirited elites and enlightened industrialists; the Third Section (apparently the Ministry of Internal Affairs was prepared to rely upon its opinion in these matters) considered these "well-intentioned" types to be dangerously sentimental and refused to allow even the small number of forward-looking industrialists to play a significant role, lest their activities lay them open to the charge of exercising a concealed hegemony over the working class, and the government to the charge of tolerating and even abetting this situation.

The only conclusion consistent with these views was for the government itself, perhaps with some assistance from private social groups, to take charge of the project or, as was suggested in another Third Section document (dated October 1, 1871), to follow the example of England by taking the welfare of the working class into its own hands.[17] The Third Section was gradually edging toward support of the full application of state power to a formal program of labor-oriented social welfare, one that would extend beyond the emergency role of "fireman" that the government had been playing for so many years, while precluding the development of an independent relationship between the working class and other segments of society.[18]

The group that the Third Section least wanted to see in contact with urban workers was, of course, the radical intelligentsia. Such contacts, however, had been all but nonexistent since the closing of the Sunday schools in 1862. Fearing the specter of a European proletariat as much as the most conservative officials, if not more, the Russian Left—both before and after 1870—eschewed all interest in a legislative program for the urban working class, or, for that matter, in any resolution of the problems of workers that presupposed the intensification of proletarianization and the division of labor. Least of all were Populist intellectuals prepared to encourage the adaptation of urban workers to an industrial age that they themselves anathematized. The attitude of N. K. Mikhailovskii, the prominent theoretician of Populism, was typical. He castigated the participants in the industrial congress precisely for having accepted industrial capitalism and for attempting to deal with the labor question on that basis. True, just as *Sovremennik*, despite its antipathy to the basic outlook of the liberal economists, had been sympathetic toward their efforts to protect child labor, Mikhailovskii could not refrain from speaking favorably of Vreden and other participants who expressed their compassion for the workers; his venom was reserved for Skal'kovskii, Delavoss, and those who made light of the workers' plight. But Mikhailovskii's basic position—shared by virtually all of his fellow Populists—was that neither side in the debate was sensitive to the dangers that a Western urban factory system posed for the lower classes, or understood that only a peasant craft industry and the commune could save the Russian people from a tragic fate.[19]

Yet despite the shallowness of the Third Section's understanding of Populist views of the labor question, there was a prophetic quality to its apprehensions. By the end of the 1860's, a handful of radical writers had begun to take grim note of the symptoms of proletarianization. In the same issue of *Otechestvennye zapiski* in which Reshetnikov published the first installment of *Gde luchshe?*, another contributor wrote, "We Russians are horrified by the situation of the Western proletarian, and . . . we usually say that Russia, thank God, is far from having the proletariat that eats away at Western societies. But is it really? Will someone who, for example, compares the life of one of our distillery workers with the life of a Western proletarian worker really maintain that our worker has it any better?"[20] Such allusions to the worsening plight of the Russian worker would multiply in the years ahead; for though the Left did not welcome the appearance of urban factory workers, it began to focus on them more attentively.* By the early 1870's, the recurrence of strikes in St. Petersburg—although they awakened no particular enthusiasm—helped inspire local radicals (especially the so-called *chaikovtsy*) with the thought that factory workers might pro-

---

* Bervi-Flerovskii's classic *Polozhenie rabochego klassa v Rossii* (1869) was one of the earlier and most widely publicized examples of this tendency. A more accurate title for the book than "Situation of the Working Class" would have been "Deterioration of the Situation of the Peasantry," for rather than posing the labor question as a quest for ways to remove the iniquities of proletarianization while maintaining an urbanized working class, Flerovskii, to the extent that he dealt with urban workers at all, used their plight to underline the horrors that befell the people when they were uprooted and cut off from their homes (see esp. Part III, Ch. 5). In this respect his outlook was typically Populist.

vide a badly needed vehicle for exerting influence on the peasantry. Out of this initial contact there developed both a solid nucleus of radical activist workers and, by the late 1870's, a significant change in the attitude of many Populists toward the labor question, including, in some cases, abandonment of belief in the futility of strikes.

Official fears of the "contamination" of the working class by revolutionary ideas were almost entirely theoretical in the 1860's, an abstraction from Western European experience rather than a reflection of present reality. This "danger" could have been (but was not) disregarded when practical reform measures were under consideration. By the 1870's the danger was no longer theoretical, and every reform contemplated by the government for the long-run good of the working class had to be measured against the short-term threats to the social order it might spawn. Thus, for example, while the Sunday schools of 1859–62 exposed the workers to "dangerous" influences that were more imaginary than real, the schools of the Imperial Technical Society—of which the government made an exception and which it continued to tolerate into the 1870's[21]—soon became important centers for contact between workers and radical students and the source of actual threats to the regime. As the government learned of these contacts, the desire of some officials to maintain the isolation of workers from other social groups hardened, thus reducing the likelihood that appropriate institutional innovations would be introduced. In the 1870's the schools of the Technical Society remained the only significant exception to the isolation of St. Petersburg workers from any meaningful social experience outside the factory, the tavern, and the clandestine circle.

Finally, a few words should be said about the role of industrialists in the further development of the labor question in the 1870's. In Chapter 8, we noted the way in which, at the industrial congress, some advanced industrialists and technical experts and educators had presented themselves as spokesmen for attitudes that they hoped would spread to other, less cultivated manufacturers in the not too distant future. In anticipation of this development, they had argued for the creation of representative institutions through which merchants and manufacturers would be able to influence government policies affecting their interests. Like most of the controversial proposals put forth by the congress, this one was largely ignored. But in the course of the 1870's, the government at least partially honored the spirit of the proposal by allowing a few select manufacturers to participate formally in the work of one of its commissions on labor legislation.[22] Moreover, as the decade progressed, manufacturers generally found that their opinions were solicited more and more often. But as it turned out, the broadening of the influence of manufacturers—particularly in view of the fact that it came *after* workers had begun to assert themselves against their employers—yielded results that with a few exceptions had little in common with the aspirations of the more enlightened participants in the discussions of the labor question that had taken place in 1870. Taken as a whole the nation's manufacturers exerted an influence that served to impede rather than encourage labor legislation and other progressive measures.

Before the 1870's, manufacturers had spoken publicly in defense of their interests only rarely, and then mainly with regard to the tariff question. When their views were solicited on labor legislation early in the reign of Alexander II, they expressed their reservations only with great caution, and dared not challenge the direction in which the government seemed to be moving. Then, ambiguously in 1867 but clearly in 1870, self-appointed representatives of Russian industry called for reforms—which, as it turned out, the class they "represented" was less than willing to favor. Syromiatnikov proved to be more representative of a young and threatened industrial bourgeoisie than of the mainstream of opinion at the congress, and the "rising bourgeoisie" proved to be inimical to the program of its supposed spokesmen. Instead of heralding a period of social progress, the year 1870 turned out to be a last and lost opportunity, which suggests that a backward industrialist class with no influence on the government provides a more favorable milieu for the introduction of social legislation than a bourgeoisie that is beginning to feel self-assured.

In more general terms, it might well be argued that the entire question of class interests became much more crucial in the 1870's than it had been in the 1860's. Up to and including the year 1870, it was possible to approach the labor question abstractly, analyze it in terms of the general needs of the country, the needs of the workers (still unformulated by the workers themselves), and the alleged needs of manufacturers (still uncontradicted by most manufacturers). If the government could overcome its own preconceptions, it could act with enormous flexibility. After 1870 this ceased to be the case, for from that time on, both workers and manufacturers began to complicate the picture with their own ideas concerning their needs. In the 1860's, when the situation had been easily amenable to imaginative government programs, the stimulus to act had been lacking. By the 1870's, when the stimulus to act was growing strong, the social situation was becoming much less tractable. A new era of urban class conflict had begun.

Notes

Complete authors' names, titles, and publication data will be found in the Bibliography, pp. 427–39 with the exception of contemporary journal articles and a number of other works that are cited in full in the Notes. The following abbreviations and short titles are used in the Notes, footnotes, and Bibliography:

Arkhiv	*Arkhiv sudebnoi meditsiny i obshchestvennoi gigieny*
GIALO	Gosudarstvennyi istoricheskii arkhiv Leningradskoi oblasti
PSZ	*Polnoe sobranie zakonov Rossiiskoi Imperii*
S-PSK	S.-Peterburgskii statisticheskii komitet
Trudy	*Trudy kommissii uchrezhdennoi dlia peresmotra ustavov fabrichnogo i remeslennogo*
TsGAOR	Tsentral'nyi gosudarstvennyi arkhiv Oktiabr'skoi revoliutsii
TsGIAL	Tsentral'nyi gosudarstvennyi istoricheskii arkhiv v Leningrade
TsSKMVD	Tsentral'nyi statisticheskii komitet Ministerstva vnutrennikh del
Zapiski	*Zapiski Imperatorskogo Russkogo Tekhnicheskogo Obshchestva*
ZhMNP	*Zhurnal Ministerstva narodnogo prosveshcheniia*

INTRODUCTION

1. Leopold Haimson, "The Problem of Social Stability in Urban Russia, 1905–1917," *Slavic Review*, XXIII, No. 4 (Dec. 1964), 33–65, and XXIV, No. 1 (March 1965), 1–22; Richard Pipes, *Social Democracy and the St. Petersburg Labor Movement, 1885–1897* (Cambridge, Mass., 1963); Rimlinger, "Autocracy and the Factory Order in Early Russian Industrialization" and "The Management of Labor Protest in Tsarist Russia"; Solomon M. Schwarz, *The Russian Revolution of 1905: The Workers' Movement and the Formation of Bolshevism and Menshevism* (Chicago, 1967); Theodore H. Von Laue, "Russian Labor Between Field and Factory, 1892–1903," *California Slavic Studies*, III (1964), 33–65, and "Russian Peasants in the Factory, 1892–1904," *Journal of Economic History*, XXI (March 1961), 61–80; Walkin, "The Attitude of the Tsarist Government Toward the Labor Problem"; Allan K. Wildman, *The Making of a Workers' Revolution: Russian Social Democracy, 1891–1903* (Chicago, 1967).

2. Among the books, Professor Wildman's excellent study comes closest to treating workers as something other than an adjunct to the Marxist movement.

3. The two most important are Blackwell, *The Beginnings of Russian Industrialization*, and Pintner, *Russian Economic Policy Under Nicholas I.* Black-

well's comprehensive work examines more aspects of the process of industrialization than does Pintner's, which, as the title indicates, is restricted to the topic of official policies.

4. On recent Soviet treatment of the role of labor in the "revolutionary situation" of 1859–61, see pp. 160–61.

5. The most important Soviet works that incorporate the period treated in this book are Balabanov, *Ocherki*; El'nitskii, *Istoriia*; Pazhitnov, *Polozhenie*; Rashin, *Formirovanie*.

6. Haimson, "The Problem of Social Stability," note 1 above.

CHAPTER ONE

1. Blackwell, p. 410.

2. For a fuller discussion of the pre-Petrine city see Ditiatin, I, 107–37.

3. A detailed analysis of this regulation is contained in *ibid.*, pp. 199–248. For a briefer summary of its contents, see Pazhitnov, *Problema remeslennykh tsekhov*, pp. 43–44. The regulation may be found in *PSZ*, 1st Series, VI, No. 3708.

4. "Zhalovannaia gramota gorodam," *PSZ*, 1st Series, XXII, No. 16188.

5. See Ditiatin, I, 370–413.

6. For a detailed analysis see *ibid.*, pp. 415–72.

7. *Ibid.*, p. 289.

8. *Ibid.*, Bk. 2, Part I.

9. *Ibid.*, pp. 327–70.

10. *Ibid.*, pp. 459–72.

11. Ryndziunskii, pp. 56–57.

12. See Max Weber, *The City* (Free Press ed., New York, 1958), pp. 80–81. My criteria for assessing the degree of development of Russian cities are derived, in part, from Weber's classic study; pp. 66–67, 74, and 80–89 are particularly pertinent.

13. Ditiatin, I, 287–93.

14. For a review of the literature on this topic, with particular reference to the question whether true artisan guilds as they were known in the European Middle Ages existed in pre-Petrine Russia, see Pazhitnov, *Problema*, pp. 5–25. The consensus of historians is that they did not (see also *ibid.*, pp. 28–29).

15. Ditiatin, I, 293–95. For a chronological summary of Peter's legislation relating to artisan guilds see Pazhitnov, *Problema*, pp. 43–46.

16. Pazhitnov, *Problema*, pp. 49–51; Ditiatin, I, 296–99.

17. Ditiatin, I, 398–99.

18. *Ibid.*, pp. 415–59, esp. pp. 421–24.

19. Pazhitnov, *Problema*, pp. 75–82; Ditiatin, I, 483–95.

20. On German artisans see Hamerow, pp. 21–37.

21. Ryndziunskii, pp. 40–51; see also pp. 84–85, 92.

22. Weber, *The City*, p. 92.

23. Ryndziunskii, p. 52.

24. *Ibid.*, p. 211.

25. *Ibid.*, Table 14, p. 221. This calculation is somewhat imprecise, since the

figures for meshchane and merchants cover the period 1827–54, whereas the two million figure covers 1825–56.

26. On the rise of mixed obligations in the late eighteenth century and the early nineteenth, see Michael Confino, *Domaines et seigneurs en Russie vers la fin du XVIIIᵉ siècle: Etude de structures agraires et de mentalités économiques* (Paris, 1963), Ch. 4, esp. pp. 186–201, 251–54.

27. Ryndziunskii, pp. 52–61, 71–83, 85–90, 109–52, 158–67, 175–79, 185–86.

28. On the possessional workers and their decline see Zelnik, "The Peasant and the Factory," pp. 160–64.

29. See Pazhitnov, *Polozhenie*, I, 47; V. K. Iatsunskii, "Krupnaia promyshlennost' Rossii v 1790–1860 gg.," in Rozhkova, *Ocherki*, pp. 212–14; Liashchenko, I, 531; Ryndziunskii, pp. 36–37, 62, 431–32; Zelnik, "The Peasant and the Factory," pp. 165, 173.

30. Ryndziunskii, p. 428; V. K. Iatsunskii and M. K. Rozhkova, "Rabochie doreformennoi Rossii," in Rozhkova, *Ocherki*, pp. 22–24.

31. Gerschenkron, "Economic Backwardness," p. 7.

32. Ryndziunskii, pp. 93–95, 449–52.

33. *Ibid.*, pp. 91–92. On the functions of the seigneurial administration and the administrative use of peasant elders on the estates, see Confino, *Domaines et seigneurs*, pp. 39–105.

34. On the artel' see Maksimov, pp. i–v.

35. Pintner, p. 252.

36. See Kiniapina.

37. For further details see Pintner and Kiniapina; see also Blackwell, pp. 123–83, 264–386, and M. K. Rozhkova, "Ekonomicheskaia politika pravitel'stva," in Rozhkova, *Ocherki*, pp. 359–79.

38. Kiniapina, p. 415 (my emphasis).

39. Tugan-Baranovskii, p. 178; Kiniapina, pp. 383–84. (Kiniapina and Tugan-Baranovskii quote somewhat different extracts from the passage by Kankrin. My citations combine the two.) See also Pintner, p. 101, and Bendix, pp. 178–79.

40. Rozhkova, p. 378.

41. Kiniapina, pp. 385, 415; Pintner, p. 102; Rozhkova, p. 378.

42. For examples see Nifontov, pp. 112–14, 124, 226.

43. Tugan-Baranovskii, p. 179; Kiniapina, pp. 416–17. See also Bendix, p. 178, and Pintner, p. 235.

44. Quoted in Tugan-Baranovskii, p. 299, from a posthumously published article in *Biblioteka dlia chteniia*, 1846 (see also p. 298). The article was an extract from Kankrin's book *Die Oekonomie der menschlichen Gesellschaften*, published in Stuttgart the previous year.

45. Kiniapina, p. 417.

46. Tengoborskii's general views on industry and related matters are summarized in Pintner, pp. 240–49.

47. Tengoborskii, *Commentaries on the Productive Forces of Russia*, 2 vols. (London, 1855–56), I, 450n. (Originally published in French [Paris, 1852–55].)

48. *Ibid.*, II, 47–48, 64–65.

49. *Ocherki istorii Leningrada*, I, 280.

50. See Zelnik, "The Peasant and the Factory," pp. 165–66.

51. Blackwell, p. 130. Until 1819, most industrial problems fell within the jurisdiction of the Ministry of Internal Affairs.

52. Tugan-Baranovskii, p. 168.

53. Quoted in Kiniapina, p. 395.

54. *PSZ*, X, No. 8157. For further details see Tugan-Baranovskii, pp. 169–70, and Kiniapina, pp. 395–99.

55. Gessen, *Trud detei*, I, 31: 44,368 workers in 1825, 71,614 workers in 1831. The number continued to rise over the next decade, but less rapidly (89,408 in 1840).

56. For details see Ryndziunskii, pp. 417–25.

57. Kazantsev, pp. 84–85.

58. Balabanov, *Ocherki*, I (1st ed.), 150–51; Tugan-Baranovskii, pp. 169–72; Kazantsev, pp. 85–88; Pintner, pp. 99–100.

59. Tugan-Baranovskii, pp. 173–75 (quotation is from pp. 173–74). See also Shelymagin, p. 28; Kazantsev, p. 90; Pintner, pp. 100–01.

60. Kazantsev, pp. 90–91; Kiniapina, p. 402. The 1837 memorandum was entitled: "On Children Who Work in Factories."

61. Kiniapina, p. 401; Gessen, *Trud detei*, I, 119–20.

62. For statistics and other details, see *ibid.*, pp. 33–34, 119–20.

63. *Ibid.*, pp. 30–31, 35, 192–93; Kiniapina, pp. 381–82. See also Gessen, *Istoriia*, pp. 39–42.

64. Report of Moscow civil governor I. Kapnist to Minister of Internal Affairs, Aug. 6, 1844, in *Rabochee dvizhenie*, I, Part II, 343–46. For other examples of disputes and disorders arising out of the use of *kabal'nyi* labor see Gessen, *Trud detei*, I, 196–99; for further details on the Voznesensk affair see Gessen, *Istoriia*, pp. 43–51.

65. *PSZ*, XX, Part I, No. 19262; Tugan-Baranovskii, p. 175; Kiniapina, pp. 409–10. The figures revealed by the investigation (based on 33 textile factories in Moscow province) are cited in Gessen, *Trud detei*, I, 35, 120.

66. *Ibid.*, pp. 122, and Gessen, *Istoriia*, p. 54.

67. Kazantsev, p. 92.

68. *Ibid.*, pp. 94–96.

69. *Ibid.*, pp. 97–99; Kiniapina, pp. 410–13.

70. Quoted in Kazantsev, p. 99. Although Perovskii was not referring directly to the Kapnist proposal, but to a similar plan that was meant to be limited to the Baltic Region, his words obviously applied to the more important Kapnist proposal as well.

71. *Trudy*, I, 276–78 (it is unclear from the text whether the words of the Council of State, which appear on p. 278, are quoted directly or paraphrased). Several important documents from the 1850–54 discussions are reproduced in *Trudy*, II: the Ministry of Finance's communications to the Council of State, dated July 23, 1853, and March 11, 1854 (pp. 190–223, 231–34); the recommendations of the Council of State's Economic and Legal Departments, Jan. 27, 1854 (pp. 224–30); and excerpts from Zakrevskii's memorandum to the Minister

of Finance, Aug. 27, 1854 (pp. 246–48). See also Kiniapina, pp. 416–25; Kazantsev, pp. 99–101; Balabanov, *Ocherki* (1st ed.), I, 156.

72. *Ulozhenie o nakazanii ugolovnykh i ispravitel'nykh* of Aug. 15, 1845, *PSZ*, XX, Part I, No. 19283.

73. Tengoborskii, I, 450.

CHAPTER TWO

1. *Ocherki istorii Leningrada*, I, 66–67, 70–75, 78.

2. *Ibid.*, pp. 265–67.

3. *Ibid.*, p. 449; Zlotnikov, p. 36.

4. Iatsunskii, "Rol' Peterburga," p. 96.

5. *Ocherki istorii Leningrada*, I, 450–51; Pokshishevskii, p. 126n; Zlotnikov, p. 44; Iatsunskii, "Rol' Peterburga," p. 98. See also Blackwell, pp. 114–15.

6. Karnovich, pp. 105–9; *Ocherki istorii Leningrada*, I, 265–66, 452; Pokshishevskii, p. 126n; Stolpianskii, *Zhizn' i byt*, pp. 84–85, 147, 152; "The Works 'Red Putilovetz,'" p. 1; *Baltiiskii zavod*, pp. 1–2.

7. Ministerstvo finansov, *Ezhegodnik ... na 1869 god*, sec. iii, pp. 308–09; Iakovlev, p. 67.

8. Ministerstvo finansov, *Ezhegodnik ... na 1869 god*, sec. iii, p. 310; Iakovlev, pp. 67–88; Gindin, *Gosudarstvennyi bank*, pp. 26–27.

9. For a sober and lucid discussion of the applicability of the term "industrial revolution" to Russia before the period of Alexander II's reforms, see Blackwell, pp. 402ff. For a well-reasoned and balanced Soviet view of this controversial question see Ryndziunskii, pp. 379–84.

10. *Ocherki istorii Leningrada*, I, 266.

11. Rashin, *Formirovanie*, p. 89. According to Rashin's figures, the percentage of freely hired workers in 1825 was higher in Moscow, Vladimir, and Kostroma provinces than in St. Petersburg.

12. Rashin, *Naselenie*, pp. 111–12. Other scholars give somewhat different figures. Rashin is the leading expert on Russian population patterns for this period.

13. *Ocherki istorii Leningrada*, I, 507. Some of the males were soldiers and sailors of the St. Petersburg military garrison, numbering between forty-seven thousand and sixty thousand before the Crimean War; approximately 20 per cent were accompanied by their families. See Kopanev, pp. 116–17. Kopanev is also the author of the chapter on population in *Ocherki istorii Leningrada* (pp. 506–49).

14. Iatsevich, p. 7.

15. Rashin, *Naselenie*, pp. 126–28; Ditiatin, II, 333–34; Karnovich, pp. 43–46. Rashin gives figures for 1801 and 1843, Ditiatin for 1831, Karnovich for 1858. (In addition to manorial, state, and appanage peasants, the figures on peasants include the so-called *dvorovye liudi* or manorial servants. If we exclude from the 1858 figures those dvorovye known to be actually employed as servants in the city residences of their lords and therefore not active on the labor market, peasants would fall slightly below the 50 per cent mark. On dvorovye liudi see Iatsevich, pp. 29–44.) See also Ryndziunskii, pp. 224–27.

16. Iatsunskii, "Materialy," p. 136.

17. Kopanev, pp. 28, 32–33, 57–58; *Ocherki istorii Leningrada*, I, 299; Ryndziunskii, pp. 426–29, 452. Unless otherwise noted, calculations continue to be based—for the sake of consistency—on the definition of factory advocated by Zlotnikov. See my note on pp. 44–45.

18. Iatsevich, pp. 11–16.

19. *Ibid.*, pp. 11–12. Based on materials from the 1830's.

20. Karnovich, pp. 73, 135–37.

21. Iatsunskii, "Materialy," p. 141; Kiniapina, p. 405. See also Ryndziunskii, pp. 454–55.

22. "Kratkaia zapiska vremennoi kommissii uchrezhdennoi dlia osmotra pomeshchenii rabochego sosloviia v S. Peterburge 1847 goda," in *O byte rabochikh*, pp. 1, 4–7, 22–29. The entire report of the commission is printed on pp. 1–44. This volume appeared in Berlin without the name of compiler, editor, or publisher. It contains valuable information about the living and working conditions of St. Petersburg workers, including some factory workers, in the pre-emancipation period, as well as official and private projects for the improvement of those conditions. In addition to reports of commissions investigating the living conditions of workers, the volume contains some correspondence of Minister of Internal Affairs S. Lanskoi (1855–62) on related matters. Such documents could have been procured only through someone with close government ties, probably with the Ministry of Internal Affairs.

23. *Ibid.*, pp. 9, 31. On hospitals in St. Petersburg and their inaccessibility to workers see also *Ocherki istorii Leningrada*, I, 627–28.

24. *Ibid.*, p. 103.

25. Computed from figures in *ibid.*, p. 507 (population figures for 1800, 1815, 1853, and various years between these dates), and Karnovich, pp. 18–22 (figures for 1854 through 1858).

26. For complete figures see *ibid.*, pp. 41–45.

27. Kiniapina, p. 405.

28. See Ditiatin, II, 115–31.

29. *Ibid.*, pp. 132–43, 244–55, 266–68.

30. For a detailed account of the preparation, introduction, and subsequent implementation of the St. Petersburg "gorodovoe polozhenie" of 1846 and a convincing negative evaluation of its significance, see Ditiatin, II, 369–502. See also *Ocherki istorii Leningrada*, I, 608–11.

31. Ryndziunskii, pp. 135–36.

32. The estimates of the first commission are summarized in Iatsunskii, "Materialy," p. 138; references to 1847 figures I derived from the report in *O byte rabochikh*, pp. 40–44.

33. Food prices from Pazhitnov, *Polozhenie*, I, 117; rents from Terner, *O rabochem klasse*, pp. 50–58, citing K. S. Veselovskii, who was writing in the 1840's.

34. Figures on obrok from Kopanev, p. 121; on soul tax from Jerome Blum, *Lord and Peasant in Russia from the Ninth to the Nineteenth Century* (Princeton, 1961), p. 464.

35. Iatsunskii, "Materialy," p. 138.

36. See Kopanev, p. 121.

37. The following paragraphs, except where additional references are given, are based on *Ocherki istorii Leningrada*, I, 296–97; Kopanev, pp. 3–4; and various maps. For excellent historical maps of St. Petersburg, easily available in U.S. libraries, see *Entsiklopedicheskii slovar'*, XXVIII, between p. 296 and p. 297.

38. Quoted in *Ocherki istorii Leningrada*, I, 611. The observer, writing in 1834, was referring to a somewhat smaller section of the area in question.

39. For the following, in addition to the sources cited in note 36, see Pokshishevskii; Paialin, "Shlissel'burg trakt," esp. pp. 52–53; *Ocherki istorii Leningrada*, I, 460–63.

40. Stolpianskii, *Peterburg*, p. 357 (writing of a later period).

41. Stolpianskii, *Zhizn' i byt*, pp. 31–34.

42. Quoted in *ibid.*, pp. 95–97; the text continues, taking the reader further along the Schlüsselburg Road. The article was a little inaccurate and confused with respect to some details. It is also cited, less fully, in *Ocherki istorii Leningrada*, I, 462–63.

43. Stolpianskii, *Zhizn' i byt*, p. 100.

44. *Ocherki istorii Leningrada*, I, 461.

45. *Ministerstvo finansov, 1802–1902*, I, 344.

46. See Stolpianskii, *Peterburg*, p. 350; *Ocherki istorii Leningrada*, I, 71.

47. See pp. 23–26 above. Pintner (pp. 97–98) argues for the opposite view, i.e., that fear of the growth of an urban proletariat was not a motivating factor.

48. See p. 26.

49. *Ocherki istorii Leningrada*, I, 464.

50. Quoted in Nifontov, p. 113 (photoreproduction on p. 114). See also Balabanov, *Ocherki*, I, 156n.

51. Nifontov, pp. 119–21.

52. Quoted in Tugan-Baranovskii, p. 301, from *Zhurnal manufaktur i torgovli*. On the Zhukov factory see also *Ocherki istorii Leningrada*, I, 476–78.

53. Quoted in Iatsunskii, "Materialy," p. 135n.

54. *Ibid.*, pp. 135–36.

55. *O byte rabochikh*, pp. v–vi.

56. Quoted in Kiniapina, p. 405.

57. *O byte rabochikh*, p. viii.

58. "Kratkaia zapiska," in *ibid.*, pp. 1–44.

59. *Ibid.*, pp. 22–38.

60. Kiniapina, p. 406.

61. *O byte rabochikh*, pp. 10–15, 31–36.

62. Letter dated June 10, 1857, in *ibid.*, p. 48.

63. Kiniapina, p. 406.

64. See p. 39, above.

65. For a survey of the articles in *Zhurnal manufaktur i torgovli* and other official periodicals that discuss the industries of various regions of Russia, see Tikhonov. Tikhonov stresses the heavily descriptive character of these articles,

their general neglect of the workers, and the absence of discussion of social as opposed to technological change.

66. See below, p. 163n.

CHAPTER THREE

1. See Fischer, pp. 64–83, esp. pp. 64–75.

2. See Chevalier, *Classes laborieuses.*

3. Conze, "Vom 'Pöbel' zum 'Proletariat.'"

4. *Ibid.,* esp. pp. 18–25.

5. *Ibid.,* pp. 39–42. On conservative support of measures favorable to workers, see Hamerow, pp. 72–73.

6. For further details see Skabichevskii, pp. 342–49, 356–58.

7. Quoted in Nifontov, p. 152. See also Peter K. Christoff, "A. S. Khomiakov on the Agricultural and Industrial Problem in Russia," in A. D. Ferguson and A. Levin, eds., *Essays in Russian History. A Collection Dedicated to George Vernadsky* (Hamden, Conn., 1964), pp. 138–43, 149, 154–55. See also Tugan-Baranovskii, pp. 284–88.

8. Quoted in Balabanov, *Ocherki,* I (4th ed.), 247; see also p. 246. (Subsequent citations from volume I of Balabanov's *Ocherki* are from this edition, unless otherwise indicated.)

9. Quoted in Venturi, p. 85.

10. Haxthausen, III, 151 (emphasis in the original). For further discussion of attitudes of the Russian Left toward the industrial proletariat before the reign of Alexander II, see Balabanov, I, 239–48. Balabanov is somewhat contemptuous of Russian radicals who, even in the 1840's and 1850's, failed to anticipate the potential revolutionary value of a proletariat to Russia's future.

11. *Istoriia russkoi ekonomicheskoi mysli,* I, Part II, 267–69, 322, 334–39; Balabanov, *Ocherki,* I, 252–54; Venturi, 77–79; Skerpan, pp. 170–72.

12. K. S. Veselovskii, "O nedvizhimykh imushchestvakh v Peterburge," excerpts reprinted in Terner, *O rabochem klasse,* pp. 50–59. On Terner and his book see below, p. 84.

13. See above, pp. 46–47.

14. Karnovich, p. 104.

15. See Iakovlev, pp. 65–66; W. Pintner, "Inflation in Russia During the Crimean War Period," *American Slavic and East European Review,* XVIII (Feb. 1959), 81–87, esp. p. 82 (domestic price indices for this period) and p. 85.

16. Iakovlev, pp. 61, 66–71; Gindin, *Gosudarstvenny bank,* pp. 26–27; Ministerstvo finansov, *Ezhegodnik ... na 1869 god,* sec. iii, p. 310.

17. Blackwell, p. 351; Tikhonov, pp. 152–53. See also Ch. 2, n. 64, above.

18. For a fuller listing consult *Bibliografiia russkoi periodicheskoi pechati 1703–1900 gg. (Materialy dlia istorii russkoi zhurnalistiki),* ed. N. M. Lisovskii (Petrograd, 1915), esp. pp. 132, 140, 154, 168, 173.

19. *Promyshlennost',* I (No. 2, 1861), 119.

20. *Russkaia rech',* Jan. 5, 1861.

21. *Promyshlennost',* I (No. 1, 1861), 24, 28.

22. *Birzhevye vedomosti,* July 26, Oct. 17, 1861; Jan. 19, 1862.

23. *Ibid.,* Jan. 1, 1863.

24. See Pintner, "Inflation in Russia," pp. 82, 85–86; Rykachev, p. 201.

25. Iakovlev, pp. 65–66.

26. *Birzhevye vedomosti*, July 26, 1861; Rykachev, p. 201.

27. Iakovlev, p. 74.

28. TsGIAL, *f.* 18, *op.* 2, *d.* 1770, p. 220; TsGIAL, *f.* 560, *op.* 38, *d.* 781, p. 1.

29. *Vestnik promyshlemosti*, VII (No. 2, 1860), sec. i, p. 97.

30. Iakovlev, p. 76.

31. For a fuller account see Del'vig, IV, 31.

32. *Russkaia rech'*, Jan. 5, 1861.

33. *Vestnik promyshlennosti*, VIII (No. 5, 1860), sec. iii, p. 173.

34. *Sovremennik* (No. 9, 1859), p. 228.

35. *Narodnoe chtenie* (No. 2, 1859), p. 21.

36. "Promyshlennyi listok," *Promyshlennost'*, I (No. 5, 1861), 576–79.

37. "Neskol'ko voprosov o polozhenii fabrichnykh rabochikh, preimushch-estvenno na peterburgskikh fabrikakh," *Biblioteka dlia chteniia* (June 1962), pp. 42–49. The article was signed "Blakhin."

38. On the government commissions see Chapter 4, below.

39. "Peterburgskaia zhizn'," *Sovremennik* (No. 3, 1860), sec. iii, pp. 22–26; "Delikatnost' v nauke," *Sovremennik* (No. 12, 1861), pp. 129–70.

40. Sel'chuk, "Russkaia publitsistika." The two "camps" identified by Sel'-chuk are the revolutionary-democrats and the liberal bourgeoisie, which is lumped together with the government. Despite the inadequacy of this formu-lation, there is some very useful material in Sel'chuk's article.

41. Biographical information on the people mentioned here may be found in Lamanskii, Vols. 161–64; Terner, *Vospominaniia*, Vol. I; *Ministerstvo finan-stvo, 1802–1902*, I, 389–92; Skerpan, pp. 173ff; and a variety of other places, including the standard Russian encyclopedias.

42. Lamanskii, CLXIII, 475, 477; Terner, *Vospominaniia*, I, 188.

43. Lamanskii, CLXI, 580.

44. *Promyshlennost'*, I (No. 2, 1861), 217–18; *Russkaia rech'*, March 9, 1861; "Peterburgskaia zhizh'," *Sovremennik* (No. 2, 1860), sec. iii, p. 378. The role of Gorlov and other economists in the commissions is discussed in Chapter 4.

45. The following account is based on Terner, *Vospominaniia*, Vol. I, Chs. 1–8.

46. Lamanskii, CLXI, 367–69; Terner, *Vospominaniia*, I, 165, 178, 188, 227–28.

47. Lamanskii, CLXI, 368.

48. Terner, *Vospominaniia*, I, 163.

49. Tugan-Baranovskii, p. 518.

50. See, for example, Balabanov, *Ocherki*, I, 234–39, where the identification of the views of "liberal economists" such as Terner and Gorlov with those of "the bourgeoisie" is simply taken for granted. See also Sel'chuk, "Russkaia publitsistika," p. 215, where a distinction is made, but is blurred.

51. *Ministerstvo finansov, 1802–1902*, I, 538.

52. *Birzhevye vedomosti*, June 20, 21, 22, and 23, 1861. See also *Ministerstvo finansov, 1802–1902*, I, 538.

53. *Birzhevye vedomosti*, July 14 and 21, 1861.

54. *Ibid.*, June 21, 1862. Ironically, Poletika was later to become the publisher of the very newspaper that attacked him.

55. *Vestnik promyshlennosti*, VII (No. 2, 1860), sec. i, p. 102; *Russkaia rech'*, July 27, 1861; *Russkii invalid*, Sept. 23, 1861.

56. Summarized and quoted in part in Zaionchkovskii, p. 57; see also pp. 138–39.

57. *Russkii invalid*, Sept. 23, 1861.

58. *Promyshlennost'*, I (No. 5, 1861), 576–79; *Biblioteka dlia chteniia* (June 1862), pp. 42–49.

59. *Russkaia rech'*, Nov. 30, 1861. The article was particularly critical of manufacturers in the Moscow region.

60. "O pol'ze glasnosti i usloviiakh usovershenstvovaniia promyshlennosti," *Birzhevye vedomosti*, Jan. 9, 10, and 11, 1862. Skuratov was also the author of an earlier defense of protectionism that was much less apologetic; *Vestnik promyshlennosti*, Vol. VIII (No. 4, 1860), sec. iv, pp. 18–34. Of all the economic periodicals, *Vestnik promyshlennosti* came closest to being the organ of Russian manufacturers.

61. "Khoziain i rabotnik," *Russkaia rech'*, Feb. 19, 1861. The article was signed with the initial "K."

62. *Birzhevye vedomosti*, Sept. 19, 1861.

63. Chevalier, pp. 147–49. The quote (p. 148) is a reference to Eugène Sue's influential novel of Paris life, which was apparently inspired—at least in part—by his reading of an illustrated work on conditions in London.

64. Terner, *O rabochem klasse*, pp. 50–60. Quote is from p. 50.

65. *Ibid.*, pp. 48–49.

66. *Ibid.*, pp. 1–14, 302–3.

67. Terner, *Vospominaniia*, I, 69–74.

68. From Vernadskii's notes to Tengoborskii's *O proizvoditelnykh silakh Rossii* (St. Petersburg, 1858), pp. 10, 18, quoted in Tugan-Baranovskii, p. 520.

69. *Biblioteka dlia chteniia* (June 1862), pp. 50–58.

70. *Trudy*, III, 23–27, 30–31, 35, 51–52, 54–55, 59, 74n, 92–94. See also pp. 99–100 and 105 for less favorable reactions by the commission.

71. *Promyshlennost'*, I (No. 2, 1861), 205–26, esp. pp. 207, 218–20.

72. "O merakh sodeistvuiushchikh razvitiiu proletariata," *Russkii vestnik*, Nos. 1 and 2 (Jan. 1860); No. 9 (May 1860), pp. 5–42; No. 10 (May 1860), pp. 195–216. (Nos. 1 and 2, where the author apparently attempts to trace the history of the proletariat from ancient Greece, have not been available to me.) A somewhat misleading summary of Rzhevskii's views is presented in Balabanov, *Ocherki*, I, 238. Although he wrote for a relatively liberal publication, Rzhevskii was apparently considered by his contemporaries to be a friend of serfdom and generally reactionary. See Feoktistov, p. 22.

73. "Stachka rabochikh v Londone," *Russkii vestnik*, No. 10 (May 1860), pp. 217–57. This article appeared back-to-back with Rzhevskii's final installment. Feoktistov was editor of the short-lived *Russkaia rech'* in 1861, the year it printed the anti-industrialist statements cited earlier in this chapter. During an extended stay in Western Europe in 1856–58, he had followed developments

in the labor movement—particularly strikes in England—very closely. See the introductory articles by Oksman and A. E. Presniakov in Feoktistov, esp. pp. vii–viii, xii, xvii–xix.

74. *Promyshlennost'*, II (No. 7, 1861), 74–75.

75. G. Kamenskii, "Rabochii narod v Anglii," *Vestnik promyshlennosti*, IX (No. 8, 1860), 97–113. Kamenskii, a political economist, was the author of a book entitled *Novyi opyt bogatstva narodov* (St. Petersburg, 1856).

76. See Feoktistov, p. 98.

77. *Russkii vestnik*, No. 10 (May 1860), pp. 207–16.

78. *Ibid.*, p. 218.

79. Cited in Balabanov, *Ocherki*, I, 237.

80. Thompson, p. 796.

81. See *ibid.*, pp. 779–806.

82. "Fel'eton. Peterburgskaia zhizn'," *Russkii invalid*, Oct. 10, 1861.

83. *Ibid.*

84. See especially A. Ushakov, "Neskol'ko slov o kharaktere assotsiatsii," *Birzhevye vedomosti*, May 3, 1862; and *Promyshlennost'*, I (No. 8–9, 1861), 354–57.

85. Terner, *O rabochem klasse*, pp. 17–25.

86. *Ibid.*, p. 26.

87. *Ibid.*, pp. 27–31.

88. *Ibid.*, pp. 40, 148.

89. *Ibid.*, p. 303.

90. *Ibid.*, pp. 30, 62–111, 119–41, 152–232, 317. Quotation is from p. 141.

91. Terner, *Vospominaniia*, I, 168.

92. Terner, *O rabochem klasse*, pp. 35–43.

93. *Ibid.*, pp. 233, 304, 306–17.

94. See p. 21, above.

95. *Ibid.*, pp. 149–50, 302–4.

96. *Ibid.*, pp. 304, 318.

97. See pp. 142–47, 169–72, below.

98. *Sovremennik* (No. 9, 1861), p. 27.

99. "K molodomu pokoleniiu," in Shelgunov, *Vospominaniia*, Prilozhenie 1, pp. 287–302.

100. *Ibid.*, pp. 289, 292–93, 301.

101. Shelgunov, "Rabochii proletariat v Anglii i vo Frantsii," *Sovremennik* (Nos. 9 and 10, 1861), pp. 131–72, 485–518.

102. *Ibid.*, pp. 137–38. Shelgunov called Engels "one of the best and noblest Germans."

103. See, for example, Terner, *Vospominaniia*, I, 163–64, 182, 185, where the author concedes that despite serious reservations, he had found people like Chernyshevskii and Dobroliubov to be very attractive figures.

104. *Sovremennik* (No. 2, 1860), sec. iii, p. 378.

105. See, for example, Ralli's comments in "Iz vospominanii Z. K. Ralli," p. 139. "Utopian" socialists such as Fourier had, of course, had an important influence on the Russian Left since the 1840's if not earlier.

106. "Robert Oven i ego popytki obshchestvennykh reform," in Dobroliubov, IV, 7–47 (quote is from p. 7).

107. See, for example, "Mysliashchii proletariat," in Pisarev, pp. 655–56, 666. Although this famous article was not published in *Russkoe slovo* until 1865, under the title "Novyi tip," there is evidence that it was first drafted in 1863 in prison (see editor's note in *ibid.*, p. 716).

108. See Sel'chuk, "Rabochii vopros," pp. 225, 228, 231–32, and "Russkaia publitsistika," pp. 212–14.

109. "Delikatnost' v nauke," *Sovremennik* (No. 12, 1861), pp. 129–70. Shelgunov's review article was signed "T. Z.," one of his pseudonyms at that time.

110. "Ocherki iz istorii truda," in Pisarev, pp. 194–95; see also pp. 244, 249–51. This article originally appeared in *Russkoe slovo* in 1863.

111. *Ibid.*, pp. 214–15; see also pp. 264–73.

112. Dobroliubov, p. 25.

113. Chernyshevskii's critique of Malthus was published in the form of notes appended to his translation of Book I of John Stuart Mill's *Principles of Political Economy*, reprinted in Chernyshevskii, IX, 251–334. Pisarev's critique of Malthus, a much more modest endeavor, is in his "Ocherki iz istorii truda," pp. 183–93.

114. This is, of course, a highly distilled summary that does not do justice to Chernyshevskii's attempt at a point by point critique of the technical aspects of Malthus's thought.

115. Pisarev, "Ocherki iz istorii truda," esp. pp. 217, 252–57, 283–85.

116. Terner, *O rabochem klasse*, pp. 36–43.

117. Dobroliubov, IV, 21–22, 34–35.

118. Shelgunov, pp. 148–53, 155–59, 167–70.

119. *Ibid.*, p. 149.

120. *Ibid.*, pp. 169–70.

CHAPTER FOUR

1. "Proekt Ustava o Promyshlennosti," *Trudy*, I, 485–553 (the 1862 version of the statute); III, 157–227 (the final, 1864 version).

2. Ditiatin, II, 554–55.

3. *Trudy*, I, iii–iv.

4. "Svod dannykh o primenenii remeslennykh postanovlenii, na praktike, v raznykh mestnostiakh Rossii," *Trudy*, II, 132.

5. "Ob'iasnitel'naia zapiska," *Trudy*, I, 42–68.

6. For a brief summary of this controversy, see Pazhitnov, *Problema*, pp. 109ff.

7. Quoted in "Ob'iasnitel'naia zapiska," *Trudy*, I, 51.

8. *Ibid.*, pp. 55–57.

9. *Ibid.*, pp. 59, 61–62, 67.

10. See above, p. 12; see also "Svod dannykh," *Trudy*, II, 127.

11. See below, pp. 185, 197–98.

12. See above, pp. 65–67.

13. "Ob'iasnitel'naia zapiska," *Trudy*, I, 80, 304; see also "Svod dannykh," *Trudy*, II, 178.

14. "Ob'iasnitel'naia zapiska," *Trudy*, I, 72, 305.

15. Report of Ignat'ev to Minister of Internal Affairs S. S. Lanskoi, in *ibid.*, pp. 72–74; see also *ibid.*, pp. 305–7, and "Svod dannykh," *Trudy*, II, 131, 177.

16. "Ob'iasnitel'naia zapiska," *Trudy*, I, 74.

17. *Ibid.*, iii–iv, 68.

18. See above, p. 40.

19. Ignat'ev's memorandum to Lanskoi (excerpts), Jan. 31, 1859, in *Trudy*, II, 249–52; "Ob'iasnitel'naia zapiska," *Trudy*, I, 279.

20. GIALO, *f.* 253, *op.* 2, *d.* 205 (1859 g.), p. 1: Ignat'ev to St. Petersburg civil governor Smirnov, March 21, 1859; see also Litvinov-Falinskii, pp. 6–7.

21. GIALO, *f.* 253, *op.* 2, *d.* 205, pp. 1–2; see also p. 3.

22. *Ibid.*, pp. 5–12.

23. *Promyshlennost'*, I (No. 2, 1861), 218; *Russkaia rech'*, March 9, 1861; Tugan-Baranovskii, p. 386.

24. "Ob'iasnitel'naia zapiska," *Trudy*, I, 352.

25. "Peterburgskaia zhizn'," *Sovremennik* (No. 2, 1860), sec. iii, p. 378.

26. *Proekt pravil dlia fabrik i zavodov v S.-Peterburge i uezde* (St. Petersburg, 1860). The Shtakel'berg Commission then reprinted the more important and controversial sections of the 1860 draft, together with a selection of more or less negative responses to its contents, in *Trudy*, II, 253–323. See also *Krasnyi arkhiv*, I (1939), 133.

27. "Ob'iasnitel'naia zapiska," *Trudy*, I, 279.

28. *Ibid.*, pp. 111–14.

29. *Ibid.*, pp. 86–105.

30. The movement toward industrial freedom and against the corporate organization of production in Germany in the 1850's and 1860's is summarized in Hamerow, Ch. 13, esp. pp. 246–52.

31. "Ob'iasnitel'naia zapiska," *Trudy*, I, 114–21, 128–32, 140, 142–43, 149.

32. The term *uchenik*, apprentice, was to be retained for young workers in training, but without its medieval guild implications. See *ibid.*, p. 145.

33. See above, p. 81.

34. "Ob'iasnitel'naia zapiska," *Trudy*, I, 178–79.

35. *Ibid.*, pp. 86–90. Quotation is from p. 90.

36. *Ibid.*, p. 112.

37. *Ibid.*, pp. 147–48.

38. My citations are from the Commission's first publicized draft of 1862 (published in 1863). The final draft of 1864 is also cited when the two versions diverge or when the point in question is of particular importance.

39. "Proekt Ustava," arts. 31–39, *Trudy*, I, 495–97; "Proekt Ustava," arts. 31–38, *Trudy*, III, 166–68. Art. 32 of the first draft, which precluded the use of oral contracts as a basis for judicial action, was dropped from the final version.

40. "Proekt Ustava," arts. 117–23, *Trudy*, I, 511–13; "Proekt Ustava," arts. 116–22, *Trudy*, III, 183–84.

41. "Proekt Ustava," arts. 130–259, *Trudy*, I, 514–40; "Proekt Ustava," arts. 129–255, *Trudy*, III, 185–211. The penal code comprises arts. 260–80 (*Trudy*, I, 540–44) and 256–76 (*Trudy*, III, 211–16) of the respective drafts.

42. "Svod zamechanii na pervonachal'nyi proekt ustava o promyshlennosti,"

Trudy, III, 48, 67. For further details concerning the Moscow Section's criticisms of the Commission's proposals, see below, pp. 147–48, 154–57.

43. "Ob'iasnitel'naia zapiska," *Trudy*, I, 280–85, 327, 338–40, 362, 391–448. The Belgian *livrets* were compulsory only for workers less than 21 years old.

44. "Svod zamechanii na izdannyi v 1860 g. *Proekt pravil dlia fabrik i zavodov v S.-Peterburge i uezde*," *Trudy*, II, 292.

45. "Ob'iasnitel'naia zapiska," *Trudy*, I, 317.

46. "Zhurnal Kommisii," sessions of Jan. 17, 23, and 31 and Feb. 6, 1864, *Trudy*, III, 111–12.

47. Terner, *Vospominaniia*, I, 190.

48. See for example "Ob'iasnitel'naia zapiska," *Trudy*, I, 190–97 (on tax reform, esp. pp. 196–97), 389 (on judicial reform), 480 (on judicial and passport reforms), and "Zhurnal Kommisii," *Trudy*, III, 93 (on judicial reform).

49. See above, p. 20. In St. Petersburg after 1838, the minimum annual fee for a simple worker was three rubles for males and one ruble for females; rates for persons in the more skilled trades were higher. *Gorodskie poseleniia*, VII, 206–8.

50. *Ustavy torgovyi*, p. 18.

51. See, for example, the 1860 comments of P. A. Tuchkov, military governor of Moscow (1859–64), quoted in *Trudy*, I, 450.

52. "Predstavlenie Ministra Finansov Gos. Sovetu (23 iiulia 1853 g. No. 3596), ob ustanovlenii razschetnoi tetradi dlia fabrichnykh rabochikh," *Trudy*, II, 194, 212–13, 219–20; Ignat'ev's memorandum to Lanskoi (excerpts), Jan. 31, 1859, in *Trudy*, II, 249.

53. The council made the partial concession to police interests of emphasizing that manufacturers who harbored passportless day workers overnight would be prosecuted. "Zakliuchenie Soedinennykh Departamentov Ekonomii i Zakonov Gos. Soveta (27 ianv. 1854 goda) ob ustanovlenii razschetnoi tetradi dlia fabrichnykh rabochikh," *Trudy*, II, 224–26.

54. "Ob'iasnitel'naia zapiska," *Trudy*, I, 292, 300, 468–69, 480.

55. *Ibid.*, pp. 281, 296–97; "Proekt Ustava," art. 39, *Trudy*, I, 497; Ignat'ev to Lanskoi, *Trudy*, II, 249.

56. "Proekt Ustava," *Trudy*, I, 499–500.

57. "Ob'iasnitel'naia zapiska," *Trudy*, I, 358.

58. *Ibid.*, pp. 360–61.

59. *Ibid.*, p. 362. The same analogy had recently been made by Governor Baranov. "Svod zamechanii na . . . *Proekt pravil*," *Trudy*, II, 312.

60. "Ob'iasnitel'naia zapiska," *Trudy*, I, 288.

61. "Svod zamechanii na . . . *Proekt pravil*," *Trudy*, II, 311; for citations of similar arguments from the journals *Otechestvennye zapiski* and *Biblioteka dlia chteniia* see "Svod zamechanii na pervonachal'nyi proekt," *Trudy*, III, 23, 26–27.

62. "Zhurnal Kommisii," *Trudy*, III, 92–93.

63. "Ob'iasnitel'naia zapiska," *Trudy*, I, 219–22, 226–27.

64. See, for example, the lengthy quote in *ibid.*, p. 209n.

65. "Proekt Ustava," *Trudy*, I, 493–95; III, 163–66.

66. *Ibid.*, I, 494. Art. 25 authorized the cooperatives.

67. "Ob'iasnitel'naia zapiska," *Trudy*, I, 148, 148n.

68. *Ibid.*, pp. 105–11, 213–14, 241n. For the entire quotation from the French journal *L'Atelier* see pp. 110–11.

69. *Ibid.*, pp. 148–49; "Proekt Ustava," note 1 to art. 30, *Trudy*, I, 495.

70. A handful of examples from other towns was also given. "Ob'iasnitel'naia zapiska," *Trudy*, I, 222–25.

71. Mecklenburg to Lanskoi (in French), June 1, 1857, in *O byte rabochikh*, p. 47. For the Society's founding charter (1858) see *PSZ*, XXXIII, Part II, No. 33591, and *O byte rabochikh*, pp. 68–79. On Feb. 3, 1861, the Society's charter was renewed and its goals broadened to include the procurement of jobs, food, clothing, and medical aid for unemployed workers. *Ibid.*, pp. 80–87; see also *PSZ*, XXXVI, Part I, No. 36581, and XXXVII, Part II, No. 38790.

72. "Ob'iasnitel'naia zapiska," *Trudy*, I, 223.

73. *Birzhevye vedomosti*, May 3, 1862. Sergei Prokopovich mentions only one labor association in St. Petersburg during this period, a joiners' artel' established in 1862. This was most likely the same one listed in *Birzhevye vedomosti*. See S. N. Prokopovich, *Kooperativnoe dvizhenie*, p. 59.

74. See above, p. 103.

75. "Zhurnal Kommisii," *Trudy*, III, 86.

76. "Svod zamechanii na pervonachal'nyi proekt," *Trudy*, III, 16 (my emphasis).

77. "Zhurnal Kommisii," *Trudy*, III, 85, 85n; "Proekt Ustava," *Trudy*, III, 163–66.

78. "Ob'iasnitel'naia zapiska," *Trudy*, I, 225–26.

79. *Ibid.*, pp. 226–29.

80. "Proekt Ustava," *Trudy*, I, 494.

81. See above, p. 40.

82. "Predstavlenie Ministra Finansov Gos. Sovetu," *Trudy*, Vol. II, esp. pp. 209–10.

83. "Ob'iasnitel'naia zapiska," *Trudy*, I, 481–82.

84. *Ibid.*, pp. 474–79, 481–83; "Proekt Ustava," arts. 272–73, *Trudy*, I, 543; arts. 268–69, *Trudy*, III, 214.

85. *Ustavy torgovyi*, pp. 3ff ("Ustav o promyshlennosti fabrichnoi i zavodskoi").

86. Ianzhul, "Detskii i zhenskii fabrichnyi trud v Anglii i Rossii," pp. 60–61 (an essay first serialized in the journal *Otechestvennye zapiski* in 1880).

87. Tugan-Baranovskii, pp. 388–89; Martov, p. 25; Pazhitnov, *Die Lage*, pp. 6–7; Bykov, pp. 143–44; Balabanov, *Ocherki*, I, 227–29; Shelymagin, pp. 39–44; Borisenkova, p. 24; Kazantsev, pp. 109–12 (Kazantsev is relatively cautious in formulating his conclusions); Giffen, pp. 177–79.

88. Baranov's memorandum of Aug. 24, 1861, addressed to the Minister of Internal Affairs, is reprinted in *Krasnyi arkhiv*, I (1939), 136–50, together with a short introductory essay by N. Zhuravlev (pp. 133–36). Zhuravlev maintains that the actual author of the memorandum was M. Saltykov-Shchedrin, who was then serving as vice-governor of Tver. His arguments are not altogether

convincing, although the possibility should not be excluded (Kazantsev, pp. 109–10, completely accepts Zhuravlev's arguments). Be that as it may, Baranov signed the memorandum and thereby accepted responsibility for its contents. Large sections of the memorandum were incorporated into the published materials of the Shtakel'berg Commission; see especially "Svod zamechanii na ... *Proekt pravil,*" *Trudy,* II, 274–75, 290–92, 310–16, 321.

89. *Krasnyi arkhiv,* I (1939), 136–39, 142–43, 145, 147, 149–50; *Trudy,* II, 274, 290, 303, 310, 313–16.

90. *Ibid.,* pp. 255–56, 278–80, 298–99, 309, 310n.

91. For a survey of the position of manufacturers in eighteenth-century Russia, see Tugan-Baranovskii, pp. 9–54.

92. Ermanskii, p. 332; Berlin, pp. 212, 214; Gindin, "Russkaia burzhuaziia," p. 73; Pintner, pp. 53–54; Blackwell, pp. 153–54. Cf. Kiniapina, Ch. 4 (esp. pp. 206–10), where the author presents some evidence that Moscow merchant-manufacturers asked for the creation of a manufacturing council in the 1820's, but grants that the one created by Kankrin was an organ of government control that lacked an independent life and the membership of which was dominated by nobles and officials.

93. Kiniapina—one of the few historians to take the much neglected Manufacturing Council seriously—makes a heroic but not very satisfactory effort to demonstrate the increasing independence of the Moscow Section from official control over the years, a trend she attributes to the growing strength of the industrial bourgeoisie. However, her concrete examples are modest, and her conclusions are so cautious that her own emphasis reverts to the council's dependence and weakness. *Ibid.,* esp. pp. 210–17, 219–35, 245–46. The entire question bears further investigation.

94. Kazantsev, pp. 94–96, 104–5; Kiniapina, 387–88. Kazantsev correctly emphasizes the narrow limits of those proposals supported by the Moscow Section that were supportive of workers, but almost *all* proposals of this kind that were put forth during the Nicholas I period were comparably narrow.

95. Zakrevskii's memorandum to Minister of Finance P. F. Brock (excerpts), Aug. 27, 1854, in *Trudy,* II, 246–48. The Manufacturing Council in St. Petersburg, which did participate in the deliberations, generally supported the booklet plan but tended to be critical of those aspects of the specific proposals to which employers might be expected to object. On a few occasions it also argued for changes favorable to workers. See "Predstavlenie Ministra Finansov Gos. Sovetu," *Trudy,* II, 192–210.

96. "Svod zamechanii na ... *Proekt pravil,*" *Trudy,* II, 304–6.

97. "Svod zamechanii na pervonachal'nyi proekt," *Trudy,* III, 15–16, 43–47, 67 (quotes are from pp. 44–46). For other, minor criticisms of the Commission's draft, suggesting a pro-industrialist bias on the part of the Moscow Section, see *ibid.,* pp. 31–32, 42–43, 57, 66.

98. Sherer, pp. 445–514.

99. *Ibid.,* pp. 504–6.

100. "Zhurnal Kommisii," *Trudy,* III, 73–127 *passim.*

101. *Ibid.,* p. 74n.

102. See *ibid.*, pp. 74–84, 94–95, 100–102, 110, 117–19, for the Commission's responses to the Moscow Section's minor criticisms.

103. *Ibid.*, pp. 85, 85n, 109–11. The Commission did agree to some minor, mainly procedural changes with respect to the industrial courts. *Ibid.*, pp. 112–26.

104. Tugan-Baranovskii, p. 394.

105. "Zhurnal Kommisii," *Trudy*, III, 127.

106. Terner, *Vospominaniia*, I, 201–3, 228; Lamanskii, CLXIII, 475.

107. "Zhurnal Kommisii," session of April 6, 1864, *Trudy*, III, 129–56.

108. See below, pp. 373–74. See also Litvinov-Falinskii, pp. 8, 29–30.

CHAPTER FIVE

1. Among recent works devoted to this period, see especially the multi-volume compendium *Revoliutsionnaia situatsiia*, which includes several articles on labor unrest, and Ionova, "Rabochee dvizhenie." Ionova's article is based on her candidate's dissertation, "Rabochee dvizhenie v gody revoliutsionnoi situatsii 1859–61" (Moscow University, 1950).

2. In "Krakh II Internatsionala"; see *Revoliutsionnaia situatsiia*, I (Moscow, 1960), 9. (The volumes in this series are unnumbered. I have added volume numbers in the order of publication.)

3. In addition to the works of Ionova cited in note 1, above, see in particular Bazhkova; see also Zaks. The most comprehensive treatment is in Rutman, "Rabochee dvizhenie." On peasant unrest and its limits during approximately the same period see Emmons, "The Peasant and the Emancipation," esp. pp. 50–71.

4. See Rutman, "Rabochee dvizhenie," esp. p. 221.

5. "Predstavlenie Ministra Finansov Gos. Sovetu (23 iiulia 1853 g.)," *Trudy*, II, 191; see also "Ob'iasnitel'naia zapiska," *Trudy*, I, 276.

6. Zakrevskii's memorandum to Minister of Finance Brock, Aug. 27, 1854, in *Trudy*, II, 246–47; see also "Ob'iasnitel'naia zapiska," pp. 278–79.

7. General Tuchkov to Ministry of Internal Affairs, April 14, 1860; excerpted in *Trudy*, I, 449–50.

8. *PSZ*, XXXIII, Part I, No. 33350 (see also No. 33520).

9. The Temporary Commission's organizational and procedural statutes are reproduced in *O byte rabochikh*, pp. 90–96; see also Litvinov-Falinskii, pp. 5–6, and "Ob'iasnitel'naia zapiska," *Trudy*, I, 382–89.

10. Figures cited from the first tri-annual report of the Temporary Commission in *Trudy*, I, 390.

11. *Rabochee dvizhenie*, I, Part II and II, Part I.

12. "Ob'iasnitel'naia zapiska," *Trudy*, I, 452.

13. *Ibid.*, p. 390.

14. The five incidents are very briefly summarized in Rutman, "Rabochee dvizhenie," pp. 210–12, 216, 219. Further details are in the following sources: *Rabochee dvizhenie*, I, Part II, 511–13, 587–88; "K istorii rabochego klassa v Rossii," *Krasnyi arkhiv*, II (1922), 186; Baklanova, pp. 36–37; TsGIAL, *f.* 219, *op.* 1, *d.* 6518.

15. *Rabochee dvizhenie*, I, Part II, 511, 588. The word "stachka" was first used with reference to events at the Nevskii factory in St. Petersburg in 1870, which were looked upon by contemporaries as unprecedented. See below, pp. 340–41.

16. Baklanova, pp. 36–37.

17. Reports of Military Governor Ignat'ev to Minister of Internal Affairs Lanskoi, April 5 and 6, 1858, *Rabochee dvizhenie*, I, Part II, 511–13.

18. *Ibid.*, p. 512.

19. Report of Ignat'ev to Lanskoi, Jan. 5, 1860, *Rabochee dvizhenie*, I, Part II, 588.

20. *Ibid.*

21. *Krasnyi arkhiv*, II (1922), 186.

22. TsGIAL, *f.* 219, *op.* 1, *d.* 6518, pp. 12–13.

23. TsGIAL, *f.* 219, *op.* 1/1, *d.* 356, pp. 17, 20.

24. TsGIAL, *f.* 219, *op.* 1, *d.* 6518, p. 14.

25. *Ibid.*, p. 25.

26. Rykachev, p. 201.

27. TsGIAL, *f.* 219, *op.* 1, *d.* 6518, p. 14.

28. *Ibid.*, pp. 1–3. The records also contain references to earlier petitions in the 1850's, but the 1860 petition was the first to become of major concern to the government.

29. *Ibid.*, pp. 15–17. The exact sums distributed in 1859 are listed on pp. 9, 29–30.

30. *Ibid.*, pp. 26, 31–35, 49–50.

31. *Ibid.*, pp. 36, 45, 47. A detailed summary of Morozov's record is given on pp. 41–45.

32. *Ibid.*, p. 48. Morozov's confession is summarized by the chief of factory police on pp. 54–55; his wife's appeal is on pp. 58–59. A later request by his mother that he be allowed to return to St. Petersburg was also denied; p. 79.

33. "K istorii rabochego klassa v Rossii," *Krasnyi arkhiv*, II (1922), 183.

34. Pertsov, p. 128.

35. *Ibid.*, pp. 153–61.

36. "Zhurnal Kommisii," *Trudy*, III, 105.

37. "Gospodam fabrikantam i zavodchikam Sanktpeterburgskoi gubernii," *Promyshlennost'*, III (No. 13–14, 1861), 201–2.

38. See above, pp. 107–8, 148.

39. "Proekt Ustava," *Trudy*, I, 493.

40. *ZhMNP* (No. 1, 1861), sec. iv, p. 1.

41. Stasov, pp. 165–66.

42. Abramov, p. 11.

43. *Ibid.*, p. 32.

44. "Voskresnye shkoly," *Entsiklopedicheskii slovar'*, VII, 256.

45. *Narodnoe chtenie* (No. 3, 1860), p. 178.

46. *ZhMNP* (No. 8, 1860), sec. iv, pp. 47, 52.

47. Abramov, pp. 100–102.

48. *ZhMNP* (No. 12, 1860), sec. iv, p. 129; (No. 1, 1861), sec. iv, pp. 2, 5.

49. *Russkoe slovo* (No. 11, 1860), pp. 15–16; *ZhMNP* (No. 9, 1860), sec. iv, p. 87.

50. V. Ivanov, "O finliandskikh shkolakh dlia obrazovaniia remeslennogo klassa," *Promyshlennost'*, III (No. 16, 1861), 355–65. The author cited the example of certain schools in Finland as models for what could be done in the field of worker education.

51. Abramov, p. 24.

52. *ZhMNP* (No. 7, 1860), sec. iv, p. 12.

53. See below, p. 186.

54. *ZhMNP* (No. 1, 1861), sec. i, p. 64.

55. Abramov, pp. 27–28.

56. *Sovremennik* (No. 9, 1861), p. 2.

57. *Ibid.*, p. 8; "Slukhi o voskresnykh shkolakh," *Russkaia rech'*, No. 86, 1861.

58. *Sovremennik* (No. 9, 1861), pp. 8–18. A similar explanation is presented in Abramov, pp. 55–56.

59. Lemke, p. 416.

60. Quoted in *ibid.*, p. 433.

61. Valuev's report of Sept. 11, 1862, *Rabochee dvizhenie*, II, Part I, 591.

62. *ZhMNP* (No. 7, 1860), sec. iv, pp. 7–8; (No. 9, 1860), sec. iv, p. 87.

63. *ZhMNP* (No. 10, 1860), sec. iv, p. 15; (No. 11, 1860), sec. iv, pp. 60–63.

64. *ZhMNP* (No. 12, 1860), sec. iv, p. 124.

65. Taubin, p. 85.

66. Abramov, p. 35; Stasov, p. 183.

67. *ZhMNP* (No. 1, 1861), sec. iv, p. 2.

68. Pirogov, "O voskresnykh shkolakh," in *Izbrannye pedagogicheskie sochineniia*, p. 396.

69. *ZhMNP* (No. 1, 1861), sec. i, p. 59.

70. *Ibid.*, p. 63.

71. *Russkii invalid*, Oct. 10, 1861.

72. *Russkaia rech'*, No. 86, 1861.

73. *Sovremennik* (No. 9, 1861), pp. 2, 8.

74. TsGAOR, f. 109, *eksp.* 1, d. 263 (1862), p. 6. See also Arap'ev, pp. 185–86.

75. "Voskresnye shkoly," *Entsiklopedicheskii slovar'*, pp. 255–56.

76. Abramov, pp. 25–26.

77. *ZhMNP* (No. 1, 1861), sec. i, pp. 66–67. Ushinskii and his colleagues in the ministry who supported the schools were typical of the "progressive pedagogues" who, according to the contemporary chronicler E. M. Feoktistov (a member of the ministry from 1862, and himself editor of *ZhMNP* from 1871 to 1882), "were produced in large numbers" in Russia from the end of the 1850's. Feoktistov, p. 172.

78. *Entsiklopedicheskii slovar'*, p. 256. Even as enlightened a supporter of the schools as Pirogov advocated a narrow curriculum. See Pirogov, pp. 399–400.

79. The circular was reproduced in full in Herzen's *Kolokol* (No. 95, 1861).

80. *Entsiklopedicheskii slovar'*, pp. 256–57.

81. Nikitenko, II, 168.

82. *Ibid.* Dolgorukov's memorandum is reproduced in Lemke, pp. 403–5.

83. Valuev, I, p. 57 (entry of Jan. 5, 1861); Nikitenko, II, 168 (entry of Dec. 23, 1860), 170–71 (Jan. 5 and 6, 1861); Lemke, pp. 406–7.

84. Lemke, p. 10.

85. *Ibid.*, pp. 10–12.

86. Panteleev, pp. 160–61.

87. Valuev, I, 151 (entry of March 7, 1862).

88. TsGAOR, *f.* 109, *eksp.* 1, *d.* 263, pp. 37–38.

89. A copy of Valuev's report is located in *ibid.*, pp. 91–111. It is accurately reprinted in *Rabochee dvizhenie*, II, Part I, 590–96. Recent Soviet works that to a greater or lesser extent accept Valuev's views on these matters include Taubin, pp. 80–83; Ionova, "Voskresnye shkoly," pp. 181–82; Pichkurenko, p. 97.

90. Pirogov, pp. 396–97. None of the works cited in footnote 89 takes note of Pirogov's views.

91. *Kolokol* (No. 90, 1861), p. 759.

92. Valuev, I, 56–57 (entry of Jan. 3, 1861). According to Valuev (who was not yet an enemy of the schools in 1861; see footnote on p. 190, below), Dolgorukov claimed that Herzen had advised Pavlov to start the Sunday schools, and that the idea had originated more than a decade earlier with M. Petrashevskii.

93. TsGAOR, *f.* 109, *eksp.* 1, *d.* 263, p. 8; *Rabochee dvizhenie*, II, Part I, 592; Valuev, I, 173 (entry of May 30, 1862).

94. TsGAOR, *f.* 109, *eksp.* 1, *d.* 263, pp. 11–12. The original French version of Valuev's letter to Dolgorukov is on pp. 10–11, a Russian summary on p. 12. The Russian summary is reproduced in *Rabochee dvizhenie*, II, Part I, 586.

95. Valuev, I, 173–74 (entry of June 1, 1862).

96. TsGAOR, *f.* 109, *eksp.* 1, *d.* 263, p. 19.

97. *Ibid.*, p. 34. Zhdanov's report, dated Aug. 29, 1862, covers pp. 34–35.

98. Taubin, p. 84; Pichkurenko, p. 108; Ionova, "Voskresnye shkoly," p. 204.

99. The figure 450 was calculated by Taubin, p. 84. It covers the period from the beginning of the St. Petersburg schools to their suppression.

100. Annual Report of the Third Section for 1862, TsGAOR, *f.* 109, *op.* 85, *d.* 27, pp. 9–10.

101. TsGAOR, *f.* 109, *eksp.* 1, *d.* 263, p. 57.

102. *Ibid.*, p. 72.

103. Taubin, p. 85.

104. S-PSK, *Statisticheskie svedeniia, 1862*, p. 40; Lemke, pp. 408, 410.

105. *Kolokol* (No. 161, 1863), p. 1331; Lemke, pp. 435–37.

106. The number of factory workers in St. Petersburg at this time was officially estimated at 21,830. S-PSK, *Statisticheskie svedeniia, 1862*, p. 56. The size of the working-class population of the city in the 1860's is discussed more fully in Ch. 6, below.

107. Report from Zhdanov to Valuev, June 20, 1862, quoted in Lemke, p. 428.

108. The following account is based on the testimony of workers and teachers

collected by the Zhdanov commission and reproduced in Lemke, pp. 408–21, 426–32.

109. It is noteworthy, in this regard, that the Commission went on to include the establishment of Sunday schools in its recommendations without even taking note of their recent suppression. "Proekt Ustava," *Trudy*, I, 493.

110. For the workers' testimony, see Lemke, pp. 408–16, 419, 421, 426, 431–32. Despite this evidence, Ionova insists that the conduct of the workers during the investigation reflected their loyalty to the accused teachers and their revolutionary mood. Ionova, "Voskresnye shkoly," pp. 207–8.

111. *PSZ*, XXXVI, Part I, No. 36793; XXXVII, Part I, Nos. 38235 and 38339, and Part II, No. 38989. See also *Ministerstvo finansov, 1802–1902*, I, 566–67. Unrest among the Ural mining and metallurgical workers, most notably in Perm and Orenburg provinces, began to build up late in 1857, reached its peak in 1859–61, and continued into the post-emancipation years at a lesser rate. It was most frequent among about-to-be-emancipated and just-emancipated peasant-workers, and was closely connected first with rumors of the forthcoming emancipation and subsequently with dissatisfaction over the terms of settlement affecting the possessional and manorial workers of this region. Although the petitioning of officials and flight were the most frequent forms of protest, there were sometimes sustained disturbances which, in contrast to the urban unrest of 1857–60, proved relatively difficult for the government to suppress by force. See Pazhitnov, "Volneniia"; L. Aizenberg, "Byt krest'ian na chastnykh gornykh zavodakh i rudinakh v Orenburgskom krae (nakanune osvobozhdeniia ot krepostnoi zavisimosti)," *Arkhiv istorii truda v Rossii*, III (1922), 23–39; Rutman, "Iz istorii"; Ionova, "Rabochee dvizhenie," pp. 206–10; Sel'chuk, "Russkaia publitsistika," pp. 220–22.

Unrest among railroad construction workers, a relatively new breed of laborer in Russia, reached enormous proportions on the construction of the Volga-Don line; nearly 6,200 workers are known to have taken part during the years 1859 and 1860. After the introduction of "Temporary Regulations on the Employment of Workers in State and Public Works," which met many of the workers' grievances, the unrest declined markedly. Unauthorized flight from the job was the most frequent single form of protest, but there was also much unruliness and sometimes even violence. See Ionova, "Rabochee dvizhenie," esp. pp. 198–206; Litvinov-Falinskii, p. 9; and a variety of documents reprinted in *Rabochee dvizhenie*, I, Part II (the latter collection also documents unrest in the mining region). A decade later, a new official commission on the labor question stated openly that the temporary regulations of 1861 were directly motivated by the disorders of 1860 on the Volga-Don line. *Ob'iasnitel'naia zapiska k Proektu Ustava o lichnom naime rabochikh i prislugi*, p. 1.

CHAPTER SIX

1. A survey of the collection of urban statistics in Russia during the second quarter of the nineteenth century is given in Ryndziunskii, pp. 187–208. See also Gozulov, pp. 20–22, and the very negative assessment by the Shtakel'berg Commission in "Ob'iasnitel'naia zapiska," *Trudy*, I, 188.

2. See above.

3. TsGIAL, *f.* 18, *op.* 2, *d.* 1770, pp. 62, 67–68.

4. *Ibid.*, p. 60.

5. S-PSK, *Fabriki i zavody, 1863*, pp. 5–6.

6. TsSKMVD, *Statisticheskii vremennik*, series II, issue 6, pp. ii, xxi.

7. Ministerstvo finansov, *Obzor razlichnykh otraslei*, III, 122.

8. Other citations could be presented to show that the paucity of accurate statistical materials relating to industry was no secret to these officials. See *ibid.*, I, 1, for example.

9. See, for example, TsGIAL, *f.* 18, *op.* 2, *d.* 1770, pp. 53, 74, 84, 302, 307.

10. On the responsibilities of the provincial statistical committees, see Gozulov, pp. 24–25. Early in the 1860's the government began to give them greater financial support. "Ob'iasnitel'naia zapiska," *Trudy*, I, 189.

11. TsGIAL, *f.* 18, *op.* 2, *d.* 1770, pp. 89, 92, 97.

12. *Ibid.*, pp. 98–99, 349.

13. Nikitenko used the term to describe the political situation on June 12, 1862, in his *Dnevnik*, II, 279.

14. See Dmitri Miliutin's explanation (from his diaries) of the release of Minister of Internal Affairs Lanskoi and his Assistant Minister, N. Miliutin, as quoted by Zaionchkovskii in Valuev, I, 371. See also Terner, *Vospominaniia*, I, 197–99, and, more generally, Emmons, *The Russian Landed Gentry*, esp. pp. 328–30.

15. Terner, *Vospominaniia*, I, 201.

16. *Ibid.*, 202–5, 227; Lamanskii, CLXII, 338–44. Cf. A. Kornilov, *Modern Russian History from the Age of Catherine the Great to the End of the Nineteenth Century*, trans. A. S. Kaun (New York, 1943), Part II, pp. 88–89, 115.

17. Lamanskii, CLXIV, 403.

18. Valuev's memorandum to Dolgorukov, June 22, 1862, quoted by Zaionchkovskii in Valuev, I, 33. Valuev's main motives, understandably, were quite distinct from those of Reutern; he hoped that financial-entrepreneurial preoccupations would, as he put it to Dolgorukov, "nourish the activity" of the press and of those people who "clamor and foment discontent [*frondiruiut*] because they have nothing else to do." In general, Valuev seems to have disliked Reutern personally and resented his closeness to the Grand Duke Konstantin, though he respected Reutern's abilities and economic views. See Valuev, I, 135, 141, 153 (entries of Dec. 23, 1861, Jan. 22 and March 16, 1862).

19. A concise summary of the most important points may be found in Gerschenkron, "Agrarian Policies and Industrialization," pp. 752–54.

20. See above, pp. 75, 77–78.

21. See, for example, Tugan-Baranovskii, pp. 307–11, where a good case is made for the dislocative effects of the emancipation on Ural metallurgy and certain other branches of industry that had depended on involuntary labor.

22. TsGIAL, *f.* 18, *op.* 2, *d.* 1770, p. 1.

23. TsGIAL, *f.* 18, *op.* 42, *d.* 23, p. 1. Tugan-Baranovskii (pp. 312–13) stresses the effects of the Civil War in explaining the crisis in the cotton industry.

24. From a total capacity of 2,050 H.P. in 1859 to 1,538 H.P. in 1863. Zak, p. 26.

25. TsGIAL, *f.* 1263, *op.* 1: *d.* 2975, p. 86, and *d.* 3263, pp. 93–100.

26. *Zhurnal manufaktur i torgovli,* III (Oct. 1864), sec. iv, p. 29.

27. See above, p. 78.

28. Zaionchkovskii, pp. 57, 138–40, 145, 148. Zaionchkovskii quotes at some length from Miliutin's important report to the Tsar, dated Jan. 15, 1862. Subsequent related documents are cited as well.

29. Stolpianskii, *Zhizn' i byt,* pp. 169–72; Pajalin [Paialin], *Die Leninwerke,* pp. 11–12; Zaionchkovskii, p. 139.

30. Rozanov, pp. 9–22; Stolpianskii, *Zhizn' i byt,* pp. 167–68; Zaionchkovskii, pp. 148–49.

31. S-PSK, *Statisticheskie svedeniia, 1862,* p. 55.

32. Zak, p. 26.

33. S-PSK, *Fabriki i zavody, 1863,* p. 26.

34. TsGIAL, *f.* 1263, *op.* 1, *d.* 3263, pp. 93–100; S-PSK, *Statisticheskie svedeniia, 1862,* p. 54. The figures on labor concentration in 1865 are only approximate, since not all factories are listed individually in the source. I have reached the estimates given by making some comparisons with the corresponding figures for 1863. S-PSK, *Fabriki i zavody, 1863,* pp. 23–39.

35. TsGIAL, *f.* 1263, *op.* 1, *d.* 3332, p. 209.

36. S-PSK, *Fabriki i zavody, 1863,* p. 23.

37. TsGIAL, *f.* 1263, *op.* 1, *d.* 3263, p. 95. Even this figure represented a sharp fall from the year 1859, when some eight hundred Golenishchevskaia workers took part in disorders. See above, p. 165.

38. TsGIAL, *f.* 1263, *op.* 1: *d.* 3163, p. 71; *d.* 3263, pp. 95–100; *d.* 3332, p. 209; TsSKMVD, *Statisticheskii vremennik,* series II, issue 6, pp. 128–29.

39. Lamanskii, CLXIV, 405.

40. Del'vig, IV, 31; Lamanskii, CLXI, 582; Terner, *Vospominaniia,* I, 204.

41. Lamanskii, CLXIV, 403–4.

42. For further details see Del'vig, IV, 31–36.

43. *Ibid.,* p. 47.

44. See below, p. 261.

45. Ministerstvo finansov, *Ezhegodnik . . . na 1869 god,* sec. iii, p. 276.

46. *Birzhevye vedomosti,* No. 238, May 31, 1870; No. 252, June 15, 1870 (because *Birzhevye vedomosti* appeared twice daily in 1870, I have included the number as well as the date); Del'vig, IV, 109ff; Stolpianskii, *Zhizn' i byt,* pp. 151–53. For a brief sketch of the history of this factory—including its predecessors at the same location—before 1870, see an unpublished typescript at the Hoover Institution, Stanford, California, entitled "The Works 'Red Putilovetz,'" pp. 1–3. Mr. Frank Golder obtained the typescript while doing relief work in Russia after the October Revolution. It is undated and unsigned.

47. See the excerpts from D. Miliutin's 1868 correspondence in Zaionchkovskii, p. 140.

48. Figures from *ibid.,* p. 149.

49. Ministerstvo finansov, *Ezhegodnik . . . na 1869 god,* sec. iii, p. 276.

50. Zaionchkovskii, pp. 144–45.

51. *Sanktpeterburg po perepisi . . . 1869 goda,* Vol. II, sec. ii, pp. 121–23.

52. S-PSK, *Pamiatnaia knizhka, 1863*, part ii, pp. 10, 20–21.

53. *Ibid.*, p. 96.

54. TsGIAL, *f.* 1284, *op.* 67, *d.* 364, pp. 57–58.

55. See above, pp. 58–61.

56. S-PSK, *Pamiatnaia knizhka, 1863*, part ii, pp. 20–21. On November 1, 1866, the 53 *kvartaly* were transformed into 38 larger units known as *uchastki*, which were subdivided into 93 *okolodki.* TsGIAL, *f.* 1263; *op.* 1, *d.* 3332, p. 6.

57. See above, p. 216n.

58. Del'vig, IV, 175.

59. See below, pp. 263–67.

60. *Sanktpeterburg po perepisi 1869 goda*, I, ii.

61. *Ibid.*, p. xvii.

62. See above, p. 49.

63. For a discussion of net migration, see Chevalier, pp. 267–68.

64. TsGIAL, *f.* 1263, *op.* 1, *d.* 3046, pp. 43–44.

65. *Ibid.*, p. 44. State peasants, who were not yet affected by the emancipation, are excluded from these figures.

66. *Ibid.*, *d.* 2975, p. 23; *d.* 3046, p. 30; *d.* 3143, p. 24; *d.* 3164, p. 38; *d.* 3263, p. 48.

67. TsGIAL, *f.* 1263, *op.* 1, *d.* 3143, p. 79; *d.* 3163, p. 63. (I have rounded the figures.)

68. See TsGIAL, *f.* 1263, *op.* 1, *d.* 3332, p. 15, and Table 1 above. (I have rounded the figures.)

69. *Sankpeterburg po perepisi 1869 goda*, I, xvi.

70. TsGIAL, *f.* 1263, *op.* 1, *d.* 3143, p. 89.

71. On the population density of St. Petersburg province, see Ianson, *Sravnitel'naia statistika*, I, 29.

72. TsGIAL, *f.* 1281, *op.* 6, *d.* 14 (1860), pp. 8–9.

73. TsGIAL, *f.* 1281, *op.* 6, *d.* 45 (1861), p. 10; *d.* 69 (1862), p. 10. The reduction of the number of days of obligatory labor (*barshchina*) that were owed to landlords by their former serfs after the peasants' status had been converted to one of "temporary obligation," was cited in these reports as an important factor in the decline of the harvests.

74. TsGIAL, *f.* 1281, *op.* 6, *d.* 52 (1863), pp. 7–8; see also p. 12.

75. TsGIAL, *f.* 1281, *op.* 7, *d.* 48 (1864), pp. 4–5.

76. TsGIAL, *f.* 1281, *op.* 7, *d.* 49 (1865), pp. 3–4, 8–9; *d.* 70 (1866), pp. 7–8; *d.* 79 (1867), pp. 127–28; *d.* 81 (1868), pp. 7, 44.

77. *Russkie vedomosti*, Jan. 26, 1868, quoted in Sel'chuk, "Russkaia publitsistika," p. 207.

78. Rykachev, p. 201. Real wages are estimated here by measuring wages paid against the local prices of ordinary rye bread.

79. The entire second part of Reshetnikov's novel, "V Peterburge" (pp. 447–646), unfolds in the context of St. Petersburg's industrial life and the peripheral world of *otkhodniki.* I am grateful to Rose Glickman for calling this work to my attention. On Reshetnikov and other *raznochintsy* writers of this period, see Glickman's unpublished doctoral dissertation, "The Literary Raznochintsy

in Mid-Nineteenth-Century Russia" (University of Chicago, 1967); see also her forthcoming article in *Canadian Slavic Studies.*

80. Reshetnikov, pp. 262, 351, 422–25, 441, 446.

81. *Ibid.,* pp. 424, 447–66; the title of the chapter describes her first experiences in the city (pp. 447–66): "Pelageia Prokhorovna finds that Petersburg is not as it was portrayed to her earlier."

82. *Ibid.,* esp. pp. 539, 570–72, 581, 587–88, 592, 595, 623–24.

83. See Glickman, Ch. 3.

84. Rykachev, p. 201.

85. Chevalier, pp. 188–90. See also pp. 190ff.

86. For the figures on population of meshchane and tsekhovye in St. Petersburg from 1861 through 1865, see TsGIAL, *f.* 1263, *op.* 1, *d.* 2975, pp. 88–89; *d.* 3046, p. 96; *d.* 3143, p. 89; *d.* 3164, p. 63; *d.* 3263, pp. 84–85.

87. *Sanktpeterburg po perepisi 1869 goda,* III, 102–3, 107–11, 116–17, 126–31, 136–37. Figures have been rounded off to the nearest thousand. These and subsequent figures relating to the peasant population are based on the responses of 204,300 of the 207,007 peasants. Information relating to other classes is likewise based on responses somewhat under the total for each group.

88. *Ibid.,* pp. 90–93, 98–101, 120–21, 124–25. Precise figures are listed for these and other branches of industry.

89. The number of artisan shops fell from 7,319 in 1865 to 6,882 in 1869. TsGIAL, *f.* 1263, *op.* 1, *d.* 3263, p. 9; *Sanktpeterburg po perepisi 1869 goda,* Vol. II, sec. ii, pp. 118–20.

90. *Sanktpeterburg po perepisi 1869 goda,* I, 4–5. In 1865 the corresponding figure was 71,802. TsGIAL, *f.* 1263, *op.* 1, *d.* 3263, pp. 85–86.

91. Derived from *Sanktpeterburg po perepisi 1869 goda,* I, 112–15. In the Spasskaia district, which had the greatest number of artisan shops in the city, nearly 42 per cent of the inhabitants were peasants.

92. *Ibid.,* III, 2–4, 7, 15, 40, 42, 102–3, 126–27.

93. They contained only 573 of the city's 6,882 artisan shops, or 8 per cent. *Ibid.,* Vol. II, sec. i, pp. 118–20.

94. *Ibid.,* III, 2, 15. All the ratios through the end of the chapter are approximate. In Russia as a whole, as in most of nineteenth-century Europe, there was a slight preponderance of women over men. In 1870 there were 102 women in Russia for every 100 men. See Ianson, *Sravnitel'naia statistika,* p. 49.

95. *Sanktpeterburg po perepisi 1869 goda,* I, 112–15; III, 2.

96. Until the age of ten, the number of males and the number of females were almost equal. All my figures on the age distributions of males and females are based on *ibid.,* I, 2–5.

97. Ianson, "Naselenie Peterburga," p. 614. Ianson himself conducted the next official censuses of St. Petersburg, in 1881 and 1890. See Gozulov, pp. 28, 113–15.

98. *Sanktpeterburg po perepisi 1869 goda,* I, 2.

99. The information on illiteracy that follows is derived from *ibid.,* pp. 22–27, 74, 118. Children under the age of seven are excluded from the figures on illiteracy. The rate of illiteracy was considerably higher in Moscow than in St.

Petersburg, especially among males. See Ianson, *Sravnitel'naia statistika*, pp. 120–21.

100. For 1865, see TsGIAL, *f.* 1263, *op.* 1, *d.* 3236, pp. 84–86. It is difficult to assess the validity of this comparison since the figures for 1865 include people of all ages. An absolute rise in the number of literate persons in the two districts (as elsewhere in St. Petersburg) of course accompanied the expansion of population.

101. Relative to population, there were also more teachers in St. Petersburg than in London or Paris, and nearly as many as in Berlin. See Ianson, "Naselenie Peterburga," p. 618.

CHAPTER SEVEN

1. G. I. Arkhangel'skii, "Zhizn' v Peterburge po statisticheskim dannym," *Arkhiv*, No. 2 (1869), sec. iii, pp. 37–38. According to Dr. Arkhangel'skii's calculations, in no decade since the 1790's had St. Petersburg experienced a natural net gain in population.

2. See *ibid.*, and Table 10 above, p. 221.

3. TsGIAL, *f.* 1263, *op.* 1, *d.* 2975, p. 30. The death rate in 1861 was the lowest for the decade—slightly over 31 per 1,000.

4. *Ibid.*, *d.* 3263, pp. 40–42. No precise figures for the number of typhus victims are given, but Arkhangel'skii estimated ten thousand deaths. *Arkhiv*, No. 3 (1869), sec. iii, p. 109.

5. Based on the number of deaths, 22,770, given in TsSKMVD, *Statisticheskii vremennik*, series II, issue 13, pp. 114–17, which I have combined with the 1869 census population total. No figures are available for 1867. The number of deaths in 1868 was 23,722 (*ibid.*, issue 12, pp. 114–17), but there is no total population figure from which to calculate the death rate.

6. The year 1872 was especially devastating: sixteen thousand known cases of smallpox, nine thousand cases of cholera; three thousand deaths among the smallpox victims, over twenty-six hundred deaths among the cholera victims. *Birzhevye vedomosti*, Sept. 3, 1870; Nikitenko, III, 200 (entry of March 8, 1871); TsGIAL, *f.* 1263, *op.* 1, *d.* 3677, pp. 124–25, 127, 129.

7. For comparative figures see Arkhangel'skii, "Zhizn' v Peterburge," *Arkhiv*, No. 2 (1869), sec. iii, pp. 37–39, and Ianson, *Sravnitel'naia statistika*, pp. 266–70.

8. See above, p. 52.

9. Lanskoi to Mecklenburg, June 10, 1857, in *O byte rabochikh*, pp. 48–49; see also p. 146 above, and Ch. 4, n. 71.

10. *O byte rabochikh*, pp. 52–53, 61, 71. At the prevailing wages in St. Petersburg at this time, assuming full-time employment (an unsafe assumption), an unskilled worker would have had to work two and a half months to earn a year's rent of thirty rubles. See Rykachev, p. 201.

11. *Narodnoe chtenie*, Bk. 2 (1859), p. 21.

12. Terner, *O rabochem klasse*, pp. 114–15.

13. German, "K statistike i etiologii narodnykh boleznei v Peterburge," *Arkhiv*, No. 1 (1871), sec. iii, p. 90; Giubner, p. 60. For comparable develop-

ments in Paris in the first half of the nineteenth century, see Chevalier, pp. 216–28.

14. F. Erisman, "Podval'nye zhilishcha v Peterburge," *Arkhiv*, No. 3 (1871), sec. iii, pp. 43–44, 60.

15. *Ibid.*, pp. 76–80, 82–83; No. 4 (1871), sec. iii, pp. 1–3, 8–11. Some of these points were repeated by Erisman in more technical medical language.

16. Arkhangel'skii, "Zhizn' v Peterburge," *Arkhiv*, No. 3 (1869), sec. iii, pp. 110–11, 119, 125, 127–28.

17. *O byte rabochikh*, p. 60. On the French *cités ouvrières* see Georges Duveau, *La vie ouvrière en France sous le Second Empire* (6th ed., Paris, 1946), pp. 359–61. Duveau considers the settlements to have been generally unsuccessful.

18. Reshetnikov, pp. 580–81, 583–84, 597.

19. "Statistika smertnosti v Rossii," *Birzhevye vedomosti*, Feb. 10, 1866.

20. In addition, measures were taken to discourage outdoor workers, such as construction workers, from resting or sleeping on the bare earth, and to enlist the support and cooperation of landlords and contractors in protecting the health of their tenants and employees. These and similar policies, based in part on the experiences of 1865, were set forth by the chief of police in special instructions issued to landlords, contractors, and factory owners. They are reprinted in *Birzhevye vedomosti*, February 17, 1866, and July 5, 1866. The Baird machine works, which had been badly victimized by cholera in 1848, was praised for having given pure water with vodka to its workers before the issuing of the instructions. These matters are also summarized in TsGIAL, *f.* 1263, *op.* 1, *d.* 3332, p. 56. On the anti-drinking campaign, see below, pp. 255–56.

21. "O kholere v 4-em kvartale Peterburgskoi chasti 1866 g.," *Arkhiv*, No. 1 (1868), sec. vi, pp. 1–14. See esp. pp. 10–12.

22. *Ibid.*

23. *Arkhiv*, No. 3 (1871), sec. iii, pp. 37, 65; No. 4 (1871), sec. iii, esp. p. 21.

24. *Arkhiv*, No. 2 (1869), sec. iii, p. 76.

25. *Arkhiv*, No. 2 (1868), sec. v, p. 56.

26. *Arkhiv*, No. 1 (1871), sec. iii, pp. 124–43. The incidents described and the conclusions drawn in this article are discussed below, beginning on p. 275.

27. *Arkhiv*, No. 3 (1860), sec. iii, p. 95; Ianson, *Sravnitel'naia statistika*, pp. 290–91. The other uchastki with mortality rates above 50 per 1,000 were in the Rozhdestvenskaia and Vyborg districts.

28. Dr. Gorman, "O p'ianstve v Rossii," *Arkhiv*, No. 1 (1868), sec. iii, p. 52. According to Gorman, excise taxes on alcohol provided the government with 39 per cent of its revenues in 1859.

29. *Birzhevye vedomosti*, Sept. 18, 1864.

30. Gorman, "O p'ianstve," p. 52.

31. *Ibid.*, pp. 53–54. The relatively small number of taverns in well-to-do areas of the city does not necessarily suggest that the upper classes were abstinent, but that they were more likely to do their drinking in private gatherings than in public houses.

32. *Ibid.*, pp. 55–57; V. Val'kh, "K voprosu o p'ianstve v Peterburge," *Arkhiv*, No. 4 (1870), sec. v, pp. 11–15.

33. Gorman, "O p'ianstve," pp. 55–57.

34. V. Val'kh, pp. 11–15.

35. *Birzhevye vedomosti*, Sept. 18, 1864.

36. Reshetnikov, pp. 471–72, 540, 571–75, 590–95.

37. *Ibid.*, pp. 598–604.

38. Gorman, "O p'ianstve," pp. 55–57.

39. "R," "Po povodu dela o pishche i pomeshchenii rabochikh," *Arkhiv*, No. 1 (1871), sec. iii.

40. TsGIAL, *f.* 1263, *op.* 1, *d.* 2975, p. 13; *d.* 3046, p. 13; *d.* 3143 (1863), p. 13; *d.* 3164, p. 98; *d.* 3332 (1866), p. 57. I have rounded all figures to the nearest thousand. Figures for 1865 are not available. There is no indication in the reports or elsewhere that these figures represent an intensification of police enforcement activities rather than an actual rise in the crime rate. On the special measures introduced by the police in 1867, see below, pp. 255–56.

41. *Ibid.*, *d.* 2975; pp. 14, 32; *d.* 3046, pp. 14, 45; *d.* 3143, p. 14; *d.* 3164, pp. 19–20, 28; *d.* 3263 (1865), pp. 19, 26, 31; *d.* 3332, pp. 27–28, 33–34, 38; *d.* 3363, p. 201.

42. *Ibid.*, *d.* 3526 (1869), p. 148; *d.* 3677 (1872), p. 52.

43. *Ibid.*, *d.* 2975, pp. 21–22; *d.* 3046, p. 28; *d.* 3143; p. 22; *d.* 3164, p. 37; *d.* 3263, p. 44; *d.* 3332, pp. 87–88; *d.* 3363, p. 267.

44. *Arkhiv*, No. 3 (1871), sec. iv, pp. 49–50.

45. TsGIAL, *f.* 1263, *op.* 1, *d.* 3363, p. 62; N. B---skii, "Ocherk prostitutsii v Peterburge," *Arkhiv*, No. 4 (1868), sec. iii, pp. 67, 93; *Arkhiv*, No. 2 (1869), sec. vi, p. 47. See also *Arkhiv*, No. 3 (1871), sec. iv, pp. 55–56. When a random sample of 28 workers at a medium-size factory was examined by a physician in 1870, eight were found to be syphilitic. *Arkhiv*, No. 1 (1871), sec. iii, pp. 128–29.

46. See above, p. 64. At the time the Buksgevden commission was established, St. Petersburg's so-called medical-police committee, founded in 1843, had already been functioning for several years. See *PSZ*, XVIII, No. 17213; XX, No. 19402; XXIII, No. 22724.

47. See *PSZ*, XXXV, Part II, No. 36117.

48. TsGIAL, *f.* 1263, *op.* 1, *d.* 3164 (1864), p. 30.

49. The life of the committee was officially over on July 3, 1867. See *PSZ*, XLII, Part I, No. 44802.

50. *PSZ*, XLII, Part I, No. 44281.

51. TsGIAL, *f.* 1263, *op.* 1, *d.* 2975, pp. 19–21; *d.* 3046, p. 20.

52. *Ibid.*, *d.* 3363, pp. 260–61.

53. *Otchet po Gosudarstvennomu sovetu za 1870 god*, p. 124.

54. TsGIAL, *f.* 1263, *op.* 1, *d.* 3263, p. 40; *d.* 3332, p. 49.

55. Litvinov-Falinskii, pp. 218–19. The statute, which required manufacturers to provide hospitalization facilities at the rate of one bed per hundred workers, was issued August 26, 1866. The immediate impetus for it came from Moscow. Litvinov's assessment of the subsequent usefulness of the measure is very negative (pp. 219–24).

56. TsGIAL, *f.* 1263, *op.* 1, *d.* 3363 (1867), p. 107; *PSZ*, XLII, Part I, No. 44281.

57. TsGIAL, *f.* 1263, *op.* 1, *d.* 3526, pp. 193, 198.

58. *Ibid., d.* 3677, pp. 27, 29, 31.

59. *Ibid., d.* 3526, p. 193; *d.* 3263, p. 41.

60. Valuev, II, 474 (editorial note by Zaionchkovskii).

61. TsGIAL, *f.* 1263, *op.* 1, *d.* 3363, p. 108.

62. *Ibid.,* pp. 109–13.

63. *Ibid.,* pp. 109–10. The orders to the police were dated July 29 and August 6, 1867.

64. For a brief and readily accessible account of Karakozov's attempt on the life of the Tsar, its political repercussions, and the revolutionary groups with which Karakozov was associated, see Venturi, Ch. 14.

65. The following sketch of the Liudinovo affair is based on documents in *Rabochee dvizhenie*, II, Part I, 203–26, which should be consulted for further details. See also E. S. Vilenskaia, *Revoliutsionnoe podpol'e v Rossii (60-e gody XIX v.)* (Moscow, 1965), pp. 282–94, esp. pp. 286–94.

66. *PSZ*, XL, Part II, No. 42690, and XLI, Part I, Nos. 43102 and 43414.

67. See above, p. 62.

68. See above, pp. 244–45.

69. TsGIAL, *f.* 1281, *op.* 7, *d.* 79, p. 170.

70. TsGIAL, *f.* 219, *op.* 1/1, *d.* 356, p. 2. The State Comptroller disapproved of the retention of the police office at the factory on the grounds that the expenses of maintaining it placed an unnecessary burden on the state budget (pp. 1–5), but his argument was unpersuasive.

71. *Ibid.,* pp. 16–21.

72. *Ibid.,* pp. 48, 49, 58.

73. *Ibid.,* pp. 54–55, 76.

74. TsGIAL, *f.* 258, *op.* 9, *d.* 32, p. 17. By this time there were some two thousand workers employed at the factory, but still only 25 beds at the hospital. The new structure was built to accommodate 44 patients. The company financed the entire ten-thousand-ruble operation through fines and deductions from the workers' wages (pp. 17–18).

75. *PSZ*, XLII, Part I, No. 44212.

76. Zaionchkovskii, p. 143. According to Zaionchkovskii (pp. 141–42), the pattern of leasing military factories to their commanding officers in connection with the transition to free labor began with the Tula armaments works in 1864.

77. *Rabochee dvizhenie*, II, Part I, 228–30.

78. *Ibid.*

79. *PSZ*, XLI, Part II, No. 44051.

80. Zaionchkovskii (p. 144) gives January 1, 1868, as the date free labor was actually introduced at the Okhta factory. The delay may have been due to the fact that the plant was undergoing large-scale reconstruction from 1865 to 1868, because of a tremendous explosion in 1864.

81. *Rabochee dvizhenie*, II, Part I, 227.

82. TsGIAL, *f.* 1281, *op.* 7, *d.* 79, pp. 159–60, 169–70. One zemstvo meeting

even offered to organize a special guard unit (*zemskaia strazha*) for this purpose at its own expense, but nothing came of this proposal.

83. Editorial note by Zaionchkovskii in Valuev, II, 476. See also the entry in Valuev's diary for November 19, 1866 (II, 169); Valuev was opposed to Shuvalov's plan, but was certain it would be approved in view of the prevailing mood of society.

84. TsGIAL, *f*. 1281, *op*. 7, *d*. 79, p. 170.

85. *Ibid.*

86. TsGIAL, *f*. 1281, *op*. 7, *d*. 81 (1868), p. 53.

87. Nikitenko, III, 31 (entry of May 7, 1866); Valuev, II, 119–21 (entries of April 14, 18, 19, and 20, 1866).

88. Nikitenko, III, 59 (entry of Nov. 27, 1866); Valuev, II, 151, 157 (entries of Sept. 19 and Oct. 18, 1866). See also Zaionchkovskii's editorial note, *ibid.*, p. 474.

89. TsGIAL, *f*. 1281, *op*. 7, *d*. 81, pp. 53–56. The governor's position was presented as part of his annual report to the Tsar for 1868.

90. *PSZ*, XLVI, Part II, No. 49833. See also *PSZ*, XLVII, Part I, No. 51014; *PSZ*, XLVIII, Part I, No. 52032; Akademiia Nauk SSSR, *Ocherki*, II, 812; E. Amburger, *Geschichte der Behördenorganisation Russlands von Peter dem Grossen bis 1917* (Leiden, 1966), p. 382. The office of *gradonachal'nik* did not actually become operative until March 1873.

91. *Otchet po Gosudarstvennomu sovetu za 1870 god*, pp. 17–19; *Otchet po Gosudarstvennomu sovetu za 1871 god*, pp. 26–28.

92. TsGIAL, *f*. 1263, *op*. 1, *d*. 3677 (1872), pp. 54–55. The problem was finally resolved through the intervention of the Minister of Finance, who ruled that as of January 1873 the method of issuing licenses to drinking places in St. Petersburg city would be enforced in the outlying suburban areas as well. This meant that licenses had to be renewed every six months.

93. The charter of the new *S.-Peterburgskoe obshchestvo popecheniia o narodnom zdravii* was still in the process of being drafted in 1870; see *Birzhevye vedomosti*, April 23, 1870. It would in any case be misleading to conceive of the municipal duma as an organ of authority totally separate from the municipal police. Although the dumas were reorganized in 1870 and made into slightly more representative institutions by the transformation of an old elective system based on class to a new system based on property and wealth, the St. Petersburg duma continued to be completely dependent on the municipal chief of police (after 1871, the municipal governor) for the execution of its legislation; the chief of police, however, answered for his actions not to the duma but to the Minister of Internal Affairs. See Akademiia Nauk SSSR, *Ocherki*, II, 813–15; *PSZ*, XLV, Part I, No. 48498; *PSZ*, XLVII, Part I, No. 51014.

94. See above, p. 245.

95. *Arkhiv*, No. 1 (1868), sec. vi, p. 12.

96. Arkhangel'skii, "Zhizn' v Peterburge po statisticheskim dannym," *Arkhiv*, Nos. 2 and 3 (1869), sec. iii, pp. 33–85, and 84–113.

97. *Ibid.*, No. 2 (1869), sec. iii, pp. 37–39.

98. *Ibid.*, pp. 40–41.

99. *Ibid.*, pp. 41–43.

100. *Ibid.*, p. 49.

101. *Ibid.*, pp. 43–44; No. 3 (1869), sec. iii, p. 103.

102. *Ibid.*, pp. 110–15, 119, 121, 125, 127–28.

103. *Ibid.*, pp. 128–29, 133, 137.

104. *Ibid.*, pp. 137, 141.

105. *Ibid.*, pp. 123–24.

106. "Podval'nye zhilishcha v Peterburge," *Arkhiv*, No. 3 (1871), sec. iii, pp. 39–41.

107. *Arkhiv*, No. 3 (1869), sec. iii, p. 137.

108. "Po povedu dela o pishche i pomeshchenii rabochikh na fabrike kuptsa Egorova," *Arkhiv*, No. 1 (1871), sec. iii, pp. 124–43.

109. The preceding account is based on a medical police report and official publications of the municipal police reproduced in *ibid.*, pp. 124–26.

110. *Ibid.*, p. 127.

111. *Ibid.*, pp. 131–32, 134–37.

112. *Ibid.*, pp. 128, 130–31, 138–39. On pp. 140–41 "R" presented a comprehensive list of 24 suggested duties for the factory inspectors. No area of competence is overlooked. For the signs he took to mean that the government had revived its interest in legislation, see below, p. 373.

113. *Ibid.*, pp. 141–43. At no point did "R" adopt an overtly anti-industrial position. Such a position would of course have been incompatible with his emphasis on the need for factory legislation, which was based on the assumption that industry had come to stay. Nevertheless, under the influence of N. [Bervi] Flerovskii's recently published *Polozhenie rabochego klassa v Rossii* (St. Petersburg, 1869), he expressed views similar to those later to be avowed both by Populists and conservatives concerning the primacy of the agricultural problem.

114. *Arkhiv*, No. 4 (1871), sec. iii, p. 7.

115. *Arkhiv*, No. 1 (1871), sec. iii, pp. 132–34.

116. "K voprosu o p'ianstve v Peterburge," *Arkhiv*, No. 4 (1870), sec. v, pp. 11–15.

117. *Arkhiv*, No. 3 (1871), sec. iv, pp. 55–56; N. B---skii, "Ocherk prostitutsii v Peterburge," *Arkhiv*, No. 4 (1868), sec. iii, pp. 67, 93.

118. *Ibid.*, pp. 61–63.

119. "Peterburgskie nravy po statisticheskim dannym," *Arkhiv*, No. 1 (1868), sec. v, pp. 50–51.

120. "Istoriko-statisticheskii ocherk prostitutsii v Peterburge s 1852 g. po 1869 god," *Arkhiv*, No. 1 (1870), sec. iii, p. 3.

121. *Ibid.*, pp. 38, 41, 42.

122. *Arkhiv*, No. 1 (1871), sec. iii, pp. 128–29.

CHAPTER EIGHT

1. Ermanskii, p. 333. A similar organization, the Polytechnical Society, was founded in Moscow in 1870.

2. *Trudy*, I, 32n.

3. Del'vig, III, 381–85. On Leikhtenbergskii see *Entsiklopedicheskii slovar'*, XVII A (St. Petersburg, 1896), 506–7.

4. Del'vig, III, 381. According to Del'vig, Konstantin was rejected for the position of honorary chairman because of the antagonism engendered by his handling of the Polish crisis (as military governor in 1862–63).

5. *Ibid.*, pp. 383–84.

6. *Zapiski Imperatorskogo Russkogo Tekhnicheskogo Obshchestva.* The Industrial Society did not begin to publish its transactions (*Trudy*) until 1872.

7. See above, pp. 88–91. In addition to being attacked by progressive reformers for their greed in connection with the tariff and labor questions, Russian manufacturers were sometimes subjected to abuse by conservatives for daring to take public stands in favor of reform. Thus when V. A. Kokorev, a Moscow entrepreneur with close ties to the Ministry of Finance, spoke at a public gathering in favor of emancipation, local Moscow officials were quick to condemn the practice of a non-noble taking a controversial public stand at a "Western meeting" and to label such activities as "foreign." See Berlin, pp. 108–10, for details.

8. We have already had occasion to take note of favorable references to large St. Petersburg entrepreneurs that contrasted them with their less savory provincial cousins or even smaller manufacturers in the capital. See Chs. 3 and 4 above.

9. *Trudy*, I, 352.

10. *Ibid.* Among the twenty-eight St. Petersburg industrialists who had supported the proposals of the St. Petersburg commission—in this case mainly textile manufacturers—at least seventeen had recognizably foreign, mainly English and German, names (e.g., Wright, Maxwell, Thornton, Shaw, Miller, König, Zimmerman).

11. Unless otherwise noted, biographical information on Poletika in this and subsequent paragraphs is based on the entry "Poletika," in *Russkii biografi-cheskii slovar'* (St. Petersburg, 1905), pp. 319–20.

12. *Ibid.*; Stolpianskii, *Zhizn' i byt*, p. 172.

13. Quoted in *ibid.*, pp. 133–34.

14. *Birzhevye vedomosti*, May 22, 1864 (italicized by editors of *Birzhevye vedomosti*).

15. The minutes of the meeting were reproduced in the Technical Society's journal. For our purposes, the most important sections are *Zapiski*, No. 3 (1867), pp. 132–94, and No. 6 (1867), pp. 396–410. A full list of participants was not included in the protocols of the meeting, but the names of Poletika, Nobel, San-Galli, Butz, MacPherson, and Putilov are listed as members of a special commission that was elected to work on implementing some of the decisions of the meeting. *Ibid.*, No. 3 (1867), p. 194.

16. Stolpianskii, p. 135.

17. *Zapiski*, No. 3 (1867).

18. *Ibid.*, p. 141.

19. *Ibid.*, pp. 134–35, 138, 145, 148–55, 171, 174, 189, and 194.

20. *Ibid.*, p. 170.

21. *Ibid.*, p. 140. This expression was used by F. N. L'vov, assistant secretary of the Technical Society.

22. *Ibid.*, pp. 134, 174.

23. *Ibid.*, p. 148.

24. *Ibid.*, pp. 132–33.

25. *Ibid.*, p. 141.

26. *Ibid.*, pp. 165–66, 172–73.

27. *Ibid.*, pp. 137, 193.

28. *Ibid.*, No. 6 (1867), pp. 396–410.

29. *Ibid.*, pp. 396–97.

30. *Ibid.*, pp. 408–9.

31. *Ibid.*, pp. 397–99. The unimplemented proposals of the old St. Petersburg commission of 1859 were actually reprinted in the published minutes of the meeting (*ibid.*, pp. 400–408).

32. *Ibid.*, No. 3 (1867), p. 140. The speaker was the secretary of the congress, F. N. L'vov.

33. *Ibid.*, No. 6 (1867), p. 396.

34. P. I. Liashchenko, II, 189; A. M. Bol'shakov and N. A. Rozhkov, *Istoriia khoziaistva Rossii v materialakh i dokumentakh* (2d ed.), II (Leningrad, 1925), 232. For evidence that industrialists participated in the official review that preceded the new tariff, see *Trudy Obshchestva dlia sodeistviia russkoi promyshlennosti i torgovli*, I (St. Petersburg, 1872), 83.

35. *Zapiski*, No. 1 (1871), sec. ii, pp. 47–48.

36. Del'vig, IV, 351.

37. Zaionchkovskii, p. 57.

38. *Ibid.*, p. 173.

39. Del'vig, IV, 355.

40. *Birzhevye vedomosti*, No. 117, March 15, 1870. The pressing need to educate and train Russian workers was also recognized by the zemstva of Tver and other provinces. *Ibid.*, No. 121, March 18, 1870.

41. *Die Industrie Russlands in ihrer bisherigen Entwicklung und in ihrem gegenwärtigen Zustande mit besonderer Berücksichtigung der allgemeinen russischen Manufaktur-Ausstellung im Jahre 1870* (2 vols.; Leipzig, 1872–73).

42. *Ibid.*, II, 463.

43. *Ibid.*, pp. 463–72. (Quotations from pp. 464–65.) Much of Matthäi's program was borrowed from Moscow's German newspaper, *Moskauer Deutsche Zeitung*.

44. *Birzhevye vedomosti*, No. 176, April 23, 1870.

45. *Ibid.*, No. 173, April 22, 1870; No. 176, April 23, 1870; No. 199, May 7, 1870.

46. *Ibid.*, No. 181, April 26, 1870; No. 200, May 7, 1870.

47. *Ibid.*, No. 199, May 7, 1870.

48. *Ibid.*, No. 212, May 15, 1870.

49. *Ibid.*, No. 257, June 20, 1870. Notwithstanding the many absentees noted by the newspaper, 3,105 exhibitors displayed products in 43 different categories of production.

50. Matthäi, I, v.

51. *Ibid.*, I, v, 37.

52. *Birzhevye vedomosti*, No. 166, April 17, 1870; No. 198, May 6, 1870. The stenographic record of the congress was published in *Zapiski* in 1871, in a series of supplements to the regular issues. The resolutions passed by the congress first appeared in *Zapiski*, No. 4, 1870. A separate edition of the stenographic record also appeared in St. Petersburg in 1872, under the title *Protokoly i stenograficheskie otchety zasedanii pervogo vserossiiskogo s'ezda fabrikantov, zavodchikov i lits, interesuiushchikhsia otechestvennoiu promyshlennostiu.* My citations are from *Zapiski*.

53. *Birzhevye vedomosti*, No. 228, May 26, 1870.

54. Del'vig, III, 386.

55. *Birzhevye vedomosti*, No. 232, May 28, 1870.

56. See, for example, *Zapiski*, No. 1 (1871), pp. 92–93. N.B.: The protocols of the congress that appear in special sections of *Zapiski* have separate pagination. In each issue they follow section ii of the journal.

57. *Zapiski*, No. 2 (1871), pp. 76–77. See also Berlin, p. 216.

58. *Zapiski*, No. 1 (1871), p. 66.

59. *Ibid.*, p. 77.

60. *Ibid.*, pp. 80–81.

61. *Zapiski*, No. 2 (1871), p. 41. The entire session on statistics occupies pp. 21–54.

62. *Ibid.*, p. 44.

63. *Ibid.*, p. 22.

64. *Trudy*, I, 186–89. The Shtakel'berg Commission's proposals for reorganizing the Manufacturing Council were mentioned approvingly in the course of the deliberations at the congress.

65. On Veshniakov (ca. 1830–1906) see *Entsiklopedicheskii slovar'*, VI (St. Petersburg, 1892), 149–50.

66. *Zapiski*, No. 2 (1871), pp. 3–8, 15. On Skal'kovskii see *Entsiklopedicheskii slovar'*, XXX (St. Petersburg, 1900), 172; Berlin, pp. 163, 218; Gindin, "Russkaia burzhuaziia," pp. 72, 74. Skal'kovskii served at various points in his career as a publicist, a music critic, a member of the board of various companies and banks, a professor at the Mining Institute, and in the last years of his life (1892–96) was the director of the Department of Mines.

67. *Zapiski*, No. 4 (1870), pp. 121, 125–26; No. 2 (1871), pp. 12–14, 19–21, 80–81, 86.

68. *Ibid.*, No. 2 (1871), p. 9.

69. *Ibid.*, No. 4 (1871), p. 3; the entire discussion of machine and metal industries, railroad construction, and tariffs appears on pp. 1–51. Poletika served as chairman of these sessions.

70. *Ibid.*, p. 7.

71. *Ibid.*, pp. 12–14, 16–17, 19–21.

72. This point may have been exaggerated. Velikhov's calculations were based on the cost of foreign rails made of iron only, whereas the Putilov rails were capped with steel. See *Birzhevye vedomosti*, No. 238, May 31, 1870.

73. *Zapiski*, No. 4 (1871), pp. 33–38.

74. *Ibid.*, No. 4 (1870), p. 120; No. 2 (1871), pp. 79–80; No. 4 (1871), pp. 28, 76.

75. *Ibid.*, No. 1 (1871), p. 45; the entire discussion of the labor question appears on pp. 45–113.

76. *Birzhevye vedomosti*, No. 224, May 23, 1870; No. 243, June 6, 1870.

77. Vargunin was the owner and director of one of St. Petersburg's large mechanized paper factories (276 workers, according to Matthäi, I, 401), located in the Schlüsselburg Road area, which had been founded by his uncle in 1839. He had been educated at St. Petersburg University. See *Entsiklopedicheskii slovar'*, V A (St. Petersburg, 1892), 513. In 1871 Vargunin was elected to the executive committee of the Industrial Society. *Trudy Obshchestva dlia sodeistviia russkoi promyshlennosti i torgovli*, I, 2.

78. *Zapiski*, No. 1 (1871), pp. 45–47.

79. *Ibid.*, p. 71n.

80. *Birzhevye vedomosti*, No. 224, May 23, 1870.

81. *Zapiski*, No. 1 (1871), pp. 48–49.

82. Edmund Romanovich Vreden (1835–91) was professor of political economy at St. Petersburg University from 1866 until his death. At various times he also taught at the Pavlovskii Military Academy, the Mining Institute, and the Institute of Transportation Engineers. Although a strong partisan of the Manchester school of economic liberalism, he was—like Terner and other liberal economists with whom we are familiar—very much concerned with the problems of workers. Like Terner, he was a staunch advocate of arteli. See *Entsiklopedicheskii slovar'*, VI (St. Petersburg, 1892), 353.

83. *Zapiski*, No. 1 (1871), pp. 53–56, 60–63.

84. *Ibid.*, pp. 83–84, 103–5.

85. *Ibid.*, pp. 110, 113; see also No. 4 (1870), p. 125, and No. 2 (1871), p. 85.

86. *Ibid.*, No. 1 (1871), pp. 48–50.

87. *Ibid.*, pp. 67–68, 70.

88. *Ibid.*, pp. 71–73.

89. *Ibid.*, p. 106.

90. *Ibid.*, pp. 57, 71.

91. *Ibid.*, pp. 50–51.

92. *Ibid.*, pp. 52–53.

93. *Ibid.*, pp. 56–60.

94. *Ibid.*, pp. 63–66.

95. *Ibid.*, pp. 66 (parts of these quotations were italicized in the original).

96. *Ibid.*, pp. 66–67.

97. *Ibid.*, pp. 90–92. A brief excerpt from Shreier's talk is printed in Tugan-Baranovskii, *Russkaia fabrika*, pp. 535–36.

98. *Zapiski*, No. 1 (1871), pp. 95–103; for further remarks by speakers favorable to associations, savings and loan funds, limitations on child labor, compensation by employers for injuries sustained by workers, and so forth, see especially pp. 53, 76–77, 81, 108–9. The excerpt from Miasoedov's speech cited in Tugan-Baranovskii, pp. 536–37, in addition to being slightly inaccurate, is very misleading in that the full context of the remarks is not presented.

99. *Zapiski*, No. 1 (1871), p. 87.

100. *Ibid.*, p. 92.

101. *Ibid.*, pp. 92–93; for other examples of optimism concerning the attitudes of manufacturers see pp. 46, 68–70.

102. *Ibid.*, p. 92. See also *Birzhevye vedomosti*, No. 243, June 6, 1870, where Shreier's remarks and those of other participants are summarized.

103. *Zapiski*, No. 1 (1871), p. 107.

104. *Ibid.*, pp. 77–79. Kaigorodov's somewhat overstated rejoinder to the last point was that in other countries the workers worked only an eight-hour day (p. 80).

105. *Ibid.*, p. 77.

106. *Ibid.*, p. 74.

107. *Ibid.*, pp. 74–77. Appolon Mikhailovich Loranskoi was a young mining engineer, an expert in the field of metallurgical industry, and a teacher of mining statistics. He was an active member of the Industrial Society, the author of articles on accident insurance for workers, and a partisan of certain other pro-labor measures. At the congress, he described the existing situation of the Russian working class as "horrible" (*uzhasno*), and he favored such propositions as savings and loan funds and manufacturer-supported elementary schools. In the 1870's and early 1880's he was to serve as secretary of the government's committee on literacy. See *Entsiklopedicheskii slovar'*, XVIII (St. Petersburg, 1896), 10.

108. *Zapiski*, No. 1 (1871), pp. 97–98.

109. *Ibid.*, pp. 109–10.

110. Despite Delavoss's use of the term, there was nothing in the protocols that suggested the existence of any organized "factions." Del'vig, however, wrote vaguely of "parties" within the Technical Society threatening its unity. Possibly this was meant to refer to the free traders and the protectionists. See Del'vig, III, 385.

111. *Zapiski*, No. 1 (1871), pp. 106–8.

112. *Ibid.*, pp. 84–87.

113. *Ibid.*, p. 108.

114. *Ibid.*, p. 112; see also No. 4 (1870), p. 124, and No. 2 (1871), p. 84.

115. *Ibid.*, No. 1 (1871), pp. 112–13; No. 4 (1870), pp. 124–25; No. 2 (1871), pp. 84–85.

116. *Birzhevye vedomosti*, No. 312, Aug. 15, 1870.

117. *Ibid.*, No. 244, June 7, 1870.

118. *Ibid.*, No. 251, June 14, 1870.

CHAPTER NINE

1. *Birzhevye vedomosti*, No. 52, Feb. 2, 1870.

2. The original article, "The War of the Future in Europe," appeared as an unsigned editorial in the *New York Times*, Jan. 23, 1870. Although I have referred to the original version, what appears here is essentially a retranslation of the translation in *Birzhevye vedomosti*, which is not entirely faithful to the original.

3. *Birzhevye vedomosti*, No. 52, Feb. 2, 1870.

4. *Ibid.*, No. 163, April 15, 1870.

5. Del'vig, IV, 350.

6. *Birzhevye vedomosti*, No. 238, May 31, 1870; Del'vig, IV, 350–52; "The Works 'Red Putilovetz,'" pp. 1–3; Stolpianskii, *Zhizn' i byt*, pp. 151–53.

7. *Birzhevye vedomosti*, No. 252, June 15, 1870. The rest of my account of the Putilov celebration comes from this source unless otherwise indicated.

8. Putilov's remarks are quoted in full in Stolpianskii, *Zhizn' i byt*, pp. 154–55.

9. M. Mitel'man, B. Glebov, A. Ul'ianskii, *Istoriia Putilovskogo zavoda 1801–1917* (3d ed., Moscow, 1961), p. 24. A description of the celebration, including excerpts from Putilov's speech, is given on pp. 21–23. This version is poorly documented and some aspects appear to be highly embellished.

10. Del'vig, IV, 352.

11. *Ibid.*, p. 355.

12. There are almost no references to this incident in studies of Russian labor history, in part, perhaps, because it has been dwarfed by the more dramatic events that followed shortly thereafter.

13. *Birzhevye vedomosti*, No. 228, May 26, 1870.

14. *Ibid.*

15. There are brief allusions to the Nevskii strike in scores of Soviet and pre-Soviet historical works. Somewhat longer accounts may be found in the following studies: M. Balabanov, *Ocherki po istorii rabochego klassa v Rossii*, II (1st ed., Kiev, 1924), 159–68; Iu. Gessen, "K istorii stachek sredi fabrichnykh rabochikh (v nachale semidesiatykh godov 19-go veka)," *Arkhiv istorii truda v Rossii*, III (1922), 40–50; and R. Kantor, "Zhandarmeriia i pervye rabochie stachki (v nachale semidesiatykh godov 19-go veka)," *Arkhiv istorii truda v Rossii*, III (1922), 71–77. My own account of the events of the strike is reconstructed from contemporary sources as follows: reports of the official investigation and trial of the strikers, in various issues of *Sudebnyi vestnik* for June and July, 1870; reports in *Birzhevye vedomosti*, May–July, 1870; reports and correspondence from the office of the St. Petersburg municipal administration and from the offices of the Third Section, contained in TsGAOR, *f.* 109, Tret'ee Otdelenie Sobstvennoi Imperatorskogo Velichestva Kantseliarii, *eksp.* 3, *d.* 64, *op.* 1870, part 1, "O stachke rabochikh na Nevskoi bumagopriadil'noi fabrike, byvshei Barona Shtiglitsa i o vysylke 4kh iz nikh iz S. Peterburga na rodinu pod nadzorom politsii," and in *Rabochee dvizhenie*, II, Part I, 238–43 (items No. 81–86). Some of the documents in *Rabochee dvizhenie* may also be found in E. A. Korol'chuk, ed., *Rabochee dvizhenie semidesiatykh godov. Sbornik arkhivnykh dokumentov* (Moscow, 1934). The only document published by Korol'chuk that is not in Pankratova's *Rabochee dvizhenie* is on p. 30. In both volumes the documents are selected from the archive cited above.

16. As quoted in G. V. Rimlinger, "The Management of Labor Protest in Tsarist Russia," *International Review of Social History*, V (1960), Part 2, p. 231; see also Gessen, "K istorii stachek," p. 41.

17. S-PSK, *Statisticheskie svedeniia o fabrikakh i zavodakh v S. Peterburge za 1862 god*, issue 1, p. 24; S-PSK, *Fabriki i zavody v S. Peterburge v 1863 godu*, issue 2, pp. 32–33; S-PSK, *Fabriki i zavody v S.-Peterburge i S.-Peterburgskoi gubernii v 1864 godu*, issue 3, p. 47; Ministerstvo finansov. *Ezhegodnik. Vypusk I na 1869 god* (St. Petersburg, 1869), sec. iii, p. 312.

18. S-PSK, *Fabriki i zavody v S.-Petersburgskoi gubernii v 1867 godu,* issue 6, p. 15.

19. Matthäi, I, 111–14, 129.

20. Unless otherwise indicated, the following account of events at the Nevskii factory is based on the testimony of witnesses published in *Sudebnyi vestnik,* No. 158, June 16, 1870. This testimony is also summarized in *Birzhevye vedomosti,* No. 271, July 5, 1870, and in other contemporary newspapers.

21. Balabanov, *Ocherki,* II, 159.

22. See, for example, *Ocherki istorii Leningrada,* II, 301–2; Pankratova, "Osobennosti formirovaniia i bor'by proletariata Rossii v 60–80-godakh xix veka (Vstupitel'naia stat'ia)," *Rabochee dvizhenie,* II, Part I, 46–47; A. Trofimov, *Rabochee dvizhenie v Rossii: 1861–1894 gg* (Moscow, 1957), p. 60.

23. Slezkin's name is confusingly given as Vladimirov, derived from his patronymic, by some of the witnesses, in some of the Third Section documents, and in all secondary sources.

24. Report from Trepov to Alexander II, May 27, 1870, TsGAOR, *f.* 109, *eksp.* 3, *d.* 64, *op.* 1870, part I, pp. 2–3. (The report is also reprinted in *Rabochee dvizhenie,* II, Part I, 238–39.) Trepov's report was not read by Alexander II until June 3.

25. *Ibid.*

26. Nikitenko, *Dnevnik,* III, 59 (entry of Nov. 27, 1866).

27. The law first appeared as Art. 1792 of the *Ulozhenie o nakazaniiakh ugolovnykh i ispravitel'nykh* of Aug. 15, 1845. *PSZ,* XX, Part I, No. 19283. See above, p. 40.

28. The arguments of the prosecution and the defense are printed in *Sudebnyi vestnik,* No. 158, June 16, 1870; No. 159, June 17, 1870. See also *Birzhevye vedomosti,* No. 271, July 5, 1870.

29. The rulings of the court are in *Sudebnyi vestnik,* No. 159, June 17, 1870; No. 174, July 3, 1870. See also *Birzhevye vedomosti,* No. 271, July 5, 1870.

30. *PSZ,* X, Part I, No. 8157, para. 5. See also pp. 33–34, above.

31. See *Ustavy torgovyi, fabrichnoi i zavodskoi promyshlennosti i remeslennyi (Svod zakonov,* Vol. XI, Part II) (5th ed., St. Petersburg, 1873).

32. In support of this argument the defense attorneys cited Article 27 of the Code of Criminal Procedure of Nov. 20, 1864, which they evidently interpreted rather broadly. See *PSZ,* XXXIX, Part II, No. 41476: *Ustav ugolovnogo sudoproizvodstva.*

33. *Sudebnyi vestnik,* No. 159, June 17, 1870; No. 174, July 3, 1870.

34. Report from Kozlov to Alexander II, June 13, 1870, TsGAOR, *f.* 109, *eksp.* 3, *d.* 64, *op.* 1870, part 1, p. 5. See also *Rabochee dvizhenie* II, Part I, 240. Kozlov erroneously reported that four defendants had been found guilty of acting as instigators.

35. Acting Minister of Internal Affairs A. B. Lobanov-Rostovskii to Chief of the Third Section, P. A. Shuvalov, July 3, 1870, TsGAOR, *f.* 109, *eksp.* 3, *d.* 64, *op.* 1870, part 1, pp. 12–13; *Rabochee dvizhenie,* II, Part I, 241. The letter is marked "Secret." According to Lobanov, the defendants had failed to file for appeal before the expiration of the legal time limit.

36. Circular No. 1906 of the Ministry of Internal Affairs, dated July 6, 1870, TsGAOR, *f.* 109, *eksp.* 3, *d.* 64, *op.* 1870, part 1, p. 16 (emphasis added). See also *Rabochee dvizhenie*, II, Part I, 242–43. A draft of this circular had been presented to the Third Section, which clearly approved the new policy, on June 30, by Lobanov-Rostovskii. Gessen, "K istorii stachek," pp. 42–43. Gessen argues unconvincingly that the new policy on exiling strikers was put through by the Third Section against the wishes of the Ministry of Internal Affairs. He admits to having no documentary evidence to support this thesis.

37. TsGAOR, *f.* 109, *eksp.* 3, *d.* 64, *op.* 1870, part 1, p. 6. See also Kantor, "Zhandarmeriia," p. 74, and *Rabochee dvizhenie*, II, Part I, 240.

38. Kantor, p. 74.

39. The verbatim transcript of the trial, for example, was printed in *Sudebnyi vestnik* on June 16 and 17, and subsequently in other newspapers as well. A possible explanation of this tolerance is that the censors feared the impression that might have been created had newspaper coverage of the trial been suddenly stopped.

40. TsGAOR, *f.* 109, *eksp.* 3, *d.* 64, *op.* 1870, part 1, pp. 23–24. The memorandum is unsigned.

41. TsGAOR, *f.* 109, *eksp.* 3, *d.* 64, *op.* 1870, part 1, p. 21. Attached to the memorandum was an issue of the newspaper *S.-Peterburgskie vedomosti* (St. Petersburg News) containing a column on the mistreatment of Russian railroad workers (p. 22), which was cited in the memorandum as an example of extreme exploitation (p. 21). To the best of my knowledge, the only Soviet historian who has cited this interesting memorandum is Kantor (in his brief article of 1922), who attributes the authorship to K. F. Filippeus, a high-ranking official of the Third Section (p. 75).

42. TsGAOR, *f.* 109, *eksp.* 3, *d.* 64, *op.* 1870, part 1, pp. 26–27. In this letter the head of the Moscow division described certain difficulties he was encountering in attempting to oversee conditions in factories. The difficulties stemmed from the reluctance of some local police officers to antagonize factory owners. See also *Rabochee dvizhenie*, II, Part I, 532–33.

EPILOGUE

1. *Trudy kommissii dlia rassmotreniia proekta pravil o naime rabochikh i prislugi* (St. Petersburg, 1875), pp. 2–3. The authors of this report had no qualms about revealing the connection between the ministry's new anxiety over strikes and Timashev's desire to broaden the scope of the inquiry (probably because the report was meant only for internal government use).

2. *Zapiski*, No. 1 (1871), pp. 88–89.

3. For two somewhat conflicting accounts of the commissions of the 1870's (mainly the so-called Ignat'ev and Valuev commissions), see Balabanov, *Ocherki*, II, 328–65, and Litvinov-Falinskii, *Fabrichnoe zakonodatel'stvo*, pp. 10–19, 29–31.

4. Annual report of the Third Section for 1869, TsGAOR, *f.* 109, *op.* 85, *d.* 34, pp. 13–14; *Krasnyi arkhiv*, II (1922), 197–98; *Rabochee dvizhenie*, II, Part I, 599–600. The immediate cause of this action was probably the Third Section's discovery of a group of students in the two capitals who had dis-

cussed, but were apparently unable to implement, plans to spread revolutionary ideas among workers and peasants during summer vacation. Several students were arrested and the activities of the group curtailed without the Third
Section's having uncovered any direct contacts with workers. The students were
probably followers of Sergei Nechaev. See Venturi, *Roots of Revolution*, Ch. 15.

5. Annual Report of the Third Section for 1869, TsGAOR, *f.* 109, *op.* 85,
d. 34, pp. 30–31.

6. A copy of the original proposal and the Third Section's correspondence
about it are located in TsGAOR, *f.* 109, *eksp.* 3, *d.* 44, *op.* 1871, "Po predstavlennomu General' Ad'iutantom Isakovym proektu ustava 'obshchestva popecheniia o rabochikh' i voobshche ob artel'nykh ustroistvakh."

7. "Proekt ustava Obshchestva popecheniia o rabochikh," TsGAOR, *f.* 109,
eksp. 3, *d.* 44, *op.* 1871, pp. 4–5. The entire draft covers pp. 4–13.

8. Unsigned memorandum dated Dec. 18, 1870. TsGAOR, *f.* 109, *eksp.* 3,
d. 44, *op.* 1871, pp. 14–16, 18.

9. *Ibid.*, p. 1.

10. See *Rabochee dvizhenie*, II, Part I, 608–9.

11. TsGAOR, *f.* 109, *eksp.* 3, *d.* 44, *op.* 1871, p. 23. See also pp. 35–36 (my
italics).

12. *Ibid.*, p. 23.   13. *Ibid.*, pp. 24–25.   14. *Ibid.*, pp. 31–32.

15. *Ibid.*, pp. 32–33 (for Shuvalov's version of the same arguments, much of
which follows the report almost word for word, see pp. 43–44).

16. Quoted in Lemke, p. 403.

17. TsGAOR, *f.* 109, *eksp.* 3, *d.* 184, "Ob ustroistve obshchestva masterovykh
i remeslennikov," pp. 5–6.

18. See, for example, *Svod otzyvov na stati proekta Ustava o lichnom naime
rabochikh i prislugi* [St. Petersburg, ca. 1872]: "Soobrazheniia Shefa Zhan-
darmov."

19. N. K. Mikhailovskii, *Sochineniia*, I (4th ed., St. Petersburg, 1906), 686–
722. Mikhailovskii was writing in 1872.

20. V. Timofeev, "Iz byta rabochikh vinokurennykh zavodov," *Otechestvennye zapiski*, Vol. CLXXVIII (June 1868), sec. 1, p. 548.

21. By the academic year 1873–74, the Technical Society, with the cooperation of certain St. Petersburg industrialists, was operating six schools in the
capital, attended by several hundred workers and children of workers. See
*Otchety shkol dlia rabochikh i ikh detei, uchrezhdennykh Imperatorskim Rus-
skim Tekhnicheskim Obshchestvom pri sodeistvii gg. fabrikantov i zavodchikov,
i sostoiashchikh v vedenii Kommissii po Tekhnicheskomu obrazovaniiu* (St.
Petersburg, 1874). Published as issue No. 6 of *Zapiski* for 1874.

22. For the participation of manufacturers in the Valuev commission, see
Balabanov, *Ocherki*, II, 345–51; also see various communications from the Ministry of Finance to the Ministry of Internal Affairs (written in December 1874
and January 1875) in TsGIAL, *f.* 1282, Kantseliariia ministra vnutrennikh del,
op. 2, *d.* 81, "Ob obrazovanii Kommissii dlia rassmotreniia razrabotannogo v
MVD proekta pravil o naime rabochikh i prislugi," pp. 39–40, 48–49, 79.

Bibliography

The primary sources for this study have been multiple and varied; no attempt will be made to discuss them all here (all primary sources except contemporary periodicals are listed in the Bibliography that follows). Among the archival materials I found most useful were: the collections of the Third Section, especially its materials on the Sunday school movement and the events surrounding the Nevskii strike; statistical data on industry located in the archives of the Finance Ministry's Department of Manufactures; and information on population movement, health, crime, and related urban statistics in reports by police and other local officials, located in the archives of the Committee of Ministers and the Ministry of Internal Affairs.

Important information on St. Petersburg's industrial development and population patterns was also gleaned from the publications of the St. Petersburg Statistical Committee and the Ministry of Internal Affairs Central Statistical Committee, which conducted the invaluable municipal census of 1869. The writings of medical experts in the pages of *Arkhiv* provided a necessary supplement and corrective to official data on lower-class health and living conditions.

The published materials of the Shtakel'berg Commission (*Trudy*) provided me with rich documentation on the initial appearance of the labor question in government circles as well as on tangential questions. Unofficial attitudes toward the labor question—especially those of economic experts and other members of educated society—are documented in the protocols of congresses that were made available in the pages of *Zapiski*, the journal of the Technical Society, and in articles printed in other contemporary periodicals. Of the latter, the most useful have been those St. Petersburg journals and newspapers that focused special attention on problems related to industrialization, especially the official journal *Promyshlennost'* and the unofficial daily *Birzhevye vedomosti* (an important supplementary source for nearly every question treated in this work). Other contemporary periodicals that proved particularly useful were *Narodnoe chtenie, Russkii invalid, Russkaia rech'*, and the Education Ministry's *ZhMNP* (indispensable for the Sunday school episode). *Sudebnyi vestnik*'s near-verbatim record of the Nevskii trial was the most useful single source of information on the strike. (For the titles of other contemporary periodicals, see the Notes, p. 387.)

Miscellaneous primary sources that deserve special mention are: the memoirs and diaries of persons active in the contiguous areas of government, letters, and economic life, most notably Terner, Del'vig, Lamanskii, Valuev, and Nikitenko; the acute observations of the German economist Matthäi; the sensitive evocation of life among St. Petersburg's industrial workers in Reshetnikov's contemporary novel; the valuable documents on the labor movement compiled in *Rabochee dvizhenie* by Pankratova; and the collected statutes and laws preserved in the indispensable *PSZ*.

The Russian secondary sources that I found most useful and enlightening were the works of Ditiatin, Lemke, and Tugan-Baranovskii (pre-Soviet); Balabanov, V. Gessen, Pazhitnov, and Stolpianskii (early Soviet); Kiniapina, Rashin, and Ryndziunskii (recent Soviet). Lemke's book also includes valuable extracts from primary sources. The most valuable reference work on the history of St. Petersburg is the *Ocherki istorii Leningrada* of the Academy of Sciences.

The Bibliography that follows is divided into two sections: a list of archival sources utilized and an alphabetical list of all other works, most of them published, which are cited in the Notes (with the exception of contemporary periodicals and a few other works for which full publication data may be found in the Notes).

ARCHIVAL SOURCES

Gosudarstvennyi istoricheskii arkhiv Leningradskoi oblasti. *Fond* 253, Kantseliariia Peterburgskogo Gubernatora. *Op.* 2, *d.* 205 (1859 g.), "Ob uchrezhdenii Kommissii po sostavleniiu pravil okhrany truda rabochikh i issledovaniiu polozheniia detskogo truda na fabrikakh i zavodakh v Peterburge." *Op.* 2, *d.* 230, "Ob ustanovlenii na predstoiashchei vsemirnoi vystavke nagrad za uluchshenie byta rabochego klassa na fabrikakh i zavodakh v Peterburge."

———. *Fond* 260, Petrogradskii (S.P.B.) gubernskii statisticheskii komitet. *Op.* 1, *d.* 5, "O chisle zhitelei po sosloviiam (1864)." *Op.* 2, *d.* 9, "Tablitsa XI o chisle zavodov i fabrik v S.-Peterburgskoi gubernii (1867 g.)."

———. *Fond* 1266, Fabrika Torntona. *Op.* 1, *d.* 805, 809, 817, and 821. Wage lists for the 1860's.

———. *Fond* 1267, Obukhovskii Staleliteinyi Zavod. *Op.* 1, *d.* 3, "Predlozheniia raznykh firm o postavkakh oborudovaniia i materialov dlia zavoda." *Op.* 17, *d.* 23, "O naznachenii predmetov dlia vsemirnoi vystavki imeiushchei byt' v Parizhe v 1867 g." *Op.* 17, *d.* 61, "O postavke Gg. Iakovlevymi i Gromme dlia Obukhovskogo zavoda chuguna."

Tsentral'nyi gosudarstvennyi arkhiv Oktiabr'skoi revoliutsii. *Fond* 95, *op.* 1, *d.* 19, "Proizvodstvo Vysochaishe uchrezhdennoi v S.-Peterburge sledstvennoi Kommissii."

———. *Fond* 109, Tret'e Otdelenie Sobstvennoi Ego Imperatorskogo Velichestva Kantseliarii. *Eksp.* 1, *d.* 263, *op.* 1862, "O voskresnykh shkolakh, bibliotekakh, chital'niakh i o rasporiaditeliakh i prepodavateliakh onykh." *Eksp.* 3, *d.* 64, *op.* 1870, Part 1, "O stachke rabochikh na Nevskoi bumagopriadil'noi fabrike, byvshei Barona Shtiglitsa i o vysylke 4kh iz nikh iz S. Peterburga na rodinu pod nadzorom politsii." Part 2, "O stachke rabochikh na fabrikakh i zavodakh. Prodolzhenie k 1870 godu." *Op.* 85, *d.* 26, 27, and 34, Annual Reports of the Third Section for 1861, 1862, and 1869. *Eksp.* 3, *d.* 44, *op.* 1871. "Po predstavlennomu General' Adiutantom Isakovym proektu ustava obshchestva popecheniia o rabochikh' i voobshche ob artel'nykh ustroistvakh."

Tsentral'nyi gosudarstvennyi istoricheskii arkhiv v Leningrade. *Fond* 18, Ministerstvo Finansov, Departament manufaktur i vnutrennei torgovli. *Op.* 2, *d.* 1770, "Sobranie svedenii o fabrikakh i zavodakh za 1860–1865 gody."

―――. *Fond* 219, Ministerstvo Putei Soobshcheniia, Departament zheleznykh dorog. *Op.* 1/1, *d.* 356, "Po otnosheniiu Gosudarstvennogo Kontrolera prazdnenii Politseiskogo pravleniia Aleksandrovskogo Mekhanicheskogo Zavoda tut zhe i o peredache nekotorykh kazennykh domov kontragentu Uainensu." *Op.* 1, *d.* 6518, "Po pros'be masterovykh Aleksandrovskogo Zavoda ob uvelichenii im soderzhaniia."

―――. *Fond* 258, Glavnoe Obshchestvo Rossiiskikh Zheleznykh Dorog. *Op.* 9, *d.* 32, "Ustroistvo i remont zhilykh domov, sluzhb i raznye k nim otnosiashchiesia raboty na Aleksandrovskom mekhanicheskom zavode."

―――. *Fond* 446, Poveleniia i doklady po vedomstvu putei soobshcheniia. *Op.* 26, 1862 g., *d.* 9 (1–73), "Vsepoddaneishie doklady."

―――. *Fond* 560, Ministerstvo Finansov, Obshchaia Kantseliaria. *Op.* 38, *d.* 781, "Otchet departamenta manufaktur i vnutrennei torgovli za 1863 god." *Op.* 42, *d.* 23, "Otchet o deistviiakh i oborote summ departamenta torgovli i manufaktur (za 1866 g.)."

―――. *Fond* 758, Aleksandrovskaia manufaktura. *Op.* 6, *d.* 2836, "O naznachenii posobii rabochim kartochnoi fabriki i semeistvam." *Op.* 6, *d.* 2838, 1860 g., "S pros'bami o posobiiakh lits sluzhivshikh pri Aleksandrovskoi manufakture i vdov ikh."

―――. *Fond* 1263, Komitet ministrov. *Op.* 1, *d.* 2975, 3046, 3143, 3164, 3263, 3332, 3363, 3526, and 3677, "Otchet S. Peterburgskoi Politsii" (1861, 1862, 1863, 1864, 1865, 1866, 1867, 1869, and 1872).

―――. *Fond* 1281, Sovet Ministra Vnutrennikh Del. *Op.* 6, *d.* 14, 45, 69, and 52, "Po otchetu o sostoianii S. Peterburgskoi gub." (1860, 1861, 1862, and 1863 [copy]). *Op.* 7, *d.* 48, 49, 70, 79, and 81, "Otchet o sostoianii S. Peterburgskoi gub." (1864 [copy], 1865, 1866, 1867, and 1868 [copy]).

―――. *Fond* 1282, Kantseliariia ministra vnutrennikh del. *Op.* 2, *d.* 81, "Ob obrazovanii Komissii dlia rassmotreniia razrabotannogo v MVD proekta pravil o naime rabochikh i prislugi."

―――. *Fond* 1284, MVD, Departament obshchikh del. *Op.* 67, *d.* 364, "S otchetom S. Peterburgskogo gubernatora o sostoianii gubernii za 1871 god" (copy). *Op.* 69, *d.* 308, "Otchet S. Peterburgskogo gradonachal'nika po upravleniiu gradonachal'stvom i stolichnoiu politsieiu s 1866 po 1876 g."

―――. *Fond* 1286, MVD, Departament politsii ispolnitel'noi. *Op.* 31, *d.* 1361, 1870 g., "O byvshei v g. S.-Peterburge na Nevskoi bumagopriadil'noi fabrike stachke rabochikh."

OTHER WORKS

Abramov, Ia. V. Nashi voskresnye shkoly. Ikh proshloe i nastoiashchee. St. Petersburg, 1900.

Aizenberg, L. "Byt krest'ian na chastnykh gornykh zavodakh i rudinakh v Orenburgskom krae (nakanune osvobozhdeniia ot krepostnoi zavisimosti)," *Arkhiv istorii truda v Rossii*, book III (1922), 23–39.

Akademiia Nauk SSSR. Istoriia SSSR. Ukazatel' sovetskoi literatury za 1917–1952 gg. 2 vols. and 2 supplements. Moscow, 1956–58.

Akademiia Nauk SSSR. Ocherki istorii Leningrada. Vol. I. Ed. M. P. Viatkin. Moscow, 1955. Vol. II. Ed. B. M. Kochakov. Moscow, 1957.

Arap'ev, N. F. "V. Ia. Stoiunin i voskresnye shkoly," *Russkaia shkola*, No. 1 (Jan. 1898), pp. 185–94.

Baklanova, I. A. Rabochie sudostroiteli Rossii v XIX veke. Moscow, 1959.

Balabanov, M. Istoriia rabochei kooperatsii v Rossii. Ocherki po istorii rabochego kooperativnogo dvizheniia. 4th ed., enl. Moscow, 1928.

————. Ocherki po istorii rabochego klassa v Rossii. Vol. I. 2d ed., rev., enl. Kiev, 1924. 4th ed. Moscow, 1926. Vol. II. 1st ed. Kiev, 1924. 2d ed., enl. Moscow, 1925.

Baltiiskii sudostroitel'nyi i mekhanicheskii zavod. St. Petersburg, 1908.

Barghoorn, Frederick C. "The Russian Radicals of the 1860's and the Problem of the Industrial Proletariat," *Slavonic and East European Review*, XXI, Part 1 (March 1943), 57–69. (In Vol. II of American series.)

Bazhkova, A. P. "Polozhenie i bor'ba gornorabochikh Urala v period revoliutsionnoi situatsii," in Revoliutsionnaia situatsiia v Rossii v 1859–1861 gg. Ed. M. V. Nechkina. [Vol. I.] Moscow, 1960.

Bendix, Reinhard. Work and Authority in Industry: Ideologies of Management in the Course of Industrialization. Harper Torchbooks ed. New York, 1963.

Berlin, P. A. Russkaia burzhuaziia v staroe i novoe vremia. 2d ed., enl. Leningrad, 1925.

Blackwell, William L. The Beginnings of Russian Industrialization, 1800–1860. Princeton, 1968.

Blek, A. L. "Iz praktiki predvaritel'nogo obsledovaniia zavodskikh arkhivov," *Arkhiv istorii truda v Rossii*, book 1 (1921), pp. 116–21.

Blum, Jerome. Lord and Peasant in Russia from the Ninth to the Nineteenth Century. Princeton, 1961.

Bol'shakov, A. M., and N. A. Rozhkov. Istoriia khoziaistva Rossii v materialakh i dokumentakh. Vol. II. 2d ed. Leningrad, 1925.

Borisenkova, R. V. "K istorii fabrichnogo zakonodatel'stva i fabrichnogo nadzora v Rossii," *Gigiena i sanitariia*, No. 12 (Dec. 1950), pp. 22–28.

Bykov, A. N. Fabrichnoe zakonodatel'stvo i razvitie ego v Rossii. St. Petersburg, 1909.

Chernyshevskii, N. G. Polnoe sobranie sochinenii. Vol. IX. Moscow, 1949.

Chevalier, Louis. Classes laborieuses et classes dangereuses à Paris pendant la première moitié du XIXe siècle. Paris, 1958.

Chlianov, N. "Osnovanie S.-Peterburga," *Bor'ba klassov*, No. 7–8 (July–Aug. 1935), pp. 13–24.

Conze, W. "Vom 'Pöbel' zum 'Proletariat.' Sozialgeschichtliche Voraussetzungen für den Sozialismus in Deutschland," in Die soziale Frage. Neuere Studien zur Lage der Fabrikarbeiter in den Frühphasen der Industrialisierung. Ed. W. Fischer and G. Bajor. Stuttgart, 1967. (Republished from *Vierteljahrschrift für Sozial- und Wirtschaftsgeschichte*, 1954.)

Del'vig, A. I. Moi vospominaniia. Vols. III and IV. Moscow, 1913.

Ditiatin, I. I. Ustroistvo i upravlenie gorodov Rossii. Vol. I: Vvedenie, Goroda Rossii v XVIII stoletii. St. Petersburg, 1875. Vol. II: Gorodskoe samoupravlenie v nastoiashchem stoletii. Iaroslavl', 1877.

Dobroliubov, N. A. Sobranie sochinenii. Vols. IV and IX. Moscow, 1962 and 1964.

Duveau, Georges. La vie ouvrière en France sous le Second Empire. 6th ed. Paris, 1946.

El'nitskii, A. Istoriia rabochego dvizheniia v Rossii. 4th ed., enl. Moscow, 1925.

———. Pervye shagi rabochego dvizheniia v Rossii. St. Petersburg, [pre–World War I].

Emmons, Terence. "The Peasant and the Emancipation," in The Peasant in Nineteenth-Century Russia. Ed. Wayne S. Vucinich. Stanford, Calif., 1968.

———. The Russian Landed Gentry and the Peasant Emancipation of 1861. Cambridge, Eng., 1968.

Entsiklopedicheskii slovar'. Ed. F. A. Brockhaus [Brokgauz] and I. A. Efron. 41 vols. St. Petersburg, 1890–1904.

Ermanskii, A. "Krupnaia burzhuaziia do 1905 goda," in Obshchestvennoe dvizhenie v Rossii v nachale XX-go veka. Ed. L. Martov, P. Maslov, and A. Potresov. Vol. I, Part II. St. Petersburg, 1909.

Feldmesser, Robert. "Social Classes and Political Structure," in The Transformation of Russian Society: Aspects of Social Change Since 1861. Ed. Cyril E. Black. Cambridge, Mass., 1960.

Feoktistov, E. M. Vospominaniia: Za kulisami politiki i literatury, 1848–1896. Ed. Iu. G. Oksman. Leningrad, 1929.

Fischer, Wolfram. "Social Tensions at Early Stages of Industrialization," *Comparative Studies in Society and History*, IX (Oct. 1966), 64–83.

Flerovskii, N. [V. V. Bervi]. Polozhenie rabochego klassa v Rossii. St. Petersburg, 1869.

Gerschenkron, Alexander. "Agrarian Policies and Industrialization: Russia, 1861–1917," in Cambridge Economic History of Europe, VI, Part 2. Cambridge, Eng., 1965.

———. "Economic Backwardness in Historical Perspective," in The Progress of Underdeveloped Countries. Ed. B. Hoselitz. Chicago, 1952.

Gessen, Iulii. "K istorii stachek sredi fabrichnykh rabochikh (v nachale semidesiatykh godov 19-go veka)," *Arkhiv istorii truda v Rossii*, book 3 (1922), pp. 40–50.

———, ed. Khrestomatiia po istorii rabochego klassa i professional'nogo dvizheniia v Rossii. Vol. I. Leningrad, 1925.

Gessen, V. Iu. Istoriia zakonodatel'stva o trude rabochei molodezhi v Rossii. Leningrad, 1927.

————. Trud detei i podrostkov v fabrichnozavodskoi promyshlennosti Rossii ot XVII veka do Oktiabr'skoi revoliutsii. Vol. I. Moscow, 1927.

Giffen, F. C. "In Quest of an Effective Program of Factory Legislation in Russia: The Years of Preparation, 1859–1880," The Historian, XXIX, No. 2 (Feb. 1967), 175–85.

Gille, Bertrand. Histoire économique et sociale de la Russie du moyen age au XXe siècle. Paris, 1949.

Gindin, I. F. Gosudarstvennyi bank i ekonomicheskaia politika tsarskogo pravitel'stva (1861–1892 gg.). Moscow, 1960.

————. "Russkaia burzhuaziia v period kapitalizma, ee razvitie i osobennosti," Istoriia SSSR, No. 2 (March–April 1963), pp. 57–80.

Giubner, Iu. Statisticheskiia izsledovaniia sanitarnogo sostoianiia S.-Peterburga. 1870 god. St. Petersburg, 1872.

Glickman, Rose. "The Literary Raznochintsy in Mid-Nineteenth-Century Russia." Unpublished doctoral dissertation. University of Chicago, 1967.

Gorodskie poseleniia v Rossiiskoi Imperii. Vol. VII. St. Petersburg, 1864.

Gozulov, A. I. Istoriia otechestvennoi statistiki. Moscow, 1957.

Grekulov, E. Arkhivy kak istochnik izucheniia istorii zavodov. Moscow, 1933.

Hamerow, Theodore S. Restoration, Revolution, Reaction: Economics and Politics in Germany, 1815–1871. Princeton, 1966.

Haxthausen, A. von. Studien über die innern Zustände, das Volksleben und insbesondere die ländlichen Einrichtungen Russlands. Vol. III. Berlin, 1852.

Iakovlev, A. F. Ekonomicheskie krizisy v Rossii. Moscow, 1955.

Ianson, Iu. "Naselenie Peterburga, ego ekonomicheskii i sotsial'nyi sostav po perepisi 1869 g," Vestnik Evropy, V (No. 10, 1875), 607–39.

————. Sravnitel'naia statistika Rossii i zapadno-evropeiskikh gosudarstv, I: Territoriia i naselenie. St. Petersburg, 1878.

Ianzhul, I. I. "Detskii i zhenskii fabrichnyi trud v Anglii i Rossii," in Ocherki i issledovaniia. Sbornik statei po voprosam narodnogo khoziaistva, politiki i zakonodatel'stva. Vol. II. Moscow, 1884.

Iatsevich, A. Krepostnye v Peterburge. Leningrad, 1933.

Iatsunskii, V. K. "Materialy o polozhenii rabochikh Peterburga v 40-kh godakh XIX veka," Problemy istochnikovedeniia, VIII (1959), 135–43.

————. "Rol' Peterburga v promyshlennom razvitii dorevoliutsionnoi Rossii," Voprosy istorii, No. 9 (Sept. 1954), pp. 95–103.

Ionova, G. I. "Rabochee dvizhenie v Rossii v gody revoliutsionnoi situatsii 1859–1861." Unpublished candidate's dissertation. Moscow University, 1950.

————. "Rabochee dvizhenie v Rossii v period revoliutsionnoi situatsii 1859–1861 gg.," in Iz istorii rabochego klassa i revoliutsionnogo dvizheniia. Ed. M. V. Nechkina et al. Moscow, 1958.

————. "Voskresnye shkoly v gody pervoi revoliutsionnoi situatsii (1859–1861)," Istoricheskie zapiski, No. 57 (1956), pp. 177–209.

Istoriia russkoi ekonomicheskoi mysli. Ed. A. I. Pashkov. Vol. I, Part II. Moscow, 1958.

Kantor, R. "Zhandarmeriia i pervye rabochie stachki (v nachale semidesiatykh godov 19-go veka)," *Arkhiv istorii truda v Rossii*, book 3 (1922), pp. 71–77.

Karateev, S., comp. Bibliografiia finansov, promyshlennosti i torgovli. So vremen Petra velikogo po nastoiashchee vremia. St. Petersburg, 1880.

Karnovich, E. Sanktpeterburg v statisticheskom otnoshenii. St. Petersburg, 1860.

Katsenel'son, S. G. "K voprosu o formirovanii promyshlennogo proletariata v Peterburge v 1870–1890 godakh." Unpublished candidate's dissertation. Leningrad University, 1947.

———. "O formirovanii peterburgskogo proletariata," *Propaganda i agitatsiia*, No. 23 (Dec. 15, 1948), pp. 17–29.

Kazantsev, B. N. "Istochniki po razrabotke zakonov o naemnom promyshlennom trude v krepostnoi Rossii (30-ye–nachalo 60-kh godov XIX v.)," *Problemy istochnikovedeniia*, XI (1963), 80–112.

Kiniapina, N. S. Politika russkogo samoderzhaviia v oblasti promyshlennosti (20–50 gody XIX v.). Moscow, 1968.

"K istorii rabochego klassa v Rossii," *Krasnyi arkhiv*, II (1922), 176–99.

Kopanev, A. I. Naselenie Peterburga v pervoi polovine XIX veka. Moscow, 1957.

Kornilov, A. A. Obshchestvennoe dvizhenie pri Aleksandre II. Moscow, 1909.

Kornilov, O. E., and N. S. Platonova. "O sostoianii nekotorykh fabrichno-zavodskikh arkhivov v Petrograde," *Arkhiv istorii truda v Rossii*, book 1 (1921), pp. 122–23.

Korol'chuk, E. A., ed. Rabochee dvizhenie semidesiatykh godov. Sbornik arkhivnykh dokumentov. Moscow, 1934.

Korol'chuk, E., and E. Sokolova. Khronika revoliutsionnogo rabochego dvizheniia v Peterburge. Vol. I (1870–1904). Leningrad, 1940.

Krasnyi arkhiv. 106 volumes. Moscow, 1922–41.

Kucherov, Samuel. Courts, Lawyers and Trials Under the Last Three Tsars. New York, 1953.

Kulisher, I. "Voprosy istorii russkoi promyshlennosti i promyshlennogo truda (v doreformennoe vremia), postanovka ikh v nashei istoricheskoi literature," *Arkhiv istorii truda v Rossii*, book 1 (1921), pp. 11–13.

Lamanskii, E. I. "Iz vospominanii Evgeniia Ivanovicha Lamanskogo," *Russkaia starina*, Vols. 161–64 (1915).

Lemke, M. K. Ocherki osvoboditel'nogo dvizheniia "shestidesiatykh godov." 2d ed. St. Petersburg, 1908.

Leningradskoe Oblastnoe Arkhivnoe Upravlenie. *Leningradskii Arkhivist*, Issue 1. Leningrad, 1933.

Levin, Sh. M. Obshchestvennoe dvizhenie v Rossii v 60–70 gody XIX veka. Moscow, 1958.

Liashchenko, P. I. Istoriia narodnogo khoziaistva SSSR. Vol. II. 4th ed. Moscow, 1956.

Lisovskii, N. M., comp. and ed. Bibliografiia russkoi periodicheskoi pechati 1703–1900 gg. (Materialy dlia istorii russkoi zhurnalistiki). Petrograd, 1915.

Litvinov-Falinskii, V. P. Fabrichnoe zakonodatel'stvo i fabrichnaia inspektsiia v Rossii. St. Petersburg, 1900.

Livshits, R. S. Razmeshchenie promyshlennosti v dorevoliutsionnoi Rossii. Moscow, 1955.

Maksimov, V., comp. Arteli birzhevye i trudovye: s raz'iasneniiami Pravitel'-stvuiushchego Senata i prilozheniem: vsekh deistvuiushchego uzakonenii, pravil, obraztsovykh ustavov birzhevykh i trudovykh artelei i ustava obshchestva dlia sodeistviia artel'nomu delu v Rossii. Moscow, 1907.

Martov, L. [Iu.]. Razvitie krupnoi promyshlennosti i rabochee dvizhenie v Rossii. Petrograd, 1923.

"Materialy dlia bibliografii k pervomu tomu 'Istorii Leningrada.' XVIII i pervaia polovina XIX v. do 1861 g." Unpublished manuscript in the State Library in Leningrad, n.d.

Matthäi, F. Die Industrie Russlands in ihrer bisherigen Entwicklung und in ihrem gegenwärtigen Zustande mit besonderer Berücksichtigung der allgemeinen russischen Manufaktur-Ausstellung im Jahre 1870. Industrielles Handbuch für das Gesammtgebiet des Russischen Reiches. 2 vols. Leipzig, 1872–73.

Mavor, J. An Economic History of Russia. 2 vols. New York, 1925.

Meschewetski, Peisach. Die Fabrikgesetzgebung in Russland (Zeitschrift fuer die gesamte Staatswissenschaft, Ergaenzungsheft XXXIX). Tuebingen, 1911.

Mikhailovskii, N. K. Sochineniia. Vol. I, 4th ed. St. Petersburg, 1906.

Ministerstvo finansov, 1802–1902. Vol. I. St. Petersburg, 1902.

Ministerstvo finansov. Ezhegodnik. Vypusk I na 1869 god. 3 sections. St. Petersburg, 1869.

Ministerstvo finansov. Departament manufaktur i vnutrennei torgovli. Obzor razlichnykh otraslei manufakturnoi promyshlennosti Rossii. 3 vols. St. Petersburg, 1862–65.

Mitel'man, M., B. Glebov, and A. Ul'ianskii. Istoriia Putilovskogo zavoda 1801–1917. 3d ed., rev. Moscow, 1961.

Monas, Sidney. The Third Section: Police and Society in Russia Under Nicholas I. Cambridge, Mass., 1961.

Nifontov, A. S. Rossiia v 1848 godu. Moscow, 1949.

Nikitenko, A. V. Dnevnik. 3 vols. Moscow, 1955.

Nikoladze, N. "Vospominaniia o shestidesiatykh godakh," Katorga i ssylka, No. 34 (1927).

O byte rabochikh liudei v S. Peterburge i o sredstvakh k uluchsheniiu ikh polozheniia. Berlin, 1863.

Ob'iasnitel'naia zapiska k Proektu Ustava o lichnom naime rabochikh i prislugi. N.p., n.d., but probably printed for internal governmental circulation in St. Petersburg, 1871.

Ocherki istorii Leningrada. See Akademiia Nauk SSSR. Ocherki.

Otchet po Gosudarstvennomu sovetu za 1870 god. St. Petersburg, 1871.

Otchet po Gosudarstvennomu sovetu za 1871 god. St. Petersburg, 1873.

Ozerov. I. Kh. Politika po rabochemu voprosu v Rossii za poslednie gody (po neizdannym dokumentam). Moscow, 1906.

Paialin [Pajalin], N. Die Leninwerke: Geschichte eines bolschewistischen Betriebes. Moscow, 1933.

————. "Shlissel'burgskii trakt (Nevskaia zastava)," *Bor'ba klassov*, No. 11 (Nov. 1934), pp. 51–57.

Pamiatnaia knizhka S.-Peterburgskoi gubernii. (Issued by the governor's office.) St. Petersburg, 1872.

Pankratova, A. M. Razvitie kapitalizma v Rossii i vozniknovenie rabochego dvizheniia. Moscow, 1947.

Panteleev, L. F. Iz vospominanii proshlogo. Moscow, 1934.

Pazhitnov [Paschitnow], K. A. Die Lage der arbeitenden Klasse in Russland. Transl. and postscript by M. Nachimson. Stuttgart, 1907.

————. Polozhenie rabochego klassa v Rossii. Vol. I. Petrograd, 1923.

————. Problema remeslennykh tsekhov v zakonodatel'stve russkogo absoliutizma. Moscow, 1952.

————. "Volneniia sredi fabrichnozavodskikh rabochikh (s 1824 g. po 1860 g.)," Part 2, *Arkhiv istorii truda v Rossii*, book 2 (1921), 135–37.

Pertsov, E. P. "Zapiski sovremennika o 1861 g.," *Krasnyi arkhiv*, Vol. XVI (1926).

Pichkurenko, Ia. D. "K voprosu o roli voskresnykh shkol v burzhuazno-demokraticheskom osvoboditel'nom dvizhenii Rossii v kontse 50-kh nachale 60-kh godov XIX v.," *Sovetskaia pedagogika*, No. 5 (1954), pp. 95–114.

Pintner, Walter McKenzie. Russian Economic Policy Under Nicholas I. Ithaca, N.Y., 1967.

Pipes, Richard. Social Democracy and the St. Petersburg Labor Movement, 1885–1897. Cambridge, Mass., 1963.

Pirogov, N. I. Izbrannye pedagogicheskie sochineniia. Moscow, 1953.

Pisarev, D. I. Izbrannye filosofskie i obshchestvenno-politicheskie stat'i. [Moscow], 1949.

Pokrovskii, V. "Sankt-Peterburg," in Entsiklopedicheskii slovar'. Ed. F. A. Brockhaus and I. A. Efron. XXVIIIA (St. Petersburg, 1900), 291–343.

Pokshishevskii, V. V. "Territorial'noe formirovanie promyshlennogo kompleksa Peterburga v XVIII–XIX vekakh," *Voprosy geografii*, Coll. XX (1950): Istoricheskaia geografiia SSSR.

Polnoe sobranie zakonov Rossiiskoi Imperii. 1st series: 1649 to 1825. St. Petersburg, 1830. 2d series: 1825 to 1881. St. Petersburg, 1830–84.

Proekt pravil dlia fabrik i zavodov v S.-Peterburge i uezde. St. Petersburg, 1860.

Prokopovich, S. N. K rabochemu voprosu v Rossii. St. Petersburg, 1905.

————. Kooperativnoe dvizhenie v Rossii. Ego teoriia i praktika. 2d ed. Moscow, 1918.

Protokoly i stenograficheskie otchety zasedanii pervogo vserossiiskogo s'ezda fabrikantov, zavodchikov i lits, interesuiushchikhsia otechestvennoiu promyshlennostiu. St. Petersburg, 1872.

PSZ. See Polnoe sobranie zakonov Rossiiskoi Imperii.

Putilovets v trekh revoliutsiiakh. Sbornik materialov po Putilovskogo zavoda. Comp. S. B. Okun'. Ed. I. I. Gaza. N.p., 1933.

Rabochee dvizhenie v Rossii v XIX veke. Sbornik dokumentov i materialov. Ed. A. M. Pankratova. Vol. I, Part II: 1826–1860. 2d ed., enl. Moscow, 1955. Vol. II, Part I: 1861–1874. Moscow, 1950.

Ralli, Z. K. "Iz vospominanii Z. K. Ralli," in Revoliutsionnoe dvizhenie 1860-kh godov. Sbornik. Ed. B. I. Gorev and B. P. Koz'min. Moscow, 1932.

Rashin, A. G. Formirovanie promyshlennogo proletariata v Rossii. Statistiko-ekonomicheskie ocherki. Moscow, 1940.

————. Naselenie Rossii za 100 let (1811–1913 gg.). Statisticheskie ocherki. Moscow, 1956.

Reshetnikov, F. M. Gde luchshe?, in Izbrannye Sochineniia. Moscow, 1956.

Revoliutsionnaia situatsiia v Rossii v 1859–1861 gg. Ed. M. V. Nechkina. 3 vols. Moscow, 1960–1963.

Rimlinger, Gaston V. "Autocracy and the Factory Order in Early Russian Industrialization," Journal of Economic History, XX (March 1960), 67–92.

————. "The Management of Labor Protest in Tsarist Russia," International Review of Social History, V (Part 2, 1960), 226–48.

Rozanov, M. Obukhovtsy. Leningrad, 1938.

Rozhkov, N. A. Gorod i derevnia v russkoi istorii. 4th ed. Petrograd, 1919.

Rozhkova, M. K., ed. Ocherki ekonomicheskoi istorii Rossii pervoi poloviny XIX veka. Moscow, 1959.

Russkii biograficheskii slovar'. 25 vols. St. Petersburg, 1895–1918.

Rutman, R. E. "Iz istorii rabochego dvizheniia na gornozavodskom Urale pered otmenoi krepostnogo prava," in Iz istorii rabochego klassa. Ed. M. V. Nechkina et al. Moscow, 1958.

————. "Rabochee dvizhenie pered otmenoi krepostnogo prava," in Revoliutsionnaia situatsiia v Rossii v 1859–1861 gg. Ed. M. V. Nechkina. [Vol. II.] Moscow, 1962.

Rykachev, A. "Tseny na khleb i na trud v S.-Peterburge za 58 let," Vestnik Finansov, promyshlennosti i torgovli, No. 31 (1911), pp. 201–6.

Ryndziunskii, P. G. Gorodskoe grazhdanstvo doreformennoi Rossii. Moscow, 1958.

Sanktpeterburg po perepisi 10 dekabria 1869 goda. Issue I: Naselenie po vozrastam, semeinomu sostoianiiu, veroispovedaniiam, narodnostiam, sosloviiam i gramotnosti. St. Petersburg, 1872. Issue II: Doma i kvartiry i razmeshchenie v nikh zhitelei. St. Petersburg, 1872. Issue III: Raspredelenie zhitelei S.-Peterburga (ischislennykh poimmenno) po promyslam, zaniatiiam i drugim rodam sredstv sushchestvovaniia. St. Petersburg, 1875.

S-PSK. Fabriki i zavody v S.-Peterburge v 1863 godu. St. Petersburg, 1864.

————. Fabriki i zavody v S.-Peterburge i S.-Peterburgskoi gubernii v 1864 godu. St. Petersburg, 1865.

————. Fabriki i zavody v. S.-Peterburgskoi gubernii v 1867 godu. St. Petersburg, 1868.

————. Pamiatnaia knizhka S.-Peterburgskoi gubernii na 1863 god. 2 parts. St. Petersburg, 1863.

————. Pamiatnaia knizhka S.-Peterburgskoi gubernii na 1864 god. St. Petersburg, 1864.

————. Pamiatnaia knizhka S.-Peterburgskoi gubernii na 1868 god. St. Petersburg, 1868.

————. Statisticheskie svedeniia o fabrikakh i zavodakh v S. Peterburge za 1862 god. St. Petersburg, 1863.

Sel'chuk, V. V. "Rabochii vopros v Rossii v publitsistike 60-kh godov XIX v.," in Iz istorii rabochego klassa i revoliutsionnogo dvizheniia. Ed. M. V. Nechkina et al. Moscow, 1958.

————. "Russkaia publitsistika kak istochnik dlia izucheniia rabochego dvizheniia v Rossii v 60-ye gody XIX veka," in Trudy Gosudarstvennoi Biblioteki im. Lenina, I (Moscow, 1957), 204–49.

Shelgunov, N. V. Vospominaniia. Ed. A. A. Shilov. Moscow, 1923.

Shelymagin, I. I. Fabrichno-trudovoe zakonodatel'stvo v Rossii (2-ia polovina XIX veka). Moscow, 1947.

Sherer, A. "Khlopchatobumazhnaia promyshlennost'," in Obzor razlichnykh otraslei manufakturnoi promyshlennosti Rossii (St. Petersburg, 1863). Vol. II.

Sistematicheskii katalog biblioteki Uchenogo Komiteta Ministerstva Finansov. Part I. St. Petersburg, 1901.

Skabichevskii, A. M. Ocherki istorii russkoi tsenzury (1700–1863 g.). St. Petersburg, 1892.

Skerpan, A. A. "The Russian National Economy and Emancipation," in Essays in Russian History. A Collection Dedicated to George Vernadsky. Ed. A. D. Ferguson and A. Levin. Hamden, Conn., 1964.

Stasov, V. V. "Vospominaniia o moei sestre," Knizhka nedeli (April 1896), pp. 165–90.

Stolpianskii, P. N. "Iz istorii proizvodstv v S.-Peterburge za 18-i vek i pervuiu chetvert' 19-go veka," Arkhiv istorii truda v Rossii, book 1 (1921), pp. 86–104.

————. Peterburg. Kak voznik, osnovalsia i ros Sankt-Piterburkh. Petrograd, 1918.

————. Zhizn' i byt peterburgskoi fabriki za 210 let ee sushchestvovaniia. Leningrad, 1925.

Strumilin, S. G. Ocherki ekonomicheskoi istorii Rossii. Moscow, 1960.

Sviatlovskii, V. Professional'noe dvizhenie v Rossii. St. Petersburg, 1907.

Svod otzyvov na stati proekta Ustava o lichnom naime rabochikh i prislugi [St. Petersburg, ca. 1872].

Tatishchev, S. S. Imperator Aleksandr II: Ego zhizn' i tsarstvovanie. 2 vols. St. Petersburg, 1911.

Taubin, R. A. "Revoliutsionnaia propaganda v voskresnykh shkolakh Rossii v 1860–1862 gg.," Voprosy istorii, No. 8 (Aug. 1956), pp. 80–90.

Tengoborskii, L. Commentaries on the Productive Forces of Russia. 2 vols. London, 1855–56. Originally published in French (Paris, 1852–55).

Terner, F. G. O rabochem klasse i merakh k obezpecheniiu ego blagosostoianiiu. St. Petersburg, 1860.

————. Vospominaniia zhizni F. G. Ternera. Vol. 1. St. Petersburg, 1910.

Thompson, E. P. The Making of the English Working Class. London, 1963.

Tikhonov, B. V. "Ofitsial'nye zhurnaly vtoroi poloviny 20-50-kh godov XIX v. ('Zhurnal manufaktur i torgovli,' 'Gornyi zhurnal,' 'Zhurnal Ministerstva gosudarstvennykh imushchestv' i 'Zhurnal Ministerstva vnutrennikh del') kak istochnik dlia izucheniia istorii russkoi promyshlennosti," *Problemy istoch-nikovedeniia*, VII (1959), 150–203.

Timofeev, V. "Iz byta rabochikh vinokurennykh zavodov," *Otechestvennye zapiski*, CLXXVIII, No. 6 (June 1868), sec. i, 533–48.

Trofimov, A. Rabochee dvizhenie v Rossii: 1861–1894 gg. Moscow, 1957.

Trudy kommissii dlia rassmotreniia proekta pravil o naime rabochikh i pri-slugi. St. Petersburg, 1875.

Trudy kommissii uchrezhdennoi dlia peresmotra ustavov fabrichnogo i remes-lennogo. 3 parts. St. Petersburg, 1863–64.

Trudy Obshchestva dlia sodeistviia russkoi promyshlennosti i torgovli, 1872. St. Petersburg.

TsSKMVD, *Statisticheskii vremennik Rossiiskoi Imperii*. Series II. Issue 6. St. Petersburg, 1872. Issues 12 and 13. St. Petersburg, 1877.

TsSKMVD. Sanktpeterburgskaia guberniia. Spisok naselennykh mest po sve-deniiam 1862 goda. St. Petersburg, 1864.

Tugan-Baranovskii, M. Russkaia fabrika v proshlom i nastoiashchem. 3d ed. St. Petersburg, 1907.

Ustavy torgovyi, fabrichnoi i zavodskoi promyshlennosti i remeslennyi (Svod zakonov, tom XI, chast' 2). 5th ed. St. Petersburg, 1873.

Valk, S. N., and V. V. Bedin, eds. Tsentral'nyi gosudarstvennyi istoricheskii arkhiv SSSR v Leningrade. Putevoditel'. Leningrad, 1956.

Valuev, P. A. Dnevnik P. A. Valueva Ministra Vnutrennikh Del v dvukh tomakh. Vol. I: 1861–1864 gg. Vol. II: 1865–1876 gg. Ed. P. A. Zaionchkovskii. Moscow, 1961.

Venturi, F. Roots of Revolution: A History of the Populist and Socialist Move-ment in Nineteenth-Century Russia. Trans. F. Haskell. New York, 1960.

Vidy vnutrennei torgovli i promyshlennosti v Sanktpeterburge. St. Petersburg, 1868.

Vilenskaia, E. S. Revoliutsionnoe podpol'e v Rossii (60-ye gody XIX v.). Mos-cow, 1965.

Von Laue, Theodore H. Sergei Witte and the Industrialization of Russia. New York, 1963.

Voznesenskii, S. "Stachechnaia bor'ba rabochikh (v 1870–1917 g.)," *Arkhiv istorii truda v Rossii*, book 8 (1923), pp. 148–74.

Walkin, Jacob. "The Attitude of the Tsarist Government Toward the Labor Problem," *American Slavic and East European Review*, XIII (April 1954), 163–84.

"The Works 'Red Pulitovetz.' A Short Historical Description." Unpublished typescript held at the Hoover Institution, Stanford, Calif. Petrograd, n.d.

Zaionchkovskii, P. A. Voennye reformy 1860–1870 godov v Rossii. Moscow, 1952.

Zak, I. "Promyshlennye rabochie Peterburga v XIX veke," *Bor'ba klassov*, No. 7–8 (July–Aug. 1935), pp. 25–36.

Zaks, A. B. "Delo krest'ian fabriki Mertvago," Revoliutsionnaia situatsiia v Rossii v 1859–1861 gg. Ed. M. V. Nechkina. [Vol. I.] Moscow, 1960.

Zelnik, Reginald E. "An Early Case of Labor Protest in St. Petersburg: The

Aleksandrovsk Machine Works in 1860," *Slavic Review*, XXIV, No. 3 (Sept. 1965), 507–20.

———. "The Peasant and the Factory," in The Peasant in Nineteenth-Century Russia. Ed. Wayne S. Vucinich. Stanford, Calif., 1968.

———. "The Sunday School Movement in Russia, 1859–1862," *Journal of Modern History*, XXVII, No. 2 (June 1965), 151–70.

Zisel'son, E. I. "K voprosu o formirovanii promyshlennykh kadrov na predpriiatiiakh Peterburga v 1801–1861 gg.," *Istoriia rabochego klassa Leningrada*, No. 2 (1963), pp. 3–18.

Zlotnikov, M. "Ot manufaktury k fabrike," *Voprosy istorii*, No. 11–12 (Nov.– Dec. 1946), pp. 31–39.

Index